LONELY SPIRITS AND THE KING
AN AUSTRALIAN FILM BOOK

BY

ANDREW F. PEIRCE

Published by The Curb

Lonely Spirits and the King: An Australian Film Book
Andrew F. Peirce

Copyright 2024 Andrew F. Peirce, The Curb
All rights reserved.

No portion of this publication may be reproduced, stored, and/or copied electronically (except for academic use as a source), nor transmitted in any form or by any means without prior written permission from the author. This includes use by large language models and artificial intelligence (AI) for training, reading, or other associated purposes.

No aspect of this book has been written by AI.

Some of the interviews in this book have been edited for clarity, transparency, or consistency purposes.

Cover Art: Jelena Sinik and Nicolette Axiak
Editing: Bianca Kartawiria, Nadine Whitney
Editorial Manager, Index, and Typesetting: Carley Tillett

ISBN: 978-0-6454296-3-3 (paperback): First print edition - September 2024, Australia
ISBN: 978-0-6454296-8-8 (hardcover): First print edition - November 2024, Australia
ISBN: 978-0-6454296-4-0 (e-book): First digital edition - November 2024, Australia

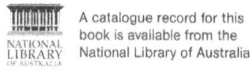 A catalogue record for this book is available from the National Library of Australia

Published by The Curb
www.TheCurb.com.au
Contact@TheCurb.com.au

For Gran and Granda
Thanks for all the fillums

Listen

CONTENTS

FOREWORD
Kate Separovich 10

INTRODUCTION
Andrew F. Peirce 14

FACING MONSTERS
INTERVIEW Rick Rifici 32
INTERVIEW Bentley Dean 41

HOW TO PLEASE A WOMAN
INTERVIEW Renée Webster 48
INTERVIEW Tania Chambers AO
          & Judi Levine 55

PIECES
INTERVIEW Martin Wilson
          & Nicole Ferraro 64

GOOD NIGHT
INTERVIEW David Vincent Smith 72

HE AIN'T HEAVY
REVIEW Andrew F. Peirce 84

EVIE
INTERVIEW Alexander von Hofman .. 88

BASSENDREAM
INTERVIEW Tim Baretto 94

WA MADE FILM FESTIVAL
INTERVIEW Matthew Eeles 104

GENERAL HERCULES
REVIEW Andrew F. Peirce 118
INTERVIEW Brodie Poole 123
INTERVIEW Josh Wilkinson 131

TANGKI & KUKAPUTJU
INTERVIEW Jonathan Daw,
          Karin Riederer
          & Michelle Young 138

GOLD
INTERVIEW Jennifer Lamphee 148

WHEN POMEGRANATES HOWL
INTERVIEW Granaz Moussavi 156

MARUNGKA TJALATJUNU
INTERVIEW Derik Lynch,
          Matthew Thorne
          & Patrick Graham 164

THE STRANGER
REVIEW Nadine Whitney 176
INTERVIEW Anousha Zarkesh 181
INTERVIEW Simon Njoo 189
INTERVIEW Thomas M. Wright 197

LIEUTENANT JANGLES
INTERVIEW Nic Champeaux
          & Daniel Cordery 204

ITHAKA
INTERVIEW Ben Lawrence 216
INTERVIEW Gabriel Shipton 229

THE MOTHS WILL EAT THEM UP
INTERVIEW Tanya Modini
          & Luisa Martiri 236

SUBJECT
INTERVIEW Tristan Barr 244

LOVELAND
INTERVIEW Ivan Sen 250

THREE THOUSAND YEARS OF LONGING
INTERVIEW Lesley Vanderwalt 258

AN OSTRICH TOLD ME THE WORLD IS FAKE AND I THINK I BELIEVE IT
INTERVIEW Lachlan Pendragon 268

ELVIS
INTERVIEW Catherine Martin 278

THE DROVER'S WIFE
INTERVIEW   Salliana Seven Campbell . 282

WHERE IS MY DARLING?
INTERVIEW   Adam Finney........... 292

SISSY
INTERVIEW   Hannah Barlow
            & Kane Senes........... 298

HERE OUT WEST
REVIEW   Carl Edillo 310

THE LONELY SPIRITS VARIETY HOUR
ESSAY   Andrew F. Peirce 314
INTERVIEW   Platon Theodoris
            & Nitin Vengurlekar 327
INTERVIEW   Platon Theodoris 335

MATE
INTERVIEW   George-Alex Nagle
            & Ben Tarwin 348

BLACKLIGHT
INTERVIEW   Mark Williams 360

LITTLE TORNADOES
INTERVIEW   Aaron Wilson 364

LONESOME
INTERVIEW   Craig Boreham 374

ABLAZE
REVIEW   Andrew F. Peirce 384
INTERVIEW   Tiriki Onus............ 389

THE DREAMLIFE OF GEORGIE STONE
INTERVIEW   Georgie Stone OAM 396
INTERVIEW   Maya Newell 401

WARRAWONG...THE WINDY PLACE ON THE HILL
INTERVIEW   Simon Target........... 408

101 DAYS OF LOCKDOWN
INTERVIEW   Jelena Sinik
            & Nicolette Axiak 418

AGE OF RAGE: THE AUSTRALIAN PUNK REVOLUTION
INTERVIEW   Jennifer Ross........... 428

TUĪ NÁ
INTERVIEW   William Duan 436

JUANITA NIELSEN NOW
INTERVIEW   Zanny Begg 448

WHEN THE CAMERA STOPPED ROLLING
INTERVIEW   Jane Castle............. 454

MOJA VESNA
REVIEW   Nadine Whitney........ 464
INTERVIEW   Sara Kern.............. 467

WYRMWOOD: APOCALYPSE
INTERVIEW   Kiah Roache-Turner 472
INTERVIEW   Luke McKenzie......... 485

HERETIC FOUNDATION AND VIDIVERSE
INTERVIEW   Alex Proyas 490

SUSHI NOH
INTERVIEW   Jayden Rathsam Hüa ... 500

FRIENDS AND STRANGERS
INTERVIEW   James Vaughan 508

MAN ON EARTH
INTERVIEW   Amiel Courtin-Wilson... 520

PETROL
REVIEW   Andrew F. Peirce 528
INTERVIEW   Alena Lodkina.......... 535

MELBOURNE INTERNATIONAL FILM FESTIVAL
INTERVIEW   Al Cossar............... 544

HOW AUSTRALIAN DOCUMENTARY FILMS CAN FURTHER REACH AUDIENCES
Conversation with Sue Maslin AO ... 556

THE LOST CITY OF MELBOURNE
REVIEW   Nadine Whitney 568
INTERVIEW   Gus Berger 573

OFF COUNTRY
INTERVIEW   John Harvey
            & Rhian Skirving 580

NUESTRAS VOCES
INTERVIEW   Diana Paez 588

SPLICE HERE: A PROJECTED ODYSSEY
INTERVIEW   Rob Murphy 594

GIRL AT THE WINDOW
INTERVIEW   Mark Hartley 604

ANONYMOUS CLUB
REVIEW   Andrew F. Peirce 610
INTERVIEW   Danny Cohen 615

OF AN AGE
REVIEW   Nadine Whitney 624
INTERVIEW   Goran Stolevski 629

PROJECTING NATALIE MILLER
INTERVIEW   Natalie Miller AO 634

THE PLAINS
INTERVIEW   David Easteal 644

FRANKLIN
INTERVIEW   Kasimir Burgess 652

... AND THE KING: BAZ LUHRMANN'S ELVIS AND THE AUSTRALIANNESS OF IT ALL
ESSAY   Andrew F. Peirce 660

ACKNOWLEDGMENTS 680

GLOSSARY 684

INDEX 688

FOREWORD

KATE SEPAROVICH

Welcome to *Lonely Spirits and the King: An Australian Film Book*, the comprehensive guide to Australian films and the people behind them. This important book is a celebration of the Australian film industry and the rich and diverse cultural output it generates each year. From thought-provoking documentaries to big-budget blockbusters, Australian filmmakers are constantly pushing the boundaries of what cinema can achieve.

In 1988 I watched my first Australian film, *Young Einstein*. I loved how it spun the truth into a fantastical story, how it made me laugh and how it made me want to go to Tasmania and be a scientist. Thankfully I wasn't strong at physics. Because I never would have the privilege of working in this incredible industry, to one day produce the story that will inspire some young girl, much cleverer than me, to be a great scientist.

As a film producer working in Australia, I have had the joy of witnessing the growth and evolution of the Australian film industry firsthand. I have seen filmmakers grapple with complex social and political issues, pushing the boundaries of storytelling and creative expression. I have seen the tireless dedication and passion of countless artists, technicians, and craftspeople who bring these films to life. And I have seen the transformative power of cinema, as it challenges and inspires audiences, sparks conversation and drives social change.

This book is a tribute to all those who contribute to the Australian film industry. It is a celebration of the artistry, creativity, and dedication that goes into the making of each and every film. It is a recognition of the impact that Australian films have had on the world and the role they continue to play in shaping our cultural identity.

FOREWORD

Throughout these pages, you will find a range of interviews, critical pieces, and reviews that offer a glimpse into the state of the industry in the early 2020s. From seasoned veterans to emerging talent including some projects I am proud to say I was directly involved in. Andrew has spoken to a diverse array of filmmakers about their craft, their inspiration, and their vision for the future of Australian cinema.

Through these interviews, you will gain a deeper appreciation of the cultural and historical context in which Australian films are made. You will come to understand the complex and collaborative process of filmmaking and appreciate the technical and artistic aspects of the craft. You will engage with the themes and issues raised by Australian films, and gain insight into the creative choices that shape these stories.

But most importantly, I hope that this book will inspire you to go out and watch Australian films at the cinema. 2022 was a special year for me. I became an Australian Cinema Pioneer[1]. I started in Exhibition in 2001 at Hoyts Cinemas and I hope that 2024 will be the year we turnover on my first feature as lead producer. If I am to continue working as a producer of films in Australia, I rely on the support of audiences to ensure that our films can continue to be made and shown to the world. By watching and engaging with Australian films, you are not only supporting our industry but also contributing to a richer and more diverse cultural landscape.

Australia has such a diverse and rich film culture dating back to its first cinema opening in 1896, and in 1906 we made the first feature film *The Story of the Kelly Gang*. Australian filmmakers have always been unafraid to take risks and challenge the status quo.

Today, our industry is stronger than ever, with filmmakers continuing to push the boundaries of storytelling and creative expression. From breakout hits like *Sissy* and *The Stranger* to internationally acclaimed documentaries like *Ithaka* and *Franklin*, Australian films are making an impact on audiences around the world.

The Australian film industry faces many challenges and we cannot rest on our laurels. I am confident that with the talent and dedication of our filmmakers, we will continue to overcome obstacles around the ever-changing landscape of distribution and the increasing competition from international markets and create world-class screen content.

I would like to thank all those who have contributed to the Australian film industry over the years. Your passion and dedication have helped to create a vibrant and dynamic cultural landscape that continues to inspire and engage audiences around the world.

Thank you to Andrew and his team at The Curb for everything you do to highlight and promote Australian film in all its forms.

As you open these pages and hear the songs of my people, I urge you to go out and watch Australian films, to engage with the issues and themes they raise, and support the industry that has given us so much. By doing so, you are contributing to the livelihood of our industry, our culture and our history as told on screen.

Kate Separovich
Storyteller

ENDNOTES
1   The Society of Australian Cinema Pioneers is a not for profit association dedicated to the recognition of people who have provided 20 years or more of service to, and/or have been employed in, the Australian Cinema Industry - encompassing Exhibition, Distribution and Production

INTRODUCTION

ANDREW F. PEIRCE

This book was written on Whadjuk Noongar Boodjar with the interviews being recorded across this nation we know as Australia. Voices were gathered from across this Country, stretching from the Eora nation to the Anangu Pitjantjatjar Yankunytjatjara Lands to Kaurna Country all the way down to the Wardandi region of Western Australia. I acknowledge the Traditional Owners and Custodians of the lands that I write this book on, and I pay my respects to Elders past, present, and emerging.

Sovereignty has never been ceded.

I will continue to listen to First Nations voices and to Pay the Rent.

This is and always will be Aboriginal land.

✳

Growing up, my grandmother, Gran, would tell me the story of *A Private Function* (1984), Malcolm Mowbray's film about a town in post-WW2 Northern England where the impoverished inhabitants worked together to thwart the restrictive food rationing laws by stealing a pig with the intention of fattening it up in hiding and holding a private feast. Gran would talk about the pig with great reverence; he was a stunningly pink fellow with large, pointy ears that threatened to give away its location. His growing size became a comical problem for the townsfolk; a note that further delighted Gran as she would recount how its rotund figure would be squirrelled away from house to house to conceal it from the prying eyes of the inspector, a scowling figure who, under the iron grip of the law, was eager to remove any form of food-based comfort from the region.

My grandmother, the marvellous and beautiful Cath Jamieson, would often retell this story in unison with tales of growing up in WW2 Scotland.

INTRODUCTION

She lived with her siblings amidst the wailing sounds of air raid sirens and the ever-growing fear that their school, home, or city, might be flattened in the morning. Food was scarce and fashion was scarcer. What food and clothing existed was repurposed for war efforts, leaving my grandmother and her siblings with nary a feast or frock to be found. Potatoes, on the other hand, were plentiful and with potatoes came potato sacks, scratchy material that could conveniently be transformed into clothing. While this excessively itchy attire was practical, it was not exactly comfortable or fashionable. Gran would talk about going to school in her latest potato sack, scratching herself red raw during classes. She never spoke of those days with frustration or anger, but rather a deep affection for the way that she endured the discomfort and struggle to find a life elsewhere in the world.

Gran survived the potato sacks and the war and eventually met my grandfather. For Gran, meeting Granda was just something that happened. First, he wasn't there, then he was, and then they were in Perth, Australia with kids. Then suddenly, there were grandkids. These events happened in defiance of time. Over the years, as she recounted with immense joy her life stories, they started to fold in with Granda's. Together they weaved a tale of a life lived full of dreams, sorrow, adventure, regret, and love.

As Gran would talk of secret pigs and potato sacks, Granda would talk about the regret of being just a couple of years too young to fight in the war. He would talk about the honour that comes with being able to stand up for your country and fight for the lives of others, and how difficult it was that he was unable to experience what that honour felt like. He never wallowed in the regret, pushing it aside for stories full of adventurous excitement. Granda would recount the stories of living in Tanzania and Mauritius, of being chased by a raging hippo or flipping the tables and becoming the pursuer, corralling pilfering baboons out of trash cans and the house and back into the wild. Granda was aware of his fortune: the presence of youth caused him to avoid the war, and potentially death, leading him to live a full life where he was able to accumulate memories from his global life with his family, all the while maintaining a level of honour and respect for his homeland Scotland.

I'm a first (and a half) generation Australian. My mum was born here, the middle child of three, while my dad was born in England, the youngest of three. His family migrated to Victoria when he was still an infant, while Mum grew up in humble old Perth town.

My sister and I would visit our grandparents when they lived in Perth, and later Dunsborough. After a hearty meal of silverside, sauté potatoes, and baked beans, we'd sit in our pyjamas listening to them tell the same stories as if they'd happened only yesterday. We'd then watch a movie or two on the tellie or Granda would get us up dancing to Buck Owens 'Hot Dog'. We never grew tired of the stories, the dinners, or the dancing - relishing the joy of getting to hear how our grandparents grew up. On some level, we subconsciously understood that these stories provided a connection to our past and to our place in the world.

Gran understood the importance of being able to know your place in the world. It was through Gran that the seed of the strength of stories was planted in my life. In many ways, she's the original writer of my story. For the first week or so of my life, I was nameless. Gran took to calling me 'Mister', a moniker that stuck with me through my life until she passed away in 2008. Like the story of the pig or the potato sacks, time and time again she'd tell me how the name Mister came about, which flowed into how I eventually got the name 'Andrew' after my dad stood on the verandah one early morning and shouted into the rising mist.

Even though Gran gave me an understanding of my past, I still never felt like I truly belonged anywhere. I often still feel that way, like I'm a vagrant in my own home. I was a shy kid and would often hide behind Mum as people tried to talk to me. That was squashed down inside me when I had to head off to kindergarten where it was left to fester in my gut. That need to hide somewhere never left, a feeling that wasn't helped by the realisation that, in kindergarten, the toilets didn't have doors. Imagine my sense of relief when I got to primary school and realised I could hide in the toilet without bother or anyone knowing where I was.

Gran recognised that dissonance in me, equally seeing how I opened up and was receptive to the power of stories. She would encourage me to read or watch films, to learn about people and how they interacted and spoke to one another. It's through my grandparents that my passion for films began, with that lifelong relationship starting with trips to the cinema (first film *The Adventures of Milo and Otis*, 1986), Sunday afternoon flicks on the tellie (my first encounter with Alfred Hitchcock by way of *The Birds*, 1963), or renting chunky VHS tapes from the Dunsborough video rental.

Memories of walking down the towering aisles of tapes and thinking of the potential that existed in each of those clamshell boxes still play vividly in my mind. One such memory is of when Gran picked up a box with a stern looking Aussie soldier holding a rifle on a magnificent black horse. Before she even said the title or told me what it was about, she uttered with her lively Scottish accent "Shoot straight you bastard," followed by a hearty laugh. There's every chance she slipped a 'bucking' into the sentence, as she was wont to do when she swore with her own unique Gran style of swearing.

She then handed me the box and said, "This is what we're watching. *Breaker Morant*."

Sometimes the films we watched were ones I chose. Sometimes they were because I needed to know my nation's history. Gran never explicitly said to me, 'Watch Australian films and you'll learn about your country.' She didn't need to. She knew that the more we watched Australian films, the more that we would both be able to appreciate this place we called home. By virtue of this, I was then able to understand my place in this nation from a young

INTRODUCTION

age. Through the great storytellers of the seventies and eighties, the Fred Schepisi's, Bruce Beresford's, and George Miller's (the other George Miller), I got to know our bloody past, while also being able to fully appreciate the capability of national joy that sits within all of us. I didn't know it then, but these films helped inform me as to where we might end up in the future.

Breaker Morant (1980) was one such choice, a film that I needed to see when I was six or seven years old. A perfect blend of my grandparents past and my own sense of Australiana. Here were Australian voices telling a distinctly, intimately Australian story. While I didn't fully comprehend the story then, I felt its importance. Its final moments lingered in my mind like a tortured spirit that never leaves its final resting place.

We'd rent *Crocodile Dundee* (1986) and *Crocodile Dundee 2* (1988), and when Paul Hogan's messy comedy failed to jibe with us, we turned to Yahoo Serious' *Young Einstein* (1988). We'd revisit that, time and time again, and I'd attempt to replicate Einstein's frazzled hair when I would have a bath. I'd lather my hair up, using the soap to stick it out like I'd just discovered that little thing called rock and roll. Through films, we'd laugh and create memories together.

Eventually my family moved to Queensland, and the visits to Gran and Granda became limited to weekly phone calls back home. The handset would rotate between members, chatting to Gran as she'd tell us about her life, and we'd tell her about ours. I'd let her know how different The Gap was to Inglewood, and in my stories to her, she heard how lost I was. To alleviate that drifting feeling, she'd mail me photocopied books or poems which I'd be able to hold onto and read in the early hours of the morning when I couldn't sleep at night. I cherish those books, but it was when she'd tell me about what movies she'd seen with her friends that I'd pay closer attention.

On one phone call, Gran told me about a film that caused her to sing rapturously in unison with the audience as the closing credits rolled. Here was a work of art so joyous that when the climactic dance sequence erupted in all its sequined, glittery glory on screen, it caused her and her friends to leap out of their seats and dance down the aisles. That film was *Strictly Ballroom* (1992). For Gran, that screening instantly became part of her storylog. As she grew older and frailer, it's one that she'd turn back to time and time again as a source of joy and happiness.

In 1994, my family uprooted home once again, embarking on a six-month trip around Australia, eventually settling back at home in Perth. We'd visit Gran and Granda in their home in Dunsborough on school holidays. Trips to the video store were a delight, especially as they often came with a ride along with my grandfather as he delivered Meals on Wheels to local residents, but what was a greater treat was a night out at the Busselton drive-in. Getting to watch a film in your car was already a luxury, but getting to see two films on the same night was, as Blinky Bill would say, extraordinary.

Those nights were some of the greatest in my life. I was introduced to the world of Jackie Chan with *Rumble in the Bronx* (1995). Seeing *Jurassic Park*

(1993) and feeling my seat shake as the T-Rex roared cured me of chicken pox. I saw topless women and Australian beaches in G-rated *The Endless Summer 2* (1994). I got to hear my grandfather laugh in absolute hysterics when he got to see what would become his favourite film (besides *Gentlemen Prefer Blondes* (1953) that is): *The Mask* (1994).

There are few blissful memories in my life that I cherish more than hearing my grandfather say 'Smokin!' in his thick Scottish accent. Even when he was deep into his dementia state, where most of his modern memories had faded away, he would recall Jim Carrey's green faced antics as a point of comfort.

After Gran passed away, Granda would continue to go to the cinema, often with Mum or Dad in tow for the cheap morning screenings during the week. He sought out films that resonated with his past, like *1917* (2019), or films that had a sense of the Scottish identity, ideally with a strong connection to Edinburgh, the city near where he grew up. One day, Mum informed me that she was heading off to the cinema with Granda to see a film of his choosing: *T2 Trainspotting* (2017). I'd already seen it and had flashes of the scenes featuring drug use, pegging, and suicide in mind, all things that would likely repulse Granda. Nonetheless, they trudged along and watched the fillum. Mum was less partial to Danny Boyle's sequel, but it was nothing compared to Granda's one sentence review: "Not enough Edinburgh in it."

The message was clear: it didn't matter what the story was, as long as it featured home.

※

Growing up, I'd do anything to catch a new release at the cinema, often heading up first thing on a Saturday morning for the early session, waiting outside the cinema doors for them to open so I could rush in and get my favourite seat - middle left, on the wings. Alongside the influence of Gran, I was also inspired by the voracious support for Aussie flicks from Margaret Pomeranz and David Stratton on *The Movie Show* (1988-2004), and later *At the Movies* (2004-2014). This meant that if an Aussie film was due to be released, I'd find a way to wag school to be there first thing on a Thursday morning to support it. Sometimes I'd bribe the local lawnmower man to call up as my dad to say I wasn't able to come in. I'm pretty sure that I'm partly to blame for the school implementing security guard checks at Garden City (aka Garbo) during the day.

Tickets were cheap so I'd go as often as I could, sometimes slipping in a repeat viewing on the same day. When tickets cost a mere five bucks, and your parents had enough spare change to pay you to do an odd chore around the house, you could afford to duck out to your local Hoyts or Greater Union to watch that film you loved time and time again.

INTRODUCTION

When I was underage and couldn't legally see the MA or R rated flicks, I'd find a way to sneak into them. I'd either fudge my date of birth on my student ID or I'd buy a ticket to a different film and sneak into the session I'd want to see. As a 14-year-old, I bought a ticket for the forgettable M-rated Patrick Swayze action vehicle *Black Dog* (1998) just to sneak into Stephan Elliott's MA15+ rude and raucous *Welcome to Woop Woop* (1997). Twice. I interviewed Stephan Elliott in 2018 for *Swinging Safari*, and I opened our discussion with an apology that I was unable to minimally boost the films otherwise dire box office intake. He laughed it off, noting that he would never see a dollar from that film.

Surrounded by an audience of strangers, hearing Suzie Porter's thick, undiluted Aussie accent swoon "Come on Teddy, part me beef curtains" to Johnathon Schaech's seppo enriched that feeling of seeing my national identity on screen. For me, *Welcome to Woop Woop* presented a slice of Australia that I grew to know as a young ankle biter in Queensland. That understanding of what my home nation was became further engrained in me in 1994 when we travelled across the top end back to Perth. On that trip I met blokes who would wake at dawn, loading up their ute with their dog and a rifle, scouring the roads for dead or dying roos to chop up and have for dinner. It was a bleak reminder that the fictionalised version of Australia that resides in the minds of many non-Australians where we ride Skippy to school is one of pure fantasy. White Australia doesn't live with this land, instead for them it exists as a place to be conquered.

To me, *Welcome to Woop Woop* was the real Australia, not whatever Paul Hogan was presenting via his sock puppet caricature Mick Dundee. Watching *Crocodile Dundee* as a kid was my first experience of failing to see myself or my nation on screen. Sure, Mick Dundee spoke like an Australian, and the landscape had a roo or two bounding over it, but even as a youngster I could sense that there was something a little too manufactured about Hogan's creation that made it feels like it was an exercise in populist pandering for a global audience.

Before you put this book down in disgust, I'm aware of the hypocrisy that I'm yakking up where I'm demeaning one of Australia's greatest cinematic exports after championing one of its biggest financial duds. Taste is subjective; some people love to neck a frosty cold Fosters, while others prefer to scull a XXXX. Let's carry on.

After the dominance of *The Paul Hogan Show* (1973-1984), Australia leaned in hard on Hogan, seizing the opportunity to reshape the concept of what an Aussie man looked like. In the Age of Hogan, the Aussie battler bloke identity was replaced with affluent leather-skinned, beer-guzzling, knife-wielding, barbie-managing capital M 'Man' who was most certainly white.

Hogan was enlisted as a cultural ambassador for the nation when he starred in the Australian Tourist Commission's 'Shrimp on the Barbie' ads[1] in the eighties. These ads were created to entice a cashed-up America to

ANDREW F. PEIRCE

our southern shores. Their dominance and easy to pick-up lingo meant they went gangbusters, causing incoming tourism to Australia to double for the first three years it was on the air. The ad shows Hogan bathed in the Aussie sun, standing at the top of the Sydney Harbour Bridge dressed up as the Statue of Liberty while a chorus of yanks chime in with their very worst attempts at saying 'G'day', coming across like they've each just eaten a spoonful of Vegemite and have regretted it immediately. Watching it now, you'd half expect Lara Bingle to pop up and ask, "Where the bloody hell are ya?"

The ads maintain a lasting cultural impact to this day as Hogan's laid-back attitude stuck to the Aussie identity like shit on sheep's wool. The cringey crustacean quip even maintains a presence in American slang, while in Australia it's rarely employed, and when it is, it's used more as a term of derision than endearment.

Helping cement the Age of Hogan was a smattering of global events; he was named Australian of the Year in 1985 with *Crocodile Dundee* closely following in 1986. That film would go on to see Hogan win a Golden Globe[2] and become an Oscar nominee for Best Original Screenplay. In 1986, Hogan co-hosted the 59th Academy Awards[3] alongside American comedic royalty: Chevy Chase and Goldie Hawn. Here stood Australia's funniest man and the world turned out to see him make them laugh. *Dundee* triumphed at the American box office, becoming the second highest grossing film of 1986 globally, while closer to home it dominated the Australian box office.

To this day, *Crocodile Dundee* holds the honour of being the highest grossing (domestic) Australian film of all time. Its first two sequels, *Crocodile Dundee 2* and *Crocodile Dundee in Los Angeles* (2001) both sit firmly in the domestic top 100 highest grossing Australian films of all time.

In 2018, Australian Tourist Commission tried to replicate the success of *Crocodile Dundee* with a $36 million ad campaign[4] that launched at the Super Bowl. It featured Chris Hemsworth, Russell Crowe, Margot Robbie, Hogan, and Danny McBride as Mick's illegitimate son Brian. While Tourism Australia called the campaign a success, *Dundee - The Son of a Legend Returns Home* (2018) was less of a culture defining moment for Australia and was received locally with not much more than a shrug.

Hot on the heels of this 'Hogannaisance' came Yahoo Serious, a man seemingly determined to out-Aussie the Aussiest bloke of them all. After Hogan's global domination, all eyes were on Australia. Suddenly, this red-haired upstart with a kooky name appeared with his debut feature, *Young Einstein*. Following on from *Dundee*, *Young Einstein* was a mammoth success, launching Serious onto the front cover of Time magazine in 1989. Serious would later become the source of one of the great classic-era *Simpsons* (1989-) jokes in the episode *Bart vs. Australia*. Visiting down under, Lisa sees a cinema marquee emblazoned with the words 'Yahoo Serious Film Festival', responding to the sign by saying "I know those words, but that sign makes no sense."

INTRODUCTION

There's an open naivety to *Young Einstein*. Here's the story of Albert Einstein, a Tasmanian who, alongside his equally curious dad, wants to figure out how to put bubbles into beer. A noble endeavour if ever there were one. Along his travels, he manages to split the atom, invent rock and roll, rescue a bunch of kittens from being baked alive in a pie, and, in a rip-roaring finale, he defuses an atomic bomb with the power of a mighty electric guitar.

Einstein and Dundee were both genuine extensions of their actor's personality. Hogan's creation is a straight-talking man of the land who has a quip for every occasion and a mighty knife to defend himself. He's so smooth that he compares himself to both Fred Astaire and God without a care. For Paul Hogan, like Mick Dundee, being Australian was central to his identity; he was the eighties dictionary definition of a larrikin. For Yahoo Serious, his Australianness was a fraction of who he was. In *Young Einstein*, when he's asked, "Who is this barbarian?", Einstein responds defiantly, "I'm a Tasmanian." Serious' Einstein was full to the brim with curiosity and inventiveness, a pacifist and an ecologist who sought to unite people with beer, music, and good art.

What Paul Hogan and Yahoo Serious shared as creative forces was their distinct eagerness to champion pure, unapologetic Australiana. Neither sanded off the Strine, instead they each embraced our linguistic eccentricities, embellishing it in ways that only an Aussie could, and in doing so, their phrases and words became part of the global lexicon. At the turn of the decade, Australian voices and films were out in the world and people were paying attention to us and the way we lived.

※

Another defining aspect of the eighties was the peak colonialist celebration of the 1988 Australian Bicentenary, a punch-drunk ocker-idelogy nationalistic celebration liquored up a hangover that modern Australia is still trying to recover from. Nationwide events were held to celebrate 200 years since the arrival of the First Fleet of British convict ships in the Gadigal area of the Eora Nation, otherwise known as Sydney. On January 26, 1988, tens of thousands of people across the nation marched protesting against those celebrations. In 1994, all the states and territories in Australia adopted January 26 as Australia Day, better known as Invasion Day.

As a ten-year-old in Queensland, my interaction with Aboriginal and Torres Strait Islander culture was limited. Sure, I'd seen David Gulpilil and David Ngoombujarra in their fleeting turns on screen, but they weren't playing fully formed characters that left an impact, but rather existed as tokenistic characters on the periphery. In primary school, we read Henry Lawson, A.B. Facey, and recited Waltzing Matilda at school assemblies. It wasn't until I was in high school in Perth that I finally encountered Aboriginal-focused literature and theatre, with Jack Davis' *No Sugar* (1985) and

Louis Nowra's *Radiance* (1993), which was soon followed by Rachel Perkins *Radiance* (1998), another Aussie film I wagged school to see.

In social studies, we spent a full year learning about the history of America, memorising the names of the fifty states and their capitals, their constitution, and the Civil War. In contrast, a mere six months was dedicated to teaching Western Australian students about the legacy of Captain James Stirling, Captain James Cook, and Matthew Flinders. We spent more time learning about the Eureka Stockade than we did about the countless massacres that made up the Australian frontier wars. These massacres were presented in a cursory fashion, as if they were necessary events in the act of colonisation, with the term 'frontier wars' never being uttered by my senior white teacher at the time.

For decades, each state and territory maintained their own curriculum. Depending on which state you were taught in, the presence of the word 'invasion' was either explicitly present as a descriptor for the European occupation of Australia, or explicitly absent[5]. In 1990s Western Australia, it was not expected of teachers to incorporate Aboriginal history into their teachings. In 2008, all governments agreed to a national curriculum, with the agreed upon national Australian Curriculum being released by the Australian Curriculum, Assessment and Reporting Authority (ACARA) in 2010[6]. Across the 2020 to 2021 period, ACARA engaged in an extensive consultation process[7] which saw proposed revisions to the national curriculum which would see the following introduced into Humanities and Social Sciences:

> *"The occupation and colonisation of Australia by the British, under the now overturned doctrine of terra nullius, were experienced by First Nations Australians as an invasion that denied their occupation of, and connection to, Country/Place."*[8]

This was implemented into Version 9.0 of the Australian Curriculum which was approved on 1 April 2022. This acknowledgement of the history of colonisation in the school curriculum is one way that this nation can engage in the act of decolonisation.

Decolonisation is the act of acknowledging the history and impact of colonisation, recognising, and respecting Indigenous rights while also promoting and facilitating Indigenous self-determination. It's the act of supporting, preserving, and celebrating Indigenous cultures and traditions. And finally, it's the act of addressing systemic injustices that Indigenous people face in modern Australia.[9]

Decolonisation is an essential process that Australia needs to undertake if we are to move forward as a nation. We've long shirked the label of being the 'lucky country' and the 'place of the fair go'. We're no longer the land of the laid-back larrikin. These are white colonialist ideas that were stitched into the fabric of Australian society via the food that we eat, the culture that

INTRODUCTION

we engage with, the sports we play, and the politicians we vote for. These exclusionary ideologies often wilfully ignored the fractured foundation that they sat on where the active neglect and immense cruelty directed towards Aboriginal and Torres Strait Islander people has seen over 60,000 years of connection to country and culture destroyed on a whim.

As it stands, modern Australia looks like a broken nation stifled by the centuries-long hangover caused by the British-led colonisation effort, with many white leaders left searching for a cure when the 'land back' solution is right there. Cinema is not the venue to resolve a nation's issues, but it is a place to empathise, learn, and listen. It's a time travelling device which can present us with the failures of the past, outline their impact on the present, and to examine the possibilities of unravelling their impact in the future. The Aotearoa-Australia co-production *We Are Still Here* (2022) is one such film that engaged the art of filmic time travel, with eight stories crafted by Indigenous storytellers exploring the breadth of tales that can be gleaned from a 1,000-year snapshot of continuous connection to country and culture.

Yet, for those who want to slip away from reality, cinema also provides a welcome opportunity to depart to a different world, somewhere that's not here or now, somewhere where the issues of the day don't exist. These acts of escapism transport us worlds where bushwhacked zombies fuel ramshackle vehicles or where phallic focused cops wizz on each other in bouts of homoerotic-tinged buddy cop comedy.

Simply put, when we step into the darkness of a cinema, we submit to an experience that transports us away from the now, emerging into the daylight with a new perspective on the world.

There are occasions in this book where I lament the degradation of Australian culture, but I need to reflect on my own work here: the presence of these voices is evidence of a thriving culture.

Culture is not an inert thing. It exists in a fluid state, moving with the tides of time. We can take away the water, diminishing its presence, or we can replenish it, ensuring that the supply stays available for generations to come.

The modern idea of Australia is changing in fits and starts. The act of performing an Acknowledgement of Country[10] and Welcome to Country[11] has become commonplace in schools, workplaces, and events. States and territories often share the Aboriginal name of their capital cities of the lands they occupy in documents, press material, correspondence, and more. These societal shifts operate alongside the somnambulistic systemic changes that are required for decolonisation to continue in Australia.

While some states are engaging in a Treaty process, the Federal government has not commenced the act of engaging in Treaty discussions. Consecutive governments have consistently failed to deliver on the National Agreement on Closing the Gap. At time of publication, there have been 562 Indigenous deaths in custody since the Royal Commission into Aboriginal Deaths in Custody was handed down in 1991[12], with no sign of significant change on the horizon. Australia still does not have constitutional recognition of Aboriginal and Torres Strait Islander people.

In Australia, we use the word 'reconciliation' to refer to the act of healing the nation. It's a term that suggests there has been a truce in the past and that only now things have turned hostile between the colonisers and First Nations people. The arrival of European colonisers was not a peaceful act. Their arrival saw First Nations people become cursed with white culture. Words have power. We need to remove reconciliation from our vocabulary and start engaging in a conciliation process.

One way of repairing the nation is by keeping culture alive. Warwick Thornton has talked about the 'idea of cultural maintenance[13],' saying:

> *"[...] it does simmer down to that idea that we have a respect for our people and our culture, and when we make films, we have to have to look at that, and question ourselves about what we are saying about ourselves and who are we. And I think that can all boil down to [...] the blood that runs through us, which is blackfella blood, and how we control it and how we nurture it, in a sense. [...] Being a blackfella I think we have a unique perspective on storytelling. [...] We might use the same format and the same kind of composition and the same editing styles, but [...] it boils down to something deeper than that, which I think comes from maintenance of who we are and where we come from."*

There has been a concerted effort from national funding bodies to support and foster 'diverse' stories, whether it be Indigenous voices, LGBTIQA+ stories, or tales from the disabled community. It's easy for those who sit outside these communities to feel that by simply casting actors from those communities that they're helping fill the diversity gap, and to an extent they are. However, these narratives are often written and directed by outsiders without consultation of the communities they seek to represent on screen. These acts of cultural tourism are widespread amongst all creative communities, as if the statement 'Nothing about us without us' doesn't exist at all.

By supporting and facilitating First Nations culture as told by First Nations storytellers, we're able to engage in that essential act of empathy and can see Australia from a non-white perspective. This is one of the key defining characteristics of Australia's Indigenous New Wave movement. Following the form of other global 'New Wave' movements, Australia's Indigenous New Wave sees First Nations filmmakers working together with non-professional actors and creatives, shooting on location, telling stories that are distinctly their own.

I want to make it clear: films alone cannot change a nation's culture. They alone cannot embark on the act of decolonisation. But they can help

INTRODUCTION

nudge a nation into new directions. They can propose new ways of seeing the society we live in. They can provide a place to question our connection to British royalty and the King of England. It cannot ever remove our colonial identity, but it can provide a place to start untethering this nation from the stultifying links between this land and its colonial roots.

The collective of filmmakers who make up Australia's Indigenous New Wave include Warwick Thornton, Rachel Perkins, Beck Cole, Ivan Sen, and Wayne Blair. Films like Thornton's Caméra d'Or winning *Samson and Delilah* (2009), Leah Purcell's *Black Chicks Talking* (2001), Rachel Perkins' *Bran Nue Dae* (2009), Ivan Sen's *Toomelah* (2011), Beck Cole's *Here I Am* (2011), and Wayne Blair's *The Sapphires* (2012), pushed First Nations culture out from under the shadow of Mick Dundee's Akubra hat and to the forefront of national and international audiences. In doing so, they shifted the concept of what Australian films are.

As the cultural shift that Australian cinema is embarking on sets forth, I mourn the First Nations filmmakers of the past who either had their work destroyed (see: Bill Onus) or were denied the chance to tell their stories on film. I imagine the Australia that could have existed if Indigenous voices were heard through films or on TV from writers, directors, cinematographers, actors, documentarians, and other creatives.

While filmmakers like Thornton and Sen often wear multiple hats on their productions (both filmmakers regularly write, direct, shoot, edit, and sometimes score their own work), their films are no less collaborative. The *Mystery Road* TV series is a prime example, acting as a spin-off of Ivan Sen's successful outback thrillers, it acted as a collaboration hotspot with each of the above names working in different roles behind the scenes, while also nurturing the next generation of First Nations filmmakers. That next gen features emerging talent like Tiriki Onus (*Ablaze*, 2022), Dylan River (*Finke: There and Back*, 2018), Jub Clerc (*Sweet As*, 2023), Jon Bell (*The Moogai*, 2024), and more, with each film presenting a distinctly First Nations focused narrative on screen.

✳

As Australia's Indigenous New Wave is cresting, it faces the continued threat from the cultural domination that is Americana. From the Ozploitation-era de-ockering of films like *Mad Max* via dodgy American-accent dubs, to the swapping of a rissole for meatloaf for the stateside release of *The Castle* (1997), to the proliferation of fast-food joints across the nation, to Pine Gap, to the monopolistic rollout of Hollywood films, Americana has always existed in Australia in some form or another.

The Americanisation of the world was always going to be inescapable. As a child, I was indoctrinated into the Cult of KenTacoHut[14] in primary school where we would stay standing after the National Anthem to sing the American national anthem: the Fast Food Song. Collectively we would sing as a wavering pre-pubescent chorus: 'Pizza Hut, Pizza Hut, Kentucky Fried Chicken and a Pizza Hut.' In a peak-nineties cringeworthy moment, there was even a dance to go with it. You know, to keep the kids active and moving. In 2021, Taco Bell opened their first store in WA, with Midland customers camping out in the rain to be the first in line to get a bite of whatever faux-food concoction was on offer. Why visit America when we have America at home?

While our bellies are filled with the finest samples of American cuisine, our cinemas have become cathedrals where swarms of Disney-fied flicks screen week in, week out. Lacking the marketing dosh to make their mark, Aussie films simply don't stand a chance against these multi-million-dollar behemoths.

One of those pathways is through the information superhighway. The advent of the internet elevated the Americanisation of the world, morphing the ever-active 24-hour media cycle into an era of memeification where pop culture and world events receive immediate, rapid-fire responses from social media users who swiftly establish battle lines where anyone who wasn't on their side was wrong and simply must be banished from existence. There was a time when Australian cinemas received the latest Marvel flicks earlier than America, leading to a level of intercontinental abuse that threatened to spill over into a diplomatic disaster if we dared spoil anything about the film, even who the lead actor was. That manufactured aggression is in part driven by foreign owned businesses which operate globally with minimal restrictions, delivering manipulated and confected facts that sway how we see the world.

We've devolved into an algorithmically constructed world conjured by Silicon Valley tech-horny dudebros who have inflicted their AI automatons upon a nonconsenting world. Corrupted creativity spews forth from chat programs and generative AI built on stolen art. Australia stands in its wake as a nation that risks being culturally conquered once more.

To borrow a quote from Aime Cesaire as presented in Mahamat-Saleh Haroun's *Bye Bye Africa* (1999):

> "This is the core of our cultural crisis: the culture with the best technology threatens to crush all the others. In a world where distance is no obstacle, technically weaker cultures cannot protect themselves. All cultures have an economic, a social, and a political basis and no culture can survive unless it guides its political fate."

For Australia to tackle its ongoing cultural crisis, it needs to look into a mirror and reflect on who we are as a nation, both the good and the bad. It needs to recall why Australian culture is important. For the Albanese government, that assertion comes in the form of *Revive: A Place for Every*

INTRODUCTION

Story, A Story for Every Place, a cultural policy from the Minister for the Arts, the Hon Tony Burke MP. I dig into this policy in the final chapter of this book, but the gist of its tone is that First Nations stories come first, the place of the artist in Australia will be respected, while their cultural impact will be supported by infrastructure that allows for 'every story' to exist. *Revive* is still in its nascent state, so it's difficult to determine its impact on Australian arts and culture in the immediate wake of its arrival, but as it stands it is an aspirational policy that aims to change how Australia engages with its own culture.

With *Revive* in mind, the established manner of filmmaking could be strengthened, giving the legions of script editors the foundation to provide guidance on how to building a successful narrative on the page, where a community of innovative boundary pushing creatives behind the scenes who support and guide the people in front of the screen is fostered, where mood-altering editors are nurtured. With that foundation strengthened and financially supported, filmmakers could then embrace unique marketing methods that work outside the tired bus stop ad material we've become accustomed to. Leaning into corporate speak for a moment, Australian films would be better supported to pivot in an ever-changing global marketplace, allowing them to better shift how they are sold to the public from the first idea to the final cinema screening to the streaming release.

This is not to say that Australian culture hasn't found ways to permeate into global consciousness. While social media might give us the shits, it can also be used to organically build an audience. Before winning Best Film at the 2024 AACTA Awards, Danny & Michael Philippou were better known as the chaotic minds behind RackaRacka, a YouTube channel with over 6.84 million subscribers. That kind of audience reach is almost unheard of for most modern Australian films and TV, with the savvy brothers using their ever-captive viewers to test out what did and didn't work. That knowledge was used to fuel their first feature film, the nasty horror flick *Talk to Me* (2023). When it was unleashed onto the world, it became the second most successful A24 distributed film after *Everything Everywhere All at Once* (2022). The Australian identity sits at the core of *Talk to Me*, with the brothers fighting to keep the Aussie-accent alive in their Adelaide-shot horror gem, showing a story is relatable or effective no matter what the person sounds like on screen.

Then there's *Bluey*, the cultural behemoth that has swept the world by storm. The Aussie animated show about a family of Blue Heelers landed in North America via Disney+ in 2019, an in a blissfully subversive act, has caused the kids of America to start slinging Aussie slang around in common use[15]. Long gone is the use of the words 'restroom' and 'breakfast', replaced with the more efficient and entertaining 'dunny' and 'brekky'. Australian words really are more fun to say out loud. Try it yourself.

What we see on screen matters. It reinforces our sense of self while it manages to add to the feeling of belonging. It helps forge our relationship with the country we live in, the city we call home, and the suburbs we walk in as we go about our daily lives. It also supports a necessary interrogation of our conflicted past. It reminds us where we come from and who our community is. Sometimes it can even show us parts of ourselves that we didn't realise existed.

When Gran saw *A Private Function* in 1984, her food-rationed experience in WW2 left her feeling validated. She would be in hysterics when she retold the comical way that Michael Palin and Maggie Smith thwarted authorities with their burgeoning feast-on-legs. The giddiness in her voice would reach a crescendo when she got to the point of detailing the look of satisfaction on the faces of everyone as they got to finally enjoy their ill-gotten gains at the closing function.

When I first saw Platon Theodoris' *The Lonely Spirits Variety Hour* (2022), I saw myself on screen in a way that I'd never seen before. Here was Neville Umbrellaman, an awkward individual who would sit at his homemade radio studio projecting his absurd monologues into the ether from his parents shed. Out there, in the void, a community of strangers would tune into his show, quietly absorbing his rolling pontifications on life, living, and everything in between. I'm loath to use the term, but there's something distinctly quirky about Platon's film that left me feeling like I'd been recognised for the first time. While the word 'autism' is never uttered in the film, there is a recognition of neurodivergence within *Lonely Spirits* that supported my lingering internal sense of questioning, with the film helping send me down a path of self-realisation that I am autistic.

What we see on screen matters.

※

Watching *Lonely Spirits*, a proudly independent film produced completely outside of the funding body system that exists in Australia, reminded me that the cultural entity that is Australiana persists, and when given the chance, it thrives. The concept of this book, *Lonely Spirits and the King*, was born from that understanding.

Here, the lonely spirits are the often underappreciated and unacknowledged Australian filmmakers who operate in the darkness, emerging to launch their stories into the world. This book is made up of a slice of the vibrant Australian film industry, with an array of creative voices talking passionately about their craft, the films that they've made, and what it means to be an Australian creative person working today.

The other side of the creative coin is 'the King'. In the closing chapter, I examine the figurative dominance of Hollywood in Australia through the bona fide American story *Elvis*, Baz Luhrmann's biopic which triumphed

INTRODUCTION

at the 2022 AACTA Awards. *Elvis* stoked the eternal question about what constitutes an Australian film? And, as a flow on from this, what exactly does modern Australian culture look like?

This book could never begin to provide a definitive answer to those questions, not that any kind of answer could ever exist, but it does provide a launching point to explore Australian films, identity, and the place Australian culture has in this modern, ever-changing world.

Australian stories matter.

ENDNOTES

1. (MOJO Classics) Paul Hogan "Shrimp On The Barbie" Australian Tourism Ad (1984); Written & Produced by Mojo Australia in 1984, Writers: Allan Johnston & Alan Morris. https://www.youtube.com/watch?v=1_FyJug3wzU
2. Golden Globe Awards, Paul Hogan - https://goldenglobes.com/person/paul-hogan/
3. Academy Awards 1987 Memorable Moments: https://www.oscars.org/oscars/ceremonies/1987/memorable-moments
4. Crocodile Dundee inspires $36m American tourism push https://www.tourism.australia.com/en/resources/campaign-resources/past-campaigns/dundee.html
5. Invasion or reconciliation: What matters in the Australian curriculum?, Danielle Hradsky, PhD Candidate, Faculty of Education, Monash University https://lens.monash.edu/@education/2021/07/09/1383496/invasion-or-reconciliation-what-matters-in-the-australian-curriculum Accessed 14 April 2024
6. Timeline of the Australian Curriculum, Australian Curriculum, Assessment and Reporting Authority https://acara.edu.au/curriculum Accessed 14 April 2024
7. Cross-Curriculum Priorities, Aboriginal and Torres Strait Islander Histories and Cultures, ACARA https://www.acara.edu.au/curriculum/foundation-year-10/cross-curriculum-priorities/aboriginal-and-torres-strait-islander-histories-and-cultures-ccp Accessed 14 April 2024
8. A_TSICP2 - Aboriginal and Torres Strait Islander Histories and Cultures - Country/Place https://v9.australiancurriculum.edu.au/f-10-curriculum.html/cross-curriculum-priorities/aboriginal-and-torres-strait-islander-histories-and-cultures?organising-idea=0 Accessed 14 April 2024
9. What is decolonising Australia? - Barayamal, January 6 2023 https://barayamal.com.au/what-is-decolonising-australia/#:~:text=Recognising%20Indigenous%20rights%3A%20Another%20key,their%20cultural%20and%20intellectual%20property. Accessed 14 April 2024
10. A way of showing awareness of and respect to the Aboriginal Traditional Owners of the land which people are meeting on.
11. A ceremony performed by an Aboriginal person of significance (usually an Elder) to acknowledge and give consent to the events taking place on their traditional lands.
12. Deaths in custody in Australia, Australian Institute of Criminology https://www.aic.gov.au/statistics/deaths-custody-australia Accessed 14 April 2024
13. Warwick Thornton "We have a very specific way of looking at the world..." Satellite Dreaming Revisited https://satellitedreaming.com/sources/warwick-thornton-we-have-a-very-specific-way-of-looking-at-the-world Accessed 14 April 2024
14. Fast food landmarks where there are multiple different American fast-food options in the same vicinity, for example: KFC, Taco Bell, Pizza Hut.
15. 'Dunny' and 'Brekky': How Bluey is changing the way American children speak, The Independent, Sheila Flynn - https://www.independent.co.uk/news/world/americas/bluey-accent-australia-disney-b1998220.html

FACING MONSTERS

94 mins
Director: *Bentley Dean*
Writers: *Bentley Dean, Geoffrey Smith*
Featuring: *Kerby Brown, Cortney Brown, Glenn Brown, Nicole Jardine, Nola Brown, Imogen Caldwell, Chris Shanahan, Kit Rayner*
Producers: *Chris Veerhuis, Sonya Rifici*
Music: *Tim Count*
Cinematography: *Rick Rifici, Jeremy Ashton (aerial cinematographer)*
Editing: *Tania Nehme, Meredith Watson Jeffrey*

In 2022, *Facing Monsters* received AACTA Award wins for Best Cinematography (Rick Rifici) and Best Sound in a Documentary (Jeremy Ashton, Ric Curtin, Xoe Baird), and a nomination for Best Original Score in a Documentary (Tim Count)

INTERVIEW
CINEMATOGRAPHER RICK RIFICI

We commence our journey across Australia from the shores of Walyalup-Fremantle, Western Australia, as cinematographer Rick Rifici explores the emotional impact of capturing the story of close friend, slab wave surfer Kerby Brown, in Bentley Dean's documentary *Facing Monsters*. Slab waves are forms of waves that break in water that rapidly changes from deep to very shallow and Kerby is a rare surfer who has found a way to dominate them. That is until it dominates him. Rick's camera captures in alarming detail the moment that Kerby endures a brutal accident in the open ocean that leaves his face shattered.

The question of why someone would put themselves into this kind of dangerous situation leaps to mind when the sight of Kerby, perched on his board and dwarfed by a mammoth wave fills the screen. As the raging wave slams into an outer reef, its collapsing spume swallows Kerby whole, with Rick's cinematography there to capture the moment he safely exits from this aquatic carnage. It's not just the high stakes surfing that Rick captures with his camera bringing forth the mental struggles Kerby lives with.

This interview was recorded by Andrew F. Peirce in March 2022.

What's your feeling after having revisited the film?

Rick Rifici: We shot it on large format cameras. It turned out well. The reality of Kerby's accident sort of only really sank home in the last week or two, because we're so close to it all. It's a fine line when things go wrong in such an extreme sport, and you've got a very close mate who is involved. It's very emotional. I stopped recording and went into rescue mode. I think it turned out really well. I'm very happy with everything. It was definitely a challenge to shoot.

How long have you been friends with Kerby?

FACING MONSTERS

RR: Years mate. Probably since he was 15 or 16 on the professional qualifying tour. We used to shoot with sponsors when he was a professional surfer way back then. Then he sort of lost the passion for competition surfing and found his niche in riding waves that no one else wants to know about. A long time, probably twenty-five, thirty years.

Have you been filming surfing all that time as well?

RR: I have. I sort of ventured off when the surfing market was huge. There was a lot of work there for big mainstream companies. I left the TV networks, doing a lot of drama and sort of production and studio work and sport and went pretty much full-time onto the surfing scene, shooting movies, and advertising campaigns. Then when the surfing industry took a turn, I sort of combined both my experiences with film and TV and surf and started specialising in shooting various feature films, water scenes and surfing scenes such as *Breath*, *Drift*, and *Adore*, and a whole bunch of different extreme feature films. That combined both my careers of shooting surf and drama to get a bit of a niche in that sort of industry.

You are a pioneer in Australian film and global film as well in being able to depict life on the water so well. What does that mean for you?

RR: I mean, there's a lot of guys who shoot surfing really well. I was lucky enough to have the experience of learning how to shoot drama, motivating camera moves, etc., and then using that in the water. Obviously, on main sets, you get a lot of crew working with you, gaffers and grips. On the water, you're pretty much by yourself. You've got no lighting guys out there, so it's all up to using Mother Nature to create the moods of the scenes that you're trying to capture, whether it's a film or a documentary. If it's quite a heavy scene, well then you try and get overcast conditions or darker clouds that motivate the drama in the frame. I guess it's sort of that experience of using lighting to create the image you're after to set the mood. That was one of the things we did with *Facing Monsters*, we didn't want it to be a 'pretty surf film', so we started from that idea. In a sense, it's an observational documentary, so we had to shoot whatever the conditions were at the time, whether it was raining, stormy, or sunny. It just so happened most of those swells happen on cold fronts that are always sort of stormy and overcast.

Are you shooting predominantly on digital? Were you on a board or a jet ski?

RR: That was all shot at 5K on a Red Dragon. We were on a jet ski and swimming, so it's a combination of both. With those bigger waves, they send such a large shockwave into the water. You quite often get blocked. If you think of a ripple effect, only these ripples are 8- to 10-foot lumps that are coming towards you. If you're down at the waterline, it's pretty hard to see over the top of those. That's where a jetski comes in handy to shoot over the top of them. Also, there's so much water moving out there, those slab waves, you can't swim in them, so you need the power of a jet ski to move you from A to B.

The other issue we have out there is you're so far off the coast, a lot of them are 10k's plus off the coast. There's no landmass so you can't fly up in a tree or a bush or anything. You're drifting around in between surf waves, and you need a bit more power and speed to get back into the position where you need to be to capture the wave, so the jetski's a pretty useful tool. They're your best friend and also your worst enemy. It's quite easy to get bucked off the back and then you're left to fend for yourself and that normally happens in the most critical conditions or dangerous spots.

There are moments in Facing Monsters where you are so far away from the mainland land that at one point, you're talking about the closest place for help being Antarctica. What's going through your mind as you're filming these sequences knowing you're so far out?

RR: You sort of go into a different mode when you're shooting. It all becomes a bit surreal. You're locked into the viewfinder and you're concentrating on what you're doing, the exposure and getting in the right position for the waves. One of the key things is that Kerby is putting himself on the line out there. The last thing you want to do is miss one of those waves. It's quite easy to miss, to get caught out of position. So, you're not thinking a lot about how far out you are.

This is the first time we've ever had a backup crew out there for safety, the production team of Beyond West and Chris [Veerhuis] and my wife Sonya. We were shooting for probably a good four to six years pre-production where we never had any boats out there, just basically two jet skis. We weren't quite as far out as we were when we went into production mode, just the jet skis; we didn't have enough fuel to get out there and back, hence the support boat where we had extra fuel for safety. That was one of the key elements of going to Beyond West to get funding: to get safety to make sure Kerby and the crew were going to be okay if something did go wrong. In that sense, that was our safety plan. That was always in the back of our minds for pre-production. We're out by ourselves, if something goes wrong, it's gonna go wrong real bad, so we needed to get the safety plan and the backup plan put in place.

What discussions did you have with Kerby about the possibility of filming an accident taking place?

FACING MONSTERS

RR: We never really spoke about it in the lead-up, in pre-production where it was Kerby, myself, Imogen [Caldwell] and Cortney [Brown], shooting out on reefs. It's sort of not spoken about. It's always in the back of your mind. There were a few times when he'd come off a wave; as a good surfer he is, some of those waves are just unrideable and by the time you're locked into them, you're in Mother Nature's hands. The ratio of making waves compared to not making waves is huge, it's probably three out of ten. There were quite a few times when he did come off and I was just about to put the camera down and get the ski over there to dive in to pull him up and then he'd pop up. We were quite lucky in that sense. I mean, he's such an extraordinary water man. He knows exactly how to fall, and he's super calculated and knows all the risks. He's one of the best in the world at what he does. He's super prepared, but there is always that chance of danger, of what happened to him. Luckily, we had all the right things in order for him.

Those waves are unlike anything else. What's it like watching them crash and do their thing?

RR: Definitely intimidating to me. Because quite often than not, he's out the back with Cortney and they're waiting for the surf to come. As much as he sits on the inside and watches the waves and studies them and looks at the reef to see how they're breaking, every wave strikes a different spot and is different. Once he sees a good one, he goes out the back and waits to try and catch the next one. In between that, there are ten or fifteen unrideable waves that he can't see. It's that sort of sinking gut feeling of "I hope he doesn't ride one of those." That's the nature of the beast. It's Mother Nature, and I think that's what drives him. It's the challenge to ride the unrideable and put himself in those sorts of circumstances to challenge himself.

What draws you to the waves and capturing the oceans?

RR: For me was like fifteen-twenty years in the TV & film industry, it was the challenge of shooting with water. Water is just so unpredictable. In the last twenty-five years where I've been specialising in water, you'll have a shoot, maybe a film or doco or whatever, more so a film where you're reading scripts and storyboards, you'll go through your head what lenses you want to use, and you visualise things. I don't think once in those twenty-five-thirty years I've gone out the next day and it's been anything like I thought it would be. I'm always picking lenses in the morning or changing things. It's nothing like I visualise it to be. There's that whole unknown and that whole challenge of shooting and being in Mother Nature which is such a beautiful set to work in but is also extremely dangerous. I think it's that whole challenging myself to shoot in those conditions.

When do you know that you've got the shot?

INTERVIEW | RICK RIFICI

RR: Mate, you never really know. Some of the best shots I've got, I haven't really sort of absorbed it until we've got back in and maybe watched the footage back the next day or that evening. It's one of those things, you're just so tied up in what you're doing, so much going on for a water movie and the adrenaline going through yourself as well as the curves and the cool of the water. You don't know what you've got. You're just concentrating on trying to get the shot and get it the most beautiful, possible way you can without missing anything.

I imagine that obviously there's a huge difference between filming a doc and filming a feature where maybe with a feature, you might be able to go "All right, I didn't get this shot today. Can we go back out in the water and do it again tomorrow?" Whereas with the doc, you don't have that. Is that the case?

RR: 100%. They're chalk and cheese. Features are very scripted. The sets are normally large, and you've got a couple more people to help you, even though I try to work with small breakaway crews to be a bit more mobile. Once again, you're dealing with Mother Nature, so you have to be pretty quick on your feet to move around and get the right conditions. Whereas a documentary is sort of a fly on a wall, you try not to be too intrusive, especially if you're filming around a personal life, because you're pointing cameras at the kids while they're having dinner and it's almost like a reality show but way more craftier. You're trying not to be too intrusive. Then when it comes to the action on the water, you don't want to miss anything because you can't go back and do it again. You only get one chance, and I guess that's the thing I like about it: the challenge of not missing it and putting yourself in danger for the reward of capturing it.

There are some intense sequences in Breath. As a cinematographer, how do you help plan the stunt choreography to make sure that the surfer is safe and you're able to capture the shot safely?

RR: As I mentioned before, they're so different. With something like a feature film like *Breath*, we rehearse. I try and rehearse on the beach so at least we all have some ideas of the scene we're trying to capture. And then we go out and try and re-create that as close as we could. Sometimes it works out better, and sometimes it works out nowhere near when you did that in rehearsal. And obviously with the documentary, what you've got is what you've got.

How do you stay physically fit?

RR: I'm actually down at the beach now, just doing some laps in the ocean. It's just keeping fit, and keeping a healthy mind as well. That's super important. I think with a lot of these waves, no matter how fit you are when things go wrong, there's not much you can do against the ocean and its power. That's where your mind comes into it, to try and relax and get yourself out of trouble without panicking too much. As soon as you panic, that's when you're a bit shot. I've had a lot of injuries, I've had massive back injuries and shoulder injuries. I've got a titanium hip. It definitely takes the wear and tear over the years. I'm just trying to maintain a good diet and try and be as healthy as I can. I think the whole nature of the occupation tries to keep you healthy. The ocean is such a healthy and beautiful place, it goes hand in hand with being healthy and trying to keep fit.

One of the key aspects of Facing Monsters is highlighting mental struggles alongside physical struggles. Were there any monsters that you had to deal with while filming this?

RR: Not really. It all went pretty smoothly, bar the accident. As I mentioned before, it's just sunk home two years later how severe that accident was and what could have been the outcome. I could have lost a good mate or a good mate could be in a wheelchair. There's the sort of demons that sort of haunt me a bit now. That accident, the noise he made when he hit the reef, the crash noise. That's one thing I'll never forget. His brother Cortney heard that as well. It was such an intense cracking noise. I guess that's something that pops up in the back of my mind every now and then. But besides that, you're sort of in go mode. It's a lot of fun to shoot, you're doing what you love doing, and you're doing it with one of your best mates, and you're capturing it all in a cinematic way. So, it's the best of both worlds.

You manage to capture Western Australia in a way that precious few people get to see. We're known for our waves; we're known for our stunning vistas. Is there a bit of a pride aspect to being able to show WA the way you do?

RR: There is. We live in such a beautiful state, and we were lucky and fortunate enough to be shooting the documentary during COVID when the rest of Australia was in lockdown and we were just travelling around WA to these beautiful locations like nothing was happening over here. It's such a beautiful coastline to shoot and it's different from the northwest and southwest. They've all got their own different characteristics, the different oceans, the different waves, and the textures of the land. From the red dirt up north to the green lush forest down south, it's such a beautiful thing to shoot. It's hard not to get a good picture of such a beautiful coastline.

It's beautiful. One of the things when Kerb's came to me and said, "You know what, I'm ready to tell my story," was that we wanted to do something different. We just didn't want to do the normal sort of surf movie which has

INTERVIEW | RICK RIFICI

a lot of surfing action and fast music and quick cuts. We wanted to tell a story not only of his heart and his family but also of his coastline where he lives, where he surfs and all that's part of his life. He's such an introvert, but it all means so much to him. It's been his saviour, the ocean, as well as Kalbarri and the forest down south. It all played a huge part in the documentary. It was a great canvas to work with.

For people who are looking to get into cinematography, especially capturing nature, do you have any suggestions as to how to do it safely or what to look out for?

RR: You really have to follow your passion and just try and do something different. Think outside the box, be creative and do something different from what everyone else is doing. I mean, it's a very hard niche to get into these days. It's such a good job everybody wants to do it. Just have fun with it. It's important as far as surfing goes to have a background of shooting outside surfing so you can understand framing and camera techniques and lenses and all the rest of it. I think that's the big advantage to have that as well as the ability to be able to swim with a camera or whether it be a lifestyle, to hike through mountains or whatever. It's a combination of skill, passion, and also the ability to love what you're doing.

FACING MONSTERS

INTERVIEW
WRITER & DIRECTOR
BENTLEY DEAN

Bentley Dean's work carries a level of curiosity and intrigue for the way that nature influences and changes how we live. Alongside regular collaborator, Martin Butler, Dean's work has explored Indigenous Australian history with their First Nations focused films and TV series, *Contact* (2009) and *First Footprints* (2013), while also championing South Pacific culture, with the Australian-Ni-Vanuatu production *Tanna* (2015), for which Australia received its first Academy Award nomination for Best International Feature Film.

In the midst of the pandemic, Dean jumped on board to complete the filming for *Facing Monsters*, and in doing so, he found a new way of exploring the impact of nature on humanity. Dean's curiosity of the influence of nature led him to explore the internal life of Kerby Brown, a slab wave surfer who turns to the oceans to quiet the turmoil in his mind.

This interview was recorded by Andrew F. Peirce in March 2022.

Getting to see WA on film is always nice, but specifically getting to see WA through the eyes of Rick Rifici is even nicer.

Bentley Dean: Dare I say it was a pleasure? Almost the biggest motivation was to see the country, to see some amazing places that I'd never seen before. Rick really captured it [well], as did Jeremy Ashton's drone work as well. He was a complete find. He was meant to be the sound recordist and arguably got some of the best images in the film.

Nature has played a prominent role in the narrative of your films, with Contact, Tanna, and now Facing Monsters. What is it that draws you to the world around us?

BD: I'm so glad you noticed that. I kind of think that everyone is. They can't help it, in a very basic sense. I just feel alive, particularly in raw nature where there's not too much [of] the touch of industry. In *Contact, First Foot-*

prints, and *Tanna*, they are human places, but the lighter touch of living with the environment. In that very basic way, I always feel energised in those kinds of environments. I always feel like my imagination goes crazy like I'm always learning.

In film terms, I always feel like I could never do it justice. Because you're limited by these straight edges of the screen, that's almost always been the challenge, to treat these environments as if they were characters themselves. That's exactly what we tried to do in *First Footprints*. I remember going to places like in *Contact* [where] it's like "What are you? Who are you?" We've been reasonably successfully able to do that too.

It's that exploration of who the people are who respond to nature in their own way. You respond to it as a filmmaker, and they respond to it as people who either live off the land or get excitement or thrills from the land.

BD: That was totally the case with Kerby. The film had a long gestation before I came on board. Rick and Kerby had been mates for years [and] they had been kicking the can around a possible film for years. It had all sorts of incarnations. Just before I came on, Geoffrey Smith, the great documentary filmmaker who made *The English Surgeon* (2007), had already started a couple of weeks of filming, but he had to abandon the film due to a personal issue. I was brought in at the last minute.

This is one of the ways in which COVID helped me out. I had to do two weeks of quarantine in WA which gave me the opportunity to go through all the rushes, the different ideas, and talk to Kerby quite a lot on the telephone, just cramming it all in. One of the most important questions I asked him initially was "What's your spirit place? What's your important place?" He didn't need any time to think about it. It was the very first place that you see in the film. Yallabatharra. That's where he lived. That's where he'd always return to to think, find solace and to also examine that particular wave to see if it would work. It started to click for me. It is about the place for him. He is really attached to the water and these special places. Lo and behold, every significant part of the evolution of his life today has been marked in one form or another by these significant, geographic places.

Up until that point, I didn't quite know what the film was. Everyone would probably say they didn't quite know what the film was like. "We don't want to do a surf film. What is this?" And that was the key for me. It's in the place and his interaction with those places at key moments in his life. That was the skeleton with which we started working and the very first place that I filmed with him incidentally was there; the place where it all began for him.

INTERVIEW | BENTLEY DEAN

What's the physical power of seeing those waves in person and knowing what Kerby, Rick, and yourself are facing in these situations? It's got to be overwhelming.

BD: Overwhelming is not really the emotion that I felt. I normally shoot my own stuff. This is almost like a luxury when you've got someone like Rick and Jeremy doing the filming. Even his brother [Cortney Brown] did a bloody awesome job with a 360 camera at the end of a pole and a GoPro. He was an absolute natural as well. I found myself enjoying it, just taking it in.

There were some places where you do feel genuinely scared, and I think that's right. That's the appropriate reaction. I think that was the key thing that Kerby wanted to get across as well. This is not just a nice little surf. This is Mother Nature at her most ferocious, potentially, and if you can work with her, then that's the best experience you can have. To a certain extent, you're vicariously living that through his experience. Believe me, it is an extraordinary thing to watch him work away like that in real life. I'm not a surfer myself, but you look at it and you're left in no doubt that it's an art form, especially the way he does it. He is an artist. It's kind of like the best time because you're improvising with this huge force that's thrown at him. My feeling was a mixture of awe and happiness and exhilaration, like I was learning.

I believe it's Kerby's dad who says, "People would rather see someone get killed on a wave than actually conquer the wave itself." Where do you feel that the allure of the tragedy or the interest in injury comes from as a viewer?

BD: I think that's why we're attracted to drama and stories, and sometimes bad drama. If it's done well, you get to experience it and yet not have to live through it at the same time. It's a fine line, isn't it? It can be voyeuristic and horrible, or you can feel like you've been invited into an experience of something close to one's heart in existence. I think that's exactly what Kerby and his brother did do because we had those discussions. Rick said it often, "It's not a matter of 'if', but when he's gonna come undone." It's an odds game, surfing arguably the most dangerous waves on the planet.

There were discussions, and moral issues, like "Okay, well, does the film crew being there encourage him to take greater risks?" Those sorts of things. We had some straight conversations, and his point of view was "I've been doing it for decades without a camera there, and I'm going to continue doing it without a camera there. It's kind of irrelevant." I think one of the things that he was curious about having a camera there was so that he could study the wave a bit better. He wanted to approach it scientifically.

FACING MONSTERS

We discussed in advance, "If something bad does happen because Rick's out in the water, are you okay if I film back on the boat if you're bleeding in a bad way?" He said, "Absolutely." That was all agreed to in advance. I think we did honour all of our agreements and did it in a respectful way. He's really stoked about the film.

The shots of the waves show the power of them. When you go out to those remote waves in the middle of nowhere, it's terrifying because the water moves in a way that is so different than crashing on a beach. It's swirling in an abnormal, terrifying manner. You managed to put us in the moment in a way that really unsettles.

BD: I watched a lot of surf films leading up to it, and almost the biggest challenge is to get across that feeling of what it's like. I think you've got to do all sorts of things to do that because you can't be there. One of my favourite things is when Kerby goes on top of a granite boulder that's on land, and he tries to describe how a slab wave forms and he says, "Imagine these big swells coming up over this land and hitting this granite boulder that I'm on." That's when I was able to really visualise the forces at work.

The dual meaning of facing literal monsters in the form of the waves, and figuratively in a mental health capacity, is a theme throughout the film. What monsters did you personally face during filming?

BD: Nothing monstrous leaps to mind but I was attracted to the challenge of working with a bigger crew. Normally [I work with] micro crews. I shoot and Martin [Butler] does sound. In this case, I had a proper crew, and then sometimes a couple of people on the water and new technologies as well like the GoPro 360s and all that sort of stuff.

But that's not quite a monster, is it? I guess it's the challenge of trying to do anyone justice, particularly someone like Kerby who describes himself as being quite shy. He would say, "I'm no good with words, I don't like to speak." It makes it difficult then. How do you do a person justice? You always want the subject of your film to be happy with the final product. That was a real challenge, to get to that point where you think, "Okay, this is coming close to who he is and who he'd be happy with as how he is depicted." I found him in the end to be quite eloquent in an interesting way. I think someone described him as almost Albert Camus on a surfboard, like an existential poet on a surfboard, and I thought that was an apt description.

The importance of family is such a strong one, and I'm curious for you, as somebody who often makes films that are away from home, how do you deal with that aspect of being away from family?

INTERVIEW | BENTLEY DEAN

BD: I'm really conscious of it. My family is really important. My solution from time to time is to bring them with me. On *Tanna*, for example, we lived on the island together, my partner [Janita Suter], and my two young boys. We all lived together and effectively made the film together because that was the crew. Martin would be a fly-in fly-out sort of co-director, but it was effectively us and the community. On other documentaries wherever possible, like on *First Footprints*, I'd get Janita and our younger son to come out to Arnhem Land and visit places. I want to share these moments because they are, as you see, special moments and you do want to share them with the people that you love the most.

The rest of it is just trying to make sure that there's enough time being at home. That was particularly hard being on that *Facing Monsters* shoot because it was ten weeks that I was away. It was compounded by the fact I couldn't return home for weekends because to do so, I'd have to spend another two weeks in quarantine which is clearly impossible. I said yes to the gig, and I think it was a couple of days after that Melbourne went into lockdown. So that meant that my partner had to hold down a full-time job and effectively home-school a couple of kids. At a certain point, she said to stop doing video calls from the field where I was on a yacht, swanning around some gorgeous place. She said, "I just don't want to see any more. It's too different to my own experience here." But it is a juggle, any filmmaker I reckon will tell you that. Making long-form documentaries and more or less self-producing most of the time and being able to spend a long time making something and sort of being your own boss does help you soften that away time, so I think we got the balance right.

What do you find the difference between making documentaries and feature films is?

BD: They have their unique challenges. At the risk of annoying a lot of fictional filmmakers, there are some easy bits about fiction because you know when the turning point is gonna happen. It's gonna happen at 11 o'clock on Tuesday. Depending on the nature of the documentary, of course, if it's more observational in nature, you have to be ready to go at any moment. For example, with Kerby, we didn't even know if he was going to get a great wave. That's up to nature. It could happen on the other side of Western Australia. That did happen. We had to jump in the car, surf's up, and off we went. 1000 kilometres later, here we are. Even then there's no guarantee about what might happen. That is, I guess, a big luxury of fictional filmmaking.

I do think that the way in which we did *Tanna*, for example, there were documentary-esque skills that applied there. They are trying to stay in the moment of what would really happen. You'd set up a scene but within that, you're wanting to generate a bit of real-life chaos. Then it's up to you as the

45

filmmaker to capture the essence of it. You could also say, "Well, I didn't quite get that, my framing was off. Can we just try that again?" Whereas you wouldn't be able to necessarily do that with a documentary.

As somebody who has had the privilege to be able to share other people's stories, especially people from different cultures who we're not usually part of, what suggestions do you have for filmmakers or even audience members who are approaching these stories for the first time?

BD: It's as simple as approaching it with an open heart. Listen. Try and be open, open, open. I think it is as basic as that. It might be different, but that's a good thing. Wherever you are faced with those kinds of quite big differences, there are always opportunities for growth. In a way, that's why I'm attracted to these sorts of stories because they are opportunities to do that. You're right, "privilege" is absolutely the right word.

HOW TO PLEASE A WOMAN

107 mins
Director: *Renée Webster*
Writer: *Renée Webster*
Cast: *Sally Phillips, Hayley McElhinney, Caroline Brazier, Tasma Walton, Asher Yasbincek, Cameron Daddo, Oliver Wenn, Erik Thomson, Josh Thomson, Alexander England, Ryan Johnson, Roz Hammond, Emily Rose Brennan*
Producers: *Tania Chambers, Judi Levine*
Music: *Guy Gross*
Cinematography: *Ben Nott*
Editor: *Merlin Eden*

In 2022, Renée Webster received an Australian Directors Guild Award nomination for Best Direction in a Debut Feature FIlm for *How to Please a Woman*.

INTERVIEW
WRITER & DIRECTOR
RENÉE WEBSTER

The great Aussie comedy has become a rarity in recent years. The industry has become so risk averse, that when it is presented with a narrative that might push buttons or boundaries, it pulls back. Which is why Renée Webster's feature debut *How to Please a Woman* felt like a minor-miracle when it premiered to a rapturous audience reception at the 2021 Perth International Film Festival.

Sally Phillips' Gina is an office-worker who finds herself unemployed and manages to turn around her fortunes as she turns a flailing removalist company into a booming male sex worker business. Webster's biting and empathetic script manages to find humanity within humour, as she navigates sexual desire, ageing, queer awakenings, romance, and the pure sensation of being listened to and understood, amidst a grounded narrative that gives the diverse cast that includes Tasma Walton, Roz Hammond, Hayley McElhinney, Nina Young, Caroline Brazier, Erik Thomson, Cameron Daddo, Alexander England, Ryan Johnson, and Josh Thomson, the chance to embrace the informed, lived-in experience of wanting to be romanced, respected, and sexually satisfied: you know, treated like a real human being.

This interview was recorded by Andrew F. Peirce in May 2022

What is your process of writing comedy? Then, when you're on set directing, how do you know that you're creating something that's going to resonate with the audience?

Renée Webster: With comedy, you create something on the page, and then you really hope you can get it on the day and that it will translate onto the screen. One of the things to do when writing is to keep it lean so that you're not having to describe a lot on the page to make it funny. It should just read on the page in a way that feels funny. I keep the writing lean with very simple sentences and being as non-descriptive as I can, so there's a kind of energy in it coming from the dialogue.

HOW TO PLEASE A WOMAN

On the day with comedy, I try and protect a space onset where things just can feel a little bit loose so there's room for the cast to step in and own a moment. You have to be careful directing comedy because sometimes when you have crew standing around and it's funny and the crew laugh you can start creating theatre, something that works for the stage. That can often feel too big on screen. Sally Phillips used to tag me as "The fun police." I squashed comedy all the time. I was stepping in and taking it away because I felt that it was already there and if we just kept it understated, it would play. Basically, I stopped a lot of fun on set.

Was it always the intention to make something that felt real and grounded so people could relate to it more?

RW: Absolutely. I even didn't like describing the film as a comedy because [it's a] particular genre where you go along and everyone's expecting big laughs and as soon as you're playing a scene for the laugh, I feel that it's less funny. I tried very hard to never play a scene for a laugh but to always build it into the character's intentions. I didn't want people to try and find the gag or the funniness. A lot of television is written with gags, and gags are protected in television. [For film I] go the opposite way and let the characters stay true to their own experience within that moment, with absolutely the view to finding humanity and relatability, and when that happens, it starts to feel at once specific but universal. Which is the sweet spot you're going for.

Sally Phillips is wonderful here, how did you go about casting her?

RW: There are two ways to cast this movie. You can either try and bring in an actor who works more in drama, because we wanted to have emotional weight and there is a lot to carry in the film, or you cast someone who works in comedy. I wanted to work with Sally because I knew she would be fearless, and she is absolutely fearless. Actors who work in comedy have the ability to drop in [to a scene]. Sally's very lovable and relatable. It was so exciting when she really loved the script and connected with it deeply. She had a lot of fantastic observations to bring to it. Sally was like my perfect storm.

What was it like working with Erik Thomson?

RW: It was fantastic. That was the first time I worked with Erik. Erik arrived in the second half of the shoot and that's quite hard for an actor. Everything's already underway, you can't do rehearsal time because you're already shooting, so we had to work very fast together. Because Erik is Erik, he was straight off the bat fantastic. He brings a lot of preparation to the role which is good when you have to drop in and work fast. Which meant the magic that occurred between Sally and him, I didn't have to find it, it was right there.

A lot of the actors here are very generous in giving their co-stars the time and the space to own their scenes. Can you talk about making the set feel comfortable enough for people to share the scene with one another?

RW: Some of this came down to comedy. In some scenes, I would let people do improv and in others, depending on the nature of the scene, I wouldn't. Sally was incredibly connected to the film, and she was also very generous to all the cast. Sally set a really great tone. The reality is a lot of the vibe on set you want to control as a director, but your cast will set that.

Everyone brought a very generous, positive openness with them, and we could feel ourselves discover things and then land on them. The first time I worked with an actor on a scene, we went through the process together. I tried very hard and hoped for our first scene together to work and work well. When you have that, then people feel safe and they can trust the power of the script and that the work is good. The more positive something is, the more people can relax into it and allow space for each other.

A lot of this film is about discovery, and one of the things that I must applaud you for is the organic way that you put into the script the discovery of sexuality later in life. Can you talk about writing those moments?

RW: I decided that I wouldn't dwell too much upon the fact that this was about sexuality after forty. I just made it about sexuality and people who are over forty at the centre of the story. Other films that do cast over forty get very caught up in themes of ageing, and that feels incredibly irrelevant because there are complex stories that go on, and those particular stories that live within marriages that are ten or twenty years or thirty years down the road. Maybe there is this common misunderstanding that people have their sexual journeys and explorations and that there is a time when that stops. I don't think that has to be true at all. These are very intimate details within a marriage you don't always hear about. It's hard to find ways to bring them to light on the screen that can still be entertaining. Again, it was just about putting these people at the centre of a sexual story.

Can you talk about working alongside Tania Chambers and Judi Levine as producers?

RW: It was terrific. I've known Tania for a really long time. When I was coming up with the concept of this film and writing the script, I knew that I wanted to take it to Tania. It feels like a Tania movie. I think I was right. Tania had seen and loved my short film work, so there was a good creative

51

connection. I also know how much integrity she has. Tania then introduced Judi to the project, and Judi produced *The Sessions* (2012) [which] is one of my favourite films and a reference for this film. That was such an exciting connection to make. Having two producers was terrific because we worked well in our triangulations between ourselves. After all, it meant sometimes one producer would lean in more than the other, and that can be helpful in your creative process.

Can you talk about the best day that you had onset?

RW: There were lots of great days on set. The reality of filmmaking is you don't always know what you're going to get. I often think of it a little bit like cooking. You have your recipe and [even] if you have very good ingredients, you're never quite sure how it's going to come together on the day. We had lots of great ingredients, and so much of that is about your casting. There is a scene in the film between Sally and Erik that involves an exercise bike, and that was something we had to find on the day. That was one of my best days on set.

What does 'find on the day' mean in practice?

RW: I think it is watching what happens when it comes to life when an actor takes on the dialogue and breathes life into it. There are so many different ways of doing it. As a director, I really like to pay attention. I watch. I don't come in and say to everyone "This is how we're going to do it." We've all talked about things, there's been some rehearsals, but there's plenty of scenes you don't get the chance to rehearse. You watch it come to life. You watch everyone jump in and inhabit it and then work out which bit you would change or tweak, and then work out what the words are you have to say to get yourself to that place.

Can you talk about your experience moving from shorts to features? What did you learn along the way?

RW: I went from shorts to feature but in between there was a lot of other filmmaking. Commercials, documentary, and television drama. What you work out is how important your instincts are. As a director, there's a craft to learn and there's all this practice. I worked out that what made my short films work and feel like they came from me were my instincts. So it's about learning how to listen to your instincts and pay attention to them, often in the heat of the moment when things are very busy and there's a lot of pressure to go a certain way, and to not be afraid to lean into your instincts, even if they are counter to what you think or the expected way of doing something. I think a director's instinct is what defines their tone.

INTERVIEW | RENÉE WEBSTER

What does it mean to be an Australian filmmaker making Australian films here?

RW: I think being an Australian filmmaker is very challenging. I'm driven by the story that I want to tell, and that will culturally always feel like an Australian story. I want to answer this politically, Andrew. It's a harrowing time in the Australian filmmaking landscape. I look at the incredible opportunity that is out there at the moment with the amount of really high-end television and streaming content [being made] and the commerce that can come with that, and I see a failure of our federal government to capture the opportunity that is there for Australian filmmaking to get our stories on screen. We need to see Australian children's television shows so our kids are growing up looking at our own stories and our own culture, not trying to be like a different culture.

HOW TO PLEASE A WOMAN

INTERVIEW
PRODUCERS
TANIA CHAMBERS AO & JUDI LEVINE

The act of desexualising the human body and celebrating sexual freedom and exploration sits at the core of Renée Webster's *How to Please a Woman*. It's a notion that attracted producers Tania Chambers and Judi Levine to the project, and helped guide them to bring a women-focused and created film to life.

Building on her work as chief executive at ScreenWest and Screen NSW, Tania created Feisty Dame Productions in 2012, bringing films like Kriv Stenders' *Kill Me Three Times* (2014) and TV series like *Invisible Boys* (2024) to life. Judi Levine has forged a global career, having produced films like *The Sessions* (2012) and the Australian-UK co-production *Falling For Figaro* (2020).

Tania was part of the Gender Matters Taskforce 2020[1], an initiative created by Screen Australia to 'address the underutilisation of female talent in key creative roles in the Australian screen industry.' In 2019, it set a KPI measure 'to have 50% of the key creatives across all projects that receive Screen Australia development <u>and</u> production funding to be women, across a three-year-average.'

This interview was recorded by Andrew F. Peirce in March 2022

What was it like to work with a local talent like Renée Webster?

Tania Chambers: To work with someone like Renée Webster whose talent was clear from when she did her short films all those years ago, *Scoff* (2003) and the subsequent ones, and then she's had a really fine award-winning career in commercials. The challenge to get a feature film script right as a writer, never mind direct it [was there]. She had exactly the right tone that we wanted. We wanted it to be heartfelt. We wanted it to be funny, but we didn't want broad comedy, we were absolutely targeting *The Full Monty* (1997) and *Calendar Girls* (2003) kind of tone. We wanted it to be something that would make you laugh, but the next minute would kick you in the guts as well. And she did that, she managed to get that tone.

HOW TO PLEASE A WOMAN

How important was that authenticity to be carried through in the story, performance, and direction?

TC: The notion of showing real people, real bodies, real women's bodies, real older women's bodies, real older men's bodies, and faces and lines and so on; you don't get to see any of that these days. It's quite shocking. It's kind of being erased from most of our screens, to be honest, never mind [our] lives sometimes. That was important to us. That's the physical side of authenticity. The emotional side was intense as well. We wanted to be able to show men, women, and non-binary people as vulnerable, and sexuality and sensuality is a way where everybody is vulnerable, and it was a vehicle to be able to explore that, wasn't it, Jude?

Judi Levine: Yes. I think that the thing that I gravitate towards, probably both Tania and I, is if something resonates with you and you feel moved by it, you hope that audiences will be as well. When I read the script, immediately there were so many things on the page that I connected with, that I'd either experienced myself or knew other people who had with men and women, and that makes for better storytelling.

In this particular genre, you want people to feel that they relate to who's on the screen and not feel that they're just watching the Ken and Barbie's of the world who are always gorgeous, and they say, "Well, that was a nice story," but not something that they even think for two minutes about when they leave. Being able to bring that sort of authenticity and depth really to a story gives people something to walk out of the cinema and think about, which is not just the storyline but also what they've seen. As Tania referred to, it is this kind of exposure of stuff that's been left off our screens, because somehow [it's] regarded as inappropriate or no one wants to see that. No one wants to see a woman walking down the beach and pulling her bathers down to cover up her bum, but that's so typical. We've all done it. We do it all the time. Maybe men don't. But women do it all the time.

I certainly do.

JL: There you go. In your budgie smugglers. We didn't want to shy away from that stuff, and just perpetuate that. We wanted to break those taboos. Renée is fantastic at doing that.

How to Please a Woman reinforces how important it is to desexualise the human body, which is so often presented in a physical, arousing manner on screen. As producers, was that a key thing to highlight while also representing the sexual desire of women, non-binary, and queer folks as well?

INTERVIEW | TANIA CHAMBERS & JUDI LEVINE

JL: Absolutely. When Gina, our character, is talking at the end of the film and she says, "It's for all those women who haven't given up on sex," and that sense of reaching a certain age and feeling that you're not desirable anymore, or you don't still have some interest in sex, or that somehow just because your body has the shape and the scars of having carried children or having worked a long time or just gravity, that those things don't make you necessarily feel disinterested in sex. We want all of that, and I think it was a real thing for Tania and me to go out there and be able to say that out loud, shout it from the rooftops, "Come on people, let's keep having an interest. It doesn't even have to be intercourse, it can just be touching, it can be intimacy in so many different ways." This was a great opportunity to say that, and I think says it succinctly.

Those sorts of difficult subjects are so much more approachable for audiences when there's humour woven in with it so that they can laugh about it because it's a little bit awkward or whatever the case might be, but it puts it out there. We've had men say, "I'm learning stuff here." You're like, "Whoa, were you just such a terrible person in bed before this?" I think that's been important for both of us to put that out there. It's interesting, because Renée's younger than me, and yet she was able to put that out there in a way, write those words and give those women that dialogue and those characters that represent that in such a terrific way.

TC: What's interesting about this film right now is that it fits into all the discussions that are going on at the moment in the context of everything from gender equality and MeToo and looking at the notion of people being able to speak out and also control and own their own bodies, the notion of consent, all sorts of things. I've been doing some discussions and talks in that space, and I was finding the thread in so many of them, lines that were coming through what is in the script and in the performances and realising that it's part of a much bigger discussion that's going on at the moment. It's timely, but again, as Jude said, so succinct.

When the beautiful character played by Hayley McElhinney says, "Is everything you've ever learned about sex from porn?" His reaction is hilarious, he doesn't even speak, he just looks at her. Then that little moment that talks about listening with your hands and so on; you could write books about that, but it's all distilled down into that little moment. There are so many other moments like that that were very carefully crafted. I'm proud that it's speaking to people of all different ages and different sexual identifications as well.

JL: We worked extremely hard to make sure that it was sensitive, that it wasn't exploitative, that there was a voice from both genders and also from people who weren't necessarily just heterosexual. We wanted to be sure that that was there. It's not entirely a thing about flipping the male gaze, it's there to give people a sense that this is a subject you can talk about, and be more open about it, let's listen to each other more when it comes to what we want and what we feel we're comfortable asking for or not asking for everywhere. At work, at home, and in the bedroom.

Mentioning this film to people in the lead-up to watching it, and the women who I've talked to have said, "This sounds like the film I need to drag my partner along to," and the men have been like, "It must be a very short film." Were there any similar reactions when in pre-production, especially with the title itself?

TC: As you would know, we're in an international marketplace seeking funding against hundreds of thousands of other scripts. We needed to stand out. We do get the privilege of going to international marketplaces, but it's not quite as glamorous as it sounds, because we're doing ten half-hour meetings and elevator pitches every time you pick up a glass of wine, all day for ten days or so, and trying to get someone to "Buy me, buy me." So, the title was quite cheekily and deliberately chosen so that you knew they would not forget you at the end of those ten days. That title is not going to go away. It did immediately get a reaction from every single person and a lot of the people that you're pitching to still in our industry are men in senior executive positions. So that was always something that, for a start, was fun for Jude and I because we're cheeky.

JL: We did have a lot of fun.

TC: Basically. The top priority in there is to have fun. Also, it did cause that reaction. As soon as you've got any kind of reaction, you've got a greater chance of getting it over the line. So, it was partly because we were passionate about the content. It was also from a business sense that we were quite acutely aware of the marketing hook in a way.

JL: Seriously, people still get the title wrong when you tell them what it is. Mostly, it's attracted an enormous amount of attention. You always get all those funny comments about "That's never going to be possible" or whatever the case might be, but it sticks, as Tania says. It really sticks.

What are some of the alternative versions of the title that you've heard?

TC: Oh god. I don't think there's any problem saying this but way back it was "Her Predilection." It was exciting as this was one of the Gender Matters Task Force[2] projects at Screen Australia that was funded. We've been working on it since 2016. It had other titles at different times. I do remember that one that we knew wouldn't stick, it was a working title. But God, it was a gobful.

How important and successful has the Gender Matters program been?

TC: I'm a little bit biased because I'm on the task force at the moment. I think what's fascinating is that the research that's been done [shows that] there have been several key interventions and levers that have led to greater gender equality in certain areas. The most dramatic of those is in scripted TV drama where Screen Australia introduced a requirement that for anything that had more than one block or in any series, there had to be at least one female director in the series. That has dramatically changed the number of female directors, and now we know we have internationally successful and multiple choices to be able to make of female directors for television.

Features, it's still a big challenge in the directing area. It's quite different in various roles of producers and writers, but in the scripted area it's still very challenging with writers; I'm mostly talking about drama here rather than factual. What is quite dramatic is the areas in which Screen Australia has not been involved and the state agencies, there are real issues. What's more, if you look at reality TV and you look at different types of content that are made that Screen Australia doesn't fund. [It's] an absolute debacle of percentages still.

The other massive thing is that when you look at heads of departments in various areas trying to get gender parity, there is a massive challenge still. The cinematographers have been great, and the Australian Cinematographers Society has got into it. They're focused on how they get people through the ranks and get people to have a chance. We're looking at all sorts of different strategies there.

For us, it was very big, because it was Renée's first feature script; certainly, first produced as a writer, and then separately as a director, and also from WA. In all of the West Coast Visions' films, there wasn't a female director until Jub Clerc's *Sweet As* (2023) and ours; there may have been producers or writers who were female, I think. [The] scheme has been running [for over a decade]. Gender Matters said, "We have picked you out of all of the talent in Australia as being a talent to watch and to back." From that point, we then had superb development support from both ScreenWest and Screen Australia and went from there. But [it took] many years and many drafts.

This is a proudly woman-driven production. Does that feed back into the production a lot? Is that as important as who's behind the camera, and what's being produced?

59

HOW TO PLEASE A WOMAN

JL: Yes. It's a broad statement to say but there's a difference between the way women perceive the world and men perceive the world and what will stand out to them when they're looking at what's available in front of the lens. There's a different atmosphere in the whole filmmaking process. When you're marrying that, bringing a woman's sensibility who's directing and writing and the rest of the women on the crew – in our case, 50% of the crew were women – as you bring all of that together, you bring results to the finished product which is likely to have been different to the way a man would have done the same thing.

That is a broad generalisation. I've known men to create very sensitive films and tell women characters perfectly well, so I don't think that you can draw a hard line. But I do think that Tania and I, – with this film in particular, which is very women-centric both in content and in the storytelling – saw all of the benefits of having all that. We did have a male DP (Ben Nott) which was an interesting balance. It just worked out that way, as so many things do. We did set out to crew with as many women as possible and have as many of the heads of department as women as possible. Pretty much all the major decision-making was by women. The sensibility of the material makes a difference when you've got a community of women working to make this project come together and succeed.

The film also manages to show off WA and Fremantle in a powerful manner.

TC: About Freo and WA on screen, what I'm aware of is [that] we are more familiar with the streets of LA and of New York – and most of the viewers in the world are – than we are of our own cities. And that's kind of nuts.

We're so spoiled in WA. One of the things that people talked about for years was in the context of not having a studio like other places did; we used to say that the locations and the extraordinary scenery was our outback studio. In a way, the point of difference [is] how we see our place as well. That was what was lovely because both Renée and I swim regularly. She's a proper swimmer, like in the film. I'm a bobber. I call it 'the slow bob.' But none of us can stay out of the water.

I think that notion of the integration of all of that, I'm sure that's got a whole lot of subconscious themes that are through the film one way or another. It's been something that gives me a massive amount of joy, putting WA locations up on the screen. In *A Few Less Men* (2017), my second feature, I couldn't get over the fact that perhaps in commercials but certainly not in features or TV then, the Pinnacles had never actually been on the big screen. For me, there are some special places in *Kill Me Three Times*. For example, apart from the extraordinary white sand dunes up at Lancelin and so on, down at Boranup Forest in Margaret River, those trees don't look like anywhere else in the world. It is with great pride that I am able to go [film there].

And it's a little bit of trying to overcome the cultural cringe. In the general creative and arts world, it's time for us to own the fact that we are world-class and at times excel beyond others. I don't know about tall poppy stuff, but at least stop having a cultural cringe as much as we can.

Watching I Met a Girl (2021), 100% Wolf (2020), and How to Please a Woman, there's something that's heart-warming about seeing Fremantle on screen. It doesn't look like any other city. It's unique.

TC: This is where politicians and others need to think and realise what a sense of pride in your place does. That's much broader than what they're thinking about in terms of taxpayer funding for culture and the arts. It is something that energises you and it's something that makes you proud of where you are. And it is something that commits you to a place which is where you do business and do your exporting from and employ people from and all that stuff.

At times, I get very frustrated that people could be so short-sighted about what's the big picture of the impact of culture and the arts in creating a sense of pride and a distinct place and who we are. And community. I mean, we throw the words around but at the end of the day, what are the values that we in our society in Australia believe about? It's those core things, that beautiful sense of community.

What does it mean to be an Australian producer making Australian films?

JL: I've just spent 25 years living somewhere else and I don't want to leave [here]. I don't want to leave. I love being an Australian producer. I'm happy being an international producer. I don't see myself boxed. I've had to be very patient as I've worked my way back into the Australian film industry. That's not always easy when you've been away quite a while and a lot of people have changed. You do come up against that tall poppy stuff still just because you've been away. [Even if you] have all this experience working in other places, it doesn't make you special, but it does mean you've got some valuable stuff to contribute. I like to bring that in.

I've just had a ball working on two Australian films back-to-back. *Falling For Figaro* (2022) we shot in Scotland, but we came here to do a post on that, and then thank heavens we got *How to Please A Woman* up because otherwise I would have had to go back to LA. I've been able to stay here for two years, probably a bit to the chagrin of my children who think that

HOW TO PLEASE A WOMAN

I ought to go back and see them. I'm doing that, but I would be happy not to, I'd be happy to stay here.

I think Australian producers should be proud of what they're achieving over here. It's a different kind of system, but every system is competitive. You learn to work the system here. There's an enormous amount of talent here and enthusiasm. We're good storytellers. We're connected to a community of people who've been telling stories for 60,000 years. We have a great sense of humour to bring to some of the stories we tell, and we can tell our own stories, and we can start telling stories that are more global or that have a broad global appeal. I certainly think that *How to Please a Woman* is something that the women I know all over the world will relate to. There's no question about it.

These sorts of things that we're talking about are without a doubt international, and that's very appealing. Australia is producing more and more great stuff. It's not always easy to get it seen overseas, there's still sort of a sense of "Oh it's *Australian*" kind of thing. Whereas the British somehow overcame that, people don't shy away so much. That seems to be shifting a little bit. And certainly, streaming makes a big difference to that. That's a whole other conversation about how many people get to see it in the theatre and how many people get to see it if you're streaming, and how do we feel about that? I'm incredibly proud to be in these movies and the rest of the ones that I've got going with other people and together, Tania and I, in the future. I love being an Australian producer.

People love Australians, too. It's something that we wear proudly overseas. It's great to be an Australian. They think very highly of us and love working with us. They love the fact that we're pretty much straight. There's no BS going on, you just want to cut to the chase, is this or isn't this going to work? Let's not tap dance around each other for ages having dinners and meetings before we make any kind of decision. They like that about us. They love our crews because they work hard but they keep a sense of humour about it. They don't complain too much, they know how to have a good time. We've got a lot going for us when it comes to the world of entertainment, whether it's film or theatre or any of those things.

TC: I love being fiercely Australian and passionately internationally at the same time. My one frustration is that a lot of younger Aussie filmmakers say, "I don't want to make an Australian film." I keep saying to them, that Australian films can be local as well as resonate internationally in the subject matter. I look at the extraordinary filmmakers that have gone before us as Australian filmmakers and I am proud to be placed amid them with three features under my belt. I look at the work and how they've touched people and been recognised for being world-class and [I'm] very, very proud to be amongst them.

JL: Also, young people don't go to Australian movies enough. From a business point of view, one of the difficulties is that you can't rely solely on an Australian box office to meet all of your needs and get a really strong return for your investors, whether it's a government funding body or private investors, and there's more and more of those coming in these days. You have to be able to make Australian films, if possible, that will have a wider reach. It's not like Finland or Greece or any of those places are necessarily making films for an international market, but they love it when they do get international recognition. But Australia, if we can be telling stories that have a wider reach, then from a business point of view, you want that and it's the best way of promoting Australia. I mean, that's the outreach, right? People see these films and then they think, "I want to go there" or "People are making movies over there like this. I want to see if I can work in the Australian industry." Maybe we can set up more partnerships and so on, keeping it going like that. I think you want to get that balance between making Australian films for Australians and having an outreach to a broader audience that's beyond New Zealand.

People are often surprised that there are as many as one hundred Australian films released each year. The awareness of them becomes a different thing altogether.

TC: I was told [there were] 600 films released in Australia last year, that's the context people don't know. Now I know some of those will be Hindi or Telugu or Cantonese or Mandarin and others, and some of those are the biggest box office of all of them. A lot of the [Australian] films didn't come through the Screen Australia or regional funding agency system, and that can be exhilarating on the one hand and laudable. On the other hand, it can also mean that there's not a pathway to get into that cinema type of release; not that cinema release is the only way to get there. It's interesting in the streaming world [where] a lot of our great directors from WA have now become very successful internationally [and] have been commissioned by streamers to make world-class films for their platforms. There seems to be a little less of an awareness of whether it's Australian or not Australian once you hit a streamer.

ENDNOTES
1 Gender Matters, Screen Australia - https://www.screenaustralia.gov.au/sa/new-directions/gender-matters - Accessed 28 April 2024
2 https://www.screenaustralia.gov.au/sa/media-centre/backgrounders/2021/10-27-gender-matters-2021

96 mins
Director: *Martin Wilson*
Writer: *Monique Wilson*
Cast: *Monique Wilson, Allegra Teo, Dalip Sondhi, Megan Aspinall, Alexander Arco, Katherine Marmion, David Genat, Luke Jai McIntosh, Stacy Teuber, Michael Ferguson, Murray Dowsett, Ashanti Suriyam, Desiree Davis*
Producers: *Nicole Ferraro, Martin Wilson*
Music: *Tim Count*
Cinematography: *Jim Frater*
Editing: *Lawrie Silvestrin*

In 2022, Pieces received AACTA Award nominations for Best Indie Film and Best Costume Design in Film (Monique Wilson, Kristie Rowe).

INTERVIEW
DIRECTOR MARTIN WILSON & PRODUCER NICOLE FERRARO

Director Martin Wilson made the unexpected jump from *Great White* (2021), a menacing shark flick, to *Pieces* (2022), a drama about a group of people who meet at an art therapy class and have their lives changed, but it was a jump made with purpose. For Martin, making the film alongside wife and producer Nicole Ferraro meant that he could honour the mental illness struggle that people like his brother live with. *Pieces* is an independent film, made with creative guidance from Helping Minds, a Western Australian based organisation that provides support to those who are impacted by mental illness.

This interview contains discussions of mental illness and trauma.

This interview was recorded by Andrew F. Peirce in September 2022

How did your relationship with Helping Minds start?

Martin Wilson: I was shooting a lot of commercial and corporate work for Helping Minds. I had directed a series of mini documentaries called *Real Stories* that depicted the raw, intimate stories of carers and their experience with mental health. I have a lived experience with my brother, who lives with schizophrenia, so I had a passion for this social topic. It seemed to be the right fit for me.

I always wanted to do a film about mental illness. I pitched an idea to Helping Minds, which was originally a series, and then it morphed into a 24-minute short film. I felt that to get this message out there; to get people talking and make an impact, a feature film was the best medium for it to be noticed. We shot most of the film within the initial five-day shoot, and then we did some pick-up shoots during post-production as the story was coming together in the edit. We kept chipping away and refining the narrative with the writer, Monique Wilson, and then I kept honing it from there.

PIECES

We didn't want it to be all bleak and dark. We wanted to put a lot of heart behind it. We also wanted it to be authentic, so it had to be confronting and raw as well. Real life is not all black, it's not all white. We tried to have nuance there.

One of the key reasons we made the film is that we wanted to take away judgement from people. We don't label the various challenges that people are going through. We want people to speak openly and honestly about their daily experiences and not be judged for it. We want people to see people that are going through the challenges as normal. That stigma really exists, and we wanted to start that conversation. I love it when people talk very openly and honestly about it and the sense that you're not going to be judged for it. People do have these moments, but it's not always going to be like that.

Nicole Ferraro: They're not defined by what they're going through or their diagnosis. The film delves into the relationships between the carers, the people living with mental illness, the friends, the people around them and those experiences.

The performances are vulnerable. How did you get the cast to that point where they were able to access those kinds of emotions?

MW: One of the biggest challenges for me was the one-week shoot constraint. I knew I had to make sure that the performances were authentic so people could believe that this was real. I worked with Annie Murtagh-Monks as the performance coach. We spent a whole week before the shoot, teasing out the characters along with Monique, going through in great detail every scene. We worked with the actors to help them research and delve into their characters, so they really knew who they were playing and why they were playing them. That was critical because a lot of the film was built around a pseudo-documentary approach. I was asking very off-the-cuff questions, but because the actors really knew their characters, the answers they gave in those pseudo-documentary moments came across as very real and raw.

I take my hat off to Monique for the research and work she did on the screenplay and how committed the actors were, working with Annie to find the truth, owning the moment, and always being authentic. We've had comments from the audience that they didn't know that these people were actors, which is the best thing for us.

You're in the film in some capacity. What was that like putting yourself in front of the camera?

MW: It was out of necessity. I'm obscured because I certainly didn't want to be a feature or obvious. It was a technique I used to move the film quickly.

INTERVIEW | MARTIN WILSON & NICOLE FERRARO

When I was in the edit suite, if there was something I said was wrong, I could just re-voice it, and change the narrative. It was easy because I was in the edit with Lawrie Silvestrin, and we could go, "Okay, how do we make this work?" I was there to be a certain type of character where I would be a bit of a provocateur, to try and incite a little bit of drama and tease out what's behind the curtain with these characters. Obviously, I'm not an actor, that's why I'm in the shadows.

Nicole, how do you balance being a producer and wrangling a production in a short period of time?

NF: Tighter parameters can often make for more succinct decision-making. We had to find ways to use the constraints in the project's favour. Communication is also always key. I tried to have a lot of transparent conversations as early as possible with people about our approach with this project. Our First AD Michael Boyle was sensational at maximising the shoot schedule and the locations with a very thoughtful approach to the story. Lauren McDonough, who was our production coordinator, was one person that works similarly to me, so we were able to bounce off each other to keep the mix of on and off-set congruent.

Marty and I sat down at the start and thought, "How are we actually going to do this?" It was ambitious. We kept the crew small and nimble. As always, planning and mitigating potential problems where I could. I spent most of a decade being crew side in the costume department, so I took that understanding into my approach with the crew's needs, knowing what slows them down and what can help them do their job more efficiently. We also worked closely with Cinematographer Jim Frater on how we could equip his department for speed to maximise coverage.

MW: I knew Jim had done *The Heights*. He's brilliantly talented with no ego. It's a nice combination to have on such a tight shoot. He's extremely generous. We went down the cinéma verité approach of handheld, and whatever we got with two cameras, we got. We blazed away and went for it.

NF: We also minimised the locations as we didn't want to waste any time moving around unnecessarily. We found an out-of-use building at the University of Western Australia that allowed us to shoot many script locations in and around the one spot.

What lessons did you learn from going from a shark flick to a film about mental health?

MW: To me, filmmaking is about a good script and good performances. I've been focusing on that for so many years and I knew that that's what a director gets judged on. What I did learn with *Great White* was that films are made in pre-production. Scriptwriting isn't the most expensive part of the process. Nicole and I had minimal locations, we workshopped the actors, and we did all those things that made the process of shooting reasonably doable.

All those craft levels that I was doing in *Great White*, which is more suspense and action, a lot of time these people are on a raft, so I had to make sure to the best of what I could do that the performances were solid. I wanted to showcase that. I didn't want to be pigeonholed as being 'that guy to make the shark film'. There's a lot more to me and a lot more to our team than that. I want to be practising directing because you don't get many opportunities at it, so the only way to get better is to just get out there and do it.

I had a passion for this because it was such a personal project. It's the one project that I was going to do on a micro-budget. I was going to throw every ounce of my 25 years at it. Fail or don't fail, I was going to have a crack at it. It was different. I didn't have the machine behind me. It was also very freeing because I just went back to my uni days at Murdoch when I had a small crew, and I could shoot really quickly. It was fun filmmaking with your friends and you're having fun, and you don't have the same pressures on you in the bigger world with a much larger team and longer schedule.

NF: Composer Tim Count and editor Lawrie Silvestrin came on board to *Pieces* after working with Marty on *Great White*. Although a very different project, knowing how well they had worked together brought us so much confidence and excitement into post-production.

MW: *Pieces* is such a Western Australian film. It is a community-based film. It's a film where we had all local actors, crew and post-production. These are all from relationships that we've built up over 25 years. Kim Lord, who did the sound design along with Ben Morris, were just amazing in what they gave to the film in terms of being so generous. The film showcases the local team's talent.

You showcase Perth in a way that we rarely get to see. The aerial shots make the city look beautiful. It makes you feel proud of the place where you live.

MW: We often get feedback about Scott Slawinski's drone footage being so cinematic. The reason I got to know Scott was because he'd done this 'May the Fourth Be with You' movie (*Cloud City Chaos*, 2022) which was shot all around WA. I thought that was amazing. I contacted him on LinkedIn and then got him into this film and had also done some commercial work with him. The other thing coming from TV commercials is that in WA you're trying to maximise production values. Doing that for years, I put that experience into film. Scott had a unique eye from an aerial perspective that I had not seen before.

The team's dynamic is an opportunity to bring different perspectives together to create something really innovative. We regularly get comments from audiences that they "Haven't seen Perth like **that**", or "It's nice to see Perth like that". It could be a different city; it just happens to be our city, Perth. When you've got no money and no time, you've got to have some X factors that you're trying to dig out of nowhere. It was like trying to give it a bit of an international lift. Because we didn't have the budget, you try and look for these little trick items in your back pocket.

NF: Kent Hosokawa graded the film and it's so beautiful and rich and also connects the palette of Kristie Rowe's artwork throughout the film. The sound design team – Benjamin Morrison, Kim Lord, and their crew – created all the sounds of the city, and it brings that urban experience when paired with the visuals.

MW: I wanted a real surreal, glossy, artsy look for the grade. Kent had also worked on *The Heights* and we just hit it off. I just can't believe how good a job they had done with some very challenging images including some very basic lighting setups. That's indie filmmaking. We even used a wheelchair at some point when we were doing some dolly shots. That's going down to the chemist and hiring a wheelchair to achieve the movement, moving and handheld.

Let's talk about the costumes, in particular the Alexander McQueen-style clothes that Tom [Luke Jai McIntosh] wears. How important was the costume design and getting it spot on?

NF: It had developed organically through the pre-production process. We discussed how to approach it and whether or not I was going to do it. Monique Wilson, the writer and lead actor, knew the characters and worked with the actors during rehearsals to explore the right pieces. She executed the majority of the costumes and collaborated with Fremantle artist Kristie Rowe, who designed and made the feathered wings, headwear and the costumes in the dance performance. There are also some of her headpieces and bits of jewellery that Tom also wears throughout the film. They both did an exceptional job. Tom, being an aspiring designer and as a key component of his character arc, required an edgier and theatrical aesthetic.

We also wanted to minimise costume changes, as they can slow things down on the shoot and can sometimes limit options in the edit. Every character has an iconic look, some more dramatic than others. Alfred Hitchcock noted the importance of identifying a character by their silhouette. That certainly comes through with our cast and their costume, together with Tess Rowe's hair and makeup design. Marty and I were so inspired by the silhouette of Luke Jai McIntosh as Tom that we engaged photographer Mauro Palmieri to shoot the stills for our key poster which was designed by Jeremy Sweeting.

How did the choreography and the discussions around presenting the dance sequence go?

MW: Monique had some dancing experience, and Ashanti Suriyam who plays Laya is a dancer and choreographer and also runs a dance studio. Monique worked with Ashanti to choreograph the dance sequence to make it as cinematic as possible. The key to constructing the dance performance was that it reflected the themes and the story of the film, including regeneration, hope, empathy, compassion, and connectivity between the community and how you get through all these challenges. We wanted it to be dynamic and reflective of the arc of the character, so there's a growth in that dance. Even though there is tragedy, the final dance is joyous. It reflects the final scene where the mother and the daughter are battling through the film and end in an embrace. It is there to imply that the relationship is never going to be perfect (like any relationship), but at that point in time, it was a common ground that was met between them, and it comes from the dance performance.

Some of my favourite movies are musicals. *Easter Parade* (1948) and *Meet Me in St Louis* (1944) come to mind. Those Hollywood musicals have big, cinematic dance sequences. They have the intensity of a chase sequence. They're cinematic in the construction because you're trying to tell a story similarly to an action sequence.

NF: Stage performance also demands a different lighting set up. The theatre location is a unique setting within the film. It brings different emotions. There's the perspective of Laya looking out to the audience and her place on the stage. There's no dialogue, it's just the movement and sound. A moment of pure vulnerability for the characters.

What does it mean to be an Australian filmmaker working right now?

MW: For Nicole and I, we do feel the isolation of where we're at in terms of connectivity with people and being able to meet them and build rapport. There are great events like CinefestOz where you can showcase your film and you get a chance to meet people who have an international perspective, and they can give you some great feedback and you go, 'Okay, maybe you're on the right track.' But we do feel our isolation. With a young family, it is not easy to jump on a plane or relocate.

I don't think there's been a more challenging time in terms of independent cinema. It's very hard for exhibitors working today. They're relying a lot on event screenings. The whole cinema experience has changed for filmmakers because of the pandemic. People are drawn to the cinema to see big Marvel-type productions, and then of course there's streaming as well. To try and get people out of their homes is the next challenge. You're not always doing an *Elvis* or *Top Gun Maverick*. They're big cinema experiences, and I certainly enjoyed them, but we're here doing much smaller productions without the $20 million P&A behind us.

Nicole and I work 24/7 because we don't have a large team behind us. It's quite daunting to be constantly trying to get your work out there. The opportunities are slim to get your next film going. I'm experiencing that now, even with some of the projects that I've got out there that are further developed, and still building a track record, there is no guarantee for your next production.

NF: The challenges and changes of the last few years have certainly been an interesting and adaptive time. Zoom calls becoming an accepted and standard form of communication was a small, yet significant shift for us being based in Perth, Western Australia. This did, for a period, help reduce the isolation. There was no expectation to get on a plane during that time. But you can never replace in-person, human connection so I think this approach has shifted back to the importance of in-person meetings.

Since we self-released *Pieces* theatrically with the support of our Executive Producers Ryan Hodgson and Melissa Kelly from Factor 30 Films and Ian Hale from Halo Films and The Backlot, we had to get creative to get people into the cinema. *Pieces* was invited to open the Western Australian Mental Health Week in 2022 and then subsequently screened regionally across the state that week which was supported by the Western Australian Association for Mental Health and the Western Australian Mental Health Commission. This affirmed the importance of the film, and we were able to reach audiences in regional cinemas such as Albany, Broome, Busselton, Geraldton, Karratha, and Kalgoorlie. We also managed to sell out seventeen, by-demand screenings at The Backlot in West Perth. As well as screenings in Melbourne, Sydney, Brisbane, Lismore, and Townsville. This was a significant, yet modest result for a film like *Pieces*. We managed all of this, from the press, promotion, and handing out flyers, to posting out posters and DCPs. It has taught us that we must think outside of the box during the process and the value of finding like-minded people to collaborate with to get the best result and experience for audiences.

GOOD NIGHT

8 mins
Director: *David Vincent Smith*
Writer: *David Vincent Smith*
Cast: *Caroline Brazier, Clarence Ryan*
Producer: *Kate Separovich*
Original Score: *Brian Kruger*
Cinematography: *Mahmudul Raz*
Editing: *Lenny Rudeberg, David Vincent Smith*

INTERVIEW
FILMMAKER
DAVID VINCENT SMITH

Perth-based filmmaker David Vincent Smith (DVS) knows what kind of filmmaker he wants to be. He knows the path that he needs to take to strengthen his filmmaking skills. And most importantly, he knows how to tell a story. For DVS, it's clear that telling stories is a personal endeavour that helps him seek out the compassion that exists in the world. In 2024, DVS released his debut feature film, *He Ain't Heavy*.

With the short film *Good Night* (2022), DVS tells the story of a sound engineer (Clarence Ryan) who accepts a late-night recording job from a desperate woman (Caroline Brazier). He's eager to get home to his family, while she is looking for someone to help create a recording in honour of her child who has passed away.

This interview was recorded by Andrew F. Peirce in February 2022

What inspired you to become a filmmaker?

David Vincent Smith: I never really thought of being a filmmaker because I'd never really imagined I could. I watched movies and the credits would come up with all these people's names. It seemed so foreign, the idea that you could possibly have a job doing that. When I was younger, I mostly read books. I wanted to be a writer and wrote stories and was encouraged by teachers. I wrote a novel when I was eighteen, an examination into my own mental health and more a journal than anything. It's terrible. That was an important stepping stone in realising I could start and complete a large project, which is the difficulty in writing feature scripts.

When I was a teenager, I started watching more obscure films, stuff that was more interesting and challenging. Then I went to university to study and get some kind of job to provide being an author. I couldn't stay in that class. I consecutively failed units. Then I enrolled in some random film course at TAFE to pass the time while I went and studied psychology. I was failing that because I was a terrible student. I wasn't rocking up. I had an

GOOD NIGHT

amazing lecturer, and he said, "I think you have something to say, I think you're not doing the right thing." He rented out a camera under his name, gave it to me and said, "If you go and make a short film with this, I'll think about letting you pass this semester."

Being given the power and being able to make all those choices in the edit suite, it lit the fire. My brain went, "Wait a minute. Filmmaking is storytelling in a visual medium." Suddenly the translation happened. It's not that I want to be an author: I want to be a storyteller. At that moment, I'd been doing a lot of storytelling, writing, and performing music. I represented WA nationally and internationally as a poet in competitions. I put a huge amount of pressure on myself. I felt, "Everyone's been doing all this stuff with filmmaking." I was only nineteen or twenty, but I felt like I was a million miles behind.

Even now, to this day, I run my own film school every night. I have books, I study, I do research. I run this program to try and build this education. I think now it's easier for kids to dream of being filmmakers because the technology is there. I didn't have smartphones when I was a teenager. For Australian film and TV, it seems more like a realistic thing as opposed to people [who go] "You're going to study film? What the hell are you going to do with that degree?"

I then went aggressively down that pathway. I started to get incredibly honest with myself, "I'm a bartender in Northbridge. I want to be a film director with films in Cannes." I'm a realistic person, "What I need to do is map the pathway from how you go from there, to there. What is my education? TAFE in Western Australia." I don't have an issue with TAFE, it's really good, but do I have the edge to be competitive on a world stage? I compare filmmaking [to] the Olympics. It's not even good enough to get into the Olympic team. It's not even good enough to get into the final. If you don't place in the medal, your film's probably not even going to get a release or going to profit. I started thinking, "I need to train like an athlete. I need to get to that level."

I Googled, "Who is the best directing tutor in the world?" I found Judith Weston. Whether it's Taika Waititi, Ava DuVernay, or Steve McQueen, they all said, "Judith Weston's the best." I emailed and asked, "How do I study with you?" Her husband got back and said, "We're running this course." I saved all my bar money, and went to LA. There were nine students in my class. Three had won best commercial at Cannes, the other was an editor for Universal Studios and cut all Will Ferrell's films, and the other was the DoP from *Parks and Recs*. I was from TAFE. "Holy shit, this is where I need to be." I went back to Perth with a lot more confidence. She demystified the directing process.

INTERVIEW | DAVID VINCENT SMITH

A lot of people treat directing like it's black magic art. 'You go into a room and write.' No, there is a series of things that you can do to help actors create a good performance. There are a series of things you can do to prepare for a movie. What are you building that's going to help you articulate your own voice? What's unique about this film as opposed to just where the camera is going to go? Why is the camera going to go there? How does it support theme and character?

The moment that I decided to take it seriously, I never looked back. I watched friends buy houses, get married, have kids. I'm closer to forty than twenty, but I know that in my heart, I'm so happy. I don't regret that. I feel good about what I'm doing. I've always landed on my feet somehow. When you care and you put in the hours and you take it seriously, it just happens.

There are so many things I've made that people have never seen. I've got four hundred private videos of all kinds of things I've shot and cut that no one's ever seen. That launched me into getting editing work. I did assembly editing on *Rams* (2020). I got to see all the rushes come in and cut scenes for that film. All those things were random. The well pays you back in a way.

What does it mean to be a Perth filmmaker and part of the Perth community?

DVS: Perth filmmaking is amazing. Everyone champions everyone because you're all on the same team. I remember thinking about when someone said to me "What's going to happen if you lose West Coast Visions[1]?" I was up against my really good friend Zoe [Pepper] who I had been sharing an office with, and we had been writing our films together that were about to go into competition. Sure, it would have been a little bit disappointing and disheartening, but at the same time, she would have probably hired my DoP and half my friends so they would have jobs. You can't be that disappointed. 'Okay, my friend got to make their first feature film and hired all my friends. That's a good thing.' You want them to do well.

Being a filmmaker in Perth, you feel super supported. I've never really felt like there's been a barrier to me speaking to people. I've always been able to communicate with people and always felt like they wanted to listen and help me. It's very different to some of my experiences in America where I was at a pitching round table. We had these successful producers – they'd had about five films at Sundance – and there were six or seven writer-directors around the table. Everyone had half an hour to do their thing. I was being nice and polite, waiting for my turn to speak. "I'm never going to speak; these people just dominate." Then I realised that one of these people had a link to an Australian film, and they had been an EP on *Buoyancy* (2019). This is the value of doing your research. I said, "I saw you were on *Buoy-*

ancy." The guy was like "Oh yeah." These two directors from LA were trying to pitch female-driven horror and were like "Have you seen *The Babadook*? You've all got to see *Babadook*." I said, "The producer of *The Babadook* is on top of our film as our mentor." You'd never seen so many people on the table go "Right." I'm like, "Now that I have something to offer you," whereas I just wanted to chat because we're all filmmakers. I think there is that real intent to sell and intent to be somebody. You don't get that in Perth as much. That's what I like about it. I'm just happy to chat with people about film. I like film and you like film and that's kind of all it needs to be.

What are you watching when you're doing your own film classes for yourself?

DVS: At the moment I'm trying to rework and educate myself back through semiotics and meaning and signs and signifiers. As directors, everything is a choice, all the things that we can pack meaning into a frame. I'm reworking my way through all the theories and all the philosophers, going back to early Eisenstein and Russian montage, and the debate between Russian film schools of theory and American film school theory. It sounds kind of weird and abstract, and does it have a purpose? Well, yes, it does.

You start to think about the choices that you're making. Usually, I'll pick a subject or a concept like an ellipsis, for example, and then I'll go through films that use that well, like *A Man Escaped* (1956) or *Cold War* (2018). These films are confident and make bold, strong cuts. I usually try and deep dive on different ideas. What I'm trying to do is roar up my brain and keep it open to the muse to come and go, "I think this is a good choice for your film."

I'll give you an example with my feature, *He Ain't Heavy*. One of the things I was interested in was point of view. I want this film to always be from the point of view of my character. What does point of view mean? Is it just what the person can see? Is it what they can see inside their mind? I'm seeing you here, but then inside my head, I might have a random flash of a frame and it's showing what the point of view looks like. What you might think is a normal dark Australian drama has scenes that question point of view. Why is the traffic light now a strobe light, and she's seeing visions of herself dancing? To me, that is how you experience life. Those scenes wouldn't exist if I hadn't done that deep dive into what point of view in a film means.

I look at different things and then I write my own essays. What happens when a film doesn't have a soundtrack? What does that do to a scene? All those kinds of things keep my brain away from the idea. I think this is the danger that directors make, they decide what the movie is and it's cut [in their mind] before they've shot a frame. What you want to do is you want to be so open that when you arrive on set, you've got all this preparation, all these plans, everything's done. Then in real life, you're like "The Sun is going down. Let's go capture that." Steve McQueen refers to that as catching butterflies. You're walking around with a net; you're waiting for those moments. If I can get three or four of those in a film, I'll be happy. To me, the greatest thing about being on set is you're there and you have all this material. You're present, you're almost inside the scene. The thing that I love about doing all that research is about giving my ability to see deeper into the moment of the opportunities that exist rather than maybe making the obvious choice, which is what I'm trying to always avoid.

What does the Australian film school mean to you?

DVS: I think lots of Australian films are about wrestling with who you are and your identity within this continent. The continent is a vast world of beaches versus rural remote versus desert. For me, they're the ingredients to strip back and get to what it means to be a human or who you are, and its place in the world. When you watch these great Australian films, – *Mad Max* (1979), *Cargo* (2017), *The Rover* (2014) – they always seem to be this opportunity to dig into who we are as people, what we believe, and why we do what we do. *Tracks* (2013) is a good example of that. "I'm just going to walk across the desert," but then it becomes such a human story. That's one of my favourite Australian films. *Samson and Delilah* (2009) had a small crew and a singular voice of a person. That's what I like about Australian cinema; it's a combat between our place in the world and the land and the history of Australia. How do you find a puzzle of 90-120 minutes that does that? That's the real frame that you have to make that portrait of Australia.

The identity of what it means to be a parent is a prominent theme in Good Night. What does the identity of being a parent mean to you?

DVS: It's huge. I have fifteen foster siblings. The transformational power of love is the biggest thing in my storytelling. How powerfully can a single act of kindness change someone's life? I watched my mum take in kids; I'm talking about some of the most traumatised children this state has. When one of my brothers came to live with me, he was mute, he's got a mental disability. As a kid, I was like, "I can't even see how this guy's gonna go to school, let alone have a job." He graduated high school and has a job now. He's one of the most inspiring people in my life. My oldest sister, she's from Jamaica. That had quite an interesting impact on me, which is why I have such a weird hip-hop, American cultural influence in my life. Being in my sister's bedroom rapping Wu-Tang when you're ten is probably not the conventional Western white lifestyle.

Being a parent, to me, is the opportunity to set up someone for life and shape them. I watched kids who had never had a birthday, and never believed in Santa Claus because Santa never came. They all lined up at birthdays, "I want a turn blowing out the candle." Everyone's lined up in the house to have a turn because they never had that. I've got twelve sisters. Some of them were teenagers thinking, "This is not going to work out for me", having that attitude and watching that change and flourish, to me that is what parenting is.

People can make kids, it's just biology. But it's the ability to raise someone and help them navigate life. It's very important, which is why I think so many of my films have parental themes. Parents; they're interesting people. You think they have all the answers, and then you get older and you realise they're just winging it as well. I think that's one of the big revelations everyone has in life. Parents don't necessarily know what they're doing, and they're only doing what their parents taught them.

We all have those moments in our lives where we suddenly realise that parents don't have their shit together or don't know everything. For some, that comes early, for others, it's later. Clarence Ryan's character is going through that realisation. I get the feeling that at the end of that night, things are starting to come into place, and he understands, "This is what I need to do as a parent, to be the best person for my kid."

When you started with this idea, did you know that it was going to be a short film?

DVS: I've had this idea for so long. When my brother was in Year One, someone in his class had a brain tumour and died. She would have been five or six. I remember my mum telling me at the funeral she read this good night bedtime story that they'd created to read when the coffin disappeared. I would have been twelve at the time and that story destroyed me. That's always stood in my mind as such a powerful moment of humanity, and this distilled love.

Four or five years ago, I thought, "I could make this film where this thing happens in a recording studio." By then I had made enough short films to kind of understand what I think a good festival short film is; a simple, clean, pitchable, articulate concept. Every time I explained it to someone, they got it. I thought, "I need to get out of short film jail and try and get into the feature world," and I just never made it. It never made sense to make it.

Then COVID happened, and I hate not filmmaking. When you're a director, it's easy to just be in development and not directing. I'm fortunate that I get to do lots of different directing things. It keeps the muscles prepared. I thought, "I just need to get some actors in a room and do some directing, even if it's with a mobile phone." I thought 'What is the simplest idea that I could execute that won't be exploitative of people's time and it's not going to cost a fortune?'. It wasn't a priority in my life to be making a short film, I just wanted to practise directing. I opened my computer and said, "We're making this short film." We were going to make [a three-minute film] for a competition. When we got into the edit, I thought, "Let's make it into more of an exercise and a better short film."

I thought, "Who are some of my friends that I've always wanted to make a film with but have never been able to? Kate Separovich, I've always wanted to make a film with her. We've always done stuff. We've developed features, but we've never had the time. Let's do it."

What's it like working with Kate?

DVS: Great. She's a really good friend of mine. Me, her, and Emma Fletcher, the production designer, have our own little chat on Messenger and we're always championing each other, sharing our accomplishments. I'd worked on a production with Kate many years ago, but they became friends and always seemed more established than me, especially Emma. Now they're very close people to me.

Working with Kate was great because I respect her work and capacity as a producer, and she respects me. The main emphasis was, "Let's not kill ourselves," because a short film can grow into an epic-scale production, depending on what you're doing. I said, "Let's make it simple, have fun. As long as we have enough people on the day to make it work, let's do that." She got it. To me, that is important, because sometimes people forget that filmmaking should be enjoyable; it shouldn't just be this process of whipping yourself to move forward. I love working with Kate.

People expect to see blood, sweat, and tears on screen. It doesn't need to be that hard.

DVS: Every morning when I wake up and write, there's enough there. The less I can avoid on set, the better. That's why I write such simple stuff in single locations because I just want to spend the time filmmaking and not worrying about problem-solving. When I'm filmmaking, I don't even like to remind myself I'm on a film set. I try to have as minimal gear as possible in front of my face, to be as close to the action. I don't even like saying "Action, cut." Everything is fake. The simpler and more distilled down the better; we can be in a moment with some characters and the more opportunity we have to explore.

You mention short film jail, what does that mean as a filmmaker?

GOOD NIGHT

DVS: Short film jail is Zoe's term. When she said it, I thought "That's the best thing I've ever heard." You start making short films when you're in film school, which is good, then it's the process of how many short films you make and how long you keep making them until you make your first feature. It's a weird concept, because for different people, someone might make a grad film that wins an award and then boom, you're making a feature. Someone else might make ten short films that do nothing at festivals or don't even play at festivals, and then they get a feature because they wrote a good script. It becomes a battle. It's hard to make a short film. It's a lot of work, and you don't want to be continually trying to lean on people and ask for favours.

For me, I really enjoy short filmmaking. I feel less like I'm in short filmmaking jail in the sense that it's always an opportunity to learn. It's about the perspective that you go into short filmmaking with. If it's just "I've got to make a film, and this is finally going to be the one that gets into the festival that launches my career," that's probably not the best career strategy. At one point, a ten-minute film will unlock a career, also, maybe a good screenplay will unlock your career or any other thing; meeting someone on the bus.

The way to get out of short film jail is, in a way, to not treat short film jail like short film jail. I treat it like going to the gym. I'm a director, I don't want to get on set on my first feature film and suddenly be learning these incredibly basic things that I probably could have learned if I just made a couple more short films. I'm going to learn a hell of a lot. At the same time, a feature is a different beast. I need that challenge and that lesson. I need the humbling of trying to do feature filmmaking to start that part of 'feature film jail' or whatever it is in terms of that learning process. I feel like I've arrived at that point where the challenge that I'm looking for in my career is in long form now.

Short films are like a testing ground where people can establish their careers, create a calling card, and then make features. They often never turn back to shorts ever again. Then I look at established feature filmmakers who have returned to short films. Do you see a future where the creative life between short films to features is fluid?

DVS: Sometimes a story is a short film. The Nash Edgerton films are a perfect example [*Spider, Bear, Shark*, 2021]; they're a great example of the container that a short film story can hold. In terms of depth, you want the story to be simple so the characters and the themes can be deeper. You don't want to try and compress a feature film into a short.

The bigger thing that probably is the roadblock to it is the market of the effort versus reward. It's time-consuming and it costs you more money than you'll gain. After a while, I can see people saying, "I could go and do this thing, but what are the positives of it versus the negatives?" Maybe there are more positives now that there's YouTube and other places where people are subscribed to short film channels. A few years ago, the market outside film festivals probably limited the value of making short films beyond trying to use it to help your career.

I saw that Park Chan-wook iPhone film (*Life is but a Dream*, 2022) the other day. How would people have watched that twenty years ago if he made that short film? I don't think anyone would be watching except at a random festival, but now I'm sure millions of people will probably watch that on YouTube. That's changed and given this whole new life to short filmmaking. Also, people are busy and [have] the ability to consume something fit for that size. The short film is its own art form because it isn't a feature film.

Where do you see the future of Australian film going?

DVS: One exciting thing is that we are entering a world of niche platforms. So, depending upon the kind of Australian film you make, you might not be held hostage to a certain pathway and a certain place to get your film to an audience. The world is opening up. We've been talking to people in Europe who make interesting films [similar to] my film. The expectation I had of where these films could go and what they could do surprised me with all the different places that exist in the world and how the market is evolving. It's about, as a filmmaker, being responsible and understanding the kind of films you're making. I'm not going to go to Screen Australia and say, "Give me $20 million." They're not going to give anyone that to make a Tarkovsky-like film. It's about recognising what you're doing. Does the market want it?

Also, understand that the market is exciting now. What that means is that Australia is going to be able to produce more diverse films. We've already started that process far better in the last few years. I think what you're going to see is there will be an encouragement from the market to keep doing that because they're going to start finding more and more homes for these movies. As an Australian filmmaker, back what you want to be doing and believe what you want to be doing and you'll find a method and a home in the world of the internet and niche platforms. It's a game-changer.

I think now with the democratisation of equipment, there's this exciting meeting of interesting new voices from different backgrounds, accessibility to equipment and resources, a supportive community – like Western Australia – and different places to market that film. If you put it into that perspective, it's exciting. I can think of so many filmmakers here who have got crazy good ideas.

GOOD NIGHT

Look at how well Australian films have been doing internationally over the last few years. Jess Parker was working in Sydney a couple of years ago on a film called *You Won't Be Alone* (2022); they smashed it at Sundance. When you get the Screen Australia reports and it shows what's playing at Berlin or Cannes, we're highly represented for what our film world in Australia is.

COVID has shown that whatever the obstacles, the arts are so important that we have to make the story whatever the cost, because the storytelling is so important, and it ends up internationally doing well as a result of that because the Australian industry wills itself into existence. Whatever doomsayers say it can't end. It's not going to end. If someone said, "It's all over, all the funding bodies are shut down", someone's gonna make a movie still. They're gonna find a way to make it happen.

ENDNOTES

1   West Coast Visions is a screen industry development program that provides production funding of $750,000 to low budget features that are to be produced in Western Australia.

HE AIN'T HEAVY

103 minutes
Director: *David Vincent Smith*
Cast: *Leila George, Sam Corlett, Greta Scacchi, Clarence Ryan, Alexandra Nell, Lawrence Murphy, Blake Richardson, Nicoletta Dimas*
Writer: *David Vincent Smith*
Producer: *Jess Parker*
Cinematography: *Lewis Potts*
Editing: *Antony Webb*

REVIEW
ANDREW F. PEIRCE

How do you break the back of a crisis? If you're writer/director David Vincent Smith (DVS) you shine a spotlight on the humanity that persists through the darkest days. In his feature debut *He Ain't Heavy*, a story of a sister who kidnaps her violent drug-addicted brother and locks him away in a last-effort attempt to force a state of sobriety onto him, DVS holds up an all-too-familiar tragedy and seeks to navigate a path out of the mess our society is in.

He Ain't Heavy opens at night in suburbia. Leila George's Jade quietly parks her car and slinks out of it, moving in the shadows towards the sound of a fist bashing against a door and a tortured man yelling at the top of his lungs. A neighbour comments to Jade that she has to do something about this or else she will. Jade manages to make her way inside the house without disrupting the figure, finding her mother Bev (Greta Scacchi) locked in her kitchen, once a vessel for nourishment and support, now a fortress with locks on the door and a roaring TV to smother the unceasing abuse from the man outside.

Through a broken window he makes his way indoors, and it's then that we properly meet Max (Sam Corlett), the broken brother and son who screams for ten bucks. Jade and Bev don't relent, denying him his request, leading Max to steal his mother's car. He doesn't get far before crashing it into a tree and fleeing on foot.

As far as openings go, *He Ain't Heavy* throws you into a disturbed suburbia and immediately forces you to question what you would do in this situation. Max is family, a fact that both Jade and Bev hold onto tightly as the importance of that status gradually diminishes in his mind. For them, the tender moments they shared as a family where they sang songs together or went on road trips play out like vivid memories which they hold onto as a buoy that acts as a reminder of who Max can be. For him, those memories have faded and all he sees in Jade and Bev is just another person to take money from and feed his habit.

Jade is at breaking point. Her friends have had kids, become scientists who travel the world, or have long term relationships to lean on; she's nearly thirty and her life has dissipated before her eyes with nothing to show for it other than an exhaustive race across Perth to clean up yet another mess that Max has left in his wake. Rehab failed, pushing him back on the street, while the seven hour wait times in hospital emergency for mental health support did nothing to alleviate the encroaching claustrophobia of a panic attack. The matchstick supports that are in place to help those in need splinter under the smallest amount of pressure, leading Jade to sedate Max and sequester him in their late grandmother's home, forcing a seven-day cleanse on him.

While Neil Armfield's *Candy* (2006) or Shannon Murphy's *Babyteeth* (2019) each present an addict's life in a compelling manner, there is an air of attention-seeking that comes with the central performances; as good as Heath Ledger and Toby Wallace are, it's hard to shake the feeling that these are two actors performing as addicts. *He Ain't Heavy* pulls away from its cinematic siblings with two central performances that are always grounded.

Leila George's Jade is a weathered soul struggling to maintain a level of self-care – the tips of her unkempt hair are tinged with faded pink; the dye run out long ago – while also trying to support the rest of her family. Jade is adrift in the world, and in the frequent moments of solitude that she gifts herself – a visit to a local swimming hole becomes a sanctuary amidst the chaos – we get a glimpse into the emotional burden she's carrying and processing. She's the kind of person who a distant friend might look at and buy a copy of *How to Keep House While Drowning* as a way of solving the problem, when really all she needs is someone to simply understand the pain she's living through.

After an impressive supporting role in *The Dry (2020)*, Sam Corlett gives Max a level of empathy and lived-in understanding that makes him more than just an 'addict'. For Corlett, Max is a sibling and a son first, a person who had dreams and desires before the grip of drugs took hold. For actors, the role of an addict carries an air of excitement about it; after all, here's a character who promises them a chance to present a range of conflicted emotions and show just how good they are as an actor. That level of ego never appears here, with Corlett echoing early Heath Ledger at times. Like Heath, Corlett acts selflessly, giving himself completely to a narrative that asks a lot of its leads.

Then there's Greta Scacchi's Bev, a single mother who has tried all she can and is now at a loss as to how to solve her own personal crisis. She is what Jade will become, alone, friendless, and scorned by a society that demands that she solve a problem she simply does not have the spoons to deal with. Without saying it, Bev only sees Max as her young boy; the sweaty figure he's turned into is a visage she simply cannot comprehend. A late moment of tenderness between Bev and Max where she bathes her sleeping boy, wiping the grime off his brow, reinforces that ever-searching spotlight of humanity that sits at the core of DVS' work.

He Ain't Heavy bleeds with raw emotion. As a storyteller, DVS draws from the personal, crawling into his memories and wrapping his arms around those uncomfortable and painful experiences in a supportive and empathetic way. He honours the tragedy, acknowledging its weight and significance, while also reminding viewers of the continuing value of compassion and empathy.

As a creative force, David Vincent Smith has shades of Ken Loach, exploring the social issues of our time and the families who are impacted by them with an uncritical lens. DVS has created a film that's deeply humanistic and delves into the need for empathy and understanding. Australian cinema has often returned to this well, but it has never been presented with such a deep level of understanding of a crisis at work. This is phenomenal filmmaking, standing as one of the great debuts in recent Australian film history.

EVIE

19 mins
Director: *Alexander von Hofmann*
Writer: *Atticus Martin, Lukas William Martin*
Cast: *Melody Rom, Ben Mortley, Paul Montague, Leon Ewing*
Producer: *Kate Separovich*
Original Score: *Dmitri Golovko*
Cinematography: *Meredith Lindsay*
Editing: *Lukas William Martin*

INTERVIEW
DIRECTOR
ALEXANDER VON HOFMAN

Evie director Alexander von Hofmann has held onto the passion for dinosaurs ever since he was a kid. When the idea of making a 'dinosaurs in the outback' film came about, he turned to his cinematic heroes, Steven Spielberg and Ridley Scott, for inspiration. However, trying to bring their sense of scale to life on a micro-budget brought about a wealth of challenges that he had to navigate with his supportive team.

Evie follows the titular young girl (Melody Rom) as she ventures into the wasteland of Australia, ruined by nuclear war and ravaged by genetically modified dinosaurs, to find medical supplies to help her ailing father. On her difficult journey, she encounters marauders and a dangerous beast.

This interview was recorded by Andrew F. Peirce in February 2022

What was it like bringing dinosaurs to the outback?

Alexander von Hofmann: Kate Separovich, the producer, brought together an amazing crew. We were both really stoked with the crew that we got together. We found a great cast and crew [who] all came together from Perth. [The shoot] happened quite smoothly. Even though we were dealing with a very low budget, it felt like a big set.

We got into editing and then part two of *Evie* came along. We planned for this dinosaur to be in the film, and I'd done a lot of work shooting quite sparingly to make sure that the dinosaur wouldn't be too big a task in post. I was influenced by *Alien* (1979). I shot it quite dark, sparingly backlit, or edge-lit [spaces]. To bring this dinosaur to life to the quality that we wanted turned into close to a two-year saga, working with a lot of different people to bring it together until we finally found the missing piece of the puzzle which was Ben Wotton. He's a VFX compositor in Sydney and an absolute genius with this stuff, and he happens to be a massive dinosaur fan. He and I got to work together during the COVID lockdown. He did the majority of post, but the one thing that he isn't is an animator, so I ended up having

EVIE

to do a little work. I learned the 3D software to do that. We use Maya. Ben gave me a lot of pointers, lots of coaching, and we got it done over about three months.

Is it a completely CGI creation with no physical aspect to it? If so, how did you create that tangible feeling?

AvH: It is. That was the real challenge. I think that's why it took us so long to get it done. Kate, Lukas [William Martin] the writer, and myself all had in our mind that what we wanted was a *Jurassic World* (2015) quality dinosaur in this film. To get that, it has to look and feel totally real.

The thing I kept talking to Ben about was "We're going to do all this work. Are we going to be able to get it there?" He rendered out a test shot and blew all of our minds with how good it could look. We were able to go forward with some confidence that we were going to get it there. That's just his lighting, compositing, texture work, and all the materials that he's able to put on those models that makes the light and the little ridges and bumps feel real.

Where did your interest in dinosaurs begin?

AvH: I suppose this all started with the velociraptors in *Jurassic Park* (1993), that's where it all started for me. I, like every kid who saw that film, went through a stage where I wanted to be a palaeontologist, and those are the ones that really stick out. We talked for a while about this being an Australovenator, which is the Australian raptor. That's a neat-looking dinosaur, and it would have been cool to have that dinosaur in this. We first started off trying to make one and then realised we weren't going to get it to where it needed to be, and then we couldn't find an existing model. In the end, we got an Allosaurus. We found one model, and Ben tweaked it because the idea was that our dinosaurs aren't one of the classic species of dinosaurs. These are slightly mutated by bringing these things to life in the future through whatever *Jurassic Park*-style experiments they're going to do. It wasn't a straight take on any of the species.

Did you have the idea that it's going to be just a short or a teaser for a feature? How do you incorporate world-building into that notion?

AvH: This was always meant to be a teaser for a feature. That was where it started. I saw the first drafts of Luke's script and I loved the idea instantly. Then we started working on 'how do we make this film feel self-contained but still like it's part of a much bigger story?' We did a few drafts together where he and I discussed what we could achieve in this short film that would be awesome, and people would leave the cinema satisfied, but at the same time be a great selling tool for the feature.

We talked a lot about how much of the world before the apocalypse we wanted to hint at. We talked a lot about having big signs out in the landscape for what used to be a theme park that you could go to *Jurassic Park*-style in the outback, and then allude to the fact that the world has collapsed because of some sort of disaster, and now those dinosaurs are free in the landscape and they're once again the apex predators; but how much of that is distracting from a short film? How much of that adds to it? There was a lot of back and forth. All that stuff is money and it's hard to put on screen on a low budget, so we had to be sparing.

What direction did you give Melody [Rom] on set?

AvH: She didn't have a lot of classic scenes where she could play off another actor, there were only a couple in there for her. A lot of it was about giving her goals to get through for each of the scenes. While a lot of it was, "You need to go into that bus and collect some maggots," it was also, "Those maggots are going to potentially save your dad's life and you've got to treat them with respect. Then you're going to have a moment with this photograph in the bus that reflects the childhood that you've missed out on." It was trying to give her motivations for each of those moments to [give depth] to the actions that she was doing.

There's a photo to show the history that she's missed out on. How important is that shorthand?

AvH: Luke and I talked a lot about those moments because they were what grounded the film. Considering that it is otherwise quite a simple story, we needed to, through devices like the photo, give the world a bit more of a grounding, to make it feel like there was more to the life of this girl beyond these actions that she's playing out and the fear of being chased by a dinosaur. We had to do that with minimal scenes. A lot of the film is about the constant danger she is in, but for you to care about somebody going through danger, you need to feel for them, you need to feel that they've got some emotional stake in the whole thing. We didn't have a lot of opportunities to build on that other than 'the dad's sick and she's trying to help him.' She's yearning for a world that's safer and has more human connection in it. We didn't have a lot of opportunities to build those elements out, but what we did was try to place some things in there that would build the world out in the audience's mind.

In Australian cinema, genre films are predominantly coming from independent filmmakers. What's it like to be able to explore genre in an independent capacity?

EVIE

AvH: It's what I want to do. All I want to do is tell genre stories. It's hard in Australia because it's hard to get funding. People don't trust [that] genre films will do well in cinemas here. Yet, they do well internationally. The way our funding is set up in this country, things have to do well in the cinema here for them to give the funding out, even though they might do well abroad. It's a strange place to be if you're a genre filmmaker. Horror films have always done well on a lower budget, and we make do with what we have. Sometimes you have to get more creative, you have to figure it out. I'm always up for that challenge. I would rather have the money. If not, then we'll make it work some other way.

When you say "get creative", what does that mean to you on the day on set?

AvH: I depend a lot on the crew around me as well as myself to come up with these solutions. A lot of people that I end up working with have more onset experience than I do, just because they're usually working crew and I've managed to get them into a short that I'm working on. Meanwhile, I'm a writer-director and the amount of time I've spent on a set is probably like a twentieth of what they spent on a set. Whenever something comes up, we've hit a wall, we can't figure out how to get around something or we have a challenge like we have one set of pig guts and you can do this take once and then you're out of guts, you just have to figure it out. I relish those challenges. They're all a part of the fun. As a result, sometimes you end up getting a shot that you never would have planned to do because you talked it through with everybody. The other thing is I try not to say "Fix it in post" too much because that becomes a nightmare. As much as possible, it's "Let's try to do this now and get it while we're on set together and find a creative solution to make it happen."

The day we spent inside the shed shooting the whole suspense sequence. We had gotten access to this shed that belonged to Kate's family. It was a big grungy-looking shed with lots of holes in the tin with light pouring through. We'd done a bunch of verge site collections and picked up every piece of trash we could find, and filled this shed with little corridors winding your way through all the trash. First Evie did a run through it, then one of the men who was chasing her goes through it, and then the dinosaur attacked. A lot is going on in that one little space. In my head, I thought, "This is my opportunity to build a really solid suspense scene that feels a bit like what you see in *Alien*." I had so much fun with it. It's my favourite scene in the film.

What's it like working with Kate as a producer?

AvH: Kate's great. She's such a mover and shaker in terms of getting projects up and running. She knows everybody in the industry, she's always got ten things on the go and has a great record of getting them up and getting them made. A shoot with Kate is great because she's got a lot of experience as a production manager. You've got a producer here who knows the shooting process inside and out, and so those sets are always wonderful. The crew that she brings on are always wonderful because she's worked with most of them and so she knows who she wants to work with next. She introduced me to people like Meredith Lindsay, the cinematographer. She's a massive talent, and I can't wait to see what she does next. She brought Ben Wotton on. We were lucky.

BASSENDREAM

80 mins
Director: *Tim Barretto*
Writer: *Tim Barretto*
Cast: *Sarah Brook, Declan Brown, Jeremy Bunny, Yasmine Caldwell, Nicolas Chapman, Benedict Chau, Oriah Chittleborough, Cezera Critti-Schnaars, Kyran Doak, Declan Driver, Olivia Dugandzic, Neve Havcercroft, Oliver Hay*
Producers: *Tim Baretto, Melanie Filler*
Music: *Sam Kuzich*
Cinematography: *Oliver Hay*

INTERVIEW
FILMMAKER
TIM BARETTO

Perth-raised filmmaker Tim Barretto has seen the world. Growing up in Bassendean, learning about film production at Edith Cowan University in Mount Lawley, Tim eventually moved over east to work on television productions. His creative life has taken him to Indonesia where he filmed documentaries as an outsider looking in. But the unremarkable suburban life of Perth was a notion that never left his mind.

Bassendream is a grand ode to Australian suburbia, to the 'dry heat' of West Aussie summers, to the winding down of the school year and the possibility of adventures over the holiday break. It's a film about the cusp of new friendships and the unexpected dissolution of hard-earned bonds, to mucking around with mates and pissing off old folks with shenanigans. It's the sound of hearing Paul Kelly's *Dumb Things* for the first time and thinking 'fuck, this song *gets me*'. It's the anger at a sibling for tearing apart your prized basketball collectors' card.

Baretto's film is an experiential one, gleaned from his mind like something that only the outer-suburbs kids can do. *Bassendream* was shot on film, evoking both the pastels of nineties attire, almost appearing at times like the faded curtains that daylight savings alarmists ranted and raved about in the letter's column of The West Australian newspaper. Australian suburban life is rarely captured on film, and with *Bassendream*, Barretto memorialises the distinct nineties sandgroper summers with a cast of locals, some WA Salvage ads, and a mix-tape of iconic Aussie songs from the likes of Jebediah, Paul Kelly, and Australian Crawl in a manner that has never been captured before.

This interview was recorded by Andrew F. Peirce in June 2022

Take me back to when you first came up with the idea for Bassendream.

Tim Barretto: It was probably ten years ago, and I was chatting with people who grew up in Bassendean. A lot of people in Perth and outside of Perth had moved on and have done quite well in their fields, and lots of them

BASSENDREAM

have come from Bassendean. I always wondered what was special about that suburb that made people have that creativity and freedom to explore ideas and not feel vulnerable in that state.

I had my dad doing Tai Chi around the backyard. I always felt like that was a unique experience, that disconnection between the adults and kids. I don't remember doing family things. I just remember being with the kids, being out on the street, and then going to bed. I thought that was an interesting dynamic to explore in Australian culture, that we hadn't really seen much on screen.

I've seen a lot of suburbia presented in a dark way. I think we get that a lot in Australia. I wanted to make a film that was fun and not so grim, even though it has a dark element at the end which pulls away quickly. It doesn't have to be honest; I wanted a heightened sense of a child's perspective of what they see as the suburb and make the suburb the central character.

The writing process has been so skewed. I wrote half of it in Taiwan. I had to get out of Australia to write about Australia. That's sort of what it felt like. I shot it over two summers in 2016 and 2017, so it wasn't a full-on one-set shoot. After I got the footage back from the first shoot, I was like, "Okay, I know how to write it from here." I gave it like a test shoot, essentially, which mostly made [into] the cut. I then developed the ideas and the characters from there and I worked out what I was missing. That was the refreshing thing about shooting on film; you've only got so much film and you can't go back and review it quickly. You have to wait two months to see it. It's a good place to be in as well as a first-time filmmaker, you can be a bit more forgiving of yourself.

You've done shorts, you've done docs. Doing a fiction feature, that's a whole new world.

TB: It is. I was trying to be super safe in the way I approached this film, to do my first feature in that I chose my hometown, the town where my granddad grew up. My family is there and there are support networks there. There are houses to film at and there are emergency levers I could pull.

In terms of story, we've got a *Magnolia*-esque style where I get to chop and throw it on the cutting room floor when I needed to. I didn't have to keep anything. That was really a nice place to be in, being the editor as well. Story-wise, you can be a bit looser, and I know that can be a challenge for some audiences. It's interesting, the wide network from different countries I showed an earlier cut to connected with different characters. That was one of our questions: what was their favourite character? They have names but they don't have memorable names, it's more just that familiarity.

INTERVIEW | TIM BARETTO

What film did you shoot it on?

TB: We shot it on 16mm on an Aaton XTR and an LTR. We managed to talk our way through TAFE and Curtin University. I went to ECU and Keith, George, Andrea, and Tanja were my film and video development lecturers. They gave me a lot of inspiration to be a filmmaker who had the confidence to do an off-centre film like this. It was shot on Kodak Vision3 500T and 50D. I wanted the daytime stuff to be as close to 35mm as possible, so fine-grained as possible, which I think it achieves. 16mm is a bit noisy, a bit grainy, and there's dirt on there. I do like to keep it as clean as possible but that is the product.

This movie wouldn't have been made if I chose to shoot on digital. I wouldn't have had the help or the seriousness or the support that came along with shooting it on film. I think we would have been bogged down with the stresses of the rushes each night, and probably felt a bit flat in what we got. You're critical at the time of performances; they're not perfect performances all the time, but there are some endearing performances that the kids have that are honest. They're two-take performances.

The whole set, they're not on their phones. We're only shooting four minutes a day of screen time; we're not shooting much. It's $1 a second. We're not doing many setups; we're not moving the camera heaps. When we do it, everyone shuts up, and then we do it as best as we can. I think you get that level of seriousness, and no one's got a split or a monitor, that's kind of refreshing. You're left with getting it later and you have to deal with what you've got. I love digital equally, I'm not one way or the other, I just think [they have] different purposes. If you gave me a choice, every time I would say shoot it on film. But I'm not anti [digital]. It just feels a bit more honest, in that sense.

Also, I wanted to make a *film*. I wanted to make a movie and that felt like the way nineties independent movies were shot back then. It was 16mm, like *Clerks* (1994). That's what they did. They got a camera from where they could and then they just put it on their shoulder or a tripod. We didn't have any dollies in the whole film. It's really simple, just be smart. You're limited by those restrictions, and they're a godsend for independent filmmakers. Don't look at them as limitations, look at the limitations as opportunities. How do you work with what you've got? We rented a house in the second year [of filming]. Ten characters used that house. That was one backyard, one front porch, one kitchen, one living room, one bedroom, another bedroom, computer room; it was also the production house, just set dressed differently. Don't overcomplicate it. Innovation is fun.

BASSENDREAM

I learned this from working on television in Sydney, the most liberating thing, like Australian telly, movie-making is not real. It's a fake land. So don't try and be too authentic. Make it work. If you have to pull the chair up really high because it looks better, just make it look better. It doesn't have to feel real in the space for the actor, it doesn't have to be fully method for the director. Some directors work that way and that's fine. But I love the playfulness and the trickery, and I always like that style.

How did you immerse the younger kids into the era? Did they understand the lingo?

TB: They embraced it. We workshopped it. We workshopped different lines, especially when we were doing the critical lines. You work out what works for them and what sounds authentic to them. We know what the objective is here, calling them a 'poncy' kid or that sort of thing. As you know, that's how we used to talk. We always used to tease each other in that way. It's not something to ignore and it's not something to celebrate, it's just something that is what it was.

I tried not to be too challenging in the dialogue. I'm not here to make a statement. It's not a film trying to make a statement about a certain culture or one culture versus another. I wanted to make something inclusive, because I think growing up as a kid, you feel like everyone's inclusive, like Indigenous people on a football team. I didn't feel there was that separation, but we still used racist language at the time, and that wasn't my fault. [We] weren't aware. I tried to keep it pretty mellow in that sense but being aware of it as well.

That certainly made me think back on growing up as a kid and the things that were just kind of commonplace for white Australians. It's a stark reminder of the racism we learn as kids, and it's kind of a relief to be able to go, "I'm not actually forgetting this stuff that happened."

TB: As long as you grow up being aware of it. You don't have to then go and punish yourself retrospectively. I think you just be aware of it, and you move on and you make choices how you direct this, and things like that. I didn't use any racist language.

With Cezera [Critti-Schnaars] who played the Indigenous friend with the two girls, I got her to write her own scenes. I want this idea that this was an Indigenous who girl grew up in the suburbs. She doesn't go on walkabout with her family out in the country or anything like that. I said, "Depict that." That's when she was like, "What do you think, I know how to like cook a kangaroo and season it with witchetty grubs?" She wrote that line. I'm so

INTERVIEW | TIM BARETTO

happy that she got to write that for herself. For the character, I think it's important to get rid of that stereotype as well, not ignore the stereotype.

I'm a nineties kid so I relate to a lot of what the kids were doing. Although I'm more like the kid who gets his bike thrown into the tree, that was me.

TB: The strict kid. The outsider.

Looking at the bullies, there's this feeling of "I want to be part of that, but also they're the worst people in the world, so I don't want to be part of that."

TB: I know, I know. You can live in your own world and the world itself, the suburb, it's a bubble, it's not specific to Bassendean. Every suburb is like a bubble. And when you exit that bubble, something feels different. You have that safe zone that when you were a kid in the nineties, you had that freedom to roam around. I always wanted to separate the adults from the children as much as possible. That was a really big thing, they don't really have scenes together, but they sort of do. I wanted to keep that.

I liked the sequence where the older woman is chasing the kids.

TB: That's sort of based on a true story, that happened to my brother. It was this crazy woman in bras and knickers.

I think we've all got that kind of story from growing up where an older person is trying to discipline strange kids who were misbehaving.

TB: Absolutely. You used to always get in trouble from other people. Everyone used to tell you, you couldn't get away with that now. You're not allowed to tell anyone's kid off apart from your own. That made you a bit scared as a kid. You treated situations like you could get told off. There's a bit more confidence now, bravado that kids have which I don't think we had so much.

There feels like a tinge of Neighbours with the font of the title of Bassendream. Then there's the cut to the WA Salvage ad. To me, the film feels like it's challenging the manufactured concept that suburbia can be so dark, while also challenging the notion on Neighbours where it's this manufactured sheen of positive suburbia. Suburbia is not super glossy, but it's also not super dark. It's just real life.

TB: The font is very *Neighbours*. It just is. I've never wanted to make something highly dramatic and highly emotionally driven. There needs to be a rawness in there that is honest and real. But then there's so much playfulness. What I wanted to achieve is something that has a bit of everything, and it's all going to be okay in the end, even when it's not okay. Life is challenging and it's not that period that's challenging. Life is probably more challenging now, it's probably simpler back then. We had our taglines before we had all the answers. Was it simpler? Or was it harder? I'm not really sure. I haven't really worked out if life was better or worse. That's just how it felt. No helmets and running around skateboarding and all of that stuff.

And just being kids where the only pressure coming towards us is the fact that it's going to be night-time soon —

TB: And then you have to deal with your parents.

How important was it for you to pull away from the glorified, rose-tinted nostalgia of the nineties?

TB: I was really scared. I didn't want to make a nostalgic piece. I wanted to make something that had its own voice. It's funny because I showed it back in 2017 and 18, and now there's been a huge wash of nostalgia and we've seen films coming out set in the nineties. I wasn't aiming to be on that wave, it just happens to be on that wave now, which is totally fine and is probably beneficial for audiences accepting the film being a period piece. I wasn't trying to just nostalgia-wash it or put things in for the sake of nostalgia.

The ads and everything, I felt, "There needs to be an ad break now. I don't know how to continue this movie right now, I just need to put in a break in." That's sort of what it felt like. It was cool exploring all these ads. I was looking at old Ansett Australia ads, but they're much harder to get. The WA Salvage one, that company doesn't exist anymore. Ansett doesn't either, but Claudio [Versaico], he's contactable, I can get approval from him. I did want to have a few ads scattered. Having tested with a few people, they were a bit [confused] at times and it still probably is a bit confusing and jarring. But I like the way you get pulled out of the film and then you have to reintroduce yourself into it.

Let's talk about the music. You've got a couple of big hits in there. How did you go about getting the approval for them?

TB: Just being very stubborn. That's why it's probably taken this long to release. Getting initial quotes, and music totals in tens of thousands of dollars, and then waiting and re-contacting them along the way. It was an independent production. We got *Dumb Things* [Paul Kelly] approved first. Once one happens, they all kind of all [happen].

[People were] like "Just make a track that sounds like it." I was like, "I just can't, it feels wrong. I'm happy just to not release it yet. I'll get some more money maybe, and then try and reapply or ask them." I always wanted to get money to handball it on. But that never happened.

It was Ian [Hale, producer] that kicked me up the bum. Ian came on and he's good like that. He was like, "No, you just do it. I get what you're trying to do." And I [went], "I'm a bit deflated, I don't know how to get to the finish line. [The movie] still needs cutting, I don't have a sound design. I can do the grade, and that's fine, but I still need a sound designer, it needs to sound like a movie." All the other bits and pieces, that EP and producing stuff is just messy. It's just hard. You need that extra person to keep you up above. Ian was that.

He's done a great job of curating and championing WA films.

TB: It's awesome. I'm a nobody in Perth. I lived in Sydney for seven years. We used to drink at the pub, when I was in ECU at the Flying Scotsman. I used to have a beer and chat with him about it. He heard about it ten years ago, "I'm gonna make this movie called *Bassendream*. I don't really know how I'm going to do it, but I'll do it." I made a short called *Before the Dream* (2013) set in the seventies in Bassendean, just to test it on 16mil. That did really well at the ATOM Awards. It was slice-of-life cuts and vignettes. It works there. I was like, "I can't believe people like that. I like that sort of movie." It's nice.

I think in Australia, and probably more specifically WA, we try and compete too much rather than try and have an authentic original voice. I was conscious of that because we tried to go too clean. That's totally cool, I love clean, and I love a good three-act structure, but if you get the opportunity to challenge it or do something different, then I'll take it. I had the support of my girlfriend-wife now. She studied film theory, and she was like, "Let's make this movie. Let's do it." I needed that support.

This kind of film is the sort that I love getting lost in because it doesn't hold your hand.

TB: Absolutely. I wish I had spent more craft trying to tell some of the stories better. But that's my learning curve as well. There's something beautiful about the shifts and the flows and the peaks and the troughs. I was just really trying to write it as a vibe, I was trying to write the edit as "What do I need next? What do I need now?" Rather than "What does the story need to give to the audience?" I was conscious of making [it as] short as I possibly could as well and not trying to over-indulge in stuff. That I find is a bit punishing and that's just a maturity thing. Probably if I cut it five or ten years ago, I probably would have over-indulged in a few things and left scenes in that probably didn't need to be there. It's good to be ruthless, in that sense.

BASSENDREAM

The title Bassendream suggests sleeping. What does that do to you, to have this film in your mind for ten years, dreaming about it, sleeping, and thinking about it?

TB: It never felt wrong. It never gave me nightmares, never kept me up at night. I was always proud of what we achieved in self-producing it. I never got haunted by it. I never felt pressured to finish it because of the way we made it. I think that was important. Sometimes you can make a film where you pull help from places where you then have to answer to people, whether that's yourself or crowdfunded or that sort of thing. The way we did it was in an honest way with the cast there. Some got paid bits and pieces.

We were generous in the way we shot, we didn't over-commit to the young kids. We didn't work them longer than eight hours, they were strict about those protocols. I think it was important that we could walk away even if we haven't got a film to show for it after five years, that everyone still had a good time in the process, and they didn't walk away feeling bitter. That was important for us. I think people have anxieties about that. I did have slight anxieties about communication, especially when you get a cast this big, but I always knew that I never did the wrong thing by them.

In terms of *Bassendream*, it was the dream. That was the dreamland. That's where ideas were developed and where we grew up. It just had the ring to it. Bassendean Council contacted me, people have made T-shirts for it, so I'm glad it's sort of been adopted by the suburb. I had felt [the film] needed a subtitle, like *A Suburban Odyssey* or something like that just so it didn't pigeonhole it for a wider audience, Australian-wide. It's just the dream. That's all it is.

I live in Booragoon. We call [the shopping centre] Garbo. There's this affectionate term that we have for our own suburbs. Bassendream fits for that.

TB: I don't know where it came from. It was us developing it and a couple of friends that lived there were chatting about it. "You're going back to the 'dream tonight?" It happened organically, that title. It was really nice.

What's it like being part of the Revelation Film Festival?

TB: It's great. I went when I was a uni student and got the gold passes back when it was at the Astor. It was the best. I got to see all those experimental films. There wasn't as much local content back then. It's nice for them to do more local content. I've always tried to be a part of it. I've been in the Super Eight competitions, and I had a couple of short films in there, but having a feature there was always in the back of my mind. I thought "It'd be a good Rev film. If I could get into Rev, I'd be happy to have that as the world premiere." Keep it in WA. That's what I wanted to do.

I think we need to bring the youth to the festival. Now that I'm an old guy, I want to see what young kids are doing. They're the ones that are not as bitter. They've still got the hope in their eyes. It's always refreshing speaking to young kids who want to be filmmakers because they have that attitude, that look in their eyes. Not that I'm old, but I feel a little bit exhausted.

What does it mean to be an Australian filmmaker for you? What does it mean to be a WA filmmaker as well?

TB: WA I have an interesting relationship [with] because I had been away from WA for eight or nine years. Coming back to WA during the COVID pandemic, I [said] to my wife "Let's not go back to Sydney, I don't want to work on any more sets, I'm done with 50–60-hour weeks. I just want to do something different." I think you can see it in a different light coming back.

WA has a lot to offer. I think we lose a lot of talent over East. There's a lot of talent that comes from WA in all forms of the arts. There is a community but it's small and it's competitive and that's what's tough. I've come back in the last two years and not even said that I'm a filmmaker. I just want to blend in and observe. I'm in observation mode. I'm not in a rush to make my next movie. I have ideas for my next movie, but I'm not in a rush. There are stories to tell everywhere and I'm all about what's achievable, what's producible. WA has a big advantage in that accessibility is easy and the cost of production is cheaper. We need to take advantage of that as independent filmmakers.

I had a big interest in Indonesia, and I made documentaries there. I think telling a story as an outsider is an interesting place to be. It's more vulnerable when you're telling your story. My idol would be Rolf de Heer. I think his approach to filmmaking has been one of the most inspirational. He did his first movie using his own family and doing it in his home. I think you can do it but be realistic about it. I probably wasn't realistic about it at the beginning of the journey. But having not been in a rush, I got to grow with the journey and then learn more about what hill that was to climb.

I don't consider being an Australian filmmaker as being patriotic. I think it's more about being real. I think Australians, when they do honest films, they're the best. That's when we thrive when we're honest about our character and who we are. The reality of the context of how Australia as a colonial state came to be here as well. It doesn't have to show that theme, but I think we just need to be honest about immigration and all that sort of thing.

WA MADE FILM FESTIVAL

INTERVIEW
FESTIVAL DIRECTOR MATTHEW EELES

Matthew Eeles was raised on a steady diet of Australian films. As a born and bred sandgroper, that filmic foundation helped inform his love for our national cinema, eventually leading to the creation of Cinema Australia, a website dedicated completely to Australian films and filmmakers. Launched in 2013, Cinema Australia has become a home for everything Australian: the shorts, the indies, the Baz Luhrmann epics, and everything in between.

In 2020, alongside fellow Aussie film buff Jasmine Leivers (Jaz), Matthew launched the WA Made Film Festival, a Perth-based film festival that celebrates the vibrant Western Australian filmmaking community with screenings, industry workshops, and more.

This interview was recorded by Andrew F. Peirce in December 2023

How did the concept of the WA Made Film Festival originate?

Matthew Eeles: I'm almost 100% certain that if Jaz was asked this question, she might have a different answer. As far as I'm concerned, Jaz launched Next Gen all those years ago, which was a monthly short film screening that played Western Australian shorts. After each screening, she would have an award ceremony where a panel would vote on awards for the films. It was a cool event.

At that time, I was thinking of launching a festival in Western Australia called WA Made and I wanted to have it at The Backlot. Ian Hale came on board because he wanted to do it as well. Unfortunately, the state funding body, ScreenWest, wouldn't allow us to have a film festival at such a small enue. Jasmine and I decided to combine our ideas together, so WA Made was basically an extension of the Next Gen screenings, and it's grown into the WA Made Film Festival which has exploded in popularity.

Was it always WA Made?

WA MADE FILM FESTIVAL

ME: It was. Honestly, and I say this to everyone, all my best ideas come to me when I'm sitting on the toilet. I specifically remember sitting on the toilet and the name 'WA Made' popping into my head. WA Made Film Festival flowed from that. Originally, someone else had come up with an idea to name it 'There's Something in the Water in Western Australia.' That was just way too long. WA Made rolls off the tongue. The name has become a brand now and everybody knows WA Made. When I hear or read somebody talk about a WA made film, I instantly think of the WA Made Film Festival. It's worked really well for us. I mean, how often are people going to say 'WA made' separate from the festival?

What does it mean for you to be able to showcase your home state on screen?

ME: I was born and bred here in Western Australia. I absolutely love this state. It's a part of my soul and who I am. I've had many opportunities to move over East, both of my brothers moved over East, but I just could not leave this state. This is my home and I want to be here forever. I get emotional watching our state on the big screen. Two of my passions are Art and Film, and another is Western Australia. I'm also a huge West Coast Eagles supporter. I love everything that comes out of WA, so to see my state transformed into an art form on the big screen, I actually get quite emotional. To see the landscape portrayed on the screen does something inside of me, it brings up so many emotions. Also, I love seeing the people behind those films succeed, especially when they get to see their films in a cinema. I absolutely love it.

As a fellow West Aussie, watching a film that's been shot here transforms how we see the city. I know that every time I drive through the Graham Farmer Freeway tunnel, I think of Stephen McCallum's 1% (2017). Or whenever I drive past The Doll's House or Leighton Beach, I think of Son of a Gun (2014). It transforms how you see your state. It stops being just a place that you live and it becomes something more.

ME: I agree with that 100%. It's funny that you talk about the city as well, because people have brought up the point that not many Western Australian films are shot in the city and that we don't get to see Perth City on the big screen very often. That's not true. It's just that we don't get to see it in mainstream films often. Pieces did an incredible job of putting Perth City on the big screen. Director John Soto does a great job at showcasing Perth City too.

In discussion with Sydney-based filmmakers, there's this idea of getting away from the Opera House and the Harbour Bridge on screen. They want to show that Sydney is more than just a tourist destination; there are the city streets and the suburbs too. I imagine for Perth people we

INTERVIEW | MATTHEW EELES

may want to show our city as being a destination to visit or to show that it's a liveable place. This leads me to address one of the criticisms that people have had about WA films: they can often feel like tourist ads. For you, as somebody who watches a lot of WA made films, what's the difference between a film that is putting tourism forward versus being a narrative-focused experience?

ME: It's a tough question. I hate the idea of using films as a tourism tool. I really don't like it. Instantly you can feel that that's what it is. It almost instantly becomes an ad, and I really don't like sitting there watching ads. Whereas with other filmmakers who don't have that ScreenWest funding or big tourism money behind them, you can feel that their films are made out of passion for the state. They really want to showcase Western Australia on the big screen, but not necessarily telling everyone 'You have to come here,' but telling people 'Look what we've got. Look where we are in the world.'

This is our place. This is our home. When you invite somebody into your home, you want to show them the things that are most precious to you and that you are passionate about. That's what WA filmmakers do on screen. That leads me to consider the films that you choose as the opening night films for the festival. How do you decide what is going to be an opening night film for WA Made?

ME: We will always choose the film that we truly believe is the best of the bunch. There's no other way to put that. We love every film that we show. Trust me, we've rejected a lot of films just purely because we didn't like them. We're not going to show everything just for the sake of showing everything.

In 2021 we received a bit of criticism from some people about having *Greenfield* (2019) open the festival because it wasn't a ScreenWest-funded film. It was originally a web series that ScreenWest then gave some money to turn into a feature film. We were criticised for that. People higher up were saying to us 'Hang on, why isn't a ScreenWest fully funded film opening the festival?' We're not going to do that. We're choosing story over that. I thought that *Greenfield* was a phenomenal film, and the audience did as well. The feedback that we got afterwards proved that. We would never pick a film to open the festival just for the sake of it. We will choose the story and the quality of the movie over anything else. Just because a film is made by ScreenWest doesn't mean we're going to show it.

We had a real lack of feature films submitted for the 2024 festival. It was probably the lowest number of feature films that we've ever had submitted. At first, we were shocked by that thinking, 'Oh my God, why aren't people submitting their feature films?' Then we brought ourselves back to reality and we realised that 'hang on, not every year we're going to have a huge stack of films being made in Western Australia.' We can't rely on six or seven feature films to be made every single year just so we can play them. It's not going to be the case. In some years we'll have more short films screened compared to feature films. 2023 was a year where there were fewer feature film productions and independent feature film productions in Western Australia. All the crews were whisked away for the new Nicolas Cage film, *The Surfer* (undated), which highlights the other aspect of making movies in Western Australia in that we have such a limited crew here that when there is a big production on, independent films suffer because of that.

For the 2022 and 2023 festivals, the opening night films were both highly anticipated films, How to Please a Woman (2022) and Sweet As (2023). These are both excellent examples of what Western Australia looks like. One is set in Fremantle and the other is set in the Kimberley. How important is it to stretch out of the city and present stories from the far north on screen?

ME: People might not believe it, but it is something that we take note of during the selection process. We really believe in the importance of that. We do want to showcase everything from Albany to Broome, but it does extend beyond that as well. The most important reason that we want to do that is because the sad reality is that not a lot of films are being made independently in regional areas. There are not a lot of independent filmmakers in Albany, Kalgoorlie, or Broome making a feature film each year. We want to put those areas onto the big screen so that the audiences will watch it and go, 'Hey, geez, we could head out there to make a film.' Or 'We could ask our friends who are down there to make a movie.' We want to try to encourage filmmaking everywhere around Western Australia, not just in Perth.

We do contact filmmakers and say, 'Hey, this looks like it was shot in Albany,' and they'll confirm, 'It was in Albany or somewhere around there.' We do put a lot of effort into the films that we select as to where they are regionally and geographically. It's really important. Also, if we've got a regional film playing, then that will encourage the regional media to get involved as well, and they'll want to talk to us about the film that's screening or want to talk to the filmmakers. It's a great way to give the filmmakers a little bit of extra publicity as well. Through us, the media companies then become interested, which makes them interested in those filmmakers who then get to have their five minutes in the spotlight.

I noticed that the line-up of films that have screened at WA Made don't always verbalise that they're stories that are set within Western Australia. Is it important that the films that you screen are stories that are

INTERVIEW | MATTHEW EELES

centred in Western Australia, or is it that they have to be shot here and can be about another place?

ME: It is important to us that they're set in WA, but every now and then one is going to slip through purely because we believe in that filmmaker, or we've been impressed by that filmmaker and what they've created. Of course, we want every single film to be set here and verbalise that they are in Western Australia, but the reality is that that's not always going to be the situation. We played *Elect Lincoln* (directed by Lincoln James Cook) in 2023, which, for its majority, was set in New Zealand, but it was written here, all the post-production was done here, and the filmmakers were from here. Actually, they were from Albany. We're not going to say no to a film like that. We have to truly believe in the filmmaker as well.

Our general rule is that the director, the producer, and the writer have to live in Western Australia and that the post-production is complete in WA as well, that's one of the criteria. We had one film that was submitted for the 2024 festival which is set in Sydney, but everything else was made here in Western Australia.

The festival itself has become a destination point for filmmakers too. I heard the story of one filmmaker who has a tattoo of a film strip where he fills in another frame for each year that he's had a film screen at WA Made. What does that mean for you as the Festival Director?

ME: That was Arnold Luke Carter. We screened his film, *Sun Moon & Thalia*, at the 2023 festival, and we screened his film *Punching Darts* at the 2021 festival. I've got such a soft spot for his filmmaking talent and him as a filmmaker. He turns out these incredibly intelligent feature films and there's something about his writing that I just love. In 2023 he came up to me while I was putting some food out onto the table. I shook his hand and said, "Welcome back," and I noticed the tattoo on his arm. I said, "What's that on your arm?" He showed me and I was almost in tears. It filled me with so much joy to see that what we're doing is working and that people are resonating with it. He's a great example of that. I said, "What are you going to do with the empty spaces?" And he said, "They're going to be for films that'll screen at WA Made in the future." How cool is that?

He's one of our favourite filmmakers. Not only does he rock up to his screenings, but he rocks up to every screening that's on. That's the case with so many other filmmakers as well. Everyone talks about tall poppy syndrome in the Australian film industry, but as far as we can tell here in Western Australia, that's just not the case. Everyone shows up to everybody's films. Everybody is so supportive. People don't just rock up and shake hands, people rock up and give each other a hug. They want to celebrate that person's filmmaking. That's what we do this for. Trust me, we don't make a lot of money out of it.

The festival started in 2020, right before the pandemic. We had no way of knowing what was going to happen. I remember the last night of that festival where WA went into a shutdown two days after the festival wrapped. Can you run through the mindset of launching a film festival during a pandemic, and being able to successfully build on it each year?

ME: It was 2020 and on the Friday night, which was our opening night, there was still some mood that COVID wasn't real and that it wasn't going to reach us. I remember on that Friday night, Jaz and I were pulling up to the cinema in the car, and we got a phone call from the producer of *Below* (2019), Kate Neylon, who told us that the director, Maziar Lahooti, didn't want to attend the festival because he was worried about COVID. The main reason that he was worried is because he had family overseas who were experiencing it much more severe than we were in WA on that night.

That's when it sunk in, 'Holy shit. This is two years of planning. Two years of blood, sweat, and tears, and we might not have a festival tomorrow.' We were really emotional about it, but we pushed through, and audiences kept rocking up. I remember Scott Morrison did a press conference that Saturday morning and said that Australia was effectively shutting down from Tuesday, not Monday, because his sports team was playing. Can you believe that? We're going to revisit that in twenty years' time and go, 'What the fuck? Our Prime Minister wanted to watch a sports game, so we didn't shut the country down.'

People kept rocking up. Everyone was in their masks. All of our sessions continued to sell out. That's proof right there that people wanted to be a part of this. We knew from that moment, watching all of those people rock up with masks on, that we had created something special, that people were willing to ignore a pandemic to come and celebrate what we were trying to achieve.

Interestingly, the 2021 and 2022 festivals were the same where we had 50% capacity for the festival. There was this weird rule in 2022 where cinemas had to be at 50% capacity, but the foyer outside the cinema could be at 100% capacity. It was the most bizarre thing, but it was a benefit for us because we thought, well, let's open up three or four cinemas and split the audience into them. We were able to attract more audiences to those films. It worked in our favour. In saying that, it was an incredible mental stress to achieve all of that.

At the end of the day, if the 2020-2022 festivals proved anything, it was that what we were doing was working because people were still attending. Every session was a sell-out. Sessions like Sarah Legg's *Cherubhead* (2022) sold out four cinemas, but everyone had to wear masks at the time. If the pandemic proved anything to us is that there was a hunger for this kind of festival. That's what will continue to drive us going forward.

WA Made has also amplified notable works of art that have typified what WA is about. I'm specifically talking about the Ship to Shore event which screened three episodes of the series and worked as a reunion event for the cast and crew. How did you pull that event off?

ME: The other important thing about WA Made is that we don't always want it to be about the future. Yes, that is our main focus, but we also want to celebrate the past.

Ship to Shore was one of the most popular kids TV shows in Australia and it was made here and down in Rockingham. It was my wife's idea. We were trying to think of something different that we could do at the festival. I remember the moment my wife and I were driving home from Northam and she said, "You should do a *Ship to Shore* reunion." Once that idea was in my head, I just could not let it go.

Fortunately, I knew some people who worked on *Ship to Shore*, specifically Ewen Leslie. He and I talk quite regularly and he kind of got the ball rolling as soon as he said, "Yes, I want to be involved, whatever you need I'll do it." He couldn't fly over because it was during COVID, but he really wanted to be a part of it, which then in turn got Paul D. Barron, the co-creator of the show involved, then Kate Hall, another actor, became involved.

It was a phenomenal experience. That session sold out quickly. Once people hear that tune, they want to be a part of that. I sat there for the first five minutes of that screening just to see how the audience would react, and instantly there was laughter. You could sense that people were feeling that wave of nostalgia as they were instantly taken back to their childhoods. It was such a special screening.

I think the most special thing about that screening was that we had the original composer, Greg Schultz, there. *Ship to Shore* isn't *Ship to Shore* without that theme song. Everyone recognises it instantly. Everybody loved that show. We were very lucky to get Greg along. There was a special moment when I sat on the stage while he told us how he came up with the tune for *Ship to Shore*. I had a tear in my eye; I used to run home from school to watch *Ship to Shore*. It was a special experience to sit there and listen to the original composer explain how he came up with the music and then play the theme live for us.

You never know what's going to become part of the public consciousness. Unlike Round the Twist, Ship to Shore is not readily available. There are some episodes on YouTube, but it's not on streaming services, so it's amazing that it still manages to permeate Aussie culture after all this time.

ME: Do you know how long it took us to find out who had the rights to this show? Everything that we screen has a screening fee. We obviously weren't going to play *Ship to Shore* illegally. We did need to know who held the rights to it. Bouncing back and forth between Umbrella, who Paul Barron thought owned the show, we discovered that no, Paul still owns the rights to it. If anyone was going to be paid to screen it, it would be Paul, not Umbrella. That was a process in itself just to get the rights to show it. I think if we didn't, we still would have screened it in some capacity. We may have just played it off a laptop or something. We weren't going to let this one pass.

Can you talk about the importance of having those pivotal events?

ME: At the first festival, we had a screening of *Hunter: For the Record* (2012) and that was going to be the launch of our retro screenings. It was another emotional screening because Hunter, the person the film was about, had passed away, and a lot of his friends and family came along to be a part of the screening.

It's about creating a community. That's what these retro and celebration screenings are about: celebrating the community around those events. The same with the *Ship to Shore*, those actors hadn't seen each other for years. It was such a special experience. That was likely the only time that that will ever happen again.

These kinds of event screenings are hard to continuously put on every year because there aren't that many opportunities out there being little old WA. There are no other shows out there like *Ship to Shore*, so we can't have an event like that each year. We do have to do some digging. But to see the community form at these kinds of special events is something special.

Something that comes up in discussions with emerging filmmakers is that some never thought they could be filmmakers. It's something that 'other people' do. Part of the joy of going to a film festival is getting to have those in-person experiences with Q&A's and realising that Tasma Walton is a real person. She's in films, but she's physically there answering your questions. Can you talk about the importance of showing the WA Made audience that the role of being a filmmaker is attainable?

INTERVIEW | MATTHEW EELES

ME: It's really important. With the Q&A's, they humanise the filmmakers. They put a face and a voice to the people who aren't there on the big screen. Part of our process is that the people who are part of the Q&A have to hang around afterwards to talk to the filmmakers. They're not going to be able to walk out the door without being mobbed, especially someone like Tasma Walton, people are going to want photos with her. Part of our agreement is that they have to hang around for one hour afterwards to talk to people.

People have approached filmmakers or actors or whoever at WA Made to have a chat with them and have gotten jobs out of it. They have ended up on a film set later down the track because of the conversation that happened there on the night. That's vitally important. We've had other filmmakers who were a part of those short film screenings who met each other for the first time who are now writing scripts together and are shooting feature films together all because of a night at the WA Made Film Festival. How special is that? You can't pay for that kind of stuff. Forget about going to Star Now trying to look for roles, these people are doing it through these networking events and Q&A's at the festival.

It's great to see a community coming together, which leads me to your other passion: Cinema Australia. This has been running strong for ten years, and through the celebration of Australian cinema, a community has formed around it. What you do with Cinema Australia has been a huge inspiration for what I do and was a driving force behind why I wanted to get into writing and covering Australian cinema. Can you reflect on the importance of ten years of Cinema Australia?

ME: It's been the most phenomenal experience of my life. I've had the most fun in my life in the last ten years. It was about 13 years ago when I was experiencing some real mental stress and suffering, anxiety, and depression. I was in the deepest black hole that a human being could ever be in. I remember lying on the lounge and an ad popped up for 'Act Belong Commit[1].' That's where the idea of Cinema Australia came from. I needed to find a community to be part of.

Unfortunately, I didn't have a foot in the door to get into the film industry. I'd always wanted to be a filmmaker when I was younger, but opportunities fall away as you get older, and you move into other things. I thought, 'Well, how am I going to get into the film industry?' The only way I could do that was to build my own door and not only open the door, but absolutely kick it down. That's what I feel like I did with Cinema Australia. I wanted to make myself known and my presence known from the very beginning. People took an instant liking to it.

There are other publications out there, like IF Magazine and Filmink, who were covering Australian films, but they weren't 100% exclusively covering Australian films. That's what I knew my point of difference would be. I started making lifelong friends from the very beginning. It's been an incredible experience ever since. I have so much fun with this thing that now it's like one of my children. I could not imagine my life without Cinema Australia. It brings so much joy to my life.

Over the past ten years, things have evolved to the point where Cinema Australia has hit a level where filmmakers, especially independent filmmakers, will ask for my opinion on a script before they start filming, or will invite me to watch a rough cut of the film for my opinion before they go into picture lock. If I could go back to 15-year-old Matt, I'd be able to pat me on the back and say, "That's what you'll be doing. It's all gonna be okay. Everything's gonna be great."

What was the point that you knew you made it?

ME: The night that I interviewed Ben Elton (for *Three Summers* - 2017) on stage in front of about 400 people. Honestly, I had this moment where I asked myself, "What the fuck am I doing on stage with Ben Elton? What the hell is happening here?" I knew in that moment that it was not so much that I had made it, but more that what I was doing was important and that it was working. That people were taking notice of it and Australian films. There may have been other experiences similar to interviewing Ben Elton before that, but that's the one that really jumped out at me.

Since then, I've sat on stage interviewing Rachel Griffiths, Bryan Brown, Simon Baker, and people like that. Sometimes I think, 'What the hell am I doing here? What's going on?' It's obviously for a purpose. I wouldn't be doing it if I wasn't passionate about it.

When you're interviewing somebody, do you ever get an out-of-body experience?

ME: All the time. Impostor syndrome kicks in quite a bit; especially with someone like Bryan Brown, who must have done hundreds and hundreds of interviews in his time, and I'm sitting there thinking 'Shit, are these questions any good? Is what I'm saying any good?'

My mum passed away in 2009. She was 48 years old. She loved Australian movies and TV shows. If she went to the video shop, she'd always bring home an Australian film. It wasn't a conscious thing, she just loved Australian actors and celebrities, which is a word that I hate. She had a big crush on a lot of these people as well, like Bryan Brown. So, a lot of the time

INTERVIEW | MATTHEW EELES

when I'm interviewing those kinds of people, I go into this zone where I start thinking about Mum and think, 'Holy shit, imagine if she was sitting here or that I could show her this. She'd be stoked about it.' A lot of the time impostor syndrome kicks in, but then the feeling in that moment of 'if only Mum could see this,' kicks in as well, and that calms me down and makes me feel great.

Did your love for Australian films come from your mum?

ME: Yeah, I'd say so. I could never put a finger on it. I've always loved Australian screen film and television. When I was younger it was mostly TV, because Australian television series were on TV every night in primetime. 8:30pm you'd have *Water Rats*, *Blue Heelers*, or *Stingers*. Any of those shows would be on a Monday, Tuesday, Wednesday, Thursday night. To have that every night in front of your face is where that love and encouragement comes from. Now that's gone. It's completely disappeared. Every Friday night, Mum would go and get a video, and we'd watch something like *Priscilla* or *Muriel's Wedding*, things like that, so I guess that's also where it comes from.

Another thing that made me want to launch Cinema Australia was the filmmaker Sarah Watt, who made *Look Both Ways* (2005) and *My Year Without Sex* (2009). She came over to Perth for a Q&A for *My Year Without Sex*. I loved that movie. I remember looking around in the audience, and it must have been half full. I kept thinking, 'Where is everybody? Why isn't everyone flocking to the cinema to see this incredible piece of Australian art?' If it was a *Transformers* film, that screening would have sold out. So that was another reason I wanted to launch Cinema Australia.

I know you've talked to people who have since passed away. It leaves you with a strange feeling. I'm thinking of the iconic Damian Hill, who we both had great rapport with. What's it like to be a custodian for their voices and to provide a place for people to hear their stories and find out about their work after they've passed away?

ME: One of my biggest fears is if I were to pass away for some reason that these interviews that I've done would be lost. Dame Hill is one of those interviews that I continuously go back to thinking, 'How can I protect this interview so that it lives on well into the future?' Making sure that Dame's work lives on through that interview, as well. I haven't listened to that interview for quite a while now, but I think it opens with him talking about how he had to go and drop his kids off at school. He was such a casual person and was so happy to share stories with you. What I love about doing these interviews is being able to capture that kind of stuff.

WA MADE FILM FESTIVAL

Part of why I do what I do is to remind people that we do make good films. Even today, there's still a stigma against Australian film. Is part of your mindset with Cinema Australia a challenge to those people who share the notion that Australian cinema is not good?

ME: Look, honestly, it's not. The truth is, I believe that people aren't going to see Australian films at the cinema just because people aren't going to the cinema anymore in general. When they are, they're going to big blockbusters. It's not like when we were younger when people would run to the cinema to see independent films on the big screen. That's what I want to happen through Cinema Australia, but the reality of the situation is that it's not going to happen immediately.

I always say that I run Cinema Australia for future generations to learn and enjoy down the track. Watching a film like *Call Me Mr. Brown* (1990), for example, and seeing Chris Haywood's performance, all I could think about was 'Imagine if I could listen to a podcast from that time and hear Chris and Scott Hicks talking about the movie and how they made it.' What a thrill that would have been. My priority is to capture these Australian filmmaking stories so that people can listen back in the future and hear these great Australian filmmaking stories. People like you and me are really the only ones out there doing it.

The thing is that you and I are independent. We get to decide what we cover. Even though independent films are thriving more than ever in Australia, they don't get coverage because they don't get clicks or it's not sexy enough or something like that. That's the fire that keeps me going. I'm sure it's part of the fire that keeps you going as well, because unearthing something that's great, and then shining a light on it, is like nothing else.

ME: It does. I should go back to what I said before about it not being my priority. If it does put a bum on a seat at the time, then excellent, that's fantastic. I've done my job.

Back when I was in high school, all I wanted to do was make films. Opportunities fell away for one reason or another, so to see people succeeding in this industry, which is a really tough industry to succeed in, fills me with so much joy. I love watching people succeed in this industry. That's what Australian films mean to me the most.

ENDNOTES

1   Act Belong Commit is a Western Australian state-wide mental health campaign created by Mentally Healthy WA.

GENERAL HERCULES

97 mins
Director: *Brodie Poole*
Writers: *Matthew Bate, Brodie Poole*
Featuring: *John Katahanas*
Producer: *Ruby Schmidt*
Original Score: *Josh Wilkinson*
Cinematography: *Brodie Poole, Jaydon Martin, Joe McLaren*
Editors: *Brodie Poole, Annika Damon, Nina Pavlovic*

In 2023, General Hercules was nominated at the Thessaloniki Documentary Film Festival in the International Competition for the Golden Alexander award.

REVIEW
ANDREW F. PEIRCE

Set during the 2019 Kalgoorlie-Boulder Mayoral election, *General Hercules* positions the titular John 'General Hercules' Katahanas as the David to the incumbent Mayor John Bowler's Goliath. The regular person versus the political leader is always an engaging thematic battle, but director Brodie Poole is interested in more than this, turning his gaze towards the history of Kalgoorlie, the impact of racism, and the plight of the town under the shadow of the greedy. Poole captures the inner machinations of modern Australiana in a grotesque, grotty, hilariously philosophical, occasionally despondent manner, creating one of the most gloriously engaging documentaries to emerge into the pantheon of Australian cinema in a long time.

General Hercules politico-focus initially sets itself as a rural counterpoint to Bob Connolly and Robin Anderson's touchstone doc *Rats in the Ranks* (1996), but it quickly evolves from being Rats in the Superpit into a vessel that gives the citizens of Kalgoorlie the chance to present their diverse, authentic selves on screen. Through the prism of an election, we see a great level playing field where the visionaries and the misguided sit on equal ground as those seeking quality, justice and social stability or to maintain the status quo.

Deep in election mode, Mayor John Bowler takes to the streets to fight off his four competitors. These include Pam O'Donnell, a grandmother running on the platform of family under the banner 'Nanny Pam'; local council enthusiast and documentarian in her own right, Suzie Williams, who keeps creative scrapbooks and journals of council meeting discussions, replete with aggravated drawings in response to discussion points; Ian Burt, a Libertarian-adjacent figure who would rather see the local council completely removed than anything else; and John Katahanas, a mostly shirtless, always engaging larrikin who lives on the outskirts of Kalgoorlie in his weather-beaten caravan, searching for gold, and making plans for the future of Australia.

Katahanas' desire to overthrow the Mayor of Kalgoorlie-Boulder comes with a healthy dose of scepticism about the manner he operates the council. Alongside fellow Kalgoorlie citizens, Katahanas stokes rumours of corrup-

GENERAL HERCULES

tion online and in the streets, raising salient queries about John Bowler's membership at the local golf club, which in turn owes the city hundreds of thousands of dollars. While *General Hercules* doesn't detail John's full three-hundred-plus dot-point plan of what he would enact if he were to become mayor, it does offer moments where Katahanas explains his vision for turning Kalgoorlie-Boulder into a nuclear-powered region. As soon as the words leave his mouth, he's conscientious of their perceived impact, being strenuous to define that he means a mini nuclear power station and not a Fukushima-level generator. It's the nuance that matters, after all.

Poole straddles the line of being enamoured by his main subject – Katahanas – and wrapped with curiosity about his worldview, using his existence as a conduit for the history of Kalgoorlie and the fallout of Paddy Hannan's fortuitous discovery of gold in 1893. Interspersed between moments at John's home, and following candidates out on the hustings, Poole entwines motifs that encapsulate the history of Kalgoorlie into this political event.

Alongside fellow cinematographers Jaydon Martin and Joe McLaren, Brodie Poole presents a vision of Kalgoorlie that is entrancing and horrifying, yet it is forever in awe of the transformation that is undergoing the town on a physical, spiritual, and political level. Poole's choice of contrasting imagery and scenes layers upon one another to create an, at times, gut-tightening experience of unease, and others, furious bouts of laughter and hilarity.

A captivating and unnerving shot of vomiting molten gold spewing upon the land in the dark of night plays like footage of a far-off world. That entrancing imagery reflects against the debauchery of a day at the races, where swathes of fancy-dressed men and women lose their inhibitions in a perfume of beer and wine and the promise of financial glory at the betting box. The excess of the Bacchanalia is itself contrasted by images of troupes of high-vis-adorned FIFO workers being ferried in from Perth to dig a truckload of dirt out of the Super Pit, make a bunch of money for some company that isn't Australian, then fly on home again. The wealth that is conjured from these rare earth minerals will never be spent in Kalgoorlie, instead leaving a gaping hole for which the town can further establish their empire of dirt within.

The gaping maw of a goldmine colloquially called 'The Super Pit' lingers like a carnival sideshow tourist attraction only metres from the town. Its hunger is never satiated, and its size forever growing, creeps over time, swallowing history, swallowing the town itself, and swallowing memories of the past into a void of black nothing. Kalgoorlie sits in the path of the oncoming void, with the 30,000 people who call it home trapped by the progression of the ouroboros of mining. They live their lives like yabbies being cooked alive on a barbecue, trapped by the flames and stuck to their fate. As one person comments, the town is "A walking, breathing sarcophagus."

In the Kalgoorlie museum, the spectre of Paddy Hannan is projected into the darkness, retelling his story with a voice that sounds like it's ringing from the void of the pit itself. His face moves with pain and anguish as if it's pulling against the streams of light that bring it into existence, trying to break out of its spiritual realm and into humanity once again.

Poole's fascination with humanity as a whole, comes through strong in moments where he lets the camera just roll and capture the absurdity of the voting mind, like when a man walks up to John Bower on the street asking him "Are you the guy in the posters?", and then demands that he makes the skimpies skimpier. Later, the conflicted imagery of an Aboriginal pastor dressed as Santa, preaching the words of Jesus, plays against the same pastor talking about the rampant racism and housing inequality that exists within Kalgoorlie. It's clear that Brodie isn't looking to provide an answer for the state of this mining nation we call Australia, but rather to take a look at it under a microscope and tease out the tendrils that make it whole.

From a guttural boozy karaoke event to John Kataharas' unplugged gig in the middle of nowhere, a rolling motif of The Animals' iconic tune House of the Rising Sun carries on the air of *General Hercules*. The guitar lick that opens the song is peppered throughout the film, accentuated by the sound of John's metal detector as he searches for riches under the soil, its strained wail reflecting a pained earth at its holder, crying for a reprieve, squealing like an auto-tuned baby on the cusp of wailing.

Its tortured sound harmonises alongside the anger that flurries within John, a modern man who rages against the system he's tethered to. Within *General Hercules*, we see Kalgoorlie as a town that is furious and hurting, with the riots that eventuated after continued inaction after multiple deaths of Aboriginal folk. While the societal and structural racism of Australia isn't a key focal point for the film, it is pointed that we see a town that appears to be mostly ambivalent towards assisting and supporting Aboriginal kids, and instead is keen to install a system that brings back 'the cane', all the while maintaining status quo.

The characters that Brodie captures on screen aren't sideshow attractions or laughingstock, instead, these are figures that are full of intrigue and wonder, communing together on film to summon the powerful reminder that the nation of Australia is not a homogenous entity with citizens who are alike. It's a complicated and conflicted land, wrought by unresolved history and non-existent conciliation, powered by greed and the fight for glory, and that's all reflected with alarming lucidity on screen here. *General Hercules* stands as a triumphant example of what modern documentary filmmaking can look like.

GENERAL HERCULES

INTERVIEW
FILMMAKER
BRODIE POOLE

Brodie Poole's *General Hercules* portrays the vibrant personality of the Western Australian mining town Karlkurla-Kalgoorlie as the 2019 mayoral election campaign plays out. In the thick of the race is the titular General Hercules himself, John Katahanas, a true-blue larrikin who lives off the land, challenges authority, and has a grand vision for the future of Kalgoorlie.

This interview was recorded by Andrew F. Peirce in June 2022

What drew you to this story?

Brodie Poole: Co-producer Joe [McLaren] and I were living together in Brisbane, and we went on this big road trip to Western Australia because we had a lot of time on our hands. We both knew that we wanted to tell some kind of story, but we had nothing lined up. We skipped from place to place. We were in Wittenoom for a little bit, an old asbestos mining town, and didn't find a story there, and then went to New Norcia, which is Australia's only monastic town in Western Australia. We were like, "These monks are very quiet. They don't want to talk to us." Then we ended up in Kalgoorlie.

In a hotel room, I found John Katahanas 'The General'; he does these music covers of a lot of eighties Australiana songs. I reached out to him online to get hold of some of his music, and he gave us a mud map to his property out in the desert. He was a little showman, and when we got there, he played us music for hours into the night. He even had circles drawn on the ground where he'd identified where gold was and he was like, "I'll wait till the boys get in, and we'll dig up that gold and make it a real occasion." I spent three or four days with him on that trip. At the end, he said "I'm running for mayor next year. You should come back and film that too." We'd established a friendship at this point. Joe, John Katahanas, and I all loved to sit in that caravan, enjoy ourselves, and have a few drinks. We made that plan to come back for the mayoral elections.

GENERAL HERCULES

We originally only had the intention of documenting what we thought was going to be a madman campaign. It was only when we came back that we realised there were four other candidates who were all interesting in their own ways, and that this town is this interesting dysfunctional society that we're learning to understand.

What were the surprises along the way?

BP: We were surprised by everything, really. The willingness of each of the candidates who immediately want to divulge everything. Usually with documentary, you work for a very long time to get access. In this case, we rocked up and on day one, the candidates were like, "All right, sit down, get this on camera. I'm going to tell you my vision for Kalgoorlie" and were revealing the world to us. That was a great surprise.

The election was interesting because we got into it a bit late in the game. We were a little bit behind the eight ball. We were only filming the election for two or three weeks. A lot of the filming happened after the results were announced. I stayed on for three or four months just hanging out with John in the desert a lot of the time. I was surprised to realise the extent of the life that John has lived. He's a chess champion, he worked at SeaWorld, he was a chef. He's bluffed all his way into these bizarre jobs. It was nice to intimately get to know someone like that.

Did you feel like you'd struck gold when you first met him and decided to make a film around him?

BP: It felt like there was some significance to making the story. John has this kind of deep poetry about both the way he speaks and his life. Observing him as somebody who is out there in the pursuit of gold or running for mayor; it's a beautifully poetic life that he lives. It's like striking gold. He's such a chaotic character, it felt like we were on this ride, and there was no way to control the story.

I rocked up to him some days, "John, I'd love to get a scene of us on a salt lake prospecting." John would be like, "Nah, I'm not going to do that. I don't want to go to the salt lake." "All right, well, what are you going to do?" He's like, "Well, today I think I just want to fix my bobcat for six hours." "Okay, we're making this mayoral election film but I guess I'll film the bobcat thing." We had to relinquish a lot of control and roll with things. There's some gold in that.

How do you relinquish control as a director?

BP: I spent a lot of time out there; I knew that I was always going to be getting things. I can be a very quiet person as well. A lot of my time with John out in the caravan, I was just sitting with a camera on my lap, talking about whatever. I didn't ask him too many questions. I knew in my mind when there would be a film and when things were significant. I knew some days when he was changing a tire on his car [that] might not be the most interesting thing for a mayoral election film, but maybe as he changed the tire on the car, he would go into some kind of rant about the election. You never really knew. You just had to be there. The way the film ends, I was filming the ending knowing it was the ending. "I know that I've been here long enough now, and I know that this is the ending."

With the other candidates, you're talking about them being quite comfortable with the camera. How did you get to the point where they understood that this film wasn't part of their campaign?

BP: The way we made ourselves known to the candidates was "We're interested in the politics of regional towns and we're making a documentary." We gave a vague idea of what kind of film we were making. "We don't know exactly what it is yet, but we're figuring it out." Given that I present passively, the Mayor John Bowler was like, "[It] doesn't matter what film he's making, I guess I'll stand up now and I'll give to you what I deem to be suitable for such a documentary." People were given a lot of space to decide what the documentary was. Some people are performative. Other people are less performative. It's interesting to see what people will do when there's a camera around.

What was it like capturing the drone imagery of the Super Pit?

BP: I did all the drone stuff. That was behind little alleyways, popping it up, flying it over the Super Pit. To stand at the edge of the Super Pit, it's surreal because you're like looking deep into the bowels of the earth. The whole operation has this humming drone sound of the many trucks turning over. It's this kind of bassy sound that you feel in your belly. It's hard to grasp the idea of scale as well because the trucks look so tiny. You feel like you're living in this cartoon world, as the General might put it himself. I liked the idea of [using drone imagery to] try to emphasise the scale of these operations as best I could.

You talk to the other townspeople about the history of the Super Pit as well.

BP: Talking to the pastor, Geoffrey Stokes, raised the stakes. There was a gravity to what he was saying. The blue crosses on the houses and the impending demolition made the talking points of the town not theoretical or hypothetical when you can see this moving machine approaching the community of Ninga Mia. Then I started getting interested in the history of the Super Pit. One of the candidates, Suzie [Williams], talks about living in the neighbourhoods that were consumed by the Super Pit. One thing we were obsessed with was this idea of an event that happened in time – the finding of gold in the region – and there being this churning machine that is like history repeating itself over and over and over.

Did you find a similarity in Kalgoorlie-Boulder to other towns that you visited around Australia?

BP: I think there are similarities. One thing that Kalgoorlie does quite well is it's like a little *Simpsons* town, Springfield, where it felt like all of Australia's hot topic talking points existed on the street. We'd sit above the pub we were staying at, looking out from the verandah, and every night would be like a theatre playing out in front of you, the race relation problems of Australia or the marching capitalism of mining. You've got the FIFO people. Every contentious point existed in this hot pot of Kalgoorlie. It was glaringly obvious. You can find that stuff across all regional towns.

Did that excite you when you knew that you had this microcosm in this one town that you could capture?

BP: It was exciting, but it was deeply, personally disturbing as well. The film did really affect me. As you're filming, [you know] this is a significant story to tell. The stories I was hearing are deeply troubling to me. I was having my own ideologies ripped apart as I was hearing the words of those I was interviewing. It wasn't entirely celebratory when I was living and spending time in Kalgoorlie. I was also really sick at the time as well. I had an autoimmune disease that I was being diagnosed with. I had to fly a friend in to hold the camera for me because I was too weak to hold it. I lost 25 kilos or something. I was going through some kind of nightmare at the time. Sometimes you're in pain for consistent amounts of time. It really does something to you, it puts you in a headspace that you only realise after the event.

How did you keep yourself sane while you were working through your diagnosis?

BP: My friend Jaydon Martin was the cameraman I got to help, and Joe helped as well. They would take me to Perth, to the surgeries that helped me get diagnosed. How do I stay sane? I don't think I did completely stay sane, in all honesty. I think sometimes you've got to realise that you could be insane for small pockets of time, as long as you get out of it at some point. Hopefully, I have now, but we'll see.

There were good people around. The General is such a dear friend of mine, he's so compassionate. He has friends in town too. There's Kathy who is a real estate agent who took me in to stay a few weeks. There was the skimpy Saffron who was staying next to my hotel room, and we'd hang out on the deck after I'd shoot, just talking away into the early evening.

How do you find that balance of being friendly with the people that you're making a film about?

BP: It's an anxiety-inducing question, isn't it? I do deeply care about everybody that's been involved in the filming process. At the end of the day, I take the feelings away and I make a film. My observations are picked out and put on a screen to show people. I'm this judge and jury of how they are represented to the world. It's something I think about a lot and hope that I do as best as I can. I let people know that this is what I'm doing. "This is what the process of filmmaking is, it involves me doing this." Staying open has been good.

John Katahanas loves the film. His response was, "I see a great future for Brodie Poole films." Suzie likes the film as well. John Bowler hasn't watched it yet. We sent it over to him. He was kind of upset with the name of the film being *General Hercules*. I think he has this image in his mind that we've chosen to put the madman on screen because it sells out cinema seats and stuff, so he's like, "I don't think I'm gonna watch this." They did sign off saying that he's enjoyed my company. You hope you get it right. You hope you get your judgments right.

What makes a Brodie Poole film?

BP: I try to be as deeply honest as I possibly can. There's one [scene where] the General is walking around town, spruiking his policy, but distracted by a lemon tree. I like to leave moments like this in their natural state with very little cutting. Even the chronological structure of the film is very true to life. The election result is announced and then the film continues for 40 minutes. I don't enjoy twisting reality so much. I think what makes a Brodie Poole film is something that tries the best it can to be true to life.

Is that the draw to ob-docs for you, that true-to-life experience?

BP: I think this film isn't entirely ob-doc because there's so much connection between the subject and me with the camera. I'm very aware of the context. The reality is I'm a stranger in this town with a camera, and people in the world are responding to that. The observational film is sometimes very lifelike, but sometimes it feels [strange] to me to not acknowledge that someone is standing in the corner of the room holding a gigantic camera.

GENERAL HERCULES

That in itself isn't an entire representation of the truth either. I kind of like the interplay between what's being filmed and the fact that "Hello, there's a camera person in the room."

It's nice to know that you acknowledge that yes, there is a camera here. Often people suggest it doesn't exist. "Somehow this footage appeared, and I've got it and made a film out of it."

BP: As if the images were plucked out of the atmosphere. There's context for everything. [During] the racecourse scenes, maybe they [thought I was] an events photographer. If you take a close look at the way news is put together, it's incredibly strange. The way someone presents the weather in front of an LCD screen, and we believe it to be normal because it's what the news is.

Can you talk about the creation of the score?

BP: It was composed by a friend of mine, Josh Wilkinson, and a whole bunch of his musician friends. I was starting conversations with Josh early on, and we took rushes to a warehouse and projected them on the wall. Most of the music was improvised. I didn't really know how to structure the film at this point. "Here's some footage of lava gold pours, hellish scenes, what can we do for this?" Josh would start a demonic guitar thing and then Joseph Burgess on the violin would improvise something. When we knew that there was something in one of the tracks being recorded, Josh would take it away and spend a bit more time finessing and adding to it and shortening it because a lot of these session recordings were 20-minute tracks.

I think you can feel the improvised nature in some of the music. I was pacing around the warehouse and in my mind, I had an idea for a scene. That jazz track when the newspapers are swinging through the factory; as that one starts, I can hear the musicians chatting to each other, getting everything sorted. I'm interested in the way in which information passes about Kalgoorlie. "Here's some footage of newspapers, what do you reckon?" Josh just pointed to the jazz drummer, and he started [playing], and Josh was saying "Speed it up, slow it down."

A lot of decisions were made on the fly. The opening song is an incredible track. It begins with a guitarist. He tuned his guitar so that every string was in mathematically perfect tuning, which is unnatural to human hearing. Typically, a G chord is always slightly out of tune, most chords are, but this had this strange quality and then he kept plucking it in this kind of pulse. Later, Josh would add elements over the top, violin, and vocals of his wife Yofe in Thai. It was a lot of fun. Even the horse racing scene which is *The House of the Rising Sun* cover. I brought ten of my friends from Bundaberg around for that, and we were all given hammers, banging on the walls of the warehouse which had microphones placed all over the joint. Good fun.

What was the choice behind using The House of the Rising Sun?

BP: I think it began from when we recorded that fella singing the karaoke song and just got fixated on the idea. Strange thing to fixate on, really. In this town, there's so much happening but I guess we wanted to hold on to some kind of ground. I think *House of The Rising Sun* was one thing. We were like, "We can do this, you know? That can be under our control."

What does it mean to be an Australian filmmaker right now?

BP: When I began making the film, I didn't have a clear image of Australia. Australia is this dysfunctional place. I definitely did the whole 'going into the desert to try to figure it out' kind of thing. What does it mean to be an Australian filmmaker now? I think it's important to realise the absurdity of what's happening in Australia right now. I think Australia is still trying to figure itself out, and it's good to be a part of that conversation. I've not figured Australia out, but I definitely enjoy being an observer of the way in which it rolls across.

GENERAL HERCULES

INTERVIEW
COMPOSER
JOSH WILKINSON

Part of what makes General Hercules such a riveting and powerful experience is the immersive and tone-setting score by Josh Wilkinson. His score is at times otherworldlie, amplifying the feeling that Kalgoorlie is not from this world. Guitars wail like possessed goats, screaming into the night as if they're minions summoned from the maw, prowling the bush at night. Often the score for a documentary feels rudimentary, as if it is the last creative choice before pushing the film into the world, but Wilkinson's work here is truly masterful, elevating the General Hercules to even grander heights.

This interview was recorded by Andrew F. Peirce in July 2022

When did you come on board?

Josh Wilkinson: Brodie had shot mostly everything. He was in Brisbane working at this amazing building that was falling down. He got me involved as they were starting to edit. We sort of did the edit process together. The process kind of went like this, I would go into this warehouse with three guys – Joseph Burgess, Nick Lavers and drummer Caleb College – and we would put up long rushes on the wall on a projector, 10-minute shots, and just play to the shots. Then we would give those long jams to Brodie. He would stick them to things as he was editing. From there, they kind of got more and more refined.

It's so good to have a project that you just really love as a thing, as a capturing of a moment. From the first few rushes I saw, [I thought] "Yep, this is exactly what I want to see on the screen." When Brodie first asked me, there was a bit of expectation that I put on myself, because I really wanted to elevate those images. I tried as hard as I could to do that.

The score feels like a little bit of The Dirty Three. What are your influences as an artist?

GENERAL HERCULES

JW: Yeah, totally The Dirty Three. Joseph plays the violin, we saw them at Vivid [Live] the year before and we're big fans. Also, the classic Dead Man score [by Neil Young], Jim Jarmusch. The way that they did that, I was just completely copying that in the warehouse. I thought it was an interesting method because it allows you to have a space for the sound. In a lot of scores and a lot of music that I like, the bands or the artists are recording something live in a space. A lot of bands I listen to, Nick Cave stuff, [in] the recordings you can hear the room, you can hear that it's being played live, and that signature translates so well when you're making a score, because everything has the same feeling no matter the mood you're going for. If it's all from the same space, then it feels coherent. I tried hard to capture it all there and do very few overdubs.

Did Brodie give you any pointers as to what emotion he wanted for the score?

JW: Yes, and no. It's sort of obvious from the footage: very open, very empty, kinda like Australian Gothic. We didn't have to talk so much about that because it was kind of obvious. There were a few scenes that he wanted to capture, like some funny moments, and some exaltational moments. Then we had themes. When we threw up the shots on the wall, we would just kind of go "Okay, this one's got to be more happy." Brodie was there a lot of the time, just sitting on the floor playing guitar, or just hanging out, but he really didn't direct it too much. We were both on the same page. I gave him so much material that it was up to him. His role was more about choosing what went in.

The score resonates and it says Kalgoorlie so much. Have you been to Kalgoorlie?

JW: I've never been no. I was a bit sad. I've been spending a lot of time in Moree [NSW]. It's not the same, but it has a similar feeling in that town. I was sort of channelling that while I was doing it. My uncles are geologists in Perth, so I know the vibe a little bit.

I was researching some great records that have been made at a studio [Studio Asaph] in Boulder. They put out a compilation record of a few bands, like The Brownley Gospel Singers, an Indigenous gospel group. At the very start I was pushing to have a few tracks from bands in town, which didn't work out.

I was listening to a lot of that music, trying to hear what people there were making.

INTERVIEW | JOSH WILKINSON

One of the motifs that runs throughout the film is The Animals track House of The Rising Sun. Did that influence your choice of what instruments you might be playing?

JW: Yeah, that one and the harp piece. The General plays a lot of songs. At the start, in the edit, there was a lot more of him playing. We thought it would be fun to meld his style of playing those tracks with the score versions and have them meld together. His fell away and then we were just left with the score version. I think the reason *House of The Rising Sun* is in there is because he was playing it, and then I created a version in his style. It did influence [the score]. I think it's a great track, it sums up a lot of the vibe.

The whole guitar wailing, wailing violin, and like weird electronics, that stems from the environment, like this pub rock noise that just seems to be seeping out of every building. And then the extremely weird sci-fi-like towers and mining equipment that's everywhere. It's kind of like a modern Gothic sci-fi in some ways, so I wanted to capture that as well.

It felt otherworldly, like this was not a place on Earth. What instruments did you use?

JW: We had two main studio setups. One was in the warehouse. I was playing electric guitar, and then we had Joseph playing violin, and my friend Nick playing electric, banjo, bass, and drums. We were turning it up really loud in those sessions. Then in my studio, we had more of a chill [vibe]. Acoustic guitars, banjos, and acoustic violin. There were three or four main instruments. A lot of the electronicky weird stuff was Joseph [and I]. He runs his violin through like a big modular rig, and I was running through some pretty weird pedals. We were getting all these spacey sounds from that.

What kind of mindset are you in when you're creating that? What's the vibe in the room?

JW: The way I found this works is by asking people that you trust really well. Like Nick, he was my guitar teacher when I was in school. We've known each other for twenty years now. [With] this kind of thing where you just throw up a picture and go for it, it doesn't work with everyone, you have to really be in tune, and everyone has to know what you're going for.

There are two approaches. One is you sit there as a composer and you write all the notes out, and you make it all perfect, and then you get players to play it. That takes a lot of time. Then there's the other approach, which is very spontaneous, where you just put people in a room and do it. But the time in that is like building the musical communication and the trust that you know what you're doing.

GENERAL HERCULES

There wasn't much talking. It wasn't much planning. It was just kind of like doing it. The sounds help like when I was playing the guitar, or when Joseph was playing the violin, the words we were using were "This has to sound more rocky." I don't mean rock music, I mean it has to sound like rocks moving, or explosions of mines. Just trying to create soundscapes with the instrument, not like notes.

I understand that something you're really interested in is exploring what sound can do to people. The comparison between music and sound is that they are very different. Music is music. Here, sound is the sound of rocks and explosions and things like that. What draws to the emotional impact that sound can create?

JW: With film music, it's just functional music. It's completely tied to the story and the emotion that you're trying to do. If you're thinking about it like that, the gap between what is music and what is sound becomes blurry. There are some Kanye West tracks where he uses sounds to create emotions. If you apply that same mentality to a film score, you can make a screaming sound wave just going like [imitates screaming noise], which no one would put in a song, but it creates the effect that you need at that moment in the scene.

It's always a good thing, I think, to broaden the parameters of what is sound and what is music. I don't know where it comes from. When I was in uni studying this stuff, I loved the way that certain sounds just always created that emotion. You could rely on it. You can use that within music to do what needs to be done for the scene.

What's the difference for you in the process of creating something for a film, as opposed to for a song or an in-person experience like an art exhibition?

JW: Film has a lot of built-in tropes, and the people who watch films understand a lot more than say, an art exhibition, but the rules are kind of loose. In film, you can really play against the rules. Especially with this film, the role of a documentary score is just to make the pieces to the camera not boring, it's just to kind of move it along. That's all people are expecting. When you go a bit further and make the score like a character in the documentary, people will respond to that. I like playing with expectations. Those are different depending on if it's music, or if it's an interactive installation, or whatever. For music, you've got to tone it down a little bit, because genres are a thing.

Do you have a certain genre or style that you prefer to work in?

JW: With what I was just saying about my love of sound, I think that means that I don't. I like functional music and playing with that, because you can then know what the audience is expecting and how you can play with it. I work a lot with my partner helping produce her music, that's kind of indie, soft, electronic music.

I'm curious for you whether there is [an] intention to build a body of work? Is that in your mind as you're creating each song or score or is it kind of one project at a time?

JW: I'm definitely interested more and more in the projects that I say yes to. I'm not consciously thinking about creating a body of work, but I guess it's happening. The more I say no, and the more I say yes, it becomes apparent that it is very much about this Australiana-like identity pulling at the cracks of what that is. I think as an Australian moving abroad, being in Iceland now for almost two years, it's becoming more and more apparent what the Australian identity is as I have a bit of distance. It's super fun to explore that from a distance because you're not so caught up in it. You can really pinpoint that when [you don't live in] Kalgoorlie, and then you see images from there, it's so easy to be like, "This is so unique. This is so amazing." I want to highlight that. I'm saying yes to projects that go really to the core of the Australian issue.

How important is getting to pick apart the seams of Australian culture through music?

JW: One of the coolest things about this project was at the very start, as soon as Brodie told me about it, I went and did a little bit of research about Kalgoorlie and Boulder, and came across this amazing paper, which was written in the nineties. It was a collection of musical performances from Kalgoorlie-Boulder. From the beginning, it was recording the first concert that ever happened in that area in the 1890s, right through to the 1920s, when the first piano came and what songs were played. It's amazing because it tells the story of what they were thinking at times.

The first song, which is in the film, that was ever sung in Kalgoorlie was *The Man Who Broke the Bank at Monte Carlo*, a song about a guy who wins the casino in Monte Carlo, and then just walks [away] with all the money. You can imagine what they were thinking at the time for that to be the first song ever performed. There are amazing accounts of [a] father and son playing violin and piano in the first church, and the piano arriving. It's incredible. Exploring that and bringing that into a modern context and trying to talk back to those early mentalities of the people is super what I'm interested in.

GENERAL HERCULES

When you come to a place like Iceland where the culture is so absent of any guilt, let's put it that way, you realise how much stuff there is being an artist in Australia. At least for me, it's very difficult to do anything without any justification. There is so much that needs to be justified. Exploring how music or any art can fit in with that and fit in with unpacking the story of colonisation and what that means. Having a small voice in that broader discussion is really interesting to me and important.

TANGKI & KUKAPUTJU

Tangki (Donkey)
6 mins
Cultural Director: *Tjunkaya Tapaya OAM*
Cultural Advisors: *Akitiya Angkuna Tjitayi, Imuna Kenta, Carolyn Kenta*
Director, Animator, Stop-Motion DoP, and Editor: *Jonathan Daw*
Executive Producer: *Michelle Young*
Story Editor and Creative Producer: *Karin Riederer;*
Storytellers: *Akitiya Angkuna Tjitayi, Imuna Kenta, Anne Karatjari Ward;*
Character Artists: *Tjunkaya Tapaya OAM, Carolyn Kenta, Imuna Kenta, Stacia Yvonna Lewis, Atipalku Intjalki, Lynette Lewis, Elizabeth Dunn, Cynthia Burke*
Live Action Cinematography and Sound: *Pitjantjatjara Yankunytjatjara Media*
Live Action Community Producer: *Loria Heffernan*
Scene Directors: *Tjunkaya Tapaya OAM, Carolyn Kenta*
Donkey Song Composer: *Akitiya Angkuna Tjitayi*, sung by *Akitiya Angkuna Tjitayi, Katrina Tjitayi, Umatji Tjitayi*

Kukaputju (The Hunter)
6 mins
Cultural Director and Storyteller: *Yanyangkari Roma Butler*
Cultural Advisors: *Cynthia Burke, Delilah Shepherd;*
Director, Animator, Stop-Motion DoP, and Editor: *Jonathan Daw*
Executive Producer: *Michelle Young*
Creative Producer: *Karen Riederer*
Character Artists: *Yanyangkari Roma Butler, Stacia Yvonne Lewis, Diane Dawson, Yangi Yangi Fox, Rene Nelson, Lucy Nelson, Cassie-Anne Woods*
Live Action Cinematography and Sound: *Anna Cadden;*
Live Action Community Producers: *Cynthia Burke, Sally Foster*

INTERVIEW
FILMMAKER JONATHAN DAW, PRODUCERS KARIN RIEDERER & MICHELLE YOUNG

Anangu stories from the Ngaanyatjarra Pitjantjatjara Yankunytjatjara (NPY) Lands, the central desert region of South Australia, Western Australia, and the Northen Territory, are told with a joyful cheekiness in the two stop-motion animated short films *Tangki (Donkey)* and *Kukaputju (The Hunter)*. Director and Animator Jonathan Daw worked alongside the Tjanpi Desert Weavers, Creative Producer Karin Riederer, and Executive Producer Michelle Young to collaboratively bring these stories to life in the language of Pitjantjatjara.

Tangki, from the Pukatja community, sees three Anangu women of different generations, Akitiya Angkuna Tjitayi, Imuna Kenta, and Anne Karatjari Ward, talk about how the introduced species of donkeys became malpa wiru, good friends and helpers to their community. Jonathan worked with 20 Tjanpi artists, including Elizabeth Dunn and Imuna Kenta, and Cultural Director Tjunkaya Tapaya OAM, to create the various characters. The women's stories of their bonds with the donkeys come from the happy childhood memories they have of riding them in the 1950s and 60s, also known as the 'mission times.'

With *Kukaputju*, Cultural Director and Storyteller Yanyangkari Roma Butler share the tale of how she would head out into the bush to go hunting with her dog, Kungka, near the tri-state border of Western Australia, South Australia, and the Northern Territory. Together, they discover a creature that is notoriously difficult to catch: the feral cat. When they do finally catch the destructive creature, they're rewarded with a delicious meal to share with one another and their friends. Characters and props for *Kukaputju* were made by Tjanpi artists in Irrunytju and Warakurna communities in Western Australia.

The artists would use tjanpi (desert grasses) such as minarri, wangunu, and intiyanu to create the characters, desert grasses collected from their Lands. These grasses would be bound together around wire frames using string, wool, or raffia, with the outer layer being stitched and human hair being created from unspun sheep's wool. With Jonathan's collaborative methods, the energy of nature is brought to life with a vivid realisation of the creatures and people who call this land their home.

Tangki received the Yoram Gross Award for Best Animation at the 2022 Sydney Film Festival, alongside the AFTRS Craft Award.

This interview was recorded by Andrew F. Peirce in March 2023

Could you discuss the reasoning behind using animation to portray the narratives crafted by the Tjanpi Desert Weavers?

Michelle Young: As a Tjanpi manager, I was approached by Jonathan to consider doing this sort of project. We thought it was a great way of using the artwork to tell those stories. It was very experimental for us. We've never quite done anything like that before. We obviously appreciated that Jonathan had worked for other Indigenous organisations around our area here as well. We thought that it would be a good opportunity to tell stories, as artists are always trying to do differently, and to be able to tell those stories to the wider world. That began with the two animation films that we made previous to *Tangki* and *Kukaputju*.

Jonathan Daw: This project came out of the initial discussion that Michelle and I had years ago. From my point of view as a stop-motion animator, someone who is passionate about handmade animation and in-camera filmmaking, I'd been looking at Tjanpi artworks for years, and thought there's so much potential [there]. It's such a unique art form [with] so much character. I thought the two mediums had a lot of potential to work well together. I approached Michelle and we made a plan to make two short animations in Warakurna with Cynthia Burke and the other tjanpi artists in that community. The first two films (*Ngayuku Papa: Bluey and Big Boy* and *Ngayuku Papa: Tiny*), which were much simpler, and smaller budget, things went really well, and then Michelle, thought it'd be good to do something with a bit more time and budget, to do something really detailed. And that's how these two films came about.

MY: The original two films were shown at Desert Mob during the symposium there, and what struck me most profoundly was how much Aṉangu themselves enjoyed seeing them on screen, and how much humour was intrinsic to the films. I recall being quite moved by how much people loved them, and exploring it in a little bit more detail with Jonathan again because it is a very new way of working for artists. It was originally those first few films done in Warakurna, so we thought, let's maybe even tell some stories further afield. I think, given how resource-heavy it is for Tjanpi, I'm not sure I would have approached it again, but I did based on that initial response from Anangu.

Karin Riederer: I was brought in just for *Tangki* and *Kukaputju*. I was the manager of Tjanpi for a couple of years before Michelle. So, I already had a relationship with a lot of the artists, which was a great asset. Michelle brought me in once she'd secured funding for these two most recent films.

What was your first reaction when you heard that these stories were being told in this way?

KR: I was really excited. Being familiar with the properties of Tjanpi, and part of my background is in book publishing, and from the year dot, before I even joined Tjanpi, when I first encountered their work, I'd thought, "Wow, you could do an amazing kids picture book," which was actually part of this project as proposed. For me, it was both the book element and the film element. I love animation as well, particularly stop-motion. It's that handcrafted element that Jonathan has referred to and so [it's] a beautiful melding of those two. I was familiar with the *Ngayuku Papa – My Dog* films. They're such fun, and warm and quirky, embodying what Tjanpi has become renowned for.

That quirkiness and the comedy and the laughter that comes from that is organic. It's beautiful because it's part of how the story is told. This is a labour-intensive process of creating the visual aspects of these different creatures, especially the blinking of the eyes, the limb movement, and more. Can you talk through the creative process of how each of those designs were created, and what the collaboration and discussion process was like with the artists to create those different visuals?

KR: Part of the initial process was recording a bunch of stories that were offered up, and then making a selection of what might work for the medium. Once that process was [complete], there was a discussion with the artists who were present about what they wanted those films to look like. Interestingly, with both of them, in the cohorts of artists, there was a little bit of crossover. They were both very clear that they didn't want their country to appear simply as blue sky and red dirt, because it's much richer than that. They wanted the vegetation to be representative.

It was an interesting point, because part of Tjanpi's aesthetic is that it is quirky and you might go, "Gee, what's that?", but they really wanted their country to be represented. That dictated a whole bunch of things around the specificity of trees, flowers, grasses, birds and so on, as well as the colour and the colour wave for each film. Tjanpi staff, Jade Brockley on *Kukaputju* and Emma Franklin on *Tangki* were instrumental in working out the colour palette, from being in the country and looking at things and talking with the women about what colours would work, and so on.

The family of the storytellers already knew these stories, and in this visual medium, everything depicted needed to make sense to Anangu when they saw the films. The artists felt a great sense of responsibility for this. They know their country intimately of course and their assets list was marvellously long. Everyone pretty quickly realised it had to be whittled down a bit. For Tangki, for example, a stand of corkwood trees that is at Balfours Well was essential.

JD: All of the assets were made in workshops. I wasn't heavily involved in choosing the aesthetics for the models, that all came from the artists themselves, who have a lot of experience making human characters, dogs, donkeys, all the birds, and animals. As Karin was saying, a lot of work was done on the landscape and the vegetation. From my point of view, as the animator, I needed these things to be able to move, so we were introducing some things that were new to a lot of these artists. We built the artwork around armatures, so I helped Jade and Cynthia who work in Warakurna learn how to make the armatures, which are like an aluminium wire skeleton, on which the things are built around, which allows them to hold their shape when I'm moving them in small increments.

For things like talking, I wanted a variety of mouth shapes, so when you see the characters talk, I'm pulling off a mouth, pinning on another mouth. I might go from a closed mouth to an open mouth and various shapes to make them talk. I had all these specifications about what was required to make these artworks animatable, which is sort of a learning process for a lot of the artists involved in that. On the Western Australian side, Jade and Cynthia were really good at working on all of that stuff. I was in one of the workshops down in Pukatja with Karin and Emma, and we worked on all these things.

The other thing with the vegetation, artists are experienced in making trees and stuff, but we had different specifications for how that could work in set building terms. We used what we call a 'forced perspective' on our sets, so you might have various scales of trees with big ones in the foreground and small ones in the background. I had to work out how to do various scales of all the different types of plants and stuff to make it all work. The stop-motion process involved a considerable amount of trial and error, and I find the creative problem-solving aspect particularly enjoyable.

KR: With the armatures, the women are used to working on a bigger scale usually, so working smaller was quite challenging on some of the birds and so on. With the donkeys, Jonathan designed some armature that we had made by Nick Pledge in Melbourne so that they were more articulated because they were going to get a big workout so that they would survive the process. But it was a complex thing because the women have learned across the years that to make a good strong sculpture, it needs to be tightly bound and then tightly stitched, to make a high-quality sculptural piece, and for these to work with the animation with the armature, it needed to be a bit looser. So, a bit of unpicking had to happen with some of them in order for Jonathan to be able to get them to move. There was a lot of trial and error. It'd be great if you could share the level of improvisation you went to including using your carjack on set.

JD: That's often something used in stop-motion animation, because carjacks are good for moving up and down in increments. So, I had the donkeys rigged on a carjack. I could just turn the knob and move it up and down. We had Nick Pledge who's in Melbourne, he's had a lot of experience working on stop-motion projects. He made us some really good armatures, which were really helpful with those donkeys.

As Karin [mentioned], the artists had to learn to make things a bit looser than they had previously. One of the things that happened was that there were a lot of really fine bits of Tjanpi that fell out of the puppets as I was animating them. We ended up treating it as a bit of a happy accident. For example, when the character when Yanyangkari is walking, and we've got a close-up of her feet walking, you can see that loose Tjanpi falling on the set. Instead of trying to clean that up, we just left that there and it sort of forms footprints. I think that's a really nice touch and one of those happy accidents that comes from this trial and error involved in working with a new technique.

That's one of the reasons why I love stop-motion - the humanity of the creators shines through so clearly on screen. With these stories, it's that blend of the people telling them, the artists, and yourself Jonathan, bringing them to life. There is that real sense of community here. What does that sense of community mean to you, especially telling stories from Central Australia and parts of Australia that usually aren't presented on screen?

MY: I take my cues from Anangu themselves where representation matters and seeing your stories on screen is a very powerful thing. We went to the opening night of the Travelling Film Festival and *Tangki* was the first one off the ranks and we had four artists up from Pukatja to see that. They were mesmerised by it. It's really important to have these stories shared and people's narratives told, while also showcasing their artwork in a fresh perspective that conveys these stories effectively. It's a very powerful thing telling stories for women out in the region, they feel a sense of responsibility to share those stories for the benefit of their grandchildren. There's something a bit immortal about film as well that it'll be around to tell those stories well into the future. For me, it was always about how much Anangu embraced the stories, how much joy they get from seeing them, and how much humour it brings to people in what is really a very labour-intensive, arduous process. That was probably the reason for doing it for me.

KR: I would echo what Michelle has said there in terms of taking the cue from Anangu. As an example, *Tangki* has three storytellers, and that wasn't in the brief. But when those stories were being offered up, Pukatja has a very strong history through the missions with donkeys and, particularly [for] the older generation of women, there's such a fondness for donkeys. So with such a large group of women sitting there, how on earth is a story going to be selected? It wasn't just those three [stories], there were others as well. The donkey [idea took] hold, and the senior women were saying, "Well, we could choose one, or we could try and put them all together. What should we do?" that's their decision. "Let's put them all together." Then you get a story across time.

The support throughout the community was such a fabulous thing to witness. That everyone got behind it all around the community in different ways, that speaks to both an individual and a collective approach to the storytelling. It turned out to be a rather lovely thing with the three storytellers.

Another unplanned bit was that they're all in the frame when they're telling the story. I find it quite a beautiful thing in how they responded to each other's stories where you get that relational aspect through the intercutting of them telling their story.

JD: I've been lucky enough to see these films in a few different contexts now, in film festivals, and in Alice Springs. I always like seeing the reactions of the different audiences when you compare people that are hearing it as a first language as opposed to people that are reading the subtitles. There are always different things that people laugh at. It's just great to see people from those communities watching those films and picking up little bits and pieces that a broader audience might not.

MY: I really like in *Tangki* that little gesture of one of the ladies when she's pointing to people coming along to where they're going. These [are the] kinds of nuanced details that only Anangu might pick up. They've kind of suggested that's how it should be done. There [are] lots of layers to it, and everyone's reading something off it.

JD: We wanted in the process of making it to get the input of the cultural directors on those little things. Even in terms of small things like hand gestures, where people are sitting when there's a group scene and things like that, it was really important for us to get those details right. So, when the Anangu are watching it, it makes sense.

The films have travelled not just around Australia, but internationally as well. Is there a particular reaction that has stuck with you from different audiences?

JD: For me a real highlight was having the chance to go to the Sydney Film Festival and seeing Imuna get up in front of a massive audience and make a speech, almost completely in Pitjantjatjara, and how that was appreciated by that big audience of film lovers from all over the place. [For] those audiences, it's really good for them to see things in language. I remember the first time I saw *Bush Mechanics* on TV and saw people laughing in Aboriginal languages. Growing up in the suburbs, I've never really heard much Aboriginal language. I think it's great for those things to get out to a big audience, as well as being for the communities themselves at the same time.

MY: For me, it was lovely to receive the Yoram Gross Award and the AFTRS Craft Award, but also for me, on another level, it was nice that the film travelled for the NT Travelling Film Festival and went to all these tiny communities. The big acknowledgments [are lovely], but it's about making it accessible to remote communities as well, which is really important. Alice Springs is having a difficult time at the moment, and the more inspiration the creative industries can give to communities about some of the joyful, innovative, creative work that's being done, and building pride across generations is really important for us to be doing as we go forward. Giving youth a sense of pride and joy as well as not giving up hope.

KR: What's struck me more is Tjanpi staff continuing to do various workshops at the bush and sending me photos from time to time of all the artists crowded around the laptop, out bush watching the films on the laptop. That's frequently how they're in circulation out in the communities. That brings so much joy that they're watching them on repeat. All the kids rushed in and everything, and we'd get sent these photos of everyone gathered around the computer in the area watching them. There is the important, bigger picture of going out into different parts of the world, and particularly with language too. I think that that's such an important thing there are offerings that [nudge] people beyond remote areas towards an understanding of the diversity of First Nation cultures. Those openings to understanding so it's not just about talk.

As you're saying, getting to hear your own and other people's stories is so vital for the continuation of culture. One of the things I really appreciate about both of these films is that they talk about the relationship with animals across communities. There's the introduced species of donkeys and cats, and there is this fluidity to the way that communities have responded to these creatures appearing in their lands. I'm curious if you can talk about the importance of showing the relationship that these communities have with animals on screen?

JD: When Michelle and I originally spoke about this, we had the idea of doing dogs for the first two animations. It was great material for both Tjanpi artists and for stop-motion animators, so it sort of made sense, when we collaborated, that that would be the theme. We put it out there to the artists to tell stories about other animals this time and these are the stories that came out.

KR: Animals are integral to culture, whether it's meat animals or non-meat animals, that's the distinction. Some of those introduced species are meat animals, and some are not. They have very much been absorbed into the cultures of those regions, one way or another. The cat hunting one is an interesting one because obviously that is not seen as a marvellous thing by everybody. We always knew that that could be a little bit contentious, but it's a fact of life. They're not so commonly hunted now, but they certainly were back in the early 1900s, [and were] very much a feature of the diet of the hunting lifestyle there. The pride that Yanyangkari has in having managed to catch a cat with the help of her dog, because they're a notoriously difficult animal to hunt down, there's a tremendous amount of pride there, and it's like a number one hunting story as a result.

I understand the impacts of feral cats, so getting to catch one hopefully means the other animals will be safer.

KR: Yes, though the reason for hunting them is more that it's a really juicy, delicious, tasty, fatty meat. That's what makes them a great catch.

What is the importance of representing or showing the Australian identity on screen for you as filmmakers or storytellers?

JD: I think that it is important that a diverse range of people and stories are represented in Australian films. In the context of these films, I feel lucky to have had the opportunity to collaborate and work with these stories. These films are for both Anangu audiences and broader audiences and I think it's great for people from all over to hear the unique stories and humour that come out of communities.

MY: I'm always guided by one of my malpa's here, who passed away recently, and she always says that Tjanpi presents a different way of being able to tell their stories. Whatever opportunities are presented to us, I take it back to Aṉangu as another way to tell those stories. That's always a guide for me as a manager here, in giving women all sorts of opportunities to continue to tell stories and using Tjanpi as the vehicle. I think this is a really beautiful way of telling those stories, and it's very engaging for Aṉangu to see it on screen too.

KR: The whole thing of an 'Australian identity' is probably something I veer away from, rather than towards, as a hangover from the Howard era, I think, when a singular 'Australian identity' was trying to be forced upon everyone. Except that, a lot of my work is about trying to create the space for other voices and stories to enter into the mainstream, as well as serving the primary purpose of being there for people's grandchildren. Like Michelle has said, consistently, that's what I hear from Aṉangu, "We want this to be there for our grandchildren and our great grandchildren." From my personal perspective, language is such a central part of anyone's identity, and for the Pitjantjatjara language to be built into the film in the ways that it is, including in the credits, that felt really important.

GOLD

97 mins
Director: *Anthony Hayes*
Writers: *Anthony Hayes, Polly Smyth*
Cast: *Zac Efron, Susie Porter, Anthony Hayes, Akuol Ngot, Thiik Biar, Andreas Sobik, Cricknowle*
Producers: *Anthony Hayes, John Schwarz, Michael Schwarz*
Music: *Antony Partos*
Cinematography: *Ross Giardina*
Editing: *Sean Lahiff*

In 2022, Gold received an AACTA Award nomination for Best Hair and Makeup for Jennifer Lamphee and Beth Halsted.

INTERVIEW
HAIR & MAKE-UP DESIGNER JENNIFER LAMPHEE

Hair and make-up artist Jennifer Lamphee has crafted an impressive Australian-based career with work on Hollywood productions like *The Wolverine* (2013) and *Pacific Rim: Uprising* (2018), and local productions like *Wolf Creek 2* (2013) and *Ladies in Black* (2018), which she won the 2018 AACTA Award for Best Hair and Makeup alongside Anna Gray and Beth Halsted.

With Anthony Hayes' *Gold* (2022), Lamphee faced some of her biggest challenges which ranged from working in the extreme South Australian November heat and mucking up the face of Hollywood screen idol Zac Efron.

This interview was recorded by Andrew F. Peirce in February 2022

How did you come to work on Gold?

Jennifer Lamphee: I have known Hayesie for close to thirty years. I've worked with him a lot as an actor. He rang and said, "I'd like you to do *Gold*." I said, "Send it, I'll have a read." I started to read it and I was like, "Oh, this isn't the desert, is it?" He goes, "No, babe, it's the desert." I go, "Oh, where are we going, Port Augusta?" "No, further." Being Australian, you shoot out in the desert so many times, and you always think after the last time, "I'm not going back there, it's just too hard." I said, "Okay, I'll do it. I must love you or something." The desert can be its own force.

Obviously [Hayesie] was directing and acting in it and I know Susie Porter equally as well. The only one I didn't know was Zac, of course. I said to Hayesie, "Is he nice or is he going to be tricky?" Because I'm like, "If he's gonna be a [pain], it's gonna be just so difficult." He goes, "No, he's really up for everything, Jen." I was like, "Cool, then I'm sure we'll have fun." Zac is pretty much in every scene and had prosthetics on his face every day with no rest for his skin. With all the elements in the desert, it was quite a tricky process.

GOLD

Hayesie, because I know him so well and he knows my work so well, handed the whole [make-up] aspect over, "Do your thing." As a designer that's gold. I said, "I'll do it, but you tell me if you're not happy, or whatever." He handed me the ball and I went for it.

What time of the year was it shot?

JL: It was in November! I was like, "Dude, do you know how hot it's gonna be out there?" He goes, "Yeah, it's gonna be hot." I kid you not, 51 degrees [ground temperature] was probably one of the coolest days we had, to the point on that clay pan, because there was nothing to shield you from anything, it was 64 degrees on one day on the actual clay pen. It melted the soles of our shoes and the grips' tires on their utes. It was intense. Every day you just didn't know what was going to happen.

[We shot in the actual] dust storm that was in the movie. Zac said to me, that because he was weirdly off-grid, there was absolutely no way his management or agent would let him out in that. They would have just come in and gone, "Absolutely not." You know? So he said, "Let's do it." It was so gnarly and full on. At one point, I said to Hayesie, "There's no coming back from this. Whatever happens, this is how he's going to have to look for the rest of the day." He'd have to get in the shower. He was covered [in dirt]. He was such an amazing sport and never complained. He was there, he was in it.

As for me, you couldn't ask for better. We had masks on and goggles, and he did in between [takes]. We washed out his eyes and things like that. He's probably still got a lung full of the desert. He was such a trooper, that he went there. He said never in the States or anywhere else would they have allowed him to do that. Weirdly, he was quite excited by that too, I guess being off-grid and just getting amongst it.

I think he likes doing projects like that, where he is taken out of that A-list Hollywood celebrity world. Where he just can be him. We were all living away, and even the accommodation was pretty no frills. I remember we did a location move further from Leigh Creek up to Marree or further. I got the wrong address, and I rock into where Zac's accommodation was, and he's moving into this tiny, shack-like thing. I go, "Oh my god, is that your accommodation?" He goes, "Yeah," and I go, "Oh, Jesus, imagine what mine looks like." His was pretty bad. And he was laughing! Of course, mine was ten times worse. There was no accommodation with frills, but he was fine with that. He said it was nice because, on weekends, he could party or go out with the crew. He said he hadn't done that since he was about sixteen because somebody would take a photo and put it somewhere. We were all in this weird little bubble together and everyone was so respectful of his privacy and our privacy. I suppose it was more his privacy that we all were just so respectful. I think Aussies are not as starstruck.

How far away from the set were you located?

JL: Because they wanted to get 360 views, it was always a drive. Once you leave the comfort of your makeup van, you're not coming back until it's wrapped. I suppose it was always like a half an hour, forty-five-minute drive into the clay pan. You didn't have any sort of creature comforts. Even with the dust storms, you'd get these things that were called whirly whirlies and you'd see it coming, and everyone would just be holding on to the top of the [tents]. It would go through you, and you'd be hammered with dust, and then it would pass. What you don't see in the film was that [there were] bright blue skies the whole time. It was hot.

These are characters who are out in the elements for a long period of time. How did you design and build the make-up for them?

JL: Before they arrived, we did lots of tests. We had a set double. The main problem I was concerned about was if I made anything with silicone prosthetics, that [with] that amount of heat and that temperature [that] when an actor sweats, they were just going to lift off. I made them out of a hard silicone called Probondo. I also knew that being out in the elements, I had to turn over the prosthetics. We had all different stages, so I had to refill them to make sure that they would set, and we would put them on his face. They're a lot more hardy or robust than a normal prosthetic. I knew that they would probably last the heat, the sweat and all the things that go on with the elements.

I had done a lot of research with medical photos, like burns and blisters, and then there's always the creative licence as well. I had boxes of different sorts of variations. First, you get the watery blister, [which] we called stage one, and then the progression of what would happen if they just kept getting more burnt. We had done tests on a double, and I'd show Hayesie and go, "What do you think? This is when he first feels them at the back of his neck." I didn't want to waste time, so we were in good shape by the time [Zac] arrived. We knew what levels [to use] and how far to push it. Hayesie would come and see the tests of how far we could push it.

The main thing was that [Zac] is so handsome. His eyes are like crystals. His skin is so beautiful. That character [also] had a couple of old scars from an old injury. I'm thinking, "Oh I'm gonna have to really break his skin down and make him look terrible." So, it was a process of trying to knock out the perfect skin. I used a lot of inks and waterproof products because everything else was just going to melt off. It was tricky. It was hard to keep him at a level of looking fucked up, even just as his character with no burns with that amount of heat. The same with Hayesie. We had to stuff up his skin, and he's a really white boy. I was concerned about him burning more to the point because it was so hot out there. You have to do all the things with sunscreen and things like that, but then you also have to layer up all your stuff over the top. It was high maintenance, but it was fine.

The same with Susie. When we did her first camera tests, I stuffed up her skin and made her skin look broken down. I bleached out her eyebrows to just make something look a little bit unusual. Even on camera tests, being Susie, she still looked so beautiful. She'd flown back to Sydney after the test, and then she was coming back again. I rang her and I said, "Porter, you look too beautiful, hun. I'm gonna have to stuff you up more. I think you're gonna have to be full-tilt ugly." She goes, "Oh Lamphee, I might have to digest that." I'm like, "Well, you digest it and call me back." I was saying we should do a harelip or a bung eye or something. She rings me back, "Okay, I'm in."

She plays two sisters; one we just sort of bleached her eyebrows out, and she didn't have any prosthetics, and the second one, we sort of did the harelip. I couldn't do just a harelip because, in this climate, it would insult the harelip community, so it wasn't like a traditional harelip. Then I made some prosthetics that drooped one eye, and she had an old scar as well. [With] that sister, I coloured all her hair and I had made some dreadlock pieces, so it was a very subtle shift. She went with it. She's very white too, so I was concerned she was going to get burnt. She didn't. You've got those elements and then you had the dust and the wind. For blue-eyed people, when you're in the desert, it's almost like shooting in the snow. The reflection was quite hardcore on their eyes to not have sunglasses on, because they're light-coloured, so it was quite full on.

We wanted everyone to be a part of that environment. Some of it developed further as we were out there because of the actual elements and the dust, but it was very important to take the city out of them. It was really important to break them down and to make them look like they were from that land or environment.

When you're out there, shooting in the elements, how do you pivot on the go?

JL: We shot in it, to be honest. We weren't supposed to be shooting the dust storm that day. At that point, I think he had some of the bubbles and the blisters on, so we just sent the runaround to go back to the unit base to grab more prosthetics and we quickly made Zac up under a tent and shot the dust storm because we had one. At that point, because it was so full on, I was like, "Hayesie, just so you know, whatever happens is going to hap-

INTERVIEW | JENNIFER LAMPHEE

pen. I don't even know myself what's really gonna happen." He was covered [in dust]. I said, "We're not going back to what we were gonna shoot earlier. We can't."

Is it easier shooting on digital so you can see what you've got right there and then?

JL: Yeah, it does. I have my own sort of monitor. Because it was digital, we had an editor onsite too that would transfer the data and then that night you'd get emailed them. We didn't have phone reception or internet, but we all did have these device things that we could use so we could watch the dailies. That was great because it made it easy for us to track all the stages and all the details. Continuity was great because we had it right there. We even had freeze-frames of the shots. When Hayesie went into the edit, it was easy for us to have all the continuity and all the levels flowing so well, because we did have all the digital data and had access to it every day. That was a blessing. I'd be holding my breath or my fingers crossed if we didn't have that. I don't know how I would have done that, to be honest. To just keep the consistency of the continuity would have been a nightmare.

Was it shot in script order or out of sequence?

JL: It was out of sequence. We did try to shoot most of it in script order, but it was dependent on the art department and location because some of the builds, like the plane set, weren't ready. The production designer [Sam Hobbs] was often building while we were filming. He did an amazing job. For example, he used onesies for the dogs, but they had their own feet out of the thing and the onesie ended at the neck because we had to mange them up. Not me, personally. I did supply the blood but that was in their sort of territory. We couldn't shoot the dogs until they were completely ready. Some days we couldn't use the dogs because the ground was too hot for their paws. We were always ready on the fly to just throw out a call sheet and not do what we were planning to do that day because the environment wasn't going to allow us, you know?

Zac's skin was under that many prosthetics every single day, you had to be so gentle just removing it because you wanted to preserve his skin for the next day. One day, [Zac's] skin didn't take it. Like we put it on and it was stinging. I said, "Mate, we can't go there." The producers came in and they go, "What do you mean, he can't?" And I'm going, "His skin is burning underneath. His skin needs a day of rest, we're going to have to shoot something else." Which is weird, because as a makeup and prosthetic designer, normally it doesn't matter. You just do it, right? I'm like "I'm not gonna burn an A-lister's face just because. I'm telling you, we can't do it." Now we're all freaking out. They were like, "Okay, okay, okay." They were very respectful of me saying "No, we can't."

You had to do things on the fly. We all sort of weirdly chipped in as a team. Every department had at least one day where everything went to shit just because of the environment. We all just band together and no one got annoyed or frustrated. We're just like, "This is what's going to happen now, we're going to do this." For me, I had everything prepped, and everything was ready. We're in the middle of nowhere. There was no shop, like a corner store.

How do you give the actors the rest and protection that they need post-prosthetic application?

JL: Once you remove something, it normally takes twenty-four hours for the pores to close. Usually, the schedule wouldn't be so gruelling. For four weeks it was pretty much just Zac, Zac, Zac, Zac. On other shoots, they do factor that in and they get that chance for their skin to rest. I think about two to three weeks in, the day that it was stinging his skin wasn't even getting the twenty-four-hour turnaround to shut the pores off. It was only getting a maximum of twelve, to be honest. Once you took the prosthetics off, we tried to do it as gently as possible, and then moisturise, sunscreen, get him to try and have a good night's sleep, and away we'd go again. It would just be a gentle process.

As for the sunscreen, all of them were zinced up with clear zinc, head to toe first. Then we put the prosthetics on. It was hard to keep the sunscreen in that sense. Obviously, you couldn't reapply a cream over the top of the prosthetic. We did try it once and they went weirdly purple. I was like "Oh, that's not a good look." It was touch and go there for a minute. I think it was the zinc oxidising with the colours. I thought, "Christ, we can't use that." We had sunscreen sprays. Then Zac's really particular with his paraben-free stuff. I was like, "Dude, it might not be paraben-free - I'm just saying - out here because we need to use a spray which has got a paraben in it. But I need to protect your skin." He was like, "Yeah, I know, I get it." Some of those products just don't cut the mustard out there.

Then we had umbrellas, so whenever they could rest while a shot was setting up, they were under as much shade as we could find them. With all those elements, you don't want your leads to get burned, especially Porter and Hayesie because they're so fair. Zac is very olive-skinned, so he wasn't a massive concern, but Susie, I mean, she doesn't even do sun in Sydney, let alone 51 degrees.

INTERVIEW | JENNIFER LAMPHEE

Originally when she's burning in the flames, she was supposed to be in a whole silicone cover, like a bald cap. But it was too hot and too dangerous to put her in a bald cap fully. With that amount of prosthetics, it was too dangerous with that heat to have no escaping the sweat. We had to think of another way to do the bald cap. I ended up using a wig and then sticking bald bits in, because at least then the heat can escape a bit. Otherwise, she would have dehydrated and it would have been too dangerous. We had to make that call on the fly going, "Oh shit, what are we going to do?"

I have one makeup artist with me, Beth [Halsted], who I've worked with for about ten years. We work well together. She was a great wingman, she just went with it. Whatever was going to be thrown at us and what we would have to alter for the comfort of the cast and stuff, it was ambitious, to say the least.

No one complained. Sometimes it's like "Jesus, it's fucken hot." But no one complained. Everyone just dug in. I think because it was such an arthouse movie, it felt like we were making something beautiful too, because everyone was there with love, and no one had any egos, not even Zac. I think that's what made it special. Every day we came back completely hammered and you'd go, "Oh, mate, that was good."

Do you have any advice for people who are looking to move into the field of make-up design in the film and TV industry?

JL: I do. Obviously, people have done makeup courses. In fact, this is how I get all my assistants. Usually, on big films, even when I was doing *The Wolverine* [2013], I'd get the students out from the schools or people would email me their CVs, and I always say, "Do you want to come out?" Because people also don't know that it's not glamorous. It's twelve- or fourteen-hour days. Some people are cut for it, and some people just aren't. I always say to do as much work experience on everyone's shows as you can. I swear to God, if you're great at it and you've got that right temperament and you love it and you're creative, you will be hired.

I remember being an assistant and at one of my first jobs, there were all these dead bodies. The makeup artist and designer made me go see a dead body at a morgue. I was like, "Oh!" It was like [retches], but I did it because I was passionate about it. I think it slightly scarred me a little bit. Back then, there wasn't so much internet and Google, we were still using Polaroid cameras. There certainly was no playback. It was like standing behind the DoP so we knew what he was seeing. Now, at least you can Google. For *Gold*, I had to Google dog bites and attacks. Some of it was so gnarly and disgusting, but you had to pick your moments when you could reset. Definitely not over lunch.

WHEN POMEGRANATES HOWL

83 mins
Director: *Granaz Moussavi*
Writer: *Granaz Moussavi*
Cast: *Arafat Faiz, Elham Ahmad Ayazi, Saeida Sadat, Freshta Alimi, Amir Shah Talsh, Hashmatullah Fanai, Ustad din Mohammad Saqi, Andrew Quilty, Hasiba Ebrahimi, Masih Ayubi, Simagul Haidari*
Producers: *Granaz Moussavi, Sayed Jalal Rohani, Marzieh Vafamehr, Baheer Wardak, Christine Williams*
Composer: *Hossein Alizadeh*
Cinematography: *Behrouz Badrouj*
Editing: *Shima Monfared*

INTERVIEW
FILMMAKER GRANAZ MOUSSAVI

Filmmaker Granaz Moussavi's *When Pomegranates Howl* (2020) is a powerful ode to the Iranian child-focused films of the 1980s, paying homage to the aesthetic of filmmakers like Abbas Kiarostami and Amir Naderi. Here, we follow Hewad (Arafat Faiz), a young boy trying to make a life for his family by selling food and pomegranate juice on the streets. Hewad bubbles with stories, telling anyone he meets about his vision of becoming a movie star. So keen is his drive for movie stardom that Heward adorns his cart with a poster for the nineties action film *Eraser* (1996). When he encounters an Australian journalist (Andrew Quilty), that filmmaking dream moves closer to reality.

When Pomegranates Howl is inspired by the true story of the devastating attack in Kabul, Afghanistan that was carried out by Australian armed forces, killing two young boys. Granaz pulls from her wealth of knowledge of Iranian filmmakers and instills the lead character of Hewad with a hope and yearning aspiration to become a filmmaker.

This interview was recorded by Andrew F. Peirce in June 2022

The film opens with a note saying: 'This is to Amir Naderi.' Could you talk about who Amir is as a person?

Granaz Moussavi: He is a great filmmaker. He started his work in the early seventies in the south of Iran, and he's one of the pioneers in the Iranian New Wave cinema. He moved to New York and has been making films since. His film, *Vegas: Based on a True Story* (2008), [premiered] at the Venice [Film Festival]. These are his American productions outside Iran. He made great films back in the seventies and eighties while he was in Iran. I'm inspired by his work and what he's done both aesthetically and cinematically, and his relation to subject matters and children as main characters. A short film that he made that inspired me greatly is called *Waiting* [*Entezar*, 1974]. Cinematically, in this film, [I'm] inspired by his work. That's why [there is] a tribute to him.

WHEN POMEGRANATES HOWL

You did your doctoral thesis on the aesthetics of poetic cinema. Is his work part of the influence on your doctoral thesis?

GM: Yes, he's one of my reference filmmakers in my thesis and this particular film, too. I have worked extensively on [Abbas] Kiarostami cinema, which has been my main focal point throughout my academic career and as a scholar, as has Amir Naderi and Sohrab Shahid-Saless.

When it comes to working in cinema, Amir Naderi, hands down, is a source of inspiration beyond [the] aesthetics of poetic cinema [with] his way of filmmaking and energy. As a little kid, I remember watching his short films on TV and being mesmerised by his work and characters. I met him at the Vancouver Film Festival. We both had films in the festival; he had *Vegas* and I had *My Tehran for Sale* (2009). I met him one more time in New York and have spoken with him over the phone a couple of times. The informal mentorship that he has given me has energised me to do this impossible work.

I would like to relay one thing that really affected me. I hope that if other filmmakers are reading this that they would be equally inspired. I was just whinging about how difficult filmmaking is and not being supported. When you're not doing mainstream films, it's just impossible. He told me, "Stop whinging. If the door is closed, you have to go through the window. If the window is closed, you have to go through the chimney. If you can't get anywhere and you've got walls in front of you, you have to start kicking. If you can't knock down the wall, then you have to start chewing the wall brick by brick. That's what you have to do. If you're a filmmaker, you will start chewing a wall."

This idea of chewing the wall brick by brick was honestly what energised me on the most difficult days when I thought it was impossible to take one more step forward, when everything was a dead end. Then I started thinking of chewing the wall.

One of the aspects I'm curious about in your films is the role of sunglasses. Can you talk about the status or the importance of them in your films?

GM: Subconsciously that comes to me from reading and writing so much on Kiarostami's cinema. They're like little screens; a shield that gives you a little bit of privacy in public spaces, and at the same time they're like a screen with a little bit of reflection. They hide a little bit, like a mask, like a little Masquerade. That's with the sunglasses as an object.

The story in *When Pomegranates Howl* is quite different from the use of sunglasses in my first film, *My Tehran for Sale*. In that scene, I wanted to show that the little kid, even though he's so deprived, even though the pair of cheap sunglasses are a novelty to this poor kid, he doesn't forget morality. According to his Islamic beliefs, when he finds an object, he must ask three times who it belongs to, and if after three times nobody answers, then you are allowed to take it. You are not allowed to take something that you find, so this little kid sticks to his principles, even when he finds something in the middle of a street fight, he's compelled to stick to his morals. He asks three times in two languages. I don't expect people to pick that, but he asks the question in the two languages that he knows, the two main languages in Afghanistan, Dari and Pashto: "Whose sunglasses are these?" Three times he asks, and when nobody answers, then he takes them.

Because he doesn't have anything else to swap, he uses it like a token for flying kites. It becomes like a heritage that is relayed from one kid to another; life goes on and other kids are going to wear them after Hewad is killed. In the final scene, the war game continues. The imitation of killing continues. Who knows who the next kid is going to be? The sunglasses represent that physical transfer of that notion, the idea that pain, the plight, the life that goes on and everything about childhood is transferred from one to another. The other side of the coin in that situation is also the danger; is the same destiny going to happen to whoever wears them?

As soon as I saw Hewad wearing the sunglasses, I recalled the iconic image of Kiarostami wearing them. I got the feeling that they were like a baton being passed on from one filmmaker to another. Hewad never gets to actually film anything, but he does in a way. We get to experience him in the alleyways, getting to 'shoot' his friends and re-enact things. It's that transference from one storyteller to another. In many ways, you're carrying on the baton for them. Do you see yourself as somebody who is continuing that legacy of being able to pass along these kinds of stories and usher in a path for future filmmakers who might watch your films and go, "I can do that"?

GM: Definitely. I'm really glad that you raised that because it's conscious of what I was trying to do in this film. Iranian cinema was known to the West mainly in the eighties. The Iranian New Wave started earlier on, before the revolution in the seventies. By the time that films hit prestigious international stages, it was the eighties. Then the world started noticing what was happening in Iranian cinema. Kiarostami was one of the pioneers. I come from a scholarship of cinema and film studies, so I have a love for studying filmmakers. I've got a compartment in my brain that's being engaged with that, so that was definitely part of it.

By the look of it, Afghanistan is like Iran a few decades back. Iranian cinema has changed so much. It's not about children's subject matters any more. It's not about the trends, fashions, manners, and aesthetics of Iranian New

WHEN POMEGRANATES HOWL

Wave cinema in the eighties. I thought it is relevant to Afghanistan today, so I wanted to recreate or import the fashion of the [Iranian] New Wave cinema to Afghanistan today with children as main subjects. Inevitably, I had all these references in my head including Kiarostami, Sohrab Shahid Saless, and Amir Naderi. They had roles here and there and this is one of them, and that is to remind audiences of that cinema. I think this film resembles that cinema a little bit, or at least reminds people of how it was.

How does identity play into your role as a filmmaker from an Australian?

GM: The question of identity is a very complex thing. I'm definitely Iranian-Australian, or Australian-Iranian because most of my life I've been in Australia. All of my meaningful life in terms of being an adult has been in Australia. I've been in Australia since I was 20-21. In Iran, I was a student, a teenager, stepping out of my family home to the world, and then bang, I was in Australia with a whole family, including my extended family. Outside of Australia, not only do I not have any family or relatives, I don't even have graves to go to. My graves are in Australia. The people who are related to me and who are lucky and alive, they are in Australia, and my father's side is in Canada.

The graves of my loved ones are in Adelaide. Adelaide will be my shine forever. My parents, my grandmother, and my uncle are buried there. I became a filmmaker in Australia. I'm trained as a filmmaker in Australia. I did drama acting in Iran for a couple of years, but I studied film and became a filmmaker in Australia.

When I think of cinema, and when I want to express myself in cinema, I don't think in Farsi, I think in English, because I'm trained here in Australia. As much as a poet I'm Iranian, as a filmmaker I'm Australian. I'm not familiar with the Iranian film industry, I haven't worked there much. That's a mixed identity because I can't detach myself as a poet from a filmmaker. At the same time, I'm both, but one is more Iranian than Australian, which is poetry. One is more Australian than Iranian, which is filmmaking. So, it's a bit mixed up, but that's how I think a lot of first-generation immigrants are.

This is a cross-country co-production. What does that mean creatively? How do you go about establishing a film in a co-production relationship like that?

GM: It's an Afghanistan-Australian co-production. It's also Iranian too, but Iran had a smaller role. [There were] four countries: Afghanistan, Australia, Netherlands, and Iran. We had talents from Iran, but in terms of financing the film, it was Afghanistan and Australia. By finances, I mean ourselves. Because we really didn't have anything other than the Adelaide Film Festival and a little bit from SAFC. Otherwise, the film was completely self-funded by me, one of the Afghan producers, and also the Australian producer who loaned money to the film. Our producer Christine [Williams] gave her own money to the film to be able to make it. I really appreciate everyone, including her, who sacrificed for this film to be made.

I didn't have any other words other than co-production. Honestly, this film has been brutally treated in terms of support of a film. Really, a 'co-production between Australia and Afghanistan' is underestimating what we went through to make this film. I don't regret it, even though I literally lost my everyday financial life. I put everything on the line, and I lost it. I lost my life savings. I lost my apartment which I had to sell. I had to sell a little piece of land that I had overseas. The Afghan producer had to do the same, Baheer Wardak. I even sold the jewellery that my late mother had left for me. I sold shoes, bags, you name it.

I don't regret it even though it's [a] crazy path that I went through. Why? Because that's why they make it impossible. They make it this way so no one goes ahead and makes it. That's the way that this system intends to deprive the audience of narratives. They raid the ABC, and they don't try to get Julian Assange back, because they just want to shut every alternative voice [down], but in legal ways. In soft, white ways. The system doesn't support a film like this to be made for the same reasons because there are narratives that the Australian audience should not be exposed to.

It's probably a little bit 'ooh' talking about this. Why? Mainstream media and the whole system intend for us to think within boxes and certain frameworks. When I talk about reality like that, it feels so strange, but just think about it. I mean, it's just pieces of a puzzle next to one another, there are narratives, and there are facts that we as Australians should not know. When it comes to film production, and the way that the system works, because we are in a first world, Western so-called 'free country', they can't come to me put me in jail or suffocate me physically, or censor me, [in the] same way that, for example, in other countries [they could]. I am also an Iranian, and the kind of hard mechanisms that are putting people in jail - I call it 'black censorship' - all that happens in Iran where they don't claim to be a democratic country. The system doesn't claim that you are free or that there is freedom of speech. They brutally stand up there, and say, "Yes, we do censor, and you deserve it. Because it's our way or the highway."

Here in Australia, you don't expect the same result. No matter what the means are, if the result is the suffocation of narrative and people who are storytellers, who are journalists, who are whistle-blowers, then what's the difference? To me, white censorship, black censorship, it doesn't matter. The means aren't important. The result is important. If the result is that the mechanism hinders a filmmaker or a creator's path to stop them from telling Australian audiences the narrative or story that they have to say or reveal, then calling it jargon like a "co-production" is just too fancy. For a purpose, it's just too fancy, but I didn't have time to come up with another term, like 'white censorship', that I created. I need to come up with terms that apply to the saga that I for one went through. In that term, yes, it is an Afghanistan-Australian co-production.

Talking about Iranian voices being silenced, or imprisoned, not allowing these stories to be made in Australia, or not supporting the distribution of them, while not on the same level as imprisoning somebody, is effectively doing a similar thing.

GM: Exactly. In terms of the means, it's not the same. It's like capital punishment. Capital punishment is capital punishment. [It] doesn't matter if you use a guillotine or if you hang someone or if you shoot them or if you use [the] electric chair: capital punishment is capital punishment. Censorship in all shapes and forms is capital punishment to the soul of the storyteller, the narrator, the whistle-blower. Whatever you call it, the result is the same.

Yes, those three filmmakers are physically in jail [Mohammad Rasoulof, Jafar Panahi, Mostafa Al-Ahmad]. We have to object. We have to resist. We have to say no. But at least we all know in the whole world that they are physically in prison. At least it gives some credit in terms of 'this is what we did.' The whole world knows about them, cinematically they are going to be looked at. I'm not saying that there are positive outcomes, not in that term; I'm just trying to say that when something like that happens, the whole world sees, and inevitably, it's going to make what they have to say be heard.

People tend to forget easily about Julian Assange. People tend not to remember what happened to ABC three years ago. Let alone a little film like mine, and many other productions like this; no one sees us. People forget us. On this side of the world where we live, we claim freedom, supposedly, we claim that it is a first world, and we claim freedom of speech, when something like this happens, society is so quiet that nobody pays attention. This is the dark side of white censorship.

At least on that side of the world, the whole world knows about you with petitions, signatures, watching your films, retrospectives of your films, and all that. What happens here? Nothing. You just fade. You just get vaporised like in *1984* [George Orwell, 1949]. You get vaporised. Unnoticeable.

MARUNGKA TJALATJUNU
Dipped in Black

23 minutes
Directors: *Derik Lynch, Matthew Thorne*
Writers: *Derik Lynch, Matthew Thorne*
Featuring: *Derik Lynch*
Cast: *Dale Baker, Dominic Roberts, Christopher Stewart*
Producers: *Patrick Graham, Matthew Thorne*
Composer: *Jed Silver*
Cinematographer: *Andrew Gough*
Editing: *Nicola Powell*

Marungka Tjalatjunu won the Documentary Australia Award at the 2023 Sydney Film Festival, the Best Documentary Short Film award at the 2023 Melbourne International Film Festival, and received a nomination for Best Short Film at the 2023 Australian Directors Guild Awards.

INTERVIEW
FILMMAKERS
DERIK LYNCH, MATTHEW THORNE & PATRICK GRAHAM

For Yankunytjatjara artist Derik Lynch, when he dances for his family and friends in the spotlights of car in a stunning gold dress in *Marungka Tjalatjunu (Dipped in Black)*, echoing the power and strength of Tina Turner, it's a moment of liberation and a powerful expression of self. *Marungka Tjalatjunu* deservedly won the Silver Bear Jury Prize (Short Film) and Teddy queer short film prize at the 2023 Berlinale, and in doing so, it shone a global spotlight on Inma, a traditional form of storytelling from the Anangu community which uses visual, verbal, and physical communication to pass along Anangu Tjukurpa (myths) between generations.

Derik's story is one that is told after co-director Matthew Thorne and co-producer Patrick Graham forged a relationship of trust and understanding over years. There's a level of trust and understanding that also comes with sharing your story with an interviewer like myself, and I'm forever grateful for the honesty and openness that Derik, Patrick, and Matthew gifted me for this interview. It's that aspect of trust that opens up the following discussion.

This interview contains discussions of suicide.

This interview was recorded by Andrew F. Peirce in July 2023

I want to start talking about trust and the level of trust that's required to tell stories on film. There is a level of trust that you, as storytellers, give to the audience and there's a level of trust that you give to me as an interviewer sharing your story. Can you talk about the level of trust that you built with each other in telling Derik's story on screen?

MARUNGKA TJALATJUNU

Matthew Thorne: You're dealing with not only the colonial layers and the political layers at work, but also with genuinely different language bases. Those language bases have ontological, theoretical differences in the way worlds are perceived, how lives are perceived, and how time is perceived. Value structures then bring that language into culture and into family and into life. Derik has described to me growing up in some kind of traditional Aboriginal community experience, certainly from a perspective of culture and storytelling; and of course, that's the sad reality we live in under the auspice of the whitefella world, but in a cultural system that is still basically as it was for over 60,000 years.

You're working on collaboration and understanding from so many incredibly difficult layers that it's really kind of like a miracle. It speaks to whatever genuine deep and meaningful spiritual connection Derik and I have that we were able to navigate as we have tried to. It speaks to Derik's generosity as an individual and the kindness in his heart to go on that process.

Derik Lynch: When I first met Matthew, I had a trust issue from my own personal experience. I remember giving him a call one night and making friends with him and feeling comfortable having that chat with him. The trust came [when] I started having conversations [with him]. We spoke on the phone from the other side of the world from each other. That's how the script came about. I still did have a trust issue around when we first started filming. I didn't know where his direction of the storyline was heading as I had a completely different vision of telling the story on screen.

Before we shot the first half of the film, I remember him telling me, "Trust me, trust me." I did not trust him right up until when he introduced me to Patrick. Patrick and I knew of each other because we had a lot of mutual friends being in Adelaide and being actors. When we first started having those conversations, I remember Matthew coming back and saying, "We've got no money, but I really want to make this film. You're not gonna get anything out of it, but just trust me, I will make the story come to life."

I guess I just trusted him a little bit until we got home. When we got home, it was like, "Okay, so what are you doing?" I would say it took four years for me to trust Matthew in what he was saying, and now after five years we fully trust each other. He's got my back and I've got his back. From my perspective, as being a blackfella, there are a lot of trust issues. From my own personal perspective, I had huge issues with trusting people, not only white people, but also my own family, my own community, and my own people. I just had huge trust issues with every human being. Now I can move forward and have conversations around working with people and all sorts of things I want to do.

INTERVIEW | DERIK LYNCH, MATTHEW THORNE & PATRICK GRAHAM

And having people like myself throw difficult questions for the very first question in an interview is hard.

DL: [laughing] And sometimes I don't trust journalists. I'm very cautious around talking about stuff. Sometimes you'll hear me say, "Do you understand what I'm saying? Do you get what I'm saying?"

Patrick Graham: When a story is hard to share, then I think you're probably in the right spot. In terms of [being] a storyteller, when you write something, if it's hard for you to give that over, then you're probably onto something. Reiterating what Derik said, it was such a long process. Five per cent of the film that's in there now we shot in mid to late 2019. We all decided when we were up there that we would apply for money to make the film bigger and better. We thought it was a really great story, so we applied for finance, from the South Australian Film Corp and the Adelaide Film Festival.

We were set to make the film on a date that we all remember, the 17th of March 2020, when the whole world went into lockdown. We had to shut down on our last day of pre-production, our first day of production, and we held for two days. We all went home and went to bed. From then we had to raise finance, but during that period it was really like a blessing in disguise. We got a chance to deepen our relationship. Funnily, I don't know if we were ready to make the film then, so to have that extra two years of developing Derik's story and Matthew and Derik rewriting and reconnecting constantly on what shape this film is going to take, the connection got stronger and stronger and deeper and deeper and those layers of trust were opened. From a producer's perspective, and also a friend's perspective, we've all grown to know each other well.

DL: We're like a family now thanks to the shutdown.

PG: Derik sharing his community is like a dream come true. To shoot and be on country and make this kind of film has been such an incredible privilege to be introduced into Derik's family, their world, and their community.

How important is it when you're sharing a bond as co-directors to give each other the space to tell a story? Especially when considering the notion that you're sharing the honour of telling Derik's story too.

MT: Derik didn't set out to make a film with a whitefella. We met by chance, so I think the fact that it seems to have been meant to happen that way, or at least there is some genuine spiritual connection is what we relied on. We both recognise very deeply that the film would not exist without the partnership that we have. I don't have any understanding, really, of Aboriginal culture, and whatever I have is because Derik has taught me. By a similar token, Derik is not really a filmmaker; he's a storyteller. He's a performer. He's a musician. He's many things, but his art was not film.

There was this thing from Derik first of all, of Ngapartji-Ngapartji, which basically means 'you give me, I give you'. It involved us making something together. I gave Derik a doorway into filmmaking or film knowledge, [which is] also an art form of some privilege, you have to have some means to go and learn to be a filmmaker, and then he gave me a doorway into Aboriginal culture and culture in the APY lands which is where he's from. That doorway is also a great gift and privilege, of course.

We have a great respect that this was a work that is Ngapartji-Ngapartji which is my understanding that it's a really important cultural part of his community. I think we also are coming to realise that this work that we've done as a whitefella and a blackfella telling a story together is also really important work itself. Yes, we must have a place for Aboriginal people to tell their story completely independently of white interference or white voice, in the same way that it's also important that we have white Australians who try and wrestle with what it means to be a 'white Australian' independently. But there's another thing that we also have to do as part of whatever this very long process of some kind of reconciliation could be, which is to work together and find out what our shared voice is.

That's not what we set out to make, and we never thought about it in those terms. We both liked each other and wanted to go to the next level. Derik just wanted to get his story told, and I wanted to make something that really connected with the underlying mysticism of the land, which of course is in many ways Aboriginal. We've learned that what we were doing and the reason it's important was something even bigger than we could imagine.

I want to talk about the visual language of the film. It embraces the harsh lighting of the city at the beginning and then as you go on to country, it's warm. There's also a sequence of diving into the water, which brings up a notion of rebirth and renewal. Can you talk about the style of filmmaking and the choice of imagery to present on screen?

DL: I had two roles, me being in front of the camera, and talking to the families. Andy (Gough) the cinematographer and Matthew went out and scouted locations with permission from me and the families permitting them to film in certain areas. [Some of the location scouting Patrick and I went out with them too.]

The water and the diving into the water wasn't even in the original script, because the second time when we went home, it rained a lot back in the desert, so that was added on. The beautiful green sceneries wasn't all planned;

that was nature giving us a blessing to shoot in those locations. With the other locations, landscapes, and the colours, I think we reflected on a lot of the things from the first shoot in terms of the colours of the earth and the sky and the trees and all of that. Throughout lockdown, Andy and Matthew looked at all of the footage and looked at the colours and would see how the colours would look the second time when we went back, and the sound came about when we got there on country.

MT: Andy is one of the most incredible spiritual creative energies I've ever had the privilege of working with. We've worked with each other for a long time, and now we kind of have one brain together. We've now grown up somehow as artists together, so we have also influenced each other to change in certain ways. Andy just gets it. He's one of the kindest, empathetic, spiritual individuals and his ability to relate to whatever the essential is, in the land, in the community, and individuals, is very present. He's very attuned, his radar is on. I think it's that sensitivity that makes the film as spectacular in that visual language as it is.

Of course, that land is beautiful, and shooting on film is beautiful, and having a Steadicam is a beautiful thing, and all these things add [up] technically, they're like the elements. But really, it's that deep, poetic, almost metaphysical understanding of what you're seeing before you that informs the way it looks, the way that it is, and I think it's something really present in the land. That's spiritual power.

Can you talk about the first time that you got to see it in a cinema? Where was it and what was that experience like?

DL: For me, I was there throughout the editing process, so to sit in front of the screen, during all of the editing, I've seen it so many times. I guess my first big screening was last October.

PG: We had a fundraiser. That was before we got into Berlin.

DL: That was last October. That was the day after my birthday. I actually saw it in Sydney, at Dendy. That was kind of like a 'wow' factor for me because it was like, "Man, I've been spending all this time in front of this computer screen." It was a good computer screen, but to see it in an actual cinema, I totally forgot that it was my story. 'Oh, what the hell is this?' It just blew me away. To see it on the big screen, and to be in the same room as a lot of the audience and watching it I felt like I was on a flight mode. Even though it was my story, I was just so emotional seeing everything that I've always wanted to share on the big screen.

MARUNGKA TJALATJUNU

PG: Partially for the first time watching it with an audience, you get so absorbed in the film, like you're saying Derik. You've seen it so many times, and then finally, when you watch it on the big screen with an audience, you kind of become an audience member again for the first time. 'Ah, okay, that's what we made.' For me, it wasn't until after we won the Silver Bear at Berlin, and we had that second to last screening in Berlin in the International, that awesome cinema, that I felt like I watched it for the first time.

DL: Every time I watch it on the big screen, and when you're sitting there with a different audience, it takes you on a journey.

Talking about going to Berlin, I imagine being away from home would give you a different perspective of the film, seeing the film with an audience who may never have been to Australia or may never have experienced an Australian film.

DL: That was very exciting for me. To take something that's from the heart of Australia. It's five minutes down the road from the actual centre of Australia. To take it over there to a European audience, it's like looking through this little tiny window to this world where I come from, where my people are, where they still live, and where our life exists out in the desert. I wanted to share my story. I wanted it to go that far. I was super excited. I love sharing stories, so, for me, it was a privilege to go over there and share a glimpse of Australia in our Indigenous communities and culture, the oldest living culture in the world.

PG: It's pretty wild. To be accepted to such a big festival was off the charts. We were all so incredibly blown away by a festival that values art so much. Cinema is a commercial business, and there is so much of that that gets pushed onto you as a producer, but to produce something that I think is also a beautiful piece of art and that's acknowledged is really cool. As the festival progressed, it just got more and more wild, winning the Teddy, and then the night of the closing night winning the Silver Bear.

DL: It was crazy because we won the Teddy the night before, and we celebrated for the Teddy, and then we're like, 'Hang on, the big one is tomorrow night, we have to wait.' Like Patrick said, it got crazy.

Can you talk about the importance of Tina Turner for you as an artist and as somebody to dance to?

DL: Oh, Tina was my biggest inspiration growing up. Of course, she was a role model, an institution, and a driving power. She was just phenomenal. She is a legend. For me growing up, I was in grade one at the time and saw the senior kids doing the Nut Bush City Limits line dance, and the rest of the grades were not allowed. They would perform everywhere in the community. When school was over, and the senior kids were staying back to learn the dance line for Nut Bush, I remember I didn't go home, I used to run over and jump in the water fountain and peek through the window and watch the senior kids practice. I was about five at the time, and I remember putting all the routines together in my head. We had this big celebration opening up the new Women's Centre and the art centre in Aputula and the senior kids stood up to do the dance, and all of us little little kids were out sitting in the front row. I remember our teacher saying "Do not get up, just sit and watch the big kids do the dance."

I did not listen to him. I got up and I did the whole routine. I was one of those kids who just got up and danced.

For me, growing up [I listened] to a lot of Tina and [watched] a lot of Tina and [was] doing it all behind closed doors and practising singing with the brush. I started practising. I didn't have heels. We didn't have heels in Aputula, so I would do a dance, which I still do, and I would do 'invisible high heels' rather than visible heels until I wore actual heels and realised it felt very natural.

I'm a firm believer that every film is made better if there's dancing in it. The beautiful moment with all the car lights on you as you dance must have been quite a powerful experience. What was it like to shoot that sequence?

DL: Oh hell, it was a powerful moment for Patrick and Matthew and everybody else. For me, it was like "I'm not doing this!" I wanted to go out and do it somewhere out of the community, on the road, in the sunlight. I did not like it at all. I was super nervous because we shot the first bit and I did not like the heels because they were shorter. The second one in this film, I've got six-inch stilettos, so I felt comfortable with that, but at the same time, I was very nervous because I've never performed in a dress in front of my community and it's something that no one has ever seen in the remote community, ever.

People see it on television, and on stage, but to perform in a gold dress with six-inch stilettos in the dirt, for me, I felt nervous because my mum was there, my brothers were there, my entire family was there. My other cousins and sisters were telling Mum I think a day before the shoot. I was telling them, "I don't want Mum to be there, I don't want these certain families to be there when we're shooting." I remember on the day of the shoot, my sister Sharlene came and said, "I've spoken to them, and they really want to see you. They're really excited to see you. Everybody knows, your mum knows, your brothers know, everybody's really proud of you and respects you and your sexuality. This is your story." Even my mum said, "You tell your story however you want to tell your story. I'm very proud of you."

That gave me the blessing to actually finally get out there and really bust a move and do it. There's a part of me that I really wanted to express. Not that I do it all the time. It's something that I, as a child, had a dream to one day wear a gold dress like Tina and do it, but I never got the chance to do it on stage so I may as well do it through film, and why not do it back home on country in front of my people and family.

PG: When we were there in 2019, we shot a bit of that sequence, but we all knew it just had to have the community arrive and be part of it, which we wrote.

DL: When we were there, it was just [an] abandoned [building]. Then when we went back, it [had] turned into a church.

PG: It's really such an iconic scene for the film now. From a technical perspective, it was a really difficult film scene to shoot. There was such a short amount of light to get it right. It was the hardest sequence to shoot and with the shortest amount of time, so it was really hard to emotionally gauge what you were doing. "This is what we're doing and we have to get into it." Derik was far more emotionally involved at that point. Then when we saw it in the rough, we were just like 'This is phenomenal.'

MT: Navigating the relationship between being co-directors, and Derik somehow being like an educator, I'm culturally out of my depth and I don't understand what people are saying, and then also sometimes Derik had to be the subject to me and step back from being a director. It's a really interesting dynamic where in some moments, I sensed with Derik that he had a lot of fear of acceptance by his community. We all kind of shy away from moments that are tough for us, or that we feel a fear of rejection or failure. We talked a lot about it before we left, it was always an important part of the story, even from the first time we went out in 2019. When it came for us to shoot it, it was my job to support Derik and encourage him, and to be there and say, "This will be safe. We'll make sure it's safe and we'll protect you, but it is important based on everything you've told me and based on everything that I know about you, I think it really is important that you do this."

Derik was very nervous about how his community would receive it, because like anywhere, queer identity is something that has a complex reality in every community. But his community was incredibly moved and supportive, and I'm very happy that Derik got to see that.

I think he's someone whose story has come. I think in Derik's story there are a lot of important lessons for Australia. I say that obviously for white Australia, but also I think for Aboriginal Australia and for his mob. Also, in a general sense, I think he's a pretty impressive ambassador for his mob. The reality is that white people, me included, we're all learning all the time about this stuff. We're writing some kind of new book while we're also learning, and hearing him speak at the Sydney Film Festival, so many of the questions were, not intentionally, often inappropriate. Seeing Derik navigate them with so much grace, charm, and kindness was impressive. I think he's an impressive individual, and that for me is what makes the film so special.

If I can pivot to talking about one of the heavier aspects of the film, which is talking about the way that trauma acts as an echo and reverberates into the present. Actors play earlier versions of yourself Derik, and I'm curious if you can talk about presenting that fractured harmony that might have been created by the trauma that you have experienced. What was the process of representing that on-screen and seeing somebody else carry your story along?

DL: For the two young boys and one young man, they were all right into it. I was very nervous because I chose three or four of those kids, but I didn't have much interaction with those kids, because they know me, and I'm a friend of the family, so I handballed it over to Matthew and Pat to build that relationship with those young kids. From my perspective, they really enjoyed being around the camera and really enjoyed the shoot, and they did a really good job of carrying those stories from my past.

What discussions did you have on set about the story?

DL: For most of the shoot with the trauma events, I wasn't present. For the sorry camp and the hanging, I wasn't there because that was just so painful that I just wasn't around for those shoots. I would come in and tell the families about what the scene is all about, and then I walked off, and I wasn't present or else it would have taken me right back to that place where I didn't want to be anymore. I've come out of all of those dark places throughout the pandemic as well. [I've been] working on myself and [have been] really taking care of my mental health. But, I was strong at the same time. The way it turned out was perfect for me, because I remember after the shoot, the guys came back and they showed me the footage, and I was like, "Wow." I was just like, "Wow, wow, wow, wow," when I saw the footage.

I've also had a suicide experience myself, and I'm looking after myself in a mental health capacity, so getting to see that you're still here, and I'm still here, and that we can survive these events is important. I found that quite a beautiful thing to witness. Thank you for being open and sharing. It means a lot to me and I imagine to a lot of other people too.

DL: Coming out of the pandemic there were so many of my friends, Patrick's friends, your friends, people that we know that couldn't handle the pandemic who have departed. Coming out of the pandemic and regrouping and shooting this made me stronger, and to look back and to see so many people that went through it in isolation, and that couldn't handle that and have departed, and [by] defining those bits in the film, I just wanted to tell a story and to share a story that it is okay to feel the way you feel. It's okay to seek help in a professional way.

Thank you for being open and honest and for sharing your story.

Patrick, how did you help to create a safe space on set to explore these emotions and themes?

PG: In the period before we got there, and with Marcellus [Enalanga] who was our cultural adviser and a relation to Derik, it was slowly getting to know the community while we were there, and shooting at a pace that was allowed for those conversations, and not pushing anyone into a place that they didn't want to be, and just making sure that consultation was open and culturally respectful.

DL: Marcellus was very helpful. He's my nephew and a cultural producer and he worked very closely, with the family, with Patrick, with Duncan, to get everything right and getting things together, and having that awareness about the community and the team as well.

Can you talk about what it meant to have Marcellus as a cultural advisor for the film?

DL: It was a big support for me, because it was my personal story in the film, having Marcellus [there] took some of the load off to support in those dark moments I was shooting around. Also, getting the families in and helping Matthew and Andy and everybody that was shooting when I wasn't around was hands down to Marcellus. A cultural producer is important to have around because they are the bridge, they will keep the communication flowing in between and let each side know what's happening. If this side doesn't agree, then they go back and forth like a bridge, they're a person that goes between both parties.

THE STRANGER

117 mins
Director: *Thomas M. Wright*
Writer: *Thomas M. Wright*
Cast: *Joel Edgerton, Sean Harris, Jada Alberts, Steve Mouzakis, Cormac Wright, Alan Dukes, Ewen Leslie, Matthew Sunderland, Fletcher Humphrys, Gary Waddell, Andreas Sobik, Checc Musolino, Kym Wheare, Spencer Scholz, Sean Daley, Violet Rowe, Brendan Rock*
Producers: *Joel Edgerton, Iain Canning, Rachel Gardner, Kim Hodgert, Kerry Kohansky-Roberts, Emile Sherman*
Score: *Oliver Coates*
Cinematography: *Sam Chiplin*
Editing: *Simon Njoo*

In 2022, *The Stranger* was a nominee for the Un Certain Regard Award at the Cannes Film Festival. *The Stranger* won Best Screenplay and Best Supporting Actor in Film (Sean Harris) at the 2022 AACTA Awards. The film also received nominations for Best Film, Best Direction, Best Lead Actor in Film (Joel Edgerton), Best Supporting Actress in Film (Jada Alberts), Best Casting, Best Sound in Film, Best Production Design in Film, Best Editing in Film, and Best Cinematography in Film.

REVIEW
NADINE WHITNEY

Thomas M. Wright is quickly becoming the Australian master of cinematic discomfort. In his debut film 2018's *Acute Misfortune,* he created an indelible film about the Australian artist Adam Cullen and his biographer Erik Jensen that was awash with toxicity and implied violence. Essentially a two-hander that explored the damaging relationship between Cullen (Daniel Henshall) and Jensen (Toby Wallace) the film was unrelenting in its tension. Again in *The Stranger* Wright opts for a two-hander approach which concentrates on the increasingly fraught connection between its two leads – Mark Frame (Joel Edgerton) and Henry Teague (Sean Harris). The first is an embedded undercover police officer trying to find out the truth about the latter, a suspect in the kidnapping and murder of a young boy.

Based on the true crime investigative book 'The Sting' by Kate Kyriacou, the film loosely adapts the immense undercover operation to uncover the truth about one of Australia's most infamous child murders. Although Wright has changed the names of all involved the case was so prominent in the Australian media that it is clear who it is representing. Wright has stated that he struggled with the idea of adapting the book but in his approach he has done as much as he can to avoid sensationalising the violence of the case (the abduction and murder are never shown) and instead uses the piece as a psychological character study that illuminates the terror Mark undergoes as he gets closer to Henry.

The film begins on a bus in Western Australia. Two men are returning from the airport. Paul (Steve Mouzakis) strikes up a conversation with Henry. Both men are ex-cons and down on their luck. Paul soon hands Henry off to Harry who is a mid-tier handler in a crime organisation. The organisation is a godsend to Henry as they are able to scrub identities and give significant payouts to members. In one scene Paul is handed a new passport, air tickets, and ten thousand dollars to disappear for a year. Such an enterprise promises great benefit to Henry and he becomes excited to be given the opportunity to disappear from his past – all the organisation insists on is that its members are honest about their past misdeeds so they can ensure there is no blowback on them and know how to best deal with any contingencies.

Mark becomes more than Henry's handler; in Henry's eyes he is his friend. Henry doles out small portions of information about his past which Mark calmly does not react to. The point of the operation is to get Henry to admit to a heinous crime and it relies on Mark's skill to act the part of a non-judgemental criminal to eke the information out of the suspect. Mark is not a professional actor, he's just a cop doing his job and the closer he gets to Henry the more it begins to impact on his psyche. Mark has a young son of his own and his anxiety is increased as he internalises the stress of dealing with a man who could be a child murderer being his near-constant companion. His nightmares become vivid when and if he is able to sleep. He drinks almost constantly. Mark is a man living on the edge of his capabilities not only as a cop but also as a human.

Wright's film is gritty and unbearably tense. As the relationship between Henry and Mark unfolds there begins to be a sense that we don't know what either man is really capable of. Wright also chose to present Henry and Mark as looking alike; both men are bearded, grizzled and sport a ponytail. The uncanny effect adds another layer to the psychological dimension of Mark's character. During one of his nightmares, he sees a man sitting on the bed next to his son. That man is implied to be Henry, but it is himself. Mark has to fight to keep his identity his own, to breathe out the darkness he is taking in.

Wright plays with timelines in *The Stranger*. Events we assume to be contemporaneous are instead played out of order. Two investigating detectives Rylett (Jada Alberts) and Ikin (Fletcher Humphreys) are working on Henry Teagues' case. They are part of the Queensland police force and through careful investigation, they are able to prove that Henry (aka Peter Morgan) was not only capable of abducting the victim but also lied about his alibi and had a previous conviction for child kidnapping and molestation. Their investigation opens up the sting operation that recruits Mark. Wright is restrained in never showing the violence of Henry's crimes, but he does allow Rylett to read a transcript about the previous conviction in the Northern Territory that is so horrifying that the detective almost weeps as she relates it.

Wright stated that *The Stranger* depicts a country that exists on hidden violence. Cinematographer Sam Caplin's desaturated work is impeccable, but the most effective use of visual imagery is when a mountain that is used as a motif for the film is juxtaposed with Henry's profile. Violence and the land become one and it is a subtle, yet canny reminder of the violence perpetrated on First Nations people in Australia.

A standout feature of the film is its sound design. Wright and his team weave between actual conversations, to recordings of those conversations, to how those conversations are listened to. The words are forever recorded not only on tape but also in Mark's mind – the sense that he will never be able to erase what he has heard is palpable.

As with *Acute Misfortune,* the actors embodying the protagonists are key to carrying tension and veracity. Joel Edgerton is unarguably one of Australia's finest male performers. As Mark his restrained but tortured performance is outstanding. Sean Harris is one of the best character actors in the world, and in addition to playing an Australian convincingly, his subtle and not-so-subtle menace is astonishing. There are times when he is almost pitiable but then others where he is so clearly a sociopath with no concept of remorse that the audience is made to endure the 'unknowable' aspect of a criminal. Wright wraps nothing up in a neat bow but instead allows questions to linger and upset.

The Stranger will hit international audiences differently. What they will see is a twisty crime thriller (which it is) but without the knowledge of the case on which it is based the film will be viewed from a distance that Australian audiences don't have. Wright's film states from the beginning that it is based on true events, yet as the film progresses the truth of the operation (although astounding) becomes somewhat secondary to the more universal truth about trauma and its lingering effects on people involved with violent crime.

Wright's ability to capture distress yet not overstate it is incredible. *The Stranger* avoids onscreen violence, yet the film is soaked in the effects of it. Just as Justin Kurzel's *Nitram* chose not to show the massacre perpetrated by the main character yet allowed the audience to experience the horror of what happened off-screen, *The Stranger* also doesn't allow the tension of implied dreadfulness to be diminished. Both films are disquieting, distressing experiences, and are acutely confronting. *The Stranger* is a masterful film, but it's not a film that is simple to digest. Like Mark, audiences will be haunted and left without the catharsis to distance themselves from the film. *The Stranger* is partially a work of fiction but the world it is based on is not.

THE STRANGER

INTERVIEW
CASTING DIRECTOR ANOUSHA ZARKESH

Anousha Zarkesh has worked as a casting director for Australian film and TV since the late 1990s, shaping the identity of Australian stories on screen. Anousha's filmography spans from Yahoo Serious (*Mr. Accident*, 2000) to Tony Ayres (*The Home Song Stories*, 2007) to Rachel Perkins (*Jasper Jones*, 2017) and Warwick Thornton (*Sweet Country*, 2017, *The New Boy*, 2023), and to the emerging work of Thomas M. Wright with *The Stranger* (2022) and Renée Webster with *How to Please a Woman*.

There's a level of alchemy that comes with being a casting director, something that Anousha spent years learning, finessing, and crafting. Anousha carries a deep understanding of different genres which helps inform the casting process, and in turn, the conversations that she will have with the director as she helps bring their film to life.

In 2022, Anousha Zarkesh received an AACTA Award nomination for Best Casting for *The Stranger*. Anousha won the AACTA Award for Best Casting for *High Ground* (2021) and *Shayda* (2024), while also receiving nominations for *Sweet Country*, *Total Control* (2019), and *The New Boy*.

This interview was recorded by Andrew F. Peirce in November 2022

What was your journey to becoming a casting director?

Anousha Zarkesh: I had no idea what a casting director was at all. From a young age my mother and her best friend always took me to the theatre. From the minute the lights went down, I was excited by what a performer did in musical theatre. I didn't want to be an actor. I studied Anthropology and Fine Arts at university, and I thought that's where I was going to head. I was ushering at the same time at the Sydney Theatre Company, so I always had my foot in the theatre and performing arts world. I went on tour with *Les Misérables* as the production secretary for a year after uni. It was great fun doing *Les Mis* in Perth, Adelaide, and New Zealand.

THE STRANGER

When I got back, I worked for Andrew Lloyd Webber's company and then I went for a job at Mullinars Casting. I had no idea who Liz Mullinar was and what casting was, but someone recommended I go for a job. It was almost like alchemy in some sense because it was about actors and what I loved about actors, and when they said, "You'll be casting actors in television and film," I kind of went, "Oh my God, this is my dream job," because I loved what actors did. I knew all the actors because I'd grown up going to the theatre for 25 years. When I started there, it was like short cutting straight to what I loved about the business. I worked there for about 10 years as Liz's assistant, and then I naturally went on to casting on my own after that.

Because I'd studied Anthropology and Fine Arts – with Anthropology being the study of culture and people, almost like sociology – when I started casting, and I read the scripts, I [naturally] wanted to understand human beings and what made them tick. Getting a grasp on the characters, the actors' interpretations, and the underlying qualities is crucial when it comes to casting decisions. When delving into scripts and character analysis, there's a significant aspect of trying to understand people from sociological and anthropological perspectives to grasp what motivates them. I'm constantly thinking about why people want the roles, the characters, what the tone of the show is, what the story is about, and then finding the actors that fit that story and tone.

Casting is a strange alchemy. It's different for every job, every director, and every person. My job is to facilitate the director's vision by interpreting what they want. Sometimes it's really clear, and sometimes it's not. It's all to do with communication and what they're after, and hopefully being in the same zone with them. Like with all heads of department, it's communicating and getting the tone right.

It starts from the interpretation of the script, then [adding] our own flair on top, and then facilitating what the director wants. Of course, each director and producer is different, just as each set of problems is different. The alchemy and the 'X-factor' things that happen on each job are a mystery. It's a miracle because we're all creatives. You have to also be organised. There are so many different facets to a casting job, for instance, we also have to negotiate the rates, and we have to negotiate with the actors. The way we communicate with each actor is different regarding what the director wants. There are so many factors to it. Ultimately, we're part of a big ensemble of people that are thrown together to make this amazing project.

For *The Stranger* it was easy because Thomas was so clear about what he wanted. He had this beautiful vision. He's such an empath and such a gorgeous human being. He wanted to talk about every role and was invested in every character. I was on his journey with him.

INTERVIEW | ANOUSHA ZARKESH

The role of being a casting director means you not only read the script and talk to the director to get the vision, but you're effectively directing and creating the film in your mind with a group of different people. I want to talk about the experience of making sure that you cast the right people, and then, when you watch the film, what the emotional experience of seeing your choices play out feels like?

AZ: Sometimes I think, "Have we got it right?" I start to really feel sick about it. I have sleepless nights, and I wake up thinking, "Am I on the same wavelength as the director and the producers?" There might be a miscommunication between us all or between the producer and the director, or the director is not communicating properly, or I can't get the tone right or I can't find the actors that they want. A lot of the time it works, it's really good, and we get on really well. The more experience I have, the better I am able to interpret all of those factors to give the director what I think they want. Then when they make a choice, ultimately, it's the choice of the director, or the producer, the network, or whoever's investing. Sometimes they override me. I'll put on a good fight if I think they're going the wrong way. If they want to hear my opinion, I will certainly say "I think you're making the wrong choice." Or "Maybe we could try it this way." I can be quite persuasive, but ultimately, I know it's their project and if they decide to go with A as opposed to B, that's fine if that's the choice they make. A lot of the time it's right, because they've been working on their project for two or three years, so they're much more attuned and emotionally connected to it.

I come on [to a project] about three or four months before most of the other heads of department. It's a very intimate relationship between the producer, director, and myself. Sometimes the writer too. I'm very sensitive to the fact that they've worked on and tried to develop their projects for years. So I can't just immediately go, "Oh, well, I think that actors shit, so don't go with them." I'm trying to be supportive and also trying to work out where their heads at so we can tonally get the rest of the film right. Once we do that, I can be quite vocal about my personal choices. Sometimes they listen, sometimes they won't. Sometimes there's external issues going on between the producer, the networks, the investors, or the distributors. There might be ten voices all talking at the same time, and sometimes I have no choice about that. I'm very respectful of that process, and I try not to get too emotional about it. Even though I do.

When we watch the [final] film, it's really difficult for me to watch it without being critical. It's interesting going back and watching a film or a TV show with a bit of distance, because then I can go, "Actually, that works a treat. They were really good." When I first watch it, I'm very critical about if maybe I got it wrong, or we all got it wrong. It is a collaboration. There's a lot of people involved. Sometimes, with distance, I can go, "Wow, that's really good."

Watching *The Stranger* for the third time the other day, I [felt], "I'm in the world." I wasn't critical about the work and my involvement in it. I watched it as someone in the public, and I went, "There's these amazing creatures." I could see how amazing Sean Harris' performance was, and all the other smaller roles. They're freaking amazing. They're all really great. I was so proud of Thomas with the way he shot it, what he got out of the performances for each person, and the way he tonally got it right. It makes such a difference for all the actors to perform their best work because Thomas got it right. Thomas knew exactly what he wanted. That gets me excited when everything works.

How do you cast for characters who have limited screen time, but leave an impact on the rest of the film? I'm particularly thinking of Alan Dukes as John and Ewen Leslie as Asst. Commissioner Milliken, who both leave their mark on the film in small scenes.

AZ: It's totally collaborative. There were weeks of conversation about those characters. We talked more about the characters of John and that detective and what they were and what they wanted. The great thing is that Thomas, because he's an actor, he knows actors and what kind of actors he wants to work with. We were talking tonally about non-acting people, and what was so great about a lot of those characters was they were [performed by] actors, but there were people that didn't have an enormous amount of experience. We talked a lot about the character first, and then I said, "Leave it with me. Let me put my thinking cap on," and then we bandied names around.

Alan Dukes was playing Mr Big aka John. In the script, there was a lot of mention of "John, John, John," and "You're gonna meet Mr. Big," so that could have been someone who had a huge personality, or was a criminal, or a big, creepy, horrible underworld person. We bandied around names of those kinds of actors, and then we thought, actually, let's make him someone who's subtle, someone that you wouldn't think was Mr. Big if you saw him in the streets. In fact, they're all cops; we were playing against it all the time. They're half criminal, half cop. By the same token, there were undercover police, and people with vulnerability, they could make or break this sting operation, so there was a lot at stake. It could get confusing. We were going "Is that the right actor to play that character because they've got to do a lot in those scenes?" Thomas and I mulled over and had lots of conversations about what those actors were, and what the roles were first, and we kept throwing names around. That's how Alan came about.

INTERVIEW | ANOUSHA ZARKESH

The same with Ewen. It could have been any cop, but we were trying to play against type all the time. The cops were disgruntled and tired and overworked and traumatised; there was all that going on. There were a lot of conversations about that and because Thomas and I had the time to talk about that, it meant that he and I could mull it over.

What conversations did you have with Jada Alberts about playing Kate Rylett and Fletcher Humphrys as Graham Ikin?

AZ: When Thomas and I first met, and he was talking about those characters, it was about how they were rookie cops, and that they were tired. They were natural and there was nothing 'actor-y' about them. Thomas didn't want actor-y actors. He would say, "Don't act. Just be." I said, "What about Jada Alberts and Fletcher Humphrys?" He had a vague understanding of who they were. I showed him some old footage that I had, and Thomas went, "Oh my God, yes." That was how simple it was. It was our first meeting to talk about the film, and this was our gut instinct and where we connected. I immediately knew we were in sync. I knew exactly 'here's how we were going to start the project. I know exactly what actors you want.' I kind of work on that level, too.

If I was working on another project, I wouldn't necessarily go there, but I think because of the tone of the film, and what I'd read in the scripts that I've read, and then when Thomas and I talked in the initial meeting, I knew exactly where he was at, and we worked on that level. On something like *How to Please a Woman* or *Rake*, for instance, even though we're playing with truth and authenticity, because it's slightly heightened comedy or a satirical comedy, and it's wordy, and it's clever, it's a very different kind of tone. You'll meet and ask, "Okay, what actors can play in that world?" With Thomas, it was a dark, underplayed, everyone's hiding, everyone's traumatised, kind of world. I got it immediately.

That's a good transition to talking about the casting of Cormac, Thomas's son, in The Stranger. Did he come to you with that idea, or was Cormac already attached to that role when you were engaged?

AZ: There was a bit of talk about Cormac. Initially, he said, "I'm thinking about putting Cormac in there." He was very respectful, and said, "Should we do that?" I said, "Of course. He's your son. Do you want him to be in there?" He said, "I don't know." There was a lot of caution around it. Ultimately, I think he felt it was his own relationship with his son and talking about the relationship between father and son and Joel's relationship with Cormac and putting Cormac in that position. Was Cormac up to it because it was quite a big acting role? It wasn't like it was fait accompli.

THE STRANGER

That's how beautiful Thomas is. Thomas was so respectful of everyone and to everyone and was asking my opinion about it. "You want him? Let's do it. You can direct your own son." Most of the time he'll be with Joel. It was always a choice that he wanted, but he was also making sure that we were all in agreeance with that. It was Thomas being gorgeous and making sure that was the right choice. I think deep down he always wanted Cormac in there. It wasn't for the faint hearted because it's quite a brutal thing to put your son through in that relationship. Of course, working with Joel, you know he's not going to be a total asshole, and they were building their relationship up together.

When it comes to casting a comedy like How to Please a Woman versus a thriller like The Stranger, is it important to have an understanding of what the genre requires?

AZ: Your instincts go there. Sometimes it's a bit of a cliché. I'm very aware of not casting cliché wise or to stereotype. You go, "Let's think outside the box. Do we go for the cliché here or do we go with the stereotype? Or do we push against that all the time?" That's a constant conversation between the director and myself. It's almost like cooking; once you start cooking, you start throwing in different ingredients and go, "Oh, yeah, that changes that. Are you up for that? Do you like that?" That's where the creative part plays. It's a relationship with the director and producers that takes time.

I've been working with similar directors for a while. I know exactly [what they want so] we can now talk in a shortcut; we don't have to build that relationship between each other and be cautious. I'm quite a big personality, I'm quite opinionated, so sometimes I try not to impose too much of myself there initially. I'm really trying to work out what the director and the producers want, and then if I try and really understand and am empathetic to exactly where they're coming from and what they want, then we can push against the stereotypes. In some cases, I know exactly what they want and that's it. It's really important that that character is played by that actor, because then everything can slot in, and then we can start to fuck around with other things. It's like putting a huge, big puzzle together, and being able to play within it; seeing the big picture, and then seeing the little pieces that fit in. Every job is different, and every person I work with is different, and that's the exciting part.

It's really terrifying too. When I start a new job and I read something, sometimes I go, "Oh my God, I'm about to embark on this. I know it's everyone's baby, and I'm honoured to be involved in their project, and they've been struggling to get it up for years." I get nervous initially, even though I've done it a million times. I have to go, 'ok, here's the journey that we're starting.' It's building the relationships between me, the director, the writer, and the producers, initially, so that we can all be really comfortable with each other to kind of go, "I'm going to say something and just don't think I'm a dickhead," or "I'm going to question you on that and are you okay to hear that or not?" We work so intimately and so intensely for a period of time, and then we say goodbye.

You've helped pull together iconic casts for so many great Australian films. How much does the role of the Australian identity play into your choice as a casting director?

AZ: It's such a complex thing, and not something that I think about really. I'm so lucky because I've been involved in so many amazing, iconic Australian projects, from *Mystery Road* to *Rake* to *How to Please a Woman* to *The Stranger*. Identity is not something I consciously think about, necessarily. I'm so proud of being an Australian, and particularly a brown skin Australian. There's always a push against racism and our views of how the Australian identity has changed over the years, particularly with diversity and inclusion in our industry. I've been fighting for that for a long time. I'm really proud of my involvement in that over the last twenty years from *Redfern Now* to all of the Indigenous projects I've worked on.

I'm lucky to be involved in projects that have been written and produced and directed, because of the work that is already there on the page. I'm just part of the collaboration process with the filmmaker and the writer. I don't really know what it means except that I'm part of that process. I push against stereotypes when I can. It's changed. I'm really proud to be Australian. I laugh about the long socks and sandals. I laugh about the Australian colloquialisms. We're so uniquely different to the people around the rest of the world and how we're viewed from the comedy aspect of it to the serious nature of it to our stoicism and our bravery and our wild animals and the snakes and spiders and people freaking out about Australia. We're hardy people. We're funny people. We're adventurous and we're resilient. All of those things that make Australians Australian I am proud of when I travel around the world. I laugh at us, and I go, "Thank God we're Australians," which sounds very nationalistic, which I'm not, I throw up about any nationalism, but all the quirkiness or the kind of eccentricities of Australians is what I love. I think we're slowly getting away from that tall poppy syndrome. We are still the underdogs, but we still love the underdog. I kind of love the underdog, and I love telling those stories.

The work that you've done in helping get the right people to tell their stories on screen is vital. I look at your work alongside Rachel Perkins, like with her series The Australian Wars, as being extremely vital.

THE STRANGER

AZ: It's very political. I think it's changed our industry and the zeitgeist of the Australian people. I'm proud of the work that I have done with beautiful, amazing, politically strong people right from the beginning. I've just been at the right place at the right time. I'm lucky to be part of that process, and I continue to be. I'm very political, as much as I can have a bit of a giggle and laugh.

The work that Rachel and Darren [Dale] did right from the beginning of *Redfern Now* with Blackfella Films was a total game changer. It's really important work and it's led the way for incredible, new Indigenous filmmakers from that day forth. The support from great people like Sally Reily at the ABC and Erica Glynn at Screen Australia, and all the funding bodies that have invested in Indigenous filmmaking has been incredible.

Warwick [Thornton] and Dylan [River], his son, the genius from the last *Mystery Road*, just blow me away. They're incredible, and I'm forever privileged to work with those guys. I'm so lucky that when we're doing *Mystery Road*, I get to travel, and I go to Kununurra and Broome, and then when I'm up there working, I go to the communities, like Lombadina, which is where *The Beach* (2020) was shot and going up to Kooljaman Cape Leveque and working with all these Indigenous filmmakers and friends, it's just blown me away. It's changed my life completely. I worked with Warwick on *The New Boy* (2023), with Cate Blanchett and these eight incredible Indigenous kids. I travelled all around the central desert and the communities to find all the kids there. It has fundamentally changed me as a person. That's the work that I get so excited about. Every time I get a job, I go, "Oh my God, where are we going now?" The incredible Indigenous men and women and the communities that I meet have totally blown me away. That aspect of my job is probably the most thrilling.

Working on *High Ground* (2021) was also just incredible. That was three months travelling up to Arnhem Land, being on the road with Stephen [Johnson] and Witiyana Marika and flying into communities. It was fucking amazing and I'm the luckiest human being alive.

INTERVIEW
EDITOR
SIMON NJOO

From Jennifer Kent's duology of darkness, *The Babadook* (2014) and *The Nightingale* (2018), to Jon Bell's unsettling short film *The Moogai* (2020), and Jennifer Peedom's stunning documentary *River* (2021), editor Simon Njoo has managed to examine Australia's relationship with violence through the simple act of a cut. Whether it be the violence inflicted upon each other, ourselves, or the land around us, Simon's editing manages to amplify the unease of what we're seeing on screen.

The notion that good editing is invisible is realised in the way that Simon's editing manages to draw energy and emotion from somewhere other than the text itself. This is in part how he manages to explore the resonance of trauma after a violent event in Thomas M. Wright's *The Stranger*. The act of violence is pointedly absent from *The Stranger* but is so profoundly felt in the tools of filmmaking. Simon Njoo's editing acts like paper cuts in the webbing of your fingers – precise, painful, and horrifying to imagine

In 2022, Simon received AACTA Award nominations for Best Editing in Film for *The Stranger* and Best Editing in a Documentary for *River*. He has also received nominations for *The Babadook* (2015 awards), *The Nightingale* (2019 awards), and *Harley & Katya* (2024 awards).

This interview was recorded by Andrew F. Peirce in October 2022

What was your entry point into editing?

Simon Njoo: I grew up in Melbourne and studied journalism at RMIT, back in the day when the journalism courses were highly competitive. They only took 24 people a year and you had to have a cadetship, and I was the only one who didn't have it. They took me based on some of my writing.

To me, journalism is a critical pillar of civil society. I think it's a really critical Fourth Estate. I was determined to be a journalist, but I was also interested in art. I was particularly interested in art journalism, but at the time there was no crossover there.

THE STRANGER

I transferred my studies to the University of Technology in Sydney (UTS) to pick up the couple of extra credits that I needed to finish my degree in journalism. The Communications course at UTS was happy to accept me, but they required that I complete the four foundation subjects. I knew nothing about those subjects and learning them was revolutionary for me. My whole vision of the world changed - how I understood the world, which was an important change, and a big part of it was looking into films.

I was introduced to early Australian cinema, from the films of Charles Chauvel to experimental films to the magazine Film Threat. Also, 1950s avant-garde cinema from France, the Nouveau era, and all of that. It's not like I hadn't seen many films. I stayed with my father on the weekends when I was growing up, and my dad would take me to see films at a cinema in Richmond called the Valhalla. We'd see some pretty wild experimental films, but he would also take me to see the James Bond retrospective. My dad just loved cinema.

For me, it was something cool to do as a pastime, and when that intersected with my studies at UTS I thought, "I can actually do this, it's not just something that I can passively receive. I can actually be a filmmaker." I mean, it never crystallised like that. It was being given the tools to actually make a film. That's what gave me that spark.

Then the editing thing was quite simple. We all had to work on each other's films at university, as is often the case in film studies courses. It wasn't until I was in the edit suite with my film that was shot on a Bolex, with the positive kind of 16-millimetre print, at two in the morning in a crappy edit room up in UTS that I realised, 'Oh my God, I made a film.'

Editing is actually a bad name, because it's not editing, it's writing. It's direct, active, intentional creativity. That's the thing I loved about it. During the shoot, I was writing something in collaboration with my filmmaking collaborators, but here in the edit room I'm really writing something, and what I create here is what's going to go out into the world. Directors often talk about that feeling of being on set and it making sense, and for me, it's that moment in the edit room when you go, 'I'm receiving all this stuff, and I'm going to make it meaningful. This is editing.'

How do you plot out your version of the script for the film?

SN: For a feature, I work in collaboration closely with the director. I've also edited commercials when I need to feed the family, but that's a different ballgame with different constraints. The two tasks and skill sets are really different. I would say that editing for commercials is 100% craft, and the idea of that craft is the pursuit of perfection. Perfection in commercial land is ultimately what the client thinks will sell their product. Whereas in feature films and documentaries, the pursuit is not perfection, the pursuit is meaning. That's an entirely artistic pursuit, which doesn't exist in the commercial world. Which for me is the difference between the craft of editing and the art of editing.

Well before the shoot, I speak to the director to get an understanding of their vision for the film. When I receive rushes, I already have an idea of the director's vision for the film. A lot of it's quite mechanical, particularly for an assembly, 'Here's the script and these are the shots that pertain to the script, create some kind of synthesis of those elements that are a reflection of what they shot on the day.' My role is multifaceted. It's primarily to support the director in the realisation of their vision for the film; "I believe in your vision. I think that it can be really strong. Here's one way that we can go about it, and then let's go work on that."

The other part is to be sceptical, and to be the person in the room who says, "Do you think that that works as well as it can? Is what we're seeing here a true reflection of the vision that we talked about in pre-production, or is it something else? If it's something else, is that justified? Is that a development, or is it a compromise? How strong is it? How meaningful is it? How radical is that?" I'm not really interested in making films that aren't radical in some way: formally, conceptually, or narratively.

I'm interested in things that usurp the language of filmmaking because that's what interests me. I'm attracted to that kind of literature. I read *A Clockwork Orange* (by Anthony Burgess), and it's a magnificently inventive piece of writing because it completely usurps the language. I love that about filmmaking and that's the kind of film that I want to work on. I see my role in the edit room to be constantly saying to the director, "Do we need that piece of information? How long can we force the viewer to sit there and go, 'What the fuck is going on?'" and "How tantalising can we make it?" That's the sort of thing that motivates my work.

The way The Stranger plays out is all about information. It's all about who knows what and the search for the truth. What conversations did you have with Thomas about that search for the truth?

SN: I loved the experience of working on that film. Let's be clear, it was very hard work. We were working long days for a long time. I think that we were working for five and a half months on that film. At the same time, it was the most rewarding of experiences. Working with Thomas is like going for a really long walk and you're with a highly intelligent and supremely articulate human being who's constantly challenging the way that you're looking at the walk. Sometimes, you separate and go different ways, but there still is communication, and then sometimes you come back together and fall into lockstep. It's astounding how satisfying that is.

Thomas is one of the bravest directors I've ever worked with. He simply refused to be complacent about anything in his film. He was very concerned about clarity. It's a complex film, and it's dense. I'm really pleased when you say the film is about layers of truth. At what moment do you reveal the truth? There were so many iterations of those different things: when to reveal that it's an undercover operation; when to reveal the organisation is totally fictional; when to reveal that the film was not about the person you think it's about at the start, but it's actually about another person; when to reveal that there's this incredible proximity to violence; all of those things.

There was a daily discussion and dance that we engaged in. It was so cool. I'm super enriched by it. Thomas is a supremely intelligent filmmaker, but he's also highly collaborative. There's no ownership of ideas in the edit room. That's the kind of thing that you aspire to, that there should be no ownership of ideas. I can really say that Thomas was totally into that. We had this kind of unspoken pact that that's the way that it was because that's the way that we work together. He's not interested in ego and that sort of thing, which can often be the case. He's just interested in the expression of the idea, in the most meaningful and artistic sense that he can achieve. That ticks so many boxes for me and it was so satisfying to work under those conditions.

For instance, something I quite often do is sequence cards and stick them on the wall, a chronological breakdown of each scene. I think there are about 160 scenes in *The Stranger*. It took up a big wall. Thomas took those cards and cut into them and reproduced them and we'd split scenes and put half the scene at the start of the film and half of the scenes at the end of the film. By the end, the sequence cards took up three walls. A good half of the first wall were scenes that had been completely deleted from the film. It was a pretty robust but super exciting and highly rewarding experience for me.

There are no pointed elements of violence in the film, and yet, it feels like it's on the precipice of violence. That comes down to the editing. How do you create the threat of violence or the perception of violence in an edit?

SN: For me, there are two kinds of violent elements in the film: there's the character played by Sean Harris, who has obviously been capable of extreme violence in the past. Whenever you've got that, that's just a loaded gun on the table. For Thomas, a lot of the meaning of the film is centred around proximity to that loaded gun. Henry's capacity for violence is ever present and we wanted to maintain it so it is boiling and bubbling away. Then, because there's nothing actually violent on the screen, save for maybe the car crash, it was all constructed in the edit with the abrupt cuts, the pushing forward in time, the sucking down of all the sound, all of those kinds of editorial devices, which are just an extension of the language of the film.

The second element of violence that we constructed and refined and played around with was sometimes as simple as shifting volume that goes from three to 97. Sometimes it's a cut that is in the middle of something, suddenly the film will cut and will be thrown somewhere else. Or other times, you feel as though the film's going one way, and then all of a sudden, something will pull you back in another direction. Oliver Coates beautiful score allowed us to turn in a way that we wouldn't have been able to do if we didn't have that incredible music to go, "We're going this way, rather than that way." It was all of those things. That's why it was such an enjoyable experience because there was such a plasticity about it. It felt super creative. It wasn't just "I've got an idea for a film," it was a lot more three-dimensional. We were constantly holding the film up and looking at it from all sorts of different angles.

I want to pivot to River briefly where the score plays a vital role. Do you edit to a score?

SN: Jennifer Peedom and Joseph Nizeti had different chapters in the film, from genesis to the intervention of humans. It changed as we went along because there was a human element that wasn't present before I started that we brought in. I came and opened up the project, and there were bins filled with footage that was appropriate for the subject and an associated bin filled with music. Basically, Jen had the trust in me as an editor to go, "I'm gonna let you start. Here's the text for this part of the film, here are the images that we think tell the story. Here's a list of ten to twenty music tracks that we think are good." Sometimes there were four hours of selects. I built an assembly based on those elements fairly quickly, I think it took six weeks or so. We were choosing the music in the editing room. They'd already said, "These are the tracks that are good." I can't remember if we changed very many of them. They did change once Richard Tognetti and Piers Burbrook de Vere got to it because of the requirements of the ACO, as they wanted music that would also work for the chamber orchestra in a live setting.

That was an interesting point of tension because the music in the film works differently from a lot of the classical scores that are in the film. Classical scores kind of bubble along and then there's another movement that's big and bold and brassy, not all the time, but quite often; it doesn't have the tension that a cinema score often does. We weren't making a film to be played behind an orchestra while I was playing the beautiful music. We were making a film that was supposed to be standalone and have some meaning. There's no point in making a wallpaper film. Hopefully, people have an emotional response to it. I certainly do. I cry every time I watch that film because there's a sadness in there, but also this melancholy hope and a little bit of "We're going to fuck it. I know that we're going to fuck it. We always fuck it," that threads through the film very much like a river.

Can you break down the construction of the sequence of the dams being destroyed which gives this sense of renewal and melancholic hope?

SN: That has a lot to do with Radiohead's achingly beautiful music. It's an incredible piece of music. I don't think I've ever met an editor who isn't also into music. Pretty much every editor I've ever met either plays an instrument, has dabbled in several instruments, or has a record collection. It's just one of those things that we all do. There's something about rhythm and tempo and emotionality that is present in the music that we kind of aspire to when we're cutting meaningful cinema. There's something in that track that just corresponded so beautifully to this incredible footage of the dams being destroyed and the river coming back and knowing how quickly that kind of biological equilibrium is re-established. There's something so beautiful about that. I think that's pretty clear in the film and it is a moment of real hope but also tinged with the melancholy of knowing that we really do a massive amount of damage to the environment.

In the first film in the series, *Mountain* (2018), what Jen made is totally different because mountains don't move. We can throw ourselves up against them, we can jump off them. You can't get rid of a mountain. However, you can literally stop a river. They're super fragile and I think it's that fragility that suggests the melancholy of that sequence.

Before I started working on *River*, I said, "Jen, I haven't seen *Solo* (2008), you've gotta send it to me." We were working during the week, and she sent me the link and I started watching that film. It's not a long film, and I was just bawling my eyes out on a Sunday morning. She's an incredibly sensitive, beautiful person.

Having worked on a fair number of films now as an assistant and as an editor, I can say that films are a representation of the psychology of the director. You can look at a film and go 'I know something about the psychology of the director of this film.' They're not separate things that don't exist outside of the director. They are a real, psychological portrait of the director in some way. With Jen, I think that's really true. Her films are so full of empathy and love. That's the sort of person that she is.

Looking at the films that you've edited, they reflect the emotions and the thought pattern of the director so completely. The work of Jennifer

Kent, Jennifer Peedom, Thomas, and Jon Bell all say something about Australia as a whole, and their films say something about how each director sees Australia. As an editor working on Australian films, what does it mean to be presenting those ideas on screen?

SN: I love the fact that I live here. I choose to live here. I grew up here. It's a big part of my identity and who I am, but I sort of reject that idea of Australian cinema in favour of an idea about Australian filmmakers. With Jennifer Kent, quite often she would say 'I don't want to make an Australian film.' There's nothing derogatory about that. I think that she didn't make a particularly Australian film with *The Babadook* (2014).

The films that I think are interesting come from a group of filmmakers; Joel and Nash Edgerton, David Michôd, Mirrah Foulkes, they're filmmakers. They're not the Australian film industry. Thomas is the same. It's like that idea of a cottage industry. That sounds derogatory, but it's not at all. The films that I'm interested in Australia are akin to the kind of film auteur output that I sometimes had the privilege to work on in France; little films that were supported by a highly intelligent and creative producer and coming from the vision of a director who really had something to say and wanted to say it in a unique way.

I've got nothing against genre films and all that sort of stuff. It all has a role. Given the opportunity, I'd love to cut a *Bourne Identity* film, I'd love it so much. It just doesn't seem to be the road that I'm on. The people that I am meeting on this road that I'm on, are people who really love films and love the language of the sorts of films that I grew up with and that I love. I don't know if it's an Australian industry. I think it's something smaller and a little bit more modest, but potentially a little bit more universal.

THE STRANGER

INTERVIEW
WRITER & DIRECTOR THOMAS M. WRIGHT

Not since the slap-in-the-face arrival of Justin Kurzel with *Snowtown* (2011) has there been an Australian filmmaker who has presented violence on film as viscerally as Thomas M. Wright.

With his second film *The Stranger*, Thomas M. Wright examines a real-life tragedy through the perspective of the undercover police officer (Joel Edgerton's Mark) who works to ensnare Sean Harris' Henry Teague within a manufactured crime syndicate that exists solely to bring him down. The violent act that Henry has been alleged of is rarely mentioned in the film with Wright allowing the echoes of trauma to reflect through the narrative until the soul-crushing conclusion.

The Stranger is a meticulous, powerful film. It is also one that plays as another entry in the ever-growing library of Australian films that attempt to reconcile with the violence, trauma and resulting tragedy that has occurred on this broken land. For some viewers, this almost obsessive quality that some Australian filmmakers have with the acts of murderers is too much, creating a pall that hangs over the rest of Australian cinema. But for filmmakers like Thomas M. Wright, their films exist to try and make sense of the world that we live in.

Thomas M. Wright won the Best Direction in a Feature Film (Budget $1m or over) award at the Australian Directors Guild Awards for *The Stranger*.

This interview was recorded by Andrew F. Peirce in September 2022

I found Acute Misfortune to be a profoundly brilliant film, and watching you grow as a filmmaker with The Stranger has been quite the journey.

Thomas M. Wright: Thank you. I think it's an interesting conversation between those two films, [it's] probably something I'll be able to reflect on in a good two decades. There's definitely a through line there. I wasn't from a film background, so I hadn't written or directed a film at all. I hadn't made short films, music videos, or commercials or had any of that kind of that apprenticeship. When I walked on set to direct *Acute Misfortune* on the first day, it was my first day of directing a film. A steep learning curve doesn't even begin to [describe it]. It was probably more just like an absolute fucking mess. The lessons learnt were really extraordinary. *The Stranger* was an opportunity to kind of reconcile some of that, to continue on from some of those lessons, but also to resolve some of those mistakes as well.

Within these two features there is an interesting thread where you have protagonists who are questioning themselves as they're questioning others. Whether it's a journalist or a police officer, there is an interrogation of people's identities.

TMW: They're also unreliable protagonists. They're unreliable perspectives. They're both films about relationships that began on shaky footing. For me, I always describe *Acute Misfortune* as [a film] about a relationship based on theft and *The Stranger* as a relationship based on lies.

How do you see yourself factoring into that? Do you see yourself as interrogating both of those figures as a director and a writer?

TMW: Definitely. I'm not interested in uncritical relationships with protagonists. I don't have an uncritical relationship with myself. I think if you did, you'd be profoundly unwell. I am interested in that thorny terrain between the person's inner life and their actions and the whole range of complexity that begins to happen once you put two people together in a compressed situation.

I find human relationships very difficult and very complex. Stories are often a way to simplify reality and to make reality manageable and digestible. Even if you're dealing with complex and thorny stories, it's a way to meditate your way through some of those questions. On a deeper level, I think that's something that I'm really engaged in with both of those stories. I'm currently developing a couple of other films and they're completely different. They're setting out on an entirely different path to achieve something very different with a very different kind of cinematic voice. It's still going to be dark. I can't come out into the light too much.

Your work is fascinated with trauma and the way that it represents itself and emerges within people. Acute Misfortune does it in a very explicit, intense way, as does The Stranger. I'm fascinated by what you are trying to divine or maybe glean from the cinematic tea leaves that you've created.

TMW: Some of that certainly has to do with my own experience of trauma, and that is very much there in *The Stranger*. Certain parts of The Stranger are in some ways intensely autobiographical. Probably more psychologically autobiographical, than anything else. I've never actually said that before. I think there's truth in that. I think the film is a really visceral description of a psychological state. There are a lot of things about this film that feel very fated.

The film that is there is so close to the original film that I described to my collaborators. I'm very proud of that. Even though there's a lot of things that changed, it was done by the necessities of filmmaking and by working with your collaborators and taking on their contributions in a deep and very authentic way. The tunnel that that film exists in is very, very close to what was originally envisaged. It was a visceral film to make and very difficult to make. It's difficult material to deal with and to invite into your home. Obviously, nothing compared to the real trauma that people who were actually affected by these events face.

You asked about that experience of trauma and kind of unpacking trauma and lessons learned through trauma, that's in *Acute Misfortune*, and that's a stated intention of Adam [Cullen]. Adam is like, "You don't know shit until you live it. Until then it's just a fucking idea." [A] very naive thing to invite in when you're talking about the type of trauma that's involved in a film like *The Stranger*. There's a great privilege inherent in that kind of perspective that's not there for the intimacy of that trauma and the personal relationship that's present in *The Stranger*. *The Stranger* is effectively *Acute Misfortune* turned up to level 40.

Certainly, I think there's a deep feeling for victims in both of those films and a sense of moral complexity in the shade. *The Stranger* has a much stronger moral perspective, I think, than *Acute Misfortune*. *Acute Misfortune* is as much judging the protagonist as the antagonist. I was always aware that the idea of having to write the truth of another person and have some objective truth of another person was going to be a flawed idea at the centre of that film, and the way that that manifests in *The Stranger* is very different because you're dealing with these much more fundamental human aspects of chaos and the need for order and a deeper moral perspective that was there in the writing of the film.

And an unconventional moral perspective, I think, too. There's nothing in the moral rulebook that says when you're telling a story, 'don't show the victim,' 'don't represent the victim,' 'don't represent their family.' I felt that I had no right to. I felt that I could only diminish them. I did not want to, in any way, be guilty of using people's trauma to validate a story and that's why it's a story told about people who are one step away, but who do give years of their mental and physical health to resolving these sorts of cases for strangers. Because when events like this happen, they do shake the foundations of our society, they do change the way that we relate to one another.

THE STRANGER

I think when you're from a country that's defined by hidden violence and violence that's present but we're unable to reconcile ourselves to it, no wonder that makes itself so often the subject of our art, whether it's music or visual art or cinema or literature. That's why it was important for me that this film was about an attempt to make meaning in the wake of violence.

I know this is all quite oblique in some ways because I'm very conscious that on one level this is a film about a police operation, it gives you that binary nature of 'here's the good guy, and here's the bad guy.' They're the two sides of the coin, and they certainly mirror and reflect one another. But I think there are some deeper things that I wanted to engage with about the lineage of Australian crime cinema, and films about violence in this country. Also, what it is to set a film in the wake of that violence, where even though violence is the reason for that film, it's not its subject, and its subject is really an attempt to make meaning when violence threatens to render things meaningless and to find the connection between people. Those sorts of questions are what led to the casting of my own son – that's my little boy who plays Joel's son in the film, that's my little boy Cormac - because he's my stake. He's my emotional reality. [He's] everything to me. He's my only child. That's what's at stake for that central character.

I'd love to explore the sound design with you.

TMW: I could talk about the sound design of this film all day. We worked exhaustively on the sound. It comes down to a very clear, simple central concept, I won't say what that is, but the diversity of the ways that we came at that concept was really broad. Everything from Matthias Schack-Arnott's experimental percussion work that you hear. Everyone interprets that differently. Jada Alberts, who plays Detective Rylett, when they heard that sound, they said, "I'm not supposed to hear that. That's a Bullroarer. That's a war sound. Anyone who isn't a fighting individual in the community shouldn't be hearing it. It's like a curse."

For me, there was something vertical about it. When I talk about form and content in a film; it's funny that we use this awful, almost pejorative word for narrative, 'content'. It's like, content is horizontal, and form is vertical. You're forever looking for something that creates something three-dimensional, something unique and sculptural that you can plant down and turn and as different light hits at different times, you'll see the film differently. It's three-dimensional. It's a solid form. The sound in the film is hugely vertical.

It's often immersive, you're placed inside someone's head. There's the foreignness of the landscapes that they're placed in; these exposed, desolate badlands that a lot of the film takes place. That's a narrative necessity because you can't have a character like Henry in populous locations. You have to keep him remote. That pressurised quality was something that we worked extraordinarily hard with Andy Wright, the Academy Award-winning sound designer (*Hacksaw Ridge*, 2016). I know he couldn't be prouder of the work in the film, and neither could I.

Oliver Coates composition as well. He's been involved with and responsible for some of the great scores of the last decade. He's worked extensively with Jonny Greenwood. He played the cello for Mica Levi's score to Jonathan Glazer's *Under the Skin* (2013), which is one of my favourite science fiction films of all time. The nature of all that work, even the percussion that Matthias did, is all physical, there's very little electronic interference, except for when it becomes something that's experienced firsthand in the film because you're being reminded that the film is all being recorded. It's the making of a film. The film is about film; the film is the making of a film which is a story to entrap this individual, and they're recording it acoustically and visually all the time. So, when you're reminded of that, it's a kind of cognitive dissonance that you're in the middle of something while recalling it from outside of it at the same time.

There is a visual style of you – the beard, the long hair – that seems to be replicated in the two characters. Is that a pointed decision?

TMW: No. No, it's not. I don't have my full beard at the moment. To be honest, I've also got one of those faces that if I don't shave twice a day, then I've got a beard in four days. I suppose the only thing I would say about that is that we were all conscious of the fact that this was a film about hiding. Truthfully, I'm a very, very private person. I try to deal with the world through my work. The subject of that ongoing conversation that you're having through your life, and the process of talking to people about that work is difficult for me because I feel that a film should be able to say all that intends to on its own and on its own terms.

I like to hide. Which is funny, because I've worked as an actor at times too, but that's its own form of hiding, and when you look at those films, they're also about the kind of performance of the self, a presentation of a version [of the self], and usually a version of the self that's defined by work. In fact, for every one of those four central characters, it's how you're taught what to be and what to want and a kind of codified language of behaviour. That's very explicit in *The Stranger*. For me, that was also that learned behaviour of journalism, or the art world in *Acute Misfortune*. In this, it's this kind of criminal enterprise and these two people start to look more and more and more alike and start to dress like one another and sound like one another and turn into one another. I don't know whether that's some deeper nature/nurture conversation I'm having about human beings or whether it's more of a Jungian thing about shadow states and hidden aspects of the self and the subconscious, but it's a conversation without end, whatever it is. I think it's something that you can return to over and over and over.

What does it mean to be an Australian filmmaker working today and exploring the Australian identity on screen for you?

TMW: My perspective is personal. There are a lot of things that I don't understand about the way the trajectory of communication is taking place. The majority of films that I watch are from the 40s through to the 50s. I love cinema of all periods. I engage through narrative film, and literature to a lesser extent. Films have been the language of my life, it's what I return to over and over again, and that's a question of form and content.

As I said, *The Stranger* and *Acute Misfortunate* are both directly in dialogue with that lineage of film in Australia, to the point where in *Acute Misfortune* you have Adam Cullen directly in conversation with the final scene of Rowan Woods' film *The Boys* (1998). Whereas in *The Stranger*, it's probably buried in a little more visual and tactile [way], and people who engage with cinema, they'll see that there. My attitude to that has always been the personal is indivisible from the cultural from the social. We're kind of lightning rods, aren't we? To decode that and to understand how all these things make their way into our bodies and our minds is for people who are much more learned than me.

I think it's an interesting marker that this film was the first Australian film in Un Certain Regard in eight years since Rolf de Heer's *Charlie's Country* (2013). We are there in a lineage of films that includes *Ten Canoes* (2006), Warwick Thornton's *Samson and Delilah* (2009), Tracey Moffatt's *BeDevil* (1993), and Ivan Sen's *Toomelah* (2011); all these extraordinary and formative works of Indigenous cinema and filmmaking. That we're there as a psychological crime thriller is really unusual. I'm so thankful that we figure anywhere in that lineage of Australian films.

Also, for the film to be then bought worldwide by Netflix and be going out to 224 million people. I'll be fascinated to see how people respond to the film. The film had an emphatic response in places like Spain and Italy; I'd be fascinated to hear what the South Koreans make of it. For me, it feels, in some ways, more like a South Korean film, not consciously, but when I reflect on it. Maybe because on the one hand, it's highly conceptual. It's very propulsive. It has this complex narrative structure, but it's also a deeply psychological film. I was aware that I was doing that, that was part of the structural formulation of the film, to think about something that was going to be structurally complex and taut, but deeply immersive psychologically, but was using a kind of forensic language that you had to work through, that was putting the audience in the position that they're in almost more in a documentary, where you're piecing together clues to make sense of what's happening in the film.

I have to say I think it's an extraordinary time in Australian film. I think that because of the way we receive information now and the way we receive our cinema. There is an incredibly diverse body of work being created by all these filmmakers, you have Kitty Green shooting her new film *The Royal Hotel* (2023), Alena Lodkina's new film *Petrol* (2023), Goran Stolevski has three films that are all on their way out, David Michôd is making *Wizards!* (undated), Garth Davis is making *Foe* (2023), and you have Jane Campion having just made *The Power of the Dog* (2021), and there's Amiel Courtin-Wilson making a film a year. There is such a diverse range of voices out there making Australian films at the moment, and quite strange and idiosyncratic trajectories for each of those films, as well. It's a really interesting time for Australian cinema.

It's been great to talk to you. You're somebody I'd love to sit down in a decades time and talk through your body of work with.

TMW: Absolutely. That's something that I'd love to do, too. I'd love to do that with Jennifer Kent or David Michôd. I'd love to do that with Justin Kurzel. Cinema is such a flexible medium. There's nothing that you can't make a compelling story about and no way that you couldn't make that story compelling, but it's going to come down idiosyncratically to the individuals who are making that film. It's a strange alchemy.

Thanks so much for talking. I never tire of it. It was great to be at both Cannes and MIFF this year. I tried to see as many films as I could, where I used to be drawn toward films that were like what I wanted to make. I used to go and see something, and I'd be like, "That's good because that's something that I would like to try to achieve myself." Now when I go to a film festival, I want to see people who think in a completely different way, who are completely unaligned with me and what I'm trying to set out to do, whose departure point is different and whose expression is different. I love that. I love the diversity of cinema.

LIEUTENANT JANGLES

97 mins
Director: *Nic Champeaux*
Writers: *Nic Champeaux, Daniel Cordery*
Cast: *Matt Dickie, Justin Gerardin, Tamara McLaughlin, Daniel Mulhall, Jack McGirr, Harry Piaggio, Graham K. Furness, Greg Kelly, Scott Young, James Topp, Timo Bardsley, Salvatore Merenda, Chris Bridgewater, Michelle Berka, Andrew Dickens*
Producers: *Gregory Kelly, Morgan MacKay, Pernell Marsden*
Composer: *Jon Reilly*
Editing: *Daniel Cordery*
Director of Photography: *Daniel Cordery*
Lieutenant Jangles Theme Composed by: *Thomas Joly*

INTERVIEW
FILMMAKERS
NIC CHAMPEAUX & DANIEL CORDERY

Lieutenant Jangles (2019) is a film which seeks to resolve the question 'How funny is a dick?' By the time credits roll, the answer is clear: they're pretty bloody funny.

Director Nic Champeaux and fellow co-writer Daniel Cordery have crafted a spoof of eighties buddy cop flicks-cum-Ozploitation-throwback that's replete with piss-jokes, dick-jokes, drongo dialogue, more dick-jokes, over the top cartoonish violence, and one more dick-joke for good measure. Heck, the name of the actor who plays Lieutenant Jangles is Matt Dickie and another character, Dickens, is played by actor Andrew Dickens. Talk about commitment to the bit. Juvenile barely covers how deliriously idiotic and entertaining *Lieutenant Jangles* can be.

Creating an action-comedy flick on a budget isn't easy, as Champeaux and Cordery talk about in the following interview. Adding to the complicated life of *Lieutenant Jangles* is the way it struggled to gain a domestic audience in Australia, all the while receiving a rapturous reception at international genre film festivals like the GenreBlast Film Festival where it won the Jury Award and Audience Award Best Feature Film in 2018, and at the South Carolina Underground Film Festival where it won the Jury Award in 2019. *Lieutenant Jangles* went on to receive an extras-stacked Blu-ray release from boutique physical media label Umbrella Entertainment.

This interview was recorded by Andrew F. Peirce in September 2022

When did you start the film?

Nic Champeaux: 2012 I think was when the concept first popped up. It was an inside joke that became the disgusting one-hour-forty dick and fart joke that it is now. It's literally almost been a decade.

What's it like to sit with this dick and fart joke film for a decade?

LIEUTENANT JANGLES

Daniel Cordery: I think ups and downs are a good way to describe that. The main shoot was the biggest event where you're working with so many different people. We're all clumped together for months on end working on it. The following year we filmed on weekends with just a handful of people and then spent a whole year in post-production where it was just us isolated in rooms. The three years after the premiere there was nothing except for festivals. It was a long silence, and we kind of gave up on the film.

And then the Umbrella release was like a very, very delayed, delayed celebration explosion for us, which makes it feel strange because we've been silent for so long. When the Umbrella thing happened, all of a sudden it was like 'We're getting this big release, we're getting posters, we're getting talked about and interviewed.'

NC: It would have been nice five years ago, but beggars can't be choosers.

As indie filmmakers, how difficult is navigating that road of trying to get the attention of festivals and audiences?

NC: Like Dan said, we kind of give up and then would get interested in it all over again. It was up and down. The good thing about this film is because it's such a niche film it's a hard sell in itself. It's so disgusting and weird, so any attention or good feedback that it got, we know it was genuine.

The festival appreciation was all international, none of it came from Australian festivals. The first one was the GenreBlast Film Festival in America, and we flew over for that. I think it's safe to say that was the best experience we're ever going to have with the movie; getting there and then seeing the first foreign audience reaction to it and it being so good and making all these new friends and staying in a hotel next door was awesome.

DC: The irony is that going to GenreBlast was the first thing that we did with the film when it was finished and it was also the best.

NC: Nothing's gonna top that ever. That was the best shit.

What made it the best? Was it that audience reception and getting to interact with people?

DC: Getting a good crowd reaction. Also, if the guys that run the festival love your film, they treat you like royalty. We've become really good friends since.

NC: We put them on the commentary track for this special edition Blu-ray because we loved them so much.

INTERVIEW | NIC CHAMPEAUX & DANIEL CORDERY

What makes a good dick joke?

DC: That there's no thought going into it. You don't plan a dick joke. If it happens, it goes in.

NC: That's the biggest thing with the comedy of this film is there's a lot of subversion. So, dangling something that the audience is going to think is the obvious joke, but then taking a hard left turn at it. Like Wheels (Daniel Mulhall), the character in a wheelchair, everyone thinks 'They're going to make fun of him being in a wheelchair,' but no, the joke is that he's too young to be a cop, and ironically he's the only useful cop in the entire film.

That, and the absence of comedy too. That was what Matt Dickie brought to the film, where he's saying something that doesn't even make sense and that just being so fucking funny in itself that it's like, 'Oh, this is what it is now.'

DC: In terms of dick preparation, I think Dickens (Andrew Dickens) getting his dick shot off in the opening shoot-out was the only thing that was actually planned because that was part of the script. Other than that, anytime Matt as Jangles says dick in any other instance, Matt said "What are you going to do? Change it?" Dinosaur dicks chief.

NC: I think he did a lot of that on purpose, especially "Find a dick in a dick stack."

DC: Which doesn't even make sense, but it's too funny to say 'Come up with something else.'

NC: The biggest inspirations for the script were *Team America* and films like that. *Freddy Got Fingered* (2001) was a big one. If you watch that movie with the commentary track, Tom Green is talking about it as a satire of Hollywood movies in general. On its surface, it looks like the dumbest, most disgusting movie ever just made to piss people off, but there's a lot of smart things in it. I think *Jangles* has a little bit of that. It is very dumb and very disgusting, but there are little sprinkles of clever satire in there.

What direction did you give the actors for the comedy? Was it an improv-friendly set?

NC: Yes. Dan shot it, edited it, did all the visual effects, all of the poster art, everything, so on set there were a lot of times where he was simultaneously ripping his hair out, but also being like, that's pretty fucking funny. We would just come up with things on the spot or change scenes entirely from what was in the script.

LIEUTENANT JANGLES

DC: Also, we didn't have rehearsals. Imagine what a pipe dream that would have been. Imagine planning.

NC: Matt's kind of an improv machine. You let him do his own thing, even if he's following the script, he's usually loosely following it. A lot of the stuff that happens in the movie is stuff he came up with. For example, the character Dino Spaghetti was merely his concept of a man deeply passionate about spaghetti. There was a lot of improv stuff happening.

How did you stage the action if there was so much improvisation taking place?

DC: The best example to describe it would be to look at the opening shoot-out versus the end shootout. With the opening shoot-out, we didn't really plan it. We didn't have storyboards or any rehearsals. We had so many extras that day, and it got into a weird mood where someone would come up with a joke, so we'd put that in. Then we realised that's kind of the worst way to go about it.

The end shoot was completely planned the week prior. I storyboarded everything to a tee. We did a floor plan of the warehouse we were filming at and had little maps of where the camera was going to go and where different spots of action were going to happen

Jangles fights someone in this corner, Wheels fights someone over in that corner, and Gonzales (Justin Gerardin) goes into the next room. Stuff like that. Preparation is key. You don't wing an action scene is what we learned.

The use of violence adds to the scene as well. Can you talk about the creation of the balls-to-the-wall gory style of violence and how important that was for the film?

DC: I like to say that Jangles is fuelled by juvenile immature boy humour. It's not like we're sitting here going, 'We're gonna make something with a message about violence on screen.' If Matt comes up on the spot and says, "I want to grab this hammer and go, 'It's hammer time,' and start bashing in their brains," then we film it. There's no deeper thought than that. We don't really realise that seems violent on screen because we just thought that was funny.

NC: Like him ripping the heart out. I think that the best thing about this movie is there's zero message and no agenda. Whatever we think is funny or entertaining goes in.

DC: Which is like a good mindset if you're recreating something from the Ozploitation era from the 70s and 80s. Back then they didn't have a clue about messages they were putting into the films. They thought, 'People want to see explosions, guns, hot chicks, fast cars, violence. Just shove it onto the screen and then we'll sell it and make a profit.' We went in with the same mindset, just without the profit.

NC: That's why it's so funny watching people try and find whatever messages they think the film has and then go on about it. They say, 'Oh, it's so offensive because of this and this.' Alright, if you say so.

DC: We had a Letterboxd review say that we were trying too hard to be offensive or edgy. It's like, were we trying?

NC: I was just happy they said we tried.

You mentioned the Ozploitation movement. How important was it to honour that style of Australian filmmaking?

DC: At the time we hadn't seen that many Ozploitation films because they weren't readily available. Now Umbrella is unleashing all these hidden gems onto the world through the Ozploitation classics line. At the time, all we had seen was the *Not Quite Hollywood* (2008) documentary. We'd seen *Stone* (1974) and *Turkey Shoot* (1982), but that was about it. Most of the exploitation homage and influence comes from our interest in film. *Miami Connection* (1987) was one example.

NC: That was a big thing. We were obsessed with that movie at the time of writing the script and shooting the movie. We had posters on the wall and Dragon Sound shirts and stuff.

How important is it to have a company like Umbrella release an extras-filled special edition alongside titles like Miami Connection? There is a seal of approval that comes with an Umbrella.

NC: Our first goal when we finished the movie was to get a Blu-ray by Umbrella. That's as big as my dreams went and having it happen now is fucking amazing.

DC: It's an absolute honour. Before Umbrella, we were basically gearing up to say 'Alright, it's gonna fade away now. Nothing really came from the film.' But now it's on our shelves right next to classics, and having it sit right next to *Miami Connection* and the Ozploitation films Umbrella has released is a massive honour. In the B to D grade level of Ozploitation and exploitation films, we're amongst giants.

LIEUTENANT JANGLES

NC: Whether it's an honour for them– probably not. But for us, it's pretty sweet.

Working with Umbrella has been a great experience for me personally after dealing with the bullshit of the ups and downs. They've been so good. The artwork is incredible. I'm super happy with it.

What's the draw of exploitation films for you?

NC: Hollywood stuff is so paint by numbers. Any kind of blockbuster comedy, like the Judd Apatow ones are two hours long and they're very predictable. Whereas when you watch stuff like *Black Dynamite* (2009), you never know what the fuck you're gonna get. That's what I feel we put into this film; you've seen this kind of movie before, but you've also never seen this movie before.

Can you talk about finding the artists for the score?

NC: The internet is a great place to meet dudes.

DC: Do you want to rephrase that?

NC: No, that's what I meant. There are a lot of Facebook groups where I met a lot of people. At that time, synthwave as a genre was starting to pick up after *Drive* (2011) came out. Dan and I would listen to YouTube playlists. Dan put a lot of temp music in the film, and we felt 'This is perfect. Let's message them and see if we can use it.' Or we would just get someone to create something similar.

In 2017, about six months before the premiere, we were down to the very end of post-production. We still didn't have the score for a lot of the movie. I randomly saw some dude in a music group had posted a video of his studio and he was playing stuff on his guitar and keyboard. I thought, 'Damn, that is really good.' So I played it over some of the edit Dan had given me. I reached out to him and showed him the movie and he did one track, then two tracks, and then he ended up scoring the rest of the film.

As you say, the internet is a great place for meeting guys, it's amazing who you find out there. On the same hand, what has been your experience with interacting with audiences when you attend festivals?

NC: A lot of people, like the festival runners, have become friends. They really liked the movie and wanted to show it again. It's all been positive. Even when they filmed the reactions of their audiences in Italy or the Netherlands, it was kind of weird that they got it because it's so Australian. I guess the backdrop is so familiar that they can connect with it.

With those screenings in Italy and the Netherlands, did it make your head spin to have your indie film screened there? When you started, did you ever imagine that it would be screened in countries like that?

NC: It's fucking crazy. It is shocking.

DC: I'm shocked by how more overseas people ate it up than here. We made it for ourselves.

NC: That was a bit disheartening. I think that was part of the reason we were starting to give up on it as well. It was like, the overseas audiences loved it and nobody here gave a shit. We were like, I don't know, maybe it sucks?

What does that do to you then? Are you planning on making another film or has this experience been too much?

NC: Who knows? The only thing is you need money to make a film. That's the biggest takeaway I have. We were all film students at the time fresh out of film school. This is literally almost a decade ago.

DC: We had all that piss and vinegar back then, "Let's make a big feature film."

NC: You could talk people into working for free, because it's like, "We're all gonna make a film together. It's gonna be fun."

What did you learn from the post-production journey?

DC: Get money and more people. Just because you can multitask doesn't mean you should. For both of us, the whole final year of 2017 was basically post-production. It was Nick working with all the actors for ADR, as well as the sound designer doing the full sound mix and all the composers. We'd locked off the edit by that point, but I was losing my mind doing all these visual effects shots and colour grading. I also helped out with the sound effects, as well as any little marketing posts for Facebook or whatever had to be done along the way.

It's like the blessing and curse of when you're in control of your own film without producers breathing down your neck. Yes, you're in control and have all this freedom, but then it's all on you to manage it. I would not go through that experience again.

LIEUTENANT JANGLES

What recommendations or suggestions would you have for people who want to embark on something like what you've done?

NC: Plan as much as you possibly can in pre-production. It's good to be on a set where everyone can adlib jokes, but man, you really, really, really need to have things planned. Some things can't just come up organically.

And, if you can raise as much money as possible, I'd suggest that. The whole final shoot-out looks fantastic because we spent thousands of dollars to rent that place. If you can rent stuff and locations like that for every single scene, then that's production value right there. It makes it look like a proper movie. We got the police station set for free, but then we had almost no money for the art department, so it was just boxes and little computers. We filmed in one corner and had all props there, and then we'd turn the camera that way and take all those props to reorganise over here to pretend like it's a different version of the office.

NC: You can hate the film or love the film, but you have to appreciate the amount of effort that went into it and how polished it ended up being. Often indie films look like trash, and it almost doesn't matter whether they're good or not.

The thing that impressed me was how good it looks for a micro-budget film. You've both put your blood, sweat, and tears into the film and it shows on screen. There's a lot to be proud of here.

NC: There's a lot to be ashamed of, and a lot to be proud of. It's a weird mix.

DC: I said to Nic the last time we hung out, "I'm done watching the film, I cannot watch it ever again." When you watch the film you see, 'This is footage from 2015. These visual effects are from 2016.' I could do so much better now. The jokes we thought were hysterical back then are like chainsaws on a violin now.

I love watching the doco. It makes us look like we're actual filmmakers.

NC: Watching the film brings back PTSD from making it, but for some reason watching the documentary makes it seem like it was all fun.

For a lot of Australian films, the 'making of' documentaries or supplementary materials feel like a rarity. With that in mind, how important is it to have a 'making of' documentary? It seems to be quite valuable as a reflection process.

INTERVIEW | NIC CHAMPEAUX & DANIEL CORDERY

NC: I'm glad we made it, but we didn't think it was important at the time. I think we were sick of explaining the origin story and we wanted it on the record once and for all.

DC: We had people on set taking the behind-the-scenes footage and photos, but if we were to make that documentary after the first couple of months of shooting, it would probably have been very boring. 'Look, we have some inside jokes and had some fun.' By the time it was after our first film festival that we went to, and we started to talk about the Blu-ray release, we realised this is a massive story to tell, so we might as well get as many actors back as we can interview and that we'd like to make a documentary. It turns out there was so much story to tell that I think the last cut of the doco was up to one hour forty minutes, the same length as the movie.

NC: There was over twenty hours of interview footage to go through. It was a nightmare. After doing the movie, we then shot and edited that together, so that was another bullshit process, and we were just burnt out. Then for some reason, we thought it'd be a good idea to put ourselves through that again for the Umbrella release and completely re-edit the film. I can officially say that I've caught up with everyone else who was working on it, and I'm fucking over it.

And now you're talking to me about it.

DC: Which isn't work. It's just ego-stroking.

NC: See, this is the part we were looking forward to. Not re-editing shit we shot in 2015.

Off the top of your head, what was your favourite scene?

It has to be the end shoot-out at the end and also the sad montage of when Jangles is moping through the city at night. Then I also keep coming back to the opening scene with the peeing competition. It sets up the vibe for the film right away.

DC: We don't ease you into it. You haven't even properly met the main character yet, but here he is with his partner pissing into each other's faces.

NC: I'm pretty sure that's the moment where every person who watches it either checks out or they start rubbing their hands together going 'Holy shit, I'm in for a treat.'

DC: That scene is an example of how it was probably written where the intention was, 'They're pissing on a fence and then the radio calls and they

LIEUTENANT JANGLES

have to go to a house.' And then we go to set and we start filming and before you know it it's turned into 'Now they're pissing on each other,' and 'Now they're pissing on each other's faces,' to 'Now he's getting piss directly into his mouth,' and it's still like, 'Ha ha, we're boys just having fun.' That's just me going like, "Yeah, we're trying hard to be edgy." It was on the spot stupid, we thought it was funny, and it went in. That's the story.

NC: It was just Matt had a water bottle to play with and he started spraying Dickens with it. 'Okay, we'll film it.'

The laughter Matt has sets the tone of the film too, because you can't take that kind of stuff seriously and you can't take that laughter seriously either.

DC: That was his genuine laugh. It got to the point where anytime we'd say something and he would laugh, we were like, 'Wait, does he genuinely find what we said funny or is he putting that on?'

NC: Matt is so naturally charismatic and funny that he doesn't even have to try. He always knows the right thing to say. It's incredible. The thing you would never think of in a million years, he would say it and you would just start crying with laughter.

DC: Wheels goes, "Look at the witness, she's a looker." And he goes, "She's like a beautiful pademelon." It's like, what's a pademelon? "Oh, it's like a marsupial." People love that line. Who comes up with that except for Matt Dickie?

NC: It's very strange because in the real world he's got his life together. He's married. He has a house. He has a really good job. And he is very immature, but he's also very progressive as well. So the dirtbag that he plays on screen is him but it also isn't him.

ITHAKA

111 mins
Director: *Ben Lawrence*
Writer: *Ben Lawrence*
Featuring: *John Shipton, Stella Assange, Nils Melzer, John Pilger, Ai Weiwei, Vivienne Westwood*
Producers: *Adrian Devant, Gabriel Shipton*
Composer: *Brian Eno*
Cinematography: *Niels Ladefoged*
Editing: *Karen Johnson*

In 2022, *Ithaka* received a nomination for Best Documentary at the AACTA Awards. Ben Lawrence and Gabriel Shipton were also nominated in 2022 for the Walkley Documentary Award at the Walkley Awards, while Lawrence also received a Best Direction in a Documentary Feature nomination at the 2022 Australian Directors Guild Awards.

Ithaka received the Amnesty International Award at the 2023 Thessaloniki Documentary Film Festival.

INTERVIEW
WRITER & DIRECTOR
BEN LAWRENCE

From the 2018 documentary *Ghosthunter*, to the 2019 drama *Hearts and Bones*, Ben Lawrence's films have empathetically examined the weight of trauma on the human soul. With his 2021 documentary *Ithaka*, Lawrence follows John Shipton, a retired builder, fighting in the UK for the freedom of his son Julian Assange, locked in the Belmarsh Prison without charge. At time of filming, a 175-year prison sentence loomed over Julian's future, leading John to embark on a life of tireless, unceasing activism for his son and for press freedom. *Ithaka* equally follows Julian's partner, Stella, as she grapples with Julian's continued imprisonment that has turned into an act of torture.

This interview was recorded by Andrew F. Peirce in October 2021

How did you come onto this project?

Ben Lawrence: I got a call from Gabriel [Shipton], the producer. He had this idea to make a film about his father. There was an upcoming hearing for Julian [Assange] at the end of last year. Gabriel contacted me in July 2020, and within a month, I was on a plane to London. They'd already been filming for about six to eight months prior, so there was a routine that John [Shipton] and Stella [Moris] had in being filmed, and I stepped into that. We got on a few more support in London, I was the only one who came out of Australia, and we continued to film. The focus was the hearing that started in September, and it took us a year. It happened very quickly. That's the fastest I know how to make a film in that period of time, with a turnaround of about twelve months, with six months of editing as well. The entry point was Gabriel's call to me, and I was pretty hooked from the moment he called.

Did you ever ask yourself, "Why me? What about me makes me the person to tell this story?"

BL: Definitely. Actually, the responsibility of telling it, the size of the story, the fact that it was very important to me, I knew that was important to others, but also to have that sort of access to John and Stella and that world weighed heavily on me in trying to tell a film that I felt was accessible, emotional, but also grappled with the larger global issues that are at play in Julian's story. It was all of that. I felt up to it. We had a very small team, and that was good for being in those intimate moments and jumping in a taxi and capturing stuff that was happening and allowing the characters to live their lives. I really wanted to slip into that. The cinematographer Niels [Ladefoged] had done such a wonderful job. He was trusted by the family. I felt like I needed to earn that as well, so that's what I wanted to continue with. There's a leap of faith in letting people into that inner circle, and I kind of cherished that and took that on from the very start.

How do you manage to balance the earning of trust with capturing a story?

BL: I asked a lot of questions of Niels; how the shooting had been going, what they'd established, where I felt I could help and support him. What we ended up doing was duplicating his camera kit system, and I was able to have a second camera which really helped us. I think it was a bit of a balance of earning John's trust because we were spending so much time together. We were living together for a period of time, sharing a house and stuff like that, which was fantastic for the film. It raises other issues because ultimately, you're trying to get a side of him out that he may not want to reveal and present the story in a way in which the audience feels like they're not just getting the veneer of something. John would spend a lot of time with the press, and I wanted to find a different side to the story that wasn't just the campaign message. In part, it's earning that trust, but also pushing some of the questions and subject matter is important because Gabriel and John feel like I'm also trying to push the documentary as well. They don't want it to be this thing that people don't engage with. It's a balancing act.

All three of your films have been about complex relationships with other people. Is there something that draws you to those particular narratives as a filmmaker?

BL: I think so. I'm obviously fascinated by people. I'm fascinated by what makes them tick and trying to reveal that in a way in which they're comfortable with as well. Ultimately, I want the experience for the subject to be worthwhile, but also rewarding and enriching and not damaging, and that was probably more so for the case of *Ghosthunter* (2018).

The other thing I would say is that growing up, I used to watch a lot of documentaries and wonder how they made it. How did they get themselves in that position where those people were comfortable enough? The mystery of that was like watching a magic trick that I wanted to solve. Slowly, over the years, I've worked out ways of doing that. It is a relationship, it is a genuine relationship you have with someone, and it goes to the core of what trust is, and how you earn that trust.

There are times you want to disappear and be that fly on the wall and capture something. You stop breathing and you're holding a camera. You know that something amazing is happening in front of you, you're capturing those things that you imagined you might. There are other times that you want to step in and ask a question. In the case of making this film, the challenging environment that Stella and John were placed under, particularly during the time that I was with them in that last hearing – the taxi rides were just silence –, you feel like it's very inappropriate to say anything, but ultimately, it's your role to ask that question, "What's going on? What are you thinking? Say something."

There was one interview I did with John that I knew he probably wasn't going to answer my questions in the way I wanted, but I was happy that at least he said "I don't want to talk about that. That's off-limits. No." Even his pushback was important to hear. Sometimes it's not a very pleasant role, but most of the time I was just trying to sit there and not breathe and not be noticed.

How do you balance being an empathetic human and a director and a documentarian at the same time? There are moments here where I can feel you wanting to reach out and hug them or give them a pat on the shoulder but there's the camera and the documentary between you.

BL: There's a lot that goes on off camera in the time that you spend with those people. I think simple things like doing what you say you're going to do and following through. I say it to documentary filmmakers all the time – and I'm still learning – but if you say you're going to be somewhere, simply be there on time, be there early. It's really simple in that way, and a lot of relationships fall apart for that and other reasons.

It's funny, the times when you don't want to point the camera are the times when you probably should point the camera and capture those things. It's a real balance. It probably happens in the time when you're having dinner or on a bus ride or you're just catching up at the end of a long evening or you're just trying to connect with people. It's a two-way street – they want to ask about you, and you want to ask about them, and sometimes you just want to sit there in silence.

In the case of *Ghosthunter*, there were some scenes that we filmed that were sensitive that took weeks for both of us to feel comfortable that we were going to put it on camera. There are a lot of other conversations that probably happened around those moments that are important.

There is both a wealth of anger and support for Julian Assange. Do you go into a film like Ithaka with an agenda to address Julian's story, or focus solely on John and hope the narrative falls out from there?

BL: A bit of both. When Gabriel and I started talking, he had a vision for the film and an idea of following John. The timing was critical as the court case was coming up, so we kind of had a structure. I was curious what John was like prior to meeting him. I was fishing with Gabriel, "Tell me what he's like. What I should expect?", just to prepare myself for the things to keep an eye out for so you can anticipate [what might happen]. Ultimately, you want as much information as you can get going in so you can be in the right place at the right time and you can anticipate things.

Gabriel and I met on similar territory, that the focus was going to be John. It wasn't long after that that Stella was going to be part of the documentary as well because they're both in each other's orbit and she had been filmed with Niels prior. Her situation is a little bit different in that she's so central to the court case and Julian. They had also [been together] under a long period of very intense surveillance. She'd just come out publicly months before about her and her family, the kids that she'd had with Julian. That environment still had an umbrella over it, [which was] pretty much the environment that we were living in.

The entry point was John and following and being with him. That not only opened up the narrative, but also the other relationships and stories that were going to occur, and the other characters that we also were able to cross paths with. That was the idea, who's crossing John's path along his journey?

In terms of an agenda, I was very interested in Julian's story and the work of WikiLeaks for a long time. One of the biggest compliments I've had about the film is that it's unhysterical, in that it's a view of that world, that story, that tries to present it on a human scale. That's what I wanted to do. That was my only agenda; I wanted to humanise it through John. This idea that other global issues were going to be brought up was out of that human single story.

What I was taken to is the relationship that fathers have with families. The influence that a son's legacy will have on a father or a father's legacy will have on the son. Was that the main thrust of finding out who John is as a man by exploring that paternal relationship?

BL: Definitely. The film reflects John's personality. I think that was the plan. It kind of has an intellectual flavour to it. It has also a very human and robust [feel] and [is] kind of tangible in the way that John was a builder and hands-on. I describe John as building a rocket to the moon, but he's doing it in his backyard. He's the sort of guy that's going to build a helicopter, and he tinkers away, and eventually, it'll take off. It's that ambition but it's grounded in this very single-family unit.

The idea of fathers, yes, was central to it. The fact that Julian has children that are a similar age to John's daughter, the fact that Gabriel was a producer who also steps into the film. I probably would have liked to explore a little bit more through Gabriel as well.

John never gave me the answer to questions in the way I expected. He always gave me something else. What occurred to me is that John has experienced and has come to understand the world through stories. Literally. He will talk about a novel and say, "This section of the book explains this part of the human personality." For a long time in his life, the world was very much a puzzle to him, as were other people. I think the reason that they were so puzzling is that he has spent his life deeply observing people and trying to understand them. In trying to make himself understandable, he reflects in very indirect ways but leaves you with a thought that you can ponder for a few hours or a few days.

In terms of it being about a father and son story, that was the core of it. What was John's motivation in taking this cause of campaigning for his son whom he was disconnected from for so long? Why was he stepping in now? I think the film offers something of that, but ultimately, it's too sacred. Ultimately that connection can never be described in a sit-down interview. I say to people, "If you were put in John's situation where you had your son say to you 'Dad, I'm being pursued by the CIA, can you help me?' What would you do? How do you embark on that journey?" John has taken this one step at a time. Somehow as this kind of suburban self-taught builder, he's stepped into this world of being a campaigner.

In part, I see it as noble and heroic, and I would hope that I could similarly undertake something like John has done. But John is unique. I don't think I've ever met anyone like him. In part, the story of Julian is the reason why we're there. I became so fascinated by John and the way he sees the world that I wanted to investigate that more. It illuminates who Julian is. There's a lot going on, but it presents it in a way that is as philosophical as John is.

There's a moment of John sitting in a taxi retelling a fable. That led me to wonder who came up with the title of Ithaka?

ITHAKA

BL: It was something that ultimately Gabriel and I landed on. It came from John. He will often quote poetry. He draws a lot of strength from poems and stories. He understands the world [through story]. It fuels any kind of motivation that he has. *Ithaka* [C.P. Cavafy] was one of the ones that he would recite.

I thought it was a lovely way of understanding what it means to be a campaigner, what it means to give your life to something, but more so how do you do it? How has he managed to do this, is the one question that I would have for Julian. Also, to understand it through John, how do you keep going? When all of us are happy to sit and watch Netflix and just deal with the complexity of life, [which] is difficult enough, but this next level of campaigning for a better world which I think is what ultimately John has done and is continuing to do. Where do you draw strength?

Ithaka became a message that gave him strength. It's a lovely poem. People will take out their own meanings from it, but where we draw strength from and how we get it was a constant source of fascination for me in watching John day-to-day, go out on this marathon of a campaign.

Where did you draw strength from during the filming?

BL: As a filmmaker, as a storyteller, it was just such a wonderful experience, it was easy for me. I loved every moment of it, being in that world and having a camera and having that access. [I have] very fond memories of] the people we came across spending time with John. The challenge is that John, Stella, and Gabriel are in the centre of this fight, and it's very hard to point a camera at someone who you can see day to day dealing with challenging issues of trying to save one of their family members. I wanted to do justice to that, and the responsibility weighed very heavily as well because it's such a complex story. There are people at the centre of it who are suffering a lot. The balance of earning their trust and being in a situation where they're willing to give something of themselves so that the rest of us can understand it more deeply.

Outside of the vocal supporters, it feels like the Australian media has neglected Julian Assange as a whole. I wonder for you what it means to be an Australian and get behind John and Julian's story. Is that a call to the other people working in media to say, "Let's focus on this more?"

BL: In some ways, it's a call to revisit this issue. It's been going on for more than a decade. I think some people have grown up with it and are unaware of it. I think some people who were of age and were aware of WikiLeaks when they first came to prominence in 2010, it's something they've followed. I think it's also been so confused and convoluted, and there's been so many twists and turns that people need another entry point, so I felt this particular court case was a really interesting way of showing what's at stake, what's important, and what's relevant to a general audience as to why they should understand what's going on.

There are big issues at play, and I'd hoped that this was another way to enter the story, that they could re-engage with something they may have lost track of in their normal day-to-day lives. It's not a campaign film. It's a film about a campaign. In some ways in experiencing what that campaign looks like, you do re-engage with it as well.

It's sad what's happening to Julian, it's devastating. It has a devastating impact on journalism and the freedom of information. I felt strongly about it, and trying to convey that to other people is difficult, particularly when you're bringing on other people who aren't engaged.

COVID is an organic aspect of the film, but how did you decide on what to show from the transition from [President Donald] Trump to [President Joe] Biden?

BL: That was really tricky. Even the COVID portrayal was difficult. In the end, I just thought, look, as soon as you put a story on about COVID everyone's gonna be like, "Okay, I know what's going on, you don't have to explain it." We're into that moment now, and everyone's wearing masks all of a sudden.

The transition from Trump to Biden was important in as much as where the documentary begins and ends. The court case was a natural structure, but also the transition into Biden and the capital riots felt like the closing of a decade for me. If the story started in 2010 when Collateral Murder[1] was released, and then we finish at the capital riots and the transition into Biden as a closing out to a very volatile decade, I just felt like that was the right way to do it. Certainly, when we were in that moment when [the] Biden transition team was coming in and he was about to be inaugurated, there were high hopes that either Trump was going to pardon Julian in some form, or that the Biden administration wasn't going to pursue it.

I needed to see that out in terms of the story because the high hopes were there. When they chose to continue the prosecution, that's when I felt like, okay, it doesn't matter what side of politics it was, it just felt like there was an underlying intent to continue this prosecution. It didn't sit with either president, meaning it wasn't up to them. I think holistically, Edward Snowden summed up where Julian's story sits at the moment in that he's being prosecuted for the best work that WikiLeaks has ever done. I would love people to grasp that he faces 170 years for releasing information about the Afghanistan-Iraq war and the detainee logs from Guantanamo. I think we're all better for knowing those things have gone on. Putting everything else aside, that's ultimately what we're dealing with.

As one of the activists says, none of the people who engaged in the war crimes have ever been charged. And here Julian is the person that's released the information about it all, sitting there facing 170 years in prison.

BL: It's funny, in all of that and the passion of all the supporters and all the people that devoted so many years of work to this, it's really easy to get up into that kind of stratosphere of campaigning like that. I hope that the film sits within a realm in which people can enter it and access it, [with people] that haven't been part of the story, and can still go on John's journey, and then slowly understand what's going on with Julian as well. That was the plan. In terms of what's on the news, it's really hard to absorb because it is so hysterical.

I've got a wall of notes here that I've written that are oddly introspective, and a lot of thoughts about who I am as a person and my relationship with my father. I was sitting there thinking, "No, this is not about me." But that's the kind of film this is. It forces you to reassess who you are as a person and look inward. That's your direction, and it's John as a person, too. It's a testament to how powerful it is.

BL: I feel the same way, having spent time with John, and particularly in that time in his life in that he is being presented with this insurmountable challenge. Seeing how he processes it gave me a different approach to looking at things in my own life. It's this very careful going through it and not being distracted by it – he says hope is not even worth engaging with – but this idea that there's a faith that he can just work his way through it. I guess the title of the film does speak to that a little bit, that you're doing it more than anything.

When I first engaged with John and I presented to him my ideas for what I wanted to do in the film, he came back with the Bhagavad Gita quotes, the long Indian poem about accepting noble causes. I just thought "What am I stepping into with this? This is the way this guy thinks." The film tried to incorporate that, and hopefully in the same way that that energises him, it can give us some energy in our own lives in the little problems that we have. It's inspiring in that way for me to have been part of it.

I want to take a step back and look at your work as a filmmaker, under the shadow of your father [Ray Lawrence, director of Bliss, Lantana, and Jindabyne], who has had such a great impact on Australian film. It feels like a rarity to see directors swap between documentaries and narrative features and then back to documentaries in Australian film. How do you balance the legacy of your father and then what you're working towards as a filmmaker yourself?

BL: Dad presents his career to me as a cautionary tale. As much as he's had a lot of success in the three films that he's made, he would have liked to have made a lot more. I've taken it upon myself to try and work as much as possible, and that's hard in a market like this. Doing documentaries and dramas opens up more opportunities. I'm fascinated by both. I'd love to be able to jump between the two.

I admire filmmakers like Michael Winterbottom who [are] so prolific and have been able to make a film a year for twenty years. I don't think that's gonna happen for me, but I think the most defining factor of Dad's work – apart from the amazing creative output – is the short list of films. The shame of the Australian cinema landscape is that we have wonderful filmmakers who can't necessarily make the films they want to make here. It's just the nature of economics, particularly when you're making films with your own voice. That's a real rarity.

I look at someone like Rolf de Heer who has a remarkable career and made so many films from his own voice. I'd love to have a career like that. I'm constantly looking at other filmmakers and what they're doing and how they're shifting between mediums and working in other areas to somehow have more volume in what I'm doing. Dad will constantly say to me, "I don't want you to have a career like mine." As much as I admire the work that he's done and the success, the advice is do more, do more work, engage in other projects. So, when this came up, it was perfect. The hardest thing was leaving the family for that many months to go to the UK during COVID. Apart from that, I just jumped at it.

How much does the Australian identity plays into your work as a filmmaker?

BL: Constantly. Being in the UK filming overseas, it's far more exaggerated. You're identified as an Australian. Telling Julian's story as an Australian is very different. Travelling through Europe, I felt more connected to his story as well, because he's an Australian on a global stage as well. He obviously has support around the world.

It's also at the front of my mind when I'm trying to tell stories. Even in the drama. *Ghosthunter* was distinctly Australian, it was Western Sydney, and it was the working-class, blue-collar roots of Australia. I wanted to reflect that because there's nowhere else like it in the world. Then the idea of *Hearts and Bones* (2019), for me as an Australian, I felt that I was growing up in a very disconnected country, meaning I felt very isolated from the rest of the world. I grew up under the flight path, so I'd see these planes coming in and out and just thought about the stories.

I felt like we're the first generation to have had international travel, we're brought up with it. I think the interconnectedness with the rest of the world is what interested me about the Australian experience and who we are, what's changed in my lifetime so much more, and the influx of refugees and migrants to Australia. It's what I wanted to explore. Growing up I felt so isolated from the rest of the world. I felt like everything happens in the Northern Hemisphere. And I still feel like that to a certain extent. It's still a place that we need to go to, to make our careers and do all that stuff.

With *Hearts and Bones*, *Ithaka*, and *Ghosthunter*, I wanted to tell stories that show other filmmakers and other storytellers and the rest of the world that we have rich and interesting stories here at home and to create those layers and textures and tapestry of who we are that hopefully we can further celebrate. We don't need to re-voice things; we don't need to make TV shows that pretend they're in California and stuff like that. I mean, it's a shame, I understand it. But it's important to me, those things.

Working with Hugo Weaving, he's so passionate about those issues that we connected on that level. If I can continue to make films in Sydney, in Australia, or about Australians, then I don't want to feel ashamed of that. And I think that some of us do. But hopefully, we can continue to celebrate it. It's a tricky choice to make. It's not necessarily the easiest one, but it is very important.

What do you see the future of Australian film being?

BL: I think it's gonna be two steps forward, a few steps back. There's a battle going on with the streamers in terms of content. When I was born, there were those kinds of vanguard pioneers that gave birth to the modern Australian film industry. I feel like there's a generation of directors out there who are on the cusp. I look back at the Fred Schepisi's and the Bruce Beresford's and people like Peter Weir, where are those people now? They made a catalogue of films in Australia about Australia before they went overseas. Is that possible now? I don't know. I'm hoping it is.

Every time I see a TV show that's filmed in Australia, it's for America, set in America, and they bring in [American actors]. I know the crews benefit from the amount of work that comes in, but it feels like a bit of a step backwards for Australian content.

On the other hand, I feel like we're probably the biggest and the busiest and the most energetic film industry that we've ever had in the history of

INTERVIEW | BEN LAWRENCE

Australia in terms of what we're making. The opportunity is incredible. It's just those voices. I hope that the increased money that there is now in the streamers can recognise that the voices like the directors and the writers who are writing those stories you're talking about can continue to make things. I think the volume will increase. But with it, we will bring up those other little voices. I'm just waiting for the next generation to step up and step out. And they're there. There are some amazing filmmakers out there.

You're part of it. Three films in three years. You're leading a cause that is happening.

BL: Well, hopefully, and I really want to be part of that. I want to be part of that generation that's making those films. I really admire the people like Warwick Thornton and others that are out there. Some have gone to make their fortune overseas. I hope they come back. I know Garth Davis [*Lion*] is making a new film locally, so that's fantastic. The temptation to go and make those other films is quite big and tempting.

Has that been presented to you?

BL: No, it hasn't. I had a bit of a journey back from Toronto, I went through Los Angeles. And it was kind of disheartening in a way. It reinforced what I wanted to do, meaning I wanted to come back and make films here. It also told me that the type of films I make don't fit within that system. That gave me more of an insight into the machine and working within that machine and how it operates. On one hand, it was disheartening, but it was also an education. It reminded me that making feature films is ultimately what I want to do. I love the form. I love the world and the infrastructure around it, the festivals. And meeting people like yourself who have a love of it. It's different to TV.

There's just something nostalgic and affectionate about it that is far deeper. There's a mystique to it as well. I love all of that. I grew up in it, looking at that magic, wondering what it was. Stepping into it now, it's still as strong and palpable as it's ever been. Having that here and connecting with others who feel that way is what I love. Being able to make another film now has just been amazing. Hopefully we can get back to normal.

Do you talk to other Australian directors about Australian films?

BL: I do. It's hard. I feel like the culture of Sydney probably doesn't have that community that if we were in a position that they were back in the Seventies, I don't know that that would happen. I can't imagine five or six of us getting together and giving life to this struggling film industry. What would we do now? I don't know. But look, I think it exists. I caught up with

ITHAKA

Sam Zubrycki [director of *Miguelito*] the other day who is a director and we talked about Australian documentaries. Jen Peedom [*River*] is someone I talk to. Exit Films is a company that I'm part of, and there's a wonderful team of directors there who occasionally run into each other. I think they all share a passion for it. It is rare, though. I don't think this is a regular thing. There might be an unspoken camaraderie. I don't think it existed how it used to. I feel like it exists in organisations like the Directors Guild and the Writers Guild. There are yearly events where people get together.

I think Gabriel has such a wonderful mind and a passion for films, and a unique perspective on the world. It's been wonderful working with him and meeting him. Working with editor Karen Johnson, those are the times that I relish being deep in making films as well. That's when you really connect.

INTERVIEW
PRODUCER
GABRIEL SHIPTON

Gabriel Shipton is the producer of Ben Lawrence's *Ithaka*. He is also the son of the film's subject, John Shipton, and the brother of the figure at the centre of the film: Julian Assange.

Filmed during 2019 and 2020, *Ithaka* shows the lengths a family will go to support and protect a family member in need, all the while fighting for the freedom of the press. In this interview, fresh from returning from the UK to be at the side of his family once again for the wedding of Julian and his fiancée Stella Morris, Gabriel talks about the power of documentary filmmaking helping push Julian's story to a wider audience, about how deeply Australian this story is, and the difficulty of seeing John being open in his interviews in the film itself.

Julian Assange agreed to a plea deal with US prosecutors and returned to Australia as a free man on 26 June 2024.

This interview was recorded by Andrew F. Peirce in March 2022

How did you know that Ben was the right person to tell this story?

Gabriel Shipton: I'd watched his previous films, *Ghosthunter* and *Hearts and Bones*, and from those two films, I got an impression of Ben as a human that he was somebody who loved people and had great respect for people, even if they were imperfect, and that he was a man of honour. An honourable person, an honourable filmmaker rather than somebody who's going to try and get a zinger or try and make some sort of exposé piece, something that isn't there. That was the impression I got from watching his films. Seeing the way he treats his characters hit it home for me and the rest of us. When we first spoke about *Ithaka*, we were speaking the same language, we were on the same page from the very beginning. It clicked just like that.

Was there a discussion that you had with John and Stella about getting him on board as well?

ITHAKA

GS: I remember showing John the two films. I think I sent them to Stella as well. There was definitely a conversation about getting Ben on board and what he would bring to the project. We tried to make it as collegial as possible with Stella and John as we went along.

As difficult as it will be with Julian still in prison, what was it like being across for the wedding?

GS: It was good to be there. There were five of us plus the two kids, seven family members who were able to attend the wedding in total including Stella. It was like a moment where Julian wasn't free, but it felt like we were in control of the jail for a change. Usually, you go in there and it's very oppressive and it's made clear that you're entering their space. But for an hour or so on that day, it sort of felt as normal as it could, being together. His visiting rights in the embassy were curtailed after 2017. Outside of a courtroom, there hasn't been a gathering like that for a very, very long time. It was a very special moment for everyone, especially Julian and Stella.

That's one of the things that stuck with me throughout the film is that need for human connection, and the need for familial connection between yourself, John, Julian, and Stella. As a family member, can you talk about the meaning of familial connection for Ithaka?

GS: I guess [the film] wouldn't exist to start with if there was no familial connection. I don't think anyone else would have been able to make it like this. For Julian, I don't know if he would be able to survive without Stella and John and that connection. It's a very, very, very hard situation to be in, even with the support of the family. I feel a lot of the times that they just keep him going and keep him alive in there. I would hate to think what would happen.

In terms of the film, because of the forces that we're up against and all the media and films that have been made in the past, it's very hard to give anyone your trust in this situation. And so, because of our involvement, we were able to have that sort of natural trust that we weren't going to take the story somewhere in a different direction or anything like, that it was going to be truly the perspective of the family. I think we've done that.

I understand that you and Stella were filming prior to Ben coming on board. How long had you been filming before you decided to get Ben on the project?

GS: I think we started filming in late 2019, then Ben came on six or seven months later. We had done quite a bit of observational-style filming at that point, mostly of John travelling around Europe and different things like that. We didn't start filming with Stella until after there was a court hearing because she was still Julian's secret family. She hadn't been exposed yet. But there was a court proceeding where Stella's name was in the documents and the judge wouldn't hold that name back, so she was going to be exposed through the court documents. At that time, she chose to take control of that and out herself on *60 Minutes* and other things like that.

We started originally filming with only John, and then Stella started being more active and turned into the amazing advocate that she is for Julian today. She's incredible. We were split in two at that point. We started following John and Stella. That's how we ended up with that dual **protagonists** type story. It was always going to be John. We had quite a large archive by the time Ben joined the project. We had very top-line direction, then Ben came on and really pulled it all together. He started putting together this plan for how we would film around the court proceedings, the four-week court proceedings that were in late 2020. He launched into the thirteen hours of interviews that he did with John which formed the backbone of the film.

At what point did you know that you had all the footage that you needed to tell the story?

GS: It's such an evolving thing. The persecution continues, right? That's how we leave the story. We planned to film around the court case and go from there. We had other bits that we shot, we even shot back in Australia, and we shot a lot over in the US. We've shot all around the place. We're still shooting some things. There's always something happening, so it's very hard to stop.

We knew where we were headed I think probably by the end of the court case. Karen Johnson, our fabulous editor, had pulled that backbone through the interviews and had that formulated. I would say it was around the end of 2020 that we sort of knew that we had everything we needed. There were particular court dates that we knew we had to cover, and then those went into the new year, 2021. By that time when Julian was denied bail, we knew that we had what we needed to finish a film. Some things came up, like the Trump-Biden campaign, we covered a lot of that, and slotted that in. There were things like that that we were able to slot in that we thought we needed to do to give the story some justice.

Were you feeding the footage straight through to Karen as you were filming so she was able to edit on the fly?

GS: She had a whole bunch of stuff to watch. We had like 160 days' worth of shooting by the time she started really cutting stuff, and then it just kept coming through. The interviews with John were the bits that she was able to start assembling and putting together. I think the first assembly was maybe four or five hours.

There are moments where you feel that John is pushing back against Ben's questions in a way which really highlights his personality. It shows his tenacity too. Can you talk about your experience sitting there, watching those interviews take place?

GS: I didn't sit through any of the interviews. I was sometimes in another room, and I could hear them. Even when I watch the film in the theatre, it's my family on the screen, you have inside this sort of weird feeling like, "Oh my god, how are people going to feel about this? How are people going to react?" I think you get that with every film. But when it's your own family, it's much more personal in that way. I find it a little bit painful to watch personally with an audience. I'm much better at watching it on my own or with the team and talking about the story and how that unfolds, and the different emotional points and information that we convey to the audience. Whenever I'm watching with an audience, I get that sort of scratchy feeling, like "Uh oh."

With that in mind, for a family in a political and global place like this, you're really putting yourself out there in a way that a lot of Australian families would struggle with. As you're saying, it's very difficult - this is your family on screen. How do you deal with that personally? Is it having that recognition that this is Julian's story that you're working to get out to a larger audience?

GS: Yes, I think that's always the intention. How can we get a different narrative about Julian out there to audiences? That was always the goal behind the film, how can we tell a different side of the story, how Julian and his family experience the persecution that is happening to him? I think what we do in a way as family members, as advocates, what John and Stella are always trying to do is get out there and do media and use your personal connection to tell a different side of the story. That's essentially what John and Stella do. They have this sort of superpower in their familial relationship with Julian that gives them a platform to be able to tell Julian's side of the story.

We're trying to do that with the film as well. There's always this trade-off, this balance that you play. Your personal connection is what people want, but you also have the chance to give them some other information that they might not get otherwise. It's always a bit of a balancing act and a trade-off. Sometimes I see John or Stella do an interview and there'll be two or three questions about their personal feelings or how Julian's doing and things like that, and then there'll be some other questions about the case and different aspects, and you'll then go and watch the interview on TV or wherever it appears and they don't include what we think would be the substance, they include all the personal information and all that sort of stuff, and then use other interviews, other narration or something to include the substance that they believe should be shared with the audience. It's good to be able to do both and sort of have it rounded and inclusive of John and Stella giving the personal side, but also including their perspective of the case and Julian's persecution and his work.

As a producer on this, how do you balance that personal story with making an engaging film?

GS: Well, I think the sort of personal story is the superpower, basically the big door, if you will, that we get people in through. That's how we engage audiences emotionally, through this father fighting for his son, or a fiancée fighting for her now husband. That is the thread that we have running through the film, and it's a balance, we still want to feel connected to these characters and connected to their emotional journey. Even through the editing process, it was always a balance, working with Ben and Karen, "Are we getting too far away from our characters? Are we losing touch with the characters if we dive into the case more?" It was always a back-and-forth.

I think it's that personal story, for me anyway. My background is more in drama-producing. The approach is always through this emotional journey from our characters that would grab the audience and take them on the journey, and then we're able to put parts of the case in. It's always a balance, that we don't lose the connection with the characters but get as much information to the audience about the case as we can.

I understand this is a film term, of course, but talking about people in documentaries as 'characters', when we're talking about your family, how do you bridge that connection between a 'character' versus a brother, a father, a sister-in-law?

GS: Yeah, it is very hard. I have a very deep understanding of their intention and what they're trying to achieve because we're all trying to do the same thing. We're all trying to free Julian. I think I bring that aspect to it: what is their goal? Their goal is to free Julian. You're always trying to respect that as well. But oh God, it's not easy.

How do you look after yourself when you're going through this? What kind of mental health strategies do you have in place for yourself? If you don't mind me asking, that is.

ITHAKA

GS: I guess the usual ones that people have, exercise and things like that. It can be all-consuming. This thing is so big that if you don't take any time off at all, you become really worn down. You need to take breaks and keep a routine. John puts it well in the film, "All the energy you give if you get nothing back, then we couldn't continue on." But because of all the actions that John does, that Stella does, there is some flow back. You get some flow back, and that gives you the energy to keep going as well. All the supporters around the world that are all backing John and Stella, it's this huge community, that gives you a lot of energy to keep going. We couldn't do any of this without them either.

The score here is quite beautiful. Having that connection there with somebody as prominent as Brian Eno, is that an act of support and active protest?

GS: I think for Brian Eno it is. He wears his politics on his sleeve. His support is definitely an act of his activism as well.

I'm curious about what it means to be an Australian filmmaker for you. Is that part of your identity?

GS: I think it is. For me, I grew up around filmmakers. My mother worked for Kennedy Miller. They're called Kennedy Miller Mitchell now. She worked there for thirty-odd years. I grew up going on sets and looking up to these amazing producers and directors and seeing them work and thinking maybe that's something that I want to do one day. It was definitely something that I was drawn to from a very, very early age. Being a filmmaker has been a dream of mine since I was a child. Being part of that sort of Australian film history and growing up around that was [great]. They've had great success overseas, but that is a very important part of the Australian film world and, hopefully we can continue it and make stories about Australians and our experiences and our sort of outlook.

This is an Australian film. It might take place mostly overseas, but we wouldn't have been able to make it without the support in Australia. We've based our whole launch around showing it in Australian cinemas, and Australian festivals. I don't know if the rest of the world is ready for this movie. But Australia definitely is. It's definitely an Australian project. The support here for this sort of film we couldn't find anywhere else.

ENDNOTES

1   Collateral Murder is the name of the WikiLeaks video that showed U.S. Army soldiers firing upon civilians, killing them, while they laughed. https://en.wikipedia.org/wiki/July_12,_2007,_Baghdad_airstrike

THE MOTHS WILL EAT THEM UP

14 mins
Directors: *Tanya Modini, Luisa Martiri*
Writer: *Tanya Modini*
Cast: *Ling Cooper Tang, Stephen Walker, Kevin Spink, Elia Allen*
Producers: *Luisa Martiri, Kristie Yates*
Composer: *Madeleine Cocolas*
Cinematography: *Julian Panetta*
Editing: *Pip Hart*

The Moths Will Eat Them Up received a nomination for Best Short Film at the 2022 AACTA Awards.

INTERVIEW
CO-DIRECTORS
TANYA MODINI & LUISA MARTIRI

Tanya Modini and Luisa Martiri join the lineage of Australian women filmmakers (Nina Buxton's *Mwah*, 2017; Del Kathryn Barton's *Blaze*, 2022) who use the medium of films to explore the impact of violence against women. It's an issue that continues to plague Australian society, with 39% of women having experienced some form of violence since the age of 15[1], and men being the most common perpetrators of physical violence, sexual harassment, and sexual violence.

With their 2021 short film, *The Moths Will Eat Them Up*, co-directors Tanya Modini and Luisa Martiri explore the ever-present threat of violence against women. An otherwise routine train ride home at night turns into a terrifying experience for Rayne (Ling Cooper Tang) when a man looms as a threat to her existence.

This interview was recorded by Andrew F. Peirce in November 2022

What was your journey into filmmaking?

Tanya Modini: My interest in filmmaking has been lifelong. When I left school, I didn't have anybody in the family who did it, so I assumed I wasn't the sort of person who did it. I went and did a bunch of other jobs and kept on meaning to get back to it. In 2018, I won a competition to go to Copenhagen for the final series of *The Bridge* premiere, and I was hosted by the production company. SBS saw it and they asked me if I wrote, and I said yes, and I started writing for their guide, and then I started looking back into films again, and thought, 'Yeah, I need to get back into this.' That's how it happened.

Luisa Martiri: It's been lifelong for me too since I was a kid. It took me a minute to find exactly which part of filmmaking that I wanted to do. I thought I wanted to act, so during and after high school I started trying to pursue that. Then I realised it absolutely wasn't my thing. Through that process, I found directing and producing and went to film school at QUT

THE MOTHS WILL EAT THEM UP

in Brisbane. Since then, I've been producing and directing independent works and working in the industry here.

It is so important to be able to discover what you are or are not interested in doing, isn't it?

LM: I would say so. When I was younger, I loved movies and when you're young, you don't have a nuanced view on many things. You watch movies, and you think that acting is [everything], so you get enamoured by that. I got into acting because I wanted to tell stories and I loved films, but during high school when I was doing it, it took me a minute to realise I wasn't any good at it. It was like trying to fit the triangle into a square, so to speak. I think that goes for a lot of people before you delve in and understand the nuances of the industry. I teach at QUT in film, and you watch the students, and they all want to be directors and producers and writers, and it's like, you're not going to be that because you're going to figure out that there are so many different roles and nuances to the industry, and you're going to find your niche that is going to work for you.

Where did the script idea come from?

TM: A few years ago, I was on a train at night coming home, this guy got on, and from a layman's perspective, it looked like he was having some sort of psychotic episode. He was doing [to me] exactly what [the man] in the film does. The train was thinning out, and I was starting to get a bit panicked because I was getting off at a very small station in the middle of nowhere. He seemed to be waiting. I don't know and I didn't really want to find out what would happen if I got off by myself.

I started thinking this would make quite a good film because it was such a sensory experience [with] him looking through the glass, and then the buzzing of the light going on and off as he went in and out of the bathroom. That's essentially where it came from. I do have a background in the prevention of violence against women and police, so that sort of fed into it.

In that regard, how important is it to tell these kinds of stories on film?

TM: It's enormously important, but we've got to be so careful how we tell them so that we don't perpetuate the violence that's already happening in the community. It's walking the tightrope between 'this is the reality of what goes on, so we need to see it represented on screen,' but how do we authentically do that without perpetuating it in society? Essentially, there probably needs to be some guidelines around the depiction of violence against women on screen. I wanted it to be an empowering [film], rather than just another woman being terrified and not being able to do anything about it.

LM: [It's] incredibly important, and I think we're coming out of this kind of landscape of films where it's heavy and dark for the sake of being heavy and dark. I think people are getting sick of seeing that, even though that does kind of reflect reality, there are also many sides to reality in society where that's not true. This film has already brought together communities of women who have resonated with it. Women have come up to us at screenings to share with us how much the film resonated with them. Amazingly and beautifully, it's connecting women and people. A lot of men come up to us after a screening, and they say that their eyes have been opened. I think the empowering part of it is [how it's] allowed that kind of community-building aspect [to emerge].

Another aspect which I found interesting was the choice of train stops. This stop, as presented in the film, contains single light infrastructures where you get out of the train and there's nothing else there. There's no safety. There are no lights to the pathway. There's just darkness. Can you talk about choosing this particular location to isolate the characters further to show how hard it can be to safely get to your car after getting off a train?

LM: When you get closer to the city, [the stations] are reasonably well-lit. Throughout Brisbane, there are quite a lot of suburbs whose train stations are quite secluded, because they are in the middle of a suburb sometimes. As this is based on Tanya's experience, and she's from the Sunshine Coast area, which is more regional, those train stations up and down the coast are so small and secluded and isolated, so it was important to portray that on screen in general because symbolically and metaphorically, that's kind of how women feel, right? It's that feeling of isolation and seclusion, both in the context of this issue, and women as a whole fighting this themselves without much input or action from men. Also, that's how you physically feel when you are alone at a train station, even if it is well-lit.

Let's talk about casting. A lot of the script relies on the reactions of the actors. How did you cast each of the roles?

LM: We got a bunch of screen tapes, particularly for the role of Rayne. There's dialogue, very minimal. The only scene that was available for her to read was the scene with the earbuds man on the train. We asked all of the actors who were interested to read that scene just for the sake of having something to read. What we looked for in their self-tapes was the moments in between the dialogue, and what their faces looked like. Do they have a screen presence? Did they radiate energy through that self-tape in those moments? We consciously [focused on] how they were in between the dialogue moments and Ling was absolutely like a standout with that.

THE MOTHS WILL EAT THEM UP

She radiates energy and has an incredible screen presence. We knew that she could 100% carry the film, and she did amazingly.

TM: It wasn't a difficult decision to choose Ling. She was a standout. As far as Man A goes, the 'bad man', we wanted someone younger than Ling, and we didn't want somebody who looked creepy. We wanted somebody who looked like Mr. Average coming home on his way home from work. Someone who also had an understanding of the issues. Kevin [Spink] ticked all those boxes. We had a lengthy phone call with him after his self-tape. He had a great understanding and was so easy to work with as well.

I want to talk about the framing of the opening scene as Rayne is walking to the train, and that tracking shot of the guys standing there on their mobile phones. It's one of those things where until you see it getting put in front of you, you don't recognise the behaviours that you do. We stand there and we wait for a train, and we don't observe the situation around us. We don't observe what's going on. I say 'we' as in the male population, we stand there with our male distance from one another. I don't think that I've truly consciously thought about it until watching this. It was a wake-up call to be better. Can you talk about the discussions around presenting how the men were staged and the distance between them?

TM: That was a very clear image in both Louisa and my minds for that opening scene. We wanted that part to look a little bit stylised. We wanted that distance between them, to see them all doing the exact same thing of holding the phone up, but as she goes past, they lift and move their eyes to look at her, but not their head. It was very specific what we wanted going on there. I spoke to Ling beforehand and said, "You're prey here, they're checking you out. What are they going to do?"

LM: The sad thing about being a woman or a non-binary person is that you have to immediately assume everyone is potentially a bad person until you're proven otherwise, especially in that scenario or that kind of context.

TM: It shows the risk assessments that women do, she stops on that staircase, and she checks out who's down there. Am I going to be safe if I go down further into this? Then she assesses it, 'Yeah, I am,' and then goes down.

As you're going through the filming process, how did you make sure that the set was kept as a safe space?

TM: For myself, from a load of work that I've done in the past, I'm quite good at compartmentalising stuff. For me, it was a film at that point, and there was no more and no less to that. I spent a lot of time talking to the actors in between takes, making sure that everybody was okay, and creating a sense of fun and safety throughout the whole shoot. We had a great set. Everyone was calm. Everybody was happy. I think that contributed to the actors dealing with that sort of stuff really well.

LM: We wanted a majority female crew on this one, and I think that that played a very large part in creating that safe space for the women on set, and the actors, particularly Ling, because there is safety in numbers.

I want to talk about the moths in particular. Tanya, where did the motif for the moths come from?

TM: I couldn't end the script as it ended for me. The idea of simply encountering a familiar man who was disembarking at my station and sitting with him? Terribly boring. I wanted a protective element, so I started Googling protective symbols and moths kept on coming up, which I thought, 'Oh, okay, that's weird.' It's some [type of] spiritual thing that I had never heard of. I thought, 'I can run with that.' At the same time, that quote from the Bible was coming up, and I thought, 'This is actually going to work quite well,' because it was worded in such a way that it fitted perfectly with the script.

I assume that it's a blend of real and digital moths, is that correct?

LM: All visual effects. That was one of the biggest elements we were struggling with, because we didn't know many VFX artists and to get it done through a cutting-edge or a post lounge or something, it was going to cost an astronomical amount. We randomly got in contact with this guy named Tim Bahrij, who was recommended. He did all of those moths himself. He was incredible. A total legend. I have no idea how he did it, but they look absolutely brilliant.

TM: We did investigate a moth wrangler and contacted him, and he was like, "Yeah, no, that's not going to work because the lifecycle of the moth is 24 hours."

LM: Moths are hard to source in winter too, so, it was all just VFX.

What other challenges or hurdles did you have to overcome that you didn't expect?

TM: It was a lot harder for us to actually get a train. We thought that we'd be able to hire and ride a train and film it, but it turns out that's hellishly expensive, so we couldn't do that. We just did the platforms. Then we found a decommissioned train in a warehouse out back of Ipswich and happened to be the same model, ironically, that I was on that night. So that worked perfectly because it had a vestibule and then the door at the end. That was a challenge that looked difficult at one stage there until this came up. Then we had a great team around us who made that train look like it was moving, which was amazing,

LM: I very rarely get to the point where I want to give up and trying to find that train almost got me there. We explored so many different options. At one point, we were going to get a vintage train and make it this weird, vintage, nondescript time period. I'm glad that didn't end up happening. It's far better how it is.

What does it mean to be an Australian creative working today? Does the Australian identity consciously play into your work at all?

TM: I think it can't help but play into your work, regardless of whether it's conscious or unconscious. I know that with *Moths*, we didn't want the film to look Australian. We didn't want it to be bright. Sometimes there's a look that comes along with that. That's not to say that we didn't want to deal with Australian issues, because obviously, it's an issue that's massive here.

LM: In my previous films, I was very attracted to the idea of Australiana. My last film, *Pools* (2000), is quite literally a road trip across Queensland. In terms of Australian identity, I mean, what does that even really mean?

For me, I probably have a very different look. My parents are Italian immigrants, so the definition of the Australian identity is maybe different to people who aren't the children of immigrants. Identity will always be cemented in each person, and whether you're struggling with your identity, or you're very sure of your identity, subconsciously or inadvertently, everything you create as an artist will be exploring identity and history and culture in some way. By virtue of exploring an issue, a story, or an idea that is personal to you, you are in some way exploring the Australian identity, because you are Australian.

ENDNOTES

1   Our Watch is a national leader in the primary prevention of violence against women and their children in Australia. The website and information were accessed on 29 March 2024. https://www.ourwatch.org.au/quick-facts/

SUBJECT

77 mins
Director: *Tristan Barr*
Writer: *Vincent Befi*
Cast: *Stephen Phillips, Gaby Seow, Tristan Barr, David Gim, Mark Kim, Tom Uhlhorn, Nathan Barrow, Scarlett Walker, Joey Lai, Matthew Connell, Aaron Walton*
Producers: *Tristan Barr, David Gim*
Score: *Richard Labrooy, Henry Sinclair*
Cinematography: *Phil Lemon*
Editing: *Liam Selby*

INTERVIEW
FILMMAKER
TRISTAN BARR

Tristan Barr lives for a challenge. His feature debut, *Watch the Sunset* (2017), was Australia's first one-shot film and featured one of the most perfectly timed sunsets captured on screen. That wasn't enough for Tristan, leading him to co-found Continuous Pictures, an independent production company that seeks to bridge the creative divide between Australia, the US, and Asia.

This cross-cultural collaboration includes the creation of a short film initiative to support emerging filmmakers. The 2022 film *Subject* is one such project that emerged from the initiative. Barr maintains his multi hyphenate status as director-producer-actor status in this thriller that sees a prisoner (Willem Phillips) undergo an intense experiment in exchange for commuting his sentence. *Subject* is an example of how Australian indie filmmaking uses limited resources to create an effective sci-fi narrative.

This interview was recorded by Andrew F. Peirce in November 2022

Can you talk about the creative mindset of Continuous Pictures?

Tristan Barr: We basically want to become a mini studio. We want to produce films with like-minded upcoming and established filmmakers. Part of our mandate of what we're looking for is content that is outside the box and has a unique perspective. We don't let budget or restrictions get in our way, we're a bit cowboy-ish in that way. If we find something we like, and we think we can pull it together, we will make it happen. We've collaborated with quite a few people in the US, and a lot of the time it's been because of that mindset. We've both had films at a festival or something like that and then once we get to talking, it's like, "Oh, hey, you created that awesome thing? How the hell did you do that?" Shorts are a great way to explore those creatives because no one has money for shorts. Now we're in a space where we're producing one or two features a year. We want to bump that up. We're looking at bigger investments and partnerships with the relationships we've created with our films so far. Hopefully, in the coming years, we'll be able to greenlight a lot more independent Australian films alongside films in the US and Asia.

You're working cross-continent. It's not just in Australia, but in the US too, which is an integral part of the distribution process and audience reach as well. Can you talk about how important that is to have that at the forefront of your mind before a project kicks off?

TB: It's hugely important. It's so hard to sell a project that the audience isn't at the forefront of. The American market is massive, and they've got so much more money than us, and they've got more people who are going to watch it. That has to be thought of immediately. We don't want people to think, "They're selling out to the Americans." If you're going to do that sort of content, then how do you make it accessible to an American audience? Why will they buy it? I think a lot of projects that go through screen agencies are solely focused on the Australian market, which they have to be because those screen agencies are funded by government money. Essentially, we want to take it one step further and go 'What works here, but also works over there?' You find that what works over there is the start of what works here. Short films are a great way to test that out. You learn through the process [what works.] [You ask yourself], can we get a known Aussie actor involved so that we can sell it to the Americans? All of our productions at the moment, we're having those conversations with the sales agents and the distributors early on.

That's a good launching point to discuss The Secret of Mt Trolla. It started as a novella, then became a short, and I assume that you'll turn it into a feature film. Can you talk about the creative process of deciding how to test out a story?

TB: The goal was always to make a feature. I didn't know it was going to be a novella to start with. I kind of started writing a treatment, and then I was like, 'I've got a lot of words here. I should edit this and get it out.' That's kind of how that came about. I then wrote a feature script off the back of the novella. We were then able to get a couple of actors attached to it, but it was tricky to finance. It was tricky at the time to make an Australian-Korean film, it didn't have enough elements for it to be appealing to the Americans.

We thought, 'Okay, we'll shoot a short film so we can prove the concept.' We got a skeleton crew together. I went down to an auto-wrecker, and we were able to get a plane carcass and I put it on the back of my mate's ute. It was this oversized plane on the back of a little 4WD ute. We dumped it in the mountains and thought 'We could get in a lot of trouble for this,' but we shot it over one night. We learned a lot from that about the story elements and from that we went back and re-drafted the feature script, which had a whole bunch of new elements in it. I've started pitching that around, and it's started to get a bit of traction now. We got shut down and knocked back early on with the feature, and then it's gone in this full circle to kind of get it up again.

Can you talk about making grandeur affordable and workable on a lower budget?

TB: It's just trying to approach each step with what is possible and within my means. [It's] not putting limitations on things early. Technology is crazy now. There are so many things at our disposal. We can achieve a big budget film [look] on really small budgets. When people say, "You can't do that," then it's a challenge for me. For instance, for *Mt Trolla*, the way we orchestrated the plane crashes was easy. We shot a handheld sequence in the plane carcass and then we had a drone shot of the mountain and we used visual effects to make the plane go through the frame. Then it's all sound design. Something that struck me as a kid watching the behind-the-scenes of the original *Star Wars* was the fact that there were people behind the doors pushing them back and forth. When you watch the film, you buy into the visual of the futuristic warship or plane, and it's just people with strings behind the scenes. That's really what it is.

Can you talk about how you first came to Subject and the creative process of translating it from a short into a feature film?

TB: We had a script initiative that we would get screenplays and judge them, and we would make a short film out of the winner. *Subject* came through that initiative and was one of our top three finalists. We found an opportunity to finance not only the short but the feature because it was so contained. We jumped into shooting that about four months from the date that we selected it. In some ways, I wish we had given ourselves more time, but the opportunity was there. From that moment, we worked with the writer to elevate it in a way that we could shoot it within our restrictions, then we financed it, cast the film, and started rehearsals.

The night before we started shooting, one of the main actors pulled out. It was a nightmare, as it would be for any filmmaker. We spent the two or three days that we could push to reschedule the shoot searching for an actor to play that role. It was hectic. We were shooting 10- or 12-hour days and were trying to get anyone to jump in, but there were these huge dialogue sequences. No one was willing to do it. Steve [Phillips], who was one of my acting teachers at VCA, and we'd cast him earlier in the role, suggested that I play it. We drilled the script late at night when we had broken for the day. It feels like that whole section of my life I don't really know what happened, it felt like a whirlwind. "Oh, okay, we made a film, and I acted in it. Hopefully people like it."

That was a huge experiment for us. We set up 12 cameras because we wanted all the cuts to match, and we wanted the actors to have as much space [as possible.] We realised pressing record on 12 cameras at once [was not possible.] We didn't have 12 camera operators. It's one of those things that you learn the process from doing. So, we filmed each room and sequence separately. Following that, we finished the editing and sent it off to a few people. Then Umbrella Entertainment and also Cinedyne Films in the US picked it up.

What did you learn from Watch the Sunset (2017) that you were able to implement into Subject?

TB: What I learned is that performance is key to a great story. I want to continue being ambitious with what we're creating because what excites me is when we pull things off and people ask, "How did you do that?" There were so many questions with *Subject* about the writing throughout the process because it's mainly one guy speaking for 90 minutes in one room. To me, it's important to build an ensemble who is as dedicated as Steve was and we were in *Watch the Sunset*.

How do you balance wearing different hats during a production, whether it be a writer, director, producer, or actor?

TB: Writing is its own beast. That's always quite separate. Once you're on set, the work has been done in that regard. With acting, in some ways it helps being the director because you know the vision. The constant challenge is being in the moment and letting yourself play from moment to moment. That's tricky, particularly when you're directing and you're thinking about things. I try and switch off and focus on my goals for the character and try to react with the other person in the scene. Once I come out of these projects, I'm a shell of a human being and I don't know who I am. All of the negative emotions that you can ever imagine hit me. That's quite normal with any performance work like you go through the waves.

What does presenting the Australian identity on screen mean to you?

TB: Identity is so complex and there are so many different facets to it. *The Lonely Spirits Variety Hour*, that's a part of our identity, as strange and unique as that film is. Then you've got films like *The Drovers Wife*, which is equally a part of our Australian identity. To me, the similar factor in all Australian films is that it requires its makers to really go above and beyond to create whatever they're going to create because it's not easy to come by the money, even if you're going through the government system. If you're doing it privately, it's not an easy task. You have to have this burning desire to go out and make something.

Similarly, in all of our Ozploitation films, the one key factor is ambition. It's got attitude. Our stories are very unique, and across the board, they're exciting. For instance, I went out and shot a couple of shorts in Winton, Queensland. It's a 14-hour drive from the nearest city. We shot a gothic horror out there, and then a mockumentary about the dunny derby races that they do. We follow a character who wants to be a dunny derby champion. That, to me, was really exciting, because it showcases our regional towns and people. I think I'll be making a lot more films in that respect. People are amazed by the uniqueness of the locations. That's something that we have on our doorstep, whereas in LA or one of those US cities, we've seen it all before. That's what we see in almost every movie.

LOVELAND

102 mins
Director: *Ivan Sen*
Writer: *Ivan Sen*
Cast: *Ryan Kwanten, Jillian Nguyen, Hugo Weaving, David Field, Michael Chan, Rhamsy, Franck Matour, Andrew Ng, Shinji Ikefuji, Lamar Brown, Brooke Nichole Lee, Julietta Roldan*
Producers: *David Jowsey, Angela Littlejohn, Ivan Sen, Greer Simpkin*
Composer: *Ivan Sen*
Cinematography: *Ivan Sen*
Editing: *Ivan Sen*

INTERVIEW
FILMMAKER
IVAN SEN

Filmmaker Ivan Sen is a one-man production house, as he takes on the role of writing, directing, lensing, scoring, and editing films like *Toomelah* (2011), *Mystery Road* (2013), *Goldstone* (2016), and *Loveland* (2022). But don't call him an auteur.

Loveland sees Ryan Kwanten as Jack, a hired mercenary who seeks out companionship from robotic lovers. It's only when he meets Jillian Nguyen's karaoke-singer April that he starts to feel alive for the first time. *Loveland* sees Sen head abroad for the first time in his career, a point that he reflects on at the start of this interview.

This interview was recorded by Andrew F. Peirce in December 2021

Ivan Sen: *Loveland* is a bit of a step away from my past work. It's going from these rural landscapes to the opposite, mega-metropolis in science fiction and the future. I started writing this film before I started other films like *Toomelah*, *Mystery Road*, and *Goldstone*. This film actually comes before them in the order of things. It's been with me for over ten years. For me, it's not a huge departure at all.

Is this a continuation of Dreamland (2009)? Or are they associated by similar titles?

IS: *Dreamland*'s a strange thing because it could be classified as sci-fi but it's also set in contemporary time. But it's also a film I haven't actually finished. I made a version of it and then I pulled it back from being released. I felt like the story and thematic elements didn't quite hit where I wanted them to hit so I held it back. I've rewrote the whole project, the whole film, into a much bigger, wider work which I'll get to in the next year or so hopefully. It's something that needs the right actor in it. I've learnt a few things over the years; the more creative you become, the more you rely on the right talent to portray the story and the character, and to give it a wider stage.

LOVELAND

Do you buy into the auteur theory at all?

IS: No, not at all. I've always felt filmmaking for me is just like photography, which I come from. Or it's from music, being a musician, or it's similar to being a painter. I haven't really painted in my life but I just see that it's something like that. The auteur thing I don't really buy into and I think the term gets thrown around pretty easily. A lot of directors who are considered auteurs, their work is very strongly created by the team that surrounds the director, and there are a lot of influences that go into that work from the crew.

I don't call myself an auteur. I just enjoy all the elements of the process. For me, I don't think I could go through the whole struggle to make a film if I wasn't getting my hands dirty. I enjoy that. It'd be like planting a garden or something. You enjoy it because you get your hands in the dirt. I enjoy getting my hands in the dirt and getting dirty and I'm not sitting behind three TV screens with a suit on drinking a cup of coffee. I'm right in the frontline with the actors and revelling in that space.

Where does the first aspect of a film come from for you? Is it the story, or have there been instances where a score has come to you first?

IS: Not really. It can happen at the same time, but usually I get the story from the land, from the location, and the location will grow the characters. The characters will come from their location which comes pretty much from observing real life. You have a location and that location has an influence on the people that live on that location, it defines the characters because that location has all kinds of elements to it that impact the characters. For me, I consider locations like countries.

All I knew twelve years ago was that I wanted to make a film in Hong Kong. I didn't know who the characters were or what the story was. I just knew I wanted to go to that place and let a story come to me, and grow out of that location. I've created music before I've created the actual story before and it's helped. You listen to the music and then that helps the story grow. But pretty much it's the location that's given them. I think that's why in the end product, in the film, if you get a strong sense of the location and/or the place, it's because that's where the whole thing started.

Tell me about the first time that you visited Hong Kong. What was your impression when you first visited?

IS: What blew me away was the energy. I remember booking hotels and I found some hotels that weren't on Hong Kong Island, but it was on the Kowloon side. I thought, "Maybe that's not a good idea" because I want to be in the thick of it on Hong Kong Island. I just felt like it's probably some place that shuts down when the sun goes down. When I got off the plane and into a taxi and drove through Kowloon, I was blown away by the energy, the lights, and the overall what you'd call the mise-en-scène of the place. It blew me away and I couldn't believe the energy that was going on in all the small streets, in the alleys, driving across intersections and looking down the laneways and just seeing the life force.

I got so excited because it's not from my immediate experience to see that extension of energy and life force which just keeps going and going and doesn't drop away to darkness as it does here in Australia [where] cafés close at two in the afternoon, and everything shuts up shop. Over there, things open a bit later, ten or something in the morning but it goes well into midnight. That just got me going, I was so inspired by that life force and energy and that will of people to move and to live life. Here, people run away to their houses and close the doors, but in Hong Kong, the houses are so small, they want to stay outside anyway. Over there, it's the life, and to a degree, you find this throughout Asia, and mainland China as well, but Hong Kong is specific. It's got this energy that is hard to find anywhere in the world.

That's what I found in my travels throughout Asia at nighttime. You're pushed out onto the streets because that's where the food is, that's where the culture is. It feels very different. Whereas here, you finish work and you come home and then that's it for the day. It's a different energy.

IS: And it's strange because the thing about Hong Kong is that it still retains a lot of the traditional structures of a village within a city framework. The area where we filmed most of the time was around Mongkok which is largely considered to be the soul of Hong Kong. You've got glittering skyscrapers but the thing that makes it different is that it's also surrounded by neighbourhoods and markets. Hong Kong is a series of villages which has been that way since it started and modernity just kind of sprung up around it. They've managed to hold on to this village feeling which I think is what feels very real and textural. It's something that I was drawn to from the moment I first got there. It's so unique.

The visual style is drenched in neon. You clearly have fun with that colour palette. It's the opposite of what you've worked with in Goldstone and Mystery Road where you use the red of the dirt. What was it like to work with all those bright colours?

IS: I was very conscious about the whole thing because I integrated an element of it into *Goldstone*, which I consciously borrowed from *Loveland*. *Loveland* was just a script at that point when shooting *Goldstone*, and I borrowed elements of *Loveland* and filtered them into *Goldstone* so it's a first taste of that film.

Unfortunately, I feel like I'm about thirty years late for the actual neon because now it's an LED city. There are some beautiful old neon's that are left. Unfortunately, they're not given the respect that they should have and they're slowly disappearing. They draw much more electricity than LED lights and all these businesses are small scale, and they've replaced a lot of the neon with LEDs which don't have quite the same kind of atmosphere. Unfortunately, that's the way of the city. There are a lot of things in Hong Kong which are disappearing quite rapidly, including a lot of the restaurants that have been there since the Sixties. We've managed to shoot in a few of them and so I'm happy to kind of capture elements of Hong Kong on camera. Even since we shot, a few of the restaurants have been renovated or closed down and transformed into some brand-new plastic kind of ugly thing.

The whole neon approach is something that when I first saw that energy, part of that was the neon and the LED and the lighting of the place. I immediately took hundreds of stills. Using the lighting that's in existence in Hong Kong on the street as the thematic lighting approach, I was conscious of that from the beginning, and working out the best way to tell the story. There are a lot of technical things to work out as well with this type of lighting. It's not the easiest thing to film because the light that's emitted from it is very little compared to when you're looking at it when you're looking at the actual sign which can be very bright. There's this balance of lighting ratios in which you have to work out how you're going to do things. I also integrated a lot of the lighting effects through the visual effects as well which have been influenced by the location.

I've read a couple of things where the trailer reminded [people] of *Blade Runner* (1982). If you look at when *Blade Runner* was created, Ridley Scott was heavily influenced by Hong Kong and his trips to Hong Kong, and if you look at Hong Kong, if you know Hong Kong cinema, you'll know that this type of high-key neon lighting approach had the film noir feeling. This has been going on in Hong Kong forever, since filmmaking started there. It's not something that *Blade Runner* made up; I can tell you that. I see it to just talk about *Blade Runner* when you see darkly lit neon images, it's culturally insensitive.

There are images of laneways that immediately struck me as being pulled from Hong Kong cinema. You seem to have some fun there.

IS: I have such a passion for it. You see some of these old Wong Kar-Wai films or John Woo films and they throw people against those lights. The thing is in Hong Kong because they have laws there, they allow you to show brands and things on the street without too many legal issues, so that also helps. In Hong Kong, they show real things through their real life, their real presence as opposed to when Hollywood does it. They just recreate everything. That's what I love about *Loveland* is using this real base and then just adding elements to it. Everything's kind of real.

Your films are often about characters who are seeking connection, trying to find their place in the world. Here, Ryan [Kwanten]'s character is doing that. Where do you find interest in these kinds of characters who are seeking a place in their own world or the worlds that they're forced into?

IS: I just see that as the most fundamental human trait, to seek connection. We're all always doing it. In almost every action we do, you can see that we are trying to connect with our place in the universe, or we're trying to connect with our immediate people around us or people who are not even close to us. We're always trying to make some kind of connection. It's built into our evolution.

It's something that I have always been drawn to, and *Loveland* is an extension of that trait. It's largely about that. It's about this world and specifically these characters who are struggling against this erosion of human traits which are love and trust, which are part of our connection traits as human beings. In the world in *Loveland,* that world is telling us that we don't need those connection traits anymore, they're of no use anymore. The thing is these traits of connection are something that are hard to let go of.

It's the struggle against the erosion of these traits that I wanted to highlight in a future context, in a futuristic world that is largely an extension of our current world. Places like Hong Kong or China or many parts of Asia. There they are. There's a lot more competition, extreme competition, over there, which we have the luxury of not having here to the extent, not yet, but you know there'll be a point where we probably will get to that stage. They're always ahead of us over there. The number of people competing with each other from a very young age, it's at a whole different level and that's something that struck me when I was over there. So how do we connect, and keep connecting while we're competing with each other? That's something I think is the main flow of the film.

What was it like reuniting with Hugo and Ryan?

IS: The struggle for connectivity is something that I know appealed to Ryan, and losing those traits that make us human in a connected way I think appealed to both of them. They both came on board early on. They both liked the scripts, and it was just a matter of locking in the finance because it's not the easiest type of film to finance. People are scared of sci-fi because they cost so much money and they don't return very well. Not like other genres, like horror for example, where they're quite cheap and easy to make. It just took a little bit of time to get the finance moving along.

Ryan has done the whole TV thing in America; this is like a bit of a character study for him. There's a lot of nonverbal activity going on with him. I think it's refreshing to see him working this way.

Hugo and Ryan are special actors. They're one hundred per cent into their career for the reasons of art. They're not there for the fame or fortune. They're there because they're passionate storytellers and want to tell stories from the heart. This is why I'm in it as well, so we find ourselves drawn to each other for that genuine reason. We want to make art that has something to say. Ryan and Hugo are dreams to work with in every way. It doesn't stop there, even when the film is finished, they said, "Whatever you need, mate, just give us a call. I'll do whatever you want."

Did the events in Hong Kong and COVID influence how you edited the film?

IS: We finished filming in Hong Kong and then the protest movement began. I think it was February-March 2019 when we finished and then around July-August the protest movement started to become active. That wasn't part of the story or anything, but I was interested in trying to integrate an element of that, so I did go back on several occasions and found myself in the middle of the whole chaos with a camera. It subtly worked its way into the film, but it's really just a layer, and it's not really to do with anything to do with the political situation.

There [wasn't a] pressure to get the film finished, but you do have to finish it at some point. It was quite a long period of post-production and doing visual effects and sound. There were many stages where I would go back and re-edit the film, go back and remix [it], largely because of COVID.

During COVID time, people have been more flexible about expecting work to be finished on time. It's just like everything, there's a delay in everything, so I took that opportunity to put more time into the editing, the effects, the sound, and the music. I must have recomposed the music; it must have been fifty times or something. The music's gone through so many different cuts.

One of the joys of someone like John Carpenter has been he's put out a whole bunch of his unused scores. There's a part of me that asks, "I wonder if Ivan's gonna do that one day."

IS: We mixed the music in the film on several occasions. In the first two mixes, there was no music or notes from those mixes present in the film at all. And this music may end up in another film as well, as a base for another score because some of it I quite like. It's a shame, I could use it again.

You're a great composer. The Goldstone score is brilliant. I listen to it while I'm writing because it helps keep you focused on what you're doing.

IS: That was the first time I actually gave myself freedom, time, and space to concentrate on music. When I finished shooting *Goldstone*, for the first two months or six weeks, I told myself 'I'm not going to look at the film, I'm just going to make music.' So that's what I did. I had this score before I even looked at the pictures. It helped the editing go together really fast because I already had the score a hundred per cent completed.

I do have a strong appreciation for *Goldstone*. I know it doesn't go into areas that some people expect it to, but for me, it's a film that resonates emotionally with me as well as thematically. When I start to watch it, I feel myself just watching, it's hard to stop watching it. If I had to pick one, it is my favourite film up to this point.

Do you revisit your films often?

IS: I try not to. But just by accident, sometimes you start watching things. I think a lot to do with *Goldstone* is there are so many layers to it. Also, I think Aaron Pedersen grew a lot from making the *Mystery Road* film because he had never made anything like that in his life, where he just gets to walk around and quietly look at things without the blah, blah, blah. I think *Goldstone* was a chance for him to take another step into his craft, into learning about his craft.

You've got three legends of Australian film in Goldstone. Aaron, Tom (Lewis), and David (Gulpilil).

IS: It was really important for me to get those three together. The three of them are iconic. And, they're not going to be around forever. It is the only time that the three of them will be in the one film. I think Aaron might have been in a film with David once before but it wasn't released (*Mimi*, directed by Warwick Thornton in 2002). For me, it's a very special film, I think it was an incredible film to make too because we made it while living on a cattle station and there was no contact with the outside world. It was amazing because the locations were five minutes apart, some of them I walked to from my tent in the morning. Incredible process.

THREE THOUSAND YEARS OF LONGING

108 mins
Director: *George Miller*
Writers: *George Miller, Augusta Gore (Based on the short story The Djinn in the Nightingale's Eye by A.S. Byatt)*
Cast: *Tilda Swinton, Idris Elba, Erdil Yasaroglu, Sabrina Dhowre Elba, Aamito Lagum, Nicolas Mouawad, Erdil Yaşaroğlu, Ece Yüksel, Lachy Hulme, Matteo Bocelli, Megan Gale, Ogulcan Aramn Uslu, Jack Braddy, David Collins, Anna Adams, Zerrin Tekindor, Melissa Jaffar, Anna Charleston, Pia Thunderbolt*
Producers: *George Miller, Doug Mitchell*
Composer: *Tom Holkenborg*
Cinematography: *John Seale*
Editing: *Margaret Sixel*

In 2022, *Three Thousand Years of Longing* was nominated for 13 AACTA Awards: Best Film, Best Direction, Best Editing, Best Cinematography, Best Original Score in Film, Best Costume Design (Kym Barrett), Best Production Design in Film (Roger Ford), Best Sound in Film (Robert Mackenzie, Ben Osmo, Yulia Akerholt, James Ashton), Best Lead Actress, Best Lead Actor, Best Screenplay, Best Hair and Make-up, Best Visual Effects or Animation (Paul Butterworth, Eric Whipp, Jason Bath, Roy Malhi, Chris Spry, Alastair Stephen, Chris Davies).

INTERVIEW
MAKE-UP & HAIR DESIGNER
LESLEY VANDERWALT

Lesley Vanderwalt started working with George Miller in 1980 on *Mad Max 2*, marking the start of a working relationship that has spanned over four decades, and has seen the make-up and hair designer win an Academy Award for her work on *Mad Max: Fury Road*. For their 2022 collaboration, *Three Thousand Years of Longing*, partially shot in Sydney during the height of the COVID pandemic, Lesley swapped the wasteland for the mystical world of Djinn's, the Queen of Sheba, and the markets of Istanbul. This world of mysticism gave Lesley the chance to play with the possibilities of the fantasy genre and work with the actors to help them organically build their characters.

Tilda Swinton's Alithea is a scholar whose work is steeped in myths and legends. After she purchases an innocuous bottle at an Istanbul marketplace, she unleashes Idris Elba's Djinn who unironically offers her three wishes. As the Djinn recounts his stories, Alithea recognises the manner that the world is smothered by technology, creating a cloud of digital noise that permeates the mind and stifles creativity. *Three Thousand Years of Longing* is an ode to the legacy of legends and the strength of stories and the worlds that have been changed in their wake.

This interview was recorded by Andrew F. Peirce in November 2022

I was reading about your working relationship with the Kennedy Miller Mitchell group and by the looks of it, Three Thousand Years of Longing marked 40 years of the relationship.

Lesley Vanderwalt: 41.

Congratulations.

LV: It would have been 40. George and I talked about it on set, "Wow, we've been working with each other for forty years now." I'm not the only one. There's a number of people like that. He's a very loyal man. He's wonderful.

THREE THOUSAND YEARS OF LONGING

Can you reflect on what makes a working relationship like that endure so brilliantly and for so long?

LV: As I said, George is very loyal to everybody around him. It's like working with a big family. Personally, I love it. I love the way he talks about what he's going to do. Being the writer, he talks about a story and as he talks about it, I sit there and visualise what he's talking about. Sometimes I ask questions. If you spend forty years with someone, it's like shorthand. You can understand what they're aiming or looking for.

When you look at actors together, you can see how that could work or what that would be like on that actor because of their facial structure or hair colour, things like that. We don't always begin at the same point. I remember, at one stage, we talked about Tilda being grey haired, and then we discussed it further and went, "Well, people get older these days, including myself, and you do colour your hair and all that. She wouldn't have been a woman that looked after herself, like a lot of people do now." She painted her nails but just in a natural shade, so she still looked after herself and had a very precise haircut and those sorts of things that come out through talking with the director about the character.

Then you involve the actress or the actor and talk to them about the character. You're sitting around a table discussing [character stuff,] and that's when you work out if you're on the same page. We had a wonderful costume designer, Kym Barrett, and she very much led the feeling and the look of it. A lot of [the ideas] that she came up with were just absolutely brilliant, all her references. We all share folders and put together all our references and work very much as a team, which I really enjoy, because in a lot of productions you get on and the costume designer does their bit, you do your bit and the production designer does them but and they're very separate departments whereas I find working with George, he brings everybody together to work as a team. One of my favourite sayings is 'there's no I in team,' and it doesn't take one person to make a movie, that takes a whole team.

I understand that George sits with stories for a long time. From my understanding, he sat with this one for about twenty years. Does he engage with you and talk with you over the years about what stories he's thinking about to give you an idea of what to create?

LV: Not so much, because you all go off on your own journeys. You have to earn a living on other films in other parts of the world, or other parts of the country. You're always doing different things. I don't remember when we started talking about *Three Thousand Years of Longing*. When he first started talking about the film and making it, it was just before COVID, to me anyway. He's quite private, he sort of keeps a lot to himself until it's time to share it. He doesn't share unnecessarily, like a lot of people do these days. He waits till he's got it all together and it's a solid thing. Then he talks about it.

I know I was still in Sydney at that time, so it must have been about 2018, I guess. Then there was COVID happening and different things and actor availabilities, so, it was put off for a little while. Then Baz rang me to do *Elvis*, and I said, "Well, I've said yes to George, so that's my first thing, obviously." Then I went up to Queensland and worked on *Elvis* setting it up, and they said, "Can we have you until George needs you?" I worked on *Elvis* for 18 weeks with the Italian makeup and hair team, and Mark Coulier (prosthetics designer) and his special effects team from the UK. We spent 18 weeks getting *Elvis* sorted out, and then COVID stopped that.

I went back home and then they rang up to say that they were going ahead with *Three Thousand Years*, which was great. I'm going to go on to that and do the movie with George that I was always intending to do. So, I left *Elvis* to do *Three Thousand Years*. You do it like that, you go from movie to movie. I don't know ahead of time what's going to happen. None of us do. That's the great thing I love about being freelance in the film industry is you never really know what's going to happen from day to day. It can all change in a phone call, and you just don't know [what's going to happen.] A lot of people can't deal with it, they like a routine in their life and they want to know what's going on over the next month or year or whatever. I've never been that sort of person. The film industry is ideal for me, it's worked well for me.

I understand that you work a lot with mentoring emerging makeup artists and people wanting to get into the industry. What does it mean to be able to pass creative information along to a new generation?

LV: In my whole life, I've fallen into things and just did it. I never made a clear decision that I wanted to be in the film industry. In fact, I always wanted to be a dress designer or a clothes designer, so I never had a clear vision, I just sort of fell into it. From experience, I can pass on valuable lessons and information that I've learned. In Australia, we have a lot of makeup schools that take people on a junior level and give them a basic knowledge of make-up, but they don't give them any experience of what it's like to actually do a film or be on a set or how to talk to actors, how to talk to the director or the art of listening and the art of watching, looking, seeing; a lot of people don't naturally have that.

To be able to pass on or experience those things is wonderful because it's a constantly rolling thing. Even now, there are so many things going on with all these streaming platforms shooting; not always good things. I call them stocking fillers to keep the platforms going. You need so many people, and there's such a shortage of people out there. The UK one was founded a couple of years ago, so I've got one of my good girlfriends over there who runs the Creative Media Skills Institute, along with the British government, where they get subsidies and set up this [initiative] where they [support] upskilling. They've got lots of people on the junior level, the first level where you go in and you learn basic make-up and they teach you as much as they can. But we haven't got anywhere where people can then go and upskill if they've done a film or two and realise there are gaps in their training. We don't have anything like that in Australia, but in the UK they do as they started to realise what a shortage of new skilled people they had. I still feel that there's a big gap here in this industry, but I don't know how we're going to fill that gap. Maybe it's something for my retirement.

Even on this latest one I've just finished, with three movies happening in Sydney, trying to get enough people for our crowd rooms and things like that was difficult. We're flying people in from all different states. I know there's the new *Planet of the Apes*, there's *The Fall Guy*, there's *The Artful Dodger*. They're all going on at the same time. How you crew a small Australian movie or lower budget thing, I really don't know. You just couldn't match the wages and the budgets and all of that on a smaller film. I guess the good thing about that is it's an opportunity for new people to get in, as long as they've got the skills. There are a lot of really fabulous artistic young people out there, but then maybe they haven't got the other skills. Films are like a marathon, not a sprint, so it's knowing how to look after yourself and the people around you for that for that time.

Let's talk about the design of the Djinn in Three Thousand Years of Longing. He's a character who is made up of electricity. There is this buzzy-ness to him, there's almost this aspect of fire as well, that lingers throughout the film, too. What discussions took place about creating the visual look for him?

LV: That was probably the longest discussion. There were discussions before Idris came in, looking back at Djinns, we were going to have a blueish tone and a bluish tinge. Then talking with Kym, we were going to have him covered in fine feathers, peacock type colours. I've got boards of all the stuff we did. You can go ahead and work on all those ideas, you can put them forward all of that, and then reality hit: how much time have we got with that actor every morning? Because the main thing is George's time with him in front of the camera, not sitting in the makeup chair for half a day, so you have to base your designs on that.

On some films, they do huge prosthetic makeup that take over five hours, but the person isn't usually in every scene in the film, every day. When you look at someone like the , he was. So, you have to do your design but you

INTERVIEW | LESLEY VANDERWALT

also have to base it on practicality. What is the main reason that we need to film with them? He's in this many scenes and there's never going to be the right turnarounds for him. You don't want to make the actor bored sitting in a makeup chair for hours. We started planning and looking at what we could do, working really closely with Kym Barrett about where the costume would start, what the costume would be, how much of it would be costume, and how much it would be makeup. So, the discussion started off like that.

With the colour, we were leaning towards blue. George had a thing where he wanted him to have an almost an Arabic nose and be bald. At one stage there was a thought of doing a little bit of hair like other Djinns have with that flap down the back. And the ears that we did in the end. All of those discussions got thrown into the mixing pot, as I call it.

Then Idris jumped in because he was cast. We started with Zoom meetings, because it was COVID. He really didn't want to be blue. He thought that was too much of a trope, it had all been done before. He didn't want the Arabic nose, he preferred that he could be a Djinn that came from his African roots. That would go backwards and forwards in the discussion between George and him because at that point I saw that this was more personal to the actor and the character, and you guys should talk about it first and then come back to us and then we can talk about what's come out of that and where we can go from there.

We did end up getting ears and nose for Idris in London, as his first makeup tests were in London with Mark Coulier and his team, who were fabulous. They did the first test, and when I looked back at the pictures where we did the full Arabic nose and the pointy goatee, that we still kept a bit of, it just looked wrong. I think the character itself was much warmer because we had Idris' look, just his nose and his eyes, it wasn't a completely different thing. It's interesting when I look back at it now when I go back through the photos and I'm so glad we didn't go with the nose. We used the nose on George as a bit of part of the storyteller in the rowboat, and he looked great. We use everything, and never let anything go away. So, it sort of evolved like that.

With the feathers and all that and the big bird that was going to be on his costume, he had a phobia about birds. We just couldn't go there. He was like, "Get that thing away from me now." It's not just a straight thing with any person, as soon as you're involved with a human being whether it's the actor, the director, the designer, whatever, everything starts to change. He couldn't cope with any feathers, so we had to get rid of them.

Then Kym did the costumes and we made stencils to match the latex on the costume and the colours, and we would airbrush from the costume onto his torso into a sort of blend where the feathers were removed. Looking back at it now, we had no idea that the actor would have a phobia about birds. The whole thing had started initially talking about being based on skin and feathers, so it was sort of a half human half creature, but all of that went. Quite often, less is more is better. I think it looks beautiful.

We used the ears, and we had lots of gold on the tips of his ears and took away most of the blue, leaving just hints of it. With his hands, we did the fingertips and the tip of his nose all gold. With Sheba, as she was a Djinn too, we did similar stuff with her. Then George went, "You know, I think the palms of his hands and the soles of his feet should be a different colour," and then we toyed around with a few different ideas. Should they be gold as well or should they be blue? And then we went opposing [colours.] For some reason I had a bright pink there, and he went, "Let's try pink," and we put pink on. Everybody went "That's it, you've got it."

To me, everything that I do is a collaboration with George and costume and the actor. I have very rarely seen it in my 45-year career where someone comes in with a design like they do more in theatre, I guess, where they go, 'this is what you're going to look like, this is what you're going to be wearing.' It's very rarely that happens. That's usually a collaboration. It's not just telling someone that this is how they're going to do it, then they have to work out how to play it.

The Queen of Sheba's hairy legs are a visually brilliant and beautiful thing. Can you talk about the construction of that?

LV: Oh my god. That's one of the things I don't want to remember.

All the Djinn were going to have hairy legs, and it was based originally that the Djinn's costume, Idris' costume, would have hairy legs from the knees down that would be hand knotted into the costume. Then we had to figure out how to give these people [long-haired legs.] Once again, with time restraints and all that. We could have laid hair on their legs, but that would have taken hours. My feeling was that surely there was a costume manufacturer that could make stockings or pantyhose with that, but apparently there wasn't. I kept referring back to the people who make animals for theme parks, and they make those sheer fabrics that pull over them. We were really busy and tight for time. It wasn't a big budget film. I was lucky I had four- or five-weeks pre-production on it. Kym had a little bit more as a costume designer, but we literally didn't have time to investigate and go any further with that.

In the end, I had strips of hair lace knotted up with hair, and then we just glued those onto the legs. We did the same for the little kids and you don't really see those, thank goodness, because it was so hard trying to keep them on those kids who were running around and putting the clothes on and off and all of that. We did these strips and then glued them on. I've got pictures of her standing on the table tops as I was trying to organise pieces. It was like having five wigs on your legs. The time it took to make them, and the cost was probably the same as having five hand knotted wigs, because you don't realise how much space there is, especially on someone like the beautiful Aamito who has the longest legs you've ever seen. It was an enormous job. I have to close my eyes when that comes up in the film because I don't want to see it. It gave me nightmares.

A lot of research goes into these things. We had a Turkish historian work with us from Turkey, and George was saying the talk was that they had these hairy legs and that's how you knew they were Djinn's. Once again, it was his idea. I've got to say, as a woman, when we first talked about it, I went "What?" I couldn't imagine it. It was funny, because looking around the crew and talking to people, I didn't realise but it's become quite a big thing these days for young people to have quite long, hairy legs. As a 65-year-old woman, I spent my whole life getting rid of hair.

What does it mean to be working in Australia on Australian productions with Australian crews, telling both Australian and international stories as a creative person?

LV: I've been incredibly lucky in my career and my life. I don't know how else to put it. I try and teach everybody to be really careful about what they choose and don't just do something for money. Think about what you're doing because you want to steer and guide your career and not just fall into anything and then go down that rabbit hole of just doing anything that comes up.

I had opportunities when I was younger to work in other places. I think I even got a grant from the Film Commission back in the eighties to go and work or study with Dick Smith in LA. I've had lots of opportunities and lots of offers. I have gone overseas to do films in the UK and Canada. Funnily enough, Martin Campbell was a Kiwi director, but he said, "Oh darling, I'm doing this film (*Beyond Borders*, 2003), come and join me." I went, "Oh, I don't know," and he went, "No, but darling, see if you come to Canada, I'll take you to Africa." That was my first trip to Namibia before *Fury Road*.

I don't like to mouth off like some people, but I feel I sort of started some of the big scenes and big films and big crowded rooms in Australia, like *Dark City* (1998). When I did *Dark City* with all the strangers and bald guys, I spent two weeks trying to work out how I was going to run that and get three hundred people with bald heads. I started to think about it as a factory.

THREE THOUSAND YEARS OF LONGING

You can overcomplicate things, or you can simplify things. I feel all of my life, the reason I get offered things is that I obviously have a creative eye, which I don't see as much as other people. I don't see what other people see in me or my work. As someone said to me, "I've got impostor syndrome." I have obviously got a creative eye. I love to do up houses. I can make anything into anything. I guess I've got that streak.

I think you work in an industry where you like the people you want to surround yourself with. When I crew a team, I look at people and then I look at what the positive points and negative points are. I always put someone with them who fills the gaps to make sure all the gaps are covered. I try and lift and promote people at what they're good at and I don't send them down the path of doing something that they struggle with. I bring someone else in to do that. We think in life, we have to do it all, and I don't believe we do. The thing is that we want a great end product, so you do that.

I feel that Australians are very good at doing that. There are a lot of Americans who are too. I've had great support from both artists in the US and the UK. They've been wonderful. But I've never had any desire to go and live and work there like some people do. Everybody says, 'the grass is always greener,' but I still think in this country we have some of the best crews and technicians in the world. When I have been overseas to work, they're blown out by what we do. I remember producers going, "Oh my god, you do make-up and hair and prosthetics?" I go "Well, being bought up on low budget films, we had to." I think our skills are fantastic compared to what I've seen in other parts of the world. We've got a really high standard of work ethic and skills. I never had the desire to work or live anywhere else. I wanted to make this country shine rather than work with others. I've had a few opportunities, and I've really enjoyed them and met some wonderful people along the way.

I've talked to a lot of people throughout the years and there are people who see working in Australia as a stepping stone to working in America. And that's fine. But there's something powerful about hearing someone wanting to build up our industry here.

LV: I'll tell you that most of them come back. They all go off and they all come back a couple of years later. They win Green Cards and go to LA and then come back and go, "Oh my God, what was that all about?" It's a different world. There's a lot of competition. Here, it's a much nicer working environment and as professional as anywhere in the world.

One of the aspects that I appreciate about your work as a makeup artist is the visual design and style that you create linger through time. You mentioned Dark City before, and the iconic look of the characters makes the memories of the film linger even more. We think of Babe: Pig in the City, Dark City, and Mad Max Fury Road and it's the visual aspect of the make-up that we think of the film first.

LV: When I look back at my career, and I go, "God, I'm good at drawing bald whitehead people." War Boys, *Dark City*, there's always one somewhere. It's very funny. I never know where it comes from.

I remember doing *Farscape* one time at the beginning of the show, and I was sitting at home in my apartment and sort of bashing myself up trying to create another new character, because you had to create so many new ones. The prosthetics department would create a couple one week and then the next week, I'd have to come up with a couple that were non-prosthetic, and then the next week it'd be the prosthetics department again. I remember going, "What can I do this time?" Sitting in front of me on the coffee table was a Belle decoration magazine. It was one of those anniversary editions and it was all black and white, the whole thing, and I started browsing through that. And I went and got the black-and-white scale thing from one of the cameramen, and that's how I created Chiana (Gigi Edgley) for *Farscape*. I'd mix makeup colours and match them to the colour bar. I matched all the make-up colours to grayscale, and then went and made her up looking at her face. I took a photo and got them to print it in black and white for me. I followed the shadows and all the different colours of that, and then I found a wig that was a sort of silver-grey colour and we cut that and created this character that was black and white in the coloured world. It's funny, things just come to you. I never know where inspiration is going to come from, but it just does.

Thank you for sharing your stories. Sometimes people might sit at home and think, "Am I doing the right thing? Am I not doing the right thing?" Just to know that someone else has gone through that helps a lot.

LV: It's that old saying from *Strictly Ballroom* (1993), "A life lived in fear is a life half lived." We feel that all the time, all of us, and I do every single day. It's not like it gets any better. You just have to keep soldiering on through. I say it every day and I see it in my young ones, and I say "Just give it a go. If it's not working, then do it again. Just keep going." That's what I try to instil in people too, you don't always get it right the first time and we're all casually fearful when we first do a person or a thing. It's okay sometimes to make mistakes. I've learned so much over the years from the mistakes that I've made. Don't be afraid to just go with what you feel and if it doesn't work out, then try something else.

AN OSTRICH TOLD ME THE WORLD IS FAKE AND I THINK I BELIEVE IT

12 mins
Director: *Lachlan Pendragon*
Writer: *Lachlan Pendragon*
Voice Cast: *Lachlan Pendragon, John Cavanagh, Michael Richard, Jamie Trotter*
Producer: *Donna Hamilton*
Music: *Envato Market*
Sound: *Lachlan Pendragon*
Visual Effects: *Lachlan Pendragon*
Animation Department: *Lachlan Pendragon*

An Ostrich Told Me the World is Fake and I Think I Believe It received a nominated for Best Short Film at the 2022 AACTA Awards and Best Animated Film - Short at the 2023 Academy Awards.

INTERVIEW
FILMMAKER
LACHLAN PENDRAGON

Not many filmmakers can say that the film they made for their university course received an Academy Award nomination, but for Meanjin-Brisbane based creative Lachlan Pendragon, it's an honour he's able to hold with pride, alongside his win for Best Animation at the Student Academy Awards in 2022[1]. Lachlan became the sixth Australian filmmaker to be nominated for the Best Animated Short Film at the Oscars.[2]

An Ostrich Told Me the World is Fake and I Think I Believe It is a meta-comedy where a call centre employee (voiced by Lachlan) gradually discovers, thanks to a mysterious ostrich, that he might be living in a stop-motion universe. Lachlan's work as an animator is joyfully expressive and delightfully self-aware, pointedly reflected in a moment where the employee discovers a box full of facial expressions that are used to swap out how he feels.

This interview was recorded by Andrew F. Peirce in July 2022

When did your interest in animation start?

Lachlan Pendragon: I had an interest in it without really knowing that I was going down that path. I wasn't the one drawing flipbook animations in textbooks and things like that. It wasn't until the end of high school when we did an animation assignment, and I was good at it. Even then, I didn't think that that was where I was going. I thought I was going to go the live-action route of going into film. I left it up to OP [Overall Position] scores. I applied for a Bachelor in Film and then my second option was Bachelor of Animation. I didn't get into film, and I'm so glad that that happened because I don't think film was the right choice for me.

Why stop-motion as a branch of animation is another good question. It's one of those mediums that doesn't make a lot of practical sense or financial sense, but it's a much different experience making a film [as a filmmaker]. It's one that I prefer, [it] feels a bit more tactile, you get to use your hands. The problem-solving is more in line with general filmmaking, whereas something like computer animation is a lot more technical, and I just wasn't able to click with that as much.

The other thing was when I was studying, there [were] very good facilities for stop-motion that the university had that not many people were using. "Okay, I'll stick my hand up. I'll take that." It just felt right. When you start a Bachelor of Animation in the first year, they take you through every single media type. You'll do 2D, you'll do 3D, and you'll get a sense of every single type of animation. Nothing was clicking with me the same way that stop-motion did back in my high school days. It wasn't until second year that I finally got back to stop-motion [and] I was like, "Yes, this was the right thing. Okay. I'm back where I should be." I haven't wavered from there since.

What films would you look to as an influence as you're growing up?

LP: For this film, there's quite a bit of Aardman-y influence. There's *Wallace and Gromit*, and there's a bit of British humour in there. My favourite film at the moment is Greta Gerwig's *Little Women* [2019], which I thought was fantastic. Growing up, there was a film called *Son of Rambow* [2007]. It's about a bunch of school kids making films. It's fun, and there's a bit of drama in there as well. That one's more of a personal favourite [that] doesn't really have any influence. I would love to be able to say I made a film like that.

With An Ostrich Told Me the World is Fake and I Think I Believe It, where did this idea come from? This applies live-action to animation and blends the two quite comfortably.

LP: You're still using cameras. You're still using lights. You're [just] doing it a lot slower. It's the best of both worlds. The thing about this film is that it comes from a research perspective. I don't think I would have arrived at this idea if I hadn't come from trying to innovate or push something or experiment with something.

It started with the idea of 'why stop-motion?' Why should I be doing stop-motion as opposed to something more practical or efficient as CG? With CG becoming much more advanced, we've seen films that can emulate a stop-motion aesthetic. What are we still getting out of that extra effort of doing something in stop-motion?

I use a lot of 3D tools, 3D printing, that kind of thing. As I keep improving my skills and getting better and more experienced, there's nothing in the way of achieving any kind of aesthetic. There's more responsibility about "Okay, how much of this handmade quality do I want to retain?" It's more and more possible to eliminate it, to edit it out, or make any kind of artistic decision you want.

INTERVIEW | LACHLAN PENDRAGON

There are some stop-motion films out there that are very polished, almost too polished, that almost question whether they should have made it stop-motion. It's almost like you need to realise that it's been made, or you need to see the imperfections in the handmade craft to appreciate it, or to give it a reason to go to all that effort. I wanted to showcase that as much as possible, and then make sure that I don't push it too far so that we can't suspend disbelief, so we can still connect with the characters and connect to the story. It was about bouncing those two by still pushing the reflexivity of it to the extreme to where it almost breaks. I think I did a good job of that.

Some of the Aardman work nowadays, there are some interesting workarounds that they do to retain their classic plasticine look. In *Early Man* [2018], they had plasticine-looking limbs, but they had very furry costumes. Actual plasticine would be a nightmare, but they still want them to look like plasticine. They modelled [characters] in plasticine, cast it in silicone, and went to this extra effort, so it looked like plasticine but it's not actually plasticine. Using advanced techniques like that, or even with 3D printing, the consideration for me was to make sure that it looked as if I could have done it by hand, or like it had that look as though it could have been handmade, but it was 3D printed like that. I think that's a better way of staying with the handmade [look], but still utilising these new tools that can speed up processes and make it more accessible.

As you're saying there is this kind of movement to replicate stop-motion, or at least, accentuated with digital effects. Do you want to push against that in some capacity to kind of re-establish the world of stop-motion in Australia?

LP: 'Push against it,' I'm not sure that's the right word, but I do think there's something different about stop-motion. There's a different goal for stop-motion. I think it's copying the model of CG, where it's kind of chasing this hyper-realistic vision or something. Whereas I feel stop-motion is never going to get there. It's never going to be able to be better at it than computer animation. So, the goal has to be something else. I'm not sure what that is.

That's what excites me about it. It is something different that has so much potential that I feel hasn't been explored too much. There are other examples out there of this sort of reflexive stuff in animation. I wanted to be part of it and see how it would affect how I make films moving forward, as I improve and use different tools so that I still understand what I want to retain aesthetics-wise, in case it gets lost. I would like to make an imprint on the Australian animation industry in some small way. That would be amazing.

This is almost like a one-man show. You're directing. You're writing. You're voicing characters as well. I assume that your hand is in there,

AN OSTRICH TOLD ME THE WORLD IS FAKE AND I THINK I BELIEVE IT

too. I kept thinking of comic strips where the characters are yelling at the artists going, "Why are you making me do this?" What's it like pushing back at yourself creatively?

LP: That's my hand.

It's weird. Especially because you listen to your voice, [listening to] the dialogue over and over and over, and you're just sick of it. I did have other voice actors, and that was nice to be able to just be able to stand back from it and see it. Collaborating with myself is difficult in that sense. If I was animating, I would only be able to see what I animated. It's very difficult to then be the director and stand back and go, "Is this working?" I was seeing every tiny little thing.

But I kind of knew that from the previous film that I made. I was aware that I would need to know that it was working before I started animating. There wasn't a lot of time spent with the animatics and storyboards where I was just focusing on the director role, and then I could relax a little bit when I got to animation and just be the animator for that part. It was difficult to be both the animator and the director. I feel like they're just so different.

Can you define what the two roles are? I think that a lot of people see a director's name on a film, and then they go, "Oh, so they did all the animation", forgetting that for most animated films, there is a team of animators working on it.

LP: The director is like the conductor, the person where everything comes together and stops with them to make sure everything works well together. Sort of the big picture stuff, and little stuff, but mostly it's to make sure that everything ties together and works.

As the animator, usually you're focusing on one shot at a time and on the performance, the micro expression, especially in animation, you have to consider every little thing. In stop-motion, you're spending a lot of time with a very small moment, and that does something to your head. So then to be able to jump out of that for a second and be "Okay, I've got to be the director now I'll think about the whole picture", is a bit tricky to switch back and forth and see it with fresh eyes. I don't know how to get around that. Maybe with more experience, I'll get better at it.

But it's a very different role with the animator. When I'm animating, you'll spend so long with one moment that you'll watch it and notice a lot more than what the audience would end up seeing. So, it's hard to then jump back to the director and be like, "Actually, all that stuff that you think they're seeing is probably not coming across." For the animator, you moved it, you know that you moved it, and that's what you're seeing. Whereas the audience or the director should be able to see it and just see the character and what the character is performing. Towards the end of the animation, it was getting a bit like that, like I was just channelling it into the puppet a bit more, and it felt more intuitive that way. Hopefully, it goes more that way if I keep animating so that it doesn't consume me a bit too much.

[If this] was a live-action film, [the director might] be able to go home and look at the rushes for that day, and then have an idea of 'Okay, no, I've got to do this shot again tomorrow.' For stop-motion animation, time is such a big part of it. How do you know when you've got something right then?

LP: [With] the storyboards and the animatics, basically that's where we're editing the film. The editing is pretty much locked up in that stage. Before we animate a shot, or before we animate a scene – I say 'we', it's weird, I have been doing that the whole production, making it seem like I have a big team – I would shoot a lot of reference footage of myself acting out the scene. And then we'd edit that, so it's essentially a live-action version, but it's just not lit, or there are no sets or anything. That gives us a great indication if it's working.

It was pretty nice when we first got the audio locked up, then that was the moment where "Ah this is working really nice." Because it worked as a [radio drama], there's a lot of dialogue. Then when we got into shooting reference footage, we were able to add in those moments that were more about the actions of the visual moments. That was really fun. So much of that influenced the decisions that were made during animating. I shot the reference first, and then from that I was able to be the director looking at it as a director would, and then sign off on that. When I was animating, I felt like if I didn't know if this was the right call, I would rely on that reference a little bit more because I knew that I had previously signed off on it. "It was working back then, it should still be working, I think you're overthinking it." That helped.

Was it always the choice to be an ostrich?

LP: No. I read earlier scripts the other day, and I forgot that it was we were talking about how his lunch would come to life and start talking to him. It was an early idea I forgot about. It was written out and a different way to go. With the ostrich, we wanted something bigger, weirder and out of place in an office setting. We wanted a big gangly bird we thought would fit the bill. That's the ostrich.

AN OSTRICH TOLD ME THE WORLD IS FAKE AND I THINK I BELIEVE IT

There are so many moving pieces to it. It's got wings, it's got layers of feathers. I imagine there's so much more than just a changing face to keep track of.

LP: That's why it's sitting down for a lot of it. The ostrich reference footage was me with balls on my hand and just sort of like doing this [moves hand like an ostrich], to get an idea of the blocking of it, and how that was going to work. It wasn't too useful. I didn't really use that reference. It was something for me to show my supervisors, "Yes, this is what this is what I'm doing for this scene." The ostrich had replacement mouths, it had eyes that could move, and its neck was all sculpt-ey, malleable and sculptable. There was maybe one shot where it did have a full-body animation, but everything else was more selective in what I showed to make that work.

Was there a book or a guide that told you 'These are the tools that are best to work with' that helped introduce you to the world of stop-motion animation? Or was it discovering it as you go along?

LP: I feel like it's different for everyone, but for stop-motion, there always seems to be "You learn how to make a puppet before you can animate." It's always in that order, which it shouldn't have to be. In CG, you can just get a rig and then just be an animator. With stop-motion, it's harder to do that if you just want to be one.

I feel like it's more common for stop-motion animators to have some experience making puppets and things like that. There's always going to be an infinite way of going about it, it's kind of up to you in terms of what materials you want to use. It's just a collection of things I've learned from various places, things I've learnt from different people along the way, [and] I've just selected the bits that worked for me, cut corners where I've had to. I'd say generally I'm using techniques that are more or less used by stop-motion students. I know there are resources out there, but there isn't a 'go-to' place. Maybe there should be.

The entry point to filmmaking is something I always find fascinating. I've talked to filmmakers who've grown up and said, "I've got a phone so therefore I just point and shoot." For stop-motion animation, if you've got a 3D printer, that can make it much easier because then you can create it.

LP: Like an Assistant. Tell your printer to "Go and print this." You can tell it exactly what to do. You can definitely do the same thing. You can get a phone and animate objects. I did that for a while. There was one where I got a stack of Jenga and animated that. It's probably the best sort of training tool for animating stop-motion because you imagine a Jenga stack isn't designed to stay still. I made a Jenga stack, and all the pieces would move

INTERVIEW | LACHLAN PENDRAGON

in time to music. In animating it, you become very good at playing Jenga as a by-product. That was one that I enjoyed doing. That's a ramp for people who maybe aren't interested in the fabrication side of things.

I'd say that that's probably me. I did all of the fabrication stuff, but I would say I'm more interested in the animation side of things. To get to that, there needs to be fabrication. I cut a lot of corners in the fabrication because I knew that the extra time I spent there was going to eat into animation time. That's always the case. I was cautious of that and made sure that I had a big block of time that I could focus on mainly because I would prefer the animation to be more polished than the fabrication.

Now you're hitting film festivals. What's that experience like?

LP: It's crazy. When we finished the film, I showed it to my supervisors, and we were honestly thinking we were going to really hunt for some niche festivals that were going to want this. I'm very surprised that it's been picked up by the festivals that have been selecting it. Also, [it's] the best feeling to sit in an audience with your film and hear their reactions is amazing. It's really good. It's great that I did a comedy, so there is a reaction that is happening. It's a great feeling when it has that response from an audience.

Going forward, do you have an idea of what kind of work you want to create and what you want to explore in the world of animation?

LP: Stop-motion in some way, shape or form. Idea wise? I don't know. I don't think I need to explore the meta-narrative space again. I might, but I don't think that's my thing. I would be just as happy doing a different kind of story. I'm not sure yet. I'm excited to get back into it. I am currently just finalising the research write-up that accompanies the film, so I'm still in the process of getting that finished and then it's back to the ideation phase.

It's interesting, at one of the festivals I won an award for screenwriting. It was a weird moment where it's like, "Oh, I guess I am a screenwriter," because it's something that I only do at the beginning of the project. There are two years between then and when I will then write again to do something else. I'm excited to be a writer for a little while until I figure out what the next thing will be.

As we've discovered, stop-motion animation isn't a huge thing in Australia. It's exciting to see another person emerging into that field and working in stop-motion animation here.

LP: This film was a lockdown film. It was shot in my living room with whatever I had. It's a great medium for making the most of very little. And for

AN OSTRICH TOLD ME THE WORLD IS FAKE AND I THINK I BELIEVE IT

me, I want to see that happen as well, [to have] more people interested in stop-motion so one day I can gather a big team to tackle a big project or something. I want to see that happen.

When your doctorate is finished, what will you be a doctor of?

LP: A doctor of visual art.

That's exciting. How do you feel about that?

LP: I never took it up for the title. Or thinking about what use it would be afterwards. But it's there. I'll be a Doctor of Visual Arts. It was an avenue for me of how I could continue doing what I do, was how I looked at it, and still look at it. It has a degree attached to it.

ENDNOTES

1. 49th Student Academy Awards | 2022 https://www.oscars.org/saa/ceremonies/2022
2. Previous honorees: Winner - Suzanne Baker - *Leisure*, 1977
   Winner - Adam Elliot - *Harvey Krumpet*, 2003
   Nominees - Sejong Park, Andrew Gregory - *Birthday Boy*, 2004
   Nominee - Anthony Lucas - *The Mysterious Geographic Explorations of Jasper Morello*, 2005
   Winner - Shaun Tan - *The Lost Thing*, 2010.

ELVIS

159 mins
Director: *Baz Luhrmann*
Writers: *Baz Luhrmann, Sam Bromell, Craig Pearce, Jeremy Doner*
Cast: *Austin Butler, Olivia DeJonge, Tom Hanks, Helen Thomson, Richard Roxburgh, Kelvin Harrison Jr., David Wenham, Kodi Smit-McPhee, Luke Bracey, Dacre Montgomery, Leon Ford, Gary Clark Jr., Yola, Natasha Bassett, Xavier Samuel, Adam Dunn, Alton Mason, Shonka Dukureh*
Producers: *Gail Berman, Baz Luhrmann, Catherine Martin, Patrick McCormick, Schuyler Weiss*
Score: *Elliott Wheeler*
Cinematography: *Mandy Walker*
Editing: *Jonathan Redmond, Matt Villa*

At the 2022 AACTA Awards, *Elvis* won Best Film, Best Direction, Best Lead Actor in Film, Best Cinematography, Best Costume Design in Film, Best Editing in Film, Best Production Design in Film, Best Sound in Film, Best Supporting Actress in Film (Olivia DeJonge), Best Hair and Makeup (Shane Thomas, Louise Coulston, Mark Coulier, Jason Baird), and Best Visual Effects or Animation (Tom Wood, Fiona Crawford, Julian Hutchens, Josh Simmonds, Adam Hammond). It also received nominations for Best Original Score in Film, Best Casting (Nikki Barrett, Denise Chamian), Best Supporting Actor in Film (Tom Hanks), and Best Screenplay in Film.

INTERVIEW
FILMMAKER
CATHERINE MARTIN

There is no Baz Luhrmann without Catherine Martin. Their life-long creative and personal partnership has seen their films become institutions in their own right, with Baz's auterish-extravaganza style being elevated and amplified by that unique Catherine Martin touch. Martin is a nine-time Oscar nominee, and a four-time winner for her work on *Moulin Rouge!* (2001) and *The Great Gatsby* (2013). Their 2022 collaboration, *Elvis*, became one of their biggest productions yet with a budget of $US85 million. Shot in 2020 during COVID locked down Gold Coast, Queensland, *Elvis* was 'expected to employ 900 Queenslanders in behind-the-scenes roles'[1], and inject more than $AU105 million into the local economy.

Elvis turned the relatively unknown Austin Butler into an overnight star, with the film quickly received a global following, with one *Elvis*-faithful creating an 'Elvis Frame by Frame'[2] Twitter account.

Elvis was nominated for Best Motion Picture of the Year, Best Performance by an Actor in a Leading Role, Best Achievement in Cinematography, Best Achievement in Costume Design, Best Achievement in Makeup and Hairstyling (Mark Coulier, Jason Baird, Aldo Signoretti), Best Sound (David Lee, Wayne Pashley, Andy Nelson, Michael Keller), Best Achievement in Film Editing, and Best Achievement in Production Design (Catherine Martin, Karen Murphy, Beverley Dunn) at the Academy Awards.

This interview was recorded by Andrew F. Peirce in June 2022

There was a moment in the film when I momentarily forgot it was Austin on screen; I actually thought it was Elvis. That's how much he really sinks into the role.

Catherine Martin: I'm so happy because Austin put so many years of his life into lovingly interpreting Elvis' humanity that I'm so thrilled when that comes across and people are touched by it. That was tireless work and research. He's even got vestiges of the accent now. He really did a deep dive and was basically in character for two years.

ELVIS

Elvis had so many iconic suits and costumes that he wore. How do you bring that Catherine Martin touch to the Elvis attire?

CM: It starts with the story that Baz wants to tell and what his visual intent is, and how he wants to translate the story into images. My job is to do that, to listen to what he has to say and look at the images that he's torn out of magazines or done a scribble of and try and translate them into reality. To me, designing costumes is all about supporting the story. We're not telling a documentary, although we want lots of touchstones that bring the audience back to familiar images of Elvis.

It's a combination of approaches. In the *68 Special*, it's the reproduction of costumes. Albeit we discovered very early on that we couldn't just imitate, we needed to find a way of connecting the costume to Austin's interpretation. The changes were very subtle: pocket size, position, collar height, and jacket length. We weren't completely reimagining the black leather suit from the *68 Special*. Then there are other things like when he's having his last big confrontation with the Colonel in the car park. That suit is based on a suit that Elvis wore in the same year that the fictionalised scene is taking place and we've used a different fabric and a different colour to underline and to help tell the story.

There is a cinematic influence of Nightmare Alley on the production design. Can you talk about how you folded that into the production?

CM: *Nightmare Alley* was Colonel Tom Parker's favourite movie. He famously was a carny and toured carnivals in the 30s and 40s. That's kind of how he got into the country music business. It was Baz's idea to have the first real interaction between the Colonel and Elvis at the carnival, kind of in Colonel Tom Parker's comfort zone because - I mean, this is me saying it - it set him up as a kind of snake oil man, as the ultimate showman who could convince anyone of anything.

Nightmare Alley has a sort of parallel tale to some degree because it really is about the exploitation of somebody for their particular gifts at their great expense, and there certainly is a parallel in the relationship between Colonel Tom Parker and Elvis. I mean, their relationship was the struggle between the commercial and the artistic, and the toll that it can have on a performer. But at the same time, just like the geek gets the bottle of alcohol at the end of his performance, sometimes the association with the carnival lifted Elvis' career and it was beneficial to him.

ENDNOTES
1. Baz Luhrmann's Untitled Elvis Project to be filmed in Queensland: https://statements.qld.gov.au/statements/87227
2. @EveryElvis - https://twitter.com/EveryElvis

THE DROVER'S WIFE
The Legend of Molly Johnson

109 mins
Director: *Leah Purcell*
Writer: *Leah Purcell*
Cast: *Leah Purcell, Rob Collins, Sam Reid, Jessica De Gouw, Malachi Dower-Roberts, Jobe Zammit-Harvey, Nash Zammit-Harvey, Benedict Hardie, Amahlia Olsson, Magnolia Maymuru, Andrew Legg*
Producers: *David Jowsey, Angela Littlejohn, Leah Purcell, Greer Simpkin, Bain Stewart*
Composer: *Salliana Seven Campbell*
Cinematography: *Mark Wareham*
Editing: *Dany Cooper*

Leah Purcell won the Best Lead Actress in Film at the 2022 AACTA Awards. *The Drover's Wife: The Legend of Molly Johnson* also received nominations for Best Film, Best Direction in Film, Best Lead Actor in Film (Rob Collins), Best Supporting Actress in Film (Jessica De Gouw), Best Supporting Actor in Film (Malachi Dower-Roberts), Best Screenplay in Film, Best Hair and Makeup (Beth Halsted, Simon Joseph, Jennifer Lamphee), Best Cinematography, Best Original Score in Film, Best Costume Design in Film (Tess Schofield), Best Production Design in Film (Sam Hobbs), Best Sound in Film (Liam Egan, Nick Emond, Leah Katz, Robert Sullivan, Tom Heuzenroeder, Les Fiddess).

INTERVIEW
COMPOSER
SALLIANA SEVEN CAMPBELL

For Goa-Gungarri-Wakke Wakke Murri actor, writer, director Leah Purcell, rewriting Henry Lawson's The Drover's Wife was an act of reasserting the Indigenous perspective into a foundational white Australian text. In talking to The Guardian, Purcell said, "I wanted to find a new way of telling an old story, one that appreciates who we are as Australians, and one that is looking at our Indigenous Australian historical experience.[1]" For her feature debut film *The Drover's Wife: The Legend of Molly Johnson* (2022), an adaptation of her stage play of the same name, Purcell managed to flip the often colonially-focused Western genre on its head and transpose an Indigenous-focused narrative in its place.

For the score, Purcell and partner and creative collaborator, Bain Stewart, turned to multi-instrumentalist Salliana Seven Campbell to bring the score to this Meat Pie Western to life. Salliana work sees her performing with a five-string violin, nyckelharpa, octave mandolin, baritone bowed psaltery, piano, hammered dulcimer, or a hurdy gurdy. Salliana's score carries a level of swagger and heft that imbues the film with an earnest purpose that strengthens Molly Johnson's story as a woman surviving in isolation after her husband left one night to drove sheep on the high country.

This interview was recorded by Andrew F. Peirce in January 2023

When did you know that music is what you wanted to dedicate your life to?

Salliana Seven Campbell: It's crazy. I knew when I was five. People would say, 'What are you gonna be when you grow up?' I'm like, 'What do you mean?' I already am [what I want to be]. I could never see another way of doing something I didn't want to do. It seemed like insanity to go off and work somewhere. I've actually never had another job. I've just played music and gigs all my life.

My mum was a piano teacher and she also played in bands. I started playing in her bands when I was young. It was like a family bush band that sang transportation songs[2] and Irish and Scottish tunes. I also learned classical at the same time, too. I was really lucky that I had that ear experience and improvisation, as well as learning to read. Then I went to the Queensland Conservatorium of Music.

I just always knew [what I wanted to do]. I underestimated what a gift that was, when there are fully grown people now who don't know what they want to do.

Did you have a favourite instrument growing up?

SSC: I started on piano and was playing the Suzuki method, which was really popular through the eighties. That was all based on ear training. The premise was that if you have a child who can't read text, then why are you expecting them to read music? It was all based on listening, and you had these tapes that you would listen to before you went to sleep. Mum would put it on all the time. You listen and work the music out by ear rather than reading. It was designed for very small children, three- to five-year-olds, but I didn't start till I was seven. I started lessons on piano, not with my mum because I would boss her around, so she sent me somewhere else.

So I started on piano, and then my sister started playing the violin, she's really talented as well. The violin got me so bad. I was like, "Mum, I need a violin! I need a violin! You don't understand!" The Suzuki school was a lot of violin and a lot of piano. Mum said "No, you're gonna learn the piano and your sisters gonna learn the violin. One is enough." We did a bunch of other things: acting, horse riding, dancing; she had us in on everything, which was great so she could see what you liked.

I just wouldn't let it rest. So, for six weeks, every night, I begged, "I need one. I need one." It captured me. There's an older repertoire they played in the Suzuki method which was all of the Baroque stuff, Vivaldi, Corelli, Bach, Telemann, and I just loved it. So after six weeks, she bought me a violin. Then I did both the piano and the violin. I just ate it up. She would be like "You don't know when to stop practising. You don't know when to stop!"

How important was it for you to have your creativity supported by your mum?

SSC: It was my dad as well. My mum and dad both said "You're gonna be a musician. You don't have to have to fall back on anything." They just knew. I often think about my partner. He begged for a guitar, and his dad never got him one. I think, what if I was born into another family? I landed into such a good family.

INTERVIEW | SALLIANA SEVEN CAMPBELL

My dad was a patron of the arts. He's passed away now, but he actually got an Order of Australia Medal for all of his community work. He started a big music competition in Queensland. He funded the schools' music department, the art department, and put on art gallery showings. He was a real patron of the arts.

They drove me to the piano lessons all the time and bought me everything. Now you can just go on YouTube and learn so much. I had teachers, summer schools, instruments, and special workshops. They didn't doubt me. As soon as I left school, I went straight to the Conservatorium.

What was that experience like?

SSC: I wasn't a great reader of music, and in the orchestra, I was always running with a bow going the wrong way and getting lost. I value all of that because I practised really hard and [my playing] got better. The biggest thing I value about that experience is the people because you land yourself with a group of peers that are the people who want to do the same thing as you.

There were three other girls and we joined a band called Tulipan, which means tulip in Hungarian. We signed with Festival Records, played three international tours, and won a huge world music competition. I thought, "Oh, this is what you do. You just join a band and then you get grants and that kind of thing." When that disbanded, I realised I was really lucky, because we played at every major festival and received all this grant money to do things. We were just four talented female multi-instrumentalists. That was the part that I valued most.

That wasn't in a classical capacity at all, that was a World Music-fusion-folk band. The girl who led it, Virag Antel, played hurdy-gurdy, hammered dulcimer, and zither, which is what brought me to my love of these more obscure instruments that feature on the score for *The Drover's Wife*. We were chosen to go to Finland to find the world's 'best World Music band.' There were six bands from all over the world and the Swedish band there had a nyckelharpa. That's when I had a nyckelharpa made.

I loved the discipline of going to the Conservatorium. These days, you hardly ever get any one-on-one tuition. When I went through, there was so much one-on-one tuition. People come to some of these music courses now, the popular ones, and they can't even play an F major scale. I value all the techniques I had to do because they set me up. It wasn't like I ever wanted a career in classical music, but I do value that I can do both. I value all the people that I met there, but I never wanted to go that way. It wasn't where my strength was.

THE DROVER'S WIFE

I knew what my strength was right from the beginning. There was a real creative bent; I was always writing pieces on the piano. I wasn't so much a technician. I was more like, 'I hear this and I want to work it out,' 'I want to play with that person,' 'I want to play this style.' I was a lot more attracted to older folk styles, like gypsy, bluegrass, old-timey, Irish Scottish music. I am more into ear traditions, it was more exciting for me to hear something and work it out than to see it written on a page.

At what age were you writing your own music pieces?

SSC: Right from the very beginning. Our music teacher was really good because she would get you to write stuff every week. She would say, "Write a little melody for this." I was doing all of the Australian Music Examinations Board stuff, so there was lots of theory in there, so I understood all of that. I was really good at maths too, and I loved all of that theoretical stuff. I loved all the patterns. I was writing stuff from when I was a kid, mostly instrumental. I'm not so much a lyricist, although I have written a lot of songs, but I usually just write them and then I don't ever want to play them again. I just want to solve the puzzle.

One of the main themes from *The Drover's Wife* is actually a song and the words are gone. *Danny's Hope* and *Men's Business*. It has a few different titles, but it's the same piece that features a few times in the film.

What were the initial discussions you had with Leah and Bain like?

SSC: It was so exciting. One day this unknown number rang, and I don't ever usually answer them but for some reason I did and it was this girl saying, "There's this movie coming up that you've been recommended for. It's an Australian Western." A friend and colleague I work with in theatre who does sound design got offered it and he said "Oh no, you've gotta get Salliana, she'll be perfect for it." I wasn't actually talking to Leah and Bain at that stage, I was liaising with another girl, and she said there were five other people [in contention], and they were quite renowned composers. I don't know who they were. It took months for them to come to a decision.

When they did, they rang me and said, "We'd like to officially offer you the role as composer." I was like, "That's awesome, but it sounds like you're about to say, 'but.'" She said, "Yeah, but you need to give us one hour's worth of temp music. It can be from your old catalogue, it doesn't matter but it'll work in your favour, because we get temp artists, and we get so used to the temp track that it can be hard to put it in." I know some composers have in their contract that you can only use their temp music, even if it's music that gets replaced later. So, I went through all my stuff and thought 'None of this is right for it.'

INTERVIEW | SALLIANA SEVEN CAMPBELL

Right from the beginning Leah said, "I want something sparse, edgy, and non-melodic." I went, "No worries. I do mongrel and I can do edgy. I can do that." I knew she wanted this raw edge and she said that she wanted the electric guitar too. I said, "Look, if you want a big, sweeping orchestral thing, all schmicko, that's not going to be me. I can't give you that. There are a million people that are going to be able to do that heaps better." I don't like sitting on a computer. I felt like most of the scores that you hear, they're incredible. That would take me a year to do one minute of it with those huge, chromatic strings and sweeping horns and everything. [They're often] all done on virtual instruments. You listen to them, and you go, 'I cannot tell if that is real or not.' The quality of it is so good.

I said, "If you want that, go somewhere else, because with mine you'll hear me breathe. You'll hear my fingers on the piano. You'll hear the pedal noise. You'll hear everything." Everything I did was played by me and not edited. If I've got to edit something, I would rather just do it again. I hate fiddling around. It destroys my vibe.

My conversations with Leah and Bain felt so good and I trusted them so much that I went 'I'm just going to cancel my life for two weeks and just write.' I only had the screenplay, and I opened a different page every day and wrote music to that scene. At the end of the two weeks, I had 45 minutes of music that I handed in. When Leah said, 'Something sparse, edgy, non-melodic,' and I sent it back to her, and they put it up against some preliminary footage they had, it worked perfectly. It was uncanny that it fit with everything.

Right from the get-go we had a real connection. She's always really calm and asks the right questions. I never felt intimidated. I said to them, "You might want to get someone else because I've never done this before. I've never done a film before." I was completely honest because I knew her career and I know how talented she is. This was gonna be her debut film. I don't want to fuck it up for her. I think a lot of people were saying to her, "You really should get someone more experienced," which is really good advice. But she decided with her gut and went with me. The girl that I was talking to said, "Sister, whatever you're doing, keep doing it, because she loves it."

So, I sent it off and at the end of that two weeks, they hadn't filmed yet. It was months later that the final edit came back, and when it came back, they'd used everything. They'd used all the temp music that I'd done, and they used a lot of it in the places that I'd pictured it for. That made up about 60% of the film, and then the 40% had other people's music, so when it came back, I basically had 40% left to do. And that took a long time.

THE DROVER'S WIFE

I'm forever grateful to Leah and Dany Cooper (editor). In her youth, she was a violinist, so she wrapped her ears around every single melody and put it all in the right place. I had no idea that that wasn't up to me; with them cutting and editing to my music, they choose how long, where to use it, the style and the texture, everything. There were places where I went, "I don't think that should be like that. I think this is what we should be hearing," in a few cases. For the most of it, I was following their lead on it all. And when things didn't work, I was just so grateful for Leah's clarity.

It was really beautiful. I don't think that I'll get another perfect match like that. The story just ripped my heart out. I cried reading the script. I can't even watch the film now. It's too much like. If I watch something, I'll think about it forever. Obviously, I watched it so many times to do the music, and now it rips my heart out. For me, it's a story of a mother's love and I love my mum like nothing else.

Can you talk through what some of the instruments might represent in a narrative sense?

SSC: The thinking was that there would be music and instruments that would have been heard in that era, except for the electric guitar. All of that background came through to feel that era; you could imagine banjolins and hurdy-gurdies everywhere. They were tunes they would have heard then, like those folk transportation songs and Irish and Scottish tunes. Molly's father was of Scottish stock, so there was the Scottish song *Black is the Colour*. *Men's Business* was a track for an initiation process that happens with Danny (Malachi Dower-Roberts) and Yadaka (Rob Collins). It used the octave mandolin, which is a 12-string instrument that's an octave lower than a normal mandolin. *Danny's Hope* and *Men's Business* was centred around that, and Leah really wanted the electric guitar in there.

Rather than using anything electronic, like any big virtual instrument sounds, I wanted it all to be raw and real, because the film was so raw and so real. With the hurdy-gurdy you can turn the wheel, and it can increase intensity, so as I was watching it, I could increase it by giving the wheel more speed, so that was a beautiful way to create all these drones. I gave them to Liam Egan who was the sound designer so that he could use some of them throughout the film. I think there were maybe 18 instruments used; there's the nyckelharpa, there's zither, there's hammered dulcimer, and they're all instruments that I play here. I recorded it all in my room.

Is it right that you played all of the instruments?

SSC: Except for the double bass. Andrew Johnson, my dear colleague and friend, played the double bass. I played the electric guitar solo, and the other electric guitar part with my other friends David McGuire and David Logan. Most of it was me playing. I love a lot more obscure string things, I don't really delve into any woodwind or brass. So, it was pretty much all strings and a lot of hammered dulcimer, which was recorded for the resonance of it.

I did it all in my little room, which had a bed that I would pull out so I could have the piano in my bedroom because it was too noisy in the other room. It's a tiny little apartment in Kangaroo Point in Brisbane, and I recorded it all in there on just one microphone. People ask me what I did with the fiddle, and I let them know I close-miked it. They loved that they could hear me breathe, and probably hear me bleed. They could hear me cry.

When I spoke to them, I said "Look, I can't meet the technical requirements, that's going to do my head in." Daniel Denholm is a long-standing colleague of mine who has done a lot of the mixing, production, and recording, and he was the mix engineer. I was like, "I can't do that," so I sent him everything raw. I didn't do any compression or reverb or anything, I just sent it to him raw and he mixed it and put it into the surround sound.

There's a physicality to some of the instruments you play, like winding up the hurdy-gurdy, that's reflected in the music that you play. Can you talk about how much of yourself you put into playing?

SSC: My fingers aren't used to using the banjo pick, so I would just use my fingers. The sound of the banjo pick wasn't what I wanted, so my fingers would bleed from the banjo and doing lots of pizzicato as well. I could play the fiddle and the piano forever, but the electric guitar or the bass are not the normal instruments that I would play, I would only use them to record.

I think it was maybe a three-month turnaround after the final edit had been done, so I worked. I didn't stop thinking about it. I'd wake up and start doing it. I'd do 12-hour days. I wanted it to be the best it could be and to give it my best shot. I knew that this was really special. I'm a bit of a sensitive soul, and sometimes you can get treated badly, and that just makes me want to run a mile, but Leah and Bain were so good to me, and it just made me want to work as hard as I could. I have so much respect for them. I didn't take a day off and worked around the clock. I was putting in the long hours which would mean my elbow and my shoulder would get sore, but it was all worth it. I didn't care that my fingers were bleeding, I just wanted to get the part right for Leah, because the story is so much about her real family.

One of the aspects I appreciate about the score is how you can imagine Molly's movement just by listening to it. You can see her swagger and the

THE DROVER'S WIFE

weight she carries when you close your eyes. It creates her presence brilliantly. Can you talk about creating the character of Molly in the score?

SSC: I didn't think about it all too much. Like I said, I just read and then I wrote. I knew that my style was in line with what Leah wanted so I didn't really have to try. That was already there. I knew that the language and the flavours Leah loved already. I'm not too cerebral about it. They gave me the gig, I read it and then I did it.

Molly is so raw and real and has so much heart. I felt like the violin needed to not be washed out. I wanted to hear the rawness of it all. They had something completely different in mind from the temp music for the first scene where she's pregnant, it created a different vibe. I went 'No, this has got to be Molly's theme.' That was one thing that I really fought for. I was so adamant that that was hers.

I've done a lot of theatre, and a lot of that has been me as a live musician in the theatre. I record backing tracks with all my instruments, and then that gets [played] through the theatre and I play live to that. A lot of the time I will be watching a character and playing them. I did this production of *Grimm Tales*, and I was playing all the birds and the goat. To play in the theatre, it has to be non-intrusive, it has to be complementary and to support what is going on. I find that's a strength of mine.

I'm never the lead person, I'm always the side person. When I play String Quartet, I play second violin. I want to play harmony. I want to play the rhythm. I want to play support. I feel like when you are in those middle parts, you've got to be listening all the time. You're not just listening to your own part, you're super aware of everything around you. I feel like all the work I've done with the theatre has helped with this score. Some people say they don't even really hear the music when they watch *The Drover's Wife*, and I think that's awesome because it's just supporting the story.

I want to talk about the working relationships that you choose to have, whether it's with artists like Bernard Fanning or Alex Lloyd, or with Leah whose work is integral to her own history. How do you choose which people you want to work with?

SSC: I have to get a real 'Yes' in my heart. I just can't do stuff now that I'm not gonna resonate with for their and my sake. It's like you'll get people ringing you saying, "Can you play violin on this thing?" I could fake it, but you should get this person who lives and breathes that and it's their passion. I would rather be the right person for it because that's where I get the most inspiration from. If I don't like a song, it's really hard for me to drag my way through it. It's like pollution for my ears, because I'm gonna have to listen to the track over and over and over again. You just know from the get-go whether you like something or not. It's an easy decision for me.

I don't want to be in something just for money. My currency has always been to move people; if they come up to me, and you can see their sincerity and feel that I've touched them, that's worth everything. For me to be aligned with that I need to do things that resonate with me. That ends too. That's not forever. When something's finished, it's finished. I always say I love something until I don't love it anymore. I think a lot of people overstay things, but in the same vein, I'll go, 'This isn't me anymore. I'm gonna go.' It doesn't have to be a bad horrible thing. It's just like, 'That chapter is finished. I loved doing that, but now it's time to go do something else.' I'm not gonna sit and eat the same food all the time and go 'I really like this,' and then never question if you don't like it anymore. It's a very intuitive thing where I can just feel if something's not right anymore, or if I'm not in the right place. I always tell people 'Follow the spark' because the spark is your blueprint of where it's supposed to take you, and if you follow something else, it almost writes its own thing. What catches our attention is part of our personality. That's different for every person. For me, it's simple when I know what I like.

[I want] to be treated well. I don't really care about if you're gonna get all of this for free, or get major sponsorship, or this many people are going to see you here, I'd rather play music I love to ten people than be on a huge stage playing something I don't want to do. I love supporting people. I love singing harmonies and I'm a good harmony singer, but I don't have a lead singer voice, and having worked with Kate Miller Heidke and Russell Morris and Alex Lloyd and Bernard Fanning, they're born with that, they can sing. People always ask, "Why don't you go and do your own thing?" I'm like, "Because I don't have that voice." I can sing but know your strengths.

ENDNOTES

1. Interview: Leah Purcell on reinventing The Drover's Wife three times: 'I borrowed and stole from each' https://www.theguardian.com/books/2019/dec/22/leah-purcell-on-reinventing-the-drovers-wife-three-times-i-borrowed-and-stole-from-each
2. Transportation songs were a genre of ballads focused on the transportation of convict criminals to either the American or Australian colonies.

WHERE IS MY DARLING?

21 mins
Director: *Adam Finney*
Featuring: *Lanz Priestley*
Producer: *Adam Finney*
Music: *Daniel O'Brien*
Cinematography: *Cameron Dunlop*
Editing: *James Taylor*
Sound: *Nathan Turnbull*

INTERVIEW
DIRECTOR & PRODUCER
ADAM FINNEY

Adam Finney's short film *Where is My Darling?* (2022) follows Lanz Priestley, a charismatic homeless man who only has a phone and a Facebook page to his name. When Lanz hears that the drought-stricken outback has no drinking water, he organises his community to help deliver water to them. Lanz was known as the leader of 'tent city' in Sydney's Martin Place, and in 2017, he and dozens of other homeless people were evicted from the site. While Lanz lived with stage four prostate cancer, he helped establish Sydney's 24-7 Street Kitchen and Safe Space Community at Martin Place, which served meals and provided a safe space for the city's rough sleepers.

Whether it be as a director or a producer, Finney's work continually explores Australian social issues that are often talked about, but rarely directly addressed: toxic masculinity, homelessness, climate change. With *Where is My Darling?*, Finney explores the homelessness crisis, which has only gotten worse since he shot the film, and the impact of climate change. Adam Finney worked as a producer on David Robinson-Smith's *Mud Crab* (2022), a film which details the brutal masculinity in a small Australian coastal town.

This interview was recorded by Andrew F. Peirce in December 2022

You're working with editor James Taylor. How do you work together to pare back Lanz's story so that it maintained the honesty and the truth of his reality? You manage to distil so much emotion into a short runtime.

Adam Finney: It's one of the hard things about documentary filmmaking. You're embedded in somebody's life, learning about it, but then you need to translate that reality into a story structure. So, setting up the audience, and then releasing the information that punches is definitely part of it.

It starts from the script writing process. I start with a script, and that script is largely made up, but it's based on the person's life. I get to know them and I'm there with them. For instance, with the water runs, we knew that we had beats that we had to cover, so I would write a fictional example of what I expected to capture. Of course, when we went out with Lanz, things were just so wild and unpredictable that they would be completely different, but we find different places within that script, and then rewrite it into what really happened.

Then it would all change again once we got into the post-production. We'd find what I'd written was different to how things would come together, so then James and I would have notepads and we would restructure the film in different ways to make the story flow. It was a process of constant rewriting, but also making sure that we remained authentic and truthful to the reality that was taking place as well.

Was it always to be a short film?

AF: It started as a three-minute film which I used as a proof of concept. I needed to build trust with Lanz. Lanz didn't know me. I contacted him over Facebook. The first time he let me come and film him, he asked me to meet him in Bourke, about 800 km west of Sydney. When I met him he told me, "You can film me but don't ask me to do anything, and stay out of my way." I knew that I wouldn't have much access to him at this point because he was working, so we wrote a film that was very stylistic. That was just to observe him and to get this message about the water out, and to also give us the proof of concept to show that we could make something bigger, and still also prove to Lanz that we were trustworthy and that we have the same goals. This film was a proof of concept for a feature film. I didn't know it was going to be a short, the goal was always to make a bigger film with Lanz.

Lanz has a strong and clear concept of what his goal is as an activist helping the community. As a documentarian capturing somebody like that on screen, does that help your narrative in being able to stress what his goal is, as well as having somebody who is captivating and engaging?

AF: There's a lot about who I am. I was talking to my granddad, and he said, "I see a lot of you in that film." There's part of my dad in Lanz, there's a part of my mum, and there's a part of who I want to be in Lanz. I think [Lanz] also saw that similarity in me, so when it came to collaborating with him, we had that shared message and understanding.

We both want to make a change in this world, but we both have different platforms for doing it. Mine has been as a filmmaker where I can find people like Lanz and amplify his story. Whereas his was on the ground. Ultimately, that's why he let me in because he knew that I had the same passion as him. That came through in a lot of ways. I slept where Lanz would sleep as I would have to follow him on a whim. Lanz brought me food when my dad passed away and while I was in quarantine. We became really close. I think that close relationship is essential for a documentary of this nature.

There is that objective quality to filmmaking and some people might feel that having a close relationship with the subject might jeopardise the storytelling. Can you explore that thought?

AF: It's an interesting question that I grappled with a lot in making the film. It was the issue early on where I couldn't let my respect for him overwhelm the greater story. What makes a story fantastic is to show the warts and all, that not everybody's perfect. Lanz had a lot of warts as well. [There was] the understanding that what we're both trying to do is bigger than ourselves. To explore Lanz deeply and to not let that love for him take over, while making a good story that's objective and fair, is what we both wanted. There's a shared trust there. I'm not exploiting him. I've got interviews and interviews with him, and he told me some quite traumatic stories about his [parents], things that I won't say here because they're not in the film. He told me a lot and trusted me with a lot. I'm happy with the balance that we struck to still keep it authentic.

It shows the desperate nature of the Australian environment too. Annually, we're living through extreme weather events, whether it's drought, floods, bushfires. Was that a key theme that you were interested in exploring?

AF: That was the biggest thing. People would say, "It's just a film about drought." I'd say, "No it's not a film about the drought. This is not a film about the fires." Wherever we were to pick up Lanz and put him where there was an issue, he would have worked on that right now. There was the message of climate change, it doesn't matter if it's droughts, it doesn't matter if it's bushfires, it doesn't matter if it's floods. It's sending the message that our world is rapidly changing, and if you think somebody should do something about something, then remember, you are somebody. That was the key message of the film I wanted people to leave with.

That's something that Lanz mentions about signing petitions. We think that that helps, but it's putting the ownership on somebody else to implement change. It's a distanced way of helping, yet it's not really doing anything. It's the salient reminder of how we engage in support with one another. As we see with Lanz's journey, here is somebody who has got almost nothing in the world, but he's giving everything.

AF: He literally had just a bag and a phone. I was with Lanz the day before he passed away, and he was sitting there on his phone the entire time. A lot of this is during COVID, and what he ended up doing after the film is with a lot of the homeless community in Sydney who were taken off the streets

WHERE IS MY DARLING?

and put into temporary housing where they ended up in houses with no fridges or [furniture]. It was so hastily done that they had no facilities.

The day before Lanz passed away he was up in the Northern Rivers. He couldn't walk anymore, but he was still on the phone organising people back in Sydney, through Facebook, to go and pick up a couch over here and take it there. 'Look after this family who can't afford food, they can't leave the house because they're stuck in lockdown.' He was managing his little army of people to keep doing things. I didn't know it then, but I knew something was up. He was literally working until the minute he passed away.

How did you change as a person during the filming experience?

AF: I think everybody who knew Lanz and who was close to him would say that there's a bit of Lanz in them now. He was so unique in the way that he saw the world, but then also active within the world and was so vastly different from anything that we see. It was such a beautiful outlook, that once you see something, and you know how something can be done, it's impossible to go to unsee it. I think Lanz blessed us, and hopefully, it comes through enough in the film, that he showed us another way of doing things. It's a mind-frame that's so vastly different from what we hear about anywhere else. That's stuck with me. I feel like Lanz has set a standard for the sorts of subjects that I look for in my films.

With Where Is My Darling? and Mud Crab, your work focuses on social issues. One is community support, and the other is toxic masculinity. What draws you to look at the world this way?

AF: I produced *Mud Crab* and the director, David Robinson-Smith, grew up in the Central Coast, and being an artist in that area was quite hard. It's that idea of trying to do something a little bit different and being pulled down [in the process]. With Lanz or with *Mud Crab*, these are people who are living on the fringes of society, they often see the world in very unique ways, and they have a lot to teach the world, but the world wants to pull them down. Lanz never got pulled down and that's why he's such a powerful person, but there are so many people out there who have grown up in communities that support and foster that sort of creativity. We lose a lot of beautiful talent. The correlation would be in that sort of space.

Where do you see your career going forward?

AF: Ultimately, especially within the documentary space, I see my job as raising awareness. Influencing culture in a positive way and shining a light on places that don't have much light shined on them. I feel like when I look ahead, it's not an easy job where I want to go and what I want to do.

I'm only just at the beginning of it, but it's also such an important job because I see these things happening all around. Over time, we forget and lose things, and the job of a filmmaker or a journalist or a musician is to shine that light. That's where I see it in terms of style and themes. I've got my eyes on some quite heavy subjects at the moment, but I also want to make them for audiences as well.

Does the Australian identity play into your work? Is that important to you as a filmmaker?

AF: I grew up mainly in Australia, I moved over here [from New Zealand] when I was ten. Being Australian is such a complex space. As an Australian, I have a lot of work to do here in terms of the healing side of things, especially within this industry, and our Indigenous past and our colonial past. There's a lot of work to do there. Growing up in this beautiful land gives you such a special outlook on the world. I find that invaluable.

SISSY

102 mins
Directors: *Hannah Barlow, Kane Senes*
Writers: *Hannah Barlow, Kane Senes*
Cast: *Aisha Dee, Hannah Barlow, Emily De Margheriti, Daniel Monks, Yerin Ha, Lucy Barrett, Shaun Martindale, April Basdall, Camille Cumpston, Amelia Lule, Louise Barlow, Victoria Hopkins*
Producers: *John De Margheriti, Bec Janek, Lisa Shaunessy, Jason Taylor*
Composer: *Kenneth Lampl*
Cinematography: *Steve Arnold*
Editing: *Margi Hoy*

In 2022, *Sissy* received nominations for Best Film, Best Lead Actress in Film (Aisha Dee), and Best Direction in Film at the AACTA Awards.

INTERVIEW
CO-DIRECTORS & WRITERS HANNAH BARLOW & KANE SENES

Hannah Barlow and Kane Senes influencer-focused horror flick *Sissy* (2022) turned heads when it debuted at the South By South West film festival in Austin, Texas in 2022, and went on to receive international acclaim at festivals like Sitges, where it won the Midnight X-Treme Audience Award, and The Overlook Film Festival where it also received the Audience Award.

Sissy tells the story of Cecilia (Aisha Dee), a wellness guru who has a massive online following giving advice to strangers. A chance encounter with childhood friend and bride-to-be Emma (Hannah Barlow) sees Cecilia receiving a last-minute invite to Emma's bachelorette weekend away in the bush. Little does Cecilia know, her childhood bully Alex (Emily De Margheriti), is also along for the ride. Bloody chaos ensues as Cecila clashes with Emma's friends, causing a rapidly increasing body count to follow.

This interview was recorded by Andrew F. Peirce in June 2022

You work together as script writers and in directing. Where do you start your creative process?

Hannah Barlow: We watch a bunch of reference films after we determine what story we want to tell. "This is what we have to say about the world. These are the characters that are brewing. This is the story that's brewing." Then we start debating what kind of film we want to make until we arrive at the same point. That process doesn't take very long because we have a lot of the same ideas, passions, and sensibilities. It feels like jamming in a garage, like being a bit of a two-person band, just trying to figure it out.

Kane Senes: With *Sissy*, we said "We know we want to make a horror film that plays on the 'cabin in the woods' thing, and that probably is a satire. We know we want it to be funny, and we know we want it to feel like those movies that we love." It's coming from the macro down to the micro, and then getting more specific. If this is the genre space, if this is the world, then who is our main character? What are the themes? Themes will sometimes start first. It usually goes big to small, in many ways, as opposed to "I saw this person sitting in a cafe and I wrote a script about what I thought that person was doing that day." It starts in an ambiguous vague visual sense. It usually starts from a place of the film-buffery of it all. Then we realise, "Okay, at some point, we have to put words on a page here and stop just watching films and talking about cool ideas."

HB: Then we do the general Blake Snyder method. You put the cards up on the wall and change them around and then the vomit draft and tweaking from there for however many months.

What were the films you used as reference points for Sissy?

HB: *Carrie* (1976) is a huge reference. Kane took me through a lot of the Seventies, Eighties, and nineties slashers that we all know like *Halloween* (1978), *Friday the 13th* (1980), *Scream* (1995), and the giallo.

KS: I felt like I was showing Hannah a lot of genre material and a lot of slashers and Hannah was showing me things that I might have seen but are not my reference, comedies like *Bridesmaids* (2011) or *Mean Girls* (2004). *Carrie* was one of those weird ones, almost where we met in the middle where it's the 'mean girl high school film meets a horror film.'

HB: The North Star for *Sissy* is *Muriel's Wedding* (1994). If Muriel started seeking revenge on the high school bullies at the midpoint, we wouldn't be able to make *Sissy* because it would have already been made.

KS: It really was. I think *Muriel's Wedding* is great because I don't feel like the rest of the world knows that film as much as Australians. We grew up with it on TV every week.

HB: I feel like we couldn't escape that movie growing up, it was playing every Friday night. You'd get sick of it. We returned to it in the writing of *Sissy* and we're like "Wow, this is actually one of the most horrifying films I've ever seen." It's dark, but it's pitched as this broad comedy.

How did you straddle that line of creating that darkness in the comedy that works so well?

HB: I think that was the main challenge of making *Sissy*. We were working towards that the entire process. I'm glad to hear that you think that we've pulled it off.

KS: It started with saying, "Let's make a horror film," and from that going, "What scares us?" and talking about social media and the notion of the influencer as someone influencing a lot of young minds especially. Who put them there? What qualifies them to be in that position? It's like this power that's been thrust into our hands, which is our phones, social media and the internet. Anyone can make themselves into anything with just a phone if they want and that's a loaded weapon.

It started from there, the horror of it all, then very soon, it went into *Muriel's Wedding*, *Bridesmaids*, *Mean Girls*. As soon as we realised that it was about someone who was bullied when they were younger and carries that trauma around with them and hasn't addressed it and then it comes out on this weekend when she's faced with the trigger, once we knew we had that setting for her, we thought "Okay, it's an underdog story about a girl who is being harassed by bullies, both in the past and also present day."

HB: She's trying to reclaim her power. That's the trajectory of her character. We also took real-life inspiration from the inherent sort of ironic comedy of real-life con artist Belle Gibson, who is an Australian icon. She's taking advantage of one of the most vulnerable communities in Australia, cancer [patients], and profiting from them, and getting exposed and denying it. It's tragic, but it's also inherently funny.

KS: It's so crazy it's funny in an 'I can't believe it' way. We're seeing more and more of these kinds of individuals in the news all around every day. The world feels like it's getting more and more insane because everyone has a mouthpiece.

HB: Anybody can slip through the cracks and proselytise whatever they want without having a professional degree, and people that shouldn't [do] follow them, and that's really dangerous. But it's also really, really funny.

How did you both start your journey into filmmaking?

KS: I started in a pretty classic way. It wasn't growing up with the 8mm [camera] in my hand or whatever. I always loved the arts, I was always into painting, I was always into writing creatively, and I was always into acting. It wasn't until uni that I saw that "You actually can put all these things together in the format of film." I was always a film buff, my parents could never pull me out of the video store fast enough. I never really thought of it as something you could do. When I discovered film studies at UNSW, I quickly fell in love with it and decided I needed to go to film school. I was fortunate enough to go straight to LA and go to a film school there. Shout out New York Film Academy (NYFA) in Universal City. That's when it all exploded for me. That's when I was like, "There's this whole world there."

All these classmates were making short films together, and you're driving past the studios every day, watching movies all the time, sharing things, voraciously taking it all in. It's been a never-ending film class ever since.

HB: I came into the filmmaking arena as an actor. I went to NIDA and did the three-year BFA course as an actor and then moved over to LA, and that's where I met Kane. Growing up, I never even permitted myself to think I could be a writer and director because, in the nineties and the early 2000s, it was a man's arena. It just never occurred to me that that's something I could strive for, [even though] acting was.

[I] got to LA and did the whole struggling actor thing, booking some jobs, waiting around. Kane and I fell in love and then we started to go "We could make things together instead of waiting for the industry to push us along." So, in the vein of Mark Duplass, Joe Swanberg, and Lynn Shelton, that class of mumblecore filmmakers who made things for nothing on micro budgets, we decided to make *For Now* (2019), which is a road trip mumblecore dramedy about my brother and me. My brother is a professional ballet dancer and so the film's premise is we drive to San Francisco to audition for the San Francisco Ballet Company because I want him to live in America with me as an actor. It was like a blurring between fiction and reality. We shot it in seven days, we improvised the whole thing on a treatment that was all possible because of the twenty-five grand we raised on Kickstarter.

It was grassroots guerrilla-style filmmaking, we had no permits. Because of that experience, Kane and I realised that we liked working together so we moved back to Australia to take advantage of the government incentives here. We wrote *Sissy* and now we're here and I've fallen in love with writing and directing. I'm still learning so much.

Hannah, you're wearing multiple hats in this film: co-lead, co-writing, co-directing. How did you manage to balance all those roles at once?

HB: I'm very lucky that I'm in a co-directing partnership with Kane, and that we can lean on Kane's talent and tenacity and the skillset that he forged at NYFA. I'm still growing into that aspect of directing. I was fortunate enough to be in the trenches with the actors with costumes and makeup, and I got to start every day with those departments. Kane would wrangle the crew and be with the camera. Because I was acting 80% of the time, we had to trust each other. I think it worked out.

KS: It was kind of fly by the seat of our pants, figuring it out as we went because we had done *For Now* together. That was just four people in a car driving along, stopping off, getting the camera out, and shooting something. Here we had a film crew, a location shoot where we had to zip around with just outside cameras. It was a tight schedule, and we were trying to pull off a lot of practical effects and all kinds of things. I don't think we realised what we had signed up for but that's filmmaking. You figure it out as you go. I don't think it ever gets easy.

KS: As Hannah was saying, she would start the day with one department, I'd start today with another department, and that's how we prepped the film in essentially ten days. We basically had two directors working double shifts.

HB: The jamming in the garage gets harder and there are more band members. The directing isn't just production. Kane and I get to do our beautiful little writing bubble for a long time.

KS: It really starts with the writing. I feel like our ability to direct starts with the writing because we know it so well.

HB: We're talking about how we're going to direct a shot as we're putting it on the page, which is fun. Then we get to jam with our editor Margi Hoy for a couple of months. That's its own beautiful little process where the three of us are trying to turn what we've got in the can into this other thing. That's my favourite part of the whole process, creating something new from those pieces.

Can you run through the timing for the production process?

KS: We had a bit of development time which might have been say, us producers, maybe a couple of weeks with a cinematographer. It was only about eleven days of paid pre-production. We moved to Canberra, set up shop, were looking for our locations, welcomed actors, did rehearsals, storyboarding, essentially all that stuff in two weeks. That's why it was lightning fast. We were very lucky that the people we made the film with were experienced, more experienced than we were, so we leant on a lot of that experience. Steve Arnold who shot the film, has shot over thirty Australian features from *Last Cab to Darwin* (2015), *Rams*, back to some of the great Aussie films from the Eighties and Nineties even. Larry Van Duynhoven did all our practical effects, makeup, prosthetics and all that stuff.

HB: I would go into the room, and Renate Henschke, the costume designer, would ask, "What do you think about this?" She was such a genius at what she does. It was like, "That's it. You got the character." We didn't have to stretch ourselves too much because these people were giving us that talent. Michael Price, our production designer, put together Cecilia's apartment in like a day or something crazy like that. He was like, "What do you want me to do?" We're like, "Honestly, we don't have time to think about this. Can you please go ahead and spray your genius everywhere?" And he did. We walked on set and we're like, "This looks like a proper multi-million-dollar production design."

KS: We got very lucky with who we worked with. Ultimately the director's job, you've got to keep reminding people of the movie that you're making. There are so many options for everyone's choice, so as long as you point people in the direction or give them a good reference, they can go off and do amazing things because they're all so experienced and talented.

A film can live or die on the quality of the practical effects. Sissy leans into the gore and the severity of violence. Can you talk about the creation of those practical effects? There were moments where I wanted to pause and enjoy the squeamishness of it all.

KS: I'm so chuffed that you're the kind of guy that would pause an image of an exploding head. That's exactly what I do. When I watch these films from the Eighties, when there's a great practical effect, I'm always that guy who rewinds it, goes frame by frame and tries to understand how they did it. I've always loved the craft of real hands-on filmmaking, figuring out how to make something look the right way in front of the camera with whatever you have on hand. I love a good Marvel movie, as anybody does, but I am getting a little fatigued by the number of effects [in them]. Even though we've leant on the effects in many ways, they were usually just to amplify or smoothen the practical effects, or to do something that we didn't have time for like lightning striking through the sky.

HB: Or like a bullet.

KS: There was a lot of wonderful use of VFX. Our VFX coordinator Seth Larney did a lot of them by hand himself, which is remarkable. With Larry and his practical effects, it was just as simple as saying, "We want to do an exploding head in this movie. We're coming at it from this perspective or angle." He'd say, "Great. What helps is if you shoot it this way and not that way, because then we can do this or then we can do that." It was the same with Seth and VFX.

The ability to have those people on hand and say, "It says in the script that this body falls off a cliff, right? How are we going to pull that off? Are we going to do that with a stuntman? Are we going to do that with a dummy? Are we going to rotoscope an actor or do a 3d scan of an actor?" Which is what we ended up doing. We always start with how do we do this practically? If you can't do it practically, then you entertain how it can be done on the computer or how it can be done with a mix. What you end up with is a product of compromise of the original vision but not in a bad way, just tweaking things here or there, it's a mix of practical and VFX things that are always a product of their time and schedule.

In our case, we got a lot more bang for our buck than we should have because of Larry and Seth. We got to go into the creature workshop now and then and see how an actor's face had turned into a mould or how they'd started to insert all the individual hairs. "Geez, Larry, you're individually feeding these strands of hair, and we're just going to drive over this head tomorrow in one take." We can't take credit for any of that because they're the ones who did it.

HB: Larry and the boys at Scarecrew Studios are so talented.

This is the kind of film that you recommend to gorehounds because somebody's head gets run over. It's a weird thing to recommend somebody to go and see a movie for, but it's appropriate.

KS: Thank you very much for that. I think a lot of it is how much you are invested in those characters that get killed. If you watched the clips by themselves on YouTube, I wonder if it has the same effect. This was kind of a by-product of our last film which was just about this small group of friends that go on a road trip. We always said "We get to know these people and you feel like you're one of their friends. Imagine if everyone started getting killed off now in this movie in the second half." That kind of led us to "Why don't we write that next time?"

I think for us, it always came from [a viewpoint of] we want to love all these people, but not necessarily in a standard archetypal way. Like the group of friends in all slasher movies, right? Some are better than others. In *Scream*, it's wonderfully meta and they're teaching you the rules about the genre, but normally, there's the jock, the cheerleader, the nerd, so when they get killed off, you're not necessarily that emotionally invested because you never really got to know them in the first place. They just feel these tropes in your head that you've seen before. I think if you hang with the group and they're people that you might not have seen that much of on-screen or especially in that configuration or with those relationships, they're modern in that sense.

HB: Not very likable, though.

KS: Somewhat unlikable, which I guess helps it. It helps you like Cecilia [Aisha Dee] more. They have to at least feel real enough as people so that when they get killed, the actual kill scene feels like a bigger deal than just the practical effects because you're invested.

SISSY

HB: I think the kills are where lies that struggle for balance between horror and comedy because these characters are not characters that you see get killed off all the time. It's uncomfortable and you are approaching the line. We worked hard to make sure that you didn't like them but also that you were not comfortable with laughing when they died. Or laughing but being like, "Oh my god, am I a terrible person for wanting to see this person die?"

How did you cast Aisha and work with her to create what is a very complicated and conflicted person?

HB: I was a big fan of Aisha on *The Bold Type* (2017-21). There's this huge Australian fanbase apparently, that she wasn't aware of. I also remember her from *The Saddle Club* (2008-09). I've been following her work, and we reached out to her, and we had one conversation with her where she said, "I am Cecilia, I am this person, I know her because I am her." We bonded over similar childhood bullying experiences. It was just clear that she was the role. We were right to cast her because she elevated what we wrote, and that's the dream as writers. Then also as directors, she's such a pro because of the amount of experience she's had on set. She was able to nail that performance in under two takes because of how quickly we were moving. She makes us look really good as directors because it was really all her. I'm just a big fan of Aisha. I think she's got a huge career ahead of her and we're lucky that we grabbed her now.

KS: You wonder what the film would have been if we had not found her, because she just had such a specific take on that character. Even when she would have a more out-there idea, we always just loved it. We were always, "Yes, do that," and it always made us laugh behind the monitor. You keep expecting 'Maybe she's going to be wrong on one of the calls,' but she never was. As wanky as it sounds, it was like she was birthing the character in front of us. We had a lot of fun watching that and forgetting what we had written. There was the blueprint for each day, but there was this whole extra wonderful layer of unpredictability and fun bubble gum, but then also kind of hard to watch losing her mind to insanity.

HB: In terms of that tone of horror and comedy but also seeing someone have a breakdown, Aisha really brought that intuitively as a performer and that's what I mean about her elevating our material. It could have been too much of a satire where that balance wouldn't have worked. We were very lucky to have had her as the lead.

I want to talk about the song choice as well, Sister by Sister2Sister. How did you come up with that?

HB: When I was eight or nine, we were heading towards the Sydney Olympics. It's this huge cultural shift for Australia. That song was huge at the time, alongside Nikki Webster and that whole era of 'evil pop', Australian pop which was so funny. My best friend Molly and I used to dance to that and choreograph routines for hours on end. It was important to me that that song was in the film because it's so twee in an uncomfortable way, it just works. It's like David Michôd's *The Rover*. He uses that song, Keri Hilson's *Pretty Girl Rock*, and it's really twee. I remember watching it at the time, thinking that works because it was in contrast to the tone of the movie. It's got that same evil pop feeling. I just wanted to make the audience squirm a little bit.

It gave me flashbacks of The Loved Ones with Not Pretty Enough by Kasey Chambers.

HB: That was a reference.

KS: Yes, that definitely was one that we watched. Our film is not about a prom, but there was such a wonderful Eighties prom aesthetic to that horror film which I thought was awesome. We looked at that and said, "What's a millennial version of that?" I still hold that right up there as one of the best horror comedies, if you can call it a comedy. It's darkly comedic, but I love that kind of stuff.

What does it mean to be Australian filmmakers, especially Australian horror filmmakers?

KS: It's funny because yes if you look at the numbers, it seems that we don't make a lot of genre films. Yet we've got so many of these classics that if you ask diehard horror fans anywhere around the world they know about them. I'm not just talking about recent things like *The Babadook* (2014) [but] going back to like *Razorback* (1984) or *Wake in Fright* (1971) which got re-released, one of only two films to play at Cannes twice. *Wolf Creek* (2005), obviously.

Someone wrote about *Sissy* and said something like, "Man, Australians are really fucked up.[1]" I got more out of that than probably anything I had read, or anyone had said about the film. Just to even scratch the surface of that rich history that we have of these deliriously messed up horror films, like *The Loved Ones*, that makes you kind of want to vomit and laugh at the same time.

HB: I think that's all in response to our own fucked up nuanced history that we don't sit very comfortably with. If we as filmmakers can kind of point at that in what we're doing, that's the goal, I guess.

SISSY

KS: We're so far away, and we all grew up almost feeling like we exist on our own little island, which we do. If you want to shout across the seas, you've really got to shout. I think a lot of Australian filmmakers have made some bold choices, whether it be the tone of the film or the music or the colour or the subject matter, how far they go with the gore, how far they go with the laughs in the same film.

To me, I think being an Australian or being Australian horror filmmaker – or at least as far as *Sissy*, it might not be all we ever do – but that means almost more to me than just saying 'Australian filmmakers.' I think it's very cool to be Australian filmmakers on the international scene. But when you make genre films, you're always thinking niche, you're always thinking about that wonderful wacky world no one else looks at. Now there's more of an appetite for it since comic book films went big, the whole kind of 'revenge of the nerds' that we're seeing in society, which is amazing, but it also has taken away that kind of niche-ness. I don't know, I just love that the most. My favourite section of every film festival is things like Freak Me Out which is what it's called at Sydney [Film Festival] or Midnight [Film Festival]. That is always my favourite section.

When we were at South by Southwest, to be playing in that section as an Australian horror but then also meeting all these other wonderful filmmakers that had their kind of wacky versions of their cultural horror or whatever that meant, that's where I get the most enjoyment. I think it's feeling that sense of an international community for a niche thing. Being Australian, I'm proud of that. I'd rather be Australian, I think, than anything else. There are wonderful films from everywhere, but I look at the stuff we've made and I like it the most.

HB: I think the world does, too. I think the world loves Australian filmmakers because we do make bonkers stuff.

KS: The Swedes make bonkers stuff. Everyone makes fun stuff.

HB: Baz Luhrmann, he's one of our greatest, if not the greatest export, as a multifaceted artist. There's no one like him. There's so much camp, incredible magic. I remember as a nine-year-old watching *Moulin Rouge!* (2001) for the first time and falling in love with Nicole Kidman, and then also being like, "I'd love to do something like this." I had no idea that I wanted to be the person behind the camera. I think it's just cool to be called an Australian filmmaker. Just to be called a filmmaker is cool.

KS: Just to make movies always feels like a blessing.

HB: They're so hard to make.

KS: For us, it's something that you knock on wood for, and then when people like yourself ask us about Australian horror films, that's when you start to enjoy that you've made the thing because you get to have these wonderful discussions and reflect on what inspired you and other people like yourself have an understanding of the genre space and all that too. It's just wonderful.

ENDNOTES

1   https://www.austinchronicle.com/daily/screens/2022-03-12/sxsw-film-review-sissy/

HERE OUT WEST

100 mins
Directors: *Fadia Abboud, Lucy Gaffy, Julie Kalceff, Ana Kokkinos, Leah Purcell*
Cast: *Nisrine Amine, Mia-Lore Bayeh, Gladys Iturra Beiza, Shameer Birges, Kaelan Camongol, Kenneth Camongol, Gabrielle Chan, Jing Xuan Chan, Lena Cruz, Arka Das, Sukhraj Deepak, Anita Hegh, Bering Axtjärn Jackson, Thuso Lekwape, Christine Milo, Rahel Romahn, Christian Ravello, Pia Thunderbolt, Leah Vandenberg*
Writers: *Nisrine Amine, Bina Bhattacharya, Matias Bolla, Claire Cao, Arka Das, Dee Dogan, Vonne Patiag, Tien Tran*
Producers: *Annabel Davis, Sheila Jayadev, Bree-Anne Sykes*
Music: *Amanda Brown*
Cinematography: *Tania Lambert*
Editing: *Martin Connor*

Carl Edillo is an emerging filmmaker and critic based in Sydney. In 2023, Carl became a first-year student studying for a Bachelor of Arts: Screen Production at the Australian Film Television and Radio School.

REVIEW
CARL EDILLO

In 2016, The Guardian published an article[1] that talked about our postcode prejudice against Western Sydney. In it, Sydney local and filmmaker Guido Gonzalez is quoted as saying: "Where in our media do you see what you see by walking down the main street in Cabramatta, Liverpool or Parramatta?" Five years later I can immediately blurt out *"Here Out West* of course."

Here Out West features a wide array of talented people both on screen and behind the scenes, and in doing so it breaks the stigma that surrounds the western suburbs in the way it presents stories that are true to form, not the stereotypes perpetuated by sensationalist media. It's great to move on from the cultural narrative of Western Sydney as shown in *Struggle Street* (2015-2017) or *Housos* (2011-2013) and lean into a more empathetic lens of the region. In this way, *Here Out West* is the catalyst for Western Sydney cinema.

The eight writers - Nisrine Amine, Matias Bolla, Arka Das, Bina Bhattacharya, Dee Dogan, Tien Tran, Vonne Patiag and Claire Cao - each excelled in portraying the everyday experiences of living within the Western Sydney area, with myriad of experiences giving weight to themes of migration, family, sibling relationships – real and surrogate, and the way people connect to their culture and language. Notably, Bina and Vonne's segments each portray the reality of being distant from one's own culture, and how provoking that can be to one's identity.

For example, *The Long Shift* segment was empathetically and touchingly directed by Julie Kalceff and written by Vonne Patiag. We take our Filipino workers and parents for granted, and in this segment, I was reminded of how hard they have to work to ensure a better life for their kids. A friend of mine who also watched the film cried at how devastatingly relatable it was for parents to work late into the night and come home tired. Props to you Vonne, you made the Filipino community proud.

With the predicted population boom and the increased government investment in Parramatta to help it become Sydney's second CBD, there needs to be a cultural shift into what we identify as what is not only our residential but our national identity. There is the idea of the "working-class man" throughout 20th century Australia as expressed by Jimmy Barnes. The bloke with the high-vis vest and denim jeans, working in heavy machinery.

While this abstract idea of the white working-class Aussie was shot down with films like *The Boys* (1998) and *Chopper* (1999), there was no recouping or change within this identity, so to this day the majority of Australian media still see a number of migrant communities from The Area™ as sort of ghettos, shrouded in crime, and they don't give enough effort to herald such communities for their hard work and overcoming barriers to make a better life.

Here Out West brings a new idea of what it is to be working class in this nation. Their central identity does not hinge on their struggles of growing up and living in a lower socio-economic area but focuses on the ebbs and flows of living cohesively as a multicultural community. This paradigm shift in Australian cinema would hopefully empower people from such communities to tell more stories that embody true and lived experiences, and further contribute to what it means to be "Australian."

Here Out West could be better if it specifically identified what suburb and area segments took place in. It would be so gratifying to hear and read the words 'Blacktown' or 'Parramatta' on the screen instead of presenting 'a universal Western Sydney suburb.' While *Here Out West* could be more brutally honest in its portrayal of the region, many films and TV shows already achieve this; *Struggle Street* and *Little Fish* (2005), and the films made by ethnic filmmakers like George Basha with *The Combination* (2009) and Khoa Do with *The Finished People* (2003). Such projects, while controversial, are often met with critical acclaim.

Like the Jimmy Barnes song, there is a need for art that exists to wholeheartedly celebrate the positives Western Sydney has to offer. The image of a 'working class man' has changed since Barnes' anthem was released in 1985. As cheesy as it may sound, there is a need to romanticise the working-class reality of millions of people, alongside our idea of where we live, and who we are, given these concepts are still shaped by those who have the privilege within our media industry; not that many film and TV execs are willing to catch the T1 train line and go way out west to cultivate and produce new stories that is. It's more likely that projects in the same vein as *Palm Beach* (2021) will be made, so it's really up to the people from here, Western Sydney, to project their own voices and create their stories.

It's a shame that *Here Out West* was released during the Omicron variant wave and that it received minimal marketing support after its Sydney Film Festival exposure. Although Event Cinemas, Hoyts, and Dendy Cinemas did exhibit it, there is still a need for greater awareness of films like *Here Out West* through marketing campaigns. While there was a buzz around its release, it wasn't enough to build public awareness, and more importantly, public investment in the film. I sincerely believe if and when there are more voices from Western Sydney in the industry, this film would be cited as the influence and the creative stepping stone for finer and greater films to come.²

This brings me back to the impact *Here Out West* will have over time. We don't always have to be self-deprecating about where we live, make a joke about how someone got stabbed in the train station when we commute to work or uni, or be pressured to chime in when your white colleague or classmate from the north shore complains about how there are too many 'Indians,' 'Arabs,' 'Asians' or even 'eshays.' We can proudly say we're from Western Sydney, and when they say, "So what's it like living there?" we can point them straight to this film.

ENDNOTES

1   https://www.theguardian.com/culture/2016/aug/23/sydney-we-need-to-talk-about-our-postcode-prejudice, accessed 07 March 2023

2   As a flow on from the ABC release of *Here Out West*, the national broadcaster released a series called *8 Nights Out West*, which saw actor Arka Das and fellow actors from the film 'uncover the culinary hotspots that are shaping the culture of Western Sydney's suburbs.'

THE LONELY SPIRITS VARIETY HOUR

77 mins
Director: *Platon Theodoris*
Writers: *Platon Theodoris, Nitin Vengurlekar*
Cast: *Nitin Vengurlekar, Sabrina Chan D'Angelo, Teik-Kim Pok, Alison Bennett, Joyce Edmonds, Peter Gizariotis, Suzanne Devery, Shalvi Singh, Tina Andrews, Dinsha Palkhiwala, Poornima Bhatt*
Producers: *Brian Rapsey, Platon Theodoris*
Music: *Donald Baldie, Dimitri Vouros, Nick Wishart*
Cinematography: *Brian Rapsey*
Editing: *Brian Rapsey*

Platon Theodoris was nominated for the Australian Innovation Award at MIFF 2022.

ESSAY
ANDREW F. PEIRCE

The following essay extensively delves into the plot of Platon Theodoris' filmography, notably his first feature films, *Alvin's Harmonious World of Opposites* and *The Lonely Spirits Variety Hour*. Out of respect for Platon and his work, I urge you to seek out these films prior to reading this essay. However, as April Wolfe says, it's not what happens but how it happens that matters.

✳

The act of connection is a constant theme in director Platon Theodoris' filmography.

In his 2010 Cambodian-shot short film, *Sunrise*, Chim Sokheang's oldest child steps in as a surrogate father to his two younger sisters when their mother must leave to work on a cucumber farm to earn money for the family. Tender scenes of the brother sitting in a hammock as he tells his sisters' stories or singing and dancing for them as they clap along are contrasted with careful moments of dinner preparation, showing the young boy connecting with adulthood and maturing into the role of primary carer for the family.

That familial connection continues in his 2019 short, *Wine Lake*, where a chance encounter between two strangers reveals their Irish heritage, providing answers to lifelong questions they both have. Ailís Logan's script gives her the space to imbue her character, Peg, with the notion of floating through life untethered, and within her poems, she seeks to ground herself and gather the sense of family and purpose that seems to elude her.

In his 2022 feature *The Lonely Spirits Variety Hour,* Platon explores the type of connection that occurs between the hour of 12:00 to 12:45 am as Rabindranath Chakraborty (Nitin Vengurlekar), better known as Neville Umbrellaman when he's broadcasting from his parents shed, projects his unique style of radio show into the night to an audience of solitary listeners who go about their evening tasks as a structured absurdism flows out

THE LONELY SPIRITS VARIETY HOUR

from FFFFFFM on the AM dial. Neville hosts an array of guests: a muso who sings mournful tunes about his cat Waffles, a multi-regional Boulanger who kneads, cajoles, and beats her dough into shape, and Sabrina (Sabrina Chan D'Angelo), Rabindranath's last guest who expresses herself using the prime format of artistry for a radio show: a dance. Neville's guests connect a scattered audience of disparate strangers through a unique brand of absurdity and surrealism. I'll explore *Lonely Spirits* in more depth later.

With his first feature film, 2015's *Alvin's Harmonious World of Opposites*, Platon Theodoris held a kaleidoscope up to the light and invited audiences to peer through the lens into an apartment full of panda-shaped absurdity in an occasionally surreal, continually thought-provoking indie film that proudly defies genre-trappings. Over a brisk 73-minute runtime, we follow the titular Alvin (a captivating Teik-Kim Pok) as he works remotely from his secluded apartment, operating on a strict routine of plant watering, panda sitting, Skype meetings, and linguistic management. Initially, Alvin's story appears to reject any sense of connection as he leads an insular life, treating the world outside of his apartment as one filled with hostility and contempt, with the hyper-vigilant figure refusing to stray into the outside world as he treats his doorstep like it's the edge of a precipice that if breached would guarantee certain doom. That is, until he's forced by the outside world that starts seeping through the ceiling of his trinket-laden-sanctuary.

Platon chooses to introduce us to Alvin with an immediately conflicted image of the reclusive figure crouched over a hole in his floor, peering on his downstairs neighbour going about her day. From his limited viewpoint, he watches her prepare for her day, and when he is seemingly content that her processes are complete, he puts a cover over the hole, breaths a sigh of relief, and allows his day to commence. Filmic tradition suggests that we should be able to empathise or relate to the lead character of a film, utilising them as an audience surrogate of sorts and finding some kind of commonality with their narrative, but within the construction of Alvin, we're presented with a prime contradiction.

Instantly, we're searching for that connection point, yet, watching a grown man peer on his female neighbour as she gets dressed and goes about her day, causes us to be instantly distanced from Alvin. It's a risky move to open a film with a tone of unease, especially for a film that seeks to put the audience firmly in its lead character's mind, but it's a confident and assured choice that pays off.

Alvin's Harmonious World of Opposites is a film that delights in contrasting complicated ideas and themes. While never excusing Alvin's behaviour, the film reveals him to be less of a predator, and more like an anxious dog, monitoring the parameters of their home for threats or issues, only able to return to its guard point when its concern is alleviated. In his isolated apartment life, Alvin maintains a strict, comfortable routine, of which monitoring the actions of his neighbours is a central aspect. Teik-Kim's innocent expression as Alvin goes a long way in carrying the energy of how harmless a figure he really is.

Platon presents Alvin's foul-mouthed neighbour Virginia (Vashti Hughes) as the extreme opposite of Alvin. She eagerly engages in racist behaviour, simmering with extreme paranoia and distrust for her neighbours. As an Aussie-Karen, Virginia bitterly pulls the 'please explain'-card as she complains about her downstairs neighbour who she is convinced has brought fleas into the apartment complex. Virginia exhibits a delirious look of joy after she delivers her constant abuse, with her breathless state showing how much she feeds off how unsettled and small she can make her victims feel. Hughes revels in bringing Virginia to life, adding extra pepper to each barbed retort and insult, utilising them as weapons to tear down the world around her.

Virginia's interactions with Alvin are limited, but they occur frequently enough to remind him why the boundaries of his apartment are sacred and must never be breached. Her appearances begin to interrupt his daily meditations and work-from-home routine, almost threatening his eighteen-month-long sojourn from the outside world.

Alvin works as a translator who frequently liaises with Angela (Ailís Logan), an authoritative figure who frequently questions his word choices, pushing Alvin to explain his decisions of why he chose this word over the other. On the surface, Angela likely considers her line of questioning as a form of ally-ship, ensuring that the translation of texts carries the correct authorial intent across, never considering that her amiable prodding instead acts as a manner of questioning Alvin's identity. When paired with Virginia's aggression, Angela's questions push Alvin further internally, seeking comfort in the inner peace he so desperately desires.

The thematic relevance of Alvin's translation work sits on the same line as his creepy spying on his downstairs neighbour: he is taking what is not his – the language of others, a stranger's privacy – and making it his own. He's not doing it for outward pleasure, but rather to satiate the worries of his mind.

As Alvin embarks on a solitary life, he amasses a wealth of nostalgic trinkets and toys from online purchases, each one bolstering the aesthetically pleasing nature of his apartment. His bed positively overflows with stuffed pandas, with each of their doe-eyed faces adding an element of charm and whimsy to the production design. For filmmakers who want to learn about how great production design can bring a film's personality to life, then they should look no further than the work that Mas Guntur and Shin Shin did on *Alvin's Harmonious World of Opposites*.

As we know from countless stories of isolation, no secure vessel is a sanctuary for long, as something inevitably arrives to disturb the peace. For Alvin, his domestic paradise is upturned by the presence of a curious black goop that starts seeping through his ceiling. Initially, he wipes it away, removing its presence, only for it to come back twofold the following day.

THE LONELY SPIRITS VARIETY HOUR

After he asks for the assistance of the building manager to find the problem, and they come up with nothing, Alvin is forced to take matters into his own hands, leading him to climb into the crawl space in his ceiling to seek the source of the black goop.

As he climbs through the crawl space, he emerges in a different land, falling into an odd world of ramshackle kitchens and abandoned carnival rides. Stepping into this strange world, Alvin encounters groups of little people who work operating a soy sauce factory. The labels on the bottles hold pictures of Alvin's face like he's this world's version of Paul Newman with his own line of branded sauces.[1] Notably, Platon never qualifies the importance of the soy sauce, and in doing so, he encourages the audience to find their own emotional resonance with its significance.

Perplexed by his rise to condiment-level infamy, Alvin stumbles around the world with Dessy Filtri's wonderful Vilna by his side. In an abandoned carnival, the two share a tender moment, an aspect of his life that has been absent for far too long. It's here that Alvin's centred mind and sense of peace are restored, an aspect that helps him finally breathe with calm when he manages to return home.

Back in the safety of his sanctuary, Alvin stands tall like a burden has been lifted. There's a lightness to his step, and in an act of closure and comfort, he seals the hole in his floor with tape, the anxiety of needing to monitor the actions of his neighbour now having subsided. When Virginia knocks at his front door, instead of steadying himself for the anger that he is about to endure, he simply stands in her tidal wave of hate and abuse, never giving an inch to Virginia's cruelty. Alvin endures.

Recognising that Alvin has become unperturbed by her aggression, Virginia amplifies it, leaving the last line of the film on a heightened moment of racial abuse. Knowing that only what is in his mind matters and what Virginia is saying has no consequence to him, Alvin responds with a smile. Virginia realises that her words no longer sting, and with the two standing on even ground, she smiles in kind. This is Alvin's harmonious world of opposites realised in a charming moment of finality.

I recognise the absurdity of calling a note of racial abuse and the lead character's response to it as 'charming'. It's as absurd as understanding that Alvin's snooping on his neighbour is less predatory than it may seem. With Platon's expressive dialogue and joyous plotting, we're encouraged to revel in the absurdity of our existence, to understand that we all live in our own harmonious worlds of opposites. We're also invited to strip back the notion of what our 'self' is, and how that 'self' interacts with the world around us.

Within Alvin, we see a figure who is learning to pull back on the anxieties that erupt within him that are brought forth by external forces that exist out of his control. It's only when he realises that he cannot change Virginia's behaviour by being defensive and reacting to the impact of her words that her behaviour truly changes. It's clear that *Alvin's Harmonious World of Opposites* is not a 'life lesson' film, but it is fascinating to see how

Platon presents the result of being able to differentiate between ruminating on an issue and actually problem-solving an issue. Equally so, while Alvin isn't consciously concentrating on his influence in the world, it's clear through the soy sauce cult that has made him their brand icon of choice, that his actions have subliminally impacted external forces.

I first viewed *Alvin's Harmonious World of Opposites* when Western Australia was opening its borders to the world after years of being in state-wide pandemic lockdown. Alvin's bed of pandas reminded me of a nearby house that, years later, still displays a mask-wearing teddy bear in their window, forever bringing passers-by a smile and a heart-warming burst of joy when they see it. *Alvin's* reminded me of how small actions can create curious changes in the world around us, a notion which is so familiar to many of us, yet it's one that we rarely consciously consider. The sisters in *Sunrise* will grow up with tender memories of the bond fortuitously forged with their brother at a younger age. The newly discovered familial relationship in *Wine Lake* has transformed the lives of two relative strangers completely. And, for Alvin, a chance encounter with the outside world brings him the greatest connection of all: with himself.

※

That sense of connection is amplified with a heartfelt poignancy in *The Lonely Spirits Variety Hour*, Platon's most personal film yet. Spliced between Neville's radio show are scenes of Rabindranath in a coma, hooked up to a respirator while his family gather, unsure whether he will wake or not. Neville and Rabindranath are one and the same person, portrayed by co-writer Nitin Vengurlekar with masterfully dry comedic timing.

The film is dedicated to Platon's long-time collaborator Vanna Seang, cinematographer on *Alvin's*, who passed away suddenly at the age of 35. *Lonely Spirits* then acts as a way for Platon to process the trauma and grief of having lost his close friend, as he says in the following interview (page 331):

> "In The Lonely Spirits Variety Hour, I had to come to terms with the fleeting nature of life and the ridiculous nature of death."

In the process of coming to terms with life and death, Platon and Nitin create a work of art that acts as an Aussie take on Spike Milligan or Jacques Tati, revelling in the absurdity of existence as Neville with lines of dialogue like, "Yes listeners, life is fleeting I know, but strap yourselves in for a journey through the night sky." Neville's radio show flits between parables about the metaphysical nature of life and satirical salesman pitches for everything from cyclonic vacuum cleaners ('because your life sucks') to annual subscriptions to major depressive disorders, all of which are in-

THE LONELY SPIRITS VARIETY HOUR

terspersed by the musical styling of TJ and the Snookergees with the title song of their 1962 album *Purple Carrots*.

Neville is someone who thrives in isolation, turning into a veritable wordsmith in front of the microphone, yet in the presence of another person, he falters and stumbles, struggling to find the right words. This is no clearer realised than when he's in the presence of Sabrina, Rabindranath's colleague and romantic interest, who agrees to be a guest on Neville's show. Sabrina is clearly keen on Rabindranath, but he is simply too socially awkward to act on it, leading him to stall her appearance during the variety hour. When Sabrina does finally get her radio time, she opts to present a wonderfully visual piece, a hilariously seductive dance routine, replete with multiple pairs of knickers being thrown. As one last pair of knickers are thrown onto a hapless stuffed koala, Neville stumbles as he tries to ask Sabrina for a drink, but instead fails to act on his heart's desire. It's in this moment that we're able to witness the comedic perfection of Platon's direction which he marries so comfortably with a level of pathos that feels lived in, making Neville's stumbles feel entirely relatable.

Rabindranath's attending physicians and nurses appear as guests on the variety hour, with Teik-Kim Pok's considerate nurse appearing as crooning cat-lover Kenneth Wong, or Peter Gizariotis' concerned doctor becomes a worried caller phoning in with a Schrödinger's cat story. Platon's metaphorical playfulness continues with an amusing transition that sees Rabindranath receiving the intravenous contrast for an MRI to Neville standing in his studio's toilet peeing. *Lonely Spirits* delights in dabbling in metaphors, as Platon leaves it up to the viewer to decide whether Neville's radio show exists in reality or if it is a construct of the last firing synapses of Rabindranath's brain.

Furthering the wonderful metaphorical exploration of Rabindranath's existence are interstitial moments where Neville makes pilgrimages to the mammoth tchotchkes of Australiana that litter the nation: our unique array of 'Big Things'. He disappears into the mouth of Swan Hill's Giant Murray River Cod in Victoria, stares into the distance from the eye of Goulburn's Big Merino in NSW, and is dwarfed by Big Lobster in Kingston, South Australia. Near the films close, Rabindranath and Sabrina make one final pilgrimage together to the Giant Koala of Dadswell Bridge in Victoria. There's an added ethereal quality to the metaphorical nature of the film that comes from the COVID-era shoot that provided vacant vistas, devoid of human life around these often-popular tourist destinations.

The ethereal nature of *Lonely Spirits* is furthered with Brian Rapsey's sensitive cinematography which captures emotionally enriched shots of Rabindranath laying in a field of lush, green grass, wrapped by its comforting embrace as Brian's camera slowly lifts towards the heavens. Later, Brian replicates the shot, only this time, he brings the heavens to Rabindranath in a touching act of finality.

ESSAY | ANDREW F. PEIRCE

Brian's camera brings the vastness of the outside world into Neville's booth, somehow managing to strip away any sense of claustrophobia that might come from the limited space of the shed based studio. An early dolly shot pulls back to reveal an aging studio workspace full of part time obsessions made up of trinkets and memorabilia of Princess Di, eighties Australiana, stuffed koalas, collectors' plates, and paintings of the Sydney Harbour Bridge. Some may call this environment cluttered; others would be able to recognise it as being chaotically organised with each items location no doubt meticulously catalogued in Rabindranath's mind.

The character informing set design by Platon is supported by the set dressing by Shin Shin, flowing into the rooms of Neville's listeners who we meet through an array of different radios; one woman sits on her couch, knitting in the night as towering stacks of literary tomes loom behind her, her AWA radiola valve radio sitting on a cabinet; another woman sits at her kitchen table, drink in hand as she flips through a magazine while her portable radio sits nearby; in a workshop, a man tinkers on his vehicle while his boombox hangs from a tool-laden wall; Vashti Hughes makes a cameo as a tired woman completing a jigsaw puzzle at her dining table while a giant stuffed teddy bear sits next to her as her dual tape deck radio projects the show behind her. These are people of the night who are connected by the basic commonality of being his audience, Neville's band of lonely spirits who collectively, unknowingly, body double with each other as they listen to his.

Later, Brian captures Neville at night in a field, sitting at his radio stand, a single spotlight fending of the darkness that threatens to envelope him as he encourages listeners to tune in for "two minutes of erotic sounds." As the sound of harmonic crickets call from the void of the night, Neville pauses before slowly saying "As we say goodbye, I'd just like to leave you with this thought." Neville stares into the darkness for just enough time to allow the viewer to question what that thought may be, a question that's extinguished by a crescendo of fountain fireworks bursting like explosions in the sky, illuminating Neville's existence and creating a wellspring of emotions as we realise these are the last moments of Neville's life.

In a pointed decision, we never see a funeral take place. Instead, Platon presents us with a different kind of remembrance. As the heart monitor flatlines, Sabrina retrieves a ukulele from a suitcase, strumming it as the Chakraborty family surround Rabindranath in hospital in mourning. Sabrina's strumming sways into the inevitable dilemma that families and friends face when a loved one passes away: how to manage their mountain of personal belongings.

In a heart-breaking sequence, the Chakraborty family dispose of Neville's ephemera in a skip, with the walls of his studio falling one by one, allowing the shed to return to its original form. With the studio emptied, and the skip full, Brian's camera carries us into the heavens once more, this time with the family surrounding the towering bin, looking at the residue of a life lived, reflecting on the person that impacted their lives. For many viewers, the act of discarding the remnants of existence is a painful one; after all, these artefacts are the enduring reminder that they existed, that they lived a life, and that they left a mark on the world around us. These items are extensions of their soul, of their personality, and act as a touchstone for remembering who they are. Each item carries a weight to that person's life, a memory attached to the day they bought it, or the journey they took to acquire a long sought after antique, or possibly the monumental occasion that a tea towel signifies.

I first viewed *The Lonely Spirits Variety Hour* at its world premiere screening at Perth's Revelation International Film Festival in July 2022. As I enjoyed the warmth of the film, I found a surprising symmetry between myself and Neville Umbrellaman. Here was a figure who sat in solitude in his studio, surrounded by personality reflecting trinkets as he delivered rambling monologues of absurdity into the great unknown of the world of radio. Neville isn't focused on listener stats, audience reach, or growing his 'platform'. No, Neville is simply focused on being himself: the creation of Neville Umbrellaman as presented by Rabindranath Chakraborty.

I felt transported to my own workspace, a ramshackle space replete with an array of oddities. Step into this room and you can glean the kind of person I am and how I live my life. Here is my desk, saddled with my microphone, attached to my laptop by an alarmingly long cable. Above my screen is a framed poster of *Faster, Pussycat! Kill! Kill!* (1965), signed by Russ Meyer. There is my stack of books about the idea of Australia, its politics, and the films created on this land. Next to me is a painting by Sonny Day of a banana headed man sitting on a stool smoking a cigarette. On my desk is an array of small items: a Garbage Pail Kids card parodying *Mac and Me* (1988) in a collectors slip, a selection of fidget toys I play with just out of frame as I navigate interviews, a crystal lion given to me by my Gran when I was just a kid, and a ceramic poo from when I tried out clay work. Behind me is my library of physical media, many I'll never view during my lifetime. Like Rabindranath, when I am gone, much of this ephemera will end up as detritus in a skip or forever lingering as an unsold item on an online marketplace. They carry a connection to me and me alone, yet together they build an idea of who I am as a person.

As Rabindranath's studio is dismantled, we feel that aspects of his personality are disappearing too. Who will carry on the legacy of Neville Umbrellaman that he's built up over time? Is there even a legacy to carry on? In the shadow of these questions, we're forced to reconcile with the notion of what kind of mark we will leave on this world when we are gone. As we grapple with this notion, Sabrina's voice rises, carrying forth the Neville-isms we've come to know as the Lonely Spirits Variety Hour to his disparate listeners out in the world at night.

These closing moments then strengthen the purpose behind why we dedicate a work of art to someone. When we dedicate a film, a book, a song, or

ESSAY | ANDREW F. PEIRCE

a painting to someone, we are using that work of art as a way of honouring their impact on your life. The resulting work says something about who they are as a person. It says that while embarking on this creative journey, they sat in your mind every step of the way.

For me, this book has been curated and written with the lives of my grandparents in my mind. Their presence in my life helped shape my appreciation of Australian film and culture, and I would hope that by dedicating *Lonely Spirits and the King* to them that you, the reader, gets a deeper understanding of who they were as people.

I am hesitant to say that by dedicating *The Lonely Spirits Variety Hour* to Vanna Seang, Platon has also given viewers a glimpse into the kind of person Vanna was. Yet, the feeling I am left with at the close of the film, one of warmth and comfort, enriches my understanding of who Vanna was as a person and as an artist. This film presents a group of characters who look at the world differently, and knowing that Vanna was a cinematographer, and having seen his creativity at play, I can experience how he saw the world: as someone full of curiosity and compassion for the world around him and those who live in it.

In the simple act of a dedication, we add to the collective memories of the person being recognised, and in turn, we extend their impact on the world long past the time they have left their corporeal form. Memories linger in our minds, rising to the surface at unexpected moments, washing over us as a wave of emotions. They can be spurred on by the proximity of an item that reminds us of someone, or a turn of phrase that we hear a stranger say, or it might even be the taste of food that takes us home and reminds us of our mothers cooking, they carry a weight that can never be truly measured. It is then a wholly considerate act to introduce us to a person by way of a feeling.

The art of cinema manages to do this in ways that precious few other art forms can. Filmmakers engage in extended acts of creativity, culminating in an experience like no other that goes out to an audience of strangers around the world. As these strangers sit in the darkness, surrendering to a narrative that plays out on screen in front of them, they also submit to having their moods changed, enhanced, or altered by a creative force. In rare moments, that filmic experience can broaden or change their world view. It may even reflect who they are as people back at them, leading that audience member to question who they are and how they live their life.

Cinema transports us away from the now to give us time to reflect on aspects of the world, of our world, silly or otherwise, and in doing so, it influences how we deal with the world we live in. In the act of walking out of the theatre or turning off your TV, we nestle a small part of the film in our minds, it becomes part of us. We may forget the film the moment the daylight washes over us, but it has become part of us, silently shaping us as people.

We carry great films in our minds as precious memories where they act as a touchstone moment in our life. For the rare gems, we invite them to become part of our lives, placing them in the sanctuary of our minds where we are able to return to the moments that brought forth such a strong emotional bond in the first place. The memory might not even be of the film we watched, instead it could be about the company that we had when we first saw it, or a monumental event that occurred in the vicinity of the film. As such, the memory of the film turns that moment into a time travelling device that presents us the past, present, and future all at once. This is why the first films we view carry a different weight for each person, including the person who introduced you to it. This is the power of film.

I couldn't help but feel an affinity with both Neville and Sabrina. I write about Australian films, interviewing filmmakers and storytellers, and in this act, I shine a light on the work of a productive Australian film industry. I am part of a continuing legion of writers who have written about Australian films for decades. We participate in a conversation across time that collectively creates a chorus of support for the Australian film industry that will continue long after we have faded into the dark.

As *The Lonely Spirits Variety Hour* continued, I felt the similarities between Neville and myself increase. I found a distinct familiarity in the scene that details the awkward confluence of Rabindranath's three worlds (family, work, personal) colliding when his Mum (the lovely Joyce Edwards) meets his colleague, Sabrina, who Rabindranath has invited to be on the show. As Rabindranath's Mum invites Sabrina over for dinner, he awkwardly notes, "Mum, it's Neville when I'm doing the show." Mrs Chakraborty hands Neville his favourite dish, truffle infused mushroom beetroot arancini with vegan aioli and a side of carrots, and with a raise of the eyebrows, leaves the booth, beaming with excitement that her son has invited a woman around to participate in his creative venture.

As someone who spent decades struggling to read social cues or injecting outwardly bizarre responses to otherwise normal conversations, Neville's stilted societal interactions and Milo Kerrigan neck-free stature felt all too familiar to me. While the term 'neurodivergent' is never uttered in *The Lonely Spirits Variety Hour*, Neville Umbrellaman does carry some distinctly neurodivergent traits that I resonated with. Neville's fixation with the 1962 album *Purple Carrots*, his ability to spin stories that feature aspects of philosophy and late-night shopping networks, the Australiana accoutrements that litter his studio, and his affinity with the Big Things of regional towns, all felt like distinct aspects of my own life as I carried on with my own niche, hyper-focused curiosities. It takes a certain brand of weird to maintain an unhealthy obsession with *Mac and Me*, to frequently champion the undervalued *Welcome to Woop Woop*, and to dedicate a significant amount of personal time to writing books about Australian films, but that's who I am and what I have grown into.

While I had an understanding that there was something a little bit autistic about me, it was those aspects of loneliness, a search for connection, and a hopeful desire to leave an impact on the world around me, that built a sense of familiarity between Neville and myself that sent me down a path of understanding that I am neurodivergent. On that path I found a level of comfort with existence that I had been searching for most of my life.

Cinema is filled with films that feature autistic characters that are often written or portrayed from a distinctly neuroatypical perspective. Yet, it's within the realm of cinema that the world of neurospicy folks' shine, often in stories that are labelled 'quirky' or 'unique'. To an outsider, the work of Platon Theodoris may be considered quirky, with *Lonely Spirits* operating like a Michel Gondry film with an Aussie lilt, but, to those on the spectrum, Platon's work may feel completely natural, as if he's reflecting our lives back with a level of recognition and understanding. There is nothing in his films that explicitly states that these characters are neurodiverse, however given the dearth of genuinely autistic characters in fiction-based media, it then falls to us neurodiverse folks to discover autistic-coded characters on screen and to make them our own.

The quirkiness of *Lonely Spirits* is accentuated with interstitial motifs of Sabrina and Rabindranath living a life together, whether it be visiting the Big Koala or Rabindranath reading a book while Sabrina cleans a public swimming pool. These moments are where *Lonely Spirits* sways into pure fantasy, suggesting a future the two would share if Rabindranath were to have not passed away. This fantasy is not built on deep philosophical conversations or extravagant trips around the world, but instead it's one conjured around the notion of feeling comfortable in the presence of someone you love, respect, and appreciate more than anything else in the world.

For me, there may be no greater feeling than that of comfort. A sense of comfort tells me that everything is safe, that my world is at relative ease, and for the time being, my worries and anxieties are abated. Comfort is sitting on the couch with my partner, watching naff videos on YouTube or rewatching *The X Files*. Comfort is eating our favourite foods together as we people watch the world go by. Comfort is watching a film that manages to reflect how I feel and to present that feeling in a manner that I have long struggled to articulate.

Comfort is being seen.

It's important to then remember threat to the unbridled creativity that people like Platon Theodoris hold within them that challenges the foundations of rampant commercialism that the film industry is built upon. This kind of creativity is part of the reason why cinemas are sacred places, and it's thanks to film festivals like Perth's Revelation International Film Festival or the Sydney Underground Film Festival which have both supported and nurtured Platon's creative ventures.

It's within the curated lineup of annual film festivals that fringe and niche films are given their moment in the cinematic spotlight, pushing aside the populist fare that's churned week in, week out at local multiplexes. Cura-

THE LONELY SPIRITS VARIETY HOUR

tors like Jack Sargeant and Richard Sowada throw filmmakers like Platon Theodoris a lifeline, and in doing so, they say to filmmakers and audiences alike that this form of filmmaking is valuable and important.

In the following interviews, Platon talks about the importance of receiving that recognition from film festivals like Revelation and SUFF, but I want to close this piece by saying that unknowingly, Platon has passed on the greatest gift to me, a relative stranger, that a filmmaker ever could give: the realisation of self and an understanding of what it means to live in a world where you are seen in the media you engage with. We may all be lonely spirits floating around in this world, but it's how we bump into each other in unexpected ways that matters. This film has become part of me like precious few have, and for that I will always be grateful.

ENDNOTES

1   Keen eyed viewers will note the Easter egg presence of Alvin's soy sauce in The Lonely Spirits Variety Hour

INTERVIEW
FILMMAKERS
PLATON THEODORIS & NITIN VENGURLEKAR

Platon Theodoris and Nitin Vengurlekar's absurdist comedy, *The Lonely Spirits Variety Hour*, had its world premiere at Perth's Revelation Film Festival, before screening at the Melbourne International Film Festival. In it, Nitin plays Neville Umbrellaman, a late-night radio host beaming his voice into the world from the solitude of his tiny garage studio. Occasionally guests participate in discussions, including visits from Kenneth Wong (Teik-Kim Pok), Yvette (Alison Bennett), and Neville's faithful listener Sabrina (Sabrina Chan D'Angelo). Intermixed between Neville's radio ramblings where he ponders about the ethics of household goods while attempting his best at selling overpriced goods, are moments where we see Neville's family unite around him in a hospital room in his final moments.

For a film that runs for a tight seventy-seven minutes long *The Lonely Spirits Variety Hour* is packed full of emotionality and humour, with Nitin's captivating monologues amplifying that vibe of connection with strangers. There's a grounded feel that comes from the heightened absurdity of Neville's dialogue which Nitin delivers with a straight-faced relatability. At the same time, what he says is nonsensical and makes all the sense in the world.

This interview was recorded by Andrew F. Peirce in June 2022

There is a grounded absurdity in your films, Platon. What was the joy in being able to work with that field of absurdity here?

Platon Theodoris: Life is weird. I know that word comes up a lot, but some of the best things that I've created or explored come from a weird idea that has roots in real experiences. If you look at the absurdity of life, at some of the wonderful or confronting things that can happen to ourselves or other people, it's often the most interesting. I'll see or encounter something, which will trigger me and then I'll run with it because you just can't make some shit up right?

THE LONELY SPIRITS VARIETY HOUR

This is why I was attracted to Nitin's stage show *The Lonely Spirits Variety Hour*. It came completely out of the absurd and ridiculous, yet it was grounded in real-life scenarios that I connected with. I remember the show just left me with big belly laughs. I was in stitches and was crying from laughter. Nitin did the stage show three times, at different venues, and I went every time. By the third time, I was trying to figure out a way to bring that quality to screen. I wasn't sure it was going to be possible. I was trying to imagine the sort of narrative I could overlay, how to adapt and tackle it with a film in mind, trying to squeeze what was essentially a series of gags into a three-act structure - give it some form and make it accessible using my film language. It was an interesting process.

Nitin Vengurlekar: On the subject of absurdity, I think part of it comes from this focus on loneliness and being awake in the wee hours of the night and where your mind goes at those hours. The thought processes, the trajectories, and tangents that your mind goes on at those hours in that situation where you're by yourself and there's nobody else around is part of where the absurdity comes from.

My tendency in the theatre shows was it was a string of gags, really a string of monologues, and Platon took that and added a coherent narrative to it so it would stand up as a film. When I started writing the stage show [it] came out of thinking about what I used to do as a kid and as a teenager in those hours of the night at 1am, 2am when there were only five channels on television, and on four of those five channels was the Home Shopping Network. They had the same show on every channel, you had no choice but to watch the Home Shopping Network. After that they had *This Is Your Day* with Benny Hinn, and all the televangelists' shows.

So, the time of day was at night-time and then watching this mixture of commercialism and spiritualism, they were both selling something. The Home Shopping Network was selling new diamond necklaces, or kind of the things that you used to get the little bits of fabric off your shirt, lint rollers. Then the spiritual shows were trying to sell you spirituality. These very commercial televangelists were trying to get your money, or at least he was trying to get money out of his audience members. That nexus of commercialism and spiritualism and the absurdity of that kind of official language that spanned both the commercial and the spiritual [influenced] some of the monologues in the film [which] kind of come out of that particular discursive territory.

I'm curious about implementing Platon's voice in the translation from the stage to the screen. What was that creative process like and how did you weave in the narrative of death and dying?

INTERVIEW | PLATON THEODORIS & NITIN VENGURLEKAR

NV: The theatre show came out of another show that I did in Bankstown, which was a segment of the show where I sat on a hilltop at night-time looking out into the sky, broadcasting to no one doing these monologues over a radio with a microphone. I took that and wrote a lot of other monologues. Then I had this series of monologues that I did as a theatre show, and I sent the script of the three shows to Platon. He combined the three shows, and [sequenced them] so that they made some sort of narrative. There was a logic to them in the first place, I think. Platon squeezed the best material out of all of them together, and left out some bits that I was like, "Oh, I thought that was pretty good."

He needed something to give it weight to beyond just a string of absurd monologues, [then he added this framing]. Initially, I was a little bit circumspect about the addition of this extra narrative thread because my impulse was that the show was primarily about loneliness and that was what the spine of the show should be. I initially felt like this other thing about death was not necessary. But then as it started to pick up a resonance for me, I understood [why it was there]. It also comes from a real situation that Platon can maybe elaborate on later.

The film essentially becomes about lifeforce because this figure projects a manic and relentless energy into a microphone to be sent out into the ether to be heard by these people by projecting himself out through the microphone. You see all the scenes where he's in these expansive, otherworld locations, and we can talk about whether they're metaphorical or not. That's the kind of thing that Platon and I jokingly argue about a lot, whether there's any metaphor in the film and I kind of say "No, there's no metaphor in the film. Everything's exactly what it is." But there is this idea of him projecting himself into other places. And so, the stuff in the hospital fits into that kind of imagistic territory or something. It's that line of thought that leads the film to being about lifeforce.

PT: It's interesting because early drafts did focus more on that loneliness aspect. Initially, I was taking the adaptation down the rom-com road-trip movie path. It was much more about the relationship between Sabrina and Neville and their unrequited love. Earlier passes had them on a road-trip and I incorporated this into the radio show. So, it was very different.

I got to the end of the second draft and parked it because I wanted to sit with the material and let it gestate some more. That was in mid-2018. Then what subsequently happened was that a dear friend of mine passed away - Vanna Seang - who was the cinematographer for *Alvin's Harmonious World of Opposites*, very suddenly at 35. This was a really difficult time for me. I think I was in shock for maybe three months and then the grief hit me like a truck a little bit later. It was just so unexpected. I was filming with Vanna

329

THE LONELY SPIRITS VARIETY HOUR

in the week before he went to hospital and then two and a half weeks later, he was gone. I helped him home from the hospital but then he died a few days later, unexpectedly. It wasn't supposed to happen that way.

Because I had been chatting to Vanna about shooting this new project and he had already read a draft of *The Lonely Spirits Variety Hour*, I couldn't think about making the film without him. We had chatted at length about the style of the film and my approach and were even discussing a potential shoot schedule. After he passed, I had no energy to do anything. Thankfully working on the short film *Wine Lake* helped me focus on something else. I can thank Ailis Logan for that. I was still grieving. I moved to Japan for six months and threw myself into writing my new feature project after *Wine Lake*. It was a difficult period.

And then, on the festival circuit for *Wine Lake*, at Raindance Film Festival in London, I got a little bit inspired again. It was a year after Vanna had passed, and I thought "I'm going to revisit it again." I gave Nitin a call, and he was still keen to pursue it, so I gave it another stab. But it felt like the project couldn't just stay the same. I wasn't the same person after losing Vanna.

Revisiting the early drafts of *The Lonely Spirits Variety Hour* was me coming to terms with grief. It was a year after he passed, and I was making sense of what had happened. I'd also helped Vanna's wife Krystal complete a documentary that he had shot but never finished. Vanna moved to Australia as a refugee from Cambodia and had spent many years in a Thai refugee camp on the border. Because he hadn't heard that story, he took his parents back on a journey through Cambodia to this Thai refugee camp and asked them to talk about how they escaped the Khmer Rouge, and how they made it out safely. It was a very personal experience; Vanna is in the doco asking all the questions.

I helped facilitate the post-production because the film was only rushes at the time of his passing. I was in the middle of this process when I started thinking about *The Lonely Spirits* again - working with an editor in Cambodia. We got the 30 hours of footage translated and worked through the rushes to create the story. Vanna's documentary is called *Return to K.I.D.*, and if anyone wants to watch it, they can find it on YouTube. It's Vanna's story. It's a great story of survival. After starting that process with Krystal, I seemed to find space to come to terms with his loss.

The weird thing is, and I only realised this in hindsight, in all my film work, which is always very personal, and I guess in a lot of my early music videos too, many of the ideas I run with come out of me dealing with some sort of trauma. A lot of my creative process is me working through stuff and I feel like through filmmaking - creating stories and images - I can come to terms with or accept or understand things about this world and myself and life in general. That's why I'm attracted to stories that are a little bit offbeat or absurd, because this allows me to make sense of the whimsy of life and the fleetingness of life. That line is in *The Lonely Spirits Variety Hour* actually. How fleeting and ridiculous and combustible life is.

With *Alvin*'s it was me dealing with anxiety and an abusive father. It was me dealing with obsessive-compulsive thoughts and how these thoughts can stain your sense of reality and become your reality. The menacing stains of black sludge permeating your apartment walls, which turn out to be sweet soy sauce, only to then discover that it is your own mind that is responsible for creating this reality. In *The Lonely Spirits Variety Hour*, I had to come to terms with the fleeting nature of life and the ridiculous nature of death. So, I just kind of ran with it.

Thank you for the honesty as well. I know that talking about these things is difficult.

PT: It is difficult talking about this aspect of the film. I'm just super thankful Brian Rapsey stepped in to shoot and edit both *Wine Lake* and *Lonely Spirits*. Without such a talented production partner *The Lonely Spirits Variety Hour* would not exist.

NV: Also the way those two trajectories, the loneliness and then this idea of lifeforce come together in the film, why it then made sense for me was because this idea you project and send out your life, this energy throughout your life until the time that it expires, and you hope that along the way, somewhere, it connects with somebody and resonates. That's what the character is doing throughout the film, sending this energy up hoping that somebody receives it until that energy then runs out.

PT: That sounds like a metaphor.

Let's lean into that then. Metaphor or not?

NV: Well, Platon put on the poster: 'There are no dress rehearsals.' I wanted the tagline to say, 'There are no metaphors in life.' Just to kind of throw a spanner in the works. I always joke with Platon that there are no metaphors in the film. I hate metaphors. I'm more from the kind of Plato's Republic sort of approach about poetry and image-making being bad for society. I kind of lean into that.

Of course, joking. There is this great reference from this book by Leslie Jamison called *Make It Scream, Make It Burn*, and it's this beautiful definition of metaphor as a salve for loneliness, that two terms take new resonance

THE LONELY SPIRITS VARIETY HOUR

through companionship and it's bringing two disparate things together, so that they share some new resonance. I just thought it's a beautiful definition of metaphor and its link to loneliness. Platon, what's your opinion?

PT: I agree with you. In life, it's all literal, right? Because you're living it, the feelings are real, your present state is your reality - the lived experience is not a metaphor. It's absolutely basic and without exaggeration. So, I can see how you'd want that interpretation. But sometimes a symbolic image or phrase allows you to transcend that a little bit. And I feel there is a lot of power in this because it can give you some objectivity, where you can remove yourself a little bit from the subjective.

NV: But I take great joy in situations where you can't quite resolve something into a metaphor. I hope that's the case with this film, where people are thinking, "Is this a metaphor? Or is it not, I can't resolve it. And that's frustrating to me." I don't know why I find that kind of productive territory between something not being a metaphor and being a metaphor, and the thought of thinking through all of that, [why] that territory is interesting for me to inhabit when I'm making images or meaning writing stuff.

From psychoanalytic stuff, not to get too much into that, but there's this idea that metaphor is kind of comparable or of the same structure as condensation, which Freud and Lacan talk about as an unconscious process of mashing together two things or compressing disparate things into one representational unit or package. Where that process goes awry or where it's a difficult process of condensation is when things don't quite weave perfectly together. That's the kind of metaphor that interests me more so than where the metaphor is 'this means that'.

PT: I agree with you Nitin because I think it's open to interpretation. I don't like it when it all just fits in easily. I like it when people need to interpret the work through their own life experiences, based on their own viewpoints, based on their own morals or ethical standards, and their own perspectives. It will mean something different every time. Every person will take away something different. Maybe that's the difference between arthouse and commercial films. The arthouse film allows the viewer to interpret the material, commercial films don't allow for that.

NV: That goes back to the absurdity as well, this kind of image of Sisyphus pushing the rock up [the hill] but transposed into a person trying to fit a square peg into a round hole and even though it doesn't work the first time you keep trying and trying. So, it's arrived at this final, nicely woven together, sense of meaning, which [it] can never arrive at really, and that's kind of what the whole struggle that the main character has is pointing to.

INTERVIEW | PLATON THEODORIS & NITIN VENGURLEKAR

One of the aspects I love about this film is the style of Australiana and the presence of koalas and big things. Can you talk about what that means to you creatively and to the film itself?

PT: I love Australian-ness. It's not often celebrated the way that I live and perceive it. I think a lot of Australian-made films have become vassals for American culture, and I don't like that. It offends me when I see films that have nothing visibly Australian culturally or hear no Aussie accents in them being celebrated as Australian cinema. So, I'm always trying to find a way to slot some obscure or weird Aussie reference into my films, [things that] perhaps only Australians might get or understand. For me, a lot of those 'big things' in *The Lonely Spirits Variety Hour* were about that ridiculous Australian grandeur which just isn't celebrated. I was trying to weave that in so people understood that *The Lonely Spirits Variety Hour* is a quintessential Australian film. It is set here. It is part of the landscape and fabric of this country, part of every Aussie's family road trip.

Every single prop detail is critical. I incorporated a lot of Australiana because I love the aesthetic and so does my partner. In fact, many of the props from both features live in our house. Australiana is fascinating and kitsch yet interesting and unique. I think it says a lot about who we are as a nation, our humour, our neurosis, our myth-building - and we don't see it enough on the big screen. I kept laughing during the filming and edit because there's a cushion in the back of the radio studio set in *The Lonely Spirits Variety Hour* that's been made from an old tea towel, 'Australia 1988'. It's got a badly illustrated koala on it with crazy red eyes, that I strategically placed in shots to ensure it's super visible. There are certainly a few koalas in this film, including the Giant Koala in Victoria which coincidentally also has crazy red eyes.

NV: Platon was saying how people in interviews ask him "What is this film saying about diversity and cultural heritage?" And I think the film largely avoids that. Other than to say that Platon, maybe I'm misrepresenting you, but often his answer to that is "I'd say nothing about it. I just make films with the people that I know that are in my life. And a lot of them happen to be people of colour." But the only kind of reference to any of that stuff, if you wanted to perceive it, is in this character who's from an Indian background, but he's sitting surrounded and encompassed by this colonial Australian iconography. There's plates of Prince Charles and Diana there, all of that sort of stuff. That is there purely on an image level, then there are all kinds of different contexts whether it's the philosophy or the jazz music that is feeding into this character's mind and what he's projecting out into the microphone; that's one of the elements that's there as well, so you could read it like that.

THE LONELY SPIRITS VARIETY HOUR

Can you talk about Sabrina and the dance as well as the choice of song, How Deep is Your Love?

PT: Sabrina was part of the original stage play where she performed a version of that dance, but it wasn't used as a seduction scene in the play. When Sabrina came on board for the film, we spoke about how this dance was going to be used in the context of the film narrative and her character's relationship with Neville. I gave Sabrina a lot of the parameters of how it was to work, what was motivating it all and how it was going to be shot. For instance, the dance needed to happen with a stool, in a very tiny space, and we needed to go through the many underwear changes. I wanted the whole opening to happen as one long take. Then basically Sabrina choreographed all of it herself. It's all Sabrina. She's a clown doctor in real life, that's her day job. She's an amazing performer.

The music track in the film was originally used in the stage show and thankfully, we were able to secure the publishing license for the film. I then found a great cover song we used in the soundtrack. It was about six to eight months' worth of negotiating and it was worth it. It was important that we got that particular track as it solidifies the relationship arc in the story. I was just thankful that we were able to use it.

INTERVIEW
FILMMAKER PLATON THEODORIS

This interview was recorded by Andrew F. Peirce in December 2022

What was the thing that set you off on your filmmaking journey?

Platon Theodoris: I loved movies. I had the original *Willy Wonka and the Chocolate Factory* on VHS that we had recorded from television, and I played it over and over and over again. I can't tell you how many times I've watched that film, and *The Wizard of Oz* and *Annie*. I grew up also watching Bill Collins classics and the Shirley Temple films on Saturday afternoons. I loved watching those films and films in general.

In late primary school, my dad bought one of those VHS video cameras where the recorder unit was separate and carried in a bag. Then in high school, I would ask the teachers if instead of handing in an essay, could I hand in a film? They were quite supportive. So instead of writing an essay on say *The Merchant of Venice* or *The Sword in the Stone*, I would get a bunch of my friends together and we would make all the props, design the wardrobe, and then shoot scenes from these books in my parent's living room or backyard. I would then edit the shots together using two VHS players. I got permission to hand in videos for so many assignments.

I was working with VHS early on but then I bought my own Super 8 camera in year 10, which I found easier to edit because I could splice and dice the film celluloid. I really enjoyed it. After high school I started at UNSW's College of Fine Arts here in Sydney. They had a 'time based moving image course.' I was excited at first because the school had amazing 16mm equipment like Bolex and Éclairs which I could borrow and shoot stuff over the weekends. But I didn't make any friends and I actually started to hate the course. It was in Sydney's eastern suburbs; it was really cliquey, and fashion based. I was the only kid from Sydney's western suburbs. I lasted a year. I dropped out and moved to the main UNSW campus where I studied a generalist Arts Degree with a major in political philosophy.

THE LONELY SPIRITS VARIETY HOUR

Because I'd taken an exchange in high school to Japan, and I'd studied Japanese, when I got to the main campus to study political philosophy, I also decided to enrol in Indonesian language as a double major. I wanted to learn another Asian language because I really do think language acquisition is like gaining a superpower. When I got to the Indonesian faculty, the head of the department goes, "Oh, you've just come from COFA." I go, "Yeah, I want to study film, but that course didn't quite work out." He goes, "There's an art school in Jakarta, and they have a film faculty. I've been trying to organise this student exchange, and no one wants to go." I was like "Yeah, nah, I don't know about Indonesia. I just want to learn the language." To be honest I wasn't sure about Indonesian films as I'd never heard or seen any and I was more interested in Paris or LA film schools. I was also still terrible at the Indonesian language. Anyway, this lecturer just kept persevering, and he brought back flyers from the Jakarta Institute of Arts. He kept telling me "I'll support you and UNSW will give you full credit." I was working part time to support myself through university, so I saved all this money and realised that six months in LA or Paris is bloody expensive. My savings would go much further in Jakarta. So, I jumped in.

When I got there, I was blown away. The Jakarta Institute of Arts was everything I wanted from an Arts School/Film School. After six months, I ended up extending my stay for two years and majored in film directing. I learnt Indonesian really quickly as I was the only non-Indonesian on campus, and no one could speak English. I got taught by some of Indonesia's biggest film directors at the time, Slamet Raharjo, Eros Djarot, and Garin Nugroho. I met some amazing people and made lifelong friends and collaborators. After that I came back to UNSW and did Honours in Political Philosophy and wrote my thesis on persuasion and propaganda. I plugged away in Sydney and picked up some directing work here and there, and finally had enough material for a half decent showreel with interesting content.

A couple of years later I travelled back up to Jakarta for a friend's wedding. Film school buddies were now working in production houses and loved my showreel. They encourage me to stay on and I'm like, "Fuck it, why not?" I ended up signing with a production house, and I lived and worked in Jakarta for five years directing music videos and TV commercials. It was a life changing, amazing, and wonderfully challenging experience. The directing opportunities were fantastic and being able to collaborate with the friends I'd made at the Jakarta Institute of Arts was a huge bonus.

Some of my early music videos picked up MTV Awards and I got the opportunity to direct big budget commercial campaigns all around the region. It was a great learning curve. Always shooting on 35mm or 16mm film as a stylistic choice, storyboarding, directing actors and working with some great teams in production and post. I went from being a poor art and full

INTERVIEW | PLATON THEODORIS

student to actually having an income and making a living in the film production business, which is kind of what you want and need when you've been to art school.

What's the vibe of the advertising scene in Jakarta? Is it similar to Australia?

PT: It's exactly the same. It's run by big corporate ad agencies. A lot of these agencies were staffed with expats. I was in this interesting position because I was an expat director who spoke Indonesian with a Jakartan slang and understood local culture. The advertising scene is generally high pressure, lots of money - actually obscene amounts of money - for thirty, forty-five, sixty second visual marketing campaigns. The amount of money per second of footage is ridiculous.

I burnt myself out in Jakarta and thought it might be different elsewhere but after directing commercials in Vietnam, Greece, Malaysia, India, and Australia, I realised it's the same toxic shit everywhere. Ads are just ads in any country and in any language. You're basically helping big multinationals market and sell more of their products. They pay you lots of money and exploit your aesthetic, creative vision, directing, and filmmaking skills.

After a particularly horrible experience I thought "I really need to start making films and telling my own stories." So, in 2005 I made my first short film in Jakarta called *ParaSoul* (2005), which not many people have seen. It's on my website though[1]. It was only four minutes long, but it was all mine. This was a huge moment for me, a really big thing, because it was my own work, something I'd written and conceptualised and produced. It wasn't beholden to a record label, like music videos are or to a strategic ad agency and client like tv commercials.

I made a second short film, *Lakemba*, in 2008, which was a 30-minute film. This was a realist mockumentary, a doco-style scripted music drama. *Lakemba* did quite well on the festival circuit. It was selected for the 52nd London BFI Film Festival that year and also screened at the Brisbane International Film Festival. In London it got picked up by a small distributor called Shorts International. They were able to screen the film on cable TV in Canada, Turkey, France, and Germany. It screened on French cable TV almost thirty times, I think. I was getting these royalty checks, which is really amazing for a short film.

After the London BFI Film Festival, Hoyts in Sydney's Bankstown gave the film a bespoke two-week theatrical release with reduced ticket prices - because it was only 30 minutes - probably a first for an Australian short film. Interestingly, both SBS and ABC rejected *Lakemba*. They've never screened

THE LONELY SPIRITS VARIETY HOUR

it, even though it's like, 'Hey, it's screening in all these countries and even secured a small theatrical release.' During this period, I got a hard and fast education on the Australian way of doing things and some insight into the power of gatekeepers in this country.

My third short film *Sunrise* (2010) was a commissioned work. It was shot in Cambodia. For *Lakemba* I had worked with non-professional actors, and *Sunrise* also required me to work with non-professional actors. There's an orphanage in Cambodia called The Sunrise Children's Village run by an Australian woman named Geraldine Cox AM. *Sunrise* came out of a project where they wanted to create a short film based around short stories that some of the children at the orphanage had written. The stories were all about how some kids ended up at the orphanage. There was a whole process of working with the kids to adapt a few of the stories into one coherent screenplay. We then cast within the orphanage in Phenom Penh. *Sunrise* went to over 30 film festivals including Vancouver International, Singapore International, St. Kilda, Busan, Brisbane International, so that was great.

In the middle of that, I was trying to get my own feature films up. And that's always a journey. I've had one project in development for over a decade now. It still hasn't been made. I've had a few near misses. I got contracted to direct a feature film where I was working with a writer. Finance fell through a few months before we were scheduled to shoot. Other projects have come my way, but I felt they weren't right for me. But I really needed to make a feature film I believed in, so I took a year and a half off directing commercials in 2012. I sat and wrote the screenplay for *Alvin's Harmonious World of Opposites*, which took over a year to get right, then six months of pre-production, the set build and location scouting.

Filmmakers like me have no choice but to do things independently. I shot *Alvin's Harmonious World of Opposites* in mid-late 2013 and finished post in late 2014. I broke the film shoot into three blocks; we shot most of it in Sydney, some scenes up in Kalgoorlie, and then we shot a whole block up in Indonesia. It was kind of this informal co-production. I utilised a lot of my network to make it happen, from film school friends and relationships formed whilst directing music videos and TV commercials. People were very supportive.

We premiered *Alvin's Harmonious World of Opposites* at Perth's Revelation International Film Festival in 2015, which is amazing because Sydney and Melbourne didn't pick it up. I'm not quite sure they even watched the submission actually. Anyway, Stefan from the Sydney Underground Film Festival saw it at Revelation and said "We really want to programme it. We don't normally programme Australian films." It screened at Sydney Underground where it won Best Film. I was like, "Oh wow, these are my people. These are the sorts of film festivals that can really champion the work I make." You can thank Jack Sargeant and Richard Sowada and Katherine Berger and Stefan Popescu for giving me a platform and a voice because I probably would have stopped making films had they not programmed *Alvin's*. It's so hard to get a feature up, but even harder to have it seen and showcased.

At the awards night for Sydney Underground, everyone asked, "Where are you going for your international premiere?" I was like, "Well, it didn't get into Sundance." Everyone was like, "Your film is not a Sundance film, are you stupid?" I'm like, "What do you mean? It's an independent film!" "No, films at Sundance aren't really independent. They're just not made out of a big studio, but they have a lot of money behind them. Real indie films screen at Slamdance. It's for films made with tiny budgets, under $1 million bucks, with no distribution." I went, "Really? Slamdance? What's that?" I popped online and with a day to spare, I submitted and was selected. *Alvin's Harmonious World of Opposites* was in the narrative competition at Slamdance 2016.

Then it exploded. American producers, development executives, production houses, and studios look to this little independent film festival to see what's been programmed. It was amazing because *Alvin's Harmonious World of Opposites* got a lot of eyeballs, and I was invited into a lot of interesting meetings. Another big learning curve for me. Americans actively do this research and development; they're on the lookout for new voices and creatives. Whereas that doesn't really happen in Australia. Here you need to literally bang the door down and pray the screen agencies will help you out. After Slamdance we did a bespoke theatrical release in Australia, USA and Indonesia; it's always fun to see the film perform well in cinemas.

In 2018 I made another short film *Wine Lake*, with Ailís Logan, who I'd worked with on *Alvin's*. It did really well on the festival circuit. It was while I was on the festival circuit for *Wine Lake* that I was inspired to revisit *The Lonely Spirits Variety Hour*.

Thankfully, I've got a great group of super creative collaborators who love the work we make together and love the way I work and are very supportive of my vision. Without these people, we wouldn't have these films. Brian Rapsey who shot and edited *Wine Lake* and *Lonely Spirits*, composers Dimitri Vouros and Donald Baldie who worked on both features, and editor Dave Rudd who cut both *Alvin's* and *Sunrise*.

At first, I thought *Alvin's* was ambitious because we had ten actors and we shot in three major locations, but I think *Lonely Spirits* was even more ambitious purely because we had to make it during COVID and there were thirty actors all up which made it so much bigger. We also had a lot more

THE LONELY SPIRITS VARIETY HOUR

locations to travel to but were able to get it all done. Independent films aren't perfect, but the main thing for me is to finish them as best they can be.

Once the film is out there and people see it, the pain of birthing an indie feature film seems to dissolve into great memories, wonderful collaborations and life-changing crew and cast camaraderie. Audiences can see that there are other ways of telling stories and there are also other ways of pulling together resources to create films which are funny, engaging, and entertaining.

There are some recurring motifs that run throughout your films. In Alvin's and Lonely Spirits, there is the imagery of salt flats, and the main characters are often in restricted locations like an apartment or radio booth. Do you consciously think about these connective visual images throughout your films?

PT: For me, the visual component of cinema is the most powerful thing. You can listen to a podcast or read a book, but the power of visuals, for me, is undeniable. I'm drawn to the metaphor of what a particular visual might mean; what particular enclosed or tight spaces look and feel like and what that means in the context of a character and story. For instance, in *Alvin's* it was about this single apartment location representing the character digging themselves into this metaphoric hole, so what might it mean for the character to then liberate themselves or for them to confront their fears. What does that look like visually? In the case of *Alvin's*, it was placing him in locations with more space and a horizon. They're no longer stuck in this boxy, vertical space, but they're open both spatially and physically.

I do think about this a lot. What sort of visual metaphor might work best for a character's particular emotional state and how can we incorporate this into the story? Sometimes it's the composition of a frame or the choice of a particular location or time of day or perhaps it's a particular prop and what that brings to the subtext or what feelings this prop may convey to an audience. An audience will have to work a little bit when they watch my films. They have to stay focused. My films don't give away everything so easily. Maybe that's what defines independent cinema and non-commercial cinema. With non-commercial cinema, it actually requires a little bit of work from the audience. I love that.

There is also this connection to discovering the 'self' within people. Characters explore and figure out who they are as people. It's a huge thing to realise who you are in the world. It's a theme I've seen carry out in your films where characters' worlds are completely changed and transformed around them, and they realise who they are as an individual and man-

INTERVIEW | PLATON THEODORIS

age to find their place in a world that may not always accept them. It's presented in a deeply humanistic manner.

PT: I spent a large part of my own childhood, teens, and twenties trying to discover my 'self.' Trying to understand what makes me tick and understand who I am. I think part of this process was coming to terms and accepting that I was gay. Another part of that was also understanding that my brain has the propensity to get stuck with obsessive compulsive thoughts. I've suffered from anxiety and anxious thoughts in the past. So, understanding that's how my brain works and that's how I was born was super important, in fact quite empowering really. I'm drawn to characters who might seemingly have what some might describe as 'flaws,' but equally love this process of self-analysis. It's all very personal for me and yet so much of what we experience as people are universal human traits. 'Flaws' are the default human condition.

I read a lot of philosophy and political philosophy when I was growing up. My parents were very left-wing and political activists. My mum was a feminist and actively involved in the feminist movement during the late sixties and seventies, equal pay for equal work. Dad was a wharfie and a big unionist, and they were members of the Socialist Party of Australia. They had this whole left-wing radical thing about them. I would read up on all of that just to figure out, 'Who am I in all this?' I could see that Mum and Dad had a statue of Lenin and Stalin on the mantelpiece here, but is that what I believe in? Is that what I stand for? It was a big journey. These sorts of existential questions, coupled with all the anxiety of being a teenager and wanting to understand your own attractions and what makes you tick – I needed a lot of therapy.

My life experiences make it into the films as part of my own understanding of the world around me. With *Alvin's*, it was understanding what sort of effect an abusive, dogmatic father might have on you and your personality. To be honest, I only realised that I'd written my dad into the horrible neighbours' character Virginia literally when I first heard actor Vashti Hughes read the words out loud. A lot of how her character speaks, how she swears, the cynicism, and bullying is actually how my father spoke and interacted with people.

Then, with *Lonely Spirits*, it was a different experience again. Because my friend Vanna passed away during the script development; the trauma of that loss was too great not to make its way into the work. Detaching myself from the grief was not an option. Trying to make sense of it by engaging with the pain was the only way. It was a conscious decision. I think we go through life always deeply affected by our experiences and for me that comes to the fore, for better or worse, in the way that you speak to and

THE LONELY SPIRITS VARIETY HOUR

treat people, in the way that you behave and the way that you respond to things, in the way that you give and receive love, in the way that you give and receive criticism. It's all the human condition. My films all touch on those sorts of things, and it doesn't mean they can't also be entertaining and accessible, as well.

Your films flip between drama and comedy, tragedy and absurdism, so brilliantly and so quickly and so precisely. Everything that you're putting on screen creates an emotional experience. I know that the word 'emotional' usually leads people to think of somebody sobbing in a corner, but to me, the emotionality of a film is that tonal roller coaster. It's sitting there laughing and then a minute later, you're crying. That is the emotion of life. I'm curious if you can talk about the kind of roller coaster of emotions that you put on screen?

PT: Sometimes I find that in the saddest of moments, often there's something happening within that moment that can also bring out extreme laughter as well. It would be absurd if it wasn't cutting you so deep. When I think of some dear lost friends or family and laugh about a particular moment with them, this laughter will also make me reflect on the loss. I'll think about them not being here right now and there's sadness to it, even though a particular memory has sparked the laughter. I'll be holding competing emotions in the same moment.

I think it comes from understanding that we're not around forever. We're here for a certain number of years. We may have experiences that are positive, negative, funny, sad, difficult, entertaining, or whatever, and most often they're all mashed together. That feels like the human experience for me, the way that I live and perceive it. The whole experience is all those things together. I feel like it's never just one and only one emotion. Those shades of grey and nuance are always more insightful than the black and white, which is so obvious of course.

When I'm working with actors and a script, I would ask them, "What are you saying here?" And they say, "I'm saying this." And then I'll ask "What are you really saying underneath that? What are you really feeling?" They might respond "I'm angry, but I'm feeling hurt." My response is "Then you need to bring an equal measure of anger and hurt into that delivery, because that's what's there." It's never just the outward projection of what's going on. For me, it's always about, what's prompting that emotion? What's going on underneath? How does it feed into this kind of understanding of our own psyche?

I think a big part of me learning about myself was doing lots of yoga and meditation and understanding that you can sit with seemingly contradictory things and that it's okay. Learning how to sit still and understand the rise and fall of different thoughts, they come in waves, and with that, the different emotions that might be attached to these thoughts. As I've slowly understood how I operate, I have also slowly brought that into the writing process and the characters I create and my film work, and also into how I direct actors. A lot of my directing process might feel hands-off, and every now and then I'll get in there and have a discussion about particular things and clarify or interrogate the material a little more deeply. Every so often, I can be quite strategic about ensuring we get the full spectrum of what it is that needs to be said.

For instance, in *Wine Lake*, the main character is having a seemingly light conversation with someone about art, but they're also still carrying this trauma and pain at losing a child, so how does an actor acknowledge that but be present with whatever else is going on, to acknowledge what else might be going on for the character in the performance? It's important to have these deep conversations with actors about the subtext and extract as much of that as possible.

I really struggle with films that use violence, death, and horror as modes of entertainment. I don't ever watch them or advocate for them. One time, many years ago, I made a music video with violence in it. I struggled for weeks afterwards. I kept getting flashbacks of the process, my creative process, and how tapping into that had affected me. It's toxic. You just have to watch the daily news and read the newspaper. So much of it is about violence, death, abuse, the really depraved aspects of humanity. I never understood the concept of taking that and turning it into entertainment. It's just not my thing.

I have, over time, understood this concept of being completely connected with someone on an emotional level, of being completely connected with them and yet perhaps not knowing them very well, but actually you just connect with their energy or life force, whatever that might look and feel like. It's a powerful feeling. I'm trying to make sense of your question, because it's quite profound, in some ways it goes to the heart of what drives creatives?

That's what makes art, whether it's film or TV, or if it's a painting or a book. It's never uniform. For one-person, Blue Poles by Jackson Pollock might be the most profound piece of artwork they've ever seen in their life, and for another, it's just splashes of paint on a canvas. We never know what our emotional reaction is going to be. That's what I found engaging with your work. There are precious few films that I've found that I've truly resonated with like I did with Lonely Spirits. It is a film that moves me in a way which I don't experience very often. It's heart-

THE LONELY SPIRITS VARIETY HOUR

warming and brilliant and hilarious, but then it's desperately moving at the same time.

In Times Square, there is an art piece by Max Neuhaus called 'the hum' which has been around for decades. Not many people know about it because it kind of just blends into the soundscape of the area. This art piece is a sound that emanates from under a grate. If you stand on top of the grate, the sound almost immerses you completely and swallows out the rest of the sound in Times Square, this huge place that's teeming with people and sound. I stood on that grate during Christmas once and the feeling of being consumed by the sound created a bizarre feeling, it's that perfect hum of experiencing two worlds at once.

When I watch your films, I have the same kind of emotional resonance that I had from this perfect hum that encompasses you where you're sitting in there. I can just sit with it and know 'This is right. This is the world that I want to sit in because it feels like I'm being seen in a way that I've never been seen before.' That's a really strange and beautiful feeling to have. It's so hard to put down on paper and to precisely say 'This is it,' but when you hit it, it's like nothing else.

PT: Yes, I get it. It's a feeling that something has resonated from the work, call it a vibration or an emotion or energy, but it blankets you. You don't forget yourself, but you do realise that the world is bigger, and you're connected with it. There are so many elements of the world that are unknown, but which are magical and beautiful nonetheless, and in moments which you're able to connect and access that magic or beauty, as fleeting as that might be, this is powerful, and it stays with you. Sometimes these can also plant a seed of transformation within.

I've sat and meditated for years and on two occasions, I felt a kind of out-of-body experience where this tingling and vibration [sensation] was overwhelming; it was all so amazing in the moment. For months afterwards when I sat down to meditate, I went looking for that feeling again. But you can't go looking for it. You've just got to experience it when it presents itself. That's the whole point of why you sit and meditate, you're learning to detach from all that in the hope that you'll connect with something in the present. But it's in moments of non-attachment where the real connection occurs. You can't go looking for it, you've just got to be wholly present in the current experience. There are some things like an ocean swim or particular music pieces that have done that for me.

Are there any that come to mind for you?

PT: *Mojo Pin* by Jeff Buckley. I remember listening to it and just crying. I was on the train, and I just couldn't stop crying. There are certain tracks that can do that somehow. The book *A Thousand Splendid Suns* by Khaled Hosseini, I remember reading that and just crying. Or the film *The Sea Inside* (2004) with Javier Bardem, just thinking about that film now I still get goosebumps. There's such joy in the film, but it's so deeply moving and sad as well. It really does [present] the full spectrum of life. It's amazing.

The flip side is that you've got to be open to that. You may have watched something a few times and it didn't do it, and then all of a sudden you watch it, and for the first time you're really paying attention, or your vibrations are really connected with the vibrations of the art piece. You need to be open and present to this creative communication. That changes as well because we change every day. We're growing and transforming. We're not the same person we were seven years ago. Every day is different. So how do you bring that into the equation as well?

For the first few viewings of *Lonely Spirits* with an audience, I was always watching the film with the humour in mind. Paying attention to where the audience were laughing or not laughing where I was actually expecting them to laugh. Then when I was in Saint-Tropez, at the Festival of the Antipodes (*Du Cinema Des Antipodes*) for the first time, and I don't know why, watching the film, I seemed to experience it on a whole other level; Neville being in hospital and then passing away. That's what resonated with me on that particular night. I was getting to the end of this film that I'd made, and I was crying. I'm like, 'Oh, this is why people were saying it's really emotional.'

I didn't realise that it could make you cry. I was kind of hoping it would only make you laugh, and it does, but it also makes you cry, but I hadn't experienced that. Maybe because by that stage on the festival circuit I was a bit more detached from the work. Maybe because I had to park that thread and those emotions whilst making it because they were so overwhelming, Anyway I only experienced these with an audience for the first time in Saint-Tropez.

It was interesting that after the screening in Paris, so many people came up to me who had responded to both those elements. 'It was so funny; I was laughing so much and then I was laughing and crying by the end of it.' I was really happy that *Lonely Spirits* had done that. Perhaps then the film was experienced as it's supposed to be. For me, in the first few months on the festival circuit, I think I was just waiting for the laughter, waiting for those punch lines to kick in, and that's a crucial component of the film, but it's not the whole film.

THE LONELY SPIRITS VARIETY HOUR

Is there any music that you've listened to that's brought on those sorts of emotions?

The orchestral score by Austin Wintory for the video game Journey. It's full of joy and moments of levity with these light instruments like flutes and violins that lift you up, which is paired with genuine sadness and darkness with a deep cello that resonates deeply and creates this variance in emotions. You play as a character walking in a desert with a mountain on the horizon that you need to reach. That's it. Along the way you meet other people who look just like you. You can only interact with them with wordless pings, creating a strange form of communication. In a climactic moment, you're nearing the peak of the mountain, and a blizzard starts raging, making it difficult to move. It slowly becomes harder to ping each other, with the sound and symbols fading in the blizzard until you can't see or hear them. When you reach the other side of the blizzard, you're welcomed by a blue sky and you're filled with an immense joy, but the weight of the sadness remains, even when your fellow character reappears. That's all made possible by Austin Wintory's score.

The first time I played Journey, I didn't realise that the other characters were real people. I thought that they were NPCs. At the end, you're presented with a list of all the people you've interacted with and you're able to then reflect on the moments that you've overcome or been through with strangers, like the blizzard.

PT: And you're doing this as an avatar, which is even more profound that you can sense all that and you actually haven't left your chair. You've just made me think a song called *First Breath After Coma* by Explosions in the Sky. They do this orchestral sound that moves through so many different emotions seamlessly. It's quite profound.

There are so many unknown elements to the world and if you can somehow find a way to tap into that – which could also be exhausting because you're always tapping into it – but if you can find a way to tap into that it can really shift the way that you view things, move you. Even the simplest of things like watching a bird eat in a Jacaranda tree and being so focused on that and so in tune with what's going on.

ENDNOTES
1   https://platontheodoris.com/portfolio/parasoul

MATE

33 mins
Director: *George-Alex Nagle*
Writers: *George-Alex Nagle, Ben Tarwin, Daniel Corboy*
Cast: *Joshua Brennan, Jeremy Blewitt, Melody Kiptoo, Di Smith, JR Laveta, Zoe Jensen, Nick Bolton, Juniper Ashmore*
Producers: *Nick Bolton, Daniel Corboy, Jess Milne, George-Alex Nagle, Ben Tarwin*
Composer: *Jai Pyne*
Cinematographer: *Campbell Brown*
Editing: *Kelly Cameron*

Mate received nominations for Best Short Production of the Year at the Screen Producers Australia Awards (2023), Best Direction in a Short Film at the Australian Directors' Guild Awards (2022), and Best Editing in a Drama at the Australian Screen Editors Awards (2022).

INTERVIEW
FILMMAKERS
GEORGE-ALEX NAGLE & BEN TARWIN

In *Mate*, co-writers George-Alex Nagle, Ben Tarwin, and Daniel Corboy, grapple with the complicated time in the lives of men, that transitional period when boys become men, and when men become fathers. John (Joshua Brennan) attempts to reconnect with his son Jack (Jeremy Blewitt) over a weekend. John takes Jack to his local watering hole, introducing his estranged son to his drinking 'mates'. Jack looks at his dad with a muddled combination of adoration and despair. Here's a dad who struggles to be a father-figure, instead wanting to become his son's 'mate'. Within John's desire is a hope that his son's future will be better than his own. *Mate* is a fine slice of Aussie domestic drama, steeped in the history of Western Sydney, the roots of which you can feel in every frame.

Mate is the first Australian film to win the International Grand Prix at the Clermont-Ferrand International Short Film Festival (2022). It was also recognised with wins at the Sapporo Short Fest (2022), Boston Film Festival (2022), Thessaloniki International Short Film Festival (2022), Rabat International Author Film Festival (2022), UK Film Festival (2022), Avanca Film Festival (2023), Torino Underground Cinefest (2023), and Bucharest Short Film Festival (2023).

This interview was recorded by Andrew F. Peirce in January 2023

Where did the concept of Mate come from?

George-Alex Nagle: The idea began with Daniel Corboy, the third part of our little creative trio. The intention was to do a short film that we could make for very little money, time, and resources. And it ended up being the complete opposite. He and I were collaborating on it, and it bloomed and bloomed. It was, I guess, a vessel to work through his own depression and certain negative feelings. Then Ben came into the process, and we ended up having three writers on the film. The genesis of the idea started as an exploration of depression and working from the premise of 'what would my former self think of my current self?'

MATE

Ben Tarwin: I became involved a bit later. As George said, it rapidly became a bit more of a monster than I think we initially envisioned or planned. I'll take some responsibility for that, in the sense that I don't have a background in film. By trade I'm an author, which is a lot cheaper and easier, because all you need is a pen and a piece of paper. As I quickly learned, film is a bit of a different beast. Initially, the plan was to make a 12–15-minute short film quick and easy. I thought, why would you want to do that? Let's be ambitious. Let's make it as long as you want. How hard can it be? As it turns out, extremely hard. A half hour-short film falls into this strange in-between zone. It's going to be more involved than just a short film, but not quite as big in scope as a full feature. It was an interesting canvas for us to work with, to be honest.

G-AN: I always knew that making a 30-minute film would be a bad idea, especially when it comes to festivals and programming and releasing it. But I had seen a lot of amazing European shorts that were of that length. Oddly, every time the Oscars comes around, there's always a handful of 30-plus minute shorts in there as well. So, although it's highly discouraged, there is a market for these kinds of films.

One thing that Ben solidified, and maybe it's from his own experience, was that we shouldn't be trying to make something that conforms to any kind of established, prefab form if it meant working against the story. The film should be in the shape that best tells the story. We found that although we wanted to make something small and fleeting, a collection of moments, we ended up having a bigger story than we thought that we had, and we didn't want to compromise that.

Another thing that contributed to the shape of the story was that although I love cinema, not just the medium, but the place and actual exhibition format as well, most films are consumed over the internet through streaming these days. The 8-12-minute short film or the 90-120-minute feature film really are designed for theatrical exhibition, but now with the landscape of streaming, there's really no reason as to why a film can't be 30-50 minutes or 7-hours long if it's the best way to tell that particular story. I guess we were trying to be a little bit progressive by making a film that was somewhere between a feature and a short, even though that's not entirely new at all.

BT: When you're trying to do anything that's not necessarily commercially minded, you always need an element of intransigence. You can't give people what they want all the time. There has to be an element of taking people out of their comfort zone a little bit.

INTERVIEW | GEORGE-ALEX NAGLE & BEN TARWIN

G-AN: That has been a point of difference for our film as well. I just realised the other day that it's not really a 30-minute short film, it's a 30-minute feature film.

When did the decision point to make it into a 30-minute film come into play?

G-AN: During scripting. We also flirted with the idea of it being a pilot for a TV series at one stage. We wanted to explore not necessarily the story, but similar themes in an anthology series. Stories that were tonally and thematically linked, but with different characters in different worlds.

BT: There was an attempt to decouple what we were trying to do with as many of the established norms and regular frameworks as we could, without making life too difficult for ourselves or making something unwatchable and self-indulgent. Essentially, it became the most ambitious film we could make with the resources that were available to us.

G-AN: That makes it sound as if it's a compromise, and I don't think it's a compromise. The 30-minute canvas gave us the scope to explore the characters, themes, and the story in general to a greater and richer degree than you could do in 12-15-minutes, but without necessarily committing audiences to sit through a two-hour film. I do think that there's a market for mid-length films, especially in streaming and film festival programmes. I don't know why film festivals don't have dedicated 'novella-sized' sections for films of this length. Some of the best short films I've seen are this length.

What has the experience of touring the film around the world been like?

G-AN: It's been amazing and fulfilling and validating and gratifying to see how well our film has been received both in Australia and internationally. It's amazing because there was a very real chance that no one would ever have seen this film. It's also amazing how international audiences have been able to read deeper into the film beyond just the surface and into the universality of the film. It's been great to speak to some critics and interviewers who have been able to read into the deeper themes. It's amazing how much they related to it on a personal level, even though they're not from Penrith or Australia.

BT: It was quite an extraordinary experience being able to attend the Clermont-Ferrand International Short Film Festival. COVID was still in full force. I think the festival itself was a little bit apprehensive as it was the first time in a couple of years it had been held in person. It was an absolutely extraordinary experience. We talk about the French as this sort of cinephile culture. Clermont-Ferrand is a small town with about 100,000 people. It has a

MATE

big university, and it has a Michelin tire factory. Those are the hometown industries. The festival takes over the whole town and everyone is excited about it. All the university kids volunteer at the festival when they go and see all the films. Schools don't give homework for the weeks because all the kids have gone to watch movies and are given days off to go watch short films. Almost all of the sessions were full. I think there were 900 people there for the screening of our session. We almost missed out on our premiere because they had to desperately find some seats. It was quite the honour just being there, let alone winning a prize. I cannot recommend it highly enough for any other Australian filmmakers, as well as anyone interested in film in general.

G-AN: It's amazing how this town comes to life in the dead of winter. The audience attendance is huge. The biggest theatres are 1000-1500 seat venues, and they pack out most sessions. We've gone to short film festivals around the world, but there's something about Clermont that made me realise just how much people love and respect short film as a medium in itself. Here, short films are something you do with your spare cash or your credit card, or maybe you're lucky enough to get funding, but it's not something that's seen as a viable business prospect. Over there, there are producers and distributors and companies that only specialise in short films. We met some people who have no interest at all in feature films, both audiences and filmmakers alike. They have dedicated their artistic output and endeavours to this medium. Some of the most important films in history would be classified as short films, like *La Jetée* (1962) or *Un Chien Andalou* (1929).

Ben, Daniel, and I have been friends for 20 years. So, something that's been amazing for me is that this is the first time that I've made a 'proper' released film with my mates. It became a very professional film in the end, but it was a couple of friends making a film together, which is why I think we've been fortunate to have had such a fruitful, creative experience. I don't think I'd go back to working with people I haven't been friends with for over a decade. I don't know how to do it.

Let's talk about the themes. Here is this dad who isn't a dad, he is a 'mate.' It shows how for some men, when they have a son, there is this perspective of not wanting to be a paternal figure for their child, they want someone who is their best friend. There is a real conflict within that idea because they almost work against each other. Can you talk about that conflict of a father versus being a mate?

G-AN: It's interesting that you saw it as the father who wanted to be a mate. I always saw it the other way around, John not being able to relate to his son as a son, but as a friend, due to his own insecurities, and due to his own emotional ineptness.

INTERVIEW | GEORGE-ALEX NAGLE & BEN TARWIN

BT: I would make the point that the name of the film *Mate* is not just a noun as in 'a mate,' but it also describes a relationship. What does it mean to call someone 'mate'? Yes, there's the meaning of it being like a close friend, but there's also an element of it being what you call a stranger. It's also what you call someone if it's not a tightly defined relationship. In that sense, what does that mean to have a relationship that's so vague as to be able to use a word like 'mate,' instead of what should be a far more solid grounded, concrete relationship, such as 'parent' and 'child'. In a sense, the concept of just being a 'mate' dissolves some of that sense of responsibility and reciprocity.

G-AN: I always have to tell people overseas that mate doesn't just mean friend. It also means stranger.

It's a distinctively Australian term in a lot of ways, even though it is used elsewhere in the world. It carries so many different meanings. I appreciate the dialogue too; it is so proudly and confidently Australian. There is that kind of grounded Australiana in the voice and choice of words here. Can you talk about playing with the Aussie vernacular?

G-AN: From the get-go, we didn't want to sanitise the language and the references and the world and the characters in any kind of way. Having said that, we didn't want to lean so heavily into it that it became overly self-referential.

BT: We didn't want it all 'aw strewth' and 'bloody ocker.'

G-AN: Dinky di.

BT: We didn't need Scott Morrison in the writer's room.

G-AN: There's quite a lot of contradictions in both the film and in the process of this. I'd be lying if I said it wasn't uniquely Australian, but we always knew that we may be making a film for international audiences. Although it's very Australian, it does have quite a, speaking generally, European sentiment to it. I, for one, was very worried if the film would be understood by anyone outside of Australia. To our surprise, they did. They might not have understood every single bit of the language or every little cultural reference, but I think it's something more than just the universality of the story that connects with international audiences. I think there's also a capacity for the language to be both specific and universal, even though it's highly specific because there are always other local equivalences of that. I wouldn't say the approach to language celebrates local culture, but it definitely uses it as a tool. I think that both local audiences appreciate that, and international audiences are enticed by it as well.

MATE

BT: The film is essentially a two-hander about exploring the relationship between these two characters. That's the foreground of the film. Another enormously important component of the film is there's also, in a sense, a social background to it. This isn't Beckett. These are not two characters that exist in a void. I think the language that's used in the dialogue is meant to be about reflecting some of the grounded social reality that these characters come from.

G-AN: Although it's full of colloquialisms, and specifically New South Wales and Penrith references, there's also a dated element to it as well. To me, John is a guy who's at the very least in arrested development, if not living in a bygone era, so a lot of the references and language, even some of the vulgarities that he used, are not really used today. They're placed in a fairly recent past.

BT: It is interesting that with international audiences on a couple of occasions when we've had the opportunity to travel when the film has been programmed in international festivals, looking at people's faces at some of the more talky parts, there's a couple of chuckles and also a couple of very blank expressions. We did try and make it particular to a certain part of Sydney, so even then you couldn't necessarily expect other Australians to pick up on all of the nuances, but I think it's generally understood what the language is getting at.

This is what I've enjoyed about seeing films like Mate and Here Out West. They're distinctly New South Wales stories. If I think of America, there are major cities like California and New York and then a whole variety of different cultures in the states in between. Yet in Australia, the perspective is often that somebody from Perth is exactly the same as somebody from Sydney, and that's just not the case. Watching Western Australian films versus New South Wales and Victorian films, it's clear there is a different way of talking and different forms of Australian culture on screen. It's comforting to see that, in a cultural sense, we're not a uniform country.

BT: We did try and make a point of some of the local differences. It was a mission statement of ours: there will be no shots of Sydney Harbour, none of the Opera House or the Harbour Bridge. I'm not saying that you get 20-minutes away from the harbour and everything is like Penrith, but Sydney is a city of 5 million people. Swanning about on yachts does not reflect the lived experience of the vast majority of people.

G-AN: It's interesting that you mentioned *Here Out West*. Western Sydney is something like 75% of Sydney, it's the majority of Sydney and there's a huge difference between Penrith and Campbelltown or Parramatta. Par-

INTERVIEW | GEORGE-ALEX NAGLE & BEN TARWIN

ramatta is the geographic centre of Sydney. There are different cultures and there are different worlds, and that's something that I was interested in exploring. Sydney is huge geographically, it's one of the biggest cities on earth. It's so vast.

I'm not speaking for everyone's experience, but there are a lot of people who live very localised lives in this vast landscape. In *Mate*, we were interested in a character who maybe hadn't ventured too far outside of his little local community ever. He was very much shaped by his immediate surroundings. Having said that, Western Sydney isn't all just stagnation, like it's represented in our film. Penrith is quite bougie these days. The centre of Penrith is anyway.

BT: This is also a key theme of the film, there's a changing social landscape. This is part of the sociological world that the characters exist in. When I was a kid, last century, Western Sydney was a pretty down place, you wouldn't brag about coming from there. It was a place that you either stayed in for your entire life, or you got out the second you could. That's not the case anymore. There's an enormous amount of pride in people who live out west. People don't see the need to leave. Migration has played a huge part in the story of Western Sydney and that'll be the same in Melbourne. With all of this sort of dynamic and vibrant change also comes dislocation. Hence you get a character like John, who has stayed the same whilst the world has changed around him.

Where we shot the last scene in the film was a housing development near Penrith, out on the western outskirts of Sydney. It's a relatively recent development. All these new houses have quarter-acre blocks and driveways. A key marker of these places is that they have rounded guttering in the streets. It was an interesting combination of people who live there. It was the more well-to-do side of Penrith. It was people from Penrith and the surrounds that made a bit of money and they've moved to this place, as well as more recently arrived Indian families. So, you would have Penrith locals going shopping at Coles walking past all these women in sarees and this incredibly colourful and vibrant, traditional clothing. That struck me as a lovely indication of part of the changes that are occurring.

G-AN: *Here Out West* is very much about pride and a celebration of place. We were more drawn to a critical engagement with the city, a warts-and-all exploration. With *Mate*, both characters and the world aren't wallowing in the negativity of the place, but it's also not glorifying it or painting an idealised version of it as well.

BT: We did not get a grant from Destination NSW for this film.

MATE

Touching on the set and production design, it feels fortuitous that John's house is based right next to this erupting apartment building. He's being pushed out by change, and he doesn't know it yet. But it's happening. His house is literally falling apart around him.

G-AN: That was always a theme in the story. Before we started scouting locations, I had placed him in an apartment building, so it was almost like he was in a cell in the way that he was surrounded by people but completely isolated. You'd be so isolated, but you're surrounded by people. Then our producer Nick Bolton found this place and believe it or not, it was on Airbnb. It was a house that I guess someone was sitting on, waiting for the best opportunity to sell it to the giant developer next door. That opportunity came and went, so they were stuck with this derelict house up against a sterile new build. That perfectly encapsulated one of the themes of the films for us.

There's one shot in the film in which John is swinging from the outside pergola, and we see the new build. That one image says so much more than we could have said with dialogue. It was a happy accident that we found that place. If we hadn't, I don't think that the film would have been as succinct as it could have been. I don't think we could have made the film without that location. It was one of the very many pieces of the puzzle that if we didn't have, we wouldn't have the film. Likewise, with the pub location, as well. We found this long courtyard with these timber slats on the side, and the light comes through them. It's almost like you're either on a train or in a prison cell in a way. I kind of love this long courtyard that's stuck in forever. It's almost like a cell as well.

BT: To make things weirdly grim, all the stools were bolted into the floor.

G-AN: It made it very difficult to shoot in there with all the seats locked in place. There's a lot you can read from this film. Our film was written with a lot of themes and a lot of ideas in mind, and throughout the writing process, our goal was to code a lot of deeper ideas in the locations and in the language and in the structure of the film. It's been amazing to hear when people can decode those deeper ideas and deeper themes of the film.

We've talked so much about the Australian identity of the film. How important it is to explore the Australian identity on screen? It's clearly something that you've both thought about in the creation of Mate.

G-AN: I can't speak for every film, but I do see a lot of Australian films that feel as if they need to sanitise the Australian experience. Maybe they think that's how we can appeal to broader audiences abroad. And I really disagree with that approach. With *Mate,* we had a warts and all approach, and we

INTERVIEW | GEORGE-ALEX NAGLE & BEN TARWIN

were against the idea of sanitising out our world and our experience in our society with our people. I think that's one of the reasons why it's been successful abroad is because people can recognise that in their own cultures.

BT: Your subject can never solely be the characters in a film. Those characters always operate within some kind of context. It's a question of how interested you are as a storyteller in exploring the actions of individuals in the world, rather than the actions of individuals only in relation to each other. By default, as a storyteller, you have to tell stories about the world as it exists in its social contexts. Otherwise, I think you have something that is incomplete and has too many blank spaces in it.

How did you build the relationship between Joshua and Jeremy prior to filming? Did you workshop the script, or was that distance relationship between the two of them important to maintain prior to shooting?

G-AN: Both. This was always going to be a performance-driven film. If we don't get the right people to bring these characters to life, then this is going to be a big waste of everybody's time. Miraculously, it was not a big waste. As far as the approach to working with them, firstly it comes down to casting them. We couldn't have cast these two guys without our casting director, Stevie Ray, at McGregor Casting.

We spent a long time looking for these two leads. Josh Brennan is not an unknown actor, but Jeremy Blewitt was. The casting process was long and difficult. There was quite a specific thing that we were looking for in both of them but at the same time, they also really surprised me and both actors ended up being not quite who I particularly had imagined when we wrote it. A lot of their personality and their unique characteristics became the missing piece of the puzzle.

I didn't want to over-rehearse with them because I wanted it to be very naturalistic, spontaneous, and chaotic. Having said that, we couldn't go in there completely unplanned. There were a couple of scenes that Jeremy had done several times throughout auditions, but Josh had not. We did have one day of rehearsal, but it was largely discussing the characters and the material as well. There was one day rehearsing in person, and I spent a lot of time over Zoom with each actor individually discussing the scenes, characters, and potential backstories. That was largely separate and working with them individually.

On set, I tried to keep it as loose as possible. Although we had a written script, we also deviated from that script greatly. I did give them time and space to improvise, although I did try to stick to the script where it was necessary for the story. One of my initial plans was to have the script as a guide and move freely from that, but as we wrote it, certain things needed to make sense and for the themes to kind of be apparent as well. I always tried to throw in a 'chaos take' where we get the scene down and then say, "Let's just do it completely differently," in terms of the characters, the blocking, and the camera. In the grenade take, both actors have given some amazing, incredible performances, and without them, there wouldn't have been a movie.

BLACKLIGHT

104 mins
Director: *Mark Williams*
Writers: *Nick May, Mark Williams (story by Nick May, Brandon Reavis)*
Cast: *Liam Neeson, Aidan Quinn, Taylor John Smith, Emmy Raver-Lampman, Claire van der Boom, Yael Stone, Andrew Shaw, Zac Lemons, Gabriella Sengos, Tim Draxl, Georgia Flood, Caroline Brazier, Mel Jarnson, Sunny S. Walia*
Producers: *Paul Currie, Allie Loh, Coco Xiaolu Ma, Myles Nestel, Mark Williams*
Composer: *Mark Isham*
Cinematography: *Shelly Johnson*
Editing: *Michael P. Shawver*

INTERVIEW
FILMMAKER MARK WILLIAMS

As had become the norm during the peak of COVID, Hollywood productions migrated south to Australia to seek some kind of COVID-free safety. Everyone from George Clooney and Julia Roberts (*Ticket to Paradise*, 2022) to Chris Hemsworth and Natalie Portman (*Thor: Love and Thunder*, 2022) shifted down under to keep the Hollywood-hamster wheel turning.

Another Hollywood-backed production was Mark Williams *Blacklight*, a Liam Neeson-led conspiracy thriller which was partially shot in Melbourne. It also saw Australia's capital city sub-in for America's capital city, Washington, with a major action sequence that featured Liam Neeson tearing it up through the streets of Canberra in a high-risk car chase.

This interview was recorded by Andrew F. Peirce in February 2022

What was the decision behind filming Blacklight in Australia?

Mark Williams: We were looking for the best place to shoot to make it as big and exciting as we wanted it to be. I have a friend, Paul Currie, who's a producer on the movie who lives in Melbourne and has been trying to sell me on Melbourne for about ten years. Finally, I realised, "Well this makes sense." When we chose to go to Melbourne, that was when Victoria was in total lockdown, and it was a mess.

I landed in Sydney and sat in a hotel room for two weeks, and then I went to Canberra for ten days and sat in that hotel room there because I couldn't go to Victoria. There were no guarantees that it was going to be Victoria, but it felt right. I was looking for a modern city that could double for Washington DC that had some cool buildings and a cool look, and Melbourne has that, so it made a lot of sense. The crew is fantastic, so it was a win-win for all of us.

How do you go about scouting for the locations? Do you have somebody on the ground sending you pictures of the city?

BLACKLIGHT

MW: You got it. They sent me a lot of photos. A lot of them were of other movies because they weren't allowed out of their houses. Then I would give them a feeling of "This is right, this is wrong." When I finally made it to Melbourne, we had permission to go out in the streets and drive around and look at things. It made it challenging because we couldn't necessarily go into every building we wanted to go into, but you have to stand there and feel it before you know if it's right.

There's a massive action sequence that was shot in Canberra. How do you logistically plan an action sequence in the nation's capital?

MW: I was in Canberra for ten days, and I noticed the downtown loop looked a lot like Washington DC. Guy Norris, who was our amazing stunt coordinator, who has done all the Mad Max series, flew down from Brisbane, and we walked the streets of downtown Canberra, and there's a perfect loop for us to be driving in. We said to the government officials, "Hey, do you mind if we use this? But we just need it for four days." They were very gracious and said "Sure." What we wanted to do was make it a live-action shoot with very few visual effects, we wanted to reproduce it in a way that was not fake in any possible way. We designed the chase around the streets that we were allowed to use and then figured out ways to really cause mayhem.

How do you make Australia look like America?

MW: I had a fantastic art department that would look at something and I wouldn't even see it. I wouldn't go "That looks very Australian," but they would know. They've worked on plenty of American movies and television shows, so they would know, "That's not a bench that you would see in the US." They would end up replacing a lot of things that Canberra has and make them more American. Honestly, if you're watching the background during a chase like that, you're probably missing the point. It's about keeping the audience in the action with the characters and keeping the emotion running high as opposed to analysing the backgrounds.

What are the benefits of working in a completely different time zone?

MW: I was centralised in Melbourne, so everything was Melbourne-related, except for two things. My editor was in Los Angeles because he couldn't come to Australia. We had a digital link, and we edited the entire movie over the internet with a fancy hook-up. My composer was in LA as well and he sent me files and we talked on the phone. For the shoot, I was 100% in Melbourne time doing Melbourne things. The challenge became during editing when it goes from a five-hour to a seven-hour time difference and then all of a sudden, I'm up some quirky hours in the morning trying to deal with it. It was fairly seamless a process.

INTERVIEW | MARK WILLIAMS

What was your experience working with Australian crews?

MW: I had a great time. I adore them. They worked so hard; they were eager to make the best movie possible. They had knowledge and skill sets that were as good as anybody. My art department, camera department, locations, every department was going above and beyond for what I was trying to achieve, and it was great to see. I'd walk on sets where I'd seen during location scouts, and it would be ten times better than I imagined. It was quite remarkable, and they were a joy to work with.

LITTLE TORNADOES

94 mins
Director: *Aaron Wilson*
Writers: *Aaron Wilson, Christos Tsiolkas*
Cast: *Mark Leonard Winter, Silvia Colloca, Robert Menzies, Fabio Motta, Minnie Liszukiewicz, Freddy Liszukiewicz, Anya Beyersdorf, Edwina Wren, Julie McGregor, Brian Simpson, Rory Dempsey, Khan Chittenden*
Producers: *Ian Anderson, Katrina Fleming, Christian Pazzaglia, Susan Schmidt, Aaron Wilson*
Composer: *Robert Mackenzie*
Cinematography: *Stefan Duscio*
Editing: *Cindy Clarkson*

Aaron Wilson won the Australian Directors Guild Award for Best Direction in a Feature Film (Budget under $1m) in 2022.

INTERVIEW
FILMMAKER AARON WILSON

Aaron Wilson's *Little Tornadoes* follows Leo (Mark Leonard Winter), a young father whose wife leaves him and their two kids. Leo attempts to shift to his new life as a father learning on the job. Meanwhile, he has to balance the failing state of his own father.

Set in rural Australia in the 1970s, *Little Tornadoes* envelopes the immigrant experience with narration written by Christos Tsiolkas. Cinematographer Stefan Duscio, *Little Tornadoes* presents a glimpse at the enduring search for human connection, whether it be a son and his father, a father and his children, or a young woman seeking a new life in Australia.

Little Tornadoes was shot in the early 2010s, with the film gestating for over a decade before it was unveiled at the 2021 Melbourne International Film Festival. Aaron Wilson toured *Little Tornadoes* around Australia in 2022, engaging in Q&A sessions with audiences, and bringing a devoutly independent spirit to this powerfully realised film.

This interview was recorded by Andrew F. Peirce in May 2022

You toured the film around Australia and have become your own one-person marketing machine. How did you manage that?

Aaron Wilson: I've been trying to do social media reels and whatnot, just to help better reach audiences or talk about the things that no one talks about with these sorts of films, which is how hard it is. Audiences don't know. I believe if audiences understand or appreciate the effort put into it, they might take a closer look at the film and even recommend it to friends when they say, "I'll tell my friends." Because they don't really understand the work that goes into putting a film out. "Oh, you're cutting up your own posters and putting up your own flyers?" I think if I can convey to people how much effort is going into it just to get the film to them, it might translate into a little bit more visibility.

LITTLE TORNADOES

My producers and I have been working on how we can best make use of our time. It's involved a lot of me driving around. The film is about regional Australia. I want to take it out to regional Australian audiences. I'm paying for every trip, every bit of petrol, and accommodation. Meeting audiences [is] wonderful for me, if I can have conversations with people and make the most of that time. At least I can't say I didn't try when you look back and [go] "What could we have done differently?" I was pretty hands-on with *Canopy* (2013) but this one even more so. It's hard when you've got limited cinemas and you're competing against Marvel films with a marketing budget. You've just got to try to find different ways and hope something sticks or hope audiences start to spread the word and gain some sort of traction that can slowly grow.

What's changed since 2013-14 with Canopy and now with Little Tornadoes?

AW: Social media, in particular. Lockdown happened so people are in their homes a bit more, they're reluctant to come out. Yes, they'll go and see some tentpole productions, but when it means investigating smaller films that they would otherwise have seen in a cinema for that cinematic experience, it's hard to bring them back to make them realise, "There is a reason why we love cinema." The tour has been good because it's allowed audiences to connect, especially small country towns and go "It reminds me of that communal nature of being out around people and having conversations about something that relates to us. I'm going to tell my friends about this." They wouldn't think of it until they've actually been in the situation. It's bringing the horse to water. Once they're in that room, they get it, but it's getting them there.

What surprised you with the conversations you've had with audiences?

AW: It's not so much surprising, but, interestingly, every single Q&A has been the same passionate energy around "This is an important subject. It's authentic, but in a way that we enjoy. We relate to it, it's a celebration of who we are." The conversation bounces from person to person and the Q&A goes on for an hour. It becomes a discussion. That's really what I was hoping for, using regional cinemas as cultural and social hubs that bring people out after lockdown. To celebrate not just cinema, but who we are, and have discussions about who we are as Australians. It has become more than just the film. It's hard to then disseminate that into the press and media to say, "This tour is happening and it's creating these ripples." It happens in isolation if you don't have any attention focused on it.

People are still very risk averse as to what they go out and see. They want the safe or the norm. They're afraid of going out to test something that might challenge them.

INTERVIEW | AARON WILSON

AW: It's interesting too that cinemas are cautious as well. "Oh, we don't know if audiences will connect with this. We don't know whether they'll want to see this sort of film." Every time we screen, the managers of the cinema are watching how the audience reacts. They're surprised. "Wow, they really connect to it. Maybe we should look at a season or more sessions." It's not surprising, I guess, but people are generally risk averse. I think with cinemas, [they're] doing it tough. They want to go for a safe bet. Trying to present this film was a task that, with some love and care, could transform it into more than just a 'little' film. It can be something that can grow into something more impactful. It's just trying to figure out how to kick it off, and how to best get the momentum.

How did you cast Mark?

AW: I auditioned around ten people for the role. I was recommended people by my wonderful casting director, Jane Norris. Mark was the second person that I spoke to. I think Jane pointed him out and said, "You'll come back to him," and I did. I guess it was his quiet intensity. It wasn't so much what he brought to the room, but it was just himself occupying space. I was curious about him, so I chatted further with him. From those chats came an understanding, I could see how the character would fit in the world of the film.

When we went to film, Mark turned up about three weeks early to just hang around the town. He moved into the factory space and worked there for two weeks. He got the guys to teach him how the lathes work, and he knew how to work the machinery by the end. In the film, he is working on the machinery. They were a bit worried about his long hair at the start. He's just existing in that space as if he were a factory worker. He brought authenticity and the ability to fit into that world that was already existing. He fit into the rhythm of that world. His performance was almost reflexive, reactive to the world around him. The people that are in the factory who are in the scene as extras, he was reactive to their rhythm and tone.

How much did you have to change the town to fit the era of the story?

AW: There's a lot of textures in the town that haven't changed in the last fifty to sixty years. In that factory, for example, the lathes are all 1950s vintage, with years of wear and tear and grease. On the day of filming, the factory owner came in and said, "I haven't cleaned it up yet. I haven't wiped the walls down." I said, "Do not touch the walls. Leave it." It was capturing that lived-in experience as it already exists, but then embellishing it with textures that we found from around the town. Our production designer Tim [Burgin] and our costume designer Maria [Tsoukas] would speak to the locals and source items that were in use at people's homes and place them into the scene. Then we brought in locals to get their thoughts on, "How

LITTLE TORNADOES

does this look? Is this what it looked like in 1971?" They would help with their advice and perspective. Bearing in mind that in the country, things feel a bit older because they don't renew and change things as much if it works, don't replace it, don't fix it.

Can you talk about creating that migrant story in this film?

AW: The world that the film is set in is my hometown region. It's the hometown of our director of photography Stefan Duscio. It's a naturally vibrant, diverse place. Lots of Calabrian and Sicilian Australians came across in the fifties, sixties, and seventies. There's that natural colour and energy and life from that influx of Italians. I wanted to reflect on that and comment on that being an organic part of this world, that it exists, and it just forms part of the story in the fabric of the world.

Also, trying to bring in that Murray River landscape, the river itself, the feeling of what it's like to live in that world and how it affects the characters. It's interesting that a lot of the Italians came over from similar climates, so they gravitated towards the Murray River region because it was good for growing fruit or produce that they were used to growing. It wasn't the big city, but it just felt like the ruralness of the world they came from. Now it's evolved into this great part of regional Australia that has this organic mix of diversity.

Stefan is one of the finest working cinematographers. Can you talk about working with him?

AW: When we researched the world of the film, we spent weeks wandering the spaces that we used to inhabit as kids. I grew up in Tocumwal on the north of the river, and he grew up in Cobram not more than five k's as the crow flies, as my father would say. We wandered the space of the forest and the town, the streets, the back streets. We wanted to find spaces that felt affecting to us but also helped to create and build a world as a character. How spaces in the morning look different than in the evening [and] gave you an eerie, surreal, more suspenseful feel. That way you're creating something people haven't seen before. At the same time, it captures an authenticity and a real sense of that part of regional Australia.

The crux of the narrative is that the mother has gone, but there is still a familial warmth that is created by Mark's character. Can you talk about how created that feeling in that home?

AW: The home is almost like a little bubble. With the sound design, we focused on room tone. We wanted to feel like once the doors are closed, it locks the outside out and it's this little oasis. Using the textures of the Seventies, the blankets and the bedhead, and the lighting to create worlds that feel familiar and nostalgic, but at the same time, they feel intimate. They talk about the importance of family and spaces for family to occupy, that would feel familiar for people, so they created a juxtaposition against the big landscapes outside. Once you're inside, that world is shut off. We're in the space of the characters and the sound design, everything is very intimate and quiet. We're drawn closer to the characters.

At the end, you've got the note "For My Nan." Can talk about your nan, I'd love to hear about her.

AW: She's been this presence in my life since I was born. We grew up on a farm, and my grandparents lived about 40-50 metres away until my grandfather passed away. Then my Nan moved to Melbourne when she was ninety. Even after that, when I moved to Melbourne, I would always seek her counsel. I would be able to talk to her about anything and everything in my life. She would listen and offer a perspective that was a little bit different to everyone else in my family. She was always someone who grounded me in what I was doing but gave me a strong connection to the place, that world that I came from.

Telling this story was a way of celebrating the world that I came from, that culture on the Murray River, but also recognising the importance of family, that even if you drift, it pulls you back. It's something that I'm always going to respect.

It's interesting, we had our gala screening in Melbourne, and it was five days after my Nan had passed away. That was a very bittersweet night for me, but it was a nice way for me to recognise the legacy of the impact she had on my life. I've now got this film to celebrate. It's my way of celebrating my connection to her and family and beyond that, my community that I grew up in.

It's universal, too. When I travel around different parts of the world, as I drift further away from home, I make friends. People in different cultures and different countries have a strong connection to their family members, and you look at the relationship between father and son or the grandmother and grandson or granddaughter. You look at the commonality of those experiences. What are the things at the heart of those connections that we all can relate to?

I've used that when I came back to make this film, and it's very hard. It's a story about a family dealing with trauma, overcoming obstacles, and how they adapt and move forward. For me, it's always recognising the importance of family when you're going through these sorts of things, and the universality of that experience. Hopefully, I've created a film that has a universal appreciation of family at its core.

That complexity is in the father as well. I want to talk about the visually impressive sequences in the film where he has those memories of the war. Can you talk about creating that visual style?

AW: In the research for *Canopy*, I was speaking to a lot of ex-POWs about their war experience. When they spoke to me, it wasn't so much about events that happened, it was about either the silence between events when they were free to let their mind drift and think about their predicament, or it was years later and where their mind would go to when they were out on the farm or when they're at a pharmacy by themselves. They would just drift, they would always be drifting back into those spaces that haunt them. They'd describe what that looked like, and it was the same story over and over.

I wanted to reflect [in that scene] in a visual cinematic way the feeling of what it must be like to drift back into traumatic moments. For me, it was about exploring trauma that persists from the war and many other wars, and the trauma that persists down the generations. That's very relevant in small country towns where you see the next generation of soldiers, particularly from the Second World War, who live with the resonant effects of the father's experience. How do we move forward, hindered by those traumatic elements in our family? How do we adapt and how do we move? It informed the storytelling for me. I don't linger on it for too long.

Can you talk about rural towns and the way that masculinity grows and changes in those areas?

AW: I think it's the physical isolation that really affects the emotional isolation of these characters. You've already got men who are stoic and don't say a lot. Then if there's trauma affecting them or things in their life they have to deal with, it's made harder by that physical isolation. I wanted to explore intimately what it might feel like for someone in that situation when the doors are closed when no one's looking. Looking at the vulnerability of these people and exploring things that perhaps you don't like talking about so much, but we know we have to, and it's a bit uncomfortable. These things are very personal to me, it's the world that I came from, and it's the people I know in that world.

Also, the maleness in context to the women and the absence of women, particularly at a period in the early seventies when there was a great social change happening, and society is questioning expectations of women and gender roles. It's almost "What would I have been like if I had grown up in

INTERVIEW | AARON WILSON

that time period and stayed in the country and didn't move to the city?" It's you as an individual trying to find your sense of self, your identity. It's hard enough to do at the best of times, let alone in a world where it's physically isolating. I guess all these things were at play in my head when I wanted to explore the maleness of this world.

How did you go about writing the character of Maria and discovering what role she might play within the actual story itself?

AW: Maria evolved quite a lot because, for me, she was symbolic of the change in the air and the energy that came in with the new migrants, the Italians into my hometown region. We use food as a symbol of the warmth and beauty that can bring families together. It's reflective of the change that happens to our culture and society as a consequence of new migrants coming and we grow, and we strengthen as a consequence.

Over the course of finishing the film, we decided we wanted to really strengthen Maria's voice. It was Christos [Tsiolkas] decision, coming on board in post-production, to give Maria a stronger voice through the narration, and then also mix Italian with English. We see on screen Leo, this man who is unable to speak but we see his journey, and then we hear Maria's journey through the narration. At some point in the film, these two characters converge, and we then see her on screen. It's the combination of hearing her voice commenting on the world as an outsider, and then seeing her as this bringer of colour and energy and love into the home. That creates different dimensions to her character that really speak to the beauty of the migrant experience, and looking at the world anew, looking at the world through outsider's eyes, and how that makes us re-evaluate the landscape that we live in.

What discussions did you have in post-production working with Christos to write that narration?

AW: Christos was a wonderful collaborator. He's very generous at looking at the footage and the material that was there and strengthening and enhancing it in a way that I certainly couldn't have done. He brings a delicate, intimate, and sensitive approach to that. When we were starting to develop the narration for Maria, there were a lot of park walks. It was during the pandemic in 2020, so we would be wandering and putting things out there. For example, the graves. Christos wrote about the cleaning of the graves, how that's important for Maria, and how the Australian graves are dirty, and they don't clean them. This experience and tradition of keeping the graves clean isn't just an Italian experience, it's Greek and Chinese. Qingming is a period of the year when the family goes and cleans the grave. It speaks to a greater immigrant feeling in the story. It was trying to imbue

LITTLE TORNADOES

that narration with something more than just a singular Italian point of view. As an outsider looking into this world, how does that add to the story of the film and create something multi-layered?

What kind of emotional process did you go through to allow another writer to come onto your work?

AW: I was sitting down with my editor Cindy [Clarkson] in post. We knew that we wanted to have an extra voice in the film. We didn't quite know how to bring it in. I didn't really have the skills to write it. I wanted to approach a writer who I thought had that intimacy and vulnerability in his work. For me, that was Christos. We approached him and sent him the edit, and thankfully, he responded very positively and said, "I'm in." Once that happened, it was about empowering him; sharing the vision first, but then once you share the vision, it's like any other collaborator on your project. You want them to bring something spectacular and exciting to the project that you couldn't have created. It's part of filmmaking being this is a collaborative journey, so I'm very open to sharing that journey with all of my team. Once Christos was on board, he was sculpting something that could only have come from him and made the film infinitely stronger and richer as a consequence of his collaboration.

It subverts what narration is. Narration has traditionally been treated in some ways as being just telling you what's on screen.

AW: Exactly. He was at pains to create something that enhanced what was already there. It wasn't going to repeat what you're seeing, it needed to be an extra layer. Christos' point of view is different, the son of immigrants, compared to me, I grew up in this small country town and I know this world very intimately but from the inside. You bring these two stories, these perspectives together, they create this great juxtaposition, this exploration of what it means to be Australian and the importance of our history and how it is relevant to what happens today.

There is a shot of a 'little tornado'. Can you talk about the creation of that shot?

AW: It's luck. As a kid, you grew up seeing those little dust devils, the whirly-whirlies. Depending on what part of the country you're in, you call them a different thing. But it was those little disturbances that happen in life, they pop up and they take a bit of topsoil away. You get on with life, you move on. For me, it was the symbolism of that, but I wanted to have a shot in there somewhere of that. It's like anything when you go looking for it, it's very hard to find. I remember it was around burn-off season, I'd sat on a paddock for about two or three days. Nothing happened. The day after I left, my brother sent me a video to say, "Is this what you're after?" It was the perfect dust devil. I ended up going back and we captured the shot with a drone. A bit of luck, a bit of persistence. A little bit of tumultuousness happening in life. It's just part of regional life, things that have happened, little textures and we don't draw attention to it as being a big scene. It's just an incidental moment, and then we move on.

You explore some interesting themes; Canopy with the war, and here we're talking about a multicultural Australia. How important is that to you as an Australian filmmaker? Is that what you want your identity as an Australian filmmaker to be?

AW: I think I've explored this in some of my shorts as well. For me, the beauty of Australia and our culture is that it's constantly evolving. When people come from different countries and different places, they bring this colour and energy that ultimately contributes towards the greater Australian society. We're small enough that we adjust, we shift, and we grow, and we strengthen, so each generation of people that come from a different world contributes something and adds to the cultural landscape, and we're constantly shifting and becoming something richer and more dynamic.

The film was a way of me saying, "Fifty years ago, this happened, and at the time, there was fear and caution, people were worried about these new arrivals. Ultimately, we look back and [realise] we're so much richer as a culture because of what these people have brought and contributed towards Australia." That constantly happens. It's happening again today. It's something we should be celebrating as Australians and be proud of and recognise that's what is Australian culture. That's what makes a strong part of our identity.

You've gone between shorts and features and documentaries. Is there a format that you enjoy working with the most?

AW: I do a lot of commercials as well. I do a bunch of stuff in Southeast Asia. The [work] I'm drawn to [explores] cross-cultural connection, when you've got people from different backgrounds, and you find this point of commonality that connects us. The same happened with this film inadvertently, it came about through the writing and once Christos came on board. It became a process of our collaboration. It's what I'm drawn to as someone who was born in a small country town, then travelled to Melbourne, then overseas. I've come back and reflected on my birthplace and the importance of that, but the importance of it as a microcosm for the greater Australian society. We are a land of mixed cultures and mixed peoples. But that mixing is ultimately what makes us special. My work is a quiet way of exploring that cross-cultural connection.

LONESOME

99 mins
Director: *Craig Boreham*
Writer: *Craig Boreham*
Cast: *Josh Lavery, Zarif, Mathew Waters, Ally Morgan, Liz Lin, Julian Oliver, Vincent Andriano, Adrian Jarrett, Shane Parsons, Aileen Beale, Anni Finsterer, Mark Paguio, Hendrix Lee Taylor*
Producers: *Craig Boreham, Ben Ferris, Dean Francis, Ulysses Oliver*
Composer: *Tony Buchen*
Cinematography: *Dean Francis*
Editing: *Danielle Boesenberg*

Lonesome received nominations for Best Indie Film at the 2022 AACTA Awards, Best Direction in a Feature Film (Budget under $1m) at the 2022 Australian Directors Guild Awards and received the Septimius Award for Best Oceanian Film in 2023, alongside nominations for Josh Lavery and Zarif in the Best Oceanian Actor category.

INTERVIEW
FILMMAKER
CRAIG BOREHAM

Writer-Director Craig Boreham is one of the leading voices behind the emerging Australian queer cinema movement. With his 2016 film, *Teenage Kicks*, Craig echoed the work of Ana Kokkinos' *Head On* (1998), as he followed Miles Szanto's Miklós Varga as he navigated his internal realisation of his sexuality. In *Lonesome*, Josh Lavery's Casey is a country boy arriving at the flurry of the Sydney-city streets, finding his way into the gay lifestyle and encountering Zarif's Tib.

Boreham frequently pushes masculine-presenting bodies to the forefront of his narratives, where characters explore their physical attraction with others and themselves. Desire is a key theme that is explored throughout Craig's filmography, with his characters exhibiting a sense of vulnerability that has helped establish what the Australian queer identity looks like on screen.

This interview was recorded by Andrew F. Peirce in May 2022

Josh [Lavery] is quite a striking lead. How did you cast him?

Craig Boreham: Casting was looking everywhere and turning every rock because I wanted to find a queer cast. I was trawling Grindr and Scruff. I found a video that Josh had done with a queer filmmaking group in Melbourne called Sissy Screens. It was a confessional documentary experimental piece, talking about his experience growing up isolated in the country as a gay boy and his first encounters with other gay people via sketchy webcam sites. It was a great, honest story. I hit up Josh on Instagram and then discovered that he had a really big Instagram following and it was a pretty racy one. I thought 'he'll probably be into this film.'

We chatted a bit on Instagram, and then his profile got banned. So, he disappeared off the face of the Earth. Fortunately, he got back in touch and then we started kicking the script around and talking about the character. I felt from the get-go that Josh was the right person for the film. He'd done

LONESOME

a short film called *Tasty* (2017) that did great on the queer festival circuit a few years back, but he hadn't done a lot of film [work]. He's a natural. He just took to it. We found the pace and tone of the character. It's a lot to suddenly have to carry a whole feature. A lot was riding on his performance, and he pulled it off.

What discussions did you have with [Zarif] about creating Tib as a character?

CB: I found [Zarif] on Grindr. I hit them up. You can imagine how that went down. That was a sketchy interaction. "Hey, I'm a director and we're making a movie, have you done any acting?" and they were immediately incensed. They're like "How dare you? I just finished a degree at QUT." They're completely skilled and trained and they thought I was a serial killer. I told them that Netflix had *Teenage Kicks* on it, check it out. They hit me up and then we had a coffee, and we went from there.

As soon as we met, I thought they were perfect for the role. They had a lot to bring to the character. Tib was someone who had a particular exterior and had all this other stuff going on but was really guarded. They're someone who lives in the cracks in Sydney and is maybe not as surrounded by the community as they could be or want to be, but that's become a bit of a defence mechanism for them, losing themselves in anonymous sex and hookup apps. But then I love that Tib is entrepreneurial and has got this vision for themselves and is working hard to make their life a better place. I love that about the character.

What discussions did you have on set?

CB: A lot of conversation around what was bubbling under the surface. I love those characters that don't give much away on the surface, but underneath that turmoil [is] absolute chaos and little cracks that happen in their exteriors that let that stuff seep out. It was finding that stuff.

Josh is a very different person than Casey. It's not like he was just being himself, because he's nothing like that character, but he could relate to it. His story was very similar. Before he moved to Melbourne, he lived in a very isolated small town, so we talked about that a lot. There was a lot of physical stuff in that performance, like finding the way to physicalise a lot of that walled-up exterior, but then being a very vulnerable character and an emotionally driven character who refuses to wear their emotions. We did a lot of different stuff, a lot of chatting and talking but also a lot of physical stuff.

Do you have many people on set?

INTERVIEW | CRAIG BOREHAM

CB: [It] depends on the film. The crew of *Teenage Kicks* was bigger than the crew on *Lonesome*, which was lean. Depending on what we were shooting, a lot of the time when we were out shooting on location, it was lean and mean. It's easier to manage and we don't have the resources to have a massive crew around. I kind of like working that way. There are pluses and minuses to that. The good thing is that you can move quite quickly. A massive crew is a massive beast to move around, whereas a tight little crew can get into nooks and crannies and get out real quick. We had a punishing schedule, so it was good to be able to keep everything moving fast.

We shot it in between lockdowns in Sydney. We did all the pre-production and polished the script during the first lockdown and then we came out of lockdown, and we had just enough time to shoot the film. Two weeks later, we went back into lockdown. Most of the post-production was done during that second lockdown in Sydney. The shoot was a bit of a pandemic miracle.

One of the motifs throughout the film is Casey in the fields by himself, partially clothed or naked. Were they dream sequences? Or are they remembering a time past? Was it a kind of sanctuary for him?

CB: They were a mix of that. They were half memory flashback, half torment of running this thing over and over and over in his mind. I wanted them to feel a bit somewhere between those spaces. Is it a memory? Or is it guilt and loss? It's hard to pinpoint exactly what they are. It's something that's churning in his subconscious.

It was interesting to shoot that. That was the first stuff we shot. It was pretty much Josh's first day in Sydney. It was the first time we met. Dean [Francis] who was the cinematographer, Josh, and I drove way out and looked for places to find beautiful moments. That whole sequence was very much off the cuff, and it's kind of beautiful for it.

The contrast between Tib's explosive hair and Casey effectively having nothing – besides being a visual difference between the two – helped contrast who they are as people and how they want to express themselves in life.

CB: It plays out in so many ways. Their physicality: Zarif is so tall and lanky. Also, the energy between [them], and Casey is so slow and internal, whereas Tib is bouncy and external. We played with that stuff a lot. We did a lot of hanging out in parks and getting the tone of their physical relationship together tight. They didn't actually meet until really close to the shoot because Josh was in Melbourne and couldn't come up until after the lockdown ended. It was nerve-wracking, I was hoping that they would click when they got together because a lot of the initial rehearsals, we were doing one-on-one with them. They just were magic and loved each other and had so much fun and really supported each other through it, which was wonderful to see.

For Tib, there is so much that we learn about who they are as a person in those scenes. There is a 'destructive horniness' to their actions, where it's almost self-obliteration, "I'm gonna go pick someone up, have sex and do exactly the same thing tomorrow night." If a connection happens, then that's an accident.

CB: I really like the way when they first meet, there's a real sense for Tib of that being an anonymous hook-up where you don't ask the person's name, or you don't hang around and chat. It's like a business. The business is done, it's time for you to leave. And Casey doesn't know the rules and decides to hang around. That's a nice scene, a nice exploration of that. Tib's character is someone who doesn't like to be emotionally vulnerable because they'd been hurt before, so they have the walls up. If they're gonna have sex, it's just sex and that's the way it is.

What discussions do you have about the physical and intimate moments?

CB: The film was always going to be pretty racy; it had a lot of sex scenes in it. They're not just sex scenes, there's a lot of story moments in them, emotional stuff happening in those scenes. If you removed any of them, the film would make less sense. We talked about that stuff a lot. I was quite clear in the script. If you read the script, you can see what you're gonna see. I didn't want lines saying, "They make love." You know? I wanted to be quite descriptive about what was going on in the scene so that anyone who was looking at the roles knew what they were up for. That did freak a lot of people out and the agents were like "What are you making? What is this film?"

We worked with a fantastic intimacy coordinator, Leah Pellinkhof, who was invaluable in shooting a lot of those more intimate scenes. It's such a wonderful process that intimacy coordinators work with. It removes all the awkwardness from those conversations, and it becomes a much more comfortable process. It sounds like it would stifle the electricity on the screen, but it kind of does the opposite. It makes everyone feel like they know what's what, what they're allowed to do, and what the other person is comfortable with doing, so they can go hard in those places. That was kind of brilliant.

There are quite a few sex scenes involving a lot of the cast, so we had big intimacy workshop days where we had all our people who were involved across the sex scenes in the one room, workshopping all of that stuff and setting the terms of shooting that stuff. Potentially, it can be rough stuff to shoot, and it can be really difficult for casts, so it's really important to be on top of that stuff.

Is it a bit like fight choreography in a way?

CB: Kind of. There's a similarity, I guess, in the way it's done. Sex scenes and fight choreography are probably the few times on a shoot where actors are given full rein to call cut if they feel like they're in some way in danger or vulnerable.

Male nudity on screen is such a rarity. It almost feels like "It just can't go below the waist." It's refreshing to be able to see men walking around naked.

CB: That was part of our plan. I was talking to Dean, one of the producers, early on about the beauty of doing a super independent film. You can push boundaries a little more without a whole bunch of people breathing down your neck saying, "You can't do that." That was good. We talked about it as almost part of a palette and tone of the film, like skin and body is a texture of the film we wanted to have. The film is very much sitting from a very queer gaze. We were like, "If we're going to talk about queer sex and gay sex, we should do it in a way that embraces that rather than pans away to a tree out the window during a sex scene."

Josh pees on screen, there are hairy bums here. There are different kinds of physicality and aspects of physicality which is refreshing.

CB: That was part of the conversation as well. We wanted bodies. We didn't want Instagram-perfect sculpted gym junkie bodies. We wanted all the bodies. We wanted the full gamut. It's nice to see different kinds of bodies in a horny way, it's nice to embrace all those bodies. They look great. Everyone loves it.

What conversations did you have with cinematographer Dean Francis about creating the visual style of the film?

CB: Dean is a director in his own right, he's made a couple of features as well. We met years ago in Berlin at the Berlinale Talent Camp. I'd been there a year before with a film and I got invited back to the talent camp. Bonnie Elliott was also there, so it was like we were the three bad Australian talents who were mostly drunk the whole time. We made a pact then to work together in the future, and we've been solid over the years. Dean's always a great sounding board when I'm working on something. When this project came up and I was working with Ben [Ferris] and Ulysses [Oliver] who are the producers from Breathless Films whose initial idea was to create an indie slate, I reached out to Dean and said, "Read the script. Would you be interested in coming on board?" He was really into it.

We spent a lot of time finding the look that evolved from those conversations quite a lot. It probably started a lot grittier, and where we ended up was quite a different place. It was a big job for Dean because it was a lean crew. I think he's managed to create a beautiful look for the film, it feels cohesive even though there are a lot of different spaces in the film, and you are playing with landscape versus these very urban spaces. Finding the right way to make that evolve was tricky.

Because we have known each other for so long, we had a great working relationship. It was helpful for the film and made it smooth. We didn't really shot list traditionally a lot of the time. We talked about scenes and the way we might shoot it, but a lot of the time it was very much evolving and pretty fluid on the spot. We didn't have a strict shot list as such. Well, we started one, but we ran out of time.

I like the urgency of some of the shots, especially near the end when Casey's realising where he needs to go and the camera moves with him.

CB: There's a lot of camera movement, a lot of epic shots we tried to do in single shots, which we mostly pulled off. I like that. I like containing a scene with minimal coverage and trying to keep it a bit more elegant rather than just shooting a lot. We didn't shoot a lot of stuff. Often, we only did one or two takes. We didn't have a lot of coverage options because we just didn't shoot them. We were pretty disciplined. Even though we didn't have a list, we knew what we wanted, and we were quite disciplined on set. Our poor editor Danielle often would be like "Wow, that's it. We've got two shots." It did work. It does mean it's a bit scary because you are committing to this idea, and you don't have a lot of choices to change it if it doesn't work out. Fortunately, I feel like it was mostly a success.

One of the things talked about in relation to queer cinema is how purple lighting is associated with being bisexual. Is there a colour palette that you used to signify themes and sexuality?

CB: Dean and I talked a lot about the colour. As the journey unfolds and Casey becomes more and more immersed in the city, we wanted the colours to become stronger and more vibrant. It builds to this hyper-colour space. I like contrasting that to the natural landscapes that are in the film as well. We were also playing with the Western tropes of big landscapes, solitary cowboys in big wide scapes at the beginning of the film and having that evolve and replicating those frames but in a city landscape and finding locations in the city that looked like a cement canyon. We wanted the palette

INTERVIEW | CRAIG BOREHAM

to have one foot in realism but then also nod to campness and queer cinema and heightened stuff as well, which I think is the right feel for the film.

Is there a joy in blending that Americana style with queer cinema and contrasting them in one film?

CB: I mean, cowboys are iconic for queers. We've always loved cowboys. It was nice to be able to play with that iconography. I'm originally from western Queensland, and I spent a lot of my early years in the country, and later between the country and the city. It was great to be able to tell that queer story and use that space. It's definitely nodding towards American Westerns, but also, we love playing with the Australian landscape in that way. We were looking for different Australian landscapes. Initially, we were talking about "Should it be deserty?" and we figured that Casey was from far out west. There's something beautiful about those grassy scapes that we did find around southwestern New South Wales, they're quite beautiful and we don't often see it on screens.

How did you decide on the hat?

CB: We needed to find the perfect hat. It was a process; we did look through a lot of hats to find the right one. It was hard because the pandemic made hat imports difficult, so they were in short supply. I eventually found it in a second-hand store. Immediately it was like, "Oh my God, that's our hat." The guy who ran the store was a bit of a hat aficionado, he helped us shape it and did a couple of repair jobs over the course of the shoot.

What was your interest in exploring the theme of loneliness? Did the pandemic influence the script?

CB: Oh, interesting. I've never thought about that. Possibly. Very much. My partner was away down south during a lot of the lockdown, and I was spending a lot of time alone. Possibly.

I was thinking initially about my own experience of first coming to Sydney and how Sydney can be a cold hard bitch when you arrive, and you don't know people. It's a hard city to crack in some ways until you find your tribe and settle in. But then it is a big city. I was [also] interested in the idea of people who exist but are living these solitary lives. They kind of all have this under-the-surface desire to connect in some way, but maybe are confronted by that. It's not the same for everyone.

Have you noticed that more queer stories are being shown in film festivals that aren't queer film festivals?

LONESOME

CB: More than say ten years ago. I think there is interest in queer cinema like there hasn't been for a while. Part of what we talked about when we were making this film was we wanted to make a queer film that was a queer film and didn't have to explain itself to people who maybe weren't queer. They can catch up, they can work it out, we're not going to spell stuff out. There [were] a few question marks around that, whether that would be okay or not. I think straight audiences are perfectly able to jump into that world and figure stuff out. I don't think they get lost. That's why we go to movies because we see things that are outside of our every day.

It feels like of late there is an emergence of queer cinema in Australia and we're seeing more stories being told in the queer space. Do you feel like you're somebody who is setting the style and language for Australian queer cinema?

CB: That's a nice compliment, thank you. I guess that's the reason I got into filmmaking. I wanted to tell queer stories, because I felt like they were missing, and that's the thing that drives me. I think that's why it's still my focus now. It's why I haven't gone off and done other stuff, because that is really what puts the fire under me.

I was talking to Adrian, one of the co-writers on the next project we're working on, the other day and we were just talking about that evolution of queer cinema and how we've come to this place where we can start to explore more maybe problematic characters or characters who make bad decisions. It's not as controversial as it once was where there was the weight of the entire community hanging on to every queer character, or every bit of representation had to be good. I've never liked the idea of 'if you put a gay character in a film, they have to be the perfect gay who represents everybody.' It's kind of impossible. It's nice to be in a place where we can explore different kinds of stuff in that way.

Did you manage to see soda jerk's Terror Nullius?

CB: Yeah! I fucken love those guys.

What's it like watching a film like that and then seeing a clip from Teenage Kicks in it? Did you know that it was going to be in there before you watched it?

CB: Oh god, it was so great. I didn't know. It was a total shock. It was complete piracy. They're total pirates. Miles [Szanto] the lead actor from *Teenage Kicks* was so into it. I totally loved that he had that horny moment with *The Man From Snowy River*. It was great. Those guys do amazing stuff. They invited me to the screening in Sydney which was nice. Love their work.

What does it mean to be an Australian filmmaker?

CB: You know, I always get pigeonholed in the queer filmmaker category, so I don't even think of myself as an Australian filmmaker; until I'm overseas. It was great screening our film in Seattle, to an American audience and seeing the way they perceive our place in the world. Especially in the Q&As after, it's like talking to them about certain things that were just obviously culturally different or simple. They didn't know what a paddock was. It's nice to introduce the world to our part of the world, and because I particularly work in queer stories, that part of our world as well is nice to take out there. It is different. I mean, we are our own weird little place down here so, it's nice to share that.

Every city in Australia has its own rhythm. We wanted to make Sydney another character in this film, but we didn't want it to be a postcard, 'Opera House Sydney'. We almost had it, but we canned it. It was a beautiful shot too, Dean was outraged. It's more of the back alleys of Sydney and the rooftops. That was the world we wanted to explore a bit more. Then you get all these beautiful landscape-y moments around the harbour and Botany Bay, those areas that are beautiful in their bleakness.

ABLAZE

90 mins
Directors: *Tiriki Onus, Alec Morgan*
Writer: *Tiriki Onus, Alec Morgan*
Featuring: *Bill Onus, Tiriki Onus, Jack Charles, John Hughes, Alan Hardy, Wayne Blair, Lee Perry*
Producers: *Tom Zubrycki, Tom Murray*
Composer: *Jen Anderson*
Cinematography: *Kathryn Milliss, Murray Vanderveer, Rick Kickbush*
Editing: *Tony Stevens*

Ablaze received nominations for Best Documentary and Best Editing in a Documentary at the 2022 AACTA Awards, with Alec Morgan and Tiriki Onus receiving the Awgie Award for Documentary - Public Broadcast at the 2021 Australian Writers' Guild awards, and the award for Best Direction in a Documentary Feature at the 2022 Australian Directors Guild Awards.

REVIEW
ANDREW F. PEIRCE

For Aboriginal and Torres Strait Islander readers, please note that this interview contains the names of deceased individuals.

The Australian film industry is experiencing the Indigenous New Wave as witnessed with the vibrant and considered work of Rachel Perkins, the singular vision of Ivan Sen, the towering importance of Warwick Thornton's filmography, the varied joys of Wayne Blair vision, and the emerging talent of filmmakers like Dylan River, Jub Clerc, Jon Bell, Tyson Perkins, and Travis Akbar. Collectively, these filmmakers are reshaping the identity of Australia and are reasserting the place of Aboriginal and Torres Strait Islander culture on screen. But it would be an act of wilful ignorance to think that this group of filmmakers are the first to bring Indigenous stories to the screen.

Enter the history of Bill Onus.

Thanks to his grandson, Indigenous Opera singer Tiriki Onus, and co-director Alec Morgan, the reveal of a long-hidden slice of Australian film and cultural history is displayed in the expansive documentary *Ablaze* (2022).

Hidden in the uncatalogued depths of the underfunded NFSA was a silent film featuring scenes of Aboriginal protesters at a work site demanding equality, a stage play, and other culturally important artefacts. Yorta Yorta and Wiradjuri man Bill Onus was a respected figure in the Australian civil rights movements, but this chance discovery brought forth the understanding that he was likely Australia's first Aboriginal filmmaker.

While the obliteration of Aboriginal culture was actively driven by the government of the day, it remains an enduring aspect of the cruelty of colonisation that sees all aspects of society both complicit and actively engaged in. Aboriginal history has been segregated from the world; archived, forgotten, and neglected in a manner that denies Indigenous directors like Bill Onus their place in Australian and global film history.

ABLAZE

It then falls to Tiriki Onus to revive Bill's legacy as he engages in an investigation that sees him scouring through Bill's past, through fractured and incomplete archives, and back to Country, to create a documentary that proudly honours his grandfather and reasserts his place in Australian history.

With *Ablaze*, Tiriki shows pride in his heritage and his desire to heal it after the damage inflicted upon it throughout the centuries. Not only is Tiriki striving to bring the story of his grandfather to the world, but also to remind viewers of all the different ways that white Australians sought to strip away the Aboriginality of Indigenous culture.

In conversation with Uncle Jack Charles, Tiriki hears about the possum skin wraps that would grow with the wearer as they aged. The wrap would start with one skin and each year a new pelt would be added with the wearer's life story burnt onto it. The wrap transforms into a grand wrap that would embrace their body with warmth and years of history and stories all at once. As the fur of native fauna became a desired item for the wealthy, the government of the day made it illegal for Indigenous folk to wear possum skins, furthering the erasure and destruction of Indigenous culture, practices, and the sense of community.

Ablaze weaves together multiple motifs, notably one that has Tiriki creating a possum wrap in honour of Bill, upon which he retells Bill's story as he scorches his legacy onto the skin. From Bill's role in the civil rights movement, to his desire to bring Aboriginal culture to the masses through Aboriginal-led stage plays, to his work as an assistant on Charles Chauvel's films, it's made clear that Bill's history is Australian history, and through its dormant life, present day Australia has been robbed of the potential of the past.

Another iconic figure that we meet in Bill's cultural sphere is Reg Saunders, the famous Aboriginal soldier in WW2 history. At once, *Ablaze* works in harmony alongside the Tim Anastasi's *Black ANZAC* (2018), a documentary that details the lost history of Aboriginal and Torres Strait Islander servicemen in Australian military history. Here, Saunders' appearance in the found footage shows him working as a tram operator, with Tiriki's investigation leading him to an ANZAC historian who unveils another devastating aspect of Australian history that Travis Akbar echoes in his short film *Tambo* (2023). In that powerful short, a First Nations ANZAC soldier returns home, only to find that he has been racially ostracised from his community, with those he fought alongside segregating him from the society he fought to protect.

The power within *Ablaze* sits with the way Tiriki and Alec Morgan provide their unflinching presentation of history, including the horrifying story of William Grayden's 1957 film *Manslaughter* (also known as *Their Darkest Hour*) about the impact of atomic bomb tests near Maralinga, Western Australia, the impact of which is still felt today, making the negligence and arrogance of continuous Australian governments all the more infuriating.

REVIEW | ANDREW F. PEIRCE

Along Bill's journey the ever paranoid and racist actions of ASIO marked him as a person of interest, causing Bill and his friends to be tracked by the organisation. While the majority of Bill's footage has been destroyed in the titular fire, there's a grand irony that ASIO themselves created an archive of Indigenous history and culture by secretly filming Aboriginal activists. That footage is presented here in a pristine manner that will make you wish that the NFSA was more securely funded so that footage like Bill's may be discovered and restored for the austerity of Australian history before it's lost to degradation.

ABLAZE

INTERVIEW FILMMAKER TIRIKI ONUS

For Aboriginal and Torres Strait Islander readers, please note that this interview contains the names of deceased individuals.

Ablaze is the essential documentary about Yorta Yorta and Wiradjuri filmmaker Bill Onus (formally known as William T. Onus) and the untold history of his work in Australian film. Lost films and hidden history are rediscovered and brought to vibrant life by Bill's grandson, Yorta Yorta man Tiriki Onus, alongside co-director Alec Morgan.

Executive Producer Sue Maslin talked about her involvement in *Ablaze* and the importance of extensive research for documentaries in February 2022:

> "I was really proud of being involved as an EP on Ablaze working with Alec Morgan and Tom Zubrycki because I had the privilege of working with Lin Onus who was the son of William T. Onus. I understood snippets about his story, but to see what Alec does in terms of the deep level of research required to bring all the threads together to tell a story that has such complexity and so many layers of how that man lived his life, what he was up against, both in terms of institutional racism through to just the personal story of his family. Those stories cannot be told unless you've got filmmakers like Alec Morgan with the passion and the dedication to spend hours upon hours upon hours researching and getting to the underbelly of those stories.
>
> And of course, who pays for that? Who values it? We live in an age where one hundred and forty characters

is the new norm of communication. We've seen journalism gradually become more and more impoverished as a result of people not valuing this level of research required. But as documentary filmmakers, we still stick at it because we just have this desire that we want these untold stories out there."

Tiriki Onus is an opera singer and works as the Senior Lecturer and Head of the Wilin Centre for Indigenous Arts and Cultural Development, Associate Dean (Indigenous) and Deputy Dean (Place) for the Faculty of Fine Arts and Music at Melbourne University.

This interview was recorded by Andrew F. Peirce in April 2022

I understand it was six years in production, is that correct?

Tiriki Onus: That's right. Six and a half, really, which was an awfully long time. It came from a brief conversation that Alec Morgan and I had way back when and then all of a sudden there it was. We struggled for a long time to find the funding for it, but we were convinced that this was a story that needed to be told. It was certainly a labour of love. We had to stick with it as long as we had to get it made. We knew that we had a story that we wanted to tell, and we thought was pretty compelling. After you've lived with it for that long, you start to be a bit too close to it and wonder to yourself, "Is it still cool? Is it right?" We were happy to see the way that others have embraced it. It has been quite humbling.

Whenever we got some resources, and a little bit of money, we'd come together, shoot for a week, and go away again. Some months later, find a little bit more money, come together, and shoot. It wasn't until we got some substantive support towards the end through VicScreen [that] we were able to really go on the final push to bring it all together and then to edit everything and turn it into a real proper film.

You're somebody who is tied into different aspects of art in Australia, from being an opera singer to working in documentaries. What does it mean to be an Australian artist?

TO: That's a very good question. I'm not entirely sure I've got an answer for you. For me, being an artist in this country has always been about having a voice and having an opportunity to tell stories that have been kept from us. Whether that be through visual art, whether it be through performance and now whether it be through film, there's a tremendous power and privilege that is afforded to the artist to be able to in many ways dictate the

INTERVIEW | TIRIKI ONUS

terms on how we want the world to be seen. We're given that opportunity to let others see the world around us through our own eyes.

In Australia, I think there's so much of our story which has been kept from us, both intentionally and – indeed now perhaps for many of those with whom I worked – accidentally. We still live with the legacies of a past which sought to exclude certain voices from these conversations. Sometimes we can find ourselves perpetuating those structures without even realising or understanding what we're doing. For me, being an artist is about tremendous responsibility.

Yes, there's an element of personal satisfaction, dare I say even indulgence at times, but there is a tremendous responsibility that goes along with that. Hopefully through my creative practice and collaborating with other extraordinary people like Alec Morgan, Tom Zubrycki, and everyone else who worked on this film, there's a chance for us to be able to bring others along to collaborate in these spaces, to make safe spaces where we can have these conversations, and being very grown up about being able to acknowledge what we've missed out on and start trying to redress that balance for us all.

In the past you've talked about the need for collaboration to continue that archival process and to continue the search through archives for more work from either Bill or other Aboriginal directors at the time. How has that journey continued since the film came out?

TO: The conversation certainly has continued. It does require a great deal of dedication and passion, particularly with the very limited resources that are available to our national archives, like the NFSA. It's a real challenge. We were fortunate there have been people who have been willing to support this with their own time and efforts in this space. Quite often we don't necessarily give history its due. We like to always think that we're looking toward the future. But when we are focused like a laser beam in one direction, we tend to neglect all of the lessons of our past and those who have gone before us as well.

Certainly, the conversation is ongoing. Even at showings of the film, there have been extraordinary opportunities to connect with people who have new memories and new perspectives of these times and their stories. Indeed, opinions about where we would, should and could go next. And that's a lovely, lovely space to be in, to be able to have real strength-based meaningful conversations about what we would like to see and do in the future. It will continue to grow, but it is going to be hard graft. It's going to be hard work, particularly when those who are doing this fantastic work are doing it with very little support and resources. We're fortunate for the passion and love that others have found in this space.

ABLAZE

Ablaze recontextualises Australian film history. The established history is that modern Australian films started back in 1969 and 1970, but Ablaze opens up the discussion that there are decades of work that has been neglected, lost, and cruelly abandoned. What does this recontextualisation of history mean to you as an artist?

TO: It means everything to me as an artist. I think about my own creative practice – which is quite varied and diverse, I get bored easily, so I do lots of different things – and it is very much one of lineages, of looking back at who taught me and who taught them and so on and so forth. Quite often we come up against walls or barriers. Often, we come up against the perception that something started at a certain point. Rarely do we see the whole picture.

That's something that's very much brought home to me as an artist, that I'm not doing anything in a vacuum. That in fact, I can trace the lineage and histories of the greatest practice that I have now back prior to the 1770s, back to traditions of storytelling and knowledge transmission and placemaking that have always gone on here in this place. I think that's true for many of us as artists; Black, white, brindled, wherever we come from.

In many ways, *Ablaze* is a story of allyship; of people who had power and privilege who didn't really like the world in the shape that it was and decided that they wanted to do something about that. So, they contributed to the amplification of other people's voices, contributed their knowledge and skills and privilege and ability to make these new spaces again and again and again. That is quite a powerful lineage to be part of as well.

When I think about how we look back, when I think about what it means to my own creative practice, I'm very taken with these influences. I'm enamoured with the dedication and the passion and the struggle that others have gone through before me in this space, and the thought that there will hopefully be other artists who come along behind. There isn't a start and an endpoint, particularly when you think about the life of a story when you think about the influences and the passions of people who have brought them to the screen, the stage, to the canvas, or whatever the medium might be. Again and again, we're able to trace these stories back. We do frequently only tell and are frequently only given a part of that history.

This feels like you're having a conversation with Bill as the film goes along. What was that experience like learning about his past, learning about what he filmed and created?

TO: I'm pleased that you see it like that because I certainly see it that way too. *Ablaze* was, on a very personal level for me, about reconnecting with

INTERVIEW | TIRIKI ONUS

Bill. Our lives are separated by some twelve years. At the same time, he's always figured hugely in my life; stories of Bill, stories of what he did. When going and visiting family members, you'd always be treated to a story of Bill or told how much I looked like him and even what I was doing now, how Bill would have approved of. That's come up again and again throughout my life. Bill has always existed very heavily and very strongly in my life.

All our families have these mythologies that we build up around family members who aren't there anymore. The extraordinary thing about *Ablaze* was that so much of that was reaffirmed and shown to be true. There was wonderful evidence of his work. It brought Bill and I closer. I'm pleased you see it as a conversation because it really was, and it remains that way as well. It is very much a conversation between me and Bill, and the conversations that we have with those who aren't here anymore, to ourselves and the space perhaps.

I was always asking myself as we went through this, "Is this what Bill would have done?" Trying to theorise and explain what his motivations were, and constantly grilling and questioning myself as to whether or not I was on the right path with the stories that I was telling too. I arrived at the conclusion that I was. It is an interesting and challenging space to be in when you're trying to remain true to someone's legacy and vision, particularly someone as passionate as Bill. To do that in the 21st century, wondering what his experience of the early and mid-20th century might have meant to how he would view the world as it is now; I think we've ended up at a pretty good place. I certainly think that Bill and I have grown a lot closer in the making of this film. I know him in a very different way from what I thought I knew him before. Time will tell if that if that's right or not. One day when we eventually see one another again, he can either tell me if I've done a good job or a bad job. Now I'm choosing to believe we've done an okay job by Bill, and that we have realised that vision.

What did it mean to you to take the footage back to Country and be able to screen that for the people who might have known him?

TO: Taking Bill's work back to Country was probably one of the most powerful experiences within the making of the whole of this film. I probably fought the idea for a little while, as to whether or not it was appropriate, whether we were manufacturing something there. I to and froed and wondered if it was relevant or not. Finally getting there and bringing the story, particularly the story of the film and *White Justice*, back to the Pilbara and the communities from once they had come was staggering and awe-inspiring. To think that we could bring to a close a piece of work and a relationship that had started on one side of the continent at least over seventy years beforehand, to finally bring that back full circle back to the community whose voice was being represented was quite extraordinary.

Bill had no idea what these communities in the Pilbara were going to make of this work from back then. The lives of Bill and his contemporaries and communities over in the far West were so controlled that there was never an opportunity for them to connect up. So not knowing was an interesting space to be in. Not knowing how people are going to respond, is this something that they want? But then to have such a hugely positive response, to see the way in which people celebrated not just Bill and the film, but their own stories and histories was wonderful. I think that's a big part of what Bill was about. A lot of work is, I think, very much about changing how we have conversations and changing narratives. When you look at the stuff that Bill shot in 1946 down here in Melbourne, not just the *White Justice* show, but others, it's all incredibly strength based. There's no deficit discourse, there's no 'oh poor me' stuff, it's 'look at everything that we've done, look at everything we're continuing to do. You can be a part of this if you want, but it's going to happen one way or another, anyway.' That was a part of taking that film back to the Pilbara that I really loved.

Similarly, being able to take it up to places like Cummeragunja, being able to take it to communities and elders who had lived in and around Little George Street in Fitzroy who remembered what it was like to be there was extraordinary. We came at an amazing time. Had we waited another generation for this film to be found – and it would have taken another generation for this film to be found – we would have missed out on that immediate connection. I'm so grateful that we did have that moment, that it didn't pass us by, that we were able to make those connections again. Whilst Bill may not have been there personally for it, there was a sense of bringing him and his histories back home, taking his films back to Cummeragunja, and taking his story back to the community again. It hasn't been forgotten.

In many ways, we're just playing a very, very long game here. Sometimes it takes multiple generations, but it does come around eventually. I think that's exactly what Bill and others were fighting for. They were fighting for broad change that was going to last, not just something that was going to be over and done within a matter of moments. You don't do these things for yourself. You do them for your children and your grandchildren. You have to think that many generations into the future, and it takes great genius and insight from activists of the past to be able to see that, I think, and to be able to plan and work accordingly. And great selflessness, too.

THE DREAMLIFE OF GEORGIE STONE

30 mins
Director: *Maya Newell*
Writer: *Georgie Stone*
Featuring: *Georgie Stone, Rebekah Robertson, Greg Stone, Harry Stone*
Producers: *Sophie Hyde, Matthew Bate, Lisa Sherrard*
Composer: *Amit May Cohen*
Cinematography: *Vincent Lamberti, Maya Newell*
Editing: *Bryan Mason*

The Dreamlife of Georgie Stone received a nomination in the Documentary category at the 2023 Peabody Awards.

INTERVIEW
WRITER & SUBJECT
GEORGIE STONE OAM

There's a deliberately ethereal quality to *The Dreamlife of Georgie Stone* that elevates the story of transgender rights activist Georgie Stone OAM. *The Dreamlife of Georgie Stone* is framed around Georgie's fight against the Family Court to allow transgender kids to begin hormone therapy, alongside the support Georgie's family gives her during her own transition journey. It's in the telling of these two stories we see the emergence of an activist, an icon, an emerging leader, and an actress.

Maya Newell's films celebrate the importance of identity and reinforce the need for community and familial support to allow those identities to flourish. Her work is always collaborative, acting as a facilitator to help share her subject's stories with the world, a point which is amplified by the abundance of home video footage of Georgie growing up with the support of her father. This is an all-embracing documentary that shines a light on the selfless people in the world, like Georgie, who are fighting for those who may not be able to fight for themselves.

This interview was recorded by Andrew F. Peirce in June 2022

Can you talk about Maya's collaborative approach to telling your story and coming on as a creative producer?

GS: It was always very important for Maya that I was consulted with everything, and that nothing was done without my consent. It was a really wonderful process. Throughout all of it, I felt safe and I felt heard. I knew that nothing was going to be put in there that I didn't agree with or didn't feel comfortable sharing. In the editing process and in the process of putting this film together, it was wonderful, not only having control from a story perspective but also in the way that it was told, in a creative sense; it was wonderful to be involved in [that too]. I have this newfound appreciation and love for filmmaking, and I think I can attribute that to Maya and seeing her work and seeing her creative process.

What was that discussion process around deciding how to frame your life story?

GS: It evolved over quite a few years. We started filming when I was 14 and at that point, we didn't have a plan for what we were doing, we were just filming. As I got into my late teens, we started to think about how we could tell the story, whether we wanted it to be a feature or a short. We went through a few ideas and then settled on this nonlinear dreamscape kind of thing where we used my surgery as a sort of jumping-off point to look back into memories. We had a lot of archive footage from when I was a kid and lots of home videos which helped fill out my early life. Once we had those videos, it cracked it open a bit and we were able to weave that into the footage that she had taken. It evolved [but] that idea of the dreams stuck.

Was the title a result of a joint discussion between Maya and yourself?

GS: We had a list of possible names, but it was Maya's idea. Once we started editing the film, it became clear that that was the right one.

Your family took a lot of home videos. Naturally, you can't talk for your parents, but what was their thinking behind filming the family growing up?

GS: I'm not sure why, I think it was just something that their parents had done, so it was something they did too. When we were maybe five or six, my brother and I loved making short films. I did one about *Swan Lake*, and there's me dancing in a tutu in the film. My brother did one about a superhero called Super Arno. We always loved filming stuff like that. In terms of the candid stuff of us running around, back when we were babies, I think they just wanted to document it all.

Did they have a labelled archival process?

GS: No, it was stored on a computer. It was quite messy. Maya spent a lot of time sifting through, trying to find stuff. I don't think it was thought through. It's just "The kids are doing something funny, let's film them" and then store it. I don't think there was a plan of "We're going to document everything and make a slideshow." I think Dad had this idea of "We'll show some really stupid videos at their 21st birthday." Maya loved it. It was a filmmakers dream to have all this footage as a kid, especially as the film was spanning years. We started at 14 and then realised there's all this footage of years before. Watching it feels like Maya has been there from the very beginning.

INTERVIEW | GEORGIE STONE

Then there is the footage of you being an advocate for trans youth. What was your experience revisiting that?

GS: It was interesting. I think in hindsight, I'm able to appreciate what we were able to do and what these last years have been like, and the fact that I was doing all of that at the same time as doing school. I think at the time, people would say, "The work you're doing is really good, it's powerful," and I'd kind of go like, "Whatever. They're just saying that. I don't feel like I'm doing much." Looking back, I have a different perspective on it. I'm realising how much work we did and to have done all of that at a young age and at school and to have been so open and so vulnerable.

Now I'm realising how much I value my privacy, which is kind of ironic because I released a documentary about my life, how important that is for me, and how much it has cost to be so open. I suppose looking back, those are the kinds of thoughts that are running through my head. It's very surreal. It's like an out-of-body experience watching your life on a cinema screen in front of other people. It's weird. It's very foreign. But good.

Did you feel like you were watching somebody else go through what you went through?

GS: In a way, yes, I did. But in some senses, I felt almost too connected which made me terrified, because I'm quite self-critical. It is sort of how you said, it's like an out-of-body experience. You're watching it like it's someone else. You do kind of have to watch the film not as yourself but as an audience member to appreciate what it's about. Then, at the same time, it's so emotional. I watched it and it brought me back to those emotions that I was feeling and the headspace I was at. It's kind of like looking through a diary. You're put back in your head. It's very weird.

You've got a great support network, both in your family but also with Maya as the director. Can you talk about what it means to have a support network when you're telling your life story on film?

GS: Oh, it's everything. It's everything. I wouldn't be able to do it without that, and I wouldn't do it without that. Everything I'm able to do is because of the family support I have, and I know that so many trans, gender-diverse, non-binary young people don't have that. About 66% don't have family support. I shouldn't be lucky to have it, but I am. I am incredibly lucky. That's why I've been able to do advocacy. That's why I've been able to be vulnerable in public and put myself out there because I know that I have people who will look after me when I get off the stage or when I get home.

THE DREAMLIFE OF GEORGIE STONE

Being so public and open has got to make that privacy feel even more precious and important. How have you been able to find the ability to return to that?

GS: It does. Having agency over your story and how you tell your story is also agency over what you share and what you don't share. That's something I've had to be more and more aware of. I've had to be more particular about what I want to say, what I do share with people, and then what I don't. I had to reset boundaries after a few years of advocacy, because then at Q&As people would start asking incredibly personal questions and it would be quite scary, quite exposing. Especially with starting *Neighbours* and a new kind of audience knowing who I am and being in the public eye more, I had to reassess what I was comfortable with and then set boundaries that would protect me. I'm a lot more economical now, I'm a lot more precious [with what I share].

Can you give any advice to people who might be going through something similar in their life, whether it's a trans, non-binary, or gender-diverse experience?

GS: I would say that exact thing. You don't owe people anything. You don't owe people your life story. You don't owe them an explanation or to be open. Share what you're willing to share. Share what you're open with. Share what you're comfortable sharing. But don't feel like you owe anyone anything more. Don't feel like they are entitled to everything. Share what you want to and who you feel comfortable with, and then don't be afraid to put up boundaries. You're not being mean. You're not being ungenerous.

It is absolutely enough just to exist, just to be. If you want to share things, you can but if you don't want to or you're unable to, that is absolutely okay. Boundaries are really important. Boundaries are healthy.

What does working in Australian film and TV mean to you?

GS: For me, it's incredibly exciting. I think right now there's a real appetite for under-represented voices and stories. A space has opened up for people like me to be in charge of the telling of our own stories, and I think the work that is coming out right now is quite exciting and raw and honest. It's really awesome. It's inspiring me to continue to create my own work. It's a great time right now.

INTERVIEW
DIRECTOR MAYA NEWELL

Maya Newell is a filmmaker who has managed to redefine what the label of 'director' means when it comes to documentary filmmaking. With *In My Blood It Runs* (2019), Newell utilised the knowledge and communal spirit of the Arrernte and Garrwa people of the Northern Territory to help tell the story of young leader, Dujuan, as he pushed against the colonial education system forced upon him and searches for a First Nations education for all.

With *The Dreamlife of Georgie Stone*, Maya Newell collaborates with transgender actress Georgie Stone to tell her story of activism and gender affirmation, and in doing so, they jointly create a text that calls for support for trans, gender diverse, and non-binary youth in Australia.

This interview was recorded by Andrew F. Peirce in June 2022

What was the original discussion that you had with Georgie and her family about the film?

MN: To be honest, for a long time we didn't know what form the film would take. Even when I approached Georgia and Beck [Robertson, Georgie's mum], there wasn't a formed idea. It really sparked my interest after making *Gayby Baby* (2015) and seeing transgender young people and children from same-sex families being thrown under the bus during the marriage equality debate and Safe Schools debacle and wanting to learn more about these young people. With *Gayby Baby*, I'd seen the power that children have when they speak truth to power. Those young people caught the attention of the nation and contributed to the legislative change that followed. They same with *In My Blood It Runs* (2019) seeing Dujuan, a young child like that speak up and have so much wisdom about the world; I think children have a lot to teach adults.

I was interested in meeting Georgie. As soon as I met her, she was this bubbly, warm, wise voice who was incredibly eager to be filmed, to be in front of

THE DREAMLIFE OF GEORGIE STONE

the camera. At that time, Georgie had been through a lot and had not been in the public arena at all. It was before she was on *Four Corners* and *Australian Story* (1996-). Her family were understandably protective about her doing media or being public, but she felt like she had a story that she wanted to share with the world, and that there was a lot of advocacy that she was excited about. So, we just filmed.

It was six years, but it wasn't every day. It was very observational. I'd go over maybe every two or three months and sit up at the kitchen bench and drink cups of tea and talk about all the things that had happened and what Georgie would like to film. We workshopped her messages and what she wanted to put out into the world. That guided my lens in what I was going to film and the kinds of things that I would look out for in the kind of observational style that I have. That collaboration eventually turned into Georgie holding a producer's credit on the film and a completely equal partnership in the edit putting the film together. Georgie was much older by the time we were putting it together and was an excellent storyteller in her own right.

You're more than just a director telling a story, you are working alongside your subjects to share their story. How important is that collaborative approach for you?

MN: It's absolutely paramount. I think that it should be for all filmmakers who are working with people from marginalised communities in particular. There are different kinds of films, but I think we need a bit of a revolution in documentary which honours and respects the subjects at the core of a film who are courageously sharing their lives on screen. It's incredibly important that they feel they're correctly presented. Many of the people in my films have had their stories misappropriated throughout history by the mainstream, and we cannot allow our film productions to continue that cycle of misappropriation and stealing stories.

I've had a lot of time to think about this through my films, particularly on *In My Blood It Runs*. I learned from an incredible producer, Rachel Edwardson [who] is a First Nations filmmaker on that film; with whom I spent a long time thinking about this [with] and co-ran workshops on that film between the amazing history of First Nations and people of colour, Screen Australia's Pathways & Protocols document which is a world-leading way of working, produced by their Indigenous department. There are lessons there for films about all topics.

When we were presenting the film together [at the Sydney Film Festival], Georgie watched the film and has been a part of its creation many times, there were no surprises on that big screen - apart from how scary it was to watch your film on a big screen. It meant we could both relax and celebrate together.

Georgie talked about recognising the level of privacy that she might have not been afforded by being a public figure and learning to balance the private life with the public life. Can you talk about how you as a director and a collaborator help to protect that private life on film?

MN: I think that's right, Georgie has a very strong public presence, especially now being a celebrity actor on *Neighbours*. Before this film came out, she had been on *Australian Story* and had a lot of her life used as political advocacy. I think in the making of this film, the appeal for her was that she would have control over the process and the story and the making, which meant that there are incredibly intimate moments between Georgie and her family, arguably the most amazing access and intimacy on screen compared to anything that she's done before. There were moments that she allowed me into as opposed to being pressured.

I think that sometimes with collaboration or if you have control over your own story, people think that you're not going to share private things or intimate moments or dramatic moments in filmmaking terms, but my experience time and time again is that if you hand over that power and allow subjects to decide what they would like you now to film or you genuinely give them the power to decide once things are filmed whether that goes in or out of the film, then they can choose what goes in. That means more often than not, you can share incredibly intimate moments. It just means that you create the context around that moment that makes it safe to share when they're a part of creating the context that feels correct and truthful.

Georgie's parents had a lot of home videos. What was that like getting to see that huge amount of home footage of Georgie and her brother growing up?

MN: It's so beautiful. I love archives so much. The film relies heavily on this beautiful trove of documentation from when Georgie and her brother were born. When we were allowed to look through those moments and use them, it steered the creative direction towards this idea of memory and all the moments that make us. The film launches from this point of Georgie's transition into adulthood when she's looking back on all the fights that she's been through in her teen hood, affirming her gender, fighting laws, and thinking about all these moments that made her. We've played in the film archives of her memories.

What was the decision behind making it into a short as opposed to a feature?

THE DREAMLIFE OF GEORGIE STONE

MN: We originally pitched it as three short films over the course of Georgie's life that would make a feature in 40 years. [laughs] Which was very beautiful and ambitious. I suppose it was a creative decision with Georgie, with the incredible editor Bryan Mason, and producers Sophie Hyde and Matt Bate, who all came on to help piece this quite complicated narrative structure together. It just felt like the right length.

Georgie has a number of films that tell a bigger story or that are longer, but this was a creative venture to lean into that elliptical, non-linear style, and it felt we could make something very powerful within 30 minutes. It felt right. In the end, Netflix and Screen Australia, who are our presenting partners, were very open for the film to be whatever length it needed to be, which is a creative freedom that I'm thankful for. This is the first film that I've made for a streaming platform as a Netflix Original. We were delightfully surprised when they had no notes on the length, which is often the big note you get from broadcasters and other screen agencies. It was wonderful. They consistently said, "Just let the film be whatever length it needs to be. It doesn't matter."

Because of the non-linear way that you're telling the story, it feels otherworldly in a way. Where did that otherworldly feeling come from?

MN: I think it originally came from Georgie who wanted to make something that was different to the current affairs shows that she'd done before that told her story in detail of the court battles and stuff. We wanted to make something that was creative for film festivals and for film lovers. Closer Productions and the producers there had a big influence on thinking creatively about how to use that incredible trove of archival material, which at the end of the day, when you come up with all the things you have, you must look at what you've got. We all agreed that the archive was so beautiful, that we wanted to find a structure that could reveal that.

I think the point to be made about this archive which becomes clear in the film is that Georgie has such a beautiful coherence of self from an incredible interview when she's nine when she's very capable of articulating who she is and her relationship to her gender. That consistency remained for the next ten years and has done since she was a toddler. When you're watching the film, that felt like it could visually present the story and the message that we wanted to send, holding to that as a core line.

Everyone came together to design this beautiful elliptical style. I should also mention producer Matt Bate. I'm very interested in gathering all the producers who have many, many different skills. You'll see all my films have many producers and then me running around doing a lot of the filming and doing everything else, a one-woman camera operation. Matt Bate made *Shut Up Little Man* (2011), and *Sam Klemke's Time Machine* (2015) and several other films that rely heavily on archives. He came on and was significant in finding that beautiful cutting style where you cut through ten different ages as Georgie curls her hair behind her ear.

What does that look like in the editing room?

MN: Working with the amazing editor Bryan Mason, we don't do a lot of storyboarding. It's a lot of feeling your way through it. I think because I haven't made something quite so nonlinear before, it's often a feel rather than finding all of the little bits. I rough-cutted the film and collected images throughout all of the footage, the many, many years which you can imagine there was quite a lot. It's probably the most amount of footage for a short film. We could have made a feature in some ways. We got in the edit and worked intuitively with Bryan's incredible mind.

I assume that you were filming this around the same time that you're doing In My Blood It Runs. Is that right?

MN: Yes.

How do you balance telling two different stories and creating two different stories in a documentary format at the same time?

MN: I don't know, I just sort of did it. For a long time, we didn't know where the film was going or the kind of form that Georgie wanted to take. We really only started the edit after we'd finished a year of the impact campaign on *In My Blood It Runs* so there's lots of overlap with the filming. It was nicely spaced to jump into a creative mindset after working on the impact campaign for *In My Blood It Runs* for several years.

How important are impact campaigns for films like this?

MN: I had an epiphany around impact film when I was introduced to it through Good Pitch Australia and Doc Society in the making of *Gayby Baby*. At the heart of my motivations for making these films is social justice. I've learned a lot from my colleagues Alex Kelly, Malinda Wink, and the Doc Society team that just raising awareness and playing at film festivals or in the cinema is not enough. We've spent in many cases many, many years making this film and telling the stories alongside our participants. It feels like our duty as filmmakers to ensure that that story continues on to work to change the status quo of the narratives that we're depicting on screen.

With *Dreamlife*, we're excited about the work that we're going to do. We've raised a bit of money from some amazing philanthropic supporters to do

THE DREAMLIFE OF GEORGIE STONE

a parallel campaign mostly bursting out around the Netflix release in September. There's a Dreamlife Youth Committee who will be making a publication alongside the film by and for trans people about their dreamlives presenting to politicians later in the year. We've got space to do parliamentary screenings, to support our leaders and decision-makers to better understand trans young people and their lives and challenges. Then a whole lot of work around celebrating the voices and encouraging access to services that were really being led by Transgender Australia, The Gender Centre and several trans-led organisations will be driving that campaign and who know much more than us as filmmakers. I see the work of films is to back and amplify the grassroots, those who have been fighting these campaigns for a long time and will continue to far beyond the film's release.

When you started, did you have the notion that you always wanted to tell stories about social justice?

MN: I think social justice is the heartland of documentary. I'm motivated by the beautiful coming together in documentary film of social justice and art. It's those two things that are working alongside one another that feeds my creative urge but also does good in the world.

What does it mean to you to be an Australian filmmaker working today?

MN: I feel very lucky and privileged to be a filmmaker in general. It's really hard but also a glorious and glamorous job. I love it more every day. I couldn't imagine doing anything else. I think the Australian part in particular, I think we have a very amazing continent. I also think that there are so many things that we need to come to terms with as a nation. Therefore, we as storytellers can keep society being their best selves, highlight, and amplify those voices that don't always get space, and breed empathy and understanding that holds that sort of large cultural consciousness together. I suppose that's how I see my role and the many roles of people in the arts.

WARRAWONG... THE WINDY PLACE ON THE HILL

29 mins
Director: *Simon Target*
Featuring: *Sue Armstrong, Brian Armstrong, the Country Women's Association Tooraweenah & Gilgandra*
Producer: *Beata Zatorska*
Music: *Lament - Nikoloz Rachveli, Lisa Batchiavilia & Georgian Philharmonic*

INTERVIEW
DIRECTOR SIMON TARGET

Simon Target's *warrawong... the windy place on the hill* presents the yawning farmland of the remote town of Tooraweenah in NSW with all its stark beauty and harsh glory. Target follows Sue and Brian, a couple in their seventies facing the impacts of isolation, loss, and the emotional toll of downsizing a farm in a town with an ageing population. From shots of Brian rounding up livestock, to drone footage of the oncoming grey clouds and the wind that blows 24 hours a day, Simon immerses viewers in the day-to-day life of a farm.

Time becomes obsolete and days lose their meaning as Sue and Brian become one with the land, dealing with a plague of mice by feeding their dead bodies to the voracious magpie family that lives on the farm. Sue and Brian are 60km from their nearest neighbour, 150km from a doctor, making the two-metre separation rule of COVID times almost feel like a farce, but it's their reality.

This interview contains discussion of mental health issues, suicide, and loneliness.

This interview was recorded by Andrew F. Peirce in May 2022

This is such a striking film. Even though it's only half an hour long, it forces you to sit there and be quiet and patient.

Simon Target: It's interesting, I asked Brian, the farmer who's in the film, about cows and I said, "Are they stupid?" People talk about dumb cows or slow animals, and he said, "Oh no, no Simon. They're very clever. They're very observant." He said, "All they do is watch all the time. That's what they do. They watch me if I leave a gate open. If I'm wearing a different coat, they notice from hundreds of metres away."

WARRAWONG...THE WINDY PLACE ON THE HILL

I went out before dawn each day and stood and tried to be like a cow and watch and see the story of the dawn. How one bunch of birds start singing and another group follow, they've all got their order of who makes the noise when. This is a very old landscape, the Warrambungles. I don't know when the volcanic eruption that created them happened, but it was millions of years ago. You really feel that as a human being. Personally, I feel very, very temporary. Brian and Sue are going to die and I'm going to die one day, but this place will be here forever.

It's what our country does to us, doesn't it? I'm sure other countries do.

ST: It does, you're right. No, I think Australia is particularly like that. You have a real sense of being temporary. I remember coming to Australia when I was a teenager, and just driving from Sydney to Melbourne and thinking if I walked off this road into the bush for a few hundred metres, no one would ever find me. I could just lie down in the sleepy daze-y afternoon and go to sleep, and that would be it. In England where I grew up, you walk for 500 metres, you come to a post office or a pub. There's not that sense that we are just recent visitors. First the dinosaurs, now us.

Brian talks about the trees that are on the property and he says, "They've been here for hundreds of years, and they'll be here for much longer." We look at a rock and we go "Well, that's been around for a very, very long time." It is an inert solid thing that is just going to stay there. Then we look at a tree and think, "Well, that's a living thing that we can cut down." It was comforting to hear him recognise that a lot of these trees that we have in Australia have been around for a long time.

ST: The obvious thing for him to do would be to cut them all down so he could get his header through and take his crop off. Instead, these header drivers have to go round and round in circles around the trees. He wouldn't dream of cutting them down because he loves them. He said, "The cattle can get shade under them, they can eat them, there's mistletoe in them, they've been there for a hundred years." There's no such thing as aging in nature. It just keeps regenerating, like the coronavirus. I feel in this war of man versus nature, man is always going to lose. That's what's truly humbling. You feel the power, but the trees will be there forever. Not that particular tree perhaps, but another tree will grow from its seeds.

How did you meet Sue and Brian?

ST: They invited us to talk at a CWA [Country Women's Association] event. CWA is an incredible organisation of women trying to stop each other from going bonkers when they live in great isolation in the bush. It's an amazing kind of group therapy organisation. Every year, they study a different

INTERVIEW I SIMON TARGET

country as a project. They make contact with women wherever and they share recipes and knitting patterns and they visit the countries.

One year they were doing Poland, and my wife is Polish. My wife had written a book about Poland, and they invited us to present at some events. I sat next to [Brian] after I told them all about Poland, which they knew already because they'd already been to Poland. They started telling me about their lives, and that was so interesting to me. They had just been through three years of terrible drought. Farmers were killing themselves; they were suiciding. The poor policeman from Tooraweenah said he'd had to go out to farms and dismantle these suicide machines where farmers were too frightened to put a gun to their head; they had invented some weird machine that would kill them after a certain amount of time. Unimaginable horror that we don't hear about, all because they couldn't grow a crop, because they had to shoot their cattle. Brian had to kill his herd four years ago. Couldn't feed them.

To support themselves, the CWA put on a feed at the pub in Tooraweenah every Saturday night. It was cheap, ten bucks for dinner. Every Saturday night, a hundred people would sit down and eat together. The population of Tooraweenah is one hundred so literally the whole town was eating together every Saturday. I live in Glebe [in Sydney] and I'm very pleased that my neighbours sometimes come over for a cup of tea or a drink. There's nothing like that cohesion in the country, and that's what got me interested. I went out there. Sue invited me, "Come and stay, and I'll show you around." I stayed and they let me just live with them and film them which was fantastic. I could film them in their pyjamas, I could film in my pyjamas, just get straight out of bed, and walk out into the field in my pyjamas in the dark. It was fantastic to do that.

How do you see your role in documenting this, as an observer or somebody who is curating the history of this town and the people that live there?

ST: I think we're all documentary makers now because we've all got an iPhone in our pocket. Every time we take a phone out and start filming, we're documenting what we see. I don't see my work as any different from that, to be honest. I just spend longer, and I use a more expensive camera and a bigger lens.

I enjoy the kind of non-narrative films which have no voiceover or captions. They're not telling you what it's about. You get to hopefully sit and observe up close someone's life, someone you don't know about, and understand a bit about what their life is like. Those kinds of films are kind of killed by television. Now everyone's sort of not watching television or watching streamers. As I say, it's so much easier to make a film yourself.

WARRAWONG...THE WINDY PLACE ON THE HILL

I find it too much. There are too many pixels for me. I want to slow it all down. When you watch *Fauda* (2015-) or something, one of these Netflix dramas, and there's a wide shot of Ramallah. I just want to say to them, "Stop, freeze it, just let me wait. I can wait for the story. I just want to look at Ramallah from the air for just a few more seconds." I'm probably old, that's why.

There's a whole new world of those kinds of films. They end up in festivals which I enjoy, and particularly in middle Europe, lots of those kinds of films are being made, fantastic movies made by people. Some guy with a GoPro living in a yurt in the middle of a tundra in Siberia for six months, and you get to see stuff in 4k on a huge screen that you'd never dream of seeing.

I love the drone. Everyone's got a drone now and it's like another dimension of the world. Ten years ago, we never saw the world from above, and now every single film has that angle which is lovely. With the drone shots in my movie, I made a rule that I wasn't going to move the camera, I was going to park it in the sky like it was on top of an enormous tripod. Rather than swoop and move around which is what everyone does. The swoopy shot is so exciting, to go storming above the ground. But if you just stop and hold the camera stationary and look down, you get this whole new view of the landscape, which I find fascinating. I could look at it for hours.

The two of them, Brian and Sue, live so isolated. In COVID, we were told to stay two metres apart. They are sixty kilometres from the nearest neighbour. They're together but they're silent. They don't talk to each other much. They just move around quietly. He doesn't talk to the animals, there's none of this [herding calls]. They follow him quietly, intuitively around, he's got this kind of wordless communication.

It is very quiet and all you hear is the wind blowing which blows all the time. Sue said to me, "Why did you call it *the windy place on the hill*? And I said, "Haven't you noticed the wind blows twenty-four hours?" She said, "No, I hadn't." She wrote me an email just the other day saying, "You're right. I just noticed that the wind blows all the time." They hadn't noticed. It does, it feels like you're on a ship at sea. I've kept worrying that the little house would blow off on its stump. It's got this incredibly constant, howling wind and stasis. I suppose a static world, as you say.

It feels like many filmmakers nowadays are afraid of being static, of being quiet. They've always got to be moving, always got to be cutting to something else. It's comforting to see a film that is just about sitting there and observing because it reflects the life that you're documenting. It makes it such a powerful experience.

INTERVIEW | SIMON TARGET

ST: You're right. The rule is to keep the camera moving, keep cutting, keep it busy, and keep people's attention. But it's like putting too much sugar on your cereal. You reach a limit where it doesn't work anymore. I think if you go back the other way, at first, it's a bit jarring perhaps and you feel it's a bit boring, what is this all about? If you start to look at this thing more as a series of moving paintings, I think it hopefully becomes very immersive. I just love it. I love looking at the world that way.

When do you know that you've got a shot that you want to use?

ST: Well, I'm not sure. Not till later. Not till you're in the cutting room, I think and then you can see. Hopefully, it's in focus and you haven't stuffed up. Because that's the other thing. The gear is so good, but it's so unforgiving because if it's slightly out of focus, the shot is unusable. Especially in this kind of static filming, you could argue that if you're following someone who's leaping off a cliff, then you're allowed to lose focus for a second. But not if you're staring at a huge wide landscape. It's got to be sharp.

You can't really see on location, because my vision is not that good anyway, I'm struggling to check. A lot of stuff gets wasted. There's an instinct, I think, as any filmmaker can tell you, if you look through the cameras and think, "Oh this is working, this feels good."

Even when Sue reaches up to get something out of the letterbox. She's got a letterbox behind the post office in Tooraweenah, and she's stretching up and she's a bit short and she's struggling to get into this [box]. I'm thinking as I'm watching, "This is good because it shows you that if you live here, you have to have a letterbox, no one's going to deliver to your door." It shows she's got the top letterbox; she should have the bottom one. How did that happen? It's just yet another tiny hardship to add to the list of hardships that this woman has to suffer. And she wants to.

The other thing about the film is that these are people who could sell the farm tomorrow and move to Sydney. They've got kids here who would gladly put them up, they could have a nice apartment looking at the sea somewhere. They don't want to. They want to stay. They love the farm; they want to stay there. Even though they have major health problems and are having to sell bits of farm and bits of stock all the time. They want to die standing in their boots, and that really interests me. Because it's not a choice of comfort at all.

It's their life as well. It's what they know, it's the place they know.

ST: It's what their parents did, and their grandparents did.

413

WARRAWONG...THE WINDY PLACE ON THE HILL

So often we hear these stories that when you get old, you come to the city and live in an apartment. I don't think that people fully appreciate the mental strength you need to do that. It's hard to go from your neighbour being sixty kilometres away to hearing them through the door.

ST: Yes, all day long. And you might enjoy that. I think they would enjoy the presence of others. But on the other hand, it's the natural world as well. Brian is constantly watching the weather, he showed me stuff I'd never noticed because they live next to a mountain. That's why the wind blows because of the convection currents going upside of this mountain. He would point to the weather and say, "Look, there's a rainstorm, it'll be here in about forty-five minutes." And sure enough, it would be.

We look at our phones for weather forecasts, he looks at the sky. The Coonabarabran Observatory [Sliding Springs Observatory] is just up the road, this is a perfect place for looking at the sky. It's high and not very humid. You get a sense of the closeness of the cosmos, to be honest. That's why I like it and looking up at the jet trails because you're always close to the sky. If you came to the city, you'd give all that up and they don't want to.

But the problem is they are old, he is sick, he needs a doctor. You get to a certain age in life, you need a doctor. And that doctor is 150 kilometres away. To get there, they have to go through the driving, freezing rain because they can't get off the farm in a normal car, so they arrive at the doctor's soaked to the skin. You can't keep doing that in your seventies and your eighties. What's the alternative?

They've become part of nature. They're not just people living on the land, they are people living with the land. The mouse problem is huge, but I loved the shot of Sue turfing this bucket of dead mice over the fence and then watching the magpies come along and tear them apart.

ST: Breakfast. 'Nice, thank you.' She's amazing. And there's more. Unfortunately, I wasn't able to film this but the wooden floor's got holes in it and snakes regularly come through. They were telling me some story about a brown snake that had got into the house, and it got into a chest full of kewpie dolls that she had been making. The snake was freaking out and moving around and the dolls were starting to move, and the snake thought the dolls were alive and started biting the dolls. Can you imagine? They came in, and there was this huge brown snake with his mouth wide open on the top of a doll, and Brian had to bludgeon it to death. That's normal.

I'd love to have shot that but unfortunately, snakes are very hard to film. They were telling me this story. I was in my room. "Are you afraid of snakes?" "Yes, I am afraid of snakes. I hate the bastards." "Oh, interesting because

INTERVIEW | SIMON TARGET

there was one last week in your room." "Thanks for telling me that, I'll be sleeping really well tonight." The mice are absolutely part of life, and anyone else would be revolted. They wouldn't be able to eat their breakfast when there were fifteen dead mice on the floor, but it's not a problem for them.

When was this filmed?

ST: I started in December 2020. Then I filmed all last year, and the last bit I filmed in February or March this year, so it's been shot over eighteen months, right throughout COVID. It was a great COVID project for me because no one could travel, but you could travel out west. It took eight hours to get there from Sydney, but then you stood on top of the hill and looked west, and you realised you're still only a third of the way across New South Wales, two-thirds to go, and it's an empty space, there's no one there.

As terrible as the pandemic has been, we got to see these kinds of stories of a community coming together. Would you have gone if we didn't have this kind of restriction?

ST: Well, no. The whole concept of isolation is something we've all been learning about in the cities through COVID, the idea of putting yourself on your own for a bit. These people have been isolating themselves for years as part of their lives. So, it's something we're thinking about more.

What I love about it is even though in theory, they're safe from COVID, for example, they respect nature. They vaccinate themselves; they vaccinate their cows; you see that in the film. Brian knows very well who's boss out there, and it's not him. He's the servant of the natural world around him. I love that about him. I could talk to him forever about farming, he's very interesting.

There is a moment where Sue forgets Brian's birthday, and she's devastated. But going back to what we were saying about the age of trees and rocks, it reinforces that time becomes almost irrelevant.

ST: New South Wales was the first state to set up the CWA in the 1920s. One of the first things they did was a radio schedule. Farmers had radios, and they would all come online at six o'clock at night and have a chat, or the women would have a chat. These are people who never spoke to other people, totally isolated. So, it's a great moment to talk. One couple rang in and said, "We've just got one question. Can you settle an argument we're having?" And the radio operator said "Sure." They said, "Can you tell us is it Thursday or Friday? Because my husband thinks it's Thursday? I'm sure it's Friday. We don't get the paper till the weekend. Would you please tell

WARRAWONG...THE WINDY PLACE ON THE HILL

us?" That was a hundred years ago. I think that sense of time having a different weight is very much alive today.

Very much so. And that comes down to the edit as well. Did you edit this film yourself?

ST: I did. I've been recently doing all my films myself, but I have other proper editors who have cut my films in the past who come in and have a look and give me advice. That's the way I work now. I cut it and then they say, "Hang on, have you thought of moving that scene a bit later or not opening with that?" And then I recut. I sort of do a series of screenings to wise friends to help do that. Otherwise, I'm a shot by shot, I do it myself.

This is the kind of film that I love losing myself in. It makes you feel at peace, even though we're watching something quite sad. We're seeing two people age and be pushed out of their lives because of time.

ST: Yes, you're absolutely right. I think it's not sad because they're not sad. They're quite cool about that, you know. "We're going to die soon; the kids are going to spread the ashes at the top. If they can get up there, that'll be fine." You know? I think they're together and that sort of insulates them against any sadness.

This is a film which I love to see come out of Australia because it kind of challenges the notion of what Australian culture is or what Australian cinema could be. Is that your intention as an Australian filmmaker telling these stories to readdress what Australian culture is?

ST: We have had four years of dreadful cultural leadership from Scott Morrison which is thankfully over but, I think art in Australia, filming in Australia is low on our priorities of what we think about. I think the reality of our country is it's very unusual and very different. And the differences do lie in the country really, not in the cities, which are perhaps more similar to other cities around the world.

That landscape Brian and Sue live in is extraordinary. It's original and the animals are unique, and the age of it is unique. Even the Indigenous life which is invisible in my film is unique too, [these] old, old people we have in Australia somewhere out there. We don't know anything about it. We don't see it. So yes, I'd love to see more of that. I really would. I think we haven't even started to represent Australia properly.

The idea of selling Australia as [a] beach is so, so boring, which is what Scott Morrison [did]. The 'Where the Bloody Hell Are You' ads that Scott Morrison came up with, apart from being crass and potentially offensive are just so dumb and unimaginative. Truly, I think people would love to come to Australia to find Indigenous culture, to find [the] outback, to find true Australianness of the pioneers in Australia in a way that completely isn't represented in our marketing of how we sell Australia. That's tragic. That's commerce, not art, but it's tragically cack-handed, I think. The Australia you and I love is just not sold properly to people overseas at all.

101 DAYS OF LOCKDOWN

2 mins
Director: *Jelena Sinik*
Writers: *Jelena Sinik, Nicolette Axiak*
Producers: *Jelena Sinik, Nicolette Axiak*
Animation: *Jelena Sinik, Nicolette Axiak*
Sound: *Jelena Sinik, Nicolette Axiak, Simon von Wolkenstein*

101 Days of Lockdown was recognised with First Place in the Digital Works Category at the 47th Rio Tinto & QAL Martin Hanson Memorial Art Awards in 2022.

INTERVIEW
FILMMAKERS
JELENA SINIK & NICOLETTE AXIAK

The animated film *101 Days of Lockdown* is an experimental exploration of the lives many lived during the 2021 Australian COVID lockdowns. Animators Jelena Sinik and Nicolette Axiak use a highly rendered rotoscoped style of animation to reflect on their interactions with their locked down world and with each other. Both Jelena and Nicolette live in NSW, but on opposite sides of Sydney with a 40km distance between each other, and as such, they experienced different styles of lockdown. Their film presents a series of brief visual postcards to each other about their daily activities.

During those long days living restricted lives, time felt like it would never end. *101 Days of Lockdown* compresses that stifling experience into a runtime of two minutes, utilising that brevity to amplify that sense of claustrophobia, while equally honouring the feeling of freedom that can come when societal pressure is relieved. Yet, *101 Days of Lockdown* is not a claustrophobic or depressing experience, but rather a welcoming one, acting as a reminder that while the pandemic was a traumatic event, it was something that we, as a society, managed to endure and come out on the other side of.

This interview was recorded by Andrew F. Peirce in August 2022

How long have you two been friends?

Nicolette Axiak: About four years. We met right at the end of university. Both of us were right on the tail end of doing a Master's postgrad degree and just started chatting in a university lab [UNSW Sydney] and became best friends after that.

Jelena Sinik: We're very different people with very different styles, but I think we share significant values in life. Our friendship is one that's gonna last, I'm certain about it. We live 40 kilometres [apart] and we went to the university in the city, which centralised us, so we were able to spend time together. My personal experience is that I live alone, and at the time of the

101 DAYS OF LOCKDOWN

lockdown Nicolette lived with her family, so we had very different experiences in that regard. Being in the east and west of the city made a big difference too because I'm within five kilometres of the beach because I could go swimming every day, but for Nicolette, it was a very different experience.

NA: The thing about the west is people moved there to be around big families. There's a lot of space, it's very suburban. I think that during the lockdown, a lot of that was taken away or it shifted the focus because you had to build a community around the people that you lived with if you lived with people. A part of the story is reflecting on what it was like to be in a place where community is so fundamental, but you're not able to interact with it in the way that you normally would.

There is brevity to the film, but it carries so much weight and emotion. The time goes by so quickly that in some ways it feels like it never happened at all.

JS: It's this really strange time when you think about it. 101 days is a significant amount of time. It's something that nobody talks about anymore, but it was talked about day in and day out, every minute of every day. The idea was that we would explore this rapid insight through this long, repetitive experience. We constrained the shots to one second per day, so we focused on a highlight or lowlight of the day.

We coined this term 'the disposable memory' because so little significant experience happened during that time that would be deemed noteworthy or something that you could commit to memory. Nobody remembers making a cup of tea on a Wednesday, but that seems to be something that we had to focus on at the time. These sorts of banal experiences became fixtures of the lockdown experience for us. We wanted to look into these 'postcards' of a time when we didn't travel, and we were all committed to staying home. That's the feeling we wanted to go for there.

Getting to see it in this way is beautiful and very grounded. How did you decide what imagery to include?

JS: It is 100% a true story, so nothing's made up in that experience. I mean, what would be the point of that? We recorded stuff, we observed things. It was like a search for what was meaningful for us in a day. It seems a bit sad that this is what it amounted to. I think our experiences were quite singular, we experienced different things. We went with what was organic for us. We didn't want to create a specific narrative. We wanted to explore that experimental space. Nicolette, your experience was quite domestic, wasn't it?

INTERVIEW | JELENA SINIK & NICOLETTE AXIAK

NA: Absolutely. You can see the divide in the film where there's a left and right screen. Everything that's on the left side is the story of the west, everything that's on the right is the east. There is a dialogue between the two. There are moments when the stories overlap, there are times when they're in solidarity. That's how we built the film so that there is a very distinct dialogue between the two.

JS: There is a sense of distance in the fact that they are separate screens. It is like a diary, so we're trying to diarise an experience as truthfully as possible and with the integrity of what actually happened with a stream-of-consciousness feeling. Things that we committed to memory that we now look back at and think "Gosh, that was 101 days." The lockdown was a little longer than that, but when you clock over 100, it's meaningless, senseless, it doesn't matter how many days.

I live in WA, so my perspective of what a lockdown was very different than what NSW and Victoria went through. Our lockdown was 'nobody can come into the state' and we carried on with our lives. It was a bizarre feeling; we looked east and saw people trapped in their homes.

JS: I'm sure your experience had its own difficulties. I mean, we're all on an island, right? We all had our own difficulties. I can't imagine what that would have been like not being able to have people come in and out. It must have been a very specific feeling for you guys. For us, it's crazy, really, that that's how we had to live. Everything stood still for a while, we only really had a sense of the 'now.' I couldn't see the future. I couldn't know what the future held. I had no concept of it. And I'm not like that. I'm a very forward-thinking person, so we did feel trapped.

It was very different for Nicolette because she had the police curfews. The west was under a different kind of scrutiny than the eastern suburbs. We focus a little bit on that in the Nicolette side of the story, too.

NA: As different as the experiences were, there is a universality about them. We kind of wanted to make a documentary, so we wanted to take the experience and build something that had this very strong effect on a very strange time in everyone's life. Everyone in Australia in some way experienced what we've put forward, so hopefully people can watch it and empathise with certain shots and sequences and feelings that we felt. We just wanted to remind people and just recreate some feelings that they had.

JS: We kept the shots to one second each because we wanted to work within the limitations of what we felt. We wanted it to be a limited time in the same way as we felt limited by our ability to move. We had a five-kilometre radius, I couldn't move past that. There were people I wanted to see who couldn't visit me, no one could come over to my house. There were days when I didn't even verbally speak with someone or use my language. Because I live alone, I didn't speak to anyone if I didn't have a phone call that day.

I feel like the point of making this film for us was to make something during a period where there was very little focus on connection in a universal sense. We wanted to connect with people. We wanted people to watch this and think that while our internal worlds are so complex and different as individuals, and our own experiences are going to be different, our physical experience was not that different. I'm sure while you're in Western Australia, you also felt there were things you couldn't do. It's that lack of choice or it's having that freedom taken from you, in whatever form, we all experienced that in different ways.

NA: Historically, we could have never imagined a time when you were unable to travel outside of five kilometres from where you live. We wanted to create a little snapshot of this [strange] time in history. I like to call them 'little postcards,' I think it's a nice way to encapsulate a feeling that we've created. It's like a little glimpse of 'we were here.'

JS: I think about the multitude of media at the time, we took so many photos that we sent to family and friends and said, "Look at my cat." "Look at my garden." "Look at my tea." "I cooked this today." We sent so many of them. They're our digital postcards. Our film is based on the things that we decided were memorable and worthy of sharing. When you look back at them, they're kind of silly in a way.

We're glad we found the motivation to make this because it was very difficult for creatives during that period to produce things. After all, you didn't know what the world was going to be like, and whether you'll be able to do that stuff again. There was a lot of uncertainty there.

Who initiated the conversation? Was it just an organic discussion to be like, "Hey, let's create this project together and tell this story about our experiences together?"

NA: Jelena was the director of the film. She was very much the driving force behind what you see. She invited me in [and] a lot of what you see is a dialogue between us.

JS: The films that Nicolette and I collaborate on are very much 'Nicolette and I' films. They're films that come from our friendship because as artists, we react to the world. Every day we respond to so much stuff all the time. We were just responding to a period where we felt like we needed to create something together. Because we couldn't see each other, we couldn't meet, we couldn't talk, we couldn't go for a walk in the park, we couldn't have dinner together, all the normal things that people need to have a human connection, we felt this need to produce something, to make something together, to be generative. That's where the film came from.

While I may have directed, it is very much the both of us. It's us looking for a way to bring our friendship together to create something that we're going to look back at years from now and think about, while our experiences were incredibly separate, we were there for each other every day. As a collective society, we did try to be there for each other. I find that that is the positive that came out of lockdown. It's this beautiful thing that you can be generative. You can look back at a time and see that you were supportive in ways that may seem small, but they made all the difference for us.

While not a traditionally child-focused medium, there is a consciousness that believes that animation is exclusively for kids. Is the desire to explore the personal also a way of challenging what the notion of animation can be?

NA: For me, a lot of the art that I create is purely driven by observation. Things that are important to me, things that I grew up with, things that I've observed. While [animation] can be seen as something that's targeted towards children, there's so much that you can do in animation that you just can't in live action. For instance, the biggest thing for me is fundamentally the fact that when you're the animator, you get to be the director, the producer, the writer, you can build the whole pipeline. There's something so wonderful about being able to produce an entire film by yourself. Then you can bring people in. Jelena and I love to collaborate both as animators but also as filmmakers.

There's nice fluidity that you get through animation. There are ways that people can project themselves onto an animated character in a way that they can't on a live-action character. You can see yourself in the artwork in a very different way. You can control the motion of the character. The way that a character moves fluidly is totally in the hands of the artists that are creating it. There's so much control that animation gives you. And by control, I really mean freedom. There's something so beautiful in the way that you can direct a character that's being driven by your own hands.

For me, it's something that I was drawn to when I was studying animation. "Wow, I can control this process. I can express myself in this character. I can build a narrative around what I want this person to be doing." A big part of that is just observing the world and thinking "How is this character going to move in the world that I've created for them?" There's just something nice about having that control or freedom.

JS: I think as animators or as filmmakers, we always want to tell stories that we understand, stories that are personal to us. There's no sense in making a story where you don't have your own point of view. That's what this film is for us. While we don't have a clear character, the film is animated from our perspective, it's completely our point of view. This animation feels like a film, you're not looking at it for just its animated value, you're looking at it as a story and as a cinematic experience, and what we like about animation is that it cuts the noise away. It lets you take what a film would record fully. And [as] you remove things, you paint the parts you want to focus on that express emotion.

What's your collaborative process like?

JS: For this film, what we did was we had our own stories. Nicolette had full control of what she wanted to say about the western suburbs and her input on that was purely hers, and on my side, I had my own story. I guess the magic happens when we know each other so well because we're such close friends that we understand each other's intentions and the things that are important to us. The shots that Nicolette was coming up with, as we went along, we crafted that into a story. It was very organic, it wasn't like "We're going to do ABCDEF and we're going to structure this many shots and that many shots." It was the highlight of every day for us to sit down and make a little thing and then go "Oh my God, look, I did this one." "Oh my God, that's amazing." And that's how we did it. We did it for each other and for everybody else. It was an organic process.

NA: As much as the film is a dialogue, the process was a dialogue as well. It was a conversation producing each shot where we're just like, "Okay, this is the back and forth." There was a really beautiful cohesion through this process where both of us were laying down ideas and shots and finding ways to marry them together. The result was what you see before you.

JS: While I may have pushed us and said, "Hey, let's make this into a film. Let's constrain it to a second. Let's do this structure," Nicolette very much brought her point of view to that. That's super important to say because she is equally as valuable in this process as I am because animation is like that. The roles melt a little bit into each other. It's not quite as clear cut as you might think, on perhaps a team of people working on a film.

Let's go back to the beginning, what was the kernel that kicked off your interest in animation?

JS: My undergraduate degree was in film, and I did my Masters in animation. So did Nicolette. My desire to get into animation came from this idea of being able to produce things that were metaphorical in a way that I didn't find film could provide me with. I know that film is a highly conceptual metaphorical space, but there is something really special about using your hands to create something, to produce something. There is a joy in movement, there is a joy in being able to show something to someone that you purely created on your own.

It's all about the story for me. I personally am interested in experimental filmmaking and experimental animation or utilising both animation or hybrid animation and film. Taking a narrative and then breaking it, and showing people things in unexpected ways, for me is where that excitement happens. It's kind of like magical realism, it's being able to capture things and layer on levels of meaning and ways that people can observe things. That's kind of what got me excited about it.

I fell in love with film. I always wanted to be a director, to begin with. Then I found this ability to be able to control things at a level that was so personal to me. That helped me look into animation further, because there is some amazing surreal animation. People always think animation is for kids. I remember saying once "I'm doing a Master of Animation," and someone said to me, "What? A master of cartoons? They do that?" It's funny, but people don't understand how much of an emotional medium animation is. It's been around for a very long time. It's something that people have experimented with, certainly. I find that it is in an experimental format really special.

NA: My experience was quite different. I had just come straight out of school and into animation thinking, "I love to draw." It was my favourite thing to do, to just fill sketchbooks day after day, just drawing pictures. I realised through learning about what animation truly is that it's so much more than that. It's about telling stories. It's about putting emotion into a character. For me, that was the part that I fell in love with, the ability to build a story.

Jelena and I do have very different things that we gravitate towards in our storytelling I tend to be more linear and conventional in my narratives, but through collaborating with Jelena, she's expanded the way that I think about film as a medium. Like she's saying she breaks the narrative, now I can think, "Ah, what's the way that I can set up an expectation with this film and then distort it and find new ways to encourage the audience to feel something different than I would have otherwise created." It was a love of drawing that got me into it, and it was a love of storytelling that kept me here.

JS: It's amazing to be able to visualise things. We like to think of animation as visual poetry. It's this amazing space that is magical, and you can write a story and bring it to life in a way that I think no other medium can. We both share that love.

101 DAYS OF LOCKDOWN

Where do you want to go from here as filmmakers?

JS: What does the future hold? That's a big question. Hopefully not another lockdown. What I'm thinking of doing in the future for me is all art, whether it's writing or illustration, making films, or sound, like Nicolette. She plays violin, she humbly didn't mention that. She did something in the film that has some violin. We all have different skills and things that we care about. We've both done solo films. It's where the art takes you, really. We like to make things that are current, and to make universal stories, to tap into the human story. If something is happening at the time, and it's either not observed, or it's overlooked, it's nice to tap into that space.

Sometimes a project is right to collaborate on. Sometimes it's better to do it on your own if the story is deeply personal. I think short films are a very, very interesting space. I would love to do a big feature film. I mean, everyone would love to do a feature, because there's more space and room to tell something highly complex, but short films are dear to us. It's a little bit underrated like people don't take it as seriously. There is something amazing about being able to tell a story in a short space of time. There is something about the constraint that breeds creativity, which is obviously an example of the lockdown for us, being limited and given a small part of something to work inside of which was important.

NA: Personally, I really love the short film space because there's so much story that you can keep in that. I like the idea of being an animator in the world. There's so much possibility around this [format]. There is so much that you can show in a very short period of time. It's very well suited to a short-form structure like this. We had 101 shots [each]. That's the whole film. There are not really many times where you can have an organic rhythm to go through a film that has 101 shots showing one second [each]. There's something powerful about using animation to get a lot of information across a very short period of time. There's a lot of power in the short form.

What does it mean to explore the Australian experience and identity on screen for you?

NA: For me, being Australian is fundamental to who I am. I love everything about this country. The people, the culture, nature. I feel like the Australian film industry punches above its weight. Considering how small we are, we do very well. [Being] an Australian making films [is] foundational to who I am as an artist. Every character that I've created has been Australian. It's what I know, it's all I've experienced. I think that there's something powerful in that. For me, the observed world is always going to have that bias, and I think it's a beautiful bias. There's something so wonderful about the community that we have here, where it's about how we work hard, we care about family, we've got important values. For me, it's really a nice thing to carry into my filmmaking.

JS: My experience is a bit different. I migrated to Australia. I grew up here. I speak another language. I love this country. This country is a place of possibility. It's a space where I can learn so much. Because I'm European, I bring my own perspective to this country. I create a dialogue with this space. I feel like whilst being both an Australian and an outsider, I have this ability to see things differently. Things that people who are from Australia take for granted. I can see Australia in a way that people who are Australian don't, because it's normal for them. Sometimes someone will say something funny, and I'll say, "Wow, that's a really interesting way to use the language." They'll say, "Oh yeah, you're right." It's funny because having another language gives you that perspective. It lets me see Australia in ways that are natural for Nicolette. It's nice when we work together to bring a different perspective of Australia to Australia, in a more global sense.

How does being an Australian fit with being from Europe? How's that different? That's what I like to bring to my films. I think that's what's special about Australia: we are diverse, and we have different opinions of the same thing. That's super important for us. I think the Australian industry is amazing because it has so many possibilities and it is open to hearing different voices, which is very important. We're both really proud to be Australian filmmakers.

AGE OF RAGE
The Australian Punk Revolution

82 mins
Director: *Jennifer Ross*
Writer: Jennifer Ross
Featuring: Alec Smart, Spike, Heather Anderson, Fabulous Sebastian, Andrew Leavold, Mark Zombo, Spike Depression, Liza G.A.S.H., Flea Thunderpussy, Anthony D'Ettorre, Taryne Laffar, Richie Vomit
Producer: *Jennifer Ross*
Composer: *Dale Cornelius*
Cinematography: *Mark Bakaitis, Anthony Ash Brennan, Jennifer Ross, Hugh Turral, Tom Vogel*
Editing: *Peter Pilley, Jennifer Ross*

Age of Rage received a nomination for Best Original Score in a Documentary at the 2022 AACTA Awards.

INTERVIEW
FILMMAKER JENNIFER ROSS

Jennifer Ross' *Age of Rage – The Australian Punk Revolution* is an archival documentary about the lifestyle of the Australian punk scene, detailing aspects of the history of punk in Australia. Featuring a huge array of interviews from those who made the punk scene of the eighties and nineties what it was. In the process of filming *Age of Rage*, Jenny gave space to the surviving punks of the era, capturing their stories on film for the first time. *Age of Rage* arrived alongside Andrew Leavold's *Pub the Movie* (2022), with each film complementing one another as historical documents for the Aussie music scene.

Within *Age of Rage*, there's an understanding of the ephemeral nature of music, art, and the movements that they bring forth. The punk scene in Australia is one such element of ephemera, with some of Jenny's interview subjects passing away during the creation of the film. During the creation of this book, Jenny passed away. This interview is a small piece of her enduring legacy as a creative force to be reckoned with.

This interview was recorded by Andrew F. Peirce in September 2022

Where did the idea for Age of Rage come from? Was it this desire to make sure [the punk scene was] on record in some capacity?

Jennifer Ross: That's the exact reason I did it. I wanted to document that period in time before everyone died, basically. It was 30 or 40 years ago, so I felt that it should be done just to preserve that aspect of our culture.

How important is that culture to you?

JR: I think it's important because as a young person, it shapes your view of the world. I think you wouldn't get involved in punk if you weren't already slightly an anarchist. That certainly cements that view of trying to make the world a place that is fair for everybody to live in. Which is probably an impossible task, but a noble one.

AGE OF RAGE - THE AUSTRALIAN PUNK REVOLUTION

I'm sure that a lot of people might just think that punk music is just punk music, but there is so much more to it. It's a way of life. It's politics. It's everything.

JR: That's what I wanted to convey in the film. I thought if no one had ever met a punk in their life or had only seen [the look] on the cover of a magazine, I wanted to convey that there's more to it than the music and the mohawks, that there's several different aspects to it. It's a lifestyle and a culture and an attitude and an ethos.

There's so much footage here [from] the past that wavers in quality, but there is the very low-fi, almost VHS style [imagery]. How did you go about curating the footage?

JR: It is VHS. It's not almost VHS style. It is actually VHS. Super-8. Mini DV. Anything that people gave me, I archived it. People would turn up to interviews with a box of 30 years of their life. I would scan every single element, even if it was a tiny one-inch by one-inch promo of their band in 1983 in *Beat* magazine. Every single thing I was given, I archived. Thankfully, later on, I was able to buy some hard drives that could store all the video. People were generous enough to trust me with their old footage, which I was able to digitise, and back up a couple of times. In doing this film, I became an archivist. I didn't just become a filmmaker; I became an archivist as well.

Was that an interesting revelation for you as you're making it?

JR: Yes. I didn't really know what I was in for. I didn't know how long it would take. I didn't know what people would give me. I didn't know what their stories would be. It was basically just one step at a time.

One person featured is Andrew Leavold. There is a conversation that's happening between your film and his film Pub: The Movie, which both launched at the same time. Can you discuss how important it is to have two films that are discussing similar fields at the same time?

JR: I met Andrew because I interviewed him for my film, but I became aware of him because he was doing the Fred Negro documentary. I did interview Fred Negro in about 2014 for my film. By 2016 I realised that the story was taking a particular path and that Fred wasn't necessarily aligned with that, but also that he had his own documentary.

[Andrew and I] were both so busy having nervous breakdowns and anxiety attacks. [He] was so helpful, like every single person that gave me archival flyers, photos, video footage, etc. Andrew gave me many, many folders of that. He's really organised. He had a folder for each band. He lives in the

INTERVIEW | JENNIFER ROSS

Sunshine Coast, and I live in Melbourne, and the conversation that did take place was I would contact him and one by one, online on Facebook Messenger, he would label the photos with me. He would tell me who was in them, what year, all of that. He's fantastic like that. Everyone was.

How long did it take to shoot and collate the interviews?

JR: COVID sort of paused my trajectory. I wanted to go to Brisbane, and that was the last city that I hadn't been to. I didn't go to Darwin, but I did get some Darwin stories in Adelaide. I kind of felt that that was probably going to be enough. I didn't know if the film would be enhanced by going to Darwin. Brisbane was the last city I got to and that was in the middle of COVID. I'd already spent a year editing the film. It took about 18 months to edit. Some of the people from Brisbane got in but mostly the story was already told. I am going to do a book, which can give a bit more insight into everyone's stories, so that will feature those people.

Reading about the film beforehand, there was a comparison to creating a cultural record in the same way that A.B. Facey did for A Fortunate Life.

JR: I love that's one of my favourite books. How lucky are we to have that book and get an insight into that time in Australian history?

It made me think that we lack so many different cultural touchstone moments and texts that are about really pivotal [moments] in our history. That's why I'm so grateful that you have documented this because, for a lot of things, it kind of feels ephemeral. It almost disappears in time. If somebody's not keeping it down on paper, it disappears.

JR: I'm aware that that's a very Australian thing. I read Bill Bryson's book, *Down Under*, and he was saying that he went to the site of the massacres on the Goldfields; there's no day of remembrance or anything, just a little plaque. I just thought that is so typical.

I had that in mind when I thought to make [the] film, it's something that we do as a nation. We just don't celebrate or dwell on things. You sort of keep inching forward, I guess. That's how we started.

The digital age certainly has helped us have more accessibility to that, though. Ten years before I started my film, it would have been a lot harder to make it. Just having a DSLR camera, and a digital camera made it possible. Having computers with programs, rather than cutting and pasting an edit and needing really expensive resources made it possible. I think it's partly to do with the time that we live in as well, because I didn't have to rely on

AGE OF RAGE - THE AUSTRALIAN PUNK REVOLUTION

funding to start the project. I think 20 or 30 years ago you might have had to wait to find some finance to start a project like this, or any other.

What was the instigating moment that you decided 'I need to do this'?

JR: It's funny, because when I was 15, I went to TAFE college. I studied drama, then I studied music, and I was a singer. When I was studying drama, there was a film component to the course, and I loved the idea of making a film. I was sort of involved in punk back then, [at] maybe 16-years-old. I didn't realise the importance of it at that time.

It was when I made my first short film, in 2012, that I set about making this. It was sort of always in the back of my mind for a really long time. As I said, the digital age came about, and it made it possible to start it. Otherwise, I probably would have been a filmmaker years ago. It's hard to say. I'm not sure how many stories I would have had to tell you years ago. But I really feel like this was a story worth telling.

The animation is so expressive and reflects the stories completely. How did you sequence those moments?

JR: I had a very talented animator, Juliet Rowe. I came across her on Facebook, she put a post up during COVID, saying, "I'm available for any animation gigs if anyone's interested," and I really liked her portfolio of work and I messaged her.

The animation was there to depict stories that I didn't have any actual visual reference for. So that's purely the reason that they were positioned where they are in the film. Ultimately, if I'd had a photo or a video to support the story, I probably would have gone for that first. I look back now, and if I thought about it, not so entrenched in the story, or the film or the process of making it, I might have added a little bit more animation here and there. I guess I can do that in my next film. There's always going to be some level of regret as to what you didn't do, or what you could have done mostly. I'm pretty pleased with it, though. That's purely why the animation exists in those places in the film.

As you were curating and collating the stories, was there anything that changed in your views of the punk scene?

JR: I don't think I became aware of anything new. How I think it worked well is that I could relate to the people, and I had a good starting point, because I knew them as young people. I learned a bit more about the crusty punks [who] went to live in the bush and were [on a daily basis] actively rising up against the logging companies. That's a pretty big choice to make

INTERVIEW | JENNIFER ROSS

in your life as a young person to say, "This is important for me to give up everything and fight this fight." I think that's an amazing thing to do.

I wasn't as aware of that sort of thing as far as the punks were concerned. The level of political astuteness and the basic desire to live as an anarchist. One of the guys in the film, Ian Wilson, spent a lot of time in Indonesia and was living with underground anarchist groups. They were targeted by the police, watched by the police all the time, and talked to by the police. I didn't include that in the film because it would have been sidestepping, but [there are] just some incredible stories about people attempting to undermine corrupt politics and politicians.

At the moment I'm reading a book called *The Last of the Hippies* by Penny Rimbaud from Crass, which is an anarchist punk band from England. It was written in 1974, but it's been republished. He's saying, "Fight back. Rise up. But don't be loud about it." I thought, 'Yeah, that's great advice. Just do the work. Keep your mouth shut, keep going.' I think that's really important.

What was a real surprise for me was the way that people in the scene had conversations with people in different countries. That would be by sending satchels of mixtapes and stuff like that around the world. It took me back to the age of bootlegging live concerts in the early 2000s, and late 90s. I used to be part of groups that would get live recordings of gigs, and would burn them onto a CD, which at that time would take hours, and then you'd send it on to somebody in a different country and share these live gigs that you'd never be able to go to. It felt like this form of communication. Hearing the stories of tape sharing and then finding your song on a mixtape shows the beautiful conversation that artists had with strangers on the other side of the world.

JR: That's life full circle, isn't it? When you see your own work presented back to you in a different format or a different context.

That feels like something that doesn't really exist anymore.

JR: Oh no, I think that exists. I just don't think it exists by post. I think it exists online, which is a lot cheaper, too.

There's another guy I interviewed, he's from Adelaide, and lives out past Burra. Where he lives is red dirt and one gum tree. It's quite fascinating. In the 90s he married a woman. She was originally from Eastern Europe, and they went over there and lived in a house that she inherited. He turned [the basement] into a punk rock venue. Then he had this building at the back which he turned into a radio station. He had bands touring from all over Europe. Unfortunately, it's another great story that didn't end up in the film. It's just that desire to connect with people and create a community and give people a place to go to. I think it's just an amazing thing that people continue to do.

[What] is the importance of Australian identity and being able to capture that on screen for you?

JR: It's a funny thing. When I was a kid, we used to go camping. I spent a lot of time in the bush listening to crunchy sounds and wind and dry dirt. It sort of becomes part of who you are. When you go skiing, the trees are weighed down by snow. I went to Canada skiing one time, and it was a completely different experience. The fir trees and the cedar trees, the snow sits on [them] like it's meant to be there. In Australia, it's not like that.

I grew up listening to the lawn mower on a Saturday in the suburbs and listening to the football in the background. My dad would lean out of the window with one elbow and say "Fillerup with super thanks mate." And "Where do you get your licence from? A bloody Kellogg's packet?" And "Bloody women drivers." I grew up with this sort of vernacular and I kind of wanted to preserve some of that as well, even though it's pretty old school. Women are better drivers. That's been proven. We don't have super petrol anymore, it's all unleaded and whatever else. I wanted to preserve a little bit of that aspect, of the way people spoke.

It's a dry, windswept, isolated place, where in some ways people suffered because of that isolation. In that sense, it kind of sets us apart from other people in the world. I thought it was important to acknowledge that as well. That's why I wanted it to be a truly Australian story with just Australian people that nobody knew who spoke like Australians. That was important to me. I tried not to compromise any of that.

It's getting into some festivals overseas now. I'm glad other cultures and countries are interested in seeing what it's like to be Australian. That's pretty important. Because much like the way you feel in Perth, I think, overall, Australia [is] so far away that people that don't really think about it. Although I have noticed recently while watching American content on Netflix there's always an Australian actor, there's always mention of Australia. It's becoming part of the conversation now. But it wasn't back then. It wasn't right up until the last five years. Unless you were a famous actor, like Nicole Kidman, Cate Blanchett, or Paul Hogan, it wasn't part of the daily conversation.

TUĪ NÁ

15 mins
Director: *William Duan*
Writer: *William Duan*
Cast: *Yipeng Xu, Tingting Liu, Hugh Burry, Sharley White, Aurelia St Clair, Lachlan Siu*
Producer: *Mimo Mukii*
Composer: *Kai Chen Lim*
Cinematography: *Gabriel Francis*
Editing: *Christine Cheung*

William Duan received a nomination for Best Direction in a Short Film at the 2022 Australian Directors Guild Awards and won the Best Short Film award at the 2023 Queer Screen Mardi Gras Film Festival.

INTERVIEW
WRITER & DIRECTOR
WILLIAM DUAN

William Duan's precise and precious short *Tuī Ná* tells the story of David (Yipeng Xu), a 17-year-old Chinese boy discovering his queer identity amidst his dedication to his mother and work. Immaculately shot and framed, *Tuī Ná* aches with yearning for a sense of place in the world. This feeling is paired with David's burning desire to embrace the body of another man who also craves his body.

Christine Cheung edits each motif together in a delicate and tender manner that shows ultimate compassion and consideration for the complexity of the story that Duan is showing here. Intertwined with shots of flowers and David looking straight into the camera are moments of David and his mother leaving offerings and prayers for David's grandmother who has recently passed.

This interview was recorded by Andrew F. Peirce in January 2023

Can you talk about the importance of presenting a queer narrative on screen for you?

William Duan: At its core, representation is incredibly important. That's been a movement and a general spirit that's been pervasive throughout the culture at large recently. The next stage that we're seeing now is intersectionality in our representation and in our depictions of minority identities and our experiences. Coming to *Tuī Ná*, what was important to me was exploring a queer narrative that I hadn't seen before, and that was from a Chinese lens, and one that explores the nuances of what it means to have several disparate identities in your body and what coming of age looks like for someone who feels so torn by all these kinds of different aspects of themselves.

Your filmmaking style is a show, don't tell style. Can you talk about that creative process?

TUĪ NÁ

WD: This is my first film as a director. I've mainly produced in the past. It was interesting coming into this from a director's perspective. I relied a lot on intuition, my intuiting the world, the characters, and where everything falls into. Collaboration is a major part of filmmaking and having such a strong and beautiful stunning team gave it so much depth. In terms of the 'show don't tell' aspects of the film that you're talking about, it's something that I'm probably still grasping with [and] finding that balance of. Maybe it's reductive, but sometimes I feel like if you show too much, then you're not treating your audience with as much respect as you should, but if you don't show enough, then the film isn't accessible. The reason I love film is because it's every person's art form, anyone can learn, anyone can tune in and be taken along for the ride because it's such a vehicle for empathy, right?

Do you have an idea of what your voice on screen will be?

WD: I haven't been trained [as a writer.] When I [write], a lot of it is intuitive. I write poetically, so there's a lot of prose in my writing. My big print tends to be quite chunky. When I was writing this and other scripts, I tried to immerse myself in the experience of the world. A lot of it is me trying to imagine what it feels like to be in that space as an observer, and when I'm writing about the characters specifically, also from their perspective as well.

I come from a design background. I studied design philosophy. When I write, I think a lot about the design of the world, the textures, and the feelings around everything. That was a very critical part [of writing *Tuī Ná*] and being able to think about not just the elements that are tangibly communicated through the screen in terms of audio and visual, but also the more nuanced textures that give the world body and depth and nuance in terms of I write sounds, tastes, and smells as well.

In terms of figuring out my style, when I was collaborating with our DP Gabe Francis and our production designer Ranima Montes, it was kind of indulgent in that we would have movie screenings every week and we'd watch different films that inspired us. From there, we would have a discussion afterwards and talk about the things that we loved about the film and what we didn't think worked as well. Then also what we could learn from each aspect that could possibly apply to *Tuī Ná*. I'm a bit of a romantic so a lot of life references are romantic melodrama, I love the richness of those experiences, so I think that probably is what kind of reads across tonally in the final product as well.

What films were you watching?

WD: I watch a lot of Italian cinema. A lot of Chinese Asian cinema. Those are my two biggest reference points. I love the work of Edward Yang and

INTERVIEW | WILLIAM DUAN

Zhao Zhang. *I Am Love* (2009) by Luca Guadagnino is one of my favourite films. Wong Kar-Wai's *In the Mood for Love* I think is so beautiful for exploring interior worlds. It's so distinctly Asian as well. The idea that the archetype of Asian people as being more emotionally withheld and more stoic in nature, which I think is a true thing, generally speaking. The exploration of interior worlds is pertinent within this cultural setting because we might not be able to express all the things that we want explicitly and so it's about all the things that skirt around it.

You mention that your writing process is not a traditional one. I wonder if there is even a traditional writing process. If it's something that works for you to get the story down on paper, is that not all that matters? With that in mind, what does your script look like? How much detail is there and how do you frame the narrative on the page?

WD: I feel like it's something that I've been reckoning with in the past few years. I never really felt truly a part of the film community. I always kind of reasoned it as a result of not going to film school and not building that sense of community there. And so, that insecurity leads to [feeling], "Am I writing this properly?" "Is this how you screen write?" "Is this how you direct?" "Is this how you produce?"

Recently, I've started to embrace the fact that there is no structure in creativity, it is really an expression of self. I'm trying to embrace it a little bit more. In terms of the script itself, it's not not traditional, it's got the scene titles and everything. It's just sometimes I'll listen to one of the myriad screenwriting podcasts out there, and they'll be talking about linking to it "These are your do's, and these are your don'ts." I'm like, 'Oh, my God'. One of the things that comes to mind as a faux pas is not writing from 'we see this' and 'we see that happen next.' But I do that all the time. Because, like I said, I imagined myself in this space, so 'this is what happens.'

Also, another faux pas is not being too flowery with your language. I'm guilty of that. I think [my writing] leans into the style of what I'm creating, which is melodrama. I always refer to the flower scene, the massage scene, and the car scene as fantasy scenes. They were the triptych of fantasy scenes in my head. This idea of melodrama fantasy, you can see it in the way I write.

From the visuals alone, I know what the foyer of the massage place smells like. I know what the altar smells like. I know what the smell of the kitchen is like. It's tangibly represented on screen. You put us in the moment beautifully. Then the sense of touch is there; between the person getting a massage and the movement of bodies in the nightclub, it amplifies David's place in the world. Can you talk about the warmth of

TUĪ NÁ

the bond between a mother and a son, and the yearning for the touch and embrace of a stranger?

WD: The sense of touch is really important. When I was writing the script, I thought a lot about sound, smell, and taste, but I don't think I thought that much about touch. Looking back over the script, it is hyper-present. It was probably something I did subconsciously.

Trying to break it down, Chinese people can be super stoic, and culturally speaking, in terms of the way we communicate, it's not a culture of communicating directly, showing love, or just getting any of our feelings out, really. Oftentimes, love and any of these emotions are expressed through other proxies. The stereotypes are like mothers cutting fruit for their children, which, again, is a real thing, but also through small gestures, like the one at the start of the film where Xiao Yu (Tingting Liu) was massaging David's face. That was something that my mum used to do with me all the time whilst we were growing up. There are so many other things, like doing things for the people you love, rather than just telling them 'I love you.'

What this question made me think about was the idea of *Tuī Ná* as a title, but also as a practice as well. Tuī Ná is a type of traditional Chinese medicine, it's a type of physical manipulation of the body in order to create harmony between yourself and the world around you. Tui means 'to push', and Na means 'to pull,' so that was kind of like the tension we were playing with in the film. I think what was really interesting was looking at Tuī Ná as this traditional practice of traditional Chinese medicine and how through its migration from China to Australia, it has undergone this process of cultural evanescence where the practice of it being medicinal has kind of been stripped from it. Now it's kind of just this 'idea' of Chinese massage.

When I was making *Tuī Ná*, I read something distressing about how it takes on average three generations for a migrant or migrant family's identities to lose their culture or lose access to their culture. I think that was something that was hanging in the back of my mind. Thinking about touch, beyond just Tuī Ná being massage, which is all about touch, David specifically is mirroring Xiao Yu's expression of love through his yearning for connection, so his connection with Jon (Hugh Burry) in the massage scene is a sort of reflection of that.

It's distressing to hear about how culture is lost over generations. People walk into a massage parlour, and they select something off a menu, not knowing its importance or what it means. It's not just massage parlours, restaurants are particularly vulnerable to this. There is something that a meal does to our body and our soul; there's a reason why we use those ingredients. What I love about film is that filmmakers like yourself are

INTERVIEW | WILLIAM DUAN

documenting those experiences, capturing it in the moment in a way that a painting or a book almost can't do.

WD: You're sharing that love and knowledge with other people.

The character of the mother is portrayed so tenderly and beautifully. David loves his mother, but he also clearly wants to push for his own place and sense of self in the world. How did you create the space for a coming-of-age story with the maternal bond present?

WD: The mother's character is almost the most important character in the film. It was really important for me to tell a uniquely Chinese queer story because the Chinese or even the Asian at large, queer experience is so different from what it means to be white and queer or white and gay. It's completely different. I was sick of seeing films where the narrative fulcrum lay in the relationship between the main character and some guy. As much as that is a huge part of coming out and coming of age and finding self, the key to the relationship [was] between David and his mother, because his mother is linked to his history.

David is desperately trying to find and make sense of his queerness and his Chineseness and how these two seemingly disparate identities can coexist, how they can operate simultaneously and how he can reconcile them. That's the exploration with this film. There's an entire discussion that can be held around the idea of whether Asianness or Chineseness is even compatible with the Western conception of queerness. This film, specifically, is framed around David's relationship with the idea of motherhood. It's the idea of motherhood itself.

In Chinese culture, as a collectivist culture, we're not defined so much as individuals as much as we are by the people around us. And really, no one is closer to us than family. David specifically is an only child, raised by a single mother. Family is Xiao Yu, his mother, because that's all he has. For queer people, family, and motherhood are further nuanced concepts. It's amorphous, and it isn't always biologically determined. It's something that is chosen for so many reasons, and probably one of the most important ones is for safety. Those two conceptions of motherhood and family were integral parts of *Tuī Ná*, and what I wanted to use as the device that reconciled these two identities for David.

In the final act of the film, David comes home from his rendezvous with Jon (Hugh Burry), and he experiences this moment of synthesis between his two identities. We see the roles reverse for him. He suddenly becomes the mother for Xiao Yu in that moment. Even if it's just a flash in the pan, that tiny moment at the end. When I was structuring the film, I really wanted

TUĪ NÁ

to structure it around this idea of the cyclical nature of motherhood. One where the film starts with the death of one mother, David's grandmother, Xiao Yu's Mother, and ends with the birth of another with David coming into a sort of embrace of self. I don't think he necessarily finds closure, but he finds a sense of being in that moment.

Tuī Ná was originally conceived as a feature film. When I went into the Queer-Screen funding, I adapted it as a short. There is a very similar arc in terms of that circle of motherhood in the feature, but it ends in a different place.

What guidance did you give the actors to ground them in their roles and allow them to explore their characters?

WD: In terms of working with the actors, the rehearsal process was less about rehearsing scenes within the film, and more structured around [discussing characters with the actors]. With Yipeng, who plays David, we had such an indulgent pre-production period for this film. Yipeng is a full-time dancer with the Australian ballet company. We would meet up at least once, if not twice a week, and we would just go through character. It was nice, we would just sit in the park, and we would talk about our own experiences. [We talked] about his experience as a first-generation Chinese queer person and my experience as a second-generation Chinese queer person. We would talk about where our stories crossed over and where they didn't, where our stories crossed over with David's story and where they didn't. It felt really special, those moments, being able to talk about the emotional beats, the characters' wants and desires, and digging into the experience of the characters from moment to moment.

That was the same with Tingting who plays Xiao Yu. It was based a lot on the emotional journey rather than what they say. These characters don't speak directly. They speak in a roundabout way. A lot of their ways of expressing things isn't through dialogue. Having said that, we had to block out a lot of scenes, especially the scenes between David and Jon. I think we spent at least a week just figuring out how he would move into the massage room, what he would grab, what his first move was. Then we had an intimacy coordinator [Adrienne Couper Smith] for the foot massage scene, and for the car scene as well, just to make sure everyone was safe on set, especially because they were both first-time actors.

Let's talk about the visual style of the film and working alongside Gabriel Francis. What was that process like?

WD: I was super fun and really indulgent. I've been friends with Gabe for years, he's a really good friend of mine. I've worked with him on so many of the films that I've been a producer on. It was great to collaborate with him in different capacities. With Gabe, we watched heaps of films in the lead-up [to filming].

We had a lot of discussions about what we wanted and what we didn't want to do. I came into the film with some hard boundaries I didn't want to cross, in terms of things I wanted to avoid. I wanted a dynamic camera. Even though I feel like it's split quite evenly in the final film, I wanted to try to avoid relying on a static camera where possible, like a camera on a stick. Sometimes it can be a stylistic choice that feels like a default for the genre of filmmaking that you want it to exist within. I wanted to challenge ourselves by being more dynamic.

There were other boundaries I didn't want to cross. The dynamic camera was one of them. I wanted the camera to be an observer in the film. I wanted to feel like a character. I think it's probably [best realised] in the flower sequence. I'm really happy with how the camera moves in that scene. There were scenes where it didn't work as well, namely, a classroom scene that was cut. There was this whole thing with the camera moving around, which took half a day to film but didn't end up making it in.

The other element of it, which I think helped us visually, was we also had a storyboard artist named Amy Ge, who's Sydney-based. After we shot-listed the film, we would have meetings remotely and talk through the key shots for each scene, and then she would paint them in watercolour. I have such a beautiful archive of the film as watercolour paintings. It's so stunning. That helped us a lot visually because we had a visual representation [to refer to]. By that time, we had cast our leads as well, so she was painting with our leads. It was all in blue as well, which was one of our key colours. Blue and red were some of our key colours. Ultramarine.

Ranima, our production designer, who is such a pro and an amazing director as well, had such a clear vision. She was a part of that process in watching films. I want to highlight her and also our costume designer Betty [Liu]. She studied fashion and she has a narrative sensibility, all of her references came from films that we had similar references of. She's one of the best costume designers I've worked with. Then our editor, Christine Cheung, was so good.

Kai Chen Lim, my composer, is my oldest collaborator. I've worked with him on nearly everything I've ever done. We've been collaborating for years. It was so nice to collaborate on something that I was directing and writing. I think that music and sound is at least 50, if not 70% of the film. The collaboration with Kai started before production. We were talking about the themes, and we made sketches of music that helped define the tone of what we were shooting. That's not a unique thing to us, but it was something that

TUĪ NÁ

I felt was special and added a lot of depth to our film. Kai is an absolute king, we love Kai. It was a really gorgeous, stunning team, I love them all.

How do you ensure that you've got a creative team that you can trust and that you feel confident sharing a personal narrative with?

WD: I definitely had a team that I could trust with *Tuī Ná*. It was a learning process for me because it was such a personal story. There were definitely moments where I needed to open up a bit more or be more vulnerable. All the behind-the-scenes crew were close friends of mine, people I already knew and hung out with and shared my life with socially and platonically. I think that really helped me feel safe.

I have to give the hugest shout out to my biggest collaborator, Mimo Mukii, my producer. As a producer myself, we both have a really similar perspective when it comes to creating a [safe] culture on set, in terms of who we actually bring into the fold and who we bring into the family. We're both very community-minded filmmakers in terms of bringing on the communities that could relate to the story. We found ourselves with a stunning team of creatives. If people weren't Chinese, they were queer, or PoC. It was a great experience because everyone was able to relate to at least some aspects of the film. It felt safer that way because you don't feel as alone. You feel like you're going on a journey with all these people who share some experience with you. So that was huge.

It was also really cool because we had a bilingual set, which I didn't imagine I'd be able to experience. The set was half Chinese, half English speaking. Some of our actors, like Tingting, [didn't] speak English, so all of our interactions and her interactions with Yipeng were in Mandarin. That was really special. It was a stunning experience, but it was also the hardest thing I've ever done in my life. It was like a trial by fire. It did help to have a producer's experience coming into it, because there were certain things I could pre-empt and other things that just completely blindsided me.

One of the key themes we're talking about is the role of identity on screen and you're talking about having a bilingual set and telling a story that has dual identities with a cast and crew that carry the perspective of the film. With that in mind, the notion of an Australian cultural identity on screen is one that we cannot pinpoint as being a singular thing. Different cultural identities exist within Australian culture. How important is exploring your own cultural identity on film?

WD: I think that it's super important as a filmmaker to be able to explore your cultural identity. I think the idea of what constitutes Australian identity is a really loaded one. It is an amalgam. It is incredibly rich. Australian film feels like maybe it's underdeveloped. I feel like we're still trying to gain a sense of what we are. There was a kind of idea or a shadow of what it could be in the past, but I don't think it was accurate, because it was so exclusionary. That's why it's important for people to explore intersectionality, cultural identity, or just anything through their specific, diverse lens that's unique to them.

We're really trying to establish a sense of national selfhood within our crafts. When you walk down the street, you see what Australia is: it's multicultural, it's so many things, it's so rich, and there are so many layers to our experience. It's super important because we needed to define that but also, I think that you want to speak from a place of authenticity with whatever you do, and that doesn't necessarily mean you have to write autobiographical works, but it does mean that you want to be creating work that's true to yourself. I think it's important that you do it in a way that doesn't feel like it's like PR or something, because I think a lot of the way that discourse around diversity is held within this country feels a little hollow at times.

I think it's impossible to define culture when you're living within it. That's why history and historians are so important. History is what defines our future.

JUANITA NIELSEN NOW

74 mins
Director: *Zanny Begg*
Writer: *Zanny Begg*
Cast: *Pamela Rabe, Koco Carey, Julie Cooper, Megan Drury, Erica Englert, Amala Groom, Vashti Hughes, Emma Jackson, Jennine Khalik, Ivy D'Orsogna, Maria Tran, Ebube Uba and Amelie Vanderstock, Bronwyn Penrith, Tim Burns, Saoirse Nicholson, Nicolas Hope, Taylor Wiese, Nyx Calder, Sebastian Goldspink, Warren Coulton, Adam Hilbery, Harrison Milas, Teneale Clifford*
Interviewees: *Julie Bates, Meredith Burghmann, Tyson Koh, David Farrell, Imogen Kelly, Ian Millis*
Producers: *Philippa Bateman*
Composer: *Jasmine Guffond, James Brown*
Singer: *Mara Knežević*
Cinematography: *Emma Paine*
Editing: *Zanny Begg*

INTERVIEW
FILMMAKER ZANNY BEGG

Filmmakers have long teased apart the reality of the documentary format, pushing it to its boundaries to help the truth of the story find a path out of the maze of its existence. Dharawal country-based filmmaker and artist Zanny Begg uses her creative force and brilliance to explore the truth that hides within contested histories with her film *Juanita Nielsen NOW*.

Juanita Nielsen NOW pulls from Begg's 2018 experimental video installation *The Beehive*, which displayed 1334 possible variations of the implications of the unsolved 1975 murder of Juanita Nielsen and transforms it into a compelling and moving documentary experience. Juanita Nielsen was a journalist, an activist, a style icon, and a progressive woman ahead of her time. On July 4th 1975, she entered The Carousel Club in Kings Cross, Sydney and vanished. Her death has never been solved. Begg ensures that Juanita is not defined by her death and that the mafia figures that hover in the periphery of her life story aren't given overwhelming attention to dominate her legacy.

Juanita Nielsen NOW is as much about modern gentrification and the impacts of unaffordable housing on society today. We hear from trans icons, sex workers, activists, performers, beekeepers, and members of the LGBTIQA+ community about what housing affordability means to them, their community, and their livelihood.

This interview was recorded by Andrew F. Peirce in October 2022

How did the concept of The Beehive occur?

Zanny Begg: Gentrification, affordable housing, and the process of what's happening to our cities is an issue that's been close to my heart for a long time, and that led me to the story of Juanita. Living in Sydney, I knew about Juanita, and when I dived deeper into her story, I realised how little I knew of it. The more I got into the story, the more in love with her I felt. She was such an extraordinary character, so unique and of her time in the seventies, but then also so contemporary in the ways in which she approached things.

JUANITA NIELSEN NOW

I discovered the story is complicated. Initially, I thought it was discovering who killed her, but as I got further into the research for the project, I realised what was more complicated was who she was and how her story connected to the Sydney that we've inherited the contemporary reality.

For the artwork I worked with an algorithm, there were 1334 possibilities, which allowed this spaghetti to unfurl into multiple storylines. The real challenge in making when *Juanita Nielsen NOW* was to bring all those multiple storylines back into the one timeline and find a path through it.

How did you ensure that there was depth to what happened and who Juanita was?

ZB: The aim of this story wasn't to make a traditional 'who done it' story. I feel like we know who killed Juanita, and the interesting bit is not who did it, but why no one was ever prosecuted, and why it was an open secret. In a sense, I shifted the focus from that 'who done it' approach to looking at the complexities of who she was as a person, and the way that her story is really the story of Sydney and the city that we have today.

Having twelve different people play Juanita was a way of picking up the threads of her story. What was interesting was what happens to those who come after when an injustice like her murder has taken place, and no one's ever been prosecuted for it. I was looking for the legacies and the way in which the threads of her story are picked up in the ongoing stories of Sydney. She was murdered in Les Girls, which was a very significant trans performance club, so there are multiple ways in which the story is picked up and reflected in the people who are cast to play her, who all have their stories of Kings Cross. It was an open casting call for the film and those people have their own stories of Sydney's real estate.

It's the story of Sydney. It's the story of Kings Cross. I say Sydney, but in a sense, it could be any city. The story of gentrification is something that's universal, which is the ways those inner-city areas, the affordable housing and the poor are getting pushed out. You have this homogenisation of middle-class, affluent values that takes away the character and what makes the city amazing and makes it homogenised and bland.

There's this feeling of rewriting the history books. I understand that you have an interest in contested histories. In an artistic sense where does that drive to expose those contested histories come from?

ZB: I would say that I would be working across history, because if it's a contested history, it's not settled. Therefore, it's like a little ghost or a spectre that sits in our society, and it keeps haunting us. When things are very settled, or we feel like we know what happened, we move on, but when things are contested or they're unresolved, they continue to haunt us. I think they make some of the best stories because that unsettledness is a place where storytelling can begin.

In Juanita's case, I feel like the historisation in film and TV – mostly TV, but there have been two films made about her [Donald Crombie's *The Killing of Angel Street* (1981) and Phillip Noyce's *Heatwave* (1982)] – and the media accounts of her have been quite masculine. They have tended to focus on the gangsters who killed her. What those versions of history left out or didn't quite manage to capture was how unique and special she was. I wanted to bring it into her world. I wanted to flip the focus away from the gangsters, who are there, they're part of her story.

She wasn't the only fighter in Kings Cross. Julie [Bates] and Imogen [Kelly] are fantastic women who are in this film. Julie is a sex worker activist, and Imogen is Australia's Queen of Burlesque and a stripper, they also fought to change Kings Cross. They also had death threats. It was bringing that story from the 70s through those struggles in the 80s and early 90s, which was the beginning of the AIDS epidemic, into the real estate landscape. The end of the film was about people making Sydney a home and what that's like today. All those stories haunt us, they trouble us because they're still active. There are still some angry ghosts running around inside those stories.

I love the dual meaning of the title. It's about the publication NOW and Juanita but also about the impact of Juanita now and how she lives with the people who fight for the same rights that she did. Was that the key thesis of the film and the work of The Beehive?

ZB: One hundred per cent. The title of Juanita's newspaper was a gift, *NOW*, it was so perfect. I was talking to Ian Millis, who is interviewed in the film, about the process of taking it from an artwork to a film, and it sort of came up in our conversation. We were playing on the words 'now', and I thought, "Well, that's obviously the title for the film: *Juanita Nielsen NOW*." It's a gift in lots of ways.

Juanita was a pioneer; I think she was ahead of her time. She was a unique journalist. Probably not one that I would necessarily like personally, but I think what was interesting about what she did was she really pioneered a subjective position, and in a way in the seventies that was not respected at all at the time. At the time she was considered lightweight, ridiculous, and vain.

There was a lot of snobbery and critiques of her as a journalist, but what she was doing was everything that we do in media today, so in a way, she was this incredible Avant Garde experimenter. She was taking selfies before the internet. She was blogging before the internet. She was pushing the boundaries of what journalism was. *NOW* capsulated all that because it was the name of her paper at the time but also it speaks to women who have been brave and innovative and ahead of time and [they] paid a huge price for that, but also blazed a trail for others by their actions.

I was reminded of Kitty Green's Casting JonBenet, and both films tell stories in a way that takes away the thing that has defined their titular figures in public consciousness: how they died. They reassert the story of who they were when they were alive. I'm curious if that was a conscious choice?

ZB: *Casting JonBenet* is one of my favourite films. I absolutely love it. I am one hundred percent influenced by Kitty, I think she is a fantastic filmmaker, [I have] complete adoration for her work. I am influenced by it, but it also has roots in my own practice. I made a film before *The Beehive* called *The City of Ladies* (2017), which was before *Casting JonBenet* came out, and we did a casting for *Joan of Arc* because it was a story of French feminism, so that was already in my practice.

What Kitty did was [similar to] what I was trying to do with *Juanita* and what I was doing with *The City of Ladies*. The casting process allowed for a multi-perspectival or poly-vocal approach to the story which allows you to get away from this teleological narrative. Kitty's work with *Casting JonBenet* was a story that the media had trawled so intensely to find a new angle on; I think she needed to do something like that. In *The City of Ladies*, I was dealing with feminism, and with the story of Juanita, that multi-perspectival way of telling the story allowed me to do something more interesting than just a 'who done it' or more interesting than just a 'this is a history of feminism.' It allowed for an untangling and a retangling of the storylines.

The shots of the bees are so precise and scientific to the point where they highlight how unique each bee is. Was that a creative choice to say these are all unique people and together they make a community?

ZB: One hundred per cent, yes. I didn't have any photographs of the drag queens or the trans performers from Les Girls. There is some footage of it, but I didn't have rights to it. Sam Droege took those pictures, he's an American scientist. His work is extraordinary. He was happy to share those images with me. The bees look like stage showgirls with this intense decoration. With those close-ups that open *Juanita Nielsen NOW*, I feel like in a way I had the showgirl costumes there through the incredible plumage and fluffy and sparkliness of the bees. The bees are an important metaphor throughout the whole film, with the Pamela Rabe character, the beekeeper, being Juanita's ghost.

We think of bees in quite a narrow sense, which is the honeybee. Human, urban societies have an ancient cohabitation with the European honeybee. We live in a colonised context here in Australia, and there are over 1200 different native bees which haven't been documented that well yet. We're still discovering a lot about them. Starting from that point of view of how we see bees as some sort of metaphor for human society, then pushing that further to say, "We've only looked at one particular narrow band of bees, there are the solitary bees, there are other forms of social bees, honey producing bees, and so forth." Diving into that complexity allowed me to draw out intuitively and subtly, that's not always easy to read, something about us as human beings, how we live together, and how we live in the natural world. Explaining all of it might, in a way, destroy it, because it is an intuitive metaphor that runs through the film.

You mentioned Pamela, what was working alongside her to bring the beekeeper to life like?

ZB: She was amazing. She was so great. Everyone in the project was amazing. Pamela is just so experienced and professional. She would nail it within seconds, and that was amazing because it was a tricky role. After all, playing a ghost is not that easy. I did no special effects whatsoever because I didn't want to make her ghostly. She's just meant to be there in the sense of this troubled history where timelines are out of sync because there hasn't been justice for Juanita. She sort of appears, she's dead, but she's still there. Pamela had the gravitas just to make that feel very normal and believable. It was a real treat to be able to work with her. There's another ghost there, which is Bronwyn Penrith who plays Ester, and those two together, there's something quite special about that conversation. I find it moving to look at those scenes, the way these two dead women are speaking together about their situation.

Getting to see how much care and tenderness they have for one another and respect for one another was very moving. Additionally, there's that feeling they're tending to the beehives and looking after the next generation, ensuring that they're supported and looked after. How did you script that sequence?

ZB: It is scripted, although, I hope people think it isn't because it is an experimental documentary. I was working with real peoples' stories, and Juanita's real story, but then also, I scripted the project as well. There's a real intermeshing between fiction and reality throughout the whole piece. In that conversation between Pamela and Bronwyn, Bronwyn just started to adlib when she was talking about the dances and the corroborees and the European bees. I was the editor, so I had a lot of intimate choices over what went in and what didn't. That was just so magnificent so of course it was going to stay in, [to] hear her talk about that. That was something I had no idea about til I heard her talk about that. It was fantastic to have that moment in the film.

Can you talk about the creative choices that you made there in having multiple different people playing Juanita going up the stairs and into the room?

ZB: Loretta Crawford is a receptionist at The Carousel Club, who is still around, I didn't get to interview her. She is someone who doesn't want to be found. She has also told three, that I know of, wildly different versions of the story of what happened to Juanita. Potentially, she's changed her mind, but there are three different versions. They are the only eyewitness versions that we have of what happened once she went up the stairs; the rest is left to our imagination. In that scene, I played out those three different versions of the story with different people playing them. Because it is a mystery. We don't know what happened. This is as close as we got, and that's what comes from the one eyewitness who was there. The fact that all three versions which come from the one-person play at the same time speaks in a way to the open secret of Juanita.

Why is it that, over 45 years later, no one has cracked and said what happened? Including people like Eddie [Trigg] who took it to his grave, and Loretta who is still around. That's a story of intimidation. We know some of the violence that Loretta suffered [with a] car window being blown out with a shotgun. Who knows what happened to Eddie? Apparently, he was living in a sort of exile inside one pub in Redfern or Waterloo for the rest of his days. Dark forces are around the story. The fragments that come out are a little bit ambiguous, so I allowed them to all play at the same time in that scene.

What happened in the casting was unknown because this is the integration between fiction and reality and the real-life stories of the people who were cast to play Juanita. The place where we know Juanita died was in Les Girls, which was a significant, legendary trans performance venue for a long time in Sydney. Kilia, or Koco as she's listed in the credits for *The Beehive*, was one of the Juanita's, who is a fantastic performer, an amazing dancer, and very active in the trans community in Sydney. I knew I wanted to have her story coming through and then dancing in that venue happen. When we got there, and then she did that dance – which picks up the thread of how bees communicate through dance –, it brought together the threads of the film in that moment. It made a beautiful climax.

INTERVIEW | ZANNY BEGG

What does it mean for you to be an Australian artist working today telling these kinds of stories?

ZB: I really hope that international audiences will be interested in this story. I feel like gentrification is not just an Australian problem. The term comes from Ruth Glass and European and American campaigns around gentrification. We all know the Bronx and Harlem because American culture is everywhere, but do people know Campbelltown and Mt Druitt overseas? I'm not sure. There might be something quite specific about the film. I struggled with that. I was trying to find a way that I could say, without ruining the story, "Campbelltown, that's Western Sydney, just let me explain that". I tried and I struggled in different ways. In the end, I was like, I can't do it because it will ruin the story. I have to just hope that by being immersed in the story, even if people don't know Mt Druitt or Green Valley, in the context of how people talk about them, they will understand 'low socioeconomic, ungentrified' or 'fancy bourgeois, gentrified.' Every city has those kinds of divisions. I hope that international audiences will get something out of this film.

I really like to experiment with film. I think this is an experimental documentary. You mentioned Kitty Green, there are some people really working at trying to push what a documentary is and what it can be. I find that hugely exciting. I guess there's the Brechtian in me that thinks fiction sometimes gives us as much of the truth [as reality]. Sometimes you need to make something up to tell the truth or to help the truth come forward for the viewer. That's the sort of work that I'm interested in doing.

WHEN THE CAMERA STOPPED ROLLING

75 mins
Director: *Jane Castle*
Writer: *Jane Castle*
Featuring: *Lilias Fraser*
Producer: *Pat Fiske*
Composer: *Kyls Burtland*
Cinematography: *Jane Castle*
Editing: *Ray Thomas*
Sound: *Sam Petty*

When the Camera Stopped Rolling received nominations for Best Documentary, Best Editing in a Documentary, Best Sound in a Documentary, and Best Original Score in a Documentary at the 2021 AACTA Awards.

INTERVIEW
FILMMAKER JANE CASTLE

The art of reflecting on the past with awareness of its impact on the present is a difficult thing to master, but filmmaker Jane Castle managed to do exactly that with her familial documentary *When the Camera Stopped Rolling*. Initially conceived as an intellectual film about death, *When the Camera Stopped Rolling* evolved over almost ten years of production into being a reassertion of Jane's mother, Lilias Fraser, into the history books of Australian cinema.

Autobiographical and revealing, *When the Camera Stopped Rolling* is at times a difficult watch as Jane works through her relationship with her mother through pristinely presented archival footage (which occasionally plays like a silent film) with a level of vulnerability that gives way to an emotionally enriching experience. *When the Camera Stopped Rolling* showcases a labour of love for parents and the culture that they introduce their children to, while also recognising the struggles that emerge from a crumbling mind.

This interview was recorded by Andrew F. Peirce in March 2022

There is a lot of personal footage, family footage, and a lot of family photos. What was your experience as you were building up the film and looking at those visuals?

Jane Castle: It was incredible. As we were editing and filming, I was digging through old boxes and finding all these negatives that I'd never seen before and scanning them and going, "Oh my God, this is incredible." One of the things I discovered was the wedding photos from my parent's wedding. [I'd] never seen them at all. They were in this little envelope and had never been printed. We ended up using only one in the end, but they captured the moment so perfectly. It was like this treasure trove. There were a lot of dead ends, but there were some amazing things. Some of the material had deteriorated. The paper it had been kept in had stuck to the negatives. I had to take it to the lab to get as much off as possible, and then Photoshop the rest. It was a big piece of work. Including the written material as well, I was reading through those, and we scanned them and put them in.

How long did it take to make?

JC: Ten years is a good number to put on it. Probably eight years from when we first got funding, but I was working on it for a couple of years before that. If you go back, the first film I ever made when I was seventeen is in the film. It was 1981, so in a way, you could say I've been making the film all my life. It took a long time because the way we made the film was kind of an iterative process. It was a bit more like an artwork than a film with a script. We had a script, but really it was just sitting with the material and the timeline and trying things out and me bringing in new material, and then to surrender what the film seems to want, and [realising] "It's not about this at all. It's about *this*." It was a labour of love for all of us on the team.

How much did the project shift and sway as the years went on?

JC: It started as a completely different film. I wanted to make an intellectual film about death, a bit of a spiritual investigation. In fact, in the first trailer I made, I interviewed nuns and monks and people who had died and come back, and people who were dying and all sorts of people. We had all these kinds of intellectual explorations. In the process of doing that, my producer said, "Why don't you just go off and write as well?" And I did. I wrote this story about my mum's death. It became pretty much the opening scene of the film. When we started to show this film about death to people, especially funders and Screen Australia, they were like, "I don't know about all these interviews with these people about death, but I loved that stuff about your mother, and hey, she's an Australian filmmaking pioneer." Then it was a no-brainer.

It was really the last thing I wanted to make a film about. Like 'ugh, my mother.' I was still pissed off at being abandoned when she went out on film shoots. "Giving her more attention, I can't bear it." But it was where the film took us. It ended up being a different film. I didn't want to have myself in it, but the narrative kept demanding that, to bring the conflict points and to have two characters. My mum's life wasn't enough to have a whole feature-length film, so our relationship became the kind of core narrative spine.

What's the experience of being open with your life and your family's life onscreen like?

JC: It's pretty excruciating, although also satisfying. It's a bit of a double-edged sword, but there is the satisfaction in telling the story of what

INTERVIEW | JANE CASTLE

happened, which I was never really able to articulate. In doing so, I've had to be very revealing and make myself very vulnerable. That's, of course, quite nerve-wracking because some people won't relate to it, but I really had to trust [the audience]. What I found out in the making was that the more honest I got with myself and then was able to put that into the film, the more gripping the film was and the more people could relate to it directly because I was being less superficial. In a way, I was also driven by this terror that the film was going to be a big flop. "I need to make this film work, I'm just gonna have to be more honest." I didn't want to make a confessional film. Sometimes I [feel] like it's still a bit confessional. It's tricky to do that vulnerable stuff without going into a kind of self-pity or overdoing it. I think we kind of found the balance in the end.

What's it like being able to bring Lilias' story to light in a way that is tender and caring, while acting as a beacon to say, 'People need to pay attention to these pioneers of Australian film history?'

JC: It's really touching. It covers a shift in me in the process because I think if I hadn't made the film, she'd just be gathering dust in the archives, and no one would know about her. I didn't make the film to highlight this pioneering filmmaker, because, as a kid, whatever your parents do, you just think "Big deal, whatever. They're human rights activists, they're actors. Whatever." My mum was just a filmmaker. Her making films annoyed me because it was chaotic, and they kept going away on vacation.

In the process [of making this], I do feel this tenderness about her and a new appreciation of her importance because I don't think I even realised the importance of her life and work. It's only from getting the reflection back from people after having made the film that I'm realising more and more what an important figure she was, and the gifts that she passed on to me and my sister in terms of her 'can do' attitude and the trailblazing-ness and not being affected at all by the systemic shut out of women from the industry.

It feels like when you moved from working on music videos to working on films, you had to break through that glass ceiling once again. Can you talk about the two different worlds of music videos and film in America?

JC: That's true. In Australia, I worked with my sister, Claudia Castle, on music videos, she was a director. We did come up against, in terms of crew, that kind of misogyny, a bit of resistance, a bit of disrespect. But because we were a team, because we had the power - she was producer-director, I was cinematographer - it was easy to overcome. In the US, the music video scene is much more of a fluid area. It's a bit cowboy, it's a bit creative. In the commercial sector and feature films, there was a lot more resistance from blokes. I had a lot of personal problems with crew members not respecting me. As a whole, men were supportive. But there were a few that just stood out in my memory. Once a camera assistant kept shaming me in front of the rest of the crew, telling me I didn't know what I was doing. I had some grumpy-bum grips and gaffers over the years.

Mum was great at giving me advice on that. With her, I think she wasn't as affected as me, she'd just shrug it off. She was much more optimistic than me, I'm a bit more pessimistic and introverted, and she'd fob them off and keep going her way. So, I would draw on her for advice. The main thing I learned was that I had to earn the respect of the guys, initially, once I had done that by being professional, being good at what I did, and demonstrating that I knew what I was doing, then they would genuinely come on board and be supportive. It was a work in progress. I think because of Mum's modelling to me, I'm a bit more resilient than some of the women that I knew in the industry who would be quite badly affected by the same stuff.

That highlights the importance of having role models and figures within the industry and your own family to show strength and how to push against the misogyny that is so prevalent within the industry.

JC: Absolutely. Role models are so important. Mum was a role model for the next generation of feminist filmmakers who came up near Martha Ansara, Jeni Thornley, Susan Lambert, and Sarah Gibson. At least she was there. She'd made like twenty-five films by the time she was fifty, and even if she was working in a boring old industrial documentary, she was an example that you can get behind the camera and do it.

The industrial documentaries are fascinating. These are films, which, at least from my search, are hard to find. Are they in an archive or the NFSA?

JC: Before we made the film, they were [archived] in physical form, but they hadn't been digitised. As part of the process of making the film, we got Ray Argall, who's a cinematographer and a digitiser to do these beautiful scans of them, so now most of them are available. I'm not sure what the process is to get to see them. They're not up on a website or anything like that. Hopefully, there'll be more of a demand to see that stuff, because it's great historical footage, that beautiful, gritty, grainy 16mm gives you a sense of the culture and the thinking behind the times as well as what you see in the frame.

One of the key things about this film is that there's no external archival footage in there, it's all personal footage. Can you talk through the decision process behind that choice?

INTERVIEW | JANE CASTLE

JC: It was a key decision early on when I was working with the script editor Alison Tilson, and it was about the authenticity of the film. It was quite hard to stick to that rule. The rule was that all the archival [footage] had to be either from one of the films my parents or I made or family home movie footage, or photos of them and to not go outside to get 'London in the 1950s' footage from somewhere. Even though it's not clear in the film, I think it generates this sense of trust in the authenticity of the material, and that we're not going to trick you by pretending that this footage was shot by Mum. I'm so glad that you've noticed that because I think it's got an invisible but very powerful impact on the trust that it builds in the audience.

It centres you in your parents' life and reminds us that while this footage was being shot, you were there, this is your point of view. It's why we watch films, to see somebody else's point of view. What was the conversation about you doing the narration as opposed to narrating to the camera?

JC: It's interesting you asking me that. It brings back memories. We did try that early on. We tried filming me telling the story and being interviewed, and it just was so clunky because I was so self-conscious in front of the camera. We ended up not filming any new footage of me. I filmed a lot of new contemporary footage in the parts where we didn't have archival. It's those spaces where I'm talking about the past in a very metaphorical sense as well as a storytelling sense. The images that I went out and got, they're from the contemporary world but they have a historic element to them as to what's in the frame, but also like a non-human element. I think there's only one person in one shot, it's a jogger running away in the distance and the rest is quite empty.

They are shots that allow the audience to drop into the contemplative space of the words because often images can be quite distracting. You've got to ride that fine line between the images adding to what's being said, but not distracting and overtaking from what's being said. It was a real trial and error process with Ray Thomas, the editor, and I. Often I'd have to go five different times to get the right shot. It was a painstaking process. It's not like they're spectacular shots, but they capture exactly the mood of what I'm saying and the story. I want to give a bit of a shout-out to Roen Davis who was the colourist and online editor. He lifted the film visually up. We spent a lot of time polishing the archival, but also the contemporary stuff. There was a lot of thought put into the visuals.

Watching some of the films that Ray's worked on (Molly & Mobarak, 2003, Rats in the Ranks, 1996, Namatjira Project, 2017), there is an urgency to his editing that brings us back to the original thesis that you're working on about death, it reminds us of the importance of life. What an editor

WHEN THE CAMERA STOPPED ROLLING

does with a cut is so brilliant with how it makes you feel. What was it like working with Ray as an editor?

JC: I can probably talk for hours about that. There were so many aspects to it. When you talk about this life force aspect, one of the big tussles we had was that I kept wanting to slow the film down in the beginning and put these endless pauses between words for some reason. Over the years, Ray helped get rid of that. The film has spaces for reflection, sure, but it also has this pace that is great momentum, and it keeps pulling the audience forward with the film. There's never a dull moment. That is a stroke of brilliance because it's a film that could have sunk and gotten kind of stuck in the mud. Ray kept it going perfectly.

In terms of our working relationship, it was from the very beginning because he worked on it when it was the trailer about death. We had worked on another TV documentary before that. We're quite different in our approach, and I think that that was a constructive difference. Along with getting the pacing right, he brought an emotional connection to the material. I was a bit too overwhelmed to emotionally relate to the film, even though it's quite emotional. I was struggling to manage all this material, my own autobiographic material and the biographic material of my mum. I was very focused on structure and just pulling the stories out from my insides. He had a beautiful relationship with Lilias, my mum, which kept him involved. He was committed to me, helping me tell my story as well. He brought the 'feeling' element to the film, which I was sometimes lacking.

He was also the receiver of all the stuff that I brought; I brought so much more material than is in the film. He was loyal to the film above me as a person. That would help filter out what came into the film and what got chucked out. He was deeply committed to the film, and so that commitment really shone through in terms of the film's final authenticity.

There is a colour palette throughout the film that connects the past with the present. What choices did you make when it came to making sure that you honour the original colours of the footage properly continuing that palette throughout the film?

JC: For some of the material it was difficult. These films might be like fifty years old, and even from the neg the colour had drained out, and over time it's just really thin. Roen Davis spent a lot of time with some of these films, just getting them to look decent, getting the black and white from Mum's early film crisp and dust removal and things like that. We didn't have a master plan about "Okay, it's going to be XYZ." Authenticity was the overriding factor.

INTERVIEW | JANE CASTLE

We shied away from making it chocolate boxy and too beautiful. We didn't want to just 'make it beautiful.' We wanted to make it rich and real. I think the footage that came to us dominated how we approached it rather than the other way around. I probably had an unconscious colour palette in my mind. There's this general push towards making everything look sparkly and beautiful. I was trying to go against that a little bit and go more towards authenticity. The colours of the footage that was there and what I brought in were the most important factors in deciding the colour palette for the film.

The film received four nominations at the AACTA Awards. What does that recognition from the industry and your peers mean to you as a filmmaker?

JC: It's a good feeling to be recognised. Along with that, for my mum's work to be recognised. It gives me confidence that it was the right decision to stick to the truth, as much truth as one can muster, that's available to our conscious minds, and authenticity. And making films from the heart rather than trying to make a splash. There are difficult parts of the story, and I think it's a testament to the fact that people are hungry for that kind of honesty and authenticity. I'm stoked that the other members of the team – Pat Fiske our producer, Sam Petty our incredible sound designer, Kyls Burtland our composer, and Ray - got their work acknowledged by their peers. That's such a lovely warm feeling for me because they all went way beyond what would normally be required of someone doing that.

Looking at the complexity of Australian film history and pulling from your mum's history as well, do you have any guidance or pointers for emerging cinematographers? What guidance or suggestions would you have to try and create their own voice on film?

JC: It's getting more and more competitive out there as the industry becomes more and more democratised by the digitisation of everything. I feel that authenticity and honesty in terms of telling stories, that's the way to go. That's the way to connect with audiences. In terms of technology, I encourage people not to get overwhelmed or intimidated by technicalities. It's easy for that to happen when you start to look at all the specs on these cameras and C log and all sorts of numbers.

Mum used to say, "It's the vision that counts." They told her that she wouldn't be strong enough to carry the cameras. I shot the contemporary parts of the film with a humble Canon 5D Mark II. And yes, it's got a lot of limitations, but we were able to go beyond those by focusing on composition, light, and content. Keeping it simple, keeping it honest, keeping it authentic. For me, there are so many stories. Any individual in this world has so many stories if they can connect to what's true in them.

WHEN THE CAMERA STOPPED ROLLING

What does being an Australian filmmaker mean to you?

JC: There is something particular about our Australian culture, one important aspect of which is coming to terms with our colonial history and the lack of justice still to this day for First Nations people. It also means with that colonial history and the convict history, there's an independence of thought, and there's this can-do attitude that you really see on Australian film crews compared to, say, American film crews. You can get by with a bit of gaffa tape and a piece of string, and still, we've got two Academy Award-nominated cinematographers [Ari Wegner, Greig Fraser] and one winner in 2022. Considering our population size, that's phenomenal. It's that can-do attitude. It's that rawness and innocence. I do feel we've still got a lot of work to do to come to terms with our history of invasion and survival.

How do you feel is the best way we address that on film?

JC: We need to promote First Nations filmmakers, and let them tell their stories, which is happening more and more. [For white culture to] back out of the picture. Also, to keep talking about that uncomfortable place that we inhabit as this dominant white culture, which includes making films talking about these issues, and by really supporting Indigenous voices to come up to the surface more and more.

MOJA VESNA

REVIEW
NADINE WHITNEY

Slovenian-Australian director Sara Kern has made an exquisite debut feature in her family drama *Moja Vesna*. Delicate and devastating, the film follows ten-year-old Moja (Loti Kovacic) as she desperately tries to keep her fracturing family together after the recent death of her mother – something she cannot accept. Moja tries to control her emotional turmoil by focusing her efforts on caring for her heavily pregnant sister, Vesna (Mackenzie Mazur) who is equally unwilling to accept her own pregnancy (a hint as to why comes from one of Vesna's pieces of slam poetry). Mute with inadequacy their father Milos (Gregor Bakovic) is wrestling with his own grief and cannot connect with the truculent Vesna nor convince Moja that she has to acknowledge that her mother is no longer around.

Moja, Vesna, and Milos live in an unrenovated rental in one of Melbourne's outer suburbs. The house is small and made smaller still by the family avoiding the mother's bedroom. Milos sleeps on the couch, and Vesna and Moja share a room and a bunk bed. Only Moja is trying to keep her mother alive by setting a place for her at the family table every night. Vesna is trying to force Moja to face the reality of their mother's death and she's also trying to untangle exactly how their mother died. A single car accident that was probably suicide, but Milos refuses to talk about the emotional state of his wife.

Conversely, Vesna is trying to speak about her own emotional state, except she's writing it through poetry and attempting to use metaphors to explain what she is feeling to Moja; a child for whom the adult world is weighing heavily. When Moja takes it upon herself to try to organise baby supplies for Vesna (something Milos should be doing but perhaps linguistic barriers prevent him) she meets the kindly Miranda (Claudia Karvan) and her free-spirited daughter, Danger (Flora Feldman). In Mirada and Danger, Moja sees what it is like to be just a kid with a mother, doing kid stuff without the burden of caring for others.

Sara Kern is concerned with the immigrant experience and the feeling of being on the outside. Milos works in a kitchen, and he is detached from any form of community. He speaks Slovenian with Moja, but Vesna refuses to interact with him in the language. When Miranda, in a somewhat tone-deaf manner, asks Milos if he misses home, he responds that he is home – yet what is that home with his family in such a state of distress?

With Milos mostly in the background, the story centres itself on the relationship between the two sisters. Vesna is suffering extreme depression and a listlessness that comes from carrying guilt about her mother's death ("She used to talk to me about her feelings" she tells Moja). Vesna also just wants to be a young person, which is something that she fails to notice is also one of Moja's desires. She leans on Moja but also deliberately places a barrier between them. The more Moja tries to nurture Vesna and the child she is carrying, the more distant Vesna becomes. Vesna is on her own journey of possible obliteration and there's nothing Moja can do to stop her.

Kern's film which stems from her own experiences as an immigrant in Australia is rich with symbolism that reveals emotional truths. When the voice of the actors cannot speak, she allows the camera to. There are indelible moments where the smallest gestures tell the story. Moja trying to stroke her sister's hair through a car window, the burning of a precious piece of furniture, a sister bringing her sister's hand to hold her. Kern's visual mastery is astounding. The director captures the meaning of silence and absence with an enigmatic skill and cinematographer Lev Predon Kowarski realises Kern's vision with impeccable work.

In a year that has provided audiences with exceptional breakout roles for child actors, such as Frankie Corio in Charlotte Well's *Aftersun* and Catherine Clinch in Colm Bairead's *The Quiet Girl*, Loti Kovacic as Moja is equally revelatory. Loti had never acted professionally before being cast in *Moja Vesna*, yet her screen presence is striking and haunting in its honesty. Moja's sad and searching eyes, her timid presence, her desire for her own childhood, and her fragile strength are all conveyed with such purpose by Loti Kovacic. In stories told through a child's eye it is essential that the child acting as the cinematic vessel is someone who the audience wants to spend time with. Loti Kovacic is an actor whose spellbinding natural talent brings the audience in on an intimate level to the film.

Mackenzie Mazur is a more mercurial presence as Vesna. We feel the danger she places herself in and the disregard she has for her safety, yet it is her storytelling that brings us closer to her as a character. Mazur wrote much of Vesna's poetry. Vesna's mental state is given a literal voice in those verses. Where she cannot express herself to Milos, nor Moja, who, for all her maturity, is still a child, it's in the poetry where her truth lies.

Sara Kern has made one of the best Australian feature debuts in recent memory. *Moja Vesna* (which in Slovenian translates to 'moja' being me, and Vesna being the goddess of spring and renewal, hence 'My Vesna,' or possibly 'My Renewal') is melancholy and difficult but ends on a note of hope, and yes, renewal for Moja. Moja is told by Vesna to "Hold tight, and feel it, feel it all," and Kern is conferring the same message to the audience. *Moja Vesna* will make you feel it all and you will be all the richer for doing so.

INTERVIEW
WRITER & DIRECTOR
SARA KERN

Sara Kern's debut feature *Moja Vesna* is a family drama wrapped around an engaging and powerful central performance from newcomer Loti Kovačič as Moja who gives one of the most powerful and soul-wrenching turns by a young actor in recent years. 10-year-old Moja has become the surrogate parental figure to her morose sister Vesna (Mackenzie Mazur) after the death of their mother. Equally adrift is their father Miloš (Gregor Baković) who manages to feed and house Moja and Vesna but finds it hard to navigate the additional impending life change that is awaiting the immigrant family: Vesna's late-stage pregnancy that she almost entirely ignores the notion of occurring.

The subject of loss and grief looms over *Moja Vesna*, as it has done in Sara Kern's previous short films. While the immediate notion that this would be heavy going for audiences is hard to escape, the presence of Claudia Karvan's empathetic stranger Miranda and her whirlwind daughter Danger (a joyful Flora Feldman) occasionally adds a welcome levity to the scenario. As Danger and Moja find ground for a friendship, the malaise that Vesna struggles to escape threatens to break that bond.

This interview was recorded by Andrew F. Peirce in August 2022

I was moved by the central performance from Loti [Kovačič]. What direction did you give her to be able to give Moja the depth that she needed?

Sara Kern: Working with children is something that I've been involved with for quite a while in short films, and before moving here, when I worked at TV Slovenia's children's program. It was a natural progression for me to write a feature film told from the child's point of view. There's something about working with children that I enjoy. It is a slightly different process in the way we work together to find these characters with each of these children.

We were casting for Moja for a long time. We were looking through the Australian-Slavic communities because I was hoping for someone who was bilingual and could speak one of the Slavic languages. I wasn't even hoping to find someone who's Slovenian-Australian, because the Slovenian community here is so small. It was an incredible amount of luck that we found Loti. She immediately caught our attention, her presence on screen, and her sensibility was so captivating. She had no prior acting experience. She's into soccer and coding, but she was keen to get involved. Even though she was nine at the time, she took our work very seriously, and this shows on screen.

We spent a lot of time together, doing improvisations, chatting about the character, finding out what the differences are between her personally and Moja. Getting to know each other and building mutual trust was very important, so she knew she could tell me straight away if she had a problem with something or didn't feel comfortable in the scene.

I didn't share the script with her because I wanted to keep things a little bit fresh. After all, we were shooting for 25 days. I've had experience working with children, with the longest being maybe five days on a short film working with someone. At 25 days long, I was anxious about how she was going to go, but she was so good. I think it helped that I kept explaining the story as we went along. We'd discuss before each scene what was going on and what her lines were, so she didn't have to learn anything in advance.

We mainly worked on getting her into the right emotional state and being able to be present in the moment and respond to the other actors in the scene. Loti and Mackenzie Mazur, who plays her sister Vesna, had such amazing chemistry from the first time we put them together in a room. I was so excited about this that I went and rewrote the script with Loti and Mackenzie in mind specifically. I added tender scenes between them which I find are crucial in the film now, and they were not even in the script before Loti and Mackenzie came on board.

Your work is focused on mortality, death, and grief. What draws you to explore those themes in film?

SK: In my shorts, and in this film, I've drawn heavily on my experiences growing up. I've written these fictional narratives out of something that was very real, from the emotional landscape of my childhood and the family dynamics I knew very well. There was much grief in my family, largely unprocessed grief. I was this 'mature', responsible child, like Moja is and people saw this as a good thing, a positive thing, but in fact, it was a coping mechanism. It was my way of securing closeness with the adults around me, it was my way of getting what I needed as a child. It distracted me from my own sadness. This can be a big problem later in life, so I wanted to find a way for Moja's character not to do that and explore how by the end of the film she can get to a place where she can allow herself to be present to her own emotions and not have to let that part of her be split off.

I find grief endlessly perplexing. It's such a complicated emotional state. Every single experience of loss is different for every single one of us. It's hard to make any generalised statements about it or to write one story and say, "That's it, I've dealt with that topic." As you dive deeper and deeper into it, it offers more and more layers. There's something about the nature of it that is so contradictory. You expect that you'd be sad, and you'd be crying a lot when you're in grief, but then you find yourself laughing uncontrollably or suddenly being very angry, and there are all sorts of things that one can go through. I wanted to explore that through this story and show how one family tries to navigate this experience of grief; how each one of the family members tries to find a way to live with their loss. How to find enough light to be able to live with the sadness. It is perplexing to me where we find this light, this determination to go forward, this strength to live on.

There's a moment where the father, Miloš, puts on his wife's slippers, and Moja stands there and he sees her looking at him. He says, "I don't know why I did that." In that moment it felt like he was saying that to himself, but then on the other hand, there was almost this envy, "She's gone and I've got to deal with everything." There is an emptiness left behind when someone dies. Can you talk about how characters process their grief and how important was it to have those moments in the film?

SK: It was crucial. The film is built on these details. It's this 'less is more approach' where I'm drawn to exploring these mundane things like the father putting on those slippers. It was nice hearing how you interpreted this. I was hoping for that, for people to turn a small thing like this into something bigger and more significant. The nature of grief is so surprising sometimes, you find yourself doing things that are quite strange. I see this moment with the slippers like that. It's unconscious; you find yourself trying to work through something, and you find yourself doing all sorts of things to get there.

Vesna does that throughout the film. Maybe she's the most active in this way. She almost chases death. She almost tries to become her mother in a way by doing all these self-destructive things, because she's looking to work something out; to understand her mother by following in her footsteps. In a way, she's trying to get back to her mother or trying to address something in their relationship which remains unspoken and keeps returning to haunt her.

Can you talk about the production and set design of the house and how you use that to reflect the themes of the film?

MOJA VESNA

SK: A lot of the story is set in the house because the family is closing in on itself. It's this unrenovated rental that they live in, so the house feels claustrophobic. I wanted to create a sense that they're closed in because I find that's another thing with grief, it can be so profoundly isolating. Then, when you're a migrant, especially a migrant from a country that is so small, and having this language, Slovenian, that almost no one else speaks, it can deepen the sense of isolation and I wanted to show that they're almost an island. Moja and Vesna, in their own ways, they're both trying to find a way out of this house.

I also wanted to show that the family lives in this small house while at the same time, they've got this bedroom that they're avoiding. The bedroom where the mother's bed is, with its bare mattress, is like a room frozen in time, a room devoid of life that sits right in the middle of the house, like a hole in the heart. The father is sleeping on the couch and the girls have got a bunk bed and there's clearly not enough room. It's like the mother is taking up a lot of space or has begun to take up more space than while she was alive. There are other things around the house, like the chair where the mother used to sit, which Moja now caresses and worships in a way. Vesna keeps trying to destroy these sacred objects as a way of trying to force the family out of the status quo that they're in; even though she's the one who's literally chasing death throughout the film, she's also the one who tries to force life back into this house.

The opening of the film shows Moja engaging in a ritual or burial process for Vesna on the beach. Is that a bookend scene? Is it a metaphor?

SK: Moja focuses on Vesna so much in the film because this distracts her from the reality of what happened. But through her interactions with Vesna, Moja is pushed to start to grieve for her mother, and I see this first scene as a metaphor for that. In order for Moja to grieve her mother, she also needs to let go of Vesna. Vesna is not and will not be her replacement mother.

When Moja buries her sister in the sand, it's probably something that they did when they were younger. It's a playful thing, but in this context, it turns into a burial. It is also a way for Moja to symbolically take control and not be pushed around by Vesna. This is something that happens at the end of the film. It is an indication that Moja will find the strength needed to go on, while for Vesna this process will be much more turbulent and there is no guarantee that she will find the will to live on.

The presence of poetry in the film feeds into how Vesna deals with grief. It is a visually poetic film, too. How important was it to reflect the poetry in the visuals of the film?

SK: The slam poetry was incredibly important to me from the beginning. I had different poetry in there at the script stage, which I thought was perfect for the script, and I was happy with it. But then once we cast Mackenzie, she brought something so unique and raw to the role of Vesna. We started rehearsing the poems, and it was fine, but it wasn't 100%. I didn't believe that it was really her slam poetry, you know? We kept talking and improvising and having rehearsals and then she just started writing her own poetry during rehearsals.

I like to find a unique way of working with every single one of the actors, and with Mackenzie, it revolved around poetry. That was the main anchor for us during the rehearsal period. Rehearsals became more and more just us doing slam poetry. She'd go home and get into the character and write all this slam poetry and come back and then perform and we talked about it. She ended up writing all of it herself, so that was pretty special.

There's just something about slam poetry that I really love, and I wanted to have it in the film as a contrast to the silences and all the unexpressed things and the family's general inability to communicate. I think Vesna's poetry is her way of distancing herself from the family and trying to find a way to express herself. She's trying to find a way out in some way. She's articulating something that she is unable to say, maybe to her father or even to herself. She's found her way of saying the unsayable, which then also helps Moja to finally start to talk about her own loss and feel whatever emotions saying these words brings up in her.

What does it mean to be able to tell a migrant story in Australia today?

SK: Oh, it means so much. I'm quite humbled by the whole thing, and that we managed to even get the funding for it, shoot it, and finish it. It feels special of course because it's my first feature, but it's also the first ever Australian-Slovenian film, so to see my home country represented in an Australian film, it's quite special. It felt like that was the most honest perspective or the perspective that I felt the most comfortable setting for my first feature in this migrant story.

Of course, they had to be from Slovenia because I'm from Slovenia. I've lived here for eight years and like I said before, I drew heavily on my childhood experiences in Slovenia, but I was also drawing from my experiences as a migrant here. It's amazing to be able to combine those two into a story.

WYRMWOOD: APOCALYPSE

88 mins
Director: *Kiah Roache-Turner*
Writer: *Kiah Roache-Turner, Tristan Roache-Turner*
Cast: *Luke McKenzie, Shantae Barnes-Cowan, Jake Ryan, Bianca Bradey, Tasia Zalar, Jay Gallagher, Nicholas Boshier, Tristan McKinnon, Goran D. Kleut, Dean Kyrwood, Lauren Grimson*
Producers: *Blake Northfield, Tristan Roache-Turner*
Composer: *Michael Lira*
Cinematography: *Tim Nagle*
Editing: *Brad Hurt, Kiah Roache-Turner*

Wyrmwood: Apocalypse received a nomination for Best Hair and Makeup at the 2022 AACTA Awards and won the Andrew Plain Award for Best Film Sound Editing and Best Sound for an Independent Feature Film at the 2022 Australian Screen Sound Guild awards.

INTERVIEW
DIRECTOR & CO-WRITER KIAH ROACHE-TURNER

After growing up on a wealthy diet of Ozploitation films, many of which were celebrated in Mark Hartley's *Not Quite Hollywood (2008)*, genre-fiend sibling duo Kiah and Tristan Roache-Turner flipped the Aussie film industry on its clacker with the outback-zombie flick *Wyrmwood: Road of the Dead* in 2014. With blood, guts, and a whole bunch of indie filmmaking gusto, the brothers turned their attention to the equally bloody follow-up, *Wyrmwood: Apocalypse*. This gung-ho flick builds on established lore, continuing the post-apocalyptic mayhem journey where zombies' breath has become a substitute for fuel.

This interview was recorded by Andrew F. Peirce in October 2021

Kiah Roache-Turner: Embarrassingly, *Not Quite Hollywood* taught me more about Australian [film] than almost any doco I've watched. I just didn't know a lot about the Seventies' Ozploitation era until I watched that. Even just watching the clips from those films was so exciting. Grant Page is like a crazy bristly Jackie Chan. What an interesting character.

What they used to do was nuts. There was almost no safety in some regards. It was a bit bonkers.

KR-T: A scary time. It seemed like it was almost socially acceptable to be a dangerous hero back in the Seventies in general. It's hard to make badass films now because it's such a different time. Now, it's all safety and correct and appropriate behaviour and words onset. We're policing our activities so carefully, and it's such a good thing that we are. Safety is super important. Everybody's got to be nice to each other. It's great that it's hard to be [one of] those horrible pushy directors. It looks more fun in the Seventies. You play seven rounds of cricket, drink fourteen beers, and then do the first take of the day. Those days are over.

WYRMWOOD: APOCALYPSE

That photo from the original *Mad Max* [of] a bike going 200 miles an hour, and the DoP is sitting behind the guy filming across the top of [his] helmet. It doesn't even look like he's strapped in. It's insane. Those were the days, just reckless superheroes of Australian cinema.

When I was about nine, my mum used to date a guy who was sort of close to some film industry types. I remember being at a party and meeting this giant bikie of a man with a giant beard and he had 100 stitches in his head. He looked like Frankenstein. That was from the original *Mad Max*. He was telling us stories about falling off the bike and smashing his skull open and then going back to film the next week. That was my first foray into the idea that these movies happen in reality. They're not just made in Valhalla and then cast down to us. People make these things. I remember being very affected by that conversation with that troll-like human being. I felt very near to that movie at that point.

Did that linger in your mind growing up? "Whatever happened to that man, I want to do it."

KR-T: Yeah, it lingers in my mind even now. *Mad Max* is such a mythological film for all of us. Even at age nine, I had seen it two or three times, and this is an R-rated action film. Things were different when I was a kid. To be able to talk to someone [from it] was like meeting somebody from a Celtic myth, it was like meeting Grendel. "Oh my god, you were there? You were there when they made that? Human beings made that?" I thought it was mythology or something. I got very excited.

The guy who used to put on those parties had a collection of thousands of movies. Parents would have these parties and us kids would sit there watching *Blade Runner* (1982), *Apocalypse Now* (1979), and *Mad Max* (1979) and *Mad Max 2* (1981). That's when being inundated with cinema started for me. Then you get your hands on a Hi8 camera, and you start making little movies with your brothers in the backyard. That's where it starts. It leads to harder stuff.

How do you think the accessibility to make films has changed over the years?

KR-T: Because of technology, things seem to get easier and more accessible. The one thing that doesn't get easier is once you pick up a camera and start mucking around you realise very quickly it's a lot harder than it looks. It's like somebody looking at a painting and going "I can do that," and then buying some paints and going "Okay, I'm maybe sub-Ken Done at this point, I'm not very good. It's gonna take a long time." It does take decades to even make something halfway good, let alone something great.

INTERVIEW | KIAH ROACHE-TURNER

The thing that used to get me was I'd use a Hi8 camera, but it didn't look like film and it killed me. It didn't look like *Apocalypse Now*. It didn't look like *Goodfellas* (1990). It just looked like a shitty video. It looked horrible. But that's all we could get our hands on. You [would have to] shoot and edit in camera, so I learned to edit in camera. You could only do one take because you can't do multiple takes in the editor. We'd do these little mini films and we'd have to cut in the camera and plan it as we went. If you didn't get the take right, you'd rewind and do it again. In between every edit would be this horrible kind of video distortion.

Now, a thirteen-year-old who wants to make a movie can get the latest iPhone, and they're shooting stuff that looks like the latest Michael Bay film, they can edit on their phones, they can get a version of After Effects and learn how to do visual effects swiftly. There are online tutorials to show you how to have a meteor hit earth, that used to cost hundreds of thousands of dollars for one shot, and now you can work out how to do that. The accessibility and the ability to make amazing content is so much easier than it was when I was a kid, but it still doesn't mean that you can just instantly make good stuff, because so much of it is about imagination and storytelling and having those original ideas, having the craft behind you to make something that feels visually dynamic.

How do you create a world like Wyrmwood?

KR-T: For the original *Wyrmwood*, it had almost been a couple of decades since *Mad Max Beyond Thunderdome* (1985) and we got sick of waiting for George Miller to make another *Mad Max*. Ironically, it took us so long to make *Wyrmwood* that he made and released *Fury Road* by the time we were releasing ours. We wanted to do something where we could make a *Mad Max* vehicle, dress people up in leathers, and have sawn-off shotguns and people running around in a post-apocalyptic world. We knew that we didn't have a lot of money, and we knew that if you don't have a lot of money, you're not going to make a film that's going to look very good, so the best thing is to do a horror film.

You look at cinema history and three things that pop up are George A Romero, Peter Jackson, and Sam Raimi. *Evil Dead* (1981), *Bad Taste* (1987), and *Night of the Living Dead* (1968); all are templates for how you make an awesome low-budget horror film that can also be distributed. *Bad Taste* went to Cannes. *Evil Dead* made a lot of money on its theatrical release. I think *Night of the Living Dead* was one of the most financially successful films of that time in terms of budget to box office ratio. We thought "Let's take *Mad Max* and chuck a bunch of zombies in there. Let's try and make it look like *Evil Dead* as much as we can. Let's try and make it visually dynamic to make up for the low budgets of it. And I think we're going to be okay."

475

WYRMWOOD: APOCALYPSE

We decided to do a proof of concept, just a scene. We've done that a bunch of times now. I don't know why, but for some reason, I like to make a proof of concept that doesn't have any dialogue. "Let's just see if this works visually as a world and as a concept without any kind of storytelling devices like exposition or any of that stuff. Let's just see if it works." We plotted out this idea for a scene and storyboarded it very tightly. We put in about $7,000 of our own money. We bought a vehicle and built that into a prop *Mad Max* type vehicle. We sourced the costumes by asking people to give us their old leather biker armour. A friend liked American football, and he gave us some old football shoulder pads. We got a hockey mask. We sourced makeup artists by sending them the storyboards, the concept, and a couple of short films that we made just to let them know that we knew what we were doing. Basically, everybody worked for free because they thought the concept was cool. Most of the people on the crew were friends of ours.

We shot it, I edited that together and did all the little visual effects myself, and we put it up online to see what would happen. Within a couple of weeks, it had 100,000 views. Which doesn't sound like a lot now, but back then [2009] it was huge. Within a week, it became viral. I didn't know what a viral video was back then. That's when we knew we had a film. Then we just moved forward until we finished. It took three and a half years because we funded it ourselves.

I think people missed those types of films like early Sam Raimi and Peter Jackson. People love handmade stuff. If you're good at what you do and you make it handmade, and there's an excitement and an energy, I think people get caught up cinematically in your excitement to do it. It did a similar kind of business to some of those films. I guess [it was] what the industry would call a success. It was a bit culty. It did what I was hoping it was gonna do which was to launch me into a 'career.' And here we are, seven years later, still doing the same thing.

Ironically, the opening for this film was written ten years ago to be the opening of *Wyrmwood: Road of the Dead*. We looked at it and just went "We don't have the money to do this." We decided that instead of starting the world-building a year into the apocalypse [that] it'd be more interesting to start with the guy's family on the night of the apocalypse and then work our way towards it. The opening was the first thing we wrote. The idea of this guy alone in the middle of nowhere, God's lonely man in the middle of this zombie-infested post-apocalyptic wasteland. It's such a mythical image, this guy in the middle of an electrified fenced enclosure in a caravan with a barbecue that runs on zombie breath, getting up and doing his morning routine exercises, and he's got a zombie chained to a pole that he uses for boxing exercise. All this stuff is such classic apocalyptic stuff.

INTERVIEW | KIAH ROACHE-TURNER

How do you and Tristan come up with ideas?

KR-T: We get together to do the work. We set aside a couple of days here and there and just work the boards. We get a big whiteboard and beat out all the scenes. The way we write is we try and come up with every single story beat as detailed as we can. Very rough ideas of intention for dialogue, but we don't actually write any dialogue down. We do a reasonably detailed beat-by-beat story treatment together. Then I'll go off and write a draft. I can't write with somebody sitting behind me. I just can't do that. Once I start writing scripts, it turns a little bit more into your more classic director/writer/creative producer team. He gives me notes and we discuss scenes, and he says, "I don't like this, and why does he say that?" We work through it like that. We work closely in terms of structure and story. The world comes 50/50 from his head and my head.

It's such a fully realised world. It feels like outside of the frame of the film, it continues moving, especially with the different mad scientists. You really lean on the genre tropes. Were there certain elements you just had to get in this entry?

KR-T: We had such a good run of it on the first film. Because we financed it ourselves, we had 100% creative control, and it just felt right. We made exactly the film that we wanted to make. And it was successful and people seem to like it. Even critically it did pretty well. The most important thing on this one was we had to have that same experience, and it's really hard to get the same experience once you enter the industry.

Once you enter the industry, you get into this – mostly money-based – thing where people are like, "Well, we're gonna give you a lot of money, and you have to make that money back. You're good artists but we don't really trust you to get the money back. It's not that you're not great, it's that we think our ideas are more bankable. Let's go 40% your ideas and 55% my ideas, and then the other 5% will be dictated by actors or demands of agents or whatever." You get caught up in the crap of "Oh, that's why it's hard to make a film in the industry." We didn't want to get caught up in the crap of all of that.

It was very important on this one to make sure that we found a collaborator that would have the creative respect to go, "Okay, you guys know what you're doing, I'm just going to back you up. I'm going to produce this, but I'm not going to try and write it with you." One of the only ways that we could do that was to have a really low budget. We made this for below the minimum of what we could make it for, so that we can, budget-wise, earn the right to have creative decisions just dictated by Tristan and me, like we did on the first film.

WYRMWOOD: APOCALYPSE

When we wrote it, we didn't give a shit. We went "Let's make something that we love. If every scene makes us happy creatively, then we're going to do it." This one needed to be *Mad Max 2*. If the first one's *Mad Max*, this is *Road Warrior*. "Let's make a rip-roaring action film where we put in everything that we want to see and set the budget low enough that we can get away with doing whatever the hell we want. And then we might make something original again as we did with the first one."

How hard is it to make something original in the zombie genre?

KR-T: One of the things we were hoping to do was even if you hadn't seen *Road of The Dead*, we wanted it to be an experience that could still be good for a viewer. The thing we didn't want to do, and there was a little bit of argy-bargy back and forth about was "Shouldn't you guys be a bit more specific about the rules of the world?" And we're like "No, no, no." People are smart enough to catch up. My feeling is you learn quickly that zombies are a power source, and it's obvious that she's controlling zombies, and the idea of hybrids, half human, half zombies, it's not so crazy complicated [that you] couldn't work out what's going on. Something that was important to Tristan and I was a lack of exposition. I hate exposition in a movie so much. I love a movie that doesn't assume that the audience is stupid as a bag of bricks. These are hardcore scientific concepts here. It's pretty standard genre lore. If you can't work it out, you probably should watch more movies.

I remember talking to a filmmaker years ago now, a very talented, super smart guy, and it was embarrassing. I was like, "What do you hate nowadays?" And he was like, "I hate anything zombie." And I'm like "Oh, okay. You're talking to a zombie filmmaker." People aren't bored of the zombies; they're just bored of the same old thing. If you're coming at a very tried and true repeated genre, as long as you're coming at that genre with fresh ideas and new energy, it doesn't matter if the people have seen it a million times. There's nothing new under the sun, it's just the energy behind it.

We're not really doing anything that hasn't been done before, because a lot of our style and stuff does come from Raimi, Jackson, and Romero. It's just that we're bringing a freshness to it, an originality to the same old thing. The key to the success of something is that there has to be a familiarity and a newness at the same time, and if you can bring those two things to a story, it's probably going to be successful. The familiarity means that people settle back and go, "I know what this is going to be," but the freshness is the twist that you give them in terms of concept or even scene construction or you kill a character that otherwise you'd have to let live. All that stuff comes down to good writing, but also taking risks.

INTERVIEW | KIAH ROACHE-TURNER

That's why it's hard in the industry because a lot of producers and financiers don't want to take risks. They're like, "Why are you killing the dog? Don't kill the dog. It's a rule. You can't kill the dog." It's like "Who says you can't kill the dog?" I don't agree with that. Maybe you can't kill the dog in a *Beethoven* movie, but this is a low-budget film, the risk is low. Let's kill the dog. People might not like it, but they'll talk about it, you know?

I had a wonderful compliment from a film festival critic friend of mine, Christian Burgess. In the first five minutes, we open with Brooke [Bianca Bradey] and Barry [Jay Gallagher], and it's a year into the apocalypse, they've changed a bit and the scene is really full on. He said, "In that scene, I sat up and I went, Kiah is not messing around here. This is not what I expected." He's not even sure it's what he wanted. "That's what I liked about it. I didn't expect it. I did not expect this at all from the *Wyrmwood* sequel." He said he stopped it and immediately watched it again. I mean, that never happens. Who watches a film and then watches it again? I took that as the greatest compliment. We're not sitting here kowtowing to what we think the fans want, we're just going with what we want. We're assuming that if it's what we want, it must be what the fans want. That's all we did with the first film.

I think [Darren] Aronofsky years ago did it where he said, "I make films for me, and I assume that there's going to be an audience for that." Because hey, we all grew up with the same films and cultural references. There must be an audience for what I like. I think that goes back to the idea of the singular vision. I don't like to say auteur because I think it sort of shits on everyone in the cast and all the other people who help on a film. I don't believe in auteurism, but I do believe in the idea of a singular vision. You look at Aronofsky and David Lynch and Martin Scorsese and all the greats, they all had a singular vision. They all fought the good fight in that they fought for their singular vision, and you feel that in their films. That's why when a new film of theirs comes out, it's a special occasion because you may not get what you want, but you're going to sit up and take notice because they're not messing around.

Is that harder in today's landscape and for Australian films? From what I've seen, if there's money involved, then it makes it harder to have that singular vision, but there is a freedom to being a low-budget production, a freedom to be independent.

KR-T: It's really hard. I'm very slowly learning that it's about writing. With *Wyrmwood*, we were in a very good position. We were lucky that we connected with Blake [Northfield] who had a solid financial plan for getting this up. Because we had success with the first one, we were able to get away with the idea that we had the final cut and all the creative decisions laid out for us. But that's very rare. Most of the time, you do need to write towards

479

the idea that somebody's going to give you a couple of million dollars for your project. It doesn't matter how talented or awesome you are, most of the time that's not going to happen unless somebody has confidence in the project's ability to make something financially happen in a marketplace. You can't just go in with these awesome ideas. It must feel market ready. Film doesn't happen in a vacuum.

If you want your singular vision to be purely auteurist, be a painter or a novelist. Film is collaborative, and it costs a lot of money, so there has to be a business aspect to what you're doing. That is the struggle of being a filmmaker trying desperately to make *Taxi Driver* but realising there's not a market for it, so you have to create that market through being incredibly clever and talented and a good writer and hopefully successful. Because at the end of the day, if your films don't make money, they're not going to keep financing you and you'll end up making stop-motion animation in your cupboard.

What was the point for you when you realised that you were talented and creative?

KR-T: That makes me sound like I think I'm talented and creative.

But you are.

KR-T: Thank you.

And surely because you continue going, there's got to be a self-realisation of it.

KR-T: I was stoked when I realised I could draw. I was about thirteen. I was like, "Man, I'm pretty good at this." I wanted to be a comics artist first. I always loved writing. In Year Six the teacher gave out an assignment to write a poem, and I remember sitting down and picking a style. "Okay, I'm going to write it in the style of Banjo Paterson." And it just flowed out of me so clearly. Nobody else in the class could do it. And I was like, "Oh, can't everybody just do this?" It's great, and you feel really special, and people pat you on the head and they pay you $10 to do a Christmas card or a birthday card for a relative. That's what kids want more than anything, to feel like they're special. To be able to draw and write and eventually start making cool little movies that people love and get a lot of pleasure out of. There's no other feeling in the world for a sensitive, shy little kid, you know? I was able to find my strength.

My older brother was instantly smart and just always good at socialising. I'd say that's his strength. Then my younger brother, he's just a tough

INTERVIEW | KIAH ROACHE-TURNER

dude, and was really good at sport. He had a lot of confidence; he's got clear strengths. I'm just kind of shy. When I realised I could draw and paint and I had a tendency towards art, [I knew] that was the thing that's going to give me confidence in life. That's my strength. For most of my life, I've drawn a lot of strength from the arts, and that's why I'm still here doing it when I'm forty-two.

And still going.

KR-T: Still getting away with it.

We were talking about safety on set before. One of the things that struck me as a cool invention is this air gun thing that disarms people and blasts them back with air. Where did that come from?

KR-T: The whack stick. When Tristan and I were writing the original *Wyrmwood*, we wrote part of it in the Megalong Valley, and we would take these long walks in the valley, and we would hit rocks out into the valley with a club, and the rocks would make this zizzing noise. We called that game whack stick. Anytime we couldn't be bothered writing anymore, we [would] go play a bit of whack stick and hit rocks into the valley. That name stuck with us, and it felt *Wyrmwood*-y.

We came up with this idea like a God's punch. We wanted something that could punch you, incapacitate you but not hurt you. The idea for this gun is that it knocks zombies off their feet, it incapacitates these people that our hero Rhys [Luke McKenzie] is trying to capture without killing them. We came up with this idea of a gun that fires a concentrated fist of like methane gas, this hot King Kong shaped fist of air that smashes into their chest and knocks them out, and so he can capture them.

The thing I love about the whack stick is it's just so practical. It was a pretty standard gun prop that looks amazing, but like there's no functionality to it. I said, " I want something that fires an explosion of oxygen, I want it to be practical. I don't want to do this digitally. I want it to be practical and safe." Tim [Namour] our art director bought a fire extinguisher, ran the hose through the barrel of the prop gun, and briefly activated the fire extinguisher, and this massive shot of oxygen punched out of the gun. It's huge and it's explosive and practically looks amazing. It doesn't really cost anything because fire extinguishers are really cheap. And it looks awesome.

That's how we like to do things. If there's a practical easy cheap solution, I'd rather do it practically. If you overuse digital without a big budget for your digital effects, it just ends up looking crap. You should do everything as practical as you can, and then augment it digitally. All the muzzle flashes are just one of the lighting guys flashing a quick hit of light into the actor's face while they pretend to do a back kick on the gun and then we add the muzzle flash in later.

In the *Wyrmwood* world, petrol has been nullified, and because muzzle flashes have a tendency to look a bit cheap, I was interested in the idea that there's something viral in the air that's affecting flammable substances, so when the gun fires, these embers kick out and there's a huge kick of smoke. People aren't used to seeing that done digitally and so I found that that helped sell the digital muzzle flashes. We didn't have a single real gun on set, they were all either plastic or prop built. I think we had one proper metal shotgun that's a real gun that had a blocked barrel. There's not a single gun on our set that could actually fire a blank. It was all done with a combination of lighting effects and digital muzzle flashes, smoke and embers. That's how I feel that digital stuff should be done. It should be done 80% practically, and 20% augmentation digitally. It seems to have worked well because I think a lot of it makes this film look quite good.

It wouldn't be an Australian film without any drone shots in it. You managed to make the drone shots feel new, inventive, exciting, and full of life in a way that I hadn't seen in an Australian film. How did you plan the drone shots?

KR-T: We knew this guy, Paul [Lee] who mostly shoots full-on drone footage of stock car racing. He can do a 360 of a car that's doing a 360 on a dirt road, doing jumps and stuff. The guy is like a ninja. There was a conversation about "Do we use him for some things?" Because he specialises in small drones, the footage looks droney, and we wanted the footage to look quite cinematic. We got the cinematic drone guy who's got this big expensive drone, and he looked at what he wanted him to do and said, "No way. We can't do any of this stuff. You guys are tripping. I'll crash my drone, no way." We were like "Oh, okay." Then we brought Paul out and said, "What do you think, Paul?" He goes, "Yeah, they're easy as piss. When do we start?" I said, "I think Paul's our guy."

It was dangerous because he crashed his drone six or seven times. I think he thought it was okay. Once he saw the footage, he was like, "Ah, it's worth it." He's got three or four different drones that he uses, and he's kind of used to that because he's a stunt drone operator. He's one of these guys who races drones, he's a phenomenal drone operator. He was getting these drones to fly 200 meters up and then in underneath these long archways of gum trees, and he was doing stuff that you just couldn't do with one of those big cinematic drones. You couldn't do it. That's why I think some of the drone shots look quite interesting because they swoop down near the car and through the trees and then around quite close to some of the per-

INTERVIEW | KIAH ROACHE-TURNER

formers. The only way you could do that is if you've got a very small drone being operated by a master. The drone footage doesn't fit any other movie's drone footage. Again, it has that low-budget risky semi-dangerous feel to it that is so important for a film like this.

It's something I'd never seen before. It made me sit up and go "Wow." There's an energy to it that is a rarity.

KR-T: That's what we want to do. We want to go back to that Sam Raimi throwing the camera around feel. We've got to try and build on some of the stuff that he was doing in *Evil Dead 2*. It's so funny, I went back and re-watched *Evil Dead 2* recently and I'm like, "Dude, I thought we got close. We didn't even get close." Even what that guy did in the Eighties was just like "My lord!" He was a master. But you've got to try. You've got to understand what people had, and one thing that we had that Sam didn't have is a drone. So, there you go.

What will Wyrmwood 3 be like?

KR-T: It'll be more it'll be more down and dirty Ozploitation, putting as much visual bang for buck as you can onscreen with a tiny budget stuff. I'd like to have a bit more budget than we had on *Apocalypse*. You wouldn't want to go any lower than that and you couldn't. A lot of people paid a very uncomfortable price for us to have a budget low enough to have all the creative decisions. I would hope if *Wyrmwood* does well enough, we'll be able to get a little bit more money next time just so people can be a little bit more comfortable, and I won't break so many actors. I'd probably get close to the same cast, same crew, anybody we didn't kill in this one we'll get back. And we'll continue. We're already starting to come up with ideas. It's pretty exciting. To be honest, I'd love to go straight into it. I would love for *Wyrmwood 3* to be the next thing that I write. We had such a great experience with everybody. And we ended up with a film that we love so much that I'd love to do it again. Just rinse and repeat.

I'm glad that it's not Wyrmwood 2, it's Wyrmwood: Apocalypse. It's nice to have the subtitle.

KR-T: A lot of people wanted *Wyrmwood 2*, a lot of people were fighting for that. But it didn't feel right. I like fantasy novels, and you don't get *Lord of the Rings* and *Lord of the Rings 2*, it's *The Fellowship of the Ring* and *The Two Towers*. Give it a name. Don't just call it '2'. I'm glad we finally found the right word. We just weren't sure what to call it. We were going to call the TV series *Chronicle* which was kind of unimaginative. Tristan and I, we're big fans of *Apocalypse Now*, and thought "Yeah, apocalypse. That's about right." Tristan wants to call the third one *Wyrmwood: Annihilation*. I'm like, "Yeah, that sounds about right."

That sets an expectation of what's going to happen. There's something about a word; you expect an apocalypse, you expect to see the road of the dead. When you walk into the film and you have your expectations met, you have a great time.

KR-T: That was an interesting conversation that we had with the distributors on the original film. They said, "Look, *Wyrmwood* is a title that nobody really understands. We're thinking of calling it *Wyrmwood: Road of the Undead*, and here's why: People need to know what they're clicking on, there's a genre expectation." Even a weird title like *Predestination*, the Spierig brothers' science fiction film, that's a weird word like *Wyrmwood*, but it does express what the film is. You're going to the destination previous to when you existed. It's a time travel film. That's why we sort of took it on the chin and we were like, "You know what, you're right. I don't like *Road of the Undead*, but *Road of The Dead* rolls off the tongue. Let's go with it." I do believe that a title is important in the marketplace, and you have to give and take. *Wyrmwood: Apocalypse*, even if you don't know what *Wyrmwood* means, everybody knows what an apocalypse is, you're going into an apocalyptic film. *Wyrmwood: Annihilation*, you know there's going to be guns and a lot of shit is going to explode. It's going to be carnage, so people who like onscreen carnage, click that button and buy a ticket.

INTERVIEW
ACTOR
LUKE MCKENZIE

Aussie genre cinema continued to thrive with the indie zombie-action-flick *Wyrmwood: Apocalypse*. Viewers of the first film, *Wyrmwood: Road of the Dead*, might be a little surprised to see actor Luke McKenzie return for the sequel given the death of his character, The Captain. With practical effects galore and an inventive spin on the character, Luke returned for the sequel to once again engage in some gnarly outback mayhem.

This interview was recorded by Andrew F. Peirce in February 2022

What was it like being asked to come back for the sequel? What was your reaction? Me? Again?

Luke McKenzie: Yes, that was my reaction. Anybody who's seen the first one knows there is not a big window open there to bring the Captain back. He's burnt up and devoured by zombies. When Kiah called me up and explained what their idea was and their new way in, it was really exciting. I've worked with Kiah and Tristan a bunch over the years, and a lot of the crew who came onto the *Wyrmwood*. They're part of a broader family. The brothers have brought in good people to their productions, so there was a reunion element to it that I was super excited about.

It's been so long since we did the first one that I think Kiah has had a lot of years to really hone his craft. He's already such a cinephile and such a lover of story and he's hyper-intelligent, but that extra seven or eight years really showed up on the page. The script was fantastic and tight and fast. I had all these ideas of taking Rhys this way or that way and digging deep into what was going on for him. Kiah loved all these conversations but ultimately, he said, "Rock up. Be in shape. Commit to it. It's going to be a hot as hell ride." It was less about wrenching myself internally and more about enjoying the process because every day on set was just a blast.

WYRMWOOD: APOCALYPSE

Rhys is a very physical role. How do you prepare yourself for something so physical besides exercise?

LMcK: I just think you've got to know that you're going to go into the trenches. If you're there in your first few days or your first week and you're battered and bruised and exhausted, and that's a surprise to you, then you're in a bit of trouble. Kiah said, "This is going to be an ordeal." It was summertime in Sydney with all the army gear on, in bunkers, and in black metal-clad cars, doing stunts and fight scenes all day for a ten-hour day. It was gruelling, but we knew it was going to be. You prepare as best you can. I think it was about a dozen kilos I dropped in the lead-up. And I didn't trick myself that it was gonna be easy. That was about the only prep you can do.

How did you differentiate Rhys from the Captain?

LMcK: Kiah's vision for Rhys was pretty clear, but we had a few discussions around it. There was talk about, "Do we take him and bring him into the world of the Captain, have them a bit more closely linked, be it physically and vocally?" At the end of the day, Kiah said, "Let's drop it right back and play right down the middle where you bring as much of yourself to Rhys as you can." I think just doing that differentiated [the two]. Where the Captain was pretty ruthless and sociopathic, he had his own justifications for why he was doing what he was doing, but the fact that Rhys questions them is another differentiation, to show he has a strong moral compass underneath what he's doing. I think it was reverse engineering the Captain, taking it back to just playing a bit more on my instincts.

Is there a draw for you towards genre films?

LMcK: 100%. I think they're just fun to make. It's always like enjoying your job. I think it's the energy. People who love genre love it. Kiah is a lightning rod of positive and driven energy because he loves what he does. He loves genre films. I think the big draw is that in Australia, we make a lot of different films. The model of getting films up in Australia has lent itself to making films that are geared towards going and getting a bunch of laurels overseas and then launching a writer or writer-director's career, and that's a beautiful thing. I love [those] films, but they haven't classically done well commercially.

The other type of films we make is we try and punch up to Hollywood, and we do well for it. We've got incredible crews, we've got great locations, great talent, and we try and punch up and make $5, $10, $15 million films into a $100 to $150 million film. You're just not going to have the days, you're not going to have the crew, you're not going to have the CG budgets, you're not going to have the time in development, you're not going to have the well-

INTERVIEW | LUKE MCKENZIE

worn heads that are part of the team who have been there and done it on the $150 million films. I think we fall a bit short when we try and do that.

The thing we have done since the Ozploitation days, [is that] we do genre well. We have a tongue-in-cheek humour. We can meet in the middle where we can have great types of stories and good performances and complex and interesting characters, but also punch up in action by leaning into practical effects. We are quite innovative.

Some of the stunts and the practical effects we did on *Wyrmwood* were ingenious. We had the sequence where Shantae [Barnes-Cowan] who plays Maxi and I were ejected from a pipe as it was blowing up, and you see us launching up through the tube at a million miles an hour and there's fire below us, and then we're launched into the air as we shoot out what is sold to be sixty to seventy feet of pipe. We did that laying on our side. They had this metre-and-a-half diameter tube that they cut a section out of. It was laid on its side and we were fixed in place. They put the cameras on us, and then they had five people slide that tube over us at a rip-roaring pace, with CO_2 blasting up from underneath. Shooting into that sold it well.

There was no huge CG budget, it was innovative and it was practical. It's the George Miller school of making it up as you go, and what looks good on camera. Leaning into genre allows you to bring all that creativity to it and explore and see how you can twist out a pre-existing world like the zombie world, which Kiah has done so well. There are a lot of reasons why genre is exciting.

As an actor, what does it mean when you walk on set and you have practical things to work with?

LMcK: Without getting cliche, acting is reacting. You're reacting to the stimulus and the other actors in the scene. The more stimulus you can get, the more it drops you into the moment. Our production designer, Esther Rosenberg, did a phenomenal job and I know she's launching into big stuff from here. The world that she built, the props, the textures, the fact that the guns were in our hands and we had the practical effects of shooting CO_2 out of the guns as we pulled the trigger, it gives you an authentic texture to the film, which you can't really replace. I haven't done a lot of CG stuff or green screen, so I don't really have a yardstick to measure against, I can only speak to the experience of having everything around you and it definitely drops you into the moment. I think that shows up on screen. Cameras don't lie and they pick up on when something is manufactured. The less you can do that and have authentic reactions, the better for everybody. As an actor, it makes your job so much easier.

WYRMWOOD: APOCALYPSE

The practical designs have allowed fans to be able to go home and make a costume and look like the characters from Wyrmwood. How was it seeing people dressed up as the characters from the films and the film having this second life through its fans?

LMcK: Truthfully, weird. It definitely is strange to see. It's gratifying to see that people have invested in and bought into the world that you've built, but then it's also surreal. I can only imagine how it is for Kiah. He built this thing in his brain, then put it into a camera, and then put it into the world. Having that full circle where people are saying, "Oh, we love what's in your brain!" It's been gratifying, but surreal.

HERETIC FOUNDATION AND VIDIVERSE

INTERVIEW
FILMMAKER ALEX PROYAS

As the mind behind films like *Spirits of the Air, Gremlins of the Clouds* (1987) and *Dark City* (1998), Alex Proyas has well and truly earned the label of being called a 'visionary filmmaker'. He's also a filmmaker with a certain level of clout, with films like *The Crow* (1994) and *I, Robot* (2004) to his name, and it's with that clout that Proyas established Heretic Foundation, an Australian based film studio that utilises 'the flexibility of Unreal Engine and LED screen tech', opening up the avenue for VFX creation and virtual production.

Paired with the launch of Heretic Foundation in 2020, was the launch of Vidiverse in 2022. This is a streaming platform that provides a place for genre fare, short and long format, to reach an audience. Films available on the platform include Proyas' 2020 short *Mask of the Evil Apparition* and the thriller *We're Not Here to Fuck Spiders* (2021).

After this interview, Proyas has continued to explore the realm of generative AI with an array of short form concepts that he's made available via his YouTube channel.

This interview was recorded by Andrew F. Peirce in September 2022

You've had an established career in America, and effectively are having a rebirth in a way in Australia by building up Heretic Foundation and Vidiverse, supporting filmmakers with an independent streaming service. Meanwhile, you've set up a studio. Together, these aspects appear to create some kind of revolution for filmmakers in Australia.

Alex Proyas: I hope so. We're not supposed to use words like 'revolution' in this country. We're supposed to remain humble and low-key. I often get accused of being an egomaniac, because I do like to use words like that, but I think in this case, it's nothing short of that. It's at least my vision for what I'm doing with my colleagues at the moment. I think the film industry kind of needs that. It needs a kick up the ass to shake it up. Something new is going to emerge out of the other end, so I'm trying to hit that on several fronts.

HERETIC FOUNDATION AND VIDIVERSE

I think it comes from the fact that the industry, the so-called 'mainstream Hollywood industry' is kind of broken now. It's not really working. It works in fits and starts and occasionally there's a success story, but everyone's scrambling for survival against this backdrop where there is a voracious appetite for more and more content. The more souls that are born on earth, the more people want to watch our stuff. Even in that context, the big conglomerates are struggling. They're playing with very large amounts of money and [can] very easily be undermined. For them, it's a process of survival right now.

Through that, I've seen that it's never in service of creative artists. It helps your cause as a creative individual if you're making the machine money. Films have always been a very expensive asset to create, so it needs to make its money back and that's okay, but when that starts to limit the potential for originality and creativity, then we have a problem. It's kind of toppled to that side over the last few years. At the same time, the cost of production is dropping. So, we have to reach a point where creative artists can regain their destinies again. I'm hoping we can help that cause as much as possible.

What was the impetus behind creating Vidiverse?

AP: It came from a somewhat pragmatic starting point. I've judged shorts at festivals around the world, and I was aware of how much great stuff there is out there made by really talented people. Inevitably, what happens is they have a certain lifespan on the festival circuit, they win a few laurels and awards, and then they get, I want to say, 'dumped' on YouTube or on Vimeo. Mainly YouTube, because it's going to give you the most eyes. Some of them are lucky enough to be very successfully downloaded and streamed, and they might get a few hundred bucks out of YouTube. On the other hand, YouTube makes thousands of dollars from their advertising. I thought, "Well, that's not really fair." That seems to make short films a viable commercial commodity, but the originators of that work don't see [much] of that revenue. They see a very small, unfair portion of it.

I wanted to build a more honest version of that, one that has a stamp of approval from myself initially. To this day, [we take] a curated approach so when a viewer comes to the platform, they know they're seeing work of a certain quality, rather than just anything random that YouTube might want to throw out. At the end of the day, it's to create some kind of viable alternative that brings this work to an audience's eyes. What we want to try and do [in the long term is] to start creating festivals and to start commissioning work. We've got a long, hard road ahead of us before we can afford to do those things, but hopefully, with the ongoing support of filmmakers, we'll get there in the end. Then it'll be more of a collaborative experience for filmmakers.

We are now engaged with developing features and series with the filmmakers [we've discovered]. That's a nice sideline of building [Vidiverse]. We want to try and promote what we call the 'filmmaker's own brand', [showcasing] a filmmaker's body of work. Many of them have created multiple, high-quality short films. One filmmaker is a local Aussie filmmaker by the name of Josh Tanner, who's made over the last 10 years a series of incredibly well-crafted high-production value films (*The Landing*, 2013, *Wandering Soul*, 2016, *The Rizzle* 2018, *Reverse*, 2018, *Decommissioned*, 2021), and he has not yet been able to make a feature. I think that's a crime, quite frankly, because I think he's a talented individual. We're supporting his work because he's already got a voice and identity, [and] we call that their 'brand'.

Short films were once considered to be a testing ground for filmmakers. How important is it for you to be able to work within that field and support people in being able to create a career in short films?

AP: I've always loved short films. They're like short stories to the novel. If you're a novelist, you don't need to go away from ever writing a short story again once you've written a novel. It's an equally valid art form. It's just that short films have never been monetised. We've tried to do that as much as possible. When we assemble a bunch of short films, it's become an anthology of short stories.

Look, I can't say we've made anyone millions of dollars yet, but we're hoping to move closer to that [in the future]. It takes time to build a groundswell for this sort of project. Hopefully, one day it will become a more commercially viable process. It's kind of linked in with the lower costs. A lot of the films on Vidiverse have been made on the smell of an oily rag, with friends and relatives, even the ones with professional actors. It's a more user-friendly medium than what it takes to get a feature film [off the ground], but more and more feature films are going to start being made in this way, as well. These days you can shoot a film of any sort on your phone and cut it on your laptop. If you write a great story and have good acting, you can get away with a very low production value, as long as it engages the audience.

What I'm trying to do with short films is to also use them as a proof of concept for my company, Heretic Foundation, which uses virtual production and does all sorts of other VFX as well. The short medium is more useful in that context. At the end of the day, they're still films, they still need to hold up as films with a good story and good acting. All the film content we're creating through the Heretic Foundation will end up exclusively on Vidiverse.

Not all of the work that is on Vidiverse is exclusively licensed videos, some are available on other platforms. We didn't want to limit individual filmmakers' abilities to derive an income stream from their films. There are

HERETIC FOUNDATION AND VIDIVERSE

genre-related platforms like DUST that are emerging which pay small licensing fees, so we share some of the content. Any original content is useful to bring more eyes to what we're doing. We hope to be commissioning [work] to be exclusive, but we're going to have a licensing deal. We're not going to be Netflix and we're not going to go, "We'll pay you five bucks, and then we own your work forevermore." We will always share whatever revenue is generated.

That idea comes from art galleries, which is a very straightforward business approach with artists. My wife ran an art gallery for a few years, so I had a bit of an insight into how that works; a painter will create some beautiful canvases on their own at home, and no one will tell them what to paint and how to paint. They'll deliver them to the gallery and the gallery will hang them on the wall. They'll invite people to view them and have champagne and cheese or whatever else they want to give them, and they split the proceeds. Generally speaking, most galleries split the proceeds 50/50 with the artists, so the gallery can cover their costs, and the artist covers all their costs to produce the work.

It's an honest and very straightforward situation, which is very unusual in the film world. It's all about the big corporations making as much profit out of you as possible, to the point where most people think I'm a billionaire because I've happened to have made some movies that have made a lot of money, and I don't see any of that money. There's a thing called 'creative accounting' in Hollywood, where I can have a movie like *I, Robot* (2004), which made close to a billion dollars in today's money, and I've not seen a cent of profit participation in that project. I would have to take them through a very expensive legal proceeding to get it and at the end of the day, I'd be up against Disney's lawyers now. I would have to spend a hell of a lot of money and some very sleepless nights before I achieved any satisfaction, and it systematically would destroy my career in Hollywood. No one would want to work with me ever again. I've had situations with close friends who have been in exactly that position and exactly what I've just said has happened to them. They don't like working with troublemakers.

To me, Vidiverse is my own version of what I think a streamer should look like and should function.

I imagine owning the Dark City IP allows you to play in that world and tell stories without strings attached.

AP: I actually don't own the IP to *Dark City*. That's one I'm kind of unravelling at the moment because we're talking about doing a *Dark City* series, but that's with their blessing. When I made the original film and wrote the original script, I signed all that away, of course, which is what you're ex-

INTERVIEW | ALEX PROYAS

pected to do in Hollywood, unfortunately. In the case of *Mask of the Evil Apparition* (2021), which is ostensibly in the *Dark City* universe, there is no specific element in that that is a direct correlation. It's an atmospheric thing, and it's just me using that spin to [get] more people to watch the film, which works. It's the whole Marvel franchise approach. You've got an audience, so keep feeding that same audience and you'll build [it] up as you go.

Heretic Foundation is leading into that same vision of re-imagining where your career can go from here. When you're talking about virtual production and VFX, can you explain what that looks like in practice?

AP: Virtual production is ostensibly just a way to create environments and bring those environments into the studio to film your actors within those environments, to move the camera and do whatever you want with it. In the case of using LED screens, everyone can see where you're supposed to be, unlike green screens where you've got to describe it all to people or show them on a monitor. [For a show like] *The Mandalorian*, those actors are standing there, looking at the planet that they're supposed to be on, which is useful for everybody. It means you can shoot in camera, so you don't have to do a lot of post-production, [instead] you do a lot of post-production in prep, which is [where] you have to build all the assets and environments, but you don't have to do a lot of stuff to fix things later on, so it does speed things up a little bit. Whereas if it's all on green screen, you've got to spend a year or more finessing the keys.

It means you can effectively shoot anywhere you want with a flick of a switch, and you're transported to another location. You don't have to pick up your crew and move them across town to find that other lounge room that you like miles away. It doesn't have to be set on an alien planet, [it can be used] even for contemporary world filming. If you've got a night shoot, you don't have to work at night. If your script says it's raining all the time, it can be raining all the time, or if it's sunny all the time, it can be sunny all the time, or if you want to shoot the entire movie during a fog or sunset that's all completely doable.

There's one project we're talking about shooting desert scenes in the middle of the night in the Outback. [Thinking of] the practicality of how do you shoot it and get your crew out there? There are so many logistical factors that can be removed or reduced substantially. Crews can be somewhat smaller; you don't need the army of carpenters and plasterers to build massive sets. When we made *Dark City* in the late nineties, we had to build it all. There was some miniature work as well, but anything that the actors were within was constructed at full scale. The buzz of being on a big set is fantastic, but that's gone forever. I don't think filmmakers in the future will know what that was like.

HERETIC FOUNDATION AND VIDIVERSE

Now with virtual production, you can do all that much more affordably and better. It's the way of the future. Certainly, until we go fully virtual, actors and all, which is coming. It's a few years away, we've got a good solid amount of time until virtual production will be the way to work. I keep saying it shouldn't really be called 'virtual productions', it should be called production, because that's really what it's becoming already, and it will continue to be.

We're a little bit behind the times here in Australia, as we always have been. It's always a good and bad thing. We got PAL TV because we weren't quick enough to get the NTSC form originally. I think that's the way it worked. That's the theory. PAL was a better format than NTSC, and then the US got lumped with the somewhat experimental technology, and we came in a little later with the best technology. I think that's what's happening right now with virtual production. We're shaking it all up. And by the time we've built our studio [we] will be world-class with all the stuff we're putting together.

You've talked about the collaborative difference between the US and Australia, where in Australia, people invite you to their film premiere, and after the film you've said, "I wish that you had engaged me in the process earlier. We could have had some creative discussions."[1] Why do you feel there is an apprehension to discuss, engage, and explore creatively the work that Australian filmmakers are making together?

AP: It's not just filmmakers, I think it's in the Australian psyche. I equate it to restaurants. You're an Italian restaurant and another Italian restaurant opens across the road and suddenly you feel threatened rather than embracing the idea that now with two Italian restaurants, it might give people who want Italian food more reason to come to your street. Even if the one across the street is doing better than you, if they can't get a seat there, they might come over to you and go, "We'll eat here." I think the same mentality is part of the Australian psyche.

I say a lot of bad things about Hollywood, but when I first started going to the US, the one thing that they showed me early on is how much they embrace filmmakers from other parts of the world, and they embrace any new talent. The cynical side of me goes, "Well, it's because they can make money out of you." That's fine, people at an early point in their careers are happy to be exploited. It's only when you get a bit old, and you go, "I don't know about that." Here, the lack of that sort of producorial kind of exploitation – and I use exploitation in the best possible way – of talent is really sad.

It also applies to creative people as well. I don't hear anyone ever saying anything nice about anyone else's work here. It's not all bad. There are some films that are great, but like anywhere else, there are some films that

INTERVIEW | ALEX PROYAS

are truly great. And I don't hear enough enthusiasm within the creative filmmaking community here [about them]. I think what people sadly don't realise is that by constantly downplaying other people's works, by being threatened by other people's output, it holds us all back, it doesn't raise you up as an individual. It holds everyone back. If you can find some good things to say and support other filmmakers' work, then we can all rise up together and become a potent force.

If you're going to say something bad, say it about Marvel or about the big filmmakers who can afford to have bad things said about them. Don't say it about local producers and filmmakers. It's changing slowly, but that's been my greatest frustration with being part of the Aussie film community to the point where I had to go overseas to get noticed to make my films. Now it's kind of the way things are done. When I did it, it was kind of an unusual approach. I hope we can continue to improve that approach.

It applies to everybody. There was a guy, Chris Thompson, who used to do reviews. He covered most of my films, and I met him at some point and said, "I have to thank you as someone who constantly supports local filmmakers and filmmakers generally." The simple reality is that he never gave anyone a bad review. He only showcased [one] film on his review [segment] that he had on *Behind the Scenes*. He said, "I only get to review 50 films a year. I'm not going to waste my time with films that I don't like, I'll only review stuff that I do like." Which makes complete sense. He also focused a lot on the local films, which was terrific. I just wish there were more people like him. So many reviewers and journos put all filmmaking on the same level, whether it's produced by an independent for no money at all or the latest blockbuster, and they think that is fair. I think it's unfair because you're dealing on a very uneven playing field. I think you need to support the underdog.

You've got Josh Reed's We're Not Here to Fuck Spiders (2021) on Vidiverse, a great film that cost nothing to make.

AP: That's the sort of filmmaking that I personally find really inspiring as a filmmaker. I think a lot of people are coming to Vidiverse for the same reason, because the films we're showing, we're not saying they're all high production value, there's just something about each of them that I go, "This is worth supporting." That approach to that film I find incredibly inspiring. No commercial forces could hold that film at bay. We wanted to be the almost commercial force to give it a platform because that's the sort of level of energy that you need to throw at movies to get them done. No one's going to jump up and give you money to finance a film like that. Few people are going to want to stream a film like that, but we do because it's that energy and passion for filmmaking that has made that film a reality, like many others on the platform as well. I find that incredibly inspiring as a filmmaker. That's the sort of energy you've got to channel to get stuff done, it doesn't matter what level of filmmaking you work on. It's like fighting a war, you've just got to keep at it, and you'll get there in the end.

You've been exploring the world of AI through videos and art. Can you briefly expand on where you see things progressing in that area?

AP: That's a huge area that we've just scratched the surface of. That's going to become a potent tool, I think. I've been through a bit of a roller coaster emotionally with that one. When it first appeared, I started off going "This is Armageddon for artists. This is Pandora's box." They've learned how to split the atom and now they're going to start dropping bombs on all the artists around the world. I thought, "How is this going to be subverted to the use of the big corporations when you don't need artists anymore?" I've evolved through the process to the point where I feel positive about it as a device because for the work to speak to a human being, you're always going to need that soul of the human. I've made films that may contradict what I'm about to say, I believe that the human soul is irreplaceable. That's what comes through in an artist's work. So, working alongside AI is like you've got a collaborator, but as the human being, you're still the person who shapes it into a construct that another human being can [connect with].

What does the Australian identity mean to you as a filmmaker?

AP: I think it's more pointed for us here in Australia because we are kind of an annex to the mainstream of filmmaking. Our entire industry is an indie industry, as such. We don't have the big financial concern supporting us. Yes, there's a little bit of that going on, and I hope it may get regulated and may prove to be greater. We're a country of less than 30 million people. It's not a big audience base, so our films have got to project out from Australia.

At the same time, the so-called 'market' is becoming more international by the moment. We have a great physical and I believe cultural connection with the entire Pan Pacific region, and that's something that I think we need to focus on more. The fact that a great percentage of our population is Asian and Indian now really tells you a lot about the nature of the changing cultural landscape of Australia. This is something that is being virtually ignored, even by the government authorities that should be embracing this. There's a great deal of support for Indigenous filmmakers, that's terrific and should be maintained, but I think there needs to be further support for Asian culture as well within the Australian idiom. That's hugely important.

It's a thing that marks us as being different to just being another state of the US or part of the Commonwealth or however we [have seen] ourselves in the past culturally speaking. Those sorts of forces are important to focus on. They're going to create different dramatic forms. At the end of the day, we've always used Hollywood filmmaking – I believe, much to our detriment as creative artists – to shape our own voice. I think we're starting to move away from that, but I think we need to embrace that and embrace it in a way with confidence, where we know that our Australian content – influenced by the cultures that I've mentioned – can travel internationally. Where we don't have to go via the US to be justified as a unique national voice. I don't think filmmakers or anyone in this country has even scratched the surface of what that means, and I think hopefully, that's something that we can focus on in the future.

ENDNOTES

1   https://indie-cinema.com/2021/08/interview-alex-proyas/

SUSHI NOH

18 mins
Director: *Jayden Rathsam Hüa*
Writer: *Jayden Rathsam Hüa*
Cast: *Felino Dolloso, Geneva Phan, Jodine Muir, Natasha Cheng, Georgie Davey, Matthew R. Grego*
Producers: *Jayden Rathsam Hüa, Philippa Silva*
Composer: *Scott Majidi*
Cinematography: *Sam Steinle*
Editing: *Gus O'Brien Cavanough*

INTERVIEW
FILMMAKER
JAYDEN RATHSAM HÜA

Jayden Rathsam Hüa manages to turn the rather innocuous phrase 'yummy, yummy sushi time' into an incantation that he uses to summon the unhinged genre flick *Sushi Noh* into existence. *Sushi Noh* is a violently absurd, schlocky experience that tells the story of a young girl, Ellie, (Geneva Phan) who becomes increasingly concerned about the ratcheting mania of her Uncle Donnie (Felino Dolloso) who she is trapped under the care of. With the hope of impressing a colleague (Jodine Muir), the uncle purchases a creepy kitchen appliance with a noh mask face that pushes sushi rolls out of its mouth in a gut-churning, faecal like manner. *Sushi Noh* contains enough wailing bloody mayhem to make you reconsider that sushi roll for lunch.

This interview was recorded by Andrew F. Peirce in July 2022

Where did this idea come from?

Jayden Rathsam Hüa: I made this film as a part of completing my master's program in producing at AFTRS. Doing that program put me in a position to meditate on what kind of content I wanted to make. At that stage, I had only made comedy stuff and silly web sketches. I realised that all that I was watching was thrillers, horror, and supernatural stuff and so I found myself at a crossroads as to which path I wanted to follow. It took quite a while for me to realise that the right path for me to take was to reconcile those two avenues and create something a little bit more distinct and personal to me.

Having realised that, one thing that I also really wanted to explore was the nature of children's nightmares. I was a pretty nervous kid, and I was afraid of a lot of things that I shouldn't have been afraid of. I didn't understand the artistic stylisation of things. For example, when I was shopping with my mum, I was terrified of the painted picture of a man on a bag of potato chips. Thinking back to what I would have dreamt a child, I realised that the nightmares that I had as a kid were different to the nightmares that I had as an adult. When I was a kid, they weren't grounded by real-world ex-

SUSHI NOH

perience. They weren't grounded by social anxieties or real-world danger, but rather, they were characterised by my slowly forming and incomplete understanding of the world around me.

That put me in the direction of exploring the phenomenon of the uncanny valley of that feeling of something not being quite right, but also close enough to the familiar so that it makes you just a little uneasy. I wanted to achieve that in different ways, and also be unapologetic about the style of the film. *Sushi Noh* was the result of me bringing in imagery that I thought was evocative and uncanny, and grounding that as a real-world appliance: a kitchen appliance. It came from the need to take something interesting and visual like the noh mask and make it accessible and inescapable in a household. The solution for that was not to present it simply as an ornamental mask, but something that is designed to appeal to adults as a product designed to remain in a shared residential space being a kitchen appliance, and then putting a kid in there and seeing what results from that and what happens if the results of nightmares start filtering into the world.

At a paranormal/supernatural level, that's what *Sushi Noh* is about, but also fundamental to the story is the niece/uncle relationship. I'm a firm believer that horror films are improved if the spine of the film is anchored by real-world drama and character and something that we can relate to. I wanted to explore a relationship and dynamic that was characterised as a familial bond as something that was uncomfortable where there were misunderstandings and inadequacies and communication, and for the consequences of that friction between the child and the man to eventuate in these heightened imaginative horror images that you see in the film.

There are different styles at play here, a bit of giallo, a bit of traditional Japanese horror, a touch of Australiana. It's like this cultural blend. What's the interest in being able to work in the different genres all at once?

JRH: I think light and shade are really important, and I feel as though genre shifting and bending is a great way to achieve that. When I was writing *Sushi Noh*, that was similar timing to when *Parasite* (2019) was out, and I thought that was a great example of a thriller that used comedy to great effect in terms of ramping up the suspense and making us feel all the more tense for the characters. What I thought was incredibly impressive about that film was the use of comedy to enhance the tension through contrast, as opposed to alleviating the tension with comedic relief.

I approached *Sushi Noh* intending to incorporate humour and comedic elements to provide contrast to the less funny parts. To establish that kind of rollercoaster ride, my team and I came up with a visual for how we wanted the film to feel for the audience, and that was to be strapped into one of

INTERVIEW | JAYDEN RATHSAM HÜA

those carnival rides, where you're in this [chair] and it's swivelling around and taking you on this track, and the ride determines what you're looking at. You're taken along this overwhelming miasma of colour, and you have no control over what you're forced to look at. That's the sensibility that we wanted to adopt for *Sushi Noh*.

The production design with dirty walls and the dishevelled apartment adds to that 'carnival ride' vibe. Can you talk about the creation of the apartment, the Noh mask, and the sushi machine itself?

JRH: Starting with the Noh mask, that began as a whole bunch of sketches. We spent a lot of time looking at the original designs of the Noh mask, and then we wanted to come up with something that looks like a bastardisation of the traditions behind the noh mask because of the racial stereotypes that are in the film, and the exoticisation of Oriental culture is at the forefront about the commodification of different cultures and how we use stereotypes to market and commodify objects to be more appealing and recognisable for whatever your target audiences are.

It's an intentionally tacky commodified interpretation of the Noh mark that is also in equal parts functional because we needed the mouth to be big enough for the sushi to slide through. Our production designer Calum [Wilson Austin] sculpted the mask and took several casts of it, so we had multiples of the mask. We had different versions of the mask for different parts of the film. For example, we had a mask that was more of a puppet, and it had all these controls connected to the back of it so that the eyes and the eyebrows could articulate. We had different versions that were velcroed onto the machine so that Felino Dolloso as Uncle Donnie could take it off and press it to his face.

The machine itself was a puppet too that had controls. Because of its modest size, no one could fit into it, so we needed to cut a hole in the kitchen bench, and someone had to wriggle into the kitchen bench and operate it from inside using sticks connected to wires connected to the sushi Noh puppet and feed the fish and the sushi out of the machine. Some elements worked in our favour, because in the first instance, when we were putting the sushi through the mouth, it kept disintegrating because of the friction between the damp sushi roll and the rubber that we had stretched across the mouth. Our solution was to slather the sushi in lube. That solved it but it also gave it this lovely gooey, luminous glistening quality to it, which worked really well. Happy accidents.

As for the set design, they were very much inspired by the micro homes of Hong Kong. We wanted the place to feel overwhelming, claustrophobic, and inhospitable for a child. With the clutter and the heightened colours,

SUSHI NOH

although weren't explicitly portraying a super surreal, subjective world – at least in the first half of the film – we wanted to imbue the world with a troubled quality as if it were being shown through the filter of a child's perception. That's why all the elements are so heightened. That's why there are no ceilings, and the room seems very tall and vacuous but also claustrophobic in the sense that you have all of these belongings and textures that are populating the frame at all times.

Let's talk about the advertising. The marketing and the motifs used in the ads lean into the idea of a nauseating, unsettling vibe, but still play with a kind of joyful feel of "Hey, buy this product!" Can you talk about being able to work in that tone for Sushi Noh?

JRH: I think the exercise of making the ad was a very helpful grounding experience for establishing the tone of the film. I feel as though there are some opportunities in the film to take it to extreme levels where you have the license to be as absurd as possible when you're framed as a television ad. You can be as funny and silly and loud and crazy as you can, and it still exists in a believable sense within the world of film. In doing so, it was a great way to put something in the film that could believably appeal to adults in being overwhelming, eye-catching, and colourful but also too much for a child and uncomfortable to watch. We had a lot of fun making the film in that infomercial style. We have so much B-roll of our actress, Natasha [Cheng], ripping that fish apart. We had to pull it back. It was a lot of fun filming that. I feel as though the performances were already quite heightened in the film and a way to balance that was to provide something to contrast against it which was the very cartoonish performance in the advertisement.

What direction did you give the actors to get them to the point of that level of heightened performance?

JRH: Felino is very committed. He's a wonderful actor. He's super physical with his [performance]. There was this fantastic moment after he drowns himself in the bathtub, and when he reanimates, we were talking about the nature of his movement. We described it as imagining that he was a corpse, but he had jolts of electricity activating different parts of his body, and he was a fleshy Marionette being led down the hallway. He connected with that direction. Between shots, as we were setting up for different setups, he would squirrel himself away in the corner of the studio and start rehearsing this. As he was doing this, we had two of the makeup girls going out for their lunch break. As they approached the exit, Felino with his eyes closed and [deep in] concentration started staggering out of the darkness towards them, covered in blood and in his underwear. That was a really great moment.

Working with an 11-year-old, Genna [Geneva Phan], was interesting too. On one hand, she was 11, and that comes with its challenges, but on the other hand, she was such a professional child actor. I learned a lot from that experience in the sense that my instincts had me speak to her like she was 11, compliment her, and provide her with assurances more than I would the other adult actors. I realised that as soon as I dropped that tone of speech, and spoke to her as an equal, that really helped, and she responded to that a lot better. That was an education point for me.

As far as bringing them into the zone of that heightened performance and feeling like they were inhabiting that space, I would come up with scenarios that were [easier] for a child to relate to. For example, when Genna was standing in front of the sushi Noh, and I wanted that feeling of subtle discomfort without being overtly terrified of something, I would create a scenario for her to envision in her head, but I'd let her fill in the key details. I would ask her, "What's the creepiest animal that you could think of?" Her answer was a guinea pig.

The situation that I had her imagine [was] that she was in a zoo, and then there was a guinea pig the size of a car in an enclosure. She knew for a fact that if she reached out and touched it, it would bite her hand. I said, "Imagine that you're at the zoo. The zookeeper is encouraging you to pet this guinea pig, but you know what's going to happen if it does." Putting her back in that space, I had her imagine that the ushi Noh was a guinea pig, and she was asked before we were rolling to go and pat it. That was the reaction that we got from the film.

What does it mean to be a working filmmaker in Australia right now?

JRH: I think it has a lot to do with my upbringing and identity. Being brought up in a Western society with an Eastern background has a lot to do with the way that I identify with Australian content and where I see our current slate of content and how I might want to contribute to it in my own way. I feel as though Australian stories have the potential to be so much more diverse beyond Outback mysticism and the *Crocodile Dundee-s* and the dramas that we often produce. I feel as though the genre is undersold in this market right now and that there are a lot more stories to be told.

It's a shame that many of our genre filmmakers and stories are being shipped off to the US to be reappropriated, and I feel as though there's a lot of potential in terms of exploring Australiana and our culture and imbuing that with unique imagery and experimental filmmaking as well.

I think as far as *Sushi Noh* goes, it's really mixing the waters of what I can bring from other cinematic sensibilities, most notably East Asian horror

SUSHI NOH

cinema and incorporating that into an Australian setting to see how it flies. With that creative style in mind, I intend to take that sensibility and adapt that into the projects that I'm working on now as well and shine a light on different communities and cultures that exist within the Australian landscape but also present them in unique and entertaining ways without taking them too seriously and having fun with them at the same time.

FRIENDS AND STRANGERS

84 mins
Director: *James Vaughan*
Writer: *James Vaughan*
Cast: *Fergus Wilson, Emma Diaz, Greg Zimbulis, Amelia Conway, David Gannon, Poppy Jones, Malcolm Kennard, Steve Maxwell, Victoria Maxwell, Jayden Muir, Dirk Nagel, David Nash, Jacki Rochester, Stefan Solomon*
Producers: *Rebecca Lamond, Lucy Rennick*
Cinematography: *Dimitri Zaunders*
Editing: *James Vaughan*

Vaughan's sole AACTA nomination for the film was in 2021 for Best Editing.
Friends and Strangers received wider attention outside of Australia, receiving critical praise by Sight and Sound magazine and awards attention from the Rotterdam International Film Festival, Jeonju Film Festival, and Beijing International Film Festival.

INTERVIEW
FILMMAKER JAMES VAUGHAN

If *Friends and Strangers* were to be released in the nineties, it'd likely be labelled as a 'slacker comedy'. While there certainly are comedic elements in James Vaughan's feature film debut, it instead plays out as an observational piece about Aussie millennials stuck in arrested development. Vaughan's characters, led by Fergus Wilson's amiable Ray, are stifled by cultural stagnation, meandering across NSW like they're stuck in some kind of purgatory.

This interview was recorded by Andrew F. Peirce in February 2022

Friends and Strangers ended up on the Sight and Sound Top 50 Films of 2021 poll, which is a rarity for Australian films. What did that do to you?

James Vaughan: It scrambled my mind. It was already scrambled and [that] scrambled it further. It was amazing to wake up to that on whatever day that was. I didn't quite believe it and had to go and look through it in detail. I thought they had made a mistake. It was just not on our radar at all. It wasn't something we expected. They break it down by which critics have put you in there. I guess I had had contact with some of those critics, like a lot of them. The whole list is dominated by American and British critics. I have heard from some of them saying they love the film. Probably at the time, I didn't realise how influential maybe some of those critics were, the fact that they were in that group of people being consulted. Because there were hardly any Australian critics who were invited to participate in that, it was such an honour.

To me, the film feels European in style and tone. It feels like European audiences might be more receptive to that. What audience was it made in mind for?

JV: I don't want this to be a kind of trite answer, but I probably wasn't thinking about any audience when I was making the film. I set out to make a film

FRIENDS AND STRANGERS

that I really wanted to make, the kind of film that I would want to see if I was going to see an Australian film. [I was] frustrated for years with just how parochial Australian cinema tends to be, and often talking big about how great it is, but not particularly engaged with the rest of the world, outside of some parts of Hollywood and that sort of thing.

It wasn't so much thinking about, "I want Australians or Europeans to like this," even though if I had to pick an audience that I felt this is important for, it would be Australians. For me, it's trying to probe into some questions about us and our culture. In that sense, if there was a social function that was bigger than just me and what I wanted to do, it would be for the Australian audience. But I have to say, it wasn't really part of the motivation for making the film.

That's the beautiful thing about funding something yourself; you can just do whatever the hell you want and not have to worry about audience metrics and projections and these things, which I think are the scourge of funding systems in Australia and don't help us make good films. They produce films that are risk-averse, formulaic, and out of touch with the new trends and new artistic directions that are constantly being explored overseas that we are choosing a lot of the time to separate ourselves from. Not having to bow to that was awesome.

There are people who you work alongside as collaborators in some capacity, Ted [Wilson], Amiel [Courtin-Wilson], Alena [Lodkina], who have all made fascinating films that push against what an Australian film can be and interrogate the Australian identity on screen. What's it like working alongside those kinds of creative people?

JV: It's beautiful to have those relationships because it can be very lonely at times when you're self-funding something and being told by institutions that what you're doing is wrong or not going to be liked or not what audiences want to see. If you don't have those people who are like-minded and share some of your values and creative aesthetic sympathies, I don't know, probably for all of us in different ways, we might have dropped out. I can only really speak for myself.

Meeting Amiel at a certain point around 2012 after I'd finished film school was really important because he was someone who I had huge respect for before I even knew him and even before seeing his work. Within a few seconds of the trailer for *Hail*, which was about to come out, [it was clear that] this was someone who wasn't playing by other people's rules and, whatever you think of the film, was passionately doing something his way and for reasons that I think are not just self-indulgent. They are reasons that

INTERVIEW | JAMES VAUGHAN

are trying to get at something deeper that is politically, socially, or artistically important to him.

The other thing too [was] someone [was] prepared to make sacrifices to do that. Seeing someone like that a half-generation ahead was inspiring for me and showed that this is a path that is worth [it]. I think if I hadn't had that, it might have been like, "Maybe I'm crazy. Maybe I'm just out of film school and wanting to do my own thing but wasn't inspired by a lot of the Australian films from the last twenty-odd years. Maybe there's something wrong with me. Maybe I've got something different I want to do, but maybe that's really silly. Surely there would be other people doing it if it was true."

Not like Ted, Alena, and Amiel are the only ones - there are so many -, but they were just the ones I've been lucky to get close to and become close friends with. It's so important to have those links because you can discuss ideas and strategies about how to move ahead with things which is so important. After all, there are so many barriers.

What kind of discussions do you have? Do you talk about the current state of Australian film?

JV: You know, I love Australian films, too. And I feel part of what Australian cinema is. I don't want to present myself or any of the other people I've mentioned as anti-Australian cinema or whatever. I'm only making that point because I think sometimes that's the reflex to [do so]. If you're critical or want to improve something, the political equivalent is that you're un-Australian or you're not patriotic. Not that it's totally parallel, but often the criticism that's made of people on the left is that they don't love their country. And by criticising something, you're showing a lack of unity and all these sorts of things. I reject that. I think it comes from a love of Australian cinema and where it has been in periods in the past, and where it can be again that's motivating a lot of this.

In terms of the discussions that we have, I guess it's a big mix. In each of my relationships with each of those people you mentioned, they're all different. Some are more strategic and all the institutional stuff, approaches to making a project for nothing, or purely creative discussions about films and ideas for films we've seen and loved, or ideas for new films, that sort of thing too, down to sharing links to possible opportunities to find the money for grant programs or small amounts of arts funding.

I stopped doing that sort of thing. I spent a few years going hard at that and just came up empty-handed again and again. It's hard enough not getting the money because you obviously are asking for it because you feel like you need it to do what you want to do. There are so many worthy applicants so

FRIENDS AND STRANGERS

you can never feel entitled to these things, but it's the time you spend doing them that becomes the big tax on your creativity. Already you're self-funding to a large degree, so a lot of your time is going to working so that you can eventually make something. You're also putting the limited amount of spare time you have into these funding grants, and that was starting to get me down too.

It was almost a mental health thing. I completely self-funded *Friends and Strangers* because yes, it's going to be horrible finding all that money and working for it, but at least then it's something I can control and set a timeline on. Work out how quickly I'm saving and start to be able to manage the years at it, rather than these false hopes of putting in this big application and hoping, fingers crossed, we get that so we can start shooting next year. Then, when you don't, you feel like your little sandcastle has been smashed by a wave and you're back to square one.

So yeah, I guess all kinds of conversations, anything you could imagine to do with the making of a film or the genesis and development of an idea is the stuff you end up talking about.

This leads to something that I found fascinating within Friends and Strangers, *this kernel of the idea that modern Australians have been neglected by the treatment of the First Nations people of the past. As such, we feel like we are adrift in a country that is struggling to find a cultural identity. That's what I got from seeing Ray wandering around, trying to find his place in the world. There is a sense of neglect for the First Nations people, who aren't present in the film, but we feel their absence so distinctly because of the manner which the previous generations have treated them. Can you talk about the conscious decision to bookend the film in such a colonial manner by presenting the colonial roots and then say, "This is the land that this film was made on?"*

JV: It's a great question. The only challenge I'd make to the premise of the question would be that I don't think our generation currently is off the hook either. I feel like if genocide was [started] by the very first white people that landed here, it continues up to this day. Yes, we inherit the consequences of it and in some ways, it becomes harder and harder to go back and atone. You can't atone for what happened, but at least honestly confront the reality of what happened. It does get harder and harder the longer you look away from it and ignore it.

We're at a point now where we have so many people that grow up in our cities who don't meet First Nations people or if they do, it's a rare thing. For me, I grew up on the north shore in Sydney, went to a private school which is its own very particular subsection of Sydney, but also not a tiny one. In

INTERVIEW | JAMES VAUGHAN

the north shores, there are huge numbers of people in that extended zone of the city but dominated by private schools, Catholic religious schools, and independent schools. South of Sydney and Western Sydney, [it's a] different story.

But up there, it's been a place of privilege and separation from First Nations history even though it exists on a place of profound First Nations history. There's an artificial separation of white culture from its origins here as a colony. Separation from the reality of how the colony began, but very much still connected to those origins, which always was a project of dispossession. The decision to bookend it with those colonial references just seemed to me apt, not only to tie in with the colonial aspects or the matters of racial history and politics here, but in a more general sense, as a way of positioning Sydney in touch with its own history in a full sense.

I did want the film to be a reflection on Australia, of where it's going. You can't look at where something's going without seeing where it's come from. It is very much embedded in Sydney's details in a contemporary sense. But you can't really explore those things without it being holistic. And just having those few moments, whether it's lingering on a statue or something that's been there for 150 years or including these watercolours that have been there for close to 250 years, these are reminders that cities don't just exist. They're not something to take for granted. They have their own history of development and it's a peculiar history, in the case of Australian cities.

I think when you see how something happened, it helps to maybe think about how it could be different. It's not just something we have to accept. Not that the film, I think, gives any answers or comes close to even trying to give answers to these things. I'm hoping that the film prompts [people] to think, just to take a step back and look at some of the things we assume about the present.

How do you feel as a filmmaker not being able to present an answer to the question that you're proposing?

JV: I don't know the answers to things. And I probably don't like films that present answers to things because I don't think any serious question about life has a clear answer. The best we can do is ask better questions, and that's what philosophy is about. That's what science is about. That's what politics is about. There's no city-state or political organisational grouping that's ever found the final answer to anything. Questions provoke new questions. Whether you make progress sometimes remains a mystery.

I like films in general that seem to start from that point of acknowledging that life is a mystery. In one way or another, I start from that point and move from there in and out of moments of revelation or insights, and then back into a sense of questioning or confusion or nihilism or whatever. I'm interested in those films that present knowledge itself as something elusive. The less critical you are of things, the easier it is to feel like you ever do know the answer.

A lot of films do try and wrap things up in a way, or point towards 'this is the way', 'this is the direction forward'. That's important too, and I'd say particularly with committed political or militant political filmmaking, that's just part and parcel with it, 'this is right', 'this is wrong'. I can't say I'm a connoisseur of that sort of cinema. Sometimes I watch things and, even when its subject matter is expressly political, I still probably prefer to watch something that presents information in an interesting and ordered and clear way and does let you maybe make your own conclusions rather than things that are telling you what's right and wrong from the outset.

With all that said, I do know that often audiences want you to plant your flag somewhere and point in the direction to make 'the message' clear. 'The message' is something that makes me cringe really hard, the question of "What's the message of the film", or "Well done, you succeeded, the message came across." I just don't like it when art is reduced to a telegram or a few lines that you can summarise, and everything is just this padding around pushing this straight, narrow message at the person's brain. I feel like art should be about questions and not answers. But that's not for everyone.

I guess entertainment too is another tricky word. I like entertainment. I saw *The Batman* (2022) last night and enjoyed it. I like Marvel movies, some of them anyway. There's a lot of mainstream cinema I like. I don't watch much television, but I'm not anti-entertainment either. I think what cinema suffers from a bit in Australia is the assumption that it is only entertainment. That if it has any other value, it's political. Its status as an art form is assumed away often, and it's probably the only art form in Australia that suffers from that.

You can have airplane novels, and everyone acknowledges that, but everyone also knows that a novel can be a serious art form. Whereas at least in the way things get funded and distributed and exhibited here, the art aspect is assumed away most of the time, and you have to fight to even just get it acknowledged that it can be an art form, which is another thing that I find hugely frustrating. It's not me saying "Banish all the rest. Cinema is art and art only." There are spaces for it.

In terms of getting things funded at the top level, it doesn't feel like there are. There needs to be some changes there because you can't get things funded. Australian Council for the Arts (AusCA), if you're theatre, music,

INTERVIEW | JAMES VAUGHAN

performance, dance; everything has a place at AusCA. Except film. They say "Go, we have dedicated agencies for you," and then you go and pitch a project and they say, "No, we don't fund that kind of thing. That's something else, you've got to go and get an arts grant." That's a problem.

The good thing about that is there's an easy solution, it's a kind of administrative adjustment. It does take some kind of belief or sympathy for the idea that a film is an art form too and that that has a place not just for the people working and wanting to do that, but that our country and our culture can benefit from the contribution of cinema to some of these questions about identity and our future.

A film costs a lot to get up off the ground, and inevitably what happens is we have a group of first-time filmmakers who never make a second film because they're still paying off their first one. I'd love to see Ted's next film, but he's still got to pay off Under the Cover of Cloud. We need to have a better process to allow these kinds of films to exist. In America and the UK, it's a little bit different, but in Australia, we still look at the box office as a determining factor of a film's success and not the cultural footprint or the critical reception, and that's frustrating. We should have generations of filmmakers who have had second films and who have been able to tell their stories how they want to.

JV: Yes, and third, fourth, fifth films too. People that have a lifetime of things that they'd like to explore, not just for themselves, but [for] a sense of engagement with the culture they're a part of. And those are the things that future generations I think really look back on and thank. We look back at the Seventies and we're not just glad for the television that entertained people at that time, we're glad for the serious works of art from that period. They're the ones that help us figure out who we are and where we're going and these bigger things, even if they're not always the most impactful things at the time. They are the things that stay with us. Change is possible.

There is this fascinating thread of the connection to Country here that is accentuated by two points. One where the young girl who Ray and Alice meet at the beginning of the film talks about the country that has been covered in weeds and trash. Then, in the closing moments, we see a coin sitting in the water. It feels to me like the white colonial connection to Country has become dominant and it's inescapable. And all it is is just trash, weeds, and disposed currency that we can't even use properly. Can you talk about the connection to Country in the film?

JV: There are so many ways I could answer this. I think part of me is a visceral sense of disappointment. It's not just Australian things, it's homogenised global capitalist developments where you find the cheapest materials

515

FRIENDS AND STRANGERS

from whatever part of the world you can get them and find the most efficient or a strange definition of efficient, but the cheapest way of achieving some goal. If that's moving people who want to get from Sydney to Adelaide, then it's the straightest road with the most number of lanes and the biggest airport that gets people going back and forth. Thoughts of how that system will work in ten or twenty years don't really matter. Thoughts of how it looks and how it sounds and how it smells and things like that don't matter. Even though when we look at old places, the places that are the most beautiful places to us – and the world seems to agree on what those places are – [are] these ancient cities or even older historic capitals, they're the places that are built holistically and they fit the ideas that how something looks, smells, and feels, and how it's experienced is as important as anything else. It's just a shallowness to how we develop things now.

Being someone who's done a bit of driving around New South Wales and Australia in general, I do get sad looking at how monotonous and degraded a lot of the parts of the country that have had heavy white development or use, whether it's agricultural or infrastructure or whatever, how dirty and sad a lot of those spaces are, the sides of highways, the toilets that you use at a rest stop, at a service station, at a camp caravan park. Not that these are inherently bad places, but anything that's not someone's personal, private store of wealth - being their house - is extremely vulnerable in Australia to a profound ugliness. Which I think says a lot about not just who we are generationally, but some of the broader political-economic paradigms that we're currently seemingly trapped within.

Maybe it's partly that experience of some of those spaces, but also the feeling of a profound experience. Whether or not it is, is a whole other thing as a white person here. But the feeling of profound experiences in national parks and some of our places that have been preserved and saved from development. There's a whole other discourse around the white approach to the preservation of those things which excludes Indigenous people from them, or traditionally has anyway, and that's changing with Indigenous rangers and things like that. The idea that a landscape is pristine if there are no people in it is like an overcompensation.

Clearly where we have too many people, stuff is ugly, so the way to keep things good is to keep people out. That dual dichotomy is problematic as well. [There are] multi-day hikes out in places where the beauty is just jaw-dropping often so close to where we live. Sydney is particularly lucky in that sense that the north, west, and south of the city are just amazing natural places of profound natural beauty. The harbour is obviously stunning. I think we have gotten better at looking after certain parts of our urban environments. The harbour's much cleaner than it was twenty years ago, and there's more emphasis on pollution.

INTERVIEW I JAMES VAUGHAN

I was in Iraq at the end of last year for a film festival. My heart broke. I met some film students and I was taken to a place that everyone was raving about, saying it was such a beautiful spot to go and have a picnic. The ground was covered completely ankle-deep in plastic bottles and plastic stuff that they just didn't even see. I guess some of these things are just what you're trained to see. After decades of being reminded that litter and pollution is bad, we've become very sensitive to that sort of thing. The broader polluting forces [are] you hear about ugly housing developments that are made for a quick buck as cheaply as possible, or multi-lane highways and toll roads being built. These are the more macro levels or layers of pollution and ugliness that are still being built at an alarming rate.

It's another thing I was thinking about in terms of what does our country stand for? What are we leaving to future generations? As flawed as the origin of our colony was, the urban buildings from that period are some of the most beautiful we have. The Macquarie-era sandstone buildings in the CBD are precious to us as Sydneysiders and going through the generations up to the Harbour Bridge and Opera House and modernist buildings that have been left as a gift to future generations. What is our present generation giving to future generations? Hideously ugly apartments. The phenomenon of terrace housing developments which are now so prized by people who get to live in those areas is that they're such a beautiful way of designing urban space that balances individual needs and also communal space and shared space and efficiency and visual beauty and symmetry and all these kinds of things.

What's our present generation giving? Aside from the Barangaroo Tower where squillionaires can get penthouses at the top and people can go and gamble? Some people might want to look at that building, but there's just not much by way of urban public works that is leaving more for the next generation than it's taking. That's something I find really sad. By putting that in the background of some of the scenes, again not to answer any questions about it, was something I wanted in the world and the zone of the film.

I'm excited to see where you go as a filmmaker, you've got so much you want to say.

JV: I'm really happy with the film. It's not perfect by any means. There are lots of things that I wanted to get in a deeper or better or more interesting way that I'm just not quite satisfied with, watching it back. I'm looking forward to having another crack at future things and I hope that that's possible. I feel like it is. I think a lot of what held back independent filmmakers in previous decades was the cost of everything. We're so lucky now with what you can get. It's still not cheap, but we shot the film on a 2010 ARRI Alexa, which, when that came out, was more than $100,000 to put it all together.

FRIENDS AND STRANGERS

Because it's old now, we got that for less than $10,000. I edited the film on my 2015 iMac. It was like $1,500 or two and a half, I can't remember, and ten or twenty years earlier, it just wasn't possible. The equipment you need to have was tens and tens of thousands just before you even start thinking about working on stuff. I think the quality you can get now with the right people in terms of hardware [has me] hoping there'll be more filmmakers coming through and making use of the opportunities that come from that.

INTERVIEW
FILMMAKER AMIEL COURTIN-WILSON

Amiel Courtin-Wilson's work as a filmmaker consistently operates in the realm of the emotional, presenting the rawness and reality of humanity with stark honesty like few other filmmakers. From his stunning 2011 film *Hail* which presented two characters clashing and exploding against each other in a turbulent relationship, to his character-focused documentaries on Uncle Jack Charles with 2008's *Bastardy* and musician Ben Lee with 2012's *Ben Lee: Catch My Disease*, Amiel's focus as a director has always been on that entity that thrives within us, conjuring our spirit into existence, day in, day out.

With *Man on Earth*, his most grounded and immediate film yet, Amiel follows the final seven days of Robert Rosenzweig – Bob – as he is surrounded by family and friends as he embarks on his journey to die with dignity as the impact of Parkinson's disease overwhelms his body and his quality of life diminishes. The embrace and depiction of Bob's soul is presented with profound empathy by Amiel and the crew of considdoerate filmmakers by his side that includes producers Alice Jamieson-Dowd and Chris Luscri, cinematographer Jacqueline Fitzgerald, sound recordist Steve Bond, and more.

This interview was recorded by Andrew F. Peirce in October 2022

How did you get to become part of Bob's legacy?

Amiel Courtin-Wilson: That's a beautiful way of putting it. It was a very circuitous process. We were working on another project called *Traces*, which is a feature documentary shot entirely with thermal imaging cameras looking at the human body at the moment of death, that we were researching before we got in contact with Bob. As part of that research, producers Alice Jamieson-Dowd and Chris Luscri, and a large team of associate producers and supporters, reached out to upwards of 1500 hospices, death doulas, dying with dignity groups, advocacy groups, everywhere from Canada, the UK, Europe, Mexico, and Southeast Asia. After around two and a half years, we were starting to question whether the project would go ahead

MAN ON EARTH

when we got a call from a hospice in Denver about *Traces*. In the space of one week, we also got a call from Robert Rosenzweig in Aberdeen, Washington, a gentleman who had heard about the *Traces* project through the dying with dignity non-profit group that he was working with. He contacted us with a deal, "I'll participate in this thermal imaging project if you come and spend the last seven days of my life with me and document my family, my feelings and thoughts." It was really his idea from the get-go.

That was the first time that had ever happened as a filmmaker. From the moment we spoke on the phone – only one month out from the date of his scheduled death – it was abundantly clear that Bob was an amazing human being, an amazing storyteller, very funny and self-aware, with this great acerbic wit. We had a lot in common in strange, unexpected ways. It was a no-brainer that this other feature film suddenly sprouted from this long research process.

Besides being a documentarian, what did you see your role in Bob's final days as being?

AC-W: Everything was so accelerated. Bob and I connected in an unusually unique way just in those first conversations in terms of humour and shared experiences. I was confident that we had the beginnings of some kind of burgeoning friendship outside of the usual filmmaker-subject relationship. Once we landed, it was instrumental that we had the right kind of crew with us for such a sensitive endeavour. We worked with Steve Bond who's an amazing sound recordist. I'm a great believer that sound recordists don't get enough of the limelight. I think he's the best location sound recordist in Australia. I knew that he would be amazing. I knew that Jacqueline Fitzgerald, our cinematographer, would be unbelievably sensitive. And Alice Jamieson-Dowd, our lead producer, was on the ground. I knew inevitably that not only would we be filming with Bob in his home with his son and primary carer Jesse, but we were sharing a family space, there would be dinners and breakfasts.

I think a lot of that remained unknown until we landed. Given that he had only had seven days left, we quickly realised from the way in which Bob was experiencing time and each day it was clear that there was an intensified and accelerated need for intimacy and connection with the people that he met around him, whether it was a conversation with a woman at a diner, or with this film crew suddenly arriving from Australia. There's a scene where he says, "Welcome to the family." To give you an indication of how rapid this acclimatisation [was], Bob said that 10 hours after meeting us; it felt like really being absorbed into his family. The crew and I needed to debrief each day and catch up with the intensity of how much was occurring.

INTERVIEW | AMIEL COURTIN-WILSON

Funnily enough, because Bob had instigated the project, and he had been in management for much of his life, he was an amazing second producer. He would gather the crew at the end of the shooting day, and ask us a series of questions, what we thought went well, and what we thought we could do better. He would critique us in terms of the questions I was asking. In that sense, he was leading the way, and we were just trying to be as malleable and as sensitive as we could.

That's a wonderful way of leading into discussing Bob's legacy. For many viewers, we're going to get to know Bob through the prism of his death, rather than the life that he lived. There are moments where he talks about what he's done in the past, but I'm curious about what kind of discussions you had with Bob and his family about making sure that his life resonated through this story, so he wasn't just defined by his death.

AC-W: I agree with medically assisted dying legislation. [I] didn't have any former personal experience with that in my family or with friends, but at the same time, it was important for us that we weren't going there to make an advocacy film. We weren't looking to make an overly didactic study of the American healthcare system or shifts in legislation.

From the first phone call with Bob, he struck me as being uniquely archetypal in and of a place and a generation, an American person of a certain age. His experiences in popular culture are a testament to that. Going to Woodstock at 14, being around the punk scene and in New York jamming with the Ramones in Queens in high school. It was important that we create a portrait of Bob that was a celebration of his unique electric energy, and his drive.

There's a remarkable story that his ex-wife told that isn't in the film that sums up Bob's obsessive optimism, vision, and verve. He was obsessed with owning a boat, he loved sailing. He decided in his 40s to build a boat inside his apartment. So, he built this small yacht that took up the entire apartment. It could not be taken out of the apartment, because he hadn't thought that far ahead. There were a lot of similarities in that story of someone who had made mistakes, had regrets, taken some wrong turns with relationships and certain family members, and certainly had to do a lot of work to make amends with some of those relationships. In terms of sheer vision and drive, and this zest and appetite for life, I knew that that was something that had to be the governing energy or force behind the film. His death, while it shapes every frame of the film, the outcome of those seven days was wanting to do it in a way that could allow an audience to be with him and to grow to love him in the 85 minutes prior.

MAN ON EARTH

How does the involvement of Bob's family and friends play into the editing process of the film?

AC-W: I hadn't encountered such a high-pressure [shoot before]. The first call with Bob and Jesse, who was on the initial part of the call, was three weeks out from when we landed; everything was happening very quickly. Jesse, who's a wonderful human being, was understandably sceptical of a group of strangers arriving at his home for this monumental and personal experience. We quickly negotiated a situation whereby the usual release forms wouldn't be signed by anyone until [the end]. We would bring an editor to the location and cut as much as we possibly could for Bob to watch the night before he died, which we did. We worked with an amazing Romanian editor who came to Aberdeen and worked with us because she believed in the project, and we were able to show Bob a 40-minute assembly of material. We returned a year later to show Jesse a two-hour rough cut of the film.

It was only at that point that a release was signed. While it's not the most pragmatic or practical thing from a producer's standpoint, there was no other way that it would proceed, and nor would I feel comfortable doing it any other way.

I must say, sitting next to Jesse at his home, 12 months after Bob had died, I don't think I've sweated so much until the credits rolled on that rough cut. Thankfully, Jesse was unbelievably generous and understanding, and so we proceeded with the traditional funding route from that point forward. We were invited to participate in spreading Bob's ashes as part of that trip, which is a testament to how close we became over the seven days of filming. That wasn't filmed and was not part of the story.

How did you change as a creative person during this process?

AC-W: I had been very interested in this topic prior to shooting. [I] had lost family members and seen people around me be maybe not as prepared in terms of developing a framework for the grieving process. In a secular context, that lack of framework and that lack of ritual in the lead-up to and in the aftermath of the death of a loved one hit me very hard. That was the genesis for the *Traces* project, and after that, *Man on Earth*. [I was] looking for a way to look at death in as honest and as direct a way as possible.

I'd seen other documentaries that deal with this subject matter or with death on screen, and they tended to maybe sit in a different bandwidth than our film. They either had a respectful distance at the moment of death, which I understand entirely, or a film like *Mrs. Fang* (2017) the Wang Bing documentary [which] is a far starker and graphic, confronting portrayal of death.

INTERVIEW | AMIEL COURTIN-WILSON

I was looking to find a way to navigate a film that was compassionate and intimate, yet also unflinching and didn't shy away from these very raw, almost animal-like emotions that occurred in those times.

To be honest with you, I probably underestimated the impact the film would have on me, and I knew the film would have a profound impact. Bob had wanted us to make this film, and part of his classic 'New York salesman' approach was it needed to be seen by as many people as it possible. I hadn't realised how much pressure I put on myself to make this film and bring it to the world in a way that was befitting of Bob's memory. We screened the film for the first time in the UK at the Sheffield Documentary Festival, and I think there was a delayed grieving process that occurred. In some ways, it was like seeing my friend die for the first time on screen, in a room full of strangers in the cinema. That was an unexpected emotional wave to crash on you but in a cathartic, good way.

To be perfectly honest, this film, in some ways, is five years in the making, including the long research process. The way it's changed me is I'm 43, there are only so many films you can make in a lifetime. I think it's distilled and refined my approach to the remaining stories I want to tell. One of the touchstones for me, throughout all my films, is Werner Herzog's quote, "We must create new images or perish." That resonates with me even more now because I feel like if a work isn't born of real urgency, then maybe you need to question why it is you're pursuing that particular endeavour.

There is a network of Australian creatives who overlap; James Vaughan, Alena Lodkina, and Sophie Hyde. You have become a mentor to a lot of Australian filmmakers. Does that mentality of the limited number of stories we can tell feed into how you [support] these filmmakers in Australia?

AC-W: That's very kind of you to say. The interesting thing about James Vaughan and Alena Lodkina, I met them almost 12 years ago now, and they were both unbelievably fully formed artists, amazingly sophisticated and unique, uncompromising; dare I say, visionary folk. I think the help that I, if any, gave them was a framework for being able to work outside the funding system, or how to navigate a way to tell your stories in an uncompromising way, and utilise the system we have here while not compromising your work. Certainly, James and Alena bearing witness to that, they helped us release *Hail* (2011) [theatrically]. They were working with us at that point, I was living with them in Melbourne around that time. James came with us while we shot *Ruin* (2013).

I think in some ways, it's about a philosophy of thinking of filmmakers in this country as a community rather than an industry. Trying to de-silo the various factions, not only within film but also within creative disciplines.

MAN ON EARTH

I still feel that there should be a much higher level of discourse and more interaction between the arts, visual arts community, the film community, dance, and music; there are so many fascinating conversations to be had. I would hope, if nothing else, that it was a philosophy of camaraderie and family and good times.

Can you talk about audience reach and the relationship between how people engage with Australian films?

AC-W: I don't think about making an Australian film for an international [audience] or making any film for any audience. I've been thinking a lot about the fact that government film funding [at a federal level] has existed now for almost 50 years. The cumulative impact that that has had on multiple generations of filmmakers, and maybe buying into the bureaucratic and reductive [element that comes with that] and coming back to this idea of the silos between visual arts and film, as a result of that, maybe as Australians, we're not seeing ourselves in as positive a light as we could. The good old cultural cringe is still looming in that regard.

[I grew up with] the classic experience of being 10 years old and turning on SBS at midnight on a Saturday and seeing a film I had no idea as to what it was. One of the biggest problems is the distribution of films, and this idea that a general audience won't appreciate a whole slew of types of films, where again and again, in screenings, whether it's showing *Hail* to a group of ex-prison inmates or people who wouldn't usually get to see an arthouse film and yet [are] moved and totally engaged. That's also a huge disconnect that I would love to rally to try to fight.

Most audiences aren't aware of what's available to them two or three more clicks away online, let alone at our local arthouse cinemas, and I feel as though it starts this very dangerous ouroboros-like logic that continues to feed audience-friendly material, films, television and otherwise. People are smarter and more curious and have far more complex tastes than they're given credit for. I think we should be combating the dumbing down of the media landscape at every turn.

Watching Man on Earth and getting to experience the way that The Animals House of the Rising Sun is recontextualised in it is powerful. How do you feel about that song and the energy that it creates?

AC-W: Just thinking about the song makes [my] hair stand up on end. I remember being 13 years old and going to a party, there was a jukebox there, and it had that song on repeat all night. I grew up listening to it so much around the house. The fact that it came on randomly when Jesse told the Alexa algorithm to "Play 60s Rock" at that particular moment, and for Jesse to know that about his dad for that song to come on, and then for Bob to take his last breath literally at the climax of the organ solo, is unbelievably powerful. There's a moment where the camera is noticeably moved by Jacqueline's heaving sobbing. I looked over to Steve Bond and he was managing to use his shirt as a tissue while booming because he was also in a state, beside himself.

What can you say about that? It's just a beautiful convergence. I can't think of a more perfect song really for the way Bob lived his life and how he felt about some of the decisions he made. There's this very searing, melancholy coupled with this locomotive strength and drive.

I'm grateful that these stories are being told, that fight for the right to die has been hard fought over the years.

AC-W: I'm unbelievably happy that audiences have come away from the screenings with a shared feeling of this idea of wanting to up the ante of the urgency with which they live. As several audience members have said, "Once I stop weeping, I need to call my parents, my wife, my kids." It is a film about mortality. Having been raised Buddhist, meditating on death every day, every seventh Mallah bead is a carved skull, so the idea of death being imminent, and making that – not in a morose way – part of your life is the thing that gives life its charge. I would hope if the film can contribute to that in some minuscule way, then that's remarkable.

The cut between when Bob's dying and seeing him standing in the doorway and stepping back, and then cutting back to the bed broke me. That edit is one I'm going to hold with me for a very long time.

AC-W: That means so much, man. I must admit, it does throw some people, which is kind of crazy to me, but I'm so glad that you said that because it's one of the edits that was in the very first assembly and I can't even tell you how it happens. It was one of those truly subconscious edits I tried super early, and it just stuck. I'm very glad you said that.

PETROL

95 mins
Director: *Alena Lodkina*
Writer: *Alena Lodkina*
Cast: *Hannah Lynch, Nathalie Morris, Daniel Frederiksen, Emmett Aldred, Daniel Aloiso, Inga Romantsova, Alex Menglet, Natalia Novikova, Hugh Fraser, Kit Brady-Brown, Jia Jia Chen, Brittany D'Argaville, Susan Godfrey, Blu Jay, Matthew Linde*
Producer: *Kate Laurie*
Score: *Raven Mahon, Mikey Young*
Cinematography: *Michael Latham*
Editing: *Luca Cappelli*

REVIEW
ANDREW F. PEIRCE

Alena Lodkina's second feature *Petrol* is a film that has been referred to by critics and film festivals as a riff on the work of Jacques Rivette[1] to 'the lovechild of *Round the Twist* and David Lynch'[2], both of which would suggest a film that is at once a homage or a pastiche, instead of being its own fully formed idea. Yet, allusions to these existing artists sits at the core of *Petrol* as Lodkina playfully tells the story of film student Eva (Nathalie Morris) and the enigmatic Melbourne artist Mia (Hannah Lynch). By chance and accident, the two swirl into each other's orbit; Eva is capturing ambient noise by the ocean when she stumbles upon Mia made up as a vampire, looming over her prey, laughing. One is performing, the other is absorbing the art of the world around her, letting it enrich her mind and sway her creative path forward.

It's not just *Celine and Julie Go Boating* (1974) or the comic timing of Bronson Twist that hovers in the air of *Petrol* as its influences stretch towards the literary in the form of Dostoevsky. Eva's family is from Russia, and when she's not setting the foundations for her filmic journey, she's assisting her mother with familial duties. The two blend in the bones of Eva's experimental documentary which conjures a vision of an older Russian woman (Becky Voskoboinik) and leads her university lecturer to ponder whether her film is less about the older woman and more of a personal piece.

Eva's creative life is pulled into the realm of Mia's distanced demeanour when she has a chance sighting of Mia walking in the back streets of Melbourne. Eva notices Mia drop a necklace, and like Alice and the intrigue of the white rabbit, Eva tumbles into Mia's wonderland as she seeks to return the necklace. The throb of bass spills out of an open-door apartment party, acting as an open invitation for Eva and leading her to Mia. This enticing entrance leads Eva into a bond that permeates her life as Mia offers up a spare room in her apartment for Eva to live in, giving fertile soil for Eva's profound curiosity and often one-sided passion for the friendship to flourish.

Aspects of magical realism arise throughout *Petrol*, with doppelgangers and ghosts appearing alongside other mystical elements. As Eva and Mia get to know each other on a beach walk, Mia laughs and smiles, then winks

PETROL

a full picnic spread into existence on the sand. Initially, *Petrol* feels like it will sway into thriller territory as Mia's interest in Eva's presence and companionship sways from apathetic ambivalence to playful enthusiasm, but Lodkina strikes a tonal balance of levity and playfulness that enriches the experience rather than adhering to any expected genre-stylings.

To this viewer, *Petrol* is a film full of wandering narrative threads that overlap and occasionally fray away from one another, offering untethered endings for the viewer to hold onto so they can tease out their own meaning of what they're viewing. *Petrol* is a self-reflective film and it's one that frequently calls attention to its surrealism; as Eva is editing her film, a fellow student appears, mentioning that they had watched Steven Spielberg's *Catch Me If You Can*, to which Eva notes that she'd had a dream about Leonardo DiCaprio the night before. That film tells the story of a youthful man who manages to shapeshift himself out of the reach of a potential captor. Its subtext becomes *Petrol*'s text.

Within many of the emerging filmmakers in Melbourne and Sydney, such as *Friends of Mine* (2022) director Andréas Giannopoulos (briefly appearing as a partygoer in the film), there is a tendency to craft films that skew towards the European, and as such, they are often labelled as 'intellectual', and therefore not audience friendly. In conversation with Alena, I raised the notion that *Petrol* actively encourages audiences to engage with intellectual art in a way that Australian audiences have often been perceived as rejecting outright. I note that outside of film enthusiast circles, 'intellectual' cinema is incorrectly seen as one of the 'snobbier' stylings of cinema as if you need a philosophy degree to understand the basic context of a narrative.

Alena notes, "Even in the writing and developing of the film, I was aware that having two protagonists who are young women and who are aspiring artists, [or] aspiring intellectuals you might say, is going to be a tricky sell. And many people will see it as – probably the word you're looking for – pretentious. It's something I had to grapple with because nobody wants to be as pretentious or snobbish, but I also think it's really important to see young characters with these aspirations."

In that regard, *Petrol* is a repudiation of the 'turn off your brain' mindset that has permeated throughout cinema history as a way for audiences to engage with the films they're watching. There is, at times, an inferred distinction between what we call 'entertainment' and 'art', as if the two must be kept separate and cannot be one and the same thing. Just because a film can provoke a marathon of thoughts and ideas in the viewer's mind does not mean that it is cordoned off from also being entertaining. A late high tea sequence in *Petrol* is a notably atypical entertaining moment, full of a brightness that helps usher in the film's close with a light energy that amplifies that encouragingly intellectual vibe that Lodkina has created.

Alena continues, "My way of dealing with it in my film was being playful. [These are] people who feel really strongly about something, they have these ambitions, they have pretentiousness as well, and sometimes they sound ridiculous and sometimes they don't know what they're talking about, but the crux is in their desire and their pursuit of something."

It's at this point that I should note to the readers out there that, at the time of writing, I'm yet to stumble into the world of Jacques Rivette, nor have I engaged with the work of Éric Rohmer, another European filmmaker whose work has so distinctly influenced many of the East Coast filmmakers in Australia. Just like the many countries that get thrust under the banner of 'European cinema', Australian filmmakers and filmgoers are not one homogenous entity. We react to what is made available to us, and as such, the film scenes within Sydney and Melbourne are frequently catered for with retrospective screenings of these titans of European cinema. For students who attend film schools such as AFTRS, the library of available films is broad, with a deep catalogue of European cinema available at their fingertips. The impact of this kind of filmic education and availability of European cinema can be seen in the output of filmmakers like Alena Lodkina and James Vaughan.

This is not to discount other Australian cities where flourishing film appreciation movements regularly hold screenings of American or Asian films. For a growing film culture to exist, there needs to be an avenue for audiences, students of cinema, and filmmakers to view, engage with, and learn from the deep history of cinema. While physical media can assist with bringing the work of Rivette or Rohmer into your home and streaming services like MUBI or the Criterion Channel (accessed via a VPN) can provide entry to the varied film movements through history, these domestic experiences lack the ability to conjure deep thoughts that may arise from communal conversations with fellow cinemagoers after a screening. These communal experiences are shifting across the nation, with organisations like Black Maria Film Collective in Perth, Moviejuice in Adelaide, Cinema Reborn in Sydney, Two Bit Movie Club in Brisbane, and Unknown Pleasures & Cinemaniacs in Melbourne, each engaging in their own form of retrospective screenings, and in turn, bringing cultural conversation starters to film societies.

Alena talks about how *Petrol* isn't "a story about someone making it as a filmmaker or self-eventuating," but rather "someone on a search [for the self]." Alena points to a scene where Eva is at her computer writing as one of the themes within *Petrol*, "It's about being in the process [of writing or making art] and getting lost in a world of ideas, a world of imagination and inner exploration. That is what art really is."

Yet, within Australia, the manner that films, and by extension, art, are made is often one that comes from a world of privilege or financial security. While the 'starving artist' is a figure that still exists in society, the mere concept of making a film in Australia is one that most artists need to put serious consideration into. Can they actually afford to make a film without stifling their financial future?

PETROL

Petrol isn't a film that covers that discussion, with a major element of the story focusing on film students who often have access to equipment and the support of fellow filmmakers to create films, bringing forth a reduced financial commitment, but it is a notion that hangs in Alena's mind: "It's really unfortunate that conversations about class and pretension come in. Unfortunately, I think it is a bit of an issue in Australia, that 'tall poppy' thing and dismissing things that are cultural as pretentious and European, 'it's not us.' We all kind of pretend that we're 'battlers' who are beyond all these pretentious things, but the reality is that this is a highly wealthy country that is in search of a dialogue about its identity, and culture and art are so important in this respect."

In conversation with ABC film critic Jason Di Rosso[3], Alena notes the difference between audience reception around the world, saying: "Overseas, I think that people don't ask as many questions about the portrayal of Melbourne and shooting in Melbourne and the practical challenges that come with that, they're more interested in the story and the characters and the stylistic choices, the inspirations for the film and things like that. There, people watch the film at a remove, whereas here, everyone is relating it to themselves, maybe."

While Australia is a broad country, with a land size that would cover many of the European countries that make up the filmic identity known as 'European cinema' (a nomenclature that belies just how varied and diverse that grouping of cinema truly is), it's also a country that is yet to truly reconcile with just how culturally diverse we are as a nation. I'm not just talking about its multicultural population or the 60,000 years of continuous First Nations culture that exists in and on this land, but rather how different each city is from one another on a purely basic level.

We may speak with a similar accent, but the truth is that we are a culturally divided nation looking for something to adhere to. To get reductive for a moment, if a Perthian were to go to Melbourne and order a 'long mac topped up,' they'd likely be met with a strange look and laughed out of the café. Additionally, the social pressures of day-to-day life in Sydney and Melbourne are vastly different than those of Perth; a reality that was made abundantly clear as Melbourne endured months of COVID lockdown while Perth remained socially free. But it's not just about how we drink our coffee, or what we call a potato cake or togs, it's about having respect and appreciation for art and artists, and that's something that I fear that Australia as a whole has not truly come to grips with.

When COVID shut down music venues, cinemas, and art galleries, the level of antagonism directed toward artists who were asking for financial support was stifling. As a nation, we proudly consume and engage with films and TV on a mass level, yet for some reason we fail to see the career of being an artist or a filmmaker as a genuine possibility. The word 'hobby' is thrown around a lot, a term that's morphed into the hyper-capitalis-

REVIEW | ANDREW F. PEIRCE

tic phrase 'side-gig,' both of which suggest a lack of respect for artists and their art.

Smothering that creative drive can be a toxic and painful experience, sometimes leading to destructive behaviour or cause mental anguish. In a pivotal scene midway through *Petrol*, Mia, hanging from the ceiling in a harness, presents her performance art to a crowd full of seemingly disinterested people. She observes the crowd as they stare, disinterestedly, back at her. At the bar, Mia is despondent, talking to Eva about how "Two women said it was self-indulgent or narcissistic." Eva, ever wanting to be a good friend, says "They don't know what they're talking about." It's clear from what we see in Mia's performance art that she goes to a place in her mind while it's happening that she can only reach through engaging with her art, and that's a state of mind that is driven by a passion for her craft.

Alena talked about the decision to make *Petrol* in relation to that conversation dialogue about Australia's identity, "I was like 'fuck it,' I'm gonna make a film about these artists, and everyone's going to say that it's pretentious, but I don't care because I feel really passionate about this."

But *Petrol* is not a film that Alena has made exclusively for herself, with the film carrying that invitational tone that aims to include audiences, rather than making them feel out of depth by the themes or narrative machinations. "Maybe not everyone has read Dostoevsky, but everyone has thought about expression and imagination. Everyone was once a child and played games and imagined things. It's in all of us, that's all part of our lives. I see art as this arena of play and discovery, more than anything else," Alena said.

For Alena, it was important that audiences didn't feel excluded by the film, "Because we're so used to watching films that offer us a resolution, I think that watching a film that is extremely open-ended can provoke feelings of discomfort and frustration and [being] shut out. And I very much empathise with that kind of experience. As a filmmaker, I was grappling with how to make a film that's open-ended but doesn't alienate audiences or make them feel silly or stupid or like they don't understand something. Because in truth, there's nothing to understand.

"If somebody feels with *Petrol*, 'Oh I didn't quite understand the film,' I think it's kind of the point. The themes are not the things that you can really understand completely, because the film is about things that are mysterious and will not be resolved in our lifetime. Mysterious connections between people and trying to understand yourself and others, things that don't have easy conclusions; so, it is just throwing ideas on the table, and it is what you make of it.

"I guess it asks you in a way to be a creative viewer. That may be unpleasant for some, but hopefully, it can also empower others to feel part of the process and come on a journey a little bit. That's a choice you make, not to tell people but to think but offer them ideas that they might respond to in their own way."

PETROL

I imagine this is where many are pulling that David Lynch comparison for *Petrol* from, this notion of no answers, just ideas. For me, outside of a late karaoke scene where Mia sings to an audience, the notion of *Petrol* being Lynchian is unfounded. Instead, I found myself thinking of the work of Apichatpong Weerasethakul, a filmmaker who is fascinated by sleep, saying, "It's a place where you can just be in this state or narrative, and that's when you open up to all kinds of connections and possibilities." Weerasethakul is a filmmaker who extends an invitation to his audience and asks them to take a journey in the shape of the ideas and imagery that linger in their mind after the film is long over.

It's a kind and considerate mindset for a filmmaker to have when they engage with their audience, extending an invitation to hold onto an idea and roll it over in their mind as they discover the personal connection with it. Additionally, it's comforting to see a filmmaker eagerly engage in the conversation about art and the artists who bring it to life in their own work in the way that Alena has done with *Petrol*. And even though the comparisons to Rivette or Lynch may be apt for this work, it's clear that there is a distinct vision from Lodkina going forward, making her one of the most vital Australian filmmakers working right now.

INTERVIEW
WRITER & DIRECTOR
ALENA LODKINA

Alena Lodkina's second feature film *Petrol* had its domestic launch at the Melbourne International Film Festival alongside a wealth of other Australian films that presented the Melbournian landscape on film. It tells the story of Eva (Nathalie Morris), an emerging filmmaker who encounters the enigmatic Mia (Hannah Lynch) while she is scouting for locations. Throughout the film, the two flow in and out of each other's lives, influencing, shaping, and changing each other in tense, curious, and playful ways, collectively orbiting the world of Melbourne art, ultimately questioning relationships with reality and fiction. At times, *Petrol* is charming and sweet, leaning into a whimsical view of the world, only to have characters pulled out of that mood and into the reality of the world around them.

When *Petrol* screened at the New York Film Festival in 2023, film critic Richard Brody wrote a deeply considered review about the film, closing his piece saying, "I'm impatient for whatever Lodkina will do next." That's a sentiment I wholeheartedly agree with.

This interview was recorded by Andrew F. Peirce in June 2022 & May 2023

Petrol is different to Strange Colours, but it's quite beautiful.

Alena Lodkina: Thank you. I'm curious for those who have seen *Strange Colours* how *Petrol* will come across. I think they are different, but they're also a little bit similar in some ways. Some people have told me they see so many similarities between the two.

I see similarities. These two characters are effectively looking for their place in the world, some kind of purpose or connection or realisation of who they are. In Strange Colours that's with her dad and trying to discover herself in that, and then in Petrol it's with a stranger who she gets to know and builds a relationship and friendship with. It's this bal-

PETROL

ance of darkness and then lightness and playfulness. How long did you have this idea rolling around in your mind?

AL: It's been so long. Probably some seeds of the story, the kind of world and the characters were in my mind even before *Strange Colours* or around that time. Whatever random notes [I wrote] were probably before I even wrote the script for *Strange Colours*. So, it's been a long, long stewing process for *Petrol*. The original document with the notes that I started on my computer was called *Petrol*, so I just kind of stuck with that name because I've always liked it. And it had this kind of sentimental value for me as well.

After *Strange Colours*, I almost immediately started working on the script, but it took ages and went through different iterations. When I started writing, I didn't know what kind of shape the story would take. I just knew how it would start and who the characters were. It's always similar for me starting on a project, I have to have a feeling that I have to hold on to. Then the story kind of shapes itself. I was writing the script for at least three years. We finally got the film funded, amazingly, early last year, and we were in production mid-last year. It's crazy, I can't believe I made a second film. It's such a huge challenge in Australia to get your second film funded.

You're part of a group of people who work together and in the orbit of one another alongside Amiel Courtin-Wilson. Is he a bit of a mentor for you?

AL: Yes. I guess it's relevant to say because this film is set in Melbourne, and it's like a real Melbourne film. I've been living there for ten years, if not more. I moved to Melbourne originally, because I had met Amiel, and I just graduated from uni. I came across his film *Hail*, and I thought that looked amazing. He was working in this kind of space that was exactly what I was interested in, which was working with non-professional actors and blending different stylistic documentary and non-documentary. I don't know what you would describe that as, I guess people used to use the word hybrid a lot, which I think is not used as much anymore. But this new realist kind of space.

I was like, "I need to meet this guy." I just reached out to him, and he said, "Oh, we have this big warehouse in Melbourne, you can intern. I always need collaborators [and] people to do stuff." And that just sounded great. I moved to Melbourne and ended up meeting all these people who were working with him, there was this kind of orbit around him. I also worked on his film *The Silent Eye*. I edited that actually, which was a cool experience going to New York and working on the edit and meeting Cecil Taylor and getting to know a little bit more about how Amiel works. He's been a friend and an important figure for me.

INTERVIEW | ALENA LODKINA

Is there an autobiographical tone or form to Petrol?

AL: It's a really obvious question, in a good way. In a way, it's obviously autobiographical, the similarities between the character and me are clearly there. But in reality, it's more of a personal film, rather than autobiographical. The whole story is completely fictional, but it comes from personal observations and experiences. My model for that, working with a character who's similar to you, was [that] when I was writing the script, I was reading Marcel Proust's *In Search of Lost Time*, and I really love the way that that work is so obviously his wife and his world, but it's not. The characters are, in fact, completely different to him. It is almost like an autobiography, but it's not.

I'm interested in how you can take from your experience of life, and yet create a work of fiction. I was never interested in telling my story, the migrant story or even the filmmakers' story. It's not even that. It's just the film happens to be fed by intimate and personal observations of life. The more intimate and personal aspects of the film are really tiny things like objects or some insignificant phrase that was borrowed from an overheard conversation.

The way that I was writing the film was not so much pulled from diaries, but more a diaristic process, in that I would take notes of things I've seen. I guess, [that's] the way that many writers work, probably without us knowing, that you're just kind of constantly taking notes about things you observe. Then, somehow, they enter the story, but not necessarily in the way that you think they would.

That leads into how the film plays with the notion of what film can be. Our first introduction to [the personality of the film] is the font. Can you talk about the choice of that font?

AL: We did work with a designer [and] I had a very clear [idea of] the colour. I really knew what I wanted. I guess I just love those kinds of simple big fonts in films that are classic in some way, but then also have a bit of an eighties vibe. Maybe I was watching some late seventies Brian DePalma and eighties Michael Mann films at the time. They don't use those kinds of fonts, [but] something about the style, it was like a little bit of eighties genre. I wanted to stylise the film like that at the start, so you would know that it's not a realist film. That it has an element of genre, but it's playing with genre. I love that blue colour.

The slight eighties genre influence, which is very indirect, [in that] we use a zoom lens. I had great fun having a zoom lens in the film. It was an actual eighties zoom lens, and that creates that feel that is a little bit out of time. I think I wanted to create that juncture in the film between realism and genre, which is really at the heart of the themes of the film, reality and imagination and art and life and the thing that repeats itself in various aspects of the film. To open with a very contemplative, naturalistic landscape, and then to have a stylised font just seemed really fun to me.

A lot of the elements of the film call attention to themselves. They force you to consider them. For example, I was conscious of the sound being recorded. It's interesting you mention de Palma because I got that feeling of Blow Out, where we're being made aware of what sound does to us, and how we pay attention to sound and especially choosing what sound to put in there. How did you write the sound design in the script?

AL: I was lucky enough to work with a really great sound recordist, Steve Bond. I think that the sound was a big part of the script because I remember even when Steve read the script, he was like, "This is gonna be really fun for me." I was like, "Yes, I'm glad you say that." Especially in that opening scene when it's playing with the subjective and objective sound. On set and in post I just had a great sound team. I'm very fortunate to work with Livia Ruzic who's the sound designer who did *Strange Colours*, and she did some of my short films as well. She's an iconic Australian sound designer. And our mixer Keith [Thomas]; they're just a great team.

It was so exciting because I wanted to create a world that was a little bit dissonant and I think that the sound helps because it kind of enters your experience as a viewer on a different, sometimes unconscious, level, but it can make you feel the scene in a really powerful, profound way.

We had a great challenge with the sound on set because, of course, this might sound naive, because I always think that "It'll be fine," but it's really difficult to shoot a film in the city. This is something I guess I didn't think about after *Strange Colours* because *Strange Colours* was such a dream. After all, we were in the middle of nowhere. The only problem we had was a gennie going somewhere in the background that was noisy, and we'd have to go ask them to turn it off. But that was basically it. In Melbourne, it's impossible. There's so much sound interference. It was so hard. We lost time having to pause because there's always some construction going on, something happening. Recording sound by the water is rough. The scene in Port Melbourne was a nightmare to record sound because there was traffic, water, and it was really windy in the winter. Somehow Steve managed to record sound, it's a question for him how he pulls it off.

Then in post-production, they created something really special. With Livia, she's got this amazing library of sounds that she uses. We always try to pull authentic sounds from places and create the real feeling of a place with

INTERVIEW | ALENA LODKINA

familiar sounds. Those little sounds like the beep at the traffic crossing, or particular Melbourne winds, I think they have a particular sound, and birds from the place.

It was something in the script. I talked to everyone about it, even in pre-production, that I wanted the sounds of construction and that sound of a progressive city to be a real part of the film, airplanes, a lot of construction, traffic. The sound has this slightly dirty feel. That again partially plays with inducing that kind of anxiety, even though you don't see anything particularly menacing, but there's a sense of anxiety, which is part of living in the city. Then it becomes true to living in the city, especially when you start recording sound and you realise how noisy and oppressive the sound is.

Then playing with a genre because a lot of elements, a lot of sounds of construction and airplanes sound like sounds from horror films, those kinds of industrial bones that we know from industrial music or noise music. I was interested in how that could enter a film that's not that and yet play with you on a different level. That was really fun and interesting.

You're working with the great cinematographer Michael Latham. He makes the screen feel so organic and lived in. What did you shoot on, and what's it like working with Michael?

AL: I'm very lucky to work with Michael. He shoots on an ARRI Alexa but with older lenses. When we started the conversation, I was like, "I want to use a zoom lens," and he was like, "Okay", and then he ordered this cool eighties lens, and said "I'm pretty sure Tarkovsky would have shot on this." Not that exact one, but that kind of lens. That was an exciting thing. It's still in my bedroom lying somewhere because, at the end, he was like, "I'm probably never gonna use this again, it's really heavy."

It was a real challenge to work with that lens, because it's not very fast, so you have to use a lot of light. Neither of us had worked with this lens before, so there was a lot of figuring things out on a practical level. I had to think ahead about what lens I wanted to use, and if we were going to use the zoom. Obviously, we were using primes [a fixed focal length lens], but if we were to go on zoom, it would be a whole new lighting setup, which would chew up time. It was hard to know ahead.

I think all that contributed to this slightly magical feel of the film. It's something that I talked to him about how to create. I wanted the film to be romantic, and the universe to be romantic, even though it's sort of urban and the life that's portrayed is quite melancholy and hard, [with] the kind of industrial sounds we just talked about, and that feeling of the city. But

PETROL

I wanted it to be beautiful and romantic and noirish in the way that Melbourne comes across. It was a real obsession of mine to create that on screen.

Michael went out and found the filters and little tricks that he used to create that kind of softness, that kind of effect of being soft around the edges you see more of that on film, and it's really hard to create that on a digital camera. CJ Dobson, who graded the film, also worked to create that look, to draw that look out. They did a marvellous job.

Something I think that's interesting with Michael, and on this film, you really see it, [is] he's not afraid to expose a scene like maybe any other commercial cinematographer would do. There's a sense of darkness, and it's always kind of on the edge of what's acceptable exposure. I think it's bold and cool. I guess the traditional thing to do would be like, let's overexpose it, and expose it really well because then you can grade it down. The film is shadowy, it's like this world of shadows and shadow play, and you can't always make out what you're seeing. Michael wasn't afraid of that. Sometimes, like in the scene in Flagstaff Gardens for instance, in the park at night, we barely had lights, he was just shooting with what was there in the park.

There is some beautiful dialogue here that sways between realism and fantasy. The line, "I fall in love all the time. It's just not with a real person," is glorious. Reading into it with the view of an artist and their art, and especially as somebody who consumes films, art and books, it feels like that's my relationship with it, that I'm falling in love with something that's not human. Is that kind of what you were aiming for?

AL: I think that's a wonderful observation and quite acute. I didn't even really think about that particular line, because it just felt organic to the conversation that they were having. But I think that it does capture something about those themes we were just talking about, art and life, reality and imagination, and the line at the edge of reality. I think that a lot of the melancholy in the film comes from this.

Some people have asked, "Is Mia real?" To me, she's definitely real. To me, the feeling of unreality comes from something that's part of just any relationship or being a person to start with, which is that you can't quite ever have a full grasp of reality. Just like those ancient philosophical problems, you don't really know what's outside of you, and you're very limited in your perception. There's a kind of melancholy in realising that even the people you get really close to, you can't know completely. Especially in the relationship that's explored in the film, it's messy, because so much of what you know about the other person is just you. [It] is your own imagination, or what you imagined about them. I think that's common, it's kind of the core of human relationships.

INTERVIEW | ALENA LODKINA

As you say, that relates to art and falling in love with art, which is such a big part of their bond in that world and being in this world of ideas and images and beauty and aesthetics and talking about those things. They are both artistic, romantic people who are very prone to getting confused. So, I think that's kind of what the film is really about, actually. That line of where you end and something else begins, that's very hard to grasp. That's at the root of all the confusion and disorientation in the film in general, and the style of the film and the dialogue of the film.

Strange Colours was such an intimately Australian story, and this one is very Melbournian. Is the idea of Australia something that you're interested in exploring as a filmmaker?

AL: I feel like it's probably fair to say that in this country we've never had a strong cinematic identity. We have a lot of brilliant filmmakers and even little pockets of movements, but nothing like Italian neo-realism or something like this. It's kind of more sporadic and dispersed. And now I think there's a great thirst to create something.

James, who made *Friends and Strangers*, is a really good friend of mine, so it feels like we all know each other and have conversations about films, so it feels like something. These are all different films, and even different genres and completely different styles, but I think that what unites us is that we all want to do something – I don't know how to put it politely – that appeals to the rest of the world. Maybe there's a feeling that Australian cinema has been a little bit insular [since] when I've been coming of age as a filmmaker. And we all want to be part of the global conversation about culture. And so, I think that we're all drawing influences from Europe and Asian cinema or whatever. Everyone has their own things to say about it, but I think that unites us that there's this thirst to create something that will be shown at festivals around the world and will be interesting, but at the same time, be very Australian.

How important is it to receive a review like the one Richard Brody wrote for The New Yorker?

AL: It's interesting. I often think about the relationship between the artist and the critic. From one perspective, I love reading film and literary criticism, and I admire critics, but from another perspective, as a filmmaker, because your work gets all kinds of reviews, the good and the bad, you have to take everything with a grain of salt. You have to learn to distance yourself from what is said about your work in the public domain. At the end of the day, you should be your own hardest judge and your kindest judge at the same time.

PETROL

Opinions are so unpredictable and circumstantial. There's something really inexplicable about how a work is received. It happens all the time where we see things being raved about, but then forgotten, and on the other hand being lambasted and then rediscovered a few years later. The trouble is that in the moment, it's very difficult to make out what to think of works.

I really struggle with this, because at the same time, I'm not gonna hide the fact that it was so pleasant to read that review, because I did feel like it spoke to the film. It's a hard thing to talk about, because at the end of the day, you're just a person and if people give you compliments, you get a bit embarrassed, and if they criticise you, you get upset and angry.

It's the same thing as a filmmaker. You have to try to be Zen about it all. I think at the end of the day, you have to take praise with a grain of salt, because by the same logic, if you take people who make fun of your film or are being really critical and you think it's unfair, then you learn to take that with a grain of salt and not take it personally. Take everything with a grain of salt.

Petrol is quite an experiential film, and like the title suggests, there's a reflective fluidity to the work. It changes as it progresses. In rewatching it, I was able to appreciate those aspects more as I knew where the narrative would progress. I'm curious if watching it with different audiences around the world changes how you feel about the film too?

AL: You put the film out into the world, and you kind of have to let go a little bit. I don't watch it anymore. I watched it at Locarno and MIFF, but now I just have to let go. The work acquires its own life. It's very unpredictable, and that's part of the excitement. The great honour of sharing your work with people is the kind of trust you establish with the audiences and it's the trust that they may not respond to it, they may fall in love with it, they may not understand it completely, but then it might grow on them in their own time. I try to take risks with my work, and I want the audience to be able to take risks and to trust the audience to take risks, which might be uncomfortable on both ends, but I think that's part of the excitement of the work, to leave it kind of open and to grow in unpredictable ways.

ENDNOTES

1 An Australian Standout at This Year's New Directors/New Films Series - Alena Lodkina's second feature, "Petrol," explores the metaphysical dimensions of a new friendship. The New Yorker, Richard Brody https://www.newyorker.com/culture/the-front-row/an-australian-standout-at-this-years-new-directorsnew-films-series

2 *Petrol* - MIFF Industry - https://miffindustry.com/premiere-fund-slate/petrol/

3 Two highly acclaimed features: Celine Song's Past Lives + Alena Lodkina's Petrol, The Screen Show, ABC https://www.abc.net.au/listen/programs/the-screen-show/celine-song-past-lives-alena-lodkina-petrol/102692698

MELBOURNE INTERNATIONAL FILM FESTIVAL

INTERVIEW
ARTISTIC DIRECTOR AL COSSAR

The Melbourne International Film Festival (MIFF) launched in 1952, when it was first named the Olinda Film Festival where it was held in the Dandenong Ranges. Over the decades, it's changed into one of the preeminent Southern Hemisphere film festivals with line-ups regularly showcasing over two hundred local and international feature films, documentaries, and shorts.

MIFF celebrated its 70th anniversary in 2022. It was a year that saw the festival emerge from under the COVID restrictions that hampered its in-person attendance, but with those restrictions, it allowed the festival the opportunity to pivot to a wider audience with online screenings that turned MIFF from a localised Melbourne destination event to a national experience.

With this anniversary year, MIFF took the opportunity to showcase its hometown of Melbourne on screen with two major events. The first was the book *Melbourne on Film - Cinemas That Defines Our City*, a critical exploration of the city as showcased on film, written by writers such as Christos Tsiolkas, Shaad D'Souza, Tim Rogers, Judith Lucy, John Safran, and Osman Faruqi. This book worked in unison with an expansive tour of Melbourne on screen throughout the years, spanning from the early days of Australian cinema with films like F.W. Thring's *A Ticket in Tatts* (1934), to Giorgio Mangiamele's *Clay* (1965), to Michael Pattinson's *Moving Out* (1983), to modern films like Alena Lodkina's *Petrol* (2022) and Gus Berger's *The Lost City of Melbourne* (2022).

Guiding the modern festival is Artistic Director Al Cossar. Al has previously worked as the Festival Manager for Flickerfest, as a Programmer and Board Member for the Human Rights Arts and Film Festival, Program Director for the Portable Film Festival, and has worked for ACMI within Public Programs. Prior to these roles, Al was also a broadcast film critic for ABC News Breakfast.

This interview was recorded by Andrew F. Peirce in October 2022 and July 2023

MELBOURNE INTERNATIONAL FILM FESTIVAL

Al commences this interview by reflecting on what that journey out of COVID was like for MIFF.

Al Cossar: There were so many layers as to what our return to cinemas [was going to be]. It was the first festival after three years of COVID disruption. We morphed ourselves in different directions with that mantra of 'meeting audiences where they are,' but this was our first time back within Melbourne Metropolitan cinemas. There was such a huge effort to push us into that place. Plus, the 70th anniversary overlaid that as well.

For us, in terms of thinking about what an anniversary year at this point means to us, a lot of those moments, as wonderful as they can be, can also be quite a navel gazing and quite insular in terms of how you regard yourself and your history and the path to where you are, so we wanted to do something that was themed around the relationship between MIFF as a festival and Melbourne as a city, [where] MIFFs spot [is] as part of the creative heartbeat in the creative history of our city, which we think is one of the most amazing, creative cities in the world. Regardless of whether you see one film at MIFF a year or none, there's an interesting story to be told between MIFF and what it means to the creative and cultural identity of Melbourne.

There were a number of initiatives that we developed from that. One was the Melbourne on film retrospective which included shorts and features. I think it was 42 films in total. Nothing at even at such a big scale can be definitive, but it was a very heartfelt portrait of our city, and its identity on screen right through the history of cinema, and all formats in terms of those iconic and restored works, which are lesser seen and are primed for rediscovery, or discovery for the first time, as well as the artists that you can build and present to audiences around that. That was the other thing about MIFF in 2022, it was back at full scale, at the same time as having something really centralised to celebrate.

Then to create a space for interesting contributions and responses in the format of the *Melbourne on Film* book, and people who are artists or filmmakers or commentators or different creatives who can really expand and provide context and ideas from an academic viewpoint through to more personal essays, to what those things mean to people as well.

We had our XR commission *Night Creatures* by Isobel Knowles and Van Somerwine. The idea of that event was that those 'in between' spaces at the festival could be some of the most enjoyable and definitive. They're what makes MIFF; it's huddling in lines with others in the darkest parts of winter, talking about those films and overhearing what other people are seeing and those kinds of in-between moments. Film festivals are the sum

INTERVIEW | AL COSSAR

totals of the films they screen and the moments that happen in between. *Night Creatures* was a fantastical, imaginative Memory Project in terms of those kinds of spaces, as well.

Then we had something like *Signatures*, which was three specially commissioned programmes, short format original works by incredible artists and filmmakers that we admired. We had taken inspiration from places like the Viennale or Göteborg Film Festival, who had some really untoward and fantastic festival identity work done by Lucrecia Martel; these kinds of ideas that had very little to do with promoting the festival but had a lot to do with articulating the spirit and the personality of what those places were and why they're so interesting. We worked with Justin Kurzel, Ivan Sen and soda jerk, and the brief was to create a response to that moment where an audience and film meet, which was driven by the filmmaker's imagination and response and to that, which MIFF is very much a director's voice film.

Festival Files with the University of Melbourne launched online as a Memory Project for the festival. Then Bright Horizons launched [in 2022], which was the introduction of a major feature film competition. For us, it was a perfect time in a parallel moment to introduce it as part of the 70th anniversary, because you have this moment that you're considering and celebrating your history, but we very much wanted to anchor that in a moment in which we were looking forward, and also doing the opposite of that, and trying to do that in a substantial way. It's a competition where $140,000 is awarded – supported through the State Government's VicScreen – that is geared towards first- and second-time filmmakers, breakthrough cinema with bold and distinct voices straight out of the gates. It's an Australian and international programme, with films screening through Melbourne IMAX, so a maximum cinema scale experience, with a lot of amazing guests from Australia, but also from the States and the Philippines and Costa Rica; an incredible array of artists.

One of our full circle moments was for the jury deliberations on that competition, we went to Olinda, the hall that MIFF was shown at for the very first time in 1952. That was the site of our jury deliberations, which was a bit freezing, but it's also beautiful up there. That was one of those lovely moments where you realise how far something has come.

In terms of stepping back into the world, the 70th was a big piece of the puzzle. It was ingrained right through the programme in a variety of ways. It was a massive amount of work for everyone. It took apart that moment of celebration and looked back in some really special ways. In terms of that Melbourne overlay, one of the other motivations was that we were stepping back into the city after it had been decimated culturally and financially, and hopefully creating something that's big enough and induces that sort of curiosity that brings people back and helps to reactivate and rebuild the excitement, imagination and creativity that comes with so many incredible festivals that run in the city.

Do you have any audience or filmmaker anecdotes about what it meant to see Melbourne on Film in the way that MIFF 70 presented?

AC: Some films were reintroduced through the programme that [has facilitated] additional interest and potentially restoration interest in. Some films had been completely unseen, underseen, or put to the side and aren't a foregrounded part of our cultural memory and bringing some of those back [created a] strong emotional response.

The opening film for the Melbourne on Film strand was *Love and Other Catastrophes* (1996), and there were people seeing it for the first time who loved it. Some people have grown up with those films and the capacity to revisit them from a point of view, but also to think about how their own nostalgia overlays those stories and those vistas of what the city is and how it's used on screen. Something like *A Ticket in Tatts* (1934) is from the incredible imagined past that feels so removed from us, but it's so immediate.

Melbourne is one of the birthplaces of film presentation in Victoria. In terms of IMAX itself, that's something separate and interesting. The way that we use that [is with] films that you would never see on an IMAX screen anywhere else. That is the joy of it. Thomas Wright discussed how IMAX is thought of as a vehicle for action spectacle, and that's what the scale of it is fundamental to, but when you have a different kind of a story that has incredible craft to it and has an emotional weight to it, that works and that connects, and the performances hold up to that level of scale and scrutiny, then the emotional impact of seeing a film on that screen is just as significant. It's something different and untoward and surprising. We had filmmakers attend who saw their films on that screen, and said, "I saw elements of the production design I'd never seen in my film before. I've seen it hundreds of times, but not in that way." That was encouraging to me.

The same with when we used Hoyts Melbourne Central. In some ways, it's an unusual place for MIFF to be, but then the audience acclimatised to what that setting is, and it became something special and unique [with] the films that [took] over that kind of space. I know that people love going to Melbourne Central now because of the technical qualities of the projection. It's an unlikely place to see a Lav Diaz film, but there's something quite joyful about those sorts of films finding a place in those unlikely spaces.

Richard Flanagan's *The Sound of One Hand Clapping* (1998) was presented by one of our MIFF ambassadors, Justin Kurzel. It's a film he's very pas-

INTERVIEW | AL COSSAR

sionate about. It's the sole directorial credit from Flanagan and was produced by Rolf de Heer. Essie Davis, Kerry Fox, and Richard Flanagan were all in attendance, with Justin Kurzel moderating a conversation afterwards. That's a film that was extraordinary to revisit. It was an emotional thing for everyone to see it back on-screen decades later, and to rediscover it anew. Many people were seeing or experiencing it for the first time.

Those sorts of things where you get to reclaim some fascinating and important works from the past and connect them to people or deepen the experience that people may have had with them was quite defining and central to the festival [with] that scale of repertory screenings. There was a lot of looking back. Hopefully in surprising ways in an anniversary year.

One of the films that was central to MIFF 2022 was Gus Berger's The Lost City of Melbourne, a documentary that talks about the relationship between the city itself and the art of cinema.

AC: That film had quite a special place in the programme for us. *The Lost City of Melbourne* was one of the breakout hits of the festival, and for good reason. It's a beautiful film. It has that reverence and curiosity for history, design, architecture, screen culture, and cinema-going in such an astute and articulate way. MIFF provided several opportunities to see that in some really special places like The Capitol or The Forum, [creating that] feeling like you're inside the movie is what we were going for. From memory, I think it sold out for maybe three of its four screenings, including its online screening as well. It was an absolute hit. I was so thrilled to see it go immediately into cinema release after, and I think it's going to have an extraordinary [life]. It's the kind of film that I could imagine people seeing and discovering and could see it playing at Cinema Nova for three or four months. It has that longevity to it.

I remember back in 2011, we played two programmes that were newsreel-based. They were Melbourne on Film programmes built from historical newsreels. From memory, they were the first things in the programme that year to sell out. [They were] quite unlikely, on paper, to have that sort of audience response against those big blockbuster festival titles or Cannes films, but there was this voracious appetite for them. When *The Lost City of Melbourne* came to us, I thought it might have a similar quality and a similar audience appeal, and it absolutely did and succeeded on those terms. I think Melburnians have a really developed sense of inquiry and curiosity about the city and where we've come from. That film not only has that sort of component, but it has a real contemporary relevance and resonance in terms of Whelan the Wrecker and overdevelopment and those things that are ours to lose. There's an urgency to it as a historical document that's fascinating. It's very connective to people.

MELBOURNE INTERNATIONAL FILM FESTIVAL

I can hear in your voice the passion for both the film and also the location where you experience a film and how it engages with you in the experience of watching the film. You've had different roles across different film festivals and have worked as a film critic as well. As somebody who regularly engages with films, how have you managed to build up and hone that experience for audiences?

AC: I hope that when we think about something that's fundamental to our festival, or any festival, it's that idea of 'collectivity', and the quality of 'collectivity', and what it means to bring audiences together. What does it mean to talk about the 'only at MIFF' moments, and those things that can happen with the alchemy of the festival experience and those around you? I've had many kinds of different experiences throughout the places that I've worked or been involved in or gone to as a punter, and those range from the Human Rights Arts & Film Festival to the Portable Film Festival (which was a technology-based response to the launch of the video iPod and had films distributed by PSPs and iPhones and alike), or underground cinema, where there's this real sort of world building and playfulness, in terms of what that organisation does and allows audiences to explore their imaginations in the context of the film they're screening. I perhaps thought about some of the qualities of that prior experience going into the COVID response and the development of MIFF play with Shift72 and things like that.

We're fortunate enough to also travel to different festivals, which is something that I think is quite fundamental to what we're talking about now. We do get screeners, we watch DCPs, we see things at cinemas locally and privately, but where we can financially or personally see a film on site with an audience [whether it is] at Sundance, Toronto, Cannes, Berlin, or a wide variety of other festivals, it is energising. It's also fundamental to how we think about audience development at MIFF. You see an audience's response. You see the dynamism of an audience responding to a work of storytelling and a filmmaker. We bring artists out, and then we have conversations with them, and then they can't clear the cinema foyer for 90 minutes because people just want to know [about the film], they want to connect, and they want to see behind the curtain of what this sort of film was.

Going to all of those locations is really interesting, [even though] it doesn't necessarily always translate. There are films and audience experiences that are pitched wildly differently in a place like Berlin that would never work here, and vice versa. Every festival has a particular kind of audience personality. We are very conscious in terms of the things that make MIFF different and special. Several films that we play go into cinemas for theatrical release, so why would someone choose to come and see it with us? It's the fundamental experience of that cinema going as well as the film itself, and you need to place value on both of those things. In terms of the audience experience of MIFF is that it's pertinent to scale; MIFF has 370 films, and even for hardcore cinephiles, that can be quite overwhelming and quite dense in terms of imagining how you cut through that. One of the joys of the festival is that your path through MIFF could be very different to mine. It has the scale and the scope to enable that kind of audience pathfinding.

All kinds of films are important from an audience development point of view, you have the very broad populace-focused, audience-friendly films and the festival blockbusters. They're there because we love them, but they're also welcoming, and open doors to an audience who might find the setting of a festival very challenging. Then you have films for the hardcore cinephiles, and they're formally adventurous, and they're challenging. If you go and see *La Flor* (2018), it's 14 hours long. They're the polar opposites of a festival experience, but they're both equally important.

For us, different kinds of cinema has the same weight in their craft, but they're defined through their ambition and the success of the realisation of that ambition. We love all kinds of cinema. What we want to do is bring audiences in through those open doors, and then increase their curiosity and their confidence with what's in the programme. They take a bit of a risk. They might love something or hate it. Hating something new, in the context of a festival, can also be a particular kind of joy if it's something that's wildly different to what you've seen before. Hopefully, what we're doing is enabling that pathfinding that people get more confident with our programme, but they also become more confident with the world of cinema itself.

It's a festival where you could see a Steve Carell indie film at Hoyts or you could see a short film package at ACMI, and they would both sell out. We always have a focus on collectivity. We have a focus on developing or welcoming different kinds of audiences, but it's about building paths, creating opportunity, and letting the audience own that experience of pathfinding and hopefully encouraging people not only to become people who love this festival but people who love the idea of cinema more and more.

We've been talking about the relationship between the artist and Australia on screen. What does it mean to be able to program Australian cinema?

AC: The way that MIFF pitches and presents ourselves is as the biggest purveyor and presenter of Australian cinema in the world, on sort of a screen event, screen culture annual basis. That definitely rings true in terms of contemporary films, but also the repertory and retrospective filmmaking as well. What we do is create a valuable opportunity for this country to connect with Australian cinema in ways that are substantial and meaningful and contextualised, where there can be lines drawn with other forms of

MELBOURNE INTERNATIONAL FILM FESTIVAL

contemporary Australian cinema and with what has come before. Where we are dedicated is that line of independent Australian cinema where we see bold, distinctive, and important voices that break through and can be elevated.

With the support of Blackmagic Design, one of the things that we did in 2022 was introduce the $70,000 Blackmagic Design Australian Innovation Award, and that is pitched at an individual Australian screen practitioner. It could be a director, writer, cinematographer, an editor, or a composer, or an HoD, anyone within the Australian features playing across the whole programme. The idea of that is that we want to create a valuable means of celebrating Australian cinema. We want to create a global worldwide platform where that value is cast onto our screen practitioners and where the attention is at an international level [driven towards] the incredible work that filmmakers are doing in this country.

I think different kinds of cinema can fulfil that ambition with MIFF as a presenter of screen culture, right from extraordinary works of cinema through the programme. Our opening night film *Of an Age* by Goran Stolevski, and with his story and quality of output and the establishment of his voice [as an artist] was one of the real joys of the festival this year, between *Of an Age* and *You Won't Be Alone*. He's someone who's gone through MIFF Accelerator.

In terms of our relationship with Australian cinema, talent amplification runs throughout MIFF's DNA. There's Accelerator in terms of a talent development lab to go from short filmmaking to feature filmmaking. There's a critics campus which develops that culture of response and creates professional pathways for people who are going through that critic and cultural commentator space. There is the Premiere fund, where MIFF is a minority co-financier, where it supports a slate of diverse Australian cinema every year, and those films end up having their launch with MIFF too. There are also awards like Bright Horizons and the Australian Innovation Award, which also work on that continuum of supporting and celebrating what Australia's cinema is and what happens next, in terms of who is emerging; talent like Alena Lodkina, like Thomas M Wright, like Goran Stolevski, like Lachlan Mcleod.

We want to fully represent the whole kaleidoscopic nature of what Australian cinema can be. We certainly have the scale of canvas to do it with MIFF, and we have the opportunity to present artists alongside works and to build a conversation around that in a meaningful way. Some of the most surprising and innovative films for me at the festival this year were local productions. Look at Platon Theodoris' *The Lonely Spirits Variety Hour*, as a micro budget indie feature, it has this almost Michel Gondry-kind of imagination and this vastness of imagination on a fixed budget. I can't wait to see what he does next. Those sorts of discoveries and that opportunity to champion local filmmakers is why we do what we do. It's fundamental and it's the real joy of it. When you see things like that and *The Plains*, which is just a phenomenal film, in terms of its rigour and its thoughtfulness, you feel very optimistic about what the possibilities are of Australian cinema at that kind of auteurist and art level, as well as the popular filmmaking level, and that despite the very difficult circumstances everyone is in, that imagination has endured and it's something to ensure that audiences know about, can engage with, and can celebrate. MIFF can be something that helps people along as artists and to fulfil their artistic ambition.

You're talking about building a relationship with the filmmakers over the years through the Accelerator lab and similar programs. How important it is for you as an Artistic Director to have that kind of relationship with filmmakers in showing their films and growth over the years?

AC: It's very important. It's amazing to be a part of the trajectory of someone's development as a filmmaker and a storyteller and to see where they go, not only on the world stage, but to see what kind of creative path they follow or creative risks they take. Filmmakers are eclectic, and a festival is a place where people get to take risks and try different things, so to not only see filmmakers, but also see them experiment or try different things in the context of who we are, as opposed to say a commercial release, is an interesting kind of format.

I think for [the filmmakers], wherever they go in the world with their films coming back to MIFF, there's nothing quite like it in terms of the audience, in terms of where they built their names, where they learnt [their craft] as a filmmaker. That's the thing, you learn [your] craft, you build networks, you have the experience of audience, and you take that with you as you build your work on screen. For a lot of the people who have had those trajectories, MIFF is very meaningful to them, because it was so instructive as to who they have become creatively.

Filmmakers like Goran Stolevski with *Of an Age* or Nora Niasari with *Shayda*, or someone like Justin Kurzel, who is an Accelerator alumni, and has come through with films like *Nitram* which was supported by the MIFF Premiere Fund. We also have his next film, the feature documentary Ellis Park, about Warren Ellis from The Dirty Three and his Wildlife Sanctuary in Sumatra, which is coming up via the MIFF Premiere Fund in 2024, which I think is going to be just incredible.

2023 was the tenth anniversary of the Critics Campus. How important is it to support critics as a film festival? It seems like a rarity in Australia that a film festival eagerly and actively supports film critics.

MELBOURNE INTERNATIONAL FILM FESTIVAL

AC: You're right, I don't think there's a lot in Australia like it. There are some things in an international festival context that it's possibly closer to. To me, it's about the ecosystem that we exist in. It kind of runs part and parcel [with] MIFF being a point of amplification iteratively with things like Accelerator, the Shorts Awards, Bright Horizons, and the Premiere Fund, and how all of these things interlock and create a chain and an ecosystem for people to develop professionally and be amplified and to take opportunities.

Critics Campus is an integral part of that system as well. It's parallel to it. You want to build opportunities for filmmakers, but you also simultaneously want to develop a culture of a professional response to cinema and professional development opportunities, because one is tethered to the other. They're not two different things. They exist in the same space. It's in its 10th anniversary now, and we're fortunate to have support through VicScreen to enable us to keep it going.

Eight people are chosen every year from applications to attend. It's a setting where a lot of people who have [been part of] it have gone on to do some amazing things. They get to use the festival space [in a] sort of boilerplate-like context to create content and create a response. It's an amazing setting to be mentored within because there is so much going on and there is so much potential to respond to.

It's also a way to strategically get MIFF in the global visibility of publications overseas. We get to bring over international trade critics and they get to experience MIFF, and then we get to position ourselves internationally in terms of global significance, which then has downstream benefits of getting particular films or getting particular filmmakers or building the reputation of the festival that then unlocks different things as well. People from *Variety* and *The Hollywood Reporter* attended in 2023.

It's about promoting a culture of response, and it's about promoting a culture of professional opportunity which is part and parcel to films being made and films being received. Critics Campus is something we love, but it [has the ability to] stay in the background a little bit; the general public don't really know about it, or they don't really have the opportunity to interact with it. In 2023, we wanted to bring it out more into the fore, to put it on centre stage, to sing its praises and state its importance. So, Critical Condition, a retrospective program, was something that we put together. It was programmed by our Critics Campus producer Luke Goodsell, in cooperation with a lot of the attending mentors and film critics.

The programme [focused on] films where the critical reception and conversation is an indelible part of that movie; you can't separate it. What people have [said] around a movie cannot be separated from it. It was an eventised retrospective where every session had a conversation and an intro [alongside] a panel discussion. The whole point is to bring people together and to [run] retrospective screenings [where] people talk about film and [where] the films themselves are the subject of that conversation. Films like Fassbinder's final film *Querelle*, Chantal Akerman's *Golden Eighties*, Claire Denis' *Trouble Every Day*, and of course William Greaves *Symbiopsychotaxiplasm: Take One*. A lot of conversation that flow from the events will deepen people's understanding of how you read a film and also the value of criticism itself. Hopefully that helps audiences to think more about the role of criticism or potentially becoming a film critic, and how you respond to a film full stop.

HOW AUSTRALIAN DOCUMENTARY FILMS CAN FURTHER REACH AUDIENCES

A CONVERSATION WITH SUE MASLIN AO
FEBRUARY 2023

Sue Maslin AO participated in a panel at the 2023 Australian International Documentary Conference (AIDC) alongside producer Tait Brady (*Love in Bright Landscapes*), Paul Wiegard (co-founder and CEO of Madman Entertainment), producer Charlotte Wilson (*Greenhouse by Joost*), and programmer Sasha Close (Gold Coast Film Festival & Brisbane International Film Festival), moderated by producer Chris Kamen (*Franklin*). The discussion was centred around the future of screening documentary filmmaking in cinemas.

While Australian narrative features have struggled to reach national audiences, documentary films in Australia have exploded in an impressive fashion. In early 2022, Perth was swinging in and out of COVID lockdown status, with Melbourne and Sydney in the hangover period of spending months on end in lockdown. Cinemas and filmmakers were struggling, and even though audiences were hesitant to see films with an audience, they did crave film-based storytelling. In conversation with Sue prior to AIDC, I asked her about what changes the industry had experienced in the early 2020s, noting the increase in Australian feature films and documentaries released theatrically.

"Incredibly there were 81 Australian feature films released by distributors into our market in 2022. 81! This is just unheard of. [We traditionally have around] 25 to 35 a year, [and then] we were getting up to about 55 a year. All of those releases are released by distributors. There are independent one-offs, [and] if you count those, there's another 40 or so on top of that. [Of those] 81 releases, 37 were documentary films. Which means there are a lot of documentary films being made.

"How are they performing? The vast bulk are not performing particularly well. The vast bulk of Australian feature films are not performing at the moment. But if you look at the [20] top performing [Australian films] of 2022, ten of those were documentaries."

Sue provided the box office numbers from both Numero and the Comscore list for this discussion, both of which provide a fascinating look into the reception of Australian films at the box office. We know that films like

HOW AUSTRALIAN DOCUMENTARY FILMS CAN FURTHER REACH AUDIENCES

Baz Luhrmann's *Elvis* and the third *Wog Boy* film were well received by audiences, but it was interesting to see how widely received Australian documentaries were by audiences. In the list of new Australian films released during 2022, the following ten films featured in the top 20:

> *The Lost City of Melbourne (Gus Berger), Franklin (Kasimir Burgess), Facing Monsters (Bentley Dean), This Much I Know to Be True (Andrew Dominik), River (Jennifer Peedom), Embrace: Kids (Taryn Brumfitt OAM), Blind Ambition (Robert Coe, Warwick Ross), Everybody's Oma (Jason van Genderen), and Love in Bright Landscapes (Jonathan Alley).*

Sue explained: "Documentary films are contributing significantly to the annual box office. There is no doubt about that. Around half of all the documentary films earn $10,000 or less at the box office. These films are not even recovering their own P&A or marketing costs."

Given how independent-driven the Australian film industry is and how difficult it can be for films to make their money back at the box office, it then becomes clear why filmmakers turn to streaming services to platform their films.

"Despite the reality of what's happening to Australian cinema at the moment, despite the reality of what's happening post-COVID, by and large, audiences have moved online, even more so than ever before. It's very hard to get audiences back into cinemas for independent films full stop. All of the box office is down in relation to non-Hollywood studio films."

While the Australian film output is reaching peak levels, audiences simply aren't turning out for these films, no matter how great the quality is. Sue wondered about this divide from an industry perspective, "[While] we're finding it harder to get our Australian films seen by local audiences, we've [also] now got this exponential growth in filmmakers wanting to make feature films and get them into the cinema. [The questions are then], why is it so important to make a feature doc? Where are they destined [for]? Are the films actually cinematic? Are they actually theatrical? If you run through the list, the films that perform best are the films that are the most cinematic."

One of Australia's preeminent cinematic documentarians is Jennifer Peedom, the director of acclaimed work like *Sherpa*, *Mountain*, and *River*. Sue said, "Jen has been very successful in creating an experience that sits around in the theatre. When *Mountain* came out, pre-COVID, it made more than $2 million. *River* came out in 2022, and so far it's made $200,000, a 10th of what *Mountain* made."

Part of the cinema release for *Mountain* included presentations of the film with the Australian Chamber Orchestra (ACO), with a premiere at the Sydney Opera House. This immersive theatrical experience made the cinema viewing more than just watching a film in a theatre, it became an event. Sue said, "*River* hasn't had its run as an experiential event. Once it has that run, it'll boost the box office up further. She has tapped into something that I've been saying for a long time: the film alone is not enough. You have to create the experience, the event, the social media, the impact. Everything that sits around the film, that becomes what the offering is." *River* finally received that orchestra-backed experience at Perth Festival in 2024.

Something that Sue wants more filmmakers to consider when they prepare their films for a theatrical run is to ask themselves, how do you make the experience of cinema-going grander than just watching a film? How do you get audience members to engage with non-Hollywood filmmaking in a manner that they may otherwise have not done before? In a generalised way, audiences have become attuned to the new normal of streaming everything, treating cinemas as vessels for the latest effects driven blockbuster, your James Cameron's or Marvels. For all the films that fall out of that scope, it's clear that the process of cinema-going desperately needs to be disrupted.

One such release that helped buck the trend was Jonathan Alley's *Love in Bright Landscapes* (2021), which toured Australia with a Triffids tribute band playing covers at select cinema events. Sue said, "[Tait Brady sold] the tickets for $50 a head, and he's [made] a successful release." Just like Jennifer Peedom did with ACO and her films, tying a documentary to the subject matter and the artists involved with the film helps make the screening more of an event, which is something that Sue herself had personal experience with as Danny Cohen's *Anonymous Club* launched in 2022.

"I distributed *Anonymous Club*, a beautiful film about Courtney Barnett all shot on 16mm. [It's an] incredible, theatrical space that goes into a very intimate, emotional journey. It ticks all the boxes of what in my view should be cinematic and theatrical. Yet, it didn't perform in the cinema. That's not to say that it's not going to perform over the long term."

Anonymous Club was the 34th placed Australian film at the box office, next to Duy Huynh's *How to Thrive* (2022) and Sue Thomson's *Under Cover* (2022), both of which had specialised screenings. *Anonymous Club* is another film impacted by COVID, which limited Barnett and Cohen from either running Q&A sessions or performing alongside the film. However, *Anonymous Club* has found an unexpected second wind in the form of the instrumental album release, *End of the Day*. Barnett crafted the score to her story, and in an act of transformative reflection, toured the release with fellow muso Stella Mozgawa long after the film's theatrical release ran its course.

Sue continues, "Courtney's got legions of fans, millions of followers worldwide. She has a very active social media base. Her youth audience will sell out [a concert] wherever she plays, they are there for the experience. Whenever we had screenings with Courtney present, [they] sold out, no worries. The minute that you start to screen the film as a standalone film, then you drop back [to] how most Australian films were performing; that is, the audience is not there. They all know about it, but they're not turning up. This is not just documentaries. This is right across the board.

HOW AUSTRALIAN DOCUMENTARY FILMS CAN FURTHER REACH AUDIENCES

"That leads you to say, 'well, there's other rationales.' People are making lots of feature docs, many of which hope to have a theatrical release. But of course, there's festival releases. Theatrical docs do have a very active life here in Australia, and of course, worldwide, it's just that there are more film festival opportunities for documentary films. Audiences are realising that if they want to see really good documentaries, that's where they find them. They find them in curated programmes at film festivals. It amazes me that the documentary sessions are often the first to sell out at film festivals everywhere. People know that's a destination."

Many of the documentaries that I've covered in this book were released at film festival releases first with a theatrical release second, if they received one at all. In many ways, the festival release is the awareness campaign for documentary films. If they sell out at festivals, then the theatrical run is like gravy. If they don't secure a theatrical release, they risk becoming memories, living on in the minds of the limited audience that was in attendance.

That is, unless they join the many Australian documentaries which receive a free-to-air broadcast release. Channels like ABC and SBS become a second home for documentaries, with many presented in reduced, sub-60-minute cuts or split across multiple episodes. Post-broadcast, these releases then find a home on boutique streaming services, like ABC iView and SBS On Demand. Outside of these public broadcast services exist documentary focused streaming services like Madman's DocPlay, where films like *Anonymous Club* and *The Lost City of Melbourne* are made available in their original format.

Sue talks about the online future for documentaries, "The reality is that most documentaries will probably end up either on television, on streamers, or in a cut down version used by community groups. Community groups don't tend to want to use a feature length doc because they want to have a discussion at the end of the screening. So, if you've got a 100-minute doc, and then you've got another hour or so of discussions, [that's] a really big event. They tend to want to watch a shorter, one-hour version, which is why we usually make two versions [of a documentary]."

Ultimately, the enduring question still applies:

"What is the rationale for your story to actually be targeted into a theatrical space?"

Films are artistic creations that have taken years, sometimes decades, to bring to life. People put blood, sweat, tears, and personal savings into bringing their films to life. Naturally, as filmmakers, they crave that cinema experience, the final step in validating their work.

I posed the question to Sue about how filmmakers need to approach that personal discussion within themselves about where the best place for their film is:

"It's a creative decision, but it's also a business decision. The two have to get together. We're not writing novels here. We're making mass media for audiences delivered over screens. Yes, it's a creative decision, but at all times, I can't see the point in making any work unless at the same time you're thinking about who it is that you want to talk to [in] the audience. They have to go hand in hand.

"Part of the problem is that there's too much desire to tell the story in the absence of really thinking about where that story will ultimately sit and who will ultimately see it. Because once you think about it, you have to ask yourself really tough questions. Why will [the audience] want to see that film? Why [are they] going to pay good, hard-earned money, when they can stay home and watch Netflix and all the other myriad of streamers for a fraction of the cost?

"They know perfectly well, because they've had two years of the COVID experience, that you can get a multitude of quality documentaries online. Why are you going to pay good money to go and see documentaries in a cinema now?

"Unless you can answer that question, I don't think that the creative impulse is enough to drive forward a documentary project anymore."

Now, I know that many readers may get upset or frustrated by reading that reasoning, and to be fair, I can understand that sentiment completely. After all, whether it's the eagerness of getting to work on a Monday morning to tell your colleagues at work about the weekend you've just had, or the burning desire to write the next *Ducks, Newburyport* and turn the literary form on its head, the burning desire to tell a story sits within us all.

In today's expansive market, the accessibility of picking up a camera or simply using your phone has made filmmaking seemingly effortless, almost to the point of oversimplification. Yes, there's freedom in being able to create just about anything, but there's also the need and push to have a creative force within yourself that can be met by knowing that there might be an audience on the other side who is eager to watch your film.

When I started writing my first book on Australian film, my partner asked me who the target audience was for it. I stared blankly at her, and somewhat foolishly gave her the response, 'me.' Now, that is very well true. I personally want to read books about Australian films, just like many Australian filmmakers, whether they be documentarians or genre filmmakers or beyond, want to see the story that they're making on screen. But that burning desire to see or hear or read our own stories must come with a clear answer of who the target audience is for what is being produced.

Supporting that national artistic vision was returning Minister for the Arts, Tony Burke. After a rapid tour of Australia in 2022, Tony Burke jumped on the front foot and pulled together an arts policy that sought to rectify a decade of stagnation in the industry with the Australian arts scene. The result was:

> *Revive: Australia's Cultural Policy for the next five years.*
> *A place for every story, a story for every place.*

HOW AUSTRALIAN DOCUMENTARY FILMS CAN FURTHER REACH AUDIENCES

It's an aspirational piece of work, full of hope, vision, and pure intentions. That word, 'hope,' can be a dangerous thing. It sparks a fire to creativity, but at the same time, that fire can be doused and smothered for an age.

Yet, there is a clear vision in 'Revive,' one that encompasses all aspects of the Australian arts. To be clear, this isn't an arts policy that is simply focused on filmmaking, naturally that would be awfully narrow-minded. It embraces theatre, dance, art, writing, and so much more.

It's a policy that's split into five pillars:
Pillar 1 – First Nations First
Pillar 2 – A Place for Every Story
Pillar 3 – Centrality of the Artist
Pillar 4 – Strong Cultural Infrastructure
Pillar 5 – Engaging the Audience

If we focus on that final pillar, the one that is most pertinent to this discussion of reaching audiences, it exposes one of the emerging issues with the arts policy as a whole: a lack of focus around the theatrical experience. There is welcome discussion of streaming quotas for Australian content, which makes a wealth of sense given that that is where the dominant audience share is placed, but by not mentioning the need to grow, support, and maintain the cinematic experience suggests that there is no further growth that can be attained in that space.

Commenting on the new arts policy, Sue remarks, "This is something that is obviously a much bigger question, [and] is something that with the Australian Feature Film Summit we've attempted to address and will continue to address by bringing together all sectors of the industry in one space to drive this forward: the exhibitors, the distributors, the filmmakers, and the agencies. It's a very real issue that is being driven by industry, which it should be.

"Of course, having a cultural policy gives us some additional leverage. We've seen what happens when you do proactive campaigns to celebrate Australian cinema. We saw it [with the] Summer of Cinema [campaign] at the beginning of 2021. In the middle of the pandemic, the phenomenal box office results for Australian films where people took a punt because Hollywood [films were] absent. They had to see an Australian film, but they liked them, and the figures were substantial. Every film experienced an incredible bump in box office as a result of that. We had this opportunity where people who had lost the habit of going to the movies, or don't routinely see Australian films, were coming out and they liked what they saw."

When pandemic restrictions were lifted around the world, it once again became difficult for Australian films to compete at the box office due to the sheer market domination and presence that films with marketing budgets and the ability to weather weeks in cinemas had against Aussie films which often lack a marketing budget or can only be booked into smaller arthouse cinemas.

A CONVERSATION WITH SUE MASLIN

This isn't to say that Australian films in 2022 weren't successful, they just didn't hit the same levels as they did in 2021. Sue talked about some of the films that stood out in the Australian film scene, and highlighted one of the reasons why that may be: "There's just as many interesting Australian films in the 2022 bunch. We've got everything from blockbusters like *Elvis*, through to films that targeted a more female demographic like *How to Please a Woman*, *The Drover's Wife*, *Falling For Figaro*, and *Seriously Red*. All of those female driven projects that are all sitting up in the top 10. But the box office figures are nowhere near as robust as they could be.

"So, the question is, how do we get people back into the habit again?

"I think having a cultural policy means that there's the potential for 'whole of industry' campaigns. We've got to look at having more data about audience behaviour, and that's happening as well. A high priority for us at the summit [was] to get data research into audience behaviour done, but more importantly, shared with filmmakers, which is something that has not happened in the past. That's bubbling away in the background as well.

"Then to have ground-up funding opportunities to put filmmakers together with the exhibitors who are closest to the audience and having the opportunity to test their ideas. We've been separated for too long. We've got to get filmmakers at the coalface talking to exhibitors, finding out what audience behaviour is, what is going to get them in.

"We know some things work extremely well, like anything that is event based [and] anything that involves talent. [It] doesn't have to always be music docs, it can be other experiences. This is, of course, something that is the cornerstone of impact strategies [for] social impact films where they're supported by campaigns. There are a lot of ways to engage audiences rather than just simply saying 'look, our film is out on this week, here's the poster, here's the trailer, here's a review, come and see my film.' It's got to be much, much more sophisticated than that going forward."

A social impact campaign is often something that's applied to social impact films, like *Franklin* or *How to Thrive*. These are documentaries that give the audience an actionable purpose once the screening has finished, making the film just one part of a much larger piece of the pie.

For example, Damon Gameau's *2040* made a mark in my local suburb. *2040* was released in 2019, with an awareness campaign across social media that preceded the nation-wide in-person Q&A tour with Damon and fellow climate activists in person. In 2019, I interviewed Damon in an electric vehicle on the South Perth foreshore, where he talked about the importance of those in person experiences. That in-person connection spurred someone in my suburb to pick up the *2040* book, which became a weathered tome as they read through it, taking notes and creating plans alongside their family. The film and its book then gave this family the tools and tips to create a localised climate action strategy for their suburb.

From watching *2040* in a cinema, to hearing the climate activists and the director engage in a Q&A, to then meet Damon after the screening and dis-

HOW AUSTRALIAN DOCUMENTARY FILMS CAN FURTHER REACH AUDIENCES

cuss the themes further, which led to buying the *2040* book, which helped kick the family into action during lockdown in Perth, leading to the creation of a local activist group that sought to combat climate change on the streets of our suburb. They embraced the 'think global, act local' approach, and now a couple of years on, that once small Facebook group has now spawned other groups that are pushing to create suburban tree canopies and save large trees in our suburbs.

The notable thing about this small case study is that it's one that typically only applies to documentary films, where the campaign before and after its release helps maintain the longevity of the message in the film. I asked Sue about whether the same kind of social impact campaign for a film like *2040* could be applied to other films, which gave way to an answer about her own personal experience with creating a social impact campaign for one of the biggest Australian films ever, *The Dressmaker* (2015):

"The 360 degrees methodology of conveying ideas and themes and engagement with the audience [can work]. We've got a lot to learn from social impact campaigns. Fortunately, I've worked across both documentaries and feature films for years. It was that idea of a 360 approach to engage an audience that drove how we wanted to present *The Dressmaker*. Yes, everybody will say, 'you hit the ball way out of the park,' [but] nobody expected it to do as well as it did, me included.

"I can tell you, that campaign did not start with Universal Pictures when they had the final film and the trailer, and then the release; that was not the beginning of the campaign. The beginning of the campaign started two years prior to the film going into production. When we did put together our social media strategy, we started building our fan base. We invited the fan base to audition to be extras in the film, which of course meant the socials went gangbusters because everybody wanted to be in a film with Kate [Winslet] and Liam [Hemsworth].

"It then continued through the making of the film to the strategy of creating an event and experience: 'grab your girlfriends, grab a glass of champagne, get dressed up and come to *The Dressmaker*.' That was the experience. It wasn't 'buy a ticket and come see the movie.' It meant groups of women did exactly that. And they shared dressing up and all of that stuff. That happened through the release. And then after, it continued through [when] Marion Boyce, the costume designer, and I put together the exhibition of the dresses.[1]

"So, you're thinking about it in a long arc. You build excitement [and] you build awareness not by making the film. I get this so many times from filmmakers, particularly emerging filmmakers, who ring up and say, 'I've just finished my first feature film, what do I do now? Where do I go? What do I do with this now?' And you go, 'That is such a great question, but you should have asked it two years ago or a year ago before you started making the film.' Because the 'what do I do now' should be completely answered

A CONVERSATION WITH SUE MASLIN

for you. Only half the job is done when you've made the film. The other 50% is connecting with the audience."

I commented that there is a notion that sometimes filmmakers are almost scared to connect with an audience, because it's that final validation about whether the film that they've spent years of their lives making is any good or not. These are often works of pure dedication, weekends spent away from families, or pushing to get that idea out of their mind and realised on film. It's something that filmmaker Gus Berger knows all too well, having spent much of the Melbourne lockdown period creating his expansive and historical documentary *The Lost City of Melbourne*, a film that Sue uses as a great example of connecting with an audience:

"[Looking] at the top performing documentaries, [there's] *The Lost City of Melbourne*. I take my hat off to Gus Berger for doing this. Who, in any other state, is going to go and see this movie? Yet, he's topped the list for documentary films in 2022. And that film is still screening! I saw it last weekend on a Sunday afternoon in Gus' cinema, which is a 52-seater. It was almost full, it's incredible.

"It's an archival film. [Gus] knows its audience, [and has] got a clever sort of strategy. It's kind of like the platform releases that we used to have in the old days where you build awareness of a film and keep it on and keep it running. If it's a quality film, which it is, then give the people the opportunity to see it over time. And people are seeing it. It was released on the first of September, and there's still 40 people in the cinema last Sunday afternoon seeing it. I find that extraordinary. I love it.

"Then there's music films [like] *Lee Kernaghan: Boy from the Bush*, *Love in Bright Landscapes*, and also with *This Much I Know to Be True*. Music is part of the element of getting audiences in. Then there's the campaign films: *Franklin*, *Greenhouse by Joost*, *Embrace: Kids*, *Blind Ambition*. These films are all supported by a really strong campaign. And then going down the list a bit further, you've got more music: *The Angels: Kickin' Down the Door*, *Wash My Soul in the River's Flow*, *Anonymous Club*. There are clues here about what is bringing audiences to the cinema.

"In all of this, you'd have to say that the production sector in theatrical documentary is vibrant. The best performing films are the ones that have the long tail. That is yes, they can have a theatrical release, but they go to find their audience on streamers, potentially on television, potentially in educational areas, and that is a perfectly valid strategy for making a feature doc. We've been doing it here at Film Art Media for years and managing the rights over the long tail has been the key to our sustainability."

It's worthwhile pointing out the bold words that are on the Film Art Media website:

Stories that engage.
Ideas that matter.

HOW AUSTRALIAN DOCUMENTARY FILMS CAN FURTHER REACH AUDIENCES

These are important values for filmmakers to keep in the back of their mind as they make a film. It's clear that for Sue Maslin AO, these are ideas and values that reinforce how she engages with producing, promoting, and discussing films.

That discussion is a vital point when it comes to sustaining the longevity of films beyond their initial screenings, and it's a point that Sue touches on when it comes to media coverage, "If you make a feature documentary, and it goes straight to TV or streaming, you're not going to get the editorial coverage that you get if you make a film that then goes on to cinemas. The editorial coverage is so important because unlike the TV review and 'what's on tonight' and the micro-reference that you might get in a programme guide, the editorial really addresses why we make documentaries, which is because we're trying to convey ideas to audiences, and there are important themes and subjects that we really want the Australian public to be aware of. While they may not get to see the film, they'll certainly get to read it on The Conversation or on their online news feeds or social media.

"Theatrical drives all of that."

"The work that you guys do is just so fundamental, because we can't afford the publicity, we don't have money for publicity campaigns. Every editorial piece gives us phenomenal value across media that we don't have to actually pay for. It's more than that; yes, it's promoting the film, which we love, and we really desperately need, but it's about the ideas. Getting people to seriously engage with ideas is really hard these days in our mainstream press.

"If you look at, for instance, the pages around reviews of books, they engage with ideas, they engage with the subject matter, with what the writer was setting out to do. There's a deep discussion, often controversy, but it's all about the idea. Go to the film review pages, and it's about, who's in it, what they wore at the premiere, what they ate while the interviewer was talking to them. It's just so facile. It's very hard to get ideas. With a few notable exceptions, we don't really have a film criticism culture in Australia anymore."

This point is particularly salient for me and my fellow Australian film critics. We are just as vital in championing, supporting, amplifying and valuing the work of Australian filmmakers. I know there are passionate supporters of Australian films, ones that manage the criticism (both negative and positive) of the Aussie film output with grace and style. But there used to be more of us, and it's something that Sue has noticed change in the critical field over the years.

In the period of writing this book, Metro Magazine, Australia's oldest film and media periodical, has found itself on life support, leaving many critical voices hanging in the void with an uncertainty of where their next paid work as a writer will come from.

"I'm old enough to have been around making films in the early 1980s and have been the beneficiary of all of the work that the filmmakers in the filmmaker co-ops did in the 1970s. They weren't just making film. They were building film criticism; they were building film magazines. We had Cinema Papers, there was Filmnews, there were a myriad of different avenues, and everybody wanted to engage with the culture of a brand-new Australian film industry or reborn Australian film industry for the second time. It wasn't just about making films.

"The sad thing I find in a lot of emerging filmmakers these days is the first question I ask them: 'What's the latest Australian film you've been to see?' They haven't seen any Australian films! And they're not necessarily really particularly interested in that kind of culture that underpins our production culture."

Sue's final point sits at the core of this whole discussion: getting bums in seats at movie theatres.

"The other comment I want to make is that the cinemas themselves, exhibitors, are up for it. Even though they make most of their money out of the studio pictures, they're already made campaigns, they put them up and they pretty much run themselves. It's actually the Australian films that give them their job satisfaction. The joy of seeing audiences come in, line up at the box office, and buy tickets to see a good Aussie movie [excites them]. They're desperate for more, they want them, they love working with us. I think that opportunity is there, and we just have to have a different conversation around it."

ENDNOTES

1   In 2019, the NFSA hosted a stunning exhibition that featured the costumes of The Dressmaker with backdrops that referenced locations from the film. https://www.nfsa.gov.au/collection/curated/dressmaker-making-hit-movie-and-its-costumes

THE LOST CITY
OF MELBOURNE

REVIEW
NADINE WHITNEY

Like everyone except the Indigenous people who lived in Naarm, I am an import to Melbourne. I first moved to the city in 1992 and found my spiritual home. There was something so uniquely cosmopolitan about the city that rivalled my experience of other Australian cities. I spent a good deal of time in Sydney (I was born there) but it never captured my imagination the way Melbourne did. In 2010 I moved away for personal reasons and did not return until 2018 – when I did, I found the city had changed dramatically over eight years. Cinemas and bookstores I haunted were gone. Carlton, which had been my stomping ground for many years seemed like a ghost of its previous self. I barely recognised the inner city. In eight years, my city had undergone huge transformations. Gus Berger's documentary *The Lost City of Melbourne* charts Melbourne's changing faces from the 1870s to the present day with a specific focus on what caused Melbourne to lose some of its most iconic buildings in the fifties and sixties.

Melbourne, as we know it, was founded by two bickering colonialists: John Batman and William Faulkner. One was a newspaperman, the other a publican, and neither can be called a good person. However, it seems fitting that Melbourne was built on the back of journalism and pubs. What really fuelled Melbourne's development was the post gold rush boom of wealth. By the 1870s Melbourne was the most sophisticated city in Australia. Unlike Sydney which grew organically and haphazardly, Melbourne was a planned city. It boasted some of the most progressive architecture in Australia and had buildings that rivalled cities like Chicago and New York.

The Victorian era magnate E W Cole opened the famous Cole's Book Arcade which in reality was a multifaceted department store that also provided public entertainment. Melbourne became a city where people paraded (the French would call them flaneurs) to be seen walking the streets for pleasure. It also had a decidedly seedy underbelly, there were no-go zones around Lonsdale Street and parts of Bourke Street for fear of criminal attack – however, this is no different to any major city.

Melbourne became a hub for theatre and cinema. Not only was Australia the first to produce a full-length feature film *The Story of the Kelly*

THE LOST CITY OF MELBOURNE

Gang in 1906, but Melbournians also went wild for the Lumiere brothers' invention and built multitudes of cinemas and theatrical spaces for the exhibition of the new technology. Melbourne's prosperity and fascination with the arts shaped the city. In almost every suburb there were several cinemas, and only a few survive today – notably The Rivoli, The Classic in Elsternwick, The Astor in St Kilda, and due to Berger's own work, The Thornbury Picture House.

So, what happened to Melbourne to change it from an arts metropolis filled with glorious Victorian-era buildings to a city littered with Brutalist office blocks? The answer comes down to a few factors. Firstly, the cultural cringe that was brought on by the 1956 Olympics. Melburnians saw their city as outdated and embarrassing to be featured on the world stage. This feeling was not aided by the advent of television around the same time which gave Victorians a look into the wider world, albeit a skewed one. The prevailing sentiment was "modernise" and (un)luckily there was one company more than prepared to take on the task of removing those unfashionable Victorian and Edwardian buildings; Whelan the Wrecker.

The Whelan the Wrecker company started out relatively nefariously by plundering the sites they wrecked for items they could sell on for a profit. They also recognised that there was a spectacle to be shown in the pulling down of buildings and made minor celebrities out of their workers. A Whelan family member is interviewed by a young Barry Humphries in the documentary. Humphries shows incredible restraint as the Whelan son gloats over pulling down the cultural history. As one of the talking heads in the documentary points out, what the Whelan family was doing was "vandalism." Without any form of National Trust in Australia at the time, the historic buildings of Melbourne were prey to any developer who saw profit in erecting a new office block or shopping centre.

Interweaving historical photographs, archive footage, and interviews from contemporary historians, Berger has made a love-letter to a lost city, yet he isn't without hope for Melbourne. For all that has been lost, he reminds us of what has been saved. The glass is half empty or half full depending on one's perspective, and it is important to note that cities are changing and evolving all the time. There is a sense of melancholy that Melbourne pulled down its own history not because it needed to be rebuilt after being war-torn, but because profit and cultural cringe pushed the city into destroying some of its most beautiful buildings.

Berger reminds us that the process is still going on. In 2020 developers gutted and destroyed The Palace Hotel on Swanston Street. Melburnians will know it as The Metro. I can't even count the number of gigs I went to there, it was an essential part of my Melbourne experience, as I'm sure it was to many people. It is now a luxury hotel. I'm hoping that the sweat of hundreds of thousands of young music lovers is soaked into the very foundations of the building.

The Lost City of Melbourne may have problems reaching an audience that isn't invested in the city, but it does speak to the wider issue of gentrification and capitalist greed and how those factors impact the places people live, work, and play. For the people of Melbourne, it is a wonderful glimpse of what the city was, and what remains. Collins Street still has a "Paris End," and although we've lost a lot, there are many remnants of a golden age, such as The Forum, The Regent, and so many more wondrous places. Melbourne is a city of resilience and a true capital of the Arts, and although the city's face has changed many times, what is true is that its heart hasn't.

THE LOST CITY OF MELBOURNE

INTERVIEW
FILMMAKER GUS BERGER

It takes a considerate eye to look at the destruction of a city over the decades and craft a film that carries a level of awe and wonder for the culture that lingers in the rubble of gentrification and modernity. This is what director Gus Berger has managed to do with his expansive historical documentary *The Lost City of Melbourne*. Utilising the Melbourne lockdowns to take a journey through the Victorian history books, Berger witnessed a city that is at threat of losing its cultural identity and crafted a film that calls for an end to the gaping maw of the kind of homogenised destruction that has swept through cities around the globe.

Berger reflects on what makes Melbourne unique, and in doing so shines a light on the structural ghosts that once dominated the city's skyline, highlighting the importance of communal venues like cinemas and theatres. When paired with the equally important *Splice Here: A Projected Odyssey* from fellow Melbournian Rob Murphy, *The Lost City of Melbourne* helps remind audiences what we stand to lose as we race into a future that prioritises rapid infrastructure progression over fortifying cultural identities and institutions.

This interview was recorded by Andrew F. Peirce in August 2022

What does it mean to be a Melbournian exploring the history of Melbourne architecture on screen?

Gus Berger: I've always been fascinated with photography and archival film, but it's always been focused more on cinemas and theatres, particularly in Melbourne. There was a book that was published by the local library and written by local historians that gave a detailed look at all of the cinemas and theatres that used to exist in Brunswick. It went from the first rudimentary cinemas, what they were like, what they were called. There were no photographs at that point of those cinemas. Some of the stories were from random projectionists who were showing films projected onto the sidewalls of buildings on Sydney Road in Brunswick. One guy had an oil

THE LOST CITY OF MELBOURNE

lamp projector, and he was putting random films onto walls in 1905 or '06. I think the rain got the better of him one winter and he never came back. There was a horse-shoe nail factory in Tinning Street off Sydney Road, not far from where I live, which was a big industry back then. At night, they got rid of the machinery, brought in bench seats, and showed films to a thousand people. They would clear away the projector and the seats later that night, and then it'd be back to being a factory.

I built up a collection of photographs which mainly came from the thirties onwards of the interior and exterior of some of these cinemas. We used to sometimes project it at the Thornbury Picture House if we needed to fill up some space, particularly on a film where we didn't have enough trailers or if we were showing a classic film where we've got an older audience. We'd play this little five-minute montage we called *The Last Cinemas of the North*. It had some music underneath it. It was a montage of photographs of cinemas that used to exist in the area that people will relate to because they're mainly from Thornbury, Brunswick, Coburg, and Preston. People always say, "I love that little film you play at the start."

So, it started as this development of going back and seeing if I could find more photos and films.

Then, because of the protracted length of the lockdowns, the research got deeper. I discovered more films that were not specifically about theatres and cinemas. It was more about Melbourne. I was finding footage of Bourke Street in 1910 and photographs of that early dry plate photography of Bourke Street, Swanston Street, and Collin Street. Back when the structures were being built, the photographers of that time always highlighted specific elements, which had their positives in different ways. I also would have loved there to be a few of those Henri Cartier-Bresson-type photographers wandering around in 1920, that were more interested in the people and the back streets.

The focus was on the buildings, but that was good because it brought awareness to these buildings that I was looking at. "Isn't that beautiful? What happened to that? Why isn't that still standing?" The APA Building, the Colonial Mutual Life Building, and Eastern Market. Then it prompted me to read books on Melbourne of the time and think, why were they knocked down? I discovered that a lot of them came down in a similar period of time, and there were these pressures that brought them down. It was this organic discovery of learning what Melbourne was like from 1910 to 1930.

That started to build a bit more of a picture. Eventually, [I thought] maybe there's a story here because of that link of the perfect storm of the mid-50s that created the pressure to the bring the old buildings down. It was only until that connection was made that I started to think that there potentially was a film here.

There is still that fight to restore and maintain a connected history to the original Melbourne. How do you see your film working in relation to say, trying to save something like the Curtin Hotel, for example?

GB: I think it's important for people to realise that the job's not done. There are no fail-safe measures in place to prevent things like the Curtin Hotel and the Corkman Hotel,[1] and, potentially even something like The Palace. It's important for people to realise that if they are interested in preserving these buildings, they do need to be aware that things can still fall through the cracks. It's really important to understand that having great heritage laws doesn't mean everything is automatically safe, because it's not. It's important to remind people that they do still have some power in preventing [them from being destroyed.] It is difficult.

What's interesting about The Curtin Hotel, and what would be important to take away from my film, is that yes, you can protect the exterior, but the interiors are a bit more of a grey area. Did you know that if legislation had come in a year earlier, The Palace couldn't have been gutted like it was? The City of Melbourne was trying to enact interior heritage protection whilst the building was being torn apart from the inside. It lost all its value by the time the laws came into place, which was unbelievable that that was allowed to happen. There should have at least been a moratorium or a stop work until that legislation got passed, considering the value of that building.

It's also important to realise that there's also this intangible part of a building that's harder to measure and harder to legislate, which is what value it has in terms of what value people have gained from going there. The Curtin Hotel has got a history of the trade union movement and politics in this state. The Palace Theatre had some of the best performers that have ever come to Melbourne to play. I'm a member of these funny, old cinema groups on Facebook, and when people post a photo of a cinema that no longer exists, there's a whole line of comments of stories of, "I remember going there with my grandma," or "My parents used to take me to that cinema, and I saw this film there." "I went on my first date with my wife at that cinema." It's such a shame that that's not around anymore.

People have got these really strong memories and cinemas and theatres are great places to form those memories. You go there with people you care about, you go there with friends, or you go there on your own, and you've got your own memories of seeing an amazing film that really moved you and you couldn't leave your seat until the lights came up after the end cred-

THE LOST CITY OF MELBOURNE

its. They're important places. It's hard to protect that emotional value that people put on places.

I've been wandering the city quite a bit in the last week waiting for films to start. I revisited the building site that features in the film, The Bourke Street Mall, where they've knocked down these buildings and left the facade and the amount of work that's progressed since shooting that footage, which was only probably six to eight months ago, it's just ridiculous. The facade that's left there has lost all its value. It will lose all its value once something high, right on the edge of it, is built. You may as well knock the whole thing down and just paint the facade on the front of the building.

There's a whole block on Russell Street between Flinders Lane and Bourke Street. It used to have an Aussie Disposals and a funny little 4D cinema or something like that. They were two-storey, 1940s buildings, but they've all gone. That entire block has gone. Maybe they didn't have any great heritage value in terms of Art Nouveau architecture or anything like that, but it was that streetscape. It's a part of Melbourne that people have known for a long time that's gone. When something is built there, it changes the feeling of that block. I know you can't stop it all, but I think we've just got to be careful. There's so much activity going on in the city at the moment, especially with the Metro tunnel. It's the inevitable sadness of change.

Change can't come at the cost of a city's cultural identity. I love visiting Melbourne because it feels, in some ways, like a time capsule. There is so much beautiful architecture. It's heartbreaking to see these iconic buildings be lost. As you're saying, having just the facade doesn't mean anything, it's like having a mask on. It's kind of a bit creepy in some ways because the personality of the building is gone.

GB: It's almost worse because it's like paying lip service to something that was amazing and you're being reminded of the loss. I remember reading about a cinema in Sydney called the Valhalla. It had a bit of a cult status, showing *The Rocky Horror Picture Show* (1975) and *The Blues Brothers* (1980), those sorts of big cult films. It was a beautiful single-screen cinema, bought by developers and turned into apartments. I went to see it, thinking that was still an intact cinema, not realising that it was an apartment. The apartments are called the Valhalla apartments. All you've got of the old Valhalla is just that facade, which is right up against the rest of the building which goes up ten storeys. And then the insensitivity, if you like, inside the foyer is a photo of the old Valhalla and a paragraph about what legendary status the Valhalla had in the seventies in Sydney. You can't remind people of what you've taken away from them like that.

INTERVIEW | GUS BERGER

With that in mind, MIFF 70 presented Melbourne on Film. The Lost City of Melbourne complements that look at cultural identity. How important is it to be part of that cultural conversation showcasing Melbourne's identity alongside the films that were made in a now-lost city?

GB: It helps solidify people's appreciation of what we've still got now if they're [made] aware of the rich legacy of the past. I always [knew] that *The Story of the Kelly Gang* (1906) was our first feature film, which followed quickly after The Salvation Army's *Soldiers of the Cross* (1900), but I don't think that really classifies as a film, it was more of a promotional piece for The Salvation Army. Either way, they were both shot in Melbourne.

What I loved about *The Kelly Gang*, which I wasn't aware of, was that whole vertical integration of the cinema industry [that] happened from that point, because they made a film, and they needed places to show it. So, they changed these theatres from Waterville into cinemas. They thought, "This film is really popular, it's selling out every session, how do we move it into Sydney and Perth and other places?" "Oh, we've got to strike more prints, we've got to set up a distribution company where we can truck these films to other states." It was this real necessity of getting the film out that inadvertently created the film industry in Australia.

We were world leaders in that industry at that time. I mean, we would have had to have been because it was the first feature film. So, it was the first time that a feature film was being shipped around the country and shown in different venues. And I think that by being an Australian film, it attracted a big audience of people that were still fascinated with those early short films. Then it was like, "Hang on a minute. We can go and see a film for an hour and a half, and it's got a band doing the sound effects?" It's important to remember that because it makes you appreciate venues like the Athenaeum Theatre, for example, which we've still got and is on the Heritage Register.

Knowing about your past helps protect the future. They work together. It instils a sense of pride in what we've got in Melbourne; in what we've achieved in the past that people may not have known about or may not have realised how important and how big that was.

I knew that the structure of the film would be of a different pace and a different aesthetic [as it progressed.] The first section [looking at] what Melbourne was like [was different] purely because there were different types of recording devices being used, such as dry plate photography. There wasn't film around, which is why we brought in the illustrations and stories to illustrate what it looked and was like. Then we moved into another section, which is fifties Melbourne, which is the [era of the] cultural credit

THE LOST CITY OF MELBOURNE

stagnation of the city. I wasn't sure how that was going to work, because there were going to be so many different levels of aesthetic. I think it was important for people to stick with that first bit, as we were setting the scene for what Melbourne was like.

I recommend Robyn Annear's book on Melbourne called *A City Lost and Found: When the Wrecker's Melbourne*. It's a wonderful book full of stories of groups and people, hilarious stories about things that went on. There was a story that we would have liked to put in the film, but it got cut due to timing. There were a whole lot of brothels in Little Lon, including some famous brothels like Madame Brussels. One night, the parliamentary mace went missing from the Victorian Parliament and ended up in Madame Brussels and was used in some bawdy nature in some role-playing games for a couple of weeks. Whoever stole it didn't want to be caught returning it, so it never got found. These are funny stories of funny people from a different time. It was fun to hear stories being told in a way that you're not going to get from your standard history books. You're not going to learn that at school.

It was a real pleasure to read and to learn about Melbourne at a time when Melbourne was in such a world of pain. It was so grim having a business in High Street in Thornbury, where my friends had businesses surrounding them and they were all closed. I went down to the cinema to do some maintenance one late Saturday afternoon and I remember coming out at six o'clock in the street and it was just tumbleweeds. This was unreal. Saturday night in High Street Thornbury is [usually] pumping, there's people everywhere, you can't get a park. It was really hard, for a lot of reasons, as a small business owner, particularly, but also as someone who loves Melbourne.

To see it in that level of pain and shuttered was probably what led me into that deeper journey of reading about Melbourne and looking at film and being fascinated by the photographs. What was powerful for me was to be drawn into those archives at the State Library. The dry plate photographers working at the time took photos on these big glass negatives. We've been lucky enough to have kept those glass negs, which is the original best source material you could ever get. Now we've got the technology over the last five years to do high-res scans of those plates, which means that if you find a photograph at the State Library, and you choose to download the TIFF file, the amount of detail is extraordinary. You could never match that now with digital photography unless you had a particular setting on your camera. I would bring a photo up on screen and zoom in to read the shop signs, 'JD Williams bootmaker.' There was another guy that was selling tobacco, and there was another guy selling saddles, another selling hats. You could zoom in and see the expression on these people's faces, see what they were wearing and see them smoking pipes. You get this incredible detail.

INTERVIEW | GUS BERGER

That was such a juxtaposition for me doing things like maintenance in my cinema and coming back and being surrounded by this city in lockdown. Then I came back into my studio and looked at this National Film and Sound Archive film of Bourke Street pumping, with so many people on the street, horses crisscrossing, and people dodging cable trams. There was something in there that was important for me as a Melburnian to connect with the city at that time.

My wife and I run the Thornbury Picture House, and it's a lot of work, there's a lot of admin and covering shifts. I do my programming every Monday, so it's kind of relentless. We love it, but it is pretty much seven days a week work. We're always aware of who's on and who's not on and what films are showing. If anyone calls in sick, one of us is going in, and sometimes both of us go in. We're bringing the kids in and bribing them with popcorn. It was probably the only good thing that came out of lockdown [for me] was that time to do that research and to read those books, because I would never have had that opportunity to have the time to do that research otherwise.

ENDNOTES

1   The John Curtin Hotel, better known as The Curtin was registered on the Victorian Heritage Register in April 2023. The Corkman Hotel was illegally demolished in 2016. The developers were given a hefty fine and jail time.

OFF COUNTRY

96 mins
Directors: *John Harvey, Rhian Skirving*
Writers: *John Harvey, Rhian Skirving*
Producers: *Nick Batzias, John Harvey, Rhian Skirving, Charlotte Wheaton*
Composer: *Helena Czajka*
Cinematography: *Dale Cochrane*
Editing: *Mark Atkin, Julie-Anne De Ruvo, Patrick McCabe*

INTERVIEW
WRITERS & DIRECTORS
JOHN HARVEY & RHIAN SKIRVING

Every year in Australia, over 3,000 Indigenous students receive scholarships to attend private boarding schools around the country. John Harvey and Rhian Skirving's *Off Country* is a documentary that follows the lives of six students as they start their year away from home at one of the nation's preeminent boarding schools: Geelong Grammar. Shot during 2020, *Off Country* finds the students in a turbulent world of change and uncertainty as the emerging COVID-19 pandemic unfurls across the world.

In 2022, *Off Country* was expanded into a four-part documentary series for SBS and NITV's 2022 NAIDOC week programming schedule.

This interview was recorded by Andrew F. Peirce in June 2022

What was your mindset when you set about capturing the story of boarding school life for Indigenous kids?

John Harvey: I've worked with young Indigenous people in the past and I've always felt passionate about the voice of young people getting out there. In terms of Indigenous stuff, young Indigenous people get a very hard rap in the media, often portrayed negatively. There's lots of policies and things surrounding young Indigenous people, but we rarely get to hear directly from them. That was the really exciting thing about this project: being able to hear from young people directly about their experiences through school, but also through life. For me, as a filmmaker, the opportunity to work with Rhian and to learn from her in terms of her storytelling was also wonderful as well.

Rhian Skirving: I initially came across the concept of the scholarships and immediately clicked how enormous that journey must be for a family of any student and in particular Indigenous students who might be coming from further away. I thought, "Wow, I'd love to know more about how that works for a family and to try and capture it, that rollercoaster of the experience." That's really how it started.

OFF COUNTRY

How did you select which kids to follow?

RS: That was a long process because the producing side of the film did take a couple of years. Initially, we met all the Indigenous students at the school or those who wanted to meet and had a chat with them and talked about the idea. We then filmed some of them in order to show our funding bodies and our commissioners the sorts of stories we could capture. Then of course a lot of those students had left by the time we were ready to go into production. Then we re-cast.

We were very clear that it was really for those who wanted to be involved. Obviously, you can't force something like this on anyone, let alone a teenager, so people had to opt in. We looked for a variety of locations that the kids came from and a variety of backgrounds and family stories.

Was the intention to gather a wide array of voices from all over Australia who could talk about what it's like to travel so far to Geelong?

JH: It was interesting because Wadawurrung country down there in Geelong is cold country. Then you've got students who are from Northern Territory or Queensland or Western Australia, so that in itself is pretty hard and a shock for them. Also, being so far away from family and during COVID, there [were] restrictions and border closures and a lot of complications coming up for the young people. For us, that was interesting too, because it also meant that we slightly shifted focus with the film.

We didn't get the traditional school year of starting the year with sports and musical tryouts and auditions and things like that. It meant we had to think on our feet which is the nature of doc but that gave us a focus on families and how families support young people through this process being so far away from home and the challenges that they go through. It was great how that came to the surface.

What were your initial feelings about the challenges that might arise when you heard that lockdowns would be on the cards?

RS: It was pretty bleak. We had only just started filming, and all of our characters were sent home and the school was shut down. It was scary for filmmakers. You have an expected story that you're going to follow, an expected timeline and an institution in which you have been given access, and then the institution has to shut down. It was difficult. Obviously being in Victoria, the lockdowns just seemed endless. We didn't know when we would have the students back and when the school would open.

INTERVIEW | JOHN HARVEY & RHIAN SKIRVING

For a while, we really were unsure what would happen. Slowly, as the lockdowns opened in WA, we could get a crew in WA to see our WA character, and John was in Queensland so he could see our Queensland character. Eventually I could get back down to Geelong as the school opened bit by bit. But a lot of our students couldn't come back to school. So, it definitely wasn't the year that we expected.

There's this feeling of disconnect with the story of the kids travelling to Geelong Grammar, then COVID comes along and adds to that feeling. We see some of the kids really struggle with that added disconnect.

JH: It's an interesting thing because from one perspective, it's a story of disconnect. From another perspective, it's a story about absolute reconnection with family and with culture. From the school perspective, there was definitely that sense of disconnection and all the challenges with on-line studying. We had a student who was in Western Australia who when they started the classes was on Victoria time, so they were getting up very early to just attend class online.

I think the interesting thing that kept bubbling up for me was here's this incredible, amazing opportunity at Geelong Grammar School. It's this prestigious Western institution of learning for schools, and I got the strong sense of young people [saying] "Yes, we want to walk down that path. But we also want to learn more and walk down this path of our cultural understanding and know our people, know our language, know where we're from, and know those stories." That was certainly equal, if not valued more for young people.

Sometimes being at home brings up things for young people about that connection. When they're away at school, they do have gatherings with other students and cultural gatherings with other Indigenous students there. These are things for any young person's identity, particularly for young Indigenous people. There are different levels of their own connection or finding out about who they are and who their family is. That idea of being home too brought that up to the surface.

RS: I think the extended period at home highlighted the sacrifice for some families. They hadn't had their kids home for a term or two. For some it made them realise what they were missing out on. As grateful and happy as they were and keen for the opportunity, I think COVID did do that for some families.

In between the moments of being on campus, there are moments where the kids are talking and answering questions on a set. When did that come in the filming process?

OFF COUNTRY

RS: It was towards the end and was done over a period of few weeks around kids' availability. John and I decided to go down that route after talking to the kids through the filming process and the many, many casual conversations off camera that we would have where these topics were brought up. We were quite taken with their responses, their attitudes, and the strength of their opinion. We thought we've got to capture this in a really concise way because we didn't have the opportunity of many observational scenes where you might be in the classroom at the right moment to capture the moment when they are discussing racism. We decided we would ask the kids directly, but the questions all came from our chats with them throughout the year.

The kids loved sharing their thoughts. They're never asked. They don't have an opportunity to express that in everyday life. They wanted to share their thoughts and appreciated being asked. Would that be fair, John?

JH: Yeah, absolutely. I mean, it comes back to that thing of providing a platform for young Indigenous people to speak their truth. That's a classic example of that. I think the other really interesting thing about that is it's a temperature check on where we are as a country. Some of their responses I could imagine myself saying as a young person. I was a bit shocked that today after too many years since I was that age, that kids are saying the same thing.

It's like yes, we've come forward as a nation in many ways, but there's obviously still a lot to do. I think the film also shows the cross-intergenerational effects of colonisation and trauma on the young people. We have to acknowledge that we have this intergenerational impact for non-Indigenous people in this country. These things come from some place. When things are said within the playground or whatever, it's rooted in this history of this country. That's a thing that we're constantly battling with.

To the school's credit, I thought that they were really open with our access, but also open to have those conversations and to acknowledge that they don't get everything right. The important thing is that we have these conversations and try to keep moving through together.

There's the moment where the kids object to singing the national anthem. There appears to be an awkward moment between the teachers who are standing there saying, "That's perfectly fine," but you can feel that they want the kids to be able to share the pride of singing a song about Australia. Were those moments of disconnect a surprise?

JH: I don't necessarily think that's a surprise from an Indigenous point of view, about people's reluctance or disconnect from that anthem that's supposed to represent everybody that clearly doesn't represent Indigenous people. I don't think there's a disconnect there or a surprise, rather.

On that, I went [to] a screening here in Queensland, and there was a young Indigenous person who's in grade five. He said to me afterwards, "I've always felt uncomfortable about singing the national anthem and I didn't understand why and couldn't articulate it." Again, to have these very young, very articulate Indigenous people speak about these things gave him words for his own experience. Kids right across this country are going through similar experiences. That was amazing to have them articulate that. There [were] definitely surprises in some things that were said. But for me, [I] was sort of surprised that "Oh, really? That's still an issue?"

I'd love to see where these kids are in five years' time, or to maybe revisit the school with a different group.

RS: I'd be fascinated to see where the kids end up and to follow them further or follow another group. I think it is evolving. I think the programs of scholarships in the schools are really working to improve things all the time. I hope some of the discussions are also moving forward. That's not for me to say. But I hope that hearing from young people can penetrate people who might have stopped listening. I know that there have been some non-Indigenous people watch the film and report back to me that they'd never thought about it that way. I had someone say, "Of course, we should change the day. I'd never thought about how awful that must be for an Indigenous person to celebrate that day."

JH: I think people will see Zoe's story as they go on. Zoe's now studying acting. I think she's just been cast in her first role for a professional theatre production up in Queensland. I think we're gonna hear more from Zoe and the other students, anyway. It's quite inspiring to see. Their journey is starting out. We've spoken a lot about challenges, but the incredible thing too is the resilience of the young people and the resilience of them going through some of these challenges and working with their family and with the school. There's so much positivity and hope that we can take away and go, "You know what, this place is in good hands." These young people, they're not buying into stuff. They're walking their own path. I think that's really wonderful.

RS: It was such a pleasure getting to know the students and their families and learning about their family story. They really are resilient; they're carrying a lot. They're carrying a weight with them, each family, of different policies that they've lived through. We mustn't forget that, and we mustn't underestimate that weight, and we should applaud them with every challenge that they overcome there. They really are great kids.

OFF COUNTRY

What does it mean to be an Australian filmmaker working today?

JH: I think part of this story is First People's stories first. There's over 60,000 years of stories in this country, so how we develop our identity is stemmed from that. The more connection we have with that identity that's been tens of thousands of years and is still there, I think the more confident we become as a society in ourselves and in our own identity. For me as a filmmaker, that often is something I think about.

RS: I agree. It's been fantastic working in collaboration with John to be able to explore a First Nations story. I've learned a lot and I appreciate that opportunity to collaborate into capturing these stories.

NUESTRAS VOCES

88 mins
Director: *Diana Paez*
Producer: *Latin Stories Australia*

INTERVIEW
DIRECTOR
DIANA PAEZ

Diana Paez's first feature documentary *Nuestras Voces* (*Our Voices*) sought to bring the stories of migrant and refugees from Spanish-speaking communities who arrived in Melbourne between the 1960s through to the 1980s. With personal stories and experiences, *Nuestras Voces* explores the challenges of settling into a different society, the fight against racism, the search for a foundation of their own cultural identity in Australia, and more.

Nuestras Voces was made in collaboration with the Victorian based organisation Latin Stories.

This interview was recorded by Andrew F. Peirce in April 2022

Where did the idea for Nuestras Voces come from?

Diana Paez: There's an organisation here in Victoria called Latin Stories. It was started by two Mexican women who started giving visibility to stories of Latin Americans in Australia. Everything is in English because the idea is to integrate and educate the Australian people and society. It started as a blog and then they had projects like workshops and exhibitions. That started growing and capturing more attention from people. Conversations started with important people in the Latin American community, people who have been in Parliament, or a woman who has won the Order of Australia. Latin Stories said, "It's time to do a bigger project," and the idea of *Nuestras Voces* came up, a project that included a documentary film, a report for the government, and some activities with the community. That's when I jumped onto the project because I'm a filmmaker. I made promotional videos for Latin Stories workshops and activities. They approached me and we started brainstorming, and now it's a film.

What was your journey to becoming a filmmaker?

DP: It has been very exciting. I did a couple of short documentaries; this is my first feature. I was born in Mexico, but I grew up in Colombia. I came to

NUESTRAS VOCES

Australia eight years ago to study filmmaking with a scholarship. Through that journey, and I think also because of the context of this country, I became interested in the documentary genre. I find a lot of value in films that tell stories and that make us discover other perspectives. It's a very powerful tool.

I have also been working a lot with stories from migrants and refugees. I started with smaller audio-visual projects and testimonies of human stories because that's something that really fascinates me. This country is like an unlimited source of different stories and different cultures. Then the Latin Stories project came. It's been wonderful because I was able to connect more with the history of the Latin American community in Australia, which I didn't know much about. I am a more recent migrant, and we have very different reasons for migrating. Through that process, I also learned a lot about Australia which is a very young country, really.

You're a recent migrant hearing the stories of people who have been here for decades. Did you find yourself r8elating to their stories? Did you see how things have changed since they arrived?

DP: Absolutely. I feel that that's part of the beauty of these stories. Even if you are a recent migrant who didn't come here four decades ago, you will find things that you relate to, emotional journeys that you can relate to. I believe if you haven't been a migrant, you can relate to things because at the end, it's about change, human interactions, and about Australia.

I think things have changed a lot. There are different challenges. Back then Australia was coming out of the White Australia policy, which was a big challenge. Also, when they migrated, Australia needed people, so they had a lot of services to settle. It was much easier than now where it's harder to get a visa to live here. I'm still trying to get residency here.

I came to a country that is way more open to other cultures, and where it's more normal to be different. It sounds a bit strange, which is a fascinating thing. I think Australia has succeeded a lot in being a multicultural country. It has a lot of things that we still need to work on, but the beautiful thing is that we are all part of it. I think at this point, we can't blame just one part of Australian society. We can all contribute to make it a harmonic place.

One of the stories is from a gentleman talking about how he was so excited to arrive here, that he was dancing and singing in the street, and a police officer told him off. What were the stories that you heard that surprised you throughout the filming?

INTERVIEW | DIANA PAEZ

DP: That one particularly, especially because Melbourne is such an artistic city. How come that happened in Melbourne? In the 1960s? Which is not long ago in terms of the history of a country. Even with the strong racism that some experienced, people like Spanish migrants who looked white European, they experienced a lot of racism. I was surprised by that. I was surprised and amazed to see how the music environment in Melbourne progressed, because nowadays Latin American music is very popular, it's trendy, but back then it was like a new discovery for everyone. I feel it would have been fascinating for these people to bring those roots and start seeing people interacting with different sounds. That especially resonates with me a lot, the arts, the music. It's beautiful, and it connects humans very easily.

What does it mean for you to be an emerging filmmaker here in Australia now?

DP: I feel privileged, to be honest. Maybe some people would say it's not that big an industry and somewhere else maybe there are more opportunities. Because I'm interested in life stories, it is a great place to be to tell stories. I also feel the government and different organisations are interested in investing in the arts and in listening to other stories. I guess it's becoming trendy to listen to different communities and minorities. That's something that interests me a lot. I'm curious to see what will happen, but also excited. This project is proof that it's possible to make films here in an independent way and make it sustainable because there are people that want to hear. I'm already looking for different stories, connecting with different people to see what's next.

Due to COVID, a lot of the interviews were filmed remotely. Maybe it's a happy accident, but with the people you interview, there is an invitation into their home in a different way. What was that like for you to capture those interviews remotely and to engage with the community?

DP: As you say, today I can see it as a happy accident. It also tells a story of the time we're living. While it was happening, it was pretty stressful for me as a filmmaker, because I had a creative plan of going to their houses to film with multiple cameras. I wanted to be able to also film them making a coffee, not just talking. That was a bit hard in terms of "How am I going to tell the stories if I cannot even visit them, see what they do in the morning, see what they do at night, what do they do in a normal day?" All those things that, artistic-wise, would make it more attractive or fancy stop mattering so much because the stories they're telling are the important thing. I wondered, "How am I going to find common themes to pull them together?" That was also a massive challenge because there were so many different stories. For me, that was the strongest process, editing thirty-five to forty hours of footage to short scenes that hopefully keep people engaged.

NUESTRAS VOCES

The good thing at the end [was] we had breaks from lockdown. I was able to visit a couple of them, and that was just beautiful, to see them in real life, a real person. I already knew them because I knew their whole life story, and they were beautiful with me. I was able to do that, to have a coffee, have a wine, talk about something, and go through their photos of their beginnings in Australia. I'm grateful at least that could happen with some of them. The time made it different and special. I think in a few years, we will be even more grateful that we were able to make it through COVID and we didn't wait to start the project after it finished.

There's also this beautiful array of photos. Were they from the people you interviewed, or did you have to go into the archives?

DP: There was a bit of everything. That was one of my biggest jobs and one of the things that consumed most of my time. Many of them did have photos and I went through a lot of albums that they gave me and tried to find out who is who. Many of them didn't have anything because they came [when they were] little or they moved a lot through cities, through countries, and they didn't keep things. I started researching in Australian libraries, and in the Chilean museum as well. I contacted them and told them about the project. They were super helpful. Tamara [Ortegon], who is part of Latin Stories, helped with all the admin to get photos and permission. We needed to pay rights for most of them. I think Australia has very good archival material in different places, it was just a matter of time and research to find exactly what I wanted so it could match what they were saying, so we were showing images and videos of the actual time they were talking about.

These stories feel like they're being uncovered for the first time. What does that mean to you to have that kind of responsibility to be able to share these stories?

DP: That's a big word. The funny thing is I felt it a lot through the process. It was a very independent little production. I had all the support from Latin Stories that started the project, but production-wise, it was pretty much me doing everything, of course with help from sound designers, subtitles, and some admin with Latin Stories. Then I had many sleepless nights because these stories are so fascinating that we need to honour them, and [the question was] how to honour all of them? Which is tricky because the story also needs to be engaging. We would love to tell the stories of the thirty people that participated, each story could even be a documentary itself. I feel it might sound very abstract, but it's been a bit of intuition when listening to the stories and putting them together of what feels good, and what highlights the best out of humans, in this case of these people who came to Australia decades ago, while also showcasing the challenges of how they went through it.

INTERVIEW | DIANA PAEZ

I feel that in the end, the most beautiful thing was seeing the resilience they had, and how they were not only in survival mode, but they wanted to thrive and be part of society and help in wider ways than just their own lives. For me, because I'm twenty-seven and I came here eight years ago, and I am the one listening to the stories, editing the story, deciding what frame to use, what colour to put, what music goes there, I feel very privileged, to be honest. I'm glad Latin Stories trusted me with this project, and that these people connected so much with the project, and that we can acknowledge their stories and their lives because many of them probably don't even know how much they have contributed to this country.

SPLICE HERE

A Projected Odyssey

118 mins
Director: *Rob Murphy*
Writer: *Rob Murphy*
Featuring: *Rob Murphy, Douglas Trumbull, Leonard Maltin, Quentin Tarantino, David Strohmaier, Pete Smith, Lawrence Johnston, Randy Gitsch, Dennis Bartok, Benjamin Tucker, Lee Zachariah, Michael Geoffrey Smith, Anthony Sloman, John Richards, Bill Hedges, Bill Lawrence, Alexa Raisbeck*
Producer: *Joanne Donahoe-Beckwith, Rob Murphy, Roslyn Walker*
Music: *Brett Aplin, Burkhard bon Dallwitz*
Cinematography: *Joanne Donahoe-Beckwith*
Editing: *Rob Murphy*

Splice Here was nominated at the 2024 AACTA Awards for Best Original Score in a Documentary, and at the 2023 ARIA Awards for Best Original Soundtrack, Cast or Show Album and Best Original Soundtrack/Cast/Show Recording.

INTERVIEW
FILMMAKER ROB MURPHY

Rob Murphy's ode to the museum of the flickering light and the people who keep it shining acts as both a tribute to his fellow projectionists as well as to the art of cinema itself. *Splice Here* brings forth the stories of projection booths around the world – from the remaining Cinerama screens to the Tarantino at the Sun Theatre in Yarraville to the chap running a makeshift screen in his backyard – and by doing so, reminds us why the cinema-going experience is a spiritual one. Murphy's passion for his craft is infectious, and even though the film is two hours long, it could easily do with another hour of projectionist chatter.

This interview was recorded by Andrew F. Peirce in August 2022

There is that warmth that comes with film, that's imbued in the storytelling and in the way that you talk about the importance of projection and presenting film in a cinema, alongside the different voices who break down why film is different from digital and why it's important to be able to retain that difference.

Rob Murphy: I'm glad that came through. I didn't want to get bogged down in that whole digital versus film thing. As one of my interviewees says, it doesn't really serve anything, because it's like comparing vinyl to CD to mp3. Every format is different. They all have advantages and disadvantages. Sure, digital might have replaced film in a commercial way, and it probably had to because, from an ecological point of view, every year thousands and thousands of prints were being struck for two months of life and then destroyed again. Just the machinery to orchestrate that and transport all those films around the world is massive. In that way, it's a good thing. Digital is getting better all the time, but it's still not the same as watching film.

I love the notion that film is not immortal. We live in a day and age where we have in our minds that everything is going to last forever, but the reality is that's not the case. As we see with the degradation of the nitrate prints, and how in 100 years these processes won't be around, so we have to make the most of it while we can. Has that changed your relationship with film itself when you project it?

RM: It has. Doing this whole thing has made me realise that even though the prints made may still be there, and they're probably going to be safe, that if something's been stored well, it will still be there in three hundred years, at least. But because there aren't as many labs around and the studios are reluctant to strike new prints from the assets that they have, that does mean that the prints that exist are probably the only ones that are going to exist of that title. It has certainly made me appreciate it a lot more when I get to run a rare print. It doesn't make me more careful because I'm already careful, but in the back of my mind, it does because yes, this could be the last print that exists of this title.

What's that like, projecting something that you know could be the last print of that title?

RM: It's kind of terrifying. But it really does have that sense [where] you feel like you're in touch with the people who made the film. This print has history. It might go right back to when that film was first exhibited, or it might be a re-release, but it still has this incredible history attached to it. If it's a Technicolor print, it looks beautiful when you hold it in your hand. If it's an IB technical upgrade, then it's really rare and really special. You feel that it has a smell. You're holding it in your hands, you see the characters right there in the frame in front of you, and you go, 'Wow, there was this print, there was a negative, and then in front of that was Humphrey Bogart.' You're that close to the actual event. You don't get that with digital. It's just ones and zeros.

Was there a moment making Splice Here where your notions or ideas about what you have been doing for years changed at all?

RM: As far as the evolution of the film went, I didn't know what I was making to begin with. It was probably a short film. It was the fact that now I have cinematography skills. I'm a filmmaker and I'm a projectionist. I thought, who else is more qualified to be documenting this as it was happening? Lots of other people were doing the same thing around the world, but all the other films I watched during that period were beautiful vignettes into what we were losing. They weren't about what happens after digital takes over. As I kept shooting, that began to come more and more into the narrative.

It probably wasn't until about 2014 or 2015 that I saw the bigger picture and realised how I could turn this into an adventure, not just a documentary. That was when I discovered John Mitchell in Sydney, the guy who had

INTERVIEW | ROB MURPHY

the backyard Cinerama cinema. I thought, 'Well, I have to go and see him.' I found out that there's one place in Bradford that still runs Cinerama films once a year. Then I got in touch with Dave Strohmaier, the guy that was restoring the films and he was going to be in Bradford that following year. I thought, 'What if I built the whole film off this search for Cinerama?' Because it's the ultimate projected film experience. I thought that was a great way of hanging everything else off it.

Then we heard about Tarantino. In the back of my mind, I thought, wouldn't it be incredible if he actually came to Melbourne and I got to interview him. While we were doing it, I really wanted to be part of the process. Projecting in 70mm was amazing, and using Ultra Panavision, which hadn't been done since the 60s, was extraordinary. Being involved in that was just great. But in the back of my mind was always 'What if I got to meet Tarantino? That would be perfect for my film.' And it happened. I didn't orchestrate it or push for it. It just happened. It was very exciting.

There are a bunch of filmmakers, Tarantino, Christopher Nolan, who talk about the importance of shooting on film. Is it vitally important that these pinnacle figures in filmmaking continue to talk about the value of shooting on film?

RM: Absolutely. It was the efforts of Tarantino, Paul Thomas Anderson, and Christopher Nolan that saved Kodak from oblivion. We wouldn't have any film to shoot on if they disappeared because all the other manufacturers are gone now. It was hugely important that they got behind the medium and started to push it out there. Christopher Nolan re-released *2001* (1968) and did a restoration of the prints. We have a brand-new print of *2001* at the Sun because of that. That's amazing. Their efforts have had a huge impact on re-emerging the medium as something that is a point of difference.

I can give you all the technical or artistic reasons why I think film is better than digital, and why digital is great in other ways, but at the end of the day, that's just kind of all arguments. It's all very self-reflective, it's very objective in that it's what you like to look at. Some people would say that digital looks great, particularly when you see computer animated films, that's where it really shines, because the whole world is in the computer, it's in the medium that you're working with. They can control it utterly. You get these rich, deep colours, and it's perfectly clean and bright. But it looks like it does at home. It's hyperreal. See I'm getting on going.

It's easy to get lost down that track, isn't it?

RM: It is. The biggest thing for me has always been the blacks. Digital projection just doesn't give you a good black. It's always a bit washed out. It's always a bit green. Film still gives you deep, rich, utter blacks, especially on a 70-millimeter print. The thing is that so many people haven't seen a 70-millimeter print now. There are whole generations of people that have never experienced it. Even people my age have come to see *The Hateful Eight* (2015) sessions, and they come up to me afterwards and say, "I never knew it could look like that. I had no idea cinema could look that incredible." There's already a real interest in shooting on film again and experiencing film prints by the public. There's a whole heap of people that have already embraced that. It's already happening because of those filmmakers, and hopefully because of this documentary, it will continue to show the point of difference that you have with film. Not that it's better, not that it's worse, but it is definitely different.

There's a documentary called Cinemania (2002) about film lovers in New York. They would visit different cinemas, watching four or five films a day. They built up a relationship with the projectionists. A lot of them would have the contact number of the projectionist to call on their mobile and say, "Hey, this is a bit blurry, can you fix it?" Whether we see our projectionist or not, we have a relationship with them because of what they're projecting and how they're projecting it. Can you talk about having that kind of relationship with an audience as you're projecting a film?

RM: It is kind of funny that when the projectionists were taken away, there was a disconnect with the audience, it didn't feel as special anymore. In a lot of cases, there's no one up there. Even in the last 10 years of film, there was probably no one up there for most of the film. It was all running automatically. Some people have remarked to me that they missed that very subtle sound of the projector clattering in the background. When I run a film, we make a big show and tell about it. There's two of us at The Sun and we go down for a presentation and talk about the film, like I did in the documentary. We do that with all our films now. We try and find some little interesting piece of information. I invite people up into the bio box during the film if we're on a kid's film, we run *Willy Wonka and the Chocolate Factory* (1971) and *The Wizard of Oz* (1939), we have a print of each, and I always let the kids come up during to watch it. They're always fascinated.

Having that person there, even if they don't talk to them or look back, just to know that there's a human being back there running the film for you makes it feel more like theatre. It makes it feel more like a presentation, not just something mechanical that you could do at home. All that has been lost with the whole showmanship of projectionists controlling the lighting and timing everything in the auditorium music and the curtains. That whole sense of presentation and knowing that someone is doing it for you, it feels like theatre and a sense of occasion that you've paid for a performance, and that's what you're getting. You don't get that with an empty bio box at a digital presentation.

It's the whole argument of 'I've got to sit through a half hour of ads and minutes of trailers before I get to watch the film.' It's the feeling of watching a product and not something that people have spent years and years of their lives working towards. To me, that relationship of having the projectionist there feels like it is the last step of the human touch of passing a film on to an audience. In Splice Here, you talk about the different sizes of the film in front of an audience, and it's that reminder that you're watching something tangible, people have worked hard on this. They've brought it here to entertain you. It means a lot. That's why we go to cinemas. There's something tangible, especially for something like Star Wars (1977), which feels so otherworldly. It makes it feel real and organic.

RM: It does. I don't know whether it feels that way for people who are creating their film memories in a digital world. I'd be interested to ask them in ten years how they feel about the product. The other thing is that back in those days, you could only go and see it at the movies, you couldn't see it any other way, so that memory would live in your mind, especially if the film was taken away. The film finished, and you wanted to keep watching it, all you had was the memory of that experience. It grows and festers, and it just becomes this incredible thing in your mind. People don't have that these days because everything's instantly accessible. I don't know whether it does create that nostalgia for people because they've always had access to it. Because of that, it doesn't feel special.

Nowadays, you can almost watch the whole film on social media through gifs, clips, and reels from films that launched that day in cinemas. That feeling of it being a special experience is lost. I remember growing up and seeing Saving Private Ryan (1998) sixteen times in the cinema because of that special feeling. I knew that as soon as its run was done, I wouldn't be able to get the same kind of experience at home. I could pick up the VHS, but it wouldn't be the same. It's that nostalgia, which I do feel it's kind of a dirty word in a way, but there is a warmth there which is really important.

RM: We ran *The Hateful Eight* on Monday night because it was the eighth of the eighth, and it was the highest grossing screen of the night. It just looks so incredible. You cannot get that experience at home or any other way but in a cinema with print.

SPLICE HERE: A PROJECTED ODYSSEY

With the MIFF screening, there was a David Thomas tribute. I understand that David was a key person associated with MIFF and projecting films for a long period of time. Can you talk about his work?

RM: Every projectionist I know has worked with Dave at some point, either at MIFF or at another cinema. I'm the same. I spent seven years at the Nova with Dave. He was just one of those people [that] no matter how stressed or crazy you are feeling, as soon as you went into a room with Dave, you felt instantly calm. He was just a really calming presence. He always had something understated to say about any situation, he would never freak out.

I remember walking into a bio box at one stage with him, and the pickup had failed. The whole film had been playing out onto the floor. It was still running through the projector, the audience didn't know any difference, but the bio box was knee-deep in film. I hadn't been in the job that long and I almost panicked instantly. Dave just put his hand on my shoulder, and that stopped me from jumping forward and said, "Just let it play out. Go to front of house and tell them the next session is cancelled." Like anybody else just would have gone "Oh my god. What are we going to do."

He was a lovely man. Really incredible at his craft. I used to talk to him for ages. He ran the roadshow release that came here of *Napoléon* (1927), Abel Gance's film from the twenties. He ran the triptych sequence in that. [He had] amazing passion and knowledge. He was just a lovely man. I was really thrilled when MIFF got in touch and said, "We love your film. We'd love to use it as a tribute to Dave." I thought, "That is perfect." Being a film from a projectionist point of view, I'm so glad that it's been used in this way.

Can you talk about what kind of person a projectionist is?

RM: Projectionists are all crazy, but in a lovable curmudgeon kind of way. All the projectionists I know are a bit nuts. I mean, I probably am too. But there's something about this end of the process. We're all film buffs too, but there's something about being in the bio box with that physical article. It's just this bit of plastic, it's this tiny little thing, and you put it into this machine, and then if you do everything correctly, it becomes this massive reality of beauty in front of you. That never gets old. When you open the gate and you start the film and you get it all right, you feel a wonderful sense of accomplishment of being part of the film.

I do like the word gatekeepers for projectionists, I think that's a great word. It's in the blood. It's like filmmakers, especially in this country, it's not something you do to make a lot of money. It's not something you do as a clever career path. You do it because you have to do it. You have these stories you want to tell in these ways you want to tell it and if you don't, you die.

INTERVIEW | ROB MURPHY

That's the way it is. It's a little bit the same for projectionists. It was really tough when digital came in, because even if people had the knowledge to make the transition, it just didn't feel the same. You're a computer technician now and you have no control over what the projector was doing. You started it and you stopped it.

The sort of people that are projectionists, they definitely do have similar interests. Other than projecting, they do seem to have a thing about steam trains, me included, that seems to be something that goes with this particular personality. What else? We're all crazy about finding that long-lost film print of something that's been missing for ages.

Do you have a grail that you're looking for?

RM: As with many people, I'm looking for *London After Midnight* (1927), the Lon Chaney horror film from the twenties. That's completely lost in a fire in the sixties, so nobody's seen it since then. Everything has been destroyed. There's a good chance that it could be in Australia.

A few months back, I made an effort through The Age to generate interest in locating people who might have a print. I'm sure it's out there somewhere. I'm sure there's a piece of it out there somewhere. I'm sure the person who has it knows how important it is. It's the Holy Grail for film archivists and projectionists. Because Australia was at the end of the distribution chain, a lot of prints ended up here and they never went home. So it could be out there. Being nitrate and being that old, it could have survived. The thing with nitrate is if it's not decomposing, then the image will still be perfect. Not like safety film where it slowly fades or shrinks or the colour starts to go, and the vinegar syndrome and all that. Nitrate is lasting better than anybody thought it would.

What's the best moment that you've had projecting a film?

RM: I have to say projecting *The Hateful Eight* was pretty special because it was Ultra Panavision and because it was technically Cinerama. That meant a lot to me. After Tarantino visited, we had full houses for months, and just to see the cinema full of people like that again and again and again, and see their reactions, I had people stand up and salute me or applaud me in the bio box, just because they were so impressed by it. That was a really special time, and I don't know whether that will come again. I hope the films will keep coming.

One thing I will say is it's difficult to do 70mm because a lot of films start on 35mm, and then they get blown up onto the print. People don't realise we're not in a digital world where you can copy things as many times as you like, and it all works fine. In the analogue world if something starts that big and you blow it up, it still has the resolution of the thing it was shot on.

We're seeing films like *The Murder on the Orient Express* (2017) and *The Death on the Nile* (2022) where they shot on 65, then they scan the negative and everything beyond that point as digital, but they do all the post at 4k, and then they output it to a 70mm print, so it doesn't look like 70 can look if you've gone from the negative to the print and taken away all that digital stuff in-between. They're bottlenecking. They're starting with something this big (65), then shrinking it down to do all the post (4k), and then putting it back out onto a medium that has a capacity for this (70), but it's still only that big (4k). That saddens me a little bit because people will say, "Oh yeah, it looked good. But it didn't blow my head off." It should. It has the capacity to do that. If the studios are going to shoot on 65, then they should be finishing it at that resolution.

What does it mean to be an Australian filmmaker telling this kind of story?

RM: Obviously, it's my personal story. It didn't start that way. I think it's great that I've got to make this film because it's typically not something that you'd see in an Australian cinema by an Australian filmmaker. Yes, it's a local story, but it's got a lot of nostalgia for American content. It's a bit of a film fan story. I didn't want it to be a serious, surgical study of what we're losing. I wanted to catch the tail of what we're gaining now, what's re-emerging. I want people to feel good about film. I want them to feel excited about film.

It's interesting that digital is the only way I got to tell the story. If we'd had to wait to generate the money to shoot this on film, it probably wouldn't have happened, because it just would have cost too much. It would have happened much quicker if we generated the money beforehand to make the film, we would have had to shoot it in maybe six months or something. So, the fact that I've done it the other way around, because I've had the skills and I've had the friends who have had the skills that we've just gone out and done it in our free time or when we could because it's evolved over 10 years, it's a much better story. No one could have foreseen what was going to happen in the first 10 years, that film would come back.

As a filmmaker, I don't know whether I would have gotten to make this film if I had to get the money first. That's probably as far as I want to go. I don't think it's a story that people would have bought off paper. I don't think it's a story that fits in with the typical kind of Australian movie that gets made or gets funded. Once I got it to a rough-cut stage, and then you can show it to people then they go "Wow, this is great. This is different. I haven't seen this before. This is an interesting Australian story that you wouldn't have thought of." There are a lot of great films being made now because of digital, and that's one of the fantastic advantages of it is that people can just go out and make something they don't need to wait for the money to make it.

The funding bodies are incredible, and they've really supported this film. That's all we've got. We can't generate the money any other way. It's very difficult, especially if you're making this kind of thing. It was really just me and Jo [Donahoe-Beckwith] and a camera and whatever we were filming. It's not as hard as doing a drama if you have to organise 50 people, a location, and three days of shooting. We had our complications, of course, but we could move pretty easily because it was only two or three of us at a time. And I had access to all of this when we were shooting.

What does it mean to be an Australian projectionist working today?

RM: I feel incredibly lucky and thankful that somehow our cinema has retained its film capability. That's largely to do with our boss, our fearless leader, Michael Smith. He's just as passionate about film as we all are. Of course, *The Hateful Eight* has pushed everything on. But there's really only two of us in Melbourne who are still running film on a regular basis. I feel incredibly lucky that I still get to do this. I feel great that I can show people what protected film is. And I love that people are getting excited about it again.

GIRL AT THE WINDOW

84 mins
Director: *Mark Hartley*
Writers: *Terence Hammond, Nicolette Minster*
Cast: *Radha Mitchell, Ella Newton, Karis Oka, Vince Colosimo, James Mackay, Andrew S. Gilbert, Jackson Gallagher, Sharon Johal, Lach Millar, Simone Buchanan, Lauren Goetz, Trae Robin*
Producers: *Antony I. Ginnane, Ross Hutchins, Caroline Pitcher, Andrew Wiseman*
Composer: *Jamie Blanks*
Cinematography: *Garry Richards*
Editing: *Mark Hartley, Roberta Horslie*

INTERVIEW
DIRECTOR
MARK HARTLEY

There are few minds who know as much about Australian cinema as Mark Hartley does. His pivotal and vital documentary *Not Quite Hollywood* (2008) inspired a new generation of filmmakers to pay homage to the Ozploitation movement with genre films of their own. Outside of documentaries that have celebrated cinema, Hartley remade the iconic horror film *Patrick* in 2013, and almost a decade later, his second fiction feature *Girl at the Window*.

This thriller is a throwback to the iconic thrillers of the eighties and nineties, pulling in a *Rear Window*-esque vibe alongside a Nancy Drew-alike heroine in the guise of newcomer Ella Newton as Amy, a teenager who starts to suspect that her mother's new romantic interest might also be the mysterious killer stalking her hometown.

This interview was recorded by Andrew F. Peirce in August 2022

After Not Quite Hollywood, Electric Boogaloo, Patrick, and now Girl at the Window, is there a notion of having a body of work that you're building up over the years?

Mark Hartley: I always aspired to be a hack, and I haven't quite achieved that yet. It's been a long time since I made a narrative film, and it's not through a lack of trying. In terms of a body of work, you make what you get offered, or what you can get financed. Certainly, I'm happy with every film I've made, and they're films that I've wanted to make, which has been important, but I would have loved to have made ten others.

Girl at the Window feels like it's the kind of thriller that's pulled from the peak of the genre, the 80s and 90s. How important was it for you to be able to pull from that era and bring it into a modern context?

MH: I don't even know if we did achieve bringing it into a modern context, but certainly we did set out to make a throwback or something that at least

605

GIRL AT THE WINDOW

harks back to the films that I loved when I was a kid. One of the first things I said to Tony Ginnanne, our producer, was this could easily go the way of being your typical serial killer next door Lifetime movie, but we need to put a bit of content in there that will elevate it slightly above that.

As a kid, I saw things like *American Werewolf in London* (1981) and *The Howling* (1981), the first adult horror films I saw, I remember thinking, "Oh my God, I can't believe as a kid I'm allowed to see some of the stuff I'm seeing." I wanted to introduce similar elements into this somewhere. At first, you think it's a film that's very much a Nancy Drew fun, quirky, rollicking kind of mystery, and then suddenly, there's a naked girl in a cage, there's an eye getting cut out, seen from inside the skull. I think those little things are what the target younger audience will say, "Wow, I can't believe I just saw that in this film."

There's the line, "This is not a normal teenage dilemma", how much do you enjoy being able to work within that genre trope?

MH: It doesn't happen very often. It's funny, I occasionally put some Blu-ray releases together, I promised Richard Franklin that I'd try to do my best to make sure that his films got out there, so I've been putting together the Blu-ray for *Cloak and Dagger*, the film he made in 1984. It's amazing the number of kids in peril in that film that you just couldn't do these days. Kids getting told that they'll get a gut shot and they'll hang around till they bleed out and all these kinds of things. In this age of teen shootings and all this kind of stuff, there's content that you just can't get on screen anymore. I wanted this to be a teenager in peril film as much as what the Hardy Boys was when I was a kid growing up. I think that it's fun to play with tropes that you don't see a lot of anymore.

How important is it for you to have somebody like Tony as a producer helping you bring these stories to life?

MH: I wouldn't have made the two narrative films [I have] if it hadn't been for Tony. The good thing about Tony is that he trusts that I know the genre, and he leaves me alone. He trusts my team, so I can work with the same DoP, the same production designer, etc. At least Tony knows that at the end of the day, he will get something that tells a story as well as we can in our limited schedule and budget. It's just good to have that support. It's been good with Tony as a producer when it comes to me delivering my director's cuts, and so forth, because I can talk to him about things that he's maybe a little bit unsure of, and most of the time, I get my stuff through. It's been a really great collaborative relationship.

INTERVIEW | MARK HARTLEY

What's it like also having somebody like him as a friend? He's a major figure in Australian cinema and, most importantly, Australian genre films.

MH: It's funny, I never really thought of that until recently. During the COVID lockdown, I was working on a book on Ozploitation film posters from the 1970s to 1990s. There's a whole lot of text that goes with them. Whenever we wanted a bit of information, I'd go, "I'll just ring Tony." It's funny to have that connection to that period, where you can just ring up someone who was there, who was in the trenches, and [they] can tell you whatever you need to know. I always took that for granted until I realised, I could just ring up Tony and ask him this stuff. I honestly think he's probably the last man standing in terms of his generation of producers still actively getting films financed. He's had a very remarkable career.

You're working with Garry Richards. How important is it to work with a cinematographer who understands genre cinema and gets the visual style and tone for a thriller?

MH: I guess it's important. I don't use Gary because he understands thriller or sci-fi or anything like that. I use Gary because I've always used Gary. We've worked together for 30 years now, and I couldn't think of being on a set with anyone else. We have a similar sensibility. We love the same kinds of movies. Neither of us can draw, so we didn't do storyboards. We had a shot list in a detailed fashion. I have a collaborative relationship with Gary probably closer than most director-DOP's. We get together and we shot list every single shot in the film, every single edit in the film. For both narrative films, we would talk about how we think a scene should be staged, and 99% of the time, we'd both come up with the same idea in terms of how we think things should be.

We're just lucky that we're in simpatico when it comes to these kinds of genres. I don't think it's just thrillers. We love a breadth of a lot of different genres. We've both watched a lot of films. I guess now we're finally developing our own aesthetic and style. I think *Patrick* was a lot more slavish to the filmmakers that we loved, and maybe *Girl at the Window* is a little bit more of our personal style coming to the fore.

The era of Ozploitation is generally considered to be like the seventies and eighties, and peters off into the nineties, there are a lot of filmmakers nowadays who are pulling from the aesthetics and that style.

MH: There are a lot of people that are certainly branding their low-budget horror Australian films as Ozploitation, 'Return to Ozploitation', another 'King of Ozploitation'. I'd like to remind them that Ozploitation ended with *Blood Moon* in 1990. They're certainly not part of that movement. It's amazing how much people have embraced our genre roots to some degree since *Not Quite Hollywood*.

How much does that influence you in your narrative films, the echoes of *Not Quite Hollywood*?

MH: I'm not sure if it influences me a lot. When you look at Tony's films, *Patrick* (1978), *Thirst* (1979), *Harlequin* (1980), all those films, they're made by really good filmmakers. They're traditional Hollywood-style filmmakers: Richard Franklin, Simon Wincer, Rod Hardy. When you look at those films, they are very classical in how they're mounted. I tried to do the same. We don't shoot handheld, we shoot everything off dollies and tracks, and we don't light everything overly naturalistic, we want to have a bit of a gloss to it. I think that's also my music video background as well. 99% of the clips Gary and I did, we did with artists to get on *Video Hits*, so we had to be as glossy as we possibly could on limited budgets. I guess it's the style that we like, and it's the kind of films that we like seeing.

Can you talk about the casting process for Ella, Radha, and Vince?

MH: With Radha, with all these kinds of films, you're dealing with a sales agent who's going to find finance for your film [and] without selling territories, you can't get the film made. They ultimately give you a list of actresses or actors that they know that can help. Thankfully, Radha was on that list. That was great because I figured it would be nice to make this 100% Australian rather than have an import in there. Radha was in Melbourne during lockdown, so it was great timing, and she liked the script. It's always good to work with people who are utterly professional. It was great too, because I could see how Radha and Ella could be seen, at least, photographically as mother and daughter. It was great when you see them interacting, and you go "It's not just the look," they feel like they're a family. It was a great casting coup getting Radha.

With Vince, I needed an established actor that people would believe would have a larger part than he does in the film. I also needed someone who I knew could be very charismatic and charming, but also turn that into an air of menace. I thought Vince would be perfect for that. I had a long conversation with him on the phone, he only really has one key scene in the film, and he really liked that. I was lucky that he said yes.

It was a real stroke of luck with Ella. We had young actresses sending in tapes, and I thought her performance was great. She captured exactly what we needed for the film. Then I met her and she was really lovely and was so keen to be making her debut feature film. I watched a couple of episodes of the *Seachange* (2019) reboot, where she played Siggy's [Sigrid Thornton] younger daughter and she was great in that. We did some screen tests for her best friend, and we got Karis [Kailani] and her together, they just clicked instantly. "There's my couple," casting solved. I think we were lucky to get her. Any day now, she'll do an audition for an American series, and she'll be gone and we'll never see her again.

You're intimately part of the Australian film industry, how does being an Australian filmmaker and the Australian identity influence what you create and direct?

MH: I'm not sure that my films are uniquely Australian. It's funny, people ask me what the appeal of the films in *Not Quite Hollywood* was and why I was drawn to films like *Patrick* and *Snapshot* (1979), and it was because I saw international stories in locations that I recognised as being Australian. That's what I've tried to do with my films. They tell international stories, but they're very much part of the milieu of being an Australian. It's really difficult to raise finance for a genre film in Australia, and because these films can sell internationally, that's the only way I've been able to make them. For me, it's about telling international stories or stories that cross international borders, but with an Australian sensibility.

There are so many Australian films out there that people just wouldn't know about. When we did *Not Quite Hollywood*, what was most gratifying for me was the fact that so many young filmmakers suddenly went "Wow, I didn't know we had this rich history of these kinds of films." I know that it's inspired a lot of filmmakers to know that they can make stories that aren't necessarily stories set in your own backyard.

ANONYMOUS CLUB

83 mins
Director: *Danny Cohen*
Writer: *Danny Cohen*
Featuring: *Courtney Barnett*
Producer: *Philippa Campey, Samantha Dinning*
Music: *Courtney Barnett, Stella Mozgawa*
Cinematography: *Danny Cohen*
Editing: *Ben Hall*

REVIEW
ANDREW F. PEIRCE

Danny Cohen's *Anonymous Club* is about space. It's about the air in a room feeling lighter as the anxiety of the day exhales itself out of existence. It's about feeling comfortable enough to put your thoughts down on a page, or in the case of the subject of the film, Courtney Barnett, a Dictaphone. It's about being able to feel a lack of self-judgment for sharing those thoughts. It's about being allowed to be a person, standing in the spotlight, singing songs about how you're feeling.

Courtney Barnett stands as a perceived enigmatic figure. Interview-shy, rarely maintaining a public profile outside of gigs in front of crowded rooms, she can easily be perceived as someone who is closed-off, reserved, and holds back from revealing herself to the world. By listening to her tunes and inviting them into your mind and part of your consciousness, you'll quickly realise that everything you need to know about who Courtney Barnett is as a person is right there, hanging on each emotionally fused lyric.

This is a person who has hung a masterpiece of a song about going into anaphylactic shock and the ambulance journey that came with it. This is someone who walks us through a deceased estate, embracing the history of this unknown woman, all the while acknowledging that her past is going to slip away under the grips of gentrification, overpriced housing, and the flurried stomp of civilisations' demand for progress. Barnett once asked listeners to tell her how they really felt, and by doing so, opened up herself as a conduit for our mental illnesses and ailments.

These are big things to hold on to, and even larger subjects to cut yourself open with on a regular basis when being pushed out onto the press trail to discuss her latest album. *Anonymous Club* wisely opens with Barnett's stilted, awkward response to an earnest and excoriating question about her own anxieties.

It almost feels trite to say that given the prism of the modern music celebrity feels distinctly different from the high-budget music label creations of eras long gone. Now, the manufactured music icons stand comfortably alongside self-made gems, conjured into existence like some miracle diamond created out of the pressure cooker of the mind. Barnett's label, Milk!

ANONYMOUS CLUB

Records was created with fellow artist Jen Cloher after Barnett needed a name to release music under. The grounded nature of Barnett's music makes all the more sense knowing that her grandmother loaned her money to record her first EP.

None of this history is covered in *Anonymous Club*. Instead, Danny Cohen eschews a traditional music documentary narrative, leaning into what makes Courtney Barnett's music iconic: the vulnerability, the relatability, the openness, and the mundane. "I overthink what I need to say, and then I don't say anything. Maybe it's more useful to just... talk," Courtney says in one of the exposed moments of dictation that overlays footage of a world tour, glimpses from the wings of stages, comfortably claustrophobic amongst the tight cabins of tour buses, or just stretching out tension during the pre-gig shuffle. *Anonymous Club* shows an artist trying to find their place in this world of touring.

In between gigs, Courtney finds solitude in hotel rooms, alone on a bed, testing lyrics in the dull, generic decor that could be anywhere, just not home. For Barnett, home is a suitcase, a friend's lounge for a week, it's the space where being transient is allowed. Home is also the stage, in front of a thriving group of rain-soaked people in Japan, or it's being backlit by a column of light that immerses the ever-observant silent auditorium in darkness. "I feel a confused relationship with home and being away from home," she mutters into the Dictaphone like a transient being floating around seeking a tether. The constant travel gives Courtney ample time to digest who she is as a person, never truly getting the opportunity to ground herself for longer than days, or possibly weeks, at a time.

In its opening half, *Anonymous Club* sees an artist clouded by self-doubt, performing the expected routine of a musician pointing to the audience just so they'll cheer in return. Touring the album *Tell Me How You Really Feel* (*TMHYRF*), a fury-laden release that features songs like *Nameless, Faceless* and *I'm Not Your Mother, I'm Not Your Bitch*, becomes exhausting. The songs speak for themselves, but as each city-stop comes with another interview that collides into another interview, the frustration about the album's release and her ability to 'sell' it comes forth. "I feel I've somehow let myself down with this album. It kind of got swept aside because I was too scared to talk about anything real or heavy," she says.

Cohen's direction and Ben Hall's editing give that self-conscious pressure the space to be free, allowing it to hang there, stagnant. A warm camera monitors the art of adding one more elastic band to a fist-sized rubber band ball that is *TMHYRF*, easing it into a calmer tone as the creative process of creating a freer album like *Things Take Time, Take Time* starts to take root in Courtney's mind.

The power of music is undeniable, especially when it comes to the knotted tension of that thing, we call a brain. Our minds do a wonderful job of spiralling out of control, cruelly addicted to the free-falling nature of our crippling self-doubt and a general lack of confidence, so witnessing Court-

REVIEW | ANDREW F. PEIRCE

ney Barnett's journey of processing how her mind works through her songs becomes calming and comforting. The art of self-reflection is one we all struggle to master, and yet, in searching for a way to tell Courtney's story, Danny and Courtney landed upon the Dictaphone idea, giving Courtney the space to be open with herself, with Danny, and with us, a group of strangers we can 'the audience'.

At all times, Danny feels present with Courtney, even when he's not. Courtney's eased "Hey Danny" opens some of the Dictaphone recordings like she's Margaret Simon seeking an answer from an unseen being.

Companionship and friendship and just having someone to listen to is a constant within Courtney's lyrics. For many, myself included, that someone is Courtney herself. At once, I can put on *Write a List of Things to Look Forward To* and feel like everything's going to be ok. I can listen to *Pedestrian at Best* and suddenly my anxiety disappears. Someone else knows what it feels like, and they've put it in words that manage to distil its power into a fog that quickly disappears.

Early in the film, Barnett meets a young fan, Bobby, who stutters out an awe-tinged request for Courtney to sign his shirt and write a lyric from *Nobody Really Cares If You Don't Go to the Party*. He clearly wakes up with the song in his mind, bouncing around like a Windows 95 screensaver, never hitting the corners, overlapping and intertwining in a confused criss-cross pattern. She reacts in kind, equally stilted and awkward, and in doing so, she quietly acknowledges the communal feeling is there and that it's ok.

For all the accolades, the sold-out gigs, and the talk show hype, in this moment it's made clear that Courtney Barnett is just a person.

It's funny to write that, like there's a distinction between someone famous and 'a person'. Like they both don't struggle to keep their house plants alive while living their lives. When we write that they're 'just a person,' it suggests that they're connected with the world, and the issues of the day. They know how far a dollar will go, and they know the impact they have on the life of a stranger.

Courtney Barnett is just a person.

We're intrinsically fascinated by other people's lives. How they do things. Where do they put their teabags when they're done? Do they type with two fingers or two hands? What do they do with their hands when they're having a conversation? How do they react to praise? Or how do they react when they receive an unexpected gift?

We can sit and be in awe of how people manage to do things they're skilled at – playing guitar, saving lives, interviewing people – but at the end of the day, they're just people. And that's where *Anonymous Club* excels, with Danny Cohen giving Courtney Barnett the space to just be a person existing in the world.

During an intimate, 'in the round' style gig in Somewhere, America, Courtney takes a moment to talk to the crowd, checking in with them. Someone from the balcony calls out to Courtney, offering her a gift of a handmade

ANONYMOUS CLUB

coffee mug. She smiles, receives it with thanks, and we move on. In that moment, the brief 'thanks,' Barnett registers the gift with almost incredulity, as if to say 'I'm touched you went to the effort. I don't know why I deserve it. I'm just Courtney Barnett'.

Later, that gift finds its home with Barnett in the suburbs of Melbourne, warming her spirits as she people-watches from above, commenting on how these strangers would never know she's up there. In that moment, with that footage, Barnett and Cohen have given this gift to a stranger, Emily, on the other side of the world. Emily might watch *Anonymous Club* and they might ask themselves, 'I'm touched by this so much. I don't know why I deserve it. I'm just an audience member at a Courtney Barnett concert.'

Music has a way of becoming a part of us. The right song, the right artist, creeps into your life and embraces your being completely. Almost a decade ago, Courtney Barnett crept into my life. First with *Canned Tomatoes (Whole)* from the *I've Got a Friend Called Emily Ferris* EP, then with *Avant Gardener* on the *A Sea of Split Peas* EP. Since then, Courtney Barnett's music has become part of my life.

Anonymous Club has equally become part of my life, making a transition to comfortably become a slice of my soul. For newcomers to Courtney Barnett, this will either invite you into her aural world, encouraging you to become a new fan, or it might distance you. Either reaction is perfectly fine. Not everything is meant for everyone.

For the Courtney Barnett faithful, this is a comfort watch, a warm embrace, a rare connection in the audience with a stranger across the room as you both sing in unison, tears running down your face, the lyrics to *Sunday Roast*.

After all, we are human, and Courtney Barnett is just a person. I hope she's doing ok.

INTERVIEW
FILMMAKER
DANNY COHEN

Anonymous Club is a film built for the Courtney Barnett faithfuls of the world, with director Danny Cohen eschewing the traditional music documentary narrative and relinquishing the history of its subject in service of giving Barnett a Dictaphone and asking her to follow her own album title: Tell Me How You Really Feel. The film reflects on the international tour for that 2018 release, with Barnett opening herself up to the Dictaphone in a vulnerable manner that an 'interview to the camera' style doc may have struggled to gather.

Barnett's music reflects her own anxieties and mental health, making her Dictaphone entries to Danny feel like supporting evidence to her mental state. Being open about mental illness is difficult, and for Barnett it's even more complex when that openness takes place in front of a room full of strangers. *Anonymous Club* was shot on film, giving it a similar warm, ephemeral feeling as to what you might experience at a live concert.

Outside of his work as a documentarian, Danny Cohen has crafted some of Australia's most notable music videos, having worked alongside artists like King Gizzard & the Lizard Wizard, Courtney Barnett, and Kirin J. Callinan's memefied track Big Enough, which featured a celestial Jimmy Barnes wailing in the sky.

Anonymous Club received a nomination for Best Cinematography in a Documentary at the 2022 AACTA Awards, with Danny Cohen also being recognised with a nomination for Best Direction in a Debut Feature Film at the 2022 Australian Directors Guild Awards.

This interview was recorded by Andrew F. Peirce in March 2022

Can you talk about the emotion of talking personally into a Dictaphone?

Danny Cohen: It's an easy entry point to be like, "Hey Danny," and at least it gives you that confidence that you're talking to somebody. It can be tough to speak in a room and hear your thoughts aloud, which feels a bit strange. I did it a bit to share with Courtney. It's so nerve-wracking to do that with anybody. There's no two way, it's just one way. Even if you just talk about your day and the feelings that came up and down, it's quite intense. I don't know if it was initially cathartic when she was doing it, maybe it turned into something cathartic, or just a way to check in with herself and see where she's at with things. I guess you'd only pick [the Dictaphone] up when you've got something to talk about negatively. [You're] less likely to pick it up and be like "Today was so great, this happened, this happened, this happened." You're kind of doing something else if you're in that mood. If you're solemn or you've had a rough day or something's on your mind, it's more likely that you want to reach out to somebody in whatever facet that is, even if it's just a diary. I've never really spoken to Courtney about how she felt, whether it was cathartic, or what she got out of that process. I'd be quite curious.

Regardless of whether there was going to be a film or not, how did you feel being the receptacle for how Courtney was feeling at that time? How was that for you as a friend?

DC: I was really touched and honoured. It was lovely that she put that much trust in me as a friend and as a filmmaker. But it was difficult because I saw a side of Courtney that I never knew was there. We were good friends, and we'd hang out here and there, but I don't think we'd ever really dive that deeply into how we felt about everything. We'd talk about the creative process a lot; I think that's something we bonded over, but we never go that deep.

So, when I got the first round of Dictaphone entries back, I was like, "Oh, okay. Holy shit. She's being brave and she's going for it." The Courtney I knew from having worked with her, she's naturally shy and all that sort of stuff. Which is fine. Everyone is, depending on who they're talking to. I was floored by how open she had been and how much she gave to the Dictaphone from the get-go. "This is good. She trusts me. We're digging deeper, we're gonna find something here."

It took a long time for me to figure out what the film would be about. It was weird from a friendship point of view because I'd be getting a Dictaphone every couple of months and backing it up, and then I'd hear something, a particularly fragile moment. The next time I saw her, I'd be like "Hey, so are you all right with that thing?" And she's like "What? No, that was two months ago." [I thought] maybe I shouldn't bring stuff up, because the film or that device and our friendship crosses over in such a weird way. It's very strange.

Courtney has a vulnerability in her music, and that vulnerability is in the film too. You open the film with the awkwardness of an interviewer

INTERVIEW | DANNY COHEN

asking, "Presenting anxiety in your music, how do you deal with that?" It sets the tone of why you've chosen this way of presenting her story in the film.

DC: From the get-go we needed to make sure that people were on the journey with her. Not that they would be against her, but so that the people who didn't know her could understand the situation she's in, the position she's in, both with fame but then also with how she's feeling and her confusion. I feel like you have got to set that from the outset where people can relate to her. She's very relatable and down to earth. I think with someone like her, [when] she's being that open, then you can connect.

From the outset, it was always about trying to ensure that Courtney didn't feel like she was, for lack of a better word, whinging about her position. It was important to get over that hurdle because it's quite draining. "Okay, is this what the whole film is going to be?" There's only so much you can hold an audience before they're like, "I feel so sorry for this person. I just feel depressed. It's too much." We were trying to strike a balance of wanting people to understand what she was going through.

There are those lines where she's like, "I really want to do this tour, but I don't want to do this tour and I don't know why." I think even by saying, "I don't know why," that helps the audience be like, "Okay well, she's not saying, 'I don't want to do this tour because x, y, and z is hard or whatever,' and 'I'm nervous'." She's like, "I don't know, I can't figure it out." So, the audience is like "Will she figure it out, what she's looking for, or how she'll get past it?"

This is your first feature film; how did you find your way through telling this kind of story?

DC: Partly intuition, partly endless advice from filmmaker friends and friends in general. Glendyn Ivin was our story consultant. We're at the same production company, Exit Films, together. Same with Garth Davis as well. There are people around me who are quite supportive from a narrative sense. I always wanted to frame it like a narrative. It's obviously a documentary, but it does still feel like it could be a three-act narrative film, like a drama, it's almost there. I'm not an avid documentary fan, and I never thought I'd be making one, but the opportunity presented itself and here I am.

I tried not to watch a lot of documentaries going into it too. I didn't want to be like, "Oh, that's good" and naturally, I'd just get influenced by it and suddenly, you're just making that. I've looked at *Don't Look Back*. That's what we set out [to do]. I was like, "If I'm just in the corner of a greenroom, doing my thing, documenting, we'll find a story, we'll figure out what that story is." It's such a hard one. So many things influence you and funnel through that come out in creative ways. A lot of support around me and people to bounce ideas off and all that sort of stuff. I just was trying to make it as slow and meditative as I possibly could without it feeling dry or boring.

How long did you shoot for?

DC: Three years on and off. When we started the edit, I showed the editor *Tokyo-ga* (1985), the Wim Wenders film which is about him going to Japan and he's interviewing people that worked with [Yasujiro] Osu. It's observational, poetic, and slow. It creates such a feeling. I'm a big fan of slow cinema, so I'm like "Let's just hang out with the film for a while."

I think it's different in this format, where I'm using a story based off a Dictaphone. There's no script, no talking heads. It may be a little bit more difficult to do so. I remember the first cut we did; it was so long. You can see in the film there are certain types of framing that I'm into. We got some feedback from some people who came in and they were like, "It's a long film. It felt really long." It's like "Maybe I can't get away with that sort of stuff without reason, not just for the sake of it slowing down."

Were you out on the road filming while Courtney was on tour?

DC: It was just me, there wasn't anyone else in the crew. That was on tour and back in Australia. I did sound, DP, film loader or whatever, all the fun jobs. On tour, it's so fast-moving that there's no time to sit and reflect. Every day is somewhere else, especially when you're doing the European or American tours where you're on the bus. It's pretty much unloading in the morning when you're in a new city. I'll be trying to figure out what Courtney is going to do that day and tag along. Could be press, could be just hanging out in a hotel, then rehearsal, then there's dinner, then there's a show, and you're back on the bus. Then you drive through the night. And then the whole thing happens again. Now I'm in Paris, now I'm in Belgium. It's just crazy.

You don't have any real alone time. I was saying to Courtney it's only once you close your little bunk curtain that no one's around. I can just sleep, I can read, sit on my phone, whatever it is. It's like your own zone. There wasn't much time to do any work when I was away. There would sometimes be a couple of days off here and there, but I wasn't editing or anything like that. The film took so long to get to New York and for the rushes to be uploaded or shipped back to me on a hard drive. Every few months, I'd get that footage back and just hope it was one: processed well and there are actually pictures; and two: that there are decent pictures.

I imagine there's got to be a bit tense, sitting there waiting.

INTERVIEW | DANNY COHEN

DC: It was at the beginning because I hadn't shot film on my own, I always had a DP. I was very particular about loading. I was a projectionist when I was in my teens or early twenties, so I understand how film travels around, so I was quite careful. "This has to be kept in the fridge." There are so many rules to it. Then by the end, I'm just like "Chuck it in the boot. It's fine." You know, it just works. If it was a proper narrative feature film, you might be a little different with it. But I was like, "I can't play this game like that." It went through a bunch of X-rays, it's fine. It's really, really hardy.

What type of film did you shoot on, and what was the decision to shoot on film?

DC: We shot on Kodak Vision3 500T. They're a higher ISO tungsten film, the whole thing was on the one stock. The decision was because it's the look. I feel it's more immersive. It's got a natural quality to it. It's textural, it feels alive in a way and it's softer. It doesn't have that same artificial feeling that digital has. I don't think it's a debate, digital versus film. They're just different worlds. And that's fine. I think digital is quite sharp and – not in an insulting way – sterile, very clinical. So many beautiful films are shot on digital.

I was rolling like a roll a day, ten, eleven minutes a day on film. Whereas I know on digital, I'd just be like five hours. Because you would, why not? You're there and that's your job. Then by the end, you'd have 500 hours' worth of footage which is just so difficult to go through and find those moments. I think there was something about being in greenrooms and not having a little viewfinder, and people can see when you're filming. There's light in the room and you suck this energy away from things. People seize up when they see that sort of stuff. Whereas the 16mm, you don't really know what I'm filming. It's quite compact and people get used to not knowing what you're doing.

Is there comfort in the restraint? As you're saying, you've got eleven, twelve minutes a day to shoot. Is there a comfort in knowing "I've got 24 hours and I'm only going to get minutes of footage today"?

DC: Yes, and no. Initially, for the first six months, the takes were too short. They were like ten- to thirty-second takes. I was so worried about spending money on film and chewing through it, so I was doing these really short takes. Even thirty seconds felt long to me for a take. Then you look at it when you're editing and you're like "What was I thinking? What can I say in that amount of time?" I [realised] maybe that's the vibe, that's part of the free flow stream of consciousness that it cuts and then all of a sudden, we're somewhere else and it cuts and it kind of keeps rolling.

ANONYMOUS CLUB

Over time, you become better at picking your moments and when you need to button on or not. More often than not, it's during moments when you anticipate nothing significant to occur. It's all the in-between moments. She could be playing a massive show in London and everyone's like "This is it, you've got to be there, 5,000 people." Why wouldn't that be a big moment? Then you film the gig and of course, it's a great gig and she's in a great zone, she's had an awesome gig in front of so many people. But then so has every other musician that plays at this venue. The documentary I was trying to make wasn't about those accolades or something like that. After the first few tours, I was like 'I've gotta stop shooting shows the way I was.' I was shooting so many shows. I was like, "This is great. I've got really good footage of Courtney playing, but just not enough of a story." It was a good lesson.

Can we talk through the editing process with Ben [Hall] and the decisions of what songs to include. Was that a discussion between you and Ben or was it a discussion between you and Courtney?

DC: I'll answer the songs first. Firstly, at the beginning of the film, I wanted to keep the songs from the record that she was touring, because the whole record was so reflective of her mood at the time when she was in quite a dark spot. The songs were angry and were about mental health and all that sort of stuff. That's exactly how Courtney was trying to work through those things, by putting it into that album. I wanted the songs to reflect the mood of the album and the mood of how she was on that tour. Songs like *I'm Not Your Mother, I'm Not Your Bitch*, any of those heavier angrier moments. Even when she sings *Sunday Roast* at the radio station somewhere in Europe, there's something about that song that was reflective of her mood on tour, that she has to keep on going, she's just praying for a day off. I was always trying to find songs that would match the mood or match where she'd come from. That shifted naturally to when she started writing the next record where the songs are a lot lighter because she was in a lighter place, so it felt right to show those sorts of moments.

With the editing, Ben and I went through and catalogued everything. We wrote out a script for the Dictaphone, and we wrote down what themes it's touching, and what story points it would be hitting, then the same with the footage. We'd go through and [work out] what's happening in this shot. Where could it link to? Where's appropriate? Where was it actually in time? Could we line that up with the Dictaphone? We had it on scene cards and printed out photos from every scene, and we just filled the walls basically with the film.

Then you start building it in terms of how you can see that arc and thread for people to go on the journey with her, but for there to be light and shade or start off maybe at the midpoint and kind of dip down to come back up

INTERVIEW | DANNY COHEN

to have that contrast. It was difficult to construct a story without a script. You're like "I just wish Courtney would say this." That would get us through to the next thing, we would go back to the Dictaphone, scrub through and try and find that moment that we're looking for. We went mad. In a good way. It's my favourite thing to do, but it's very difficult.

Was there ever a time that you thought, "I wish I could just call up Courtney and go 'Hey, this is what we're dealing with in this moment. Can you give us a little bit more?'"

DC: Definitely. The thought crossed our minds a lot. But then we knew it wouldn't be the same tone, wouldn't come from the same place. Those entries are so special because they're a moment in time where she was feeling x, y, z. You just hear it in her voice, in the surroundings. It wouldn't work, and you've got to try and be as truthful as possible.

What are you going to do with the recordings?

DC: I don't know. I'll definitely delete all the Dictaphone recordings. I don't think that needs to be stored. I guess it's more in Courtney's world than filmmaker's world. But there are so many shows. It's a great document of all that stuff.

I'm curious about the decision to choose Anonymous Club as the title.

DC: It was something about that line that she says early in the film - if a lot of people feel alone, then maybe they're not so alone. That resonated with me. She's just one of many people out there, but what she's experiencing, I think a lot of other people are experiencing the same thing. You do feel somewhat alone in that, but you're not. It was something that worked well.

I've always loved the song, and the words together are quite powerful. I feel like there are a lot of people alone in that club. They are anonymous, but maybe by being all together, they're not actually alone. I remember Glendyn early on when we were talking about the story, he was like "She feels like a ghost." You see her in this town, you see her quiet in a hotel room, and then she's kind of popping up everywhere. Not haunting a bad way, but just like passing through time, or time and place. I think that fed in a little bit to the *Anonymous Club*.

Do you have a favourite Courtney Barnett track?

DC: I think it'd be up there with *Small Poppies*, probably because Courtney's live performance of it shows her chops on the guitar. There's one particular one I love from the *Lotta Sea Lice* record, *Blue Cheese*. It's such a fun

ANONYMOUS CLUB

combination of Courtney and Kurt [Vile]. I had a real emotional connection to it. I was shooting some stuff for them at the time in the studio, and just seeing the vibe of that being created and then hearing it was a really special moment there. And it's got a good level of humour.

What do you want from your career as a filmmaker? Do you want to continue doing those music videos or documentaries or move to features?

DC: Features are definitely where I want to go. There's a few kicking around at the moment, just things bubbling away, same with some longer-form music docs. Definitely, [I have] wacky psychedelic features in the brain at the moment. I heard from a friend that it's good to have a bunch of films on your plate. When there's a roadblock for some reason, either creatively or funding or whatnot, you shift to something else. So, I'm just trying to load up.

I don't really want to music videos so much anymore. The budgets are just really, really low, which is no fault of anyone's, but it makes it difficult. There are only so many favours you can call in before people are like, "We've done enough, and I can't keep working for free." It's hard to wrangle people. The [music videos] have served a purpose, I think, of learning and gaining experience and getting to work with artists before doing longer form.

Leaning into one of the more prominent things that you've been part of is the Jimmy Barnes and Kirin [J Callinan] music video. What's it like for you mentally to see that become a meme?

DC: It's awesome. Kirin and I always talk about it. It's just like so special that people are still reacting to it and still enjoying it and people that have no idea who Jimmy is. Every ten minutes, there's a new comment. It's kind of awesome that all over the world, these people are just having a giggle over something and not taking it too seriously. That's what it's about, connecting with a large audience and people finding something in it. Even if that's just humour. I think that's awesome. [It's] not what anyone expected. I remember it was like sitting at 50,000 views or something, and we thought that was it.

Do you have a favourite of the memes that's out there?

DC: I think my favourite one is a *Happy Gilmore* one because he has everyone in the clouds. That was our VFX reference, putting Jimmy in there. When I was speaking to this guy Patrick who did the VFX, I was like "This sort of softness to it and opaqueness." It weirdly came full circle to be taken off in that context.

OF AN AGE

100 mins
Director: *Goran Stolevski*
Writer: *Goran Stolevski*
Cast: *Thom Green, Elias Anton, Hattie Hook, Jack Kenny, Louise Child, Toby Derrick, Verity Higgins, Matthew Page, Milijana Cancar, Jonty Reason, Kasuni Imbulana, Grace Gaznak*
Producer: *Kristina Ceyton, Samantha Jennings*
Cinematography: *Matthew Chuang*
Editing: *Goran Stolevski*

Of an Age was nominated for Best Film, Best Direction in Film, Best Lead Actor (both Elias Anton and Thom Green), and Best Screenplay in Film at the 2024 AACTA Awards.

REVIEW
NADINE WHITNEY

In the space of two years Macedonian-Australian director Goran Stolevski has emerged as a cinematic talent who can vividly craft a philosophical treatise on what it is to live wrapped in the skin of a folk horror genre piece with *You Won't Be Alone* set in 19th Century Macedonia and deliver a deeply romantic queer coming-of-age story set in Melbourne in 1999 (and again in 2010) with *Of an Age*. There are comparisons to be made between the films in Stolevski's use of a point of view from an outsider's perspective and the ache the protagonist feels to find a portal of belonging. In *You Won't Be Alone*, the silent Navena changes skin to avoid detection from the villagers who view her as a threat, so too does Kol (Elias Anton) change as much as he is able to avoid anyone gleaning his sexuality in *Of an Age*. He cannot hide his ethnicity, although he is seen as a generic "wog" by many in his working-class northern Melbourne suburb. Navena and Kol want to experience life, but they fear that they are rendered outsiders and without acceptance, they will walk alone and lonely.

Of an Age begins with Serbian-Australian Kol practicing his dance moves in a mirror. He scrutinises his body. In a few hours, he will be performing in a ballroom dance final with his friend Ebony Donegal (Hattie Hook) as his partner. That is until he gets a frenzied call from Ebony who has been out partying the night before and has woken up stranded somewhere with a beach. The beach is in Altona, and Kol is in Watsonia. If he hurries, he can get to Ebony, get her dressed, and make it to the competition. In reality, the distance between Watsonia and Altona means the trip will take hours, but Kol has been looking forward to expressing himself on the dancefloor and all Ebony really needs is a ride home from Altona.

After a flurried series of adventures to pick up Ebony's dress, Ebony's older brother Adam (Thom Green) is called in to get his sister out of whatever mess she's gotten herself in and just maybe get the pair to the dance competition.

Just out of high school, Kol is still finding his feet. Adam has just finished a degree in linguistics and is heading to Argentina to do his PhD the next day. Over the course of twenty-four hours Kol's life will be changed –

OF AN AGE

he will be seen and loved for who he is by a man who will disappear from his life for over ten years.

The drive to Altona is shot in the car by Stolevski and his cinematographer Matthew Chuang. The intimacy of the setting is palpable but made even more so by Stolevski's revelatory script. Adam sees Kol as a bright young man who has been stifled by the incurious world around him. As someone who was also a student at Watsonia College and one who kept his head down, he knows that just being bright is enough to warrant exclusion from social circles. Adam and Kol exchange jokes and Adam is genuinely impressed that Kol can make a Kafka joke. He laughs when Kol mispronounces Borges, but it is a gentle ribbing that is laced with a feeling of recognition. Adam asks why Kol would be friends with Ebony, and Kol admits that no one else would speak to him at school.

Stolevski lets the camera tease out the similarities between the two men and also the differences. Adam is calm and self-possessed. Kol is nervous and reticent. As Adam brings Kol out of his shell, Stolevski's camera stays close on their faces – the side glances they give each other. Adam is unafraid to look at Kol, but Kol is not quite ready for what Adam sees. They discuss film, literature, and music – Kol is surprised to find anyone who cares about his opinion, certainly Ebony doesn't. Other than his widowed mother who works tirelessly to provide for Kol and his little brother, the only other family Kol has are his macho uncle and cousins. From the casual and pointed racism he faces every day (including from Ebony) to the suggestion that he is a "faggot" from his peers, Kol has shrunk himself down to be as invisible as possible. When Adam deliberately lets slip that he is gay, Kol immediately 'dudes up' and pretends he is straight. Adam already knows Kol is gay, he's just waiting for him to admit it to himself.

Ebony functions as a foil between the two men. She's an entitled brat (who is nursing her own wounds and is perhaps more self-aware than she seems) and her presence gives Adam and Kol something more to bond over. Putting up with Ebony is something only saints would be required to do. Eventually, when they get back to Adam and Ebony's house Adam offers Kol some of his old clothing (Kol has been wearing his dancing outfit all day) and as Kol changes clothes he finds he is starting to resemble Adam. Looking in the mirror he sees himself, really sees himself, and with shame and frustration knows he cannot hide his sexuality for much longer.

"I bet you're the kind of person who practices words in a mirror," Adam jokes with Kol in the car. The observation is more pertinent than a casual quip. Kol's only friend and worst enemy has been the mirror. He is free to see himself in it, but it strips him bare physically and psychologically. After a disastrous house party that Adam made Ebony invite Kol to, where he is called a faggot and told to go back to Czechoslovakia by the genuinely hateful Coral (Grace Graznak), Kol storms down the road only to be picked up by Adam where they make love. In a devastating final shot that ends the 1999 section of the film the two men, almost identical in dress, look over the outer suburbs of Melbourne. Both are destined to leave, and both have found something they weren't expecting the morning they met.

The story picks up again in 2010. Kol, who now goes by Nikola is an out gay man who has spent years living in the UK working in public health. Seemingly by chance he looks over the luggage carousel at Tullamarine Airport and sees Adam. Adam has segued from linguistics and now works in a non-profit in Spain. Instantly their connection reignites. Nikola jokes that now he is an elder gay and has been told he is too old by twinks. On a more serious note, he tells Adam that in coming out he and his mother were excommunicated from the family and she now lives in rural Victoria. The seventeen-year-old Kol had a lot to lose by accepting his sexuality, perhaps more than Adam could understand.

They are both there to attend Ebony's wedding to a feckless and pedestrian man. Ebony's fate was something she understood as soon as she wasn't accepted into NIDA after high school. She would stay in Watsonia, marry someone, and play queen-bee with people like Coral (who ironically married a Serb). Nikola openly says he isn't going to be married until it is legal, leading him to find out that Adam has married. His heartbreak is profound and turns to anger. Somewhere Kol became frozen in time in the moment he was seen by Adam. Even though ten years have passed he kept up an adolescent dream that one day he would be reunited with his first love.

Dressed in their wedding suits Nikola and Adam are once again mirrors. Stolevski and Chuang reinforce the metaphor with a Bundoora Hotel reflecting their image. Throughout the film mirrors in bedrooms, cars, houses, and hotels have been reflecting the men. Glass has been smashed in anger. Shards of identity have been recognised, but as every glimpse into a mirror is fleeting even if the feeling experienced is not, it is akin to the adage that the same river can never be stepped into twice.

Goran Stolevski's *Of an Age* understands what it is to be stripped bare by a gentle gaze. It also comprehends all the confusion and panic that surrounds being seen and seeing oneself. Kol found a mentor and a lover in the space of twenty-four hours and expected that to last forever, and in a way it did. Elias Anton and Thom Green's nuanced performances make the audience believe that there is a love that never goes away even if the world moves on. Being frozen in time does not necessarily mean being trapped by it, recalling being brave enough to see what someone else sees in you and take steps to become that person is like stepping away from the lonely mirror to bask in a new reflection.

OF AN AGE

INTERVIEW
FILMMAKER GORAN STOLEVSKI

For his second feature, *Of an Age*, Macedonian Australian filmmaker Goran Stolevski turns inwards, pulling from the personal to create characters that resonate with the understanding and acceptance of what it means to be a gay man in Australia. Kol (a captivating Elias Anton) is yet to realise his queer identity, but when he meets his dancing partners brother, Adam (Thom Green), he feels the emotional cogs slipping into place: desire, yearning, affection, and the embrace of another man. *Of an Age* is split into two significant moments in time, divided by a volcano eruption and years of longing. By splitting the film into these two time periods, Stolevski gives us the weight of a passionate heart that's strained by the desire for the one you love.

Matthew Chuang's intimate cinematography creates a conversation between Annelise Hickey's *Hafekasi* (which he lensed) and *Of an Age*; both present aspects of 1990s Australia that were threatened to be lost to time. Both explore the stories of people seeking to make sense of their place in the world; stories that – if told in the Nineties – would have been directed by outsiders looking in. What makes *Of an Age* (and by extension, *Hafekasi*) resonate so strongly is how deeply informed and understanding Stolevski is of the lives that both Kol and Adam live. The strength of a beating heart resonates strong with him.

This interview was recorded by Andrew F. Peirce in August 2023

Have you had a chance to reflect on the journey you've had over the past few years as a filmmaker?

Goran Stolevski: As the film nerd I am, I'm curious how I would have felt about it if I wasn't the person who made it. When would I have heard of it? How would I have heard of it? Would I like it? I don't really have the answer to that.

OF AN AGE

Honestly, I've had a chance to reflect on the main reason I make movies, and I've distilled it down to whether 50 years after I die, will someone be watching it? It doesn't have to be many people, just anyone. That's kind of the barometer of success in my head. It's more about emotional success, rather than financial or critical. I came to the conclusion that I just have to keep making films for as long as I humanly can and create a body of work that makes people ideally want to see several of them. For now, if someone just asked me, "Do you feel successful?" or "Do you consider the film of success?", my honest response is I have no idea.

A better question might be if you're proud of the films you've made?

GS: I love them. Absolutely. I love every second of them. I had a chance to watch *Of an Age* again in New York, and I had a little bit of distance from it, and I still felt very connected to it. It reflected emotionally everything I wanted to imprint it with of myself. I had the same thing with *You Won't Be Alone*. I hadn't seen it for almost a year, and then I watched it at the London Film Festival, and I just loved it.

To me, they're perfect, including their flaws. I don't aim to make something flawless. I think works of art that are flawless are really bland. I am more interested in works of art that may have mistakes and may also have high intensity moments that make you feel them and remember them, and they stay with us. For me yeah, both of these films, I just absolutely fucking love them.

Within Of an Age there is a sense of intimacy and claustrophobia. There are intimate moments, and then moments of claustrophobia paired with awkwardness. They're presented in equal measure. Can you talk about how you personally distinguish between the two emotions on screen?

GS: Moments can hold very contradictory feelings. In the same moment, comedy and drama live together. I don't feel like you have to separate them tonally. You want to have a handle on them so that everything feels like you can just latch on to each coming moment and the energy feels like it's building, and the connection feels like it's building. Claustrophobia and sexual electricity are very conducive to awkwardness and each other and all these things. The aim is to distil every moment or beat in a story and to make sure you're loaded with as many of these kinds of feelings and adjectives as possible. If a moment is only doing one thing, then it feels like a bad exposition. It doesn't feel like art. There needs to be a subtext to things for them to feel alive and worth watching.

INTERVIEW | GORAN STOLEVSKI

Thom and Elias are wonderful. What conversations did you have with them in relation to the divide in time between the two halves of the film in 1999 and 2010 to ensure that those two time periods were distinct?

GS: That was a longer and more complex conversation with Elias than it was with Thom, partly because Thom is closer to me in age, so he understands both timeframes quite well. Whereas Elias was 23 when we were shooting, he was born in 1998 and had to play 17 and 28, with the 17-year-old growing up in a very different era. Most of the conversations happened well in advance of the shoot. With Thom, we talked about our relationships and experiences in our respective relationship histories.

Once we were filming, how I gave direction was to create an environment to nurture people rather than telling them 'Do this'. It's about giving them ideas of what they can do, and then letting them build or adjust, and most of it is about instinct, and connecting with the material emotionally rather than intellectually trying to convey things.

The conversation that was theoretical or abstract happened before the film shoot, even at the audition stage where we talked to Elias about what it would involve for him to play 17 and then 28. I brought it back to my own life, and what the difference was when I walked into a room as a 17-year-old and when I walked into a room as a 28-year-old. For me, they were distinct in the sense that when you're 17, you're very easily overwhelmed. You're not quite aware or comfortable or in control of your body or aura or energy. When you're 28, or older in general, you step into a room, and you take in a lot more much more quickly and you're less overwhelmed. It was about being a bit more comfortable in your skin.

It was more about not really thinking about these elements intellectually, but rather building a sense of feeling and a sense of how he feels in his body when he steps into a room and how he feels when someone speaks to him in a certain way. All of 2010 came down to 'start with this feeling as the basis,' and all of 1999 started with this feeling. As a person, he connected a lot more to the younger version for many reasons that I don't want to divulge, we had a lot of detailed conversations that were very personal.

You worked with Matthew Chuang again who creates a powerful representation of suburban Melbourne. What discussions did you have about presenting those landscapes on screen?

GS: He knows I start with a close-up as the establishing shot, as is abundantly clear in this film. He knows it's more of crafting the close-ups and also giving the actors a lot of space so that they have the freedom to move around in their own time. There are no marks. Discussions are more about

OF AN AGE

the general principles of the camera, in that it has to stay on one side of them so that the image is cinematic and also about how you frame in relation to the lighting source where sometimes the sunlight is what makes the image cinematic. It's about prioritising the actors but also making sure that that doesn't sacrifice visual quality.

Bethany Ryan's contribution is underrated. She's the production designer on both of these films, which are both period films. She creates a space on a very limited budget and the logistics are that it's complicated to create a space that's 360 degrees so the camera can spin around. We know how to operate with the crew, but we have to be able to point the camera in a way to retain that flexibility so that the actors can move around, and you have this documentary style of naturalism, but also, there is visual detail. They were very careful about finding locations that were accommodating for all these things to begin with so we can build on top of that. Usually, we would shoot the close-ups first on most sequences, especially ones that are quite detailed emotionally and have a lot of dialogue, and then the wide shot later on.

It's not just point and shoot, because point and shoot aren't transportive. I still want this film to be transportive in a way that movies are. It's not just meant to be gritty; you need to feel visceral and present, but it still needs to hit at a certain part of your chest that means you're about to be taken away somewhere else.

Matthew knows my compositional and framing finishes, lots of headroom, for example. We have a shorthand language now. I often talk during a take to him. We build on each other in terms of ideas. I shot list obsessively, but then on the day of shooting, I throw away the shot list. I've absorbed it. I shot list mostly so I can get my head around it and I talk him through what I've come up with. Then, it changes on the day. We're both trying to be alert to things happening in the moment that you can't really organise or rehearse for and to just capture those moments and make sure they don't go away. Because I also edit my films, I know where to find a certain detail for it to flow organically with the rest of the story, and what else we might need for coverage. Also keeping coverage to a minimum to not exhaust actors and crew, because I don't believe in doing a wide shot or a close-up if it's something I won't use in the edit.

Can you talk about the Aussie era specific dialogue? What was it like revisiting and keeping that kind of dialogue alive on film for you?

GS: It was a funny experience in the sense that I landed in Australia in '97, and I did not want to be here. I felt very disconnected from it. Everything that was specifically Australian, I would just react against in my body. The dialect annoyed me, the slang annoyed me. It's how I ended up with this mutant accent that is from nowhere and everywhere at the same time. Going back to it and trying to capture this realistically, I was now doing it from a very different relationship where the things that used to bother me, I now find fascinating. I have this kind of distance where it didn't feel as imposed upon me. All these were psychological problems. None of this was Australia's fault. All of it was mine.

It was kind of fun, because it felt like reliving some moments and elements of growing up here that I didn't properly feel present for. The words came back. Now, from a certain distance, I have friends now who I can have conversations with whom I didn't have at the time, so to revisit these words from a position of relative safety and belonging, it's fun. They're hilarious.

I also wanted to document that and preserve them. My best friend Julia Harari, who's in the film, she plays one of the bridesmaids, the most obnoxious one, we had weeks of talking via WhatsApp listing words that we definitely had to have in the script because they're from 1999 when we were in high school. She improvised a lot in the film, like in the wedding sequence. Julia came up with that herself. I wrote the role for her. She was a key part of my creative arsenal and is always. It's been a special experience for both of us

PROJECTING NATALIE MILLER

INTERVIEW
FILMMAKER NATALIE MILLER AO

The impact of Natalie Miller AO on the film industry in Australia has been felt across the decades through her work as a film distributor, exhibitor, and producer. Miller founded the film distribution house Sharmill Films and has helped establish notable arthouse cinemas like Cinema Nova and FoMo Cinemas in Melbourne, after having worked as a leader at the iconic Longford Cinema.

In 2022, Natalie's legacy and impact on the film industry was essayed in the expansive book *Projecting Natalie Miller*, a historical guide that includes stories from family and friends, interviews with those who have been impact by Natalie's work, and a welcome tour through Australian film industry history.

This interview was recorded by Andrew F. Peirce in February 2023

What was the experience like for you as you collated these wonderful images, the varied newspaper clippings, as well as the deep history of Australian film?

Natalie Miller: It was quite emotional. Fortunately, I'm a bit of a collector of memorabilia. I hate throwing things out, much to my husband's dismay. I tend to collect everything, so it was all just there. Everyone used to say to me, "You must do a book, you must do a book," I said, "I'll never have time." And then Deborah Blashki-Marks, the publisher, came to me about a book she was doing, and when I mentioned all that, she said, "I'd love to do it." So, we started on a two-year journey. She used to come to my home office every week, and apart from all the talking, we would go through all of the memorabilia, the photos, and all the letters. It was really quite an exciting experience.

Did that process of reflection transport you back to the moments when the photos were taken or the events that the clippings featured?

PROJECTING NATALIE MILLER

NM: Very much so very much. I think back to Longford Cinema days, which we ran from 1984 to about 2001. They were amazing days. We were a single-screen cinema, and we got films like *Mona Lisa* (1986) with Bob Hopkins as an exclusive. You would never see any of that today. That transported me back to a time when the industry was such a different business than what it is today, particularly for arthouse cinemas.

Over the years, what has stood out for you as a positive change in the arthouse cinema scene?

NM: The most positive thing is the fact that we now have a lot of outlets playing arthouse films. Back in the day, when I started my business, my first film was Luis Buñuel's *The Exterminating Angel* (1962), I hired the Palais Theatre in St Kilda to play it. In Melbourne, apart from the Australia Cinema[1] (active 1965-1988) and the Savoy Theatre[2] (active 1939-1963), there were no other outlets to screen arthouse films. As I continued to buy more films, we found that there was an audience for them outside of the film festivals, where they used to only play, and I realised that unless I had an exhibition outlet for them, it would be difficult to screen them. Fortunately, I had this opportunity to acquire the Longford cinema. When the previous owners of the Australian Film Institute got out, because I knew the landlord, I was at the head of the queue to be able to take it.

Having an outlet made a difference for arthouse films. Of course, now there are so-called 'art houses' all over the place, but they're not art houses in the tradition perhaps that we have at the Cinema Nova and what we were doing at the Longford. When someone says, "What's you're branding at the Nova?", I pride myself when I say, "We play everything but *Star Wars*," which means I'm either stupid or clever. I don't know which but it's all about the branding for the arthouse cinema room. The difference today is that you can take an arthouse film like *Triangle of Sadness* (2022), which is one of mine and was nominated for Best Film at the Oscars. For films like that, we had about fifty different screens we could play it on. So that is the big difference.

When it comes to watching a film that's released under the banner of Sharmill Films, or even at the Cinema Nova, there is an assurance that it will be a satisfying watch. Can you talk through the process that ensures that there is that stamp of approval and quality assurance with the companies you operate?

NM: I think it's a bit like sticking to my knitting. I've always had great respect for [great] directors, as you can see when I started off with Luis Buñuel and in recent years with Ruben Ostlund. My choices are an instinct of my own personal taste of knowing a good film and respecting the director. It's

INTERVIEW | NATALIE MILLER

getting harder and harder for the smaller arthouse films in the marketplace today. I'm not sure why, but I think that cinemas are becoming more and more commercial. At the Nova, in recent times, we had quite a few arthouse films that should have done so much better but didn't. Reflecting on the past few years as we've seen with the pandemic, maybe it's a change in the marketplace, and maybe it's because a lot of the arthouse audience is an older audience and they've been staying home. It's very hard to put one's finger on it, but it all gets back to the film; if you've got a really good film, they will come.

What was the film that got you hooked?

NM: My experiences as a teenager were that my parents had first-night seats at the Palais Theatre, which is hard to imagine now. They'd go every Saturday night and would very proudly have the front-row lounge seats. Of course, I got taken, so I saw a lot of those early films from those days. I don't think I'll say how long ago that was, but I did grow up on a lot of the MGM musicals, the Fred Astaire's, the Judy Garland's, the Esther Williams. I used to just love all those films. That's very strong in my memory. In fact, I had a crush on Peter Lawford and kept a scrapbook of every press cutting that mentioned him. And I still have it, talking of keeping things.

My career opportunities came after doing a Bachelor of Arts university course, and then I joined a small public relations firm that produced a paper and where they trained me in journalism, then I went to the ABC. After that I left, and I had my first child, I was lucky to get a position with the Melbourne Film Festival to do their public relations. I worked for many years closely with the late Erwin Rado. He was the most enormous influence on my life because he was a true believer in European cinema and arthouse cinema, particularly Hungarian cinema. I think a lot of that just got into my DNA and moulded my tastes and my love of the medium and of what I considered cinema as an art.

What stands out as a memorable cinema-going moment?

NM: Goodness, there are so many. At some stage in my career, I started going to the Cannes Film Festival, so you can imagine the number of films that I saw. My first film, Luis Buñuel's *The Exterminating Angel*, is so etched in my mind. Later, Ermanno Olmi's *The Tree of Wooden Clogs* (1978) and the Taviani brothers Palme dÓr winning *Padre Padrone* (1977), which I managed to get as a distributor, and I doubt whether I would be in the race today, it's all become a business with huge prices. I guess it was expensive at the time, but not like it is today.

What was the Cannes experience like as a distributor?

PROJECTING NATALIE MILLER

NM: In the initial days, it was fantastic. Absolutely fantastic. There weren't many buyers from Australia. I could name them on one hand. One particular memory I have is there was Sylvie Le Clezio and co, who were not big distributors, but they wanted to buy a film. That was the year I bought *The Tree of Wooden Clogs*. We each decided which film we wanted to buy and we wouldn't compete with the other person. Well, those days are gone forever. Over the years it became more and more competitive. You have to be quick to get in there.

I bought films like Andrei Tarkovsky's *The Sacrifice* (1986) and later, Nuri Bilge Ceylan's *Winter Sleep* (2014). If I see a film and I really get excited about it, then I have to go for it. I saw *Once Were Warriors* (1994), a fabulous New Zealand film, in Cannes, and I came outside and had a cup of coffee with one competitor, crying, and while I was crying, another competitor raced up the Croisette and bought the film. So, I said, "Well, I was crying, she was buying." That's how difficult it has all become. In the later years, it all became about business. There was no time to sit and reflect.

It's not just about watching the films and selecting what is best for distribution, it's also about the relationships that you create. In the book, there are a wealth of filmmakers, like Gillian Armstrong and Fred Schepisi, family members, and even politicians, who reflect on the impact you've had on the film industry. Has the realisation of what you have achieved settled in?

NM: No, I don't really think about it like that. The book has a lot of interviews from people like Joel Pearlman, Fred Schepisi, Gillian Armstrong, Jocelyn Morehouse, Alan Finney, and as you suggested a politician, Josh Frydenberg, who I happen to know personally, and I just thought it was nice to throw it in. I've always been one to sort of have my feet on the ground and just keep going, and that's what I'm still doing now. I just keep going to the next step and that's wherever life will take me. The past doesn't overwhelm me, I think it's all just there.

After the Longford, the Cinema Nova was an enormous opportunity for me exhibition-wise. When Barry Peak, who ran the Valhalla Cinema[3], came to me and said, "Would you like to go into a partnership in a cinema in Carlton?" And I said, "Of course, I'd love to talk about it." The rest is history. We're now at sixteen screens at the Nova, and we started as two. It's all just been a natural progression year after year after year. I still have some plans to look forward to happening in the future. I look to the future more than the past.

It's interesting you mentioned Gillian, she generously did a launch of my book, and she spoke so beautifully. She and I have a bond because I bought her first film *One Hundred a Day* (1973), which she made for the Australian Film and Television School, as it was based on the Alan Marshall story, *How Beautiful Are Thy Feet*. I had released the Czech version of Alan Marshall's book *I Can Jump Puddles* (1955), which was another great experience in my life taking the late author Alan Marshall around Australia.

I went to the film school and said, "I'd like to buy Gillian's short." They've never done a commercial deal before, so that was their first commercial sale. That bonded Gillian and I forever. People like Fred Schepisi, apart from his filmmaking, I've gotten to know well, because I've sat on several boards like in the early days of Film Victoria (now known as VicScreen). Of course, I follow their stellar careers, they've all gone on to do wonderful things.

Film Victoria and the Australian Centre for Moving Image (ACMI), I was on their first boards. When an organisation is starting and developing, it's very exciting to be on the board. With Film Victoria, the board had people like Fred and the late Chris Green. It was a fantastic board. We used to read the scripts and make the decisions, and of course, now all these organisations are huge with script assessors and goodness knows what else. I enjoyed being on these boards. It wasn't all at once, so I'd fit it in.

There's a great saying by Betty Friedan that I'm forever quoting, 'Women can do it all, but not all at once.' That's a very true statement. I guess I did all these things at once, it's just that they were spread out over a lot of years. I've got three sons and I used to juggle my family responsibilities among all that. Funnily enough, in the early days, I was working from home, but I've now gone full circle and started working from home again. That's how I would manage because if you work from home, you can juggle the two lives. It's all about just doing it and enjoying it to start with. Obviously, I enjoyed everything I did.

There is this great photo of you in the book, where you're wearing a wonderful shirt that says 'Gentleman and Natalie' on it. Was that made for you?

NM: That was made for me by this photographer, Sam Burke, with Rebecca Umlauf. They interviewed a whole lot of different women, and they asked me to put a motto on a shirt and I chose that one. This is probably a major thing in my career where I've sat on many boards and I'd be the only woman. This is why my assistant, Chrissy Thomson, started the Natalie Miller Fellowship, which was started in honour of my name. Initially I said, "You only do that when someone's dead." But they did it anyway. Ten years on, I'm still here.

PROJECTING NATALIE MILLER

We started that because I said, "Women need to be pushed further up in the distribution and exhibition area into becoming CEOs because it's such a male-dominated area." Would you believe that even today I sit on the board of the National Association of Cinema Operators-Australasia, and I think there was one woman with me for a while, but at the last meeting I was the only woman there. It's because all these male CEOs are in their jobs for a long time, and the chair doesn't become vacant. That's what that t-shirt was all about because someone once said, "Gentleman and Natalie" at one of these board meetings.

What can we do to instil change in the film industry?

NM: One of the things I want for my book is for women to buy it and see what women can do in the industry. To be fair, there are now a lot of women in charge of film festivals, you've got Sasha Close up there in Brisbane[4], and Caroline Pitcher is the CEO of VicScreen. I think it has come a long way, but not quite enough in the exhibition industry, because as I said, a lot of people don't leave their jobs. I do believe in years to come when many of the male CEOs retire, that women will end up in those positions. I think there's enough push and movement for women to be moved up the ladder. I really believe society has changed a lot.

What were the initial discussions about the Natalie Miller Fellowship like?

NM: As I said, I commented first that I was reluctant. Then I realised that I have this group of very enthusiastic women who banded together to do this and that I should support it. I've been more than delighted with what they've done over the years. Every year $20,000 is given to a woman who wants to take steps to further their career and really good results come out of that. Although I'm not on the board of the fellowship, I am involved every year in the choosing of the candidate, and it's just wonderful to see so many women who apply for what is a very rigid application. Our very first candidate, Rachel Okine, went overseas and attended the Women's Leadership Forum: Innovation Strategies for a Changing World at Harvard[5], and then went on to become the top person at StudioCanal, before coming back to Australia for a position with Stan. It has really had an effect over the years for all these women. I'm more than proud of what they're all doing.

It's important to note that these are not just filmmakers who can receive the fellowship, but for aspirational women in all sectors of the film industry. How important was it for you that the fellowship covered all aspects of the film industry?

NM: To be honest, my own focus and why I was delighted about it was more on the exhibition and distribution industry. There is a lot of support from Screen Australia, VicScreen, and other agencies. I want to see people climbing the ladder in the exhibition and distribution industry. Although the fellowship is now open to everybody, I am personally very focused on helping people climb the ladder in the business side of the industry.

While we're talking about the different aspects of your career, one of the ones that may not be fully understood is the role of the publicist. The role of being a publicist can often be a thankless one, can you talk about the importance of publicists?

NM: Having been one and credited with the Australian Journalists Association (now MEAA), which I've kept up with throughout the years, I'm very appreciative of what my publicists do. I know Tracey (Mair) well; back in the day at Cannes, Tracey and I went on a train to Barcelona together after the festival. They're all the nice moments of film festivals. We use NIXCO a lot now, and in my publicity campaign for *Triangle of Sadness* (2022), I said to Jillian, who was running the campaign, "Look, I'm sorry to be asking so many questions. I was a publicist and I really appreciate the work you do and the difficulties of getting interviews and all the other difficulties that go with being a publicist." I was apologising for feeling like I was interfering, but it wasn't so much interfering but taking an interest. You might see an interview in the paper, but it could have taken the publicist hours chasing up overseas to get the available time. I feel that that background has been a very useful and happy one so that I can understand it all.

I'm interested in how Cinema Nova has managed on the other side of the pandemic.

NM: During the pandemic, I said and tried to encourage my staff that we're lucky because we'll have a business to go back to. I've always had faith in the cinema. There's nothing like watching a film on the big screen. We do sit looking at TVs and films on streamers, but there's nothing like being back in the cinema. Fortunately, audiences are coming back and we're at about 80% (capacity) now. We've had an enormous success with *Aftersun* (2022), and we had an enormous success with a late-night showing of *The Room* (2004) where we had the director out. He was amazing. Even between the lockdowns we had success with screenings. People are coming out again. Hopefully, in another six months, we'll be back to normal, but it all depends on the films. Sharmill Films distributes the National Theatre and Met Opera events, and we do alternative content, like *Knowing the Score* (2023) on Simone Young. We've got faith that all of the audiences will come back for all these different events. We just have to continue doing what we do and hope that what I say is true.

PROJECTING NATALIE MILLER

How important is it for Cinema Nova to have event screenings like Q&A sessions with filmmakers or exclusive presentations?

NM: It's become enormously important. It can make the difference between a break-even week and making some money in the week because people do come out to the event screenings. We seem to be doing more and more now. It's a lot of work for the publicists and the staff, but it's how people want to do it. For documentaries, only the really good ones do well. I love documentaries. *Knowing the Score* had an event in Sydney where about 600-700 people came. People want to come out to see something special, so we will be doing a lot of those. Yes, it's important.

We co-distributed *Knowing the Score* with Bonsai Films. I think it's fabulous. It again deals with a subject that I'm interested in, women rising in their careers, which Simone Young did. She rose up to be the conductor of the Sydney Symphony Orchestra. It's very interesting to see it in relation to *Tár* (2022) because you've got Cate Blanchett who is extraordinary as Lydia Tár, but I've had some people say they sought it out after seeing Simone Young's story. It's got to be something special to bring people out. Over the years we've had some very special documentaries, but a lot of them are more suited to television than the cinema. Filmmakers love having something at the cinema, which I guess I should be happy about.

I'm grateful that the National Theatre Live productions are presented in cinemas, otherwise it would cost a small fortune to attend one of these performances. Seeing it in a cinema becomes a different sort of communal experience. I'm interested to hear what that communal experience means to you?

NM: Two examples would be *Prima Facie*, the National Theatre play, which was extraordinary. I sat with my mouth agape through that, and I have to mention *Triangle of Sadness* again, the middle section of that is hysterical. To sit in a cinema and hear people laughing their heads off gives me such joy. I love it. I just love it.

The Melbourne International Film Festival has celebrated 70 years, and as someone who lives in Melbourne, I'm interested to hear about what the importance of the festival means to you?

NM: I think it's a wonderful thing. I look back over the festival and think of Erwin Rado and think of how proud he would be to see the festival that he so long nurtured. With Melbourne on screen, there's *The Lost City of Melbourne* which played at the Nova for many, many weeks. The festival showcases and introduces us to so many experiences. I think it's all for the good of the industry.

INTERVIEW | NATALIE MILLER

What do Australian films mean to you?

NM: I am a true believer in Australia having to tell our own stories. We've had so many wonderful Australian films; I've been fortunate to dabble in a bit of production and be part of all that as well. I admire all the producers, because it's a very difficult thing to make an Australian film, in that you're competing with Hollywood. We've got lots of good stories to tell. We've got a lot of good filmmakers. We've got wonderful locations. So of course, it's terribly important.

Where do we buy the book?

NM: You can buy it at Readings Bookstore, ACMI, and the Sun Yarraville, and you can also get it online. It really is full of wonderful pictures. I must say the photos brought back the memories of all the people that I've shared my life with and the cinemas and the personalities and the filmmakers. Even when I skim through it, I thought, 'Oh my goodness, how did we do this?' And the letters from Philip Adams that he wrote to me that I've kept. It is a lovely coffee table book. The main thing is it's a legacy to my family, and most importantly, it's a history of independent cinema over decades. It's a book I feel and hope can inspire women.

ENDNOTES

1   The Australia Theatre was opened on Collins Street, Melbourne in 1965 and operated by Village Drive-In Theatres. Closed on 1st May 1988. Source: https://cinematreasures.org/theaters/52939
2   From 1939 the Savoy Theatre (previously known as the Imperial Theatre) on Russell Street, Melbourne, screened 'Continental films' with English subtitles. It was closed and demolished in 1963. Source: https://cinematreasures.org/theaters/52962
3   The Valhalla Cinema was opened as the Crown Theatre in 1913 before undergoing multiple name changes. It was eventually closed in January 1988, and was demolished in June 1988 after a fire. Source: https://cinematreasures.org/theaters/52836
4   Head of Programming Gold Coast Film Festival and Brisbane International Film Festival
5   https://nataliemillerfellowship.com/rachel-okine-inaugural-receipient-of-the-natalie-miller-fellowship/

THE PLAINS

180 mins
Director: *David Easteal*
Writer: *David Easteal*
Cast: *Andrew Rakowski, David Easteal, Cheri LeCornu, Inga Rakowski, Jon Faine, Sarah Jane Bell, Henry Belot, Julian McMahon, Christos Tsiolkas*
Producer: *David Easteal*
Cinematography: *Simon J. Walsh*
Editing: *David Easteal*

INTERVIEW
FILMMAKER
DAVID EASTEAL

David Easteal's three-hour docu-drama, *The Plains* (2022), follows his friend and colleague Andrew (Andrew Rakowski) as he drives home at five pm in congested Melbourne traffic. With the camera firmly placed in the back passenger seat, we sit with Andrew as he listens to the radio, navigates traffic, talks with his wife over the phone, and occasionally acts as a lift home for his colleague David (Easteal).

The Plains is a deliberately mundane experience, with Easteal using rudimentary methods to engage in profound acts of soul searching. There has not been anything like *The Plains* in the history of Australian cinema. If we consider *The Plains* in the age of Chantal Akerman's *Jeanne Dielman, 23, quai du commerce, 1090 Bruxelles* (1975) being crowned the Best Film of All Time by Sight & Sound, there's every chance that the cultural impact of Easteal's drive-time epic is yet to be fully realised.

This interview was recorded by Andrew F. Peirce in July 2022

I know that you're very keen for audiences to see The Plains in the cinema. Can you expand on what the cinema viewing experience means for you?

David Easteal: It's interesting how rapidly the way we view movies is changing. I think that all films are better seen in a cinema. It's not just preferable for bigger, spectacular films, but also for slower, more contemplative, quieter films. Being enveloped in the darkness and not having the distractions you do at home, to be absorbed into the film's rhythm. When watching films at home I'll catch myself reaching for my phone or something like that, even for films I really want to see, it's terrible.

With that said, I was very pleasantly surprised after we launched the film digitally. The film was meant to launch physically in Rotterdam at the start of the year, but at the last minute new COVID restrictions were implemented in the Netherlands and the festival was changed to an online event for the press and industry only. Initially, I was quite concerned about presenting

THE PLAINS

the film in this way, for the reasons just mentioned, however, it was received well through the online platform. Viewing films at home perhaps permits a unique intimacy, which is different from what occurs when viewing communally in a cinema, and it has its own merit, especially if you can be disciplined about distractions.

Can you talk about your path into filmmaking?

DE: To earn a living, I work as a lawyer. I started making short films while I was a student. I wasn't studying film, but I've always been drawn to film. I wanted to start exploring making films and I loved the process. I kept on trying it. I studied law and other humanities and at the same time, I was learning about making short films through the process of doing it.

There is an autobiographical tone to The Plains. You're in it. A colleague, Andrew, is also in it. Where did the idea of turning your experiences driving home together into a film come from?

DE: At the time of conceiving the film I had left the workplace where I had met Andrew. I was trying to think of a new film after my last short film. A character along the lines of Andrew intrigued me, and I tried to write a film based on such a character; someone in their middle age hurtling towards retirement, stuck at work in some respects, and with a heightened sense of mortality dawning upon them in the context of his mother passing away. In the year that we drove home together, I had been present as his mother's health declined and she passed away. I realised that I knew Andrew from the specific context of the commute home and the idea came to limit the film just to this context. With the imposition of this limitation, suddenly things opened up for me creatively.

There are certainly some autobiographical elements, but it's not a straight autobiography or documentary. I was working to make it a narrative work, something to be viewed from start to finish. Although it draws from reality at times, it has been manipulated and shaped for the purpose of making a film.

I approached Andrew about playing a version of himself, and thankfully, he was interested. There are many aspects unique to Andrew's personality, and how he communicates, which were important to me to retain in the film. He can be quite funny, immediately next to saying something very existential. My personal performance in the film was perhaps more pragmatic. I was concerned that combining Andrew with a professional actor would inhibit things. We had an existing friendship, which grew further over the course of the film, which I thought could help us go to more emotional places in the film. It also permitted me a way to direct the film, as I could attempt to shape the conversation and progression of topics during the long, uninterrupted takes.

There's a moment where Andrew is asking you about your relationship, and the David in the film says, "I don't really want to talk about that." Then there is a pause for maybe a minute or so, and then Andrew asks "Well, what about it then?" That's the kind of familiarity in your relationship with one another that that kind of questioning doesn't feel intrusive or awkward. It comes across so gently, almost like a brotherly figure. That is hard to imitate.

DE: Thank you. When I got to know Andrew years prior, I had been going through a breakup and he would give me advice talking about it during our drives. So, including that element in the film was true to the time, but also functionally served a purpose in the script. I wanted to start to include information about Andrew's life and his relationships, and it seemed like a natural way to be able to progress to this – for Andrew as the older colleague to start asking questions, it then worked for me to start asking him questions in reply, as part of a normal flow of a conversation.

Was there a script written or was it following key dot points of what needed to be touched on?

DE: From the outset of the project, I knew broadly where the film was going to go, which was the death of his mother and the character of the co-worker leaving the office at the end of the film, based on the time we worked together. Each month I would embark upon a process of writing what was to occur in the next month's shoot, keeping in mind the overall shape of the film. I would discuss the plan with Andrew and or Cheri. When we came to shoot the next scene, we were both on the same page, not regarding precise dialogue, which was improvised, but rather the overall content of the conversation to be filmed that day.

In writing the film in this incremental way, it began to evolve and take shape in many unexpected ways that could not have been foreseen at the start of the shoot. Events were happening in all our lives, and what started as a dramatisation of years past, began to involve the inclusion of more contemporaneous events.

Let's talk about the radio elements because that feeds into the metaphorical tone that gives you this understanding of the cycle that these people are trapped in; they're going home but never truly getting home. They hear fractured politics on the radio with people talking about being unhappy about society. Were they real radio segments or were they scripted?

THE PLAINS

DE: Obtaining the rights for real talkback radio proved to be prohibitively expensive. As a result, all of the radio was constructed in post, which turned out to be a blessing, it ended up being one of my favourite elements of the film. Talkback radio, particularly Jon Faine, was listened to by a number of my colleagues who worked at the legal centre. In that sense it seemed to speak to the character in a way - the demographic that listens to ABC talkback is largely middle class, left-leaning, and middle-aged.

I approached Jon Faine, he had just left his position at the ABC, and he thankfully agreed to be the host. We recorded a sort of fake radio show where I gave Jon a list of topics and he had a few suggestions about those topics and what might happen, and we organised several callers and ran a sort of radio show in real-time that was recorded at the sound designer's studio. The callers were great. Some of them were Andrew's friends. I had a friend who was at that time producing talkback radio in a regional city in Victoria and if they were a bit quiet on any specific day, they had a list of locals who were the regulars that they could call up, so we enlisted some of these call-back regulars. It was only scripted insofar as the topics provided, Jon can riff on whatever topic you give him, he is a professional.

The talkback did something interesting in the film. There's a sense of isolation in the commute. You're amongst all these other people moving through the city, but you're separate from them. The radio brings in a broader socio-, political-context of what's going on with others in the city. In the context of the film, whenever there's a silence, and perhaps the isolation of the commute is most acutely felt, Andrew puts the radio on.

Tara Judah wrote in Senses of Cinema [1] *"This is possibly the most authentic I've ever seen Australia depicted on screen," partially because we spend so much time in our cars. It made me think of my drive to work where an hour or more of my day is spent in the car by myself. It's a mundane aspect of our lives that we don't get to see on screen often. How important was it for you to bring that aspect of Australian life to the screen?*

DE: Realism has been important to me so far in my films. It's true that a lot of Australian films don't deal with the day-to-day reality of middle-class lives. There are exceptions of course, however a lot of films engage with a criminal underworld, or are more outback/Western type of films, or if they are contemporary there seems to be an emphasis on genre. I, like a lot of the population, am middle-class, work a job, engage with family and friends, and have to commute home at the end of the working day, amongst thousands of others, often tired. I have concerns about things in my domestic life and struggles with some relationships. I wanted to reflect life as I knew it, I wanted to make a film about characters I like. I don't know any career criminals or cowboy types. I can't really imagine writing about a killer or

INTERVIEW | DAVID EASTEAL

something like that. It's interesting that in Australia a lot of our everyday life is not often reflected in our cinema, whether that's to do with filmmakers' preferences or funding models is perhaps for a broader conversation.

I think the commute is a very interesting thing to explore. It's this sort of dead time where you're moving with this rhythm of thousands of other people through the city yet alienated from them. It is perhaps more pronounced in Australian cities which are quite sprawling. I wanted the streets of Melbourne to be a part of the film, indeed they are documented through the windscreen throughout the film, forming almost half of the frame. There is something nice about just being able to see the streets of Melbourne. Maybe in time you can look back and see what Melbourne was like. I don't want to speak too grandiosely, but it's almost like a historical record that depicts what the streets of Melbourne were like at the time we filmed. I know when I watch earlier Frederick Wiseman films, I find them quite fascinating as a document of a time.

Often, if somebody is travelling home, we see them get in the car and then it cuts to them at home. The journey is inconsequential. What I appreciated about The Plains, noting that you can't decide what gets shown on billboards along the drive, is that we see a couple of Clive Palmer billboards. One is 'Make Australia Great' hanging over this sea of traffic. It's this reinforcement of what you're exploring in the film. It feels fortuitous.

DE: Indeed, these in-between moments are often excluded from films. They form a large part of our day-to-day lives, and I seem to be drawn to exploring them. It was exciting to film this way, uninterrupted on the real streets during rush hour, as an element of the shoot was totally out of my control as the filmmaker and left to chance. There was something exciting as each time we didn't know what was going to happen on the roads, and how that would interact with what was being filmed in the more controlled environment inside the car.

For me, some extraordinary coincidences occurred during the shoot, which are visible if you pay close attention, such as the billboards. Another one that comes to mind that I liked is in that moment we talked about earlier where Andrew's probing about my relationship, a truck rolls up beside the car and it has the word 'Cope' on the side.

My commute in Perth is very different from the commute in Melbourne. We don't have tolls here, so it took me a while to realise the ping every so often was a toll charge being registered.

THE PLAINS

DE: You actually only hear the triple ping when you are running out of money on your e-tag. Even though Andrew commutes all the time, it always was a triple ping, he never seems to top up his e-tag. There was a nice moment of serendipity for me in the film regarding those pings, when the pings of the e-tag match up with the similar twinkly sounds in the Suicide song *Cheree*, when it is played in the film.

There are about 15 cuts in the film and some of them are a little bit jarring. We get set into the rhythm of him leaving the office, entering the car, and driving, and then sometimes he'll already be on the drive home. Can you talk about the choice of where to place the edit?

DE: We didn't shoot to have coverage so were always limited with editing choices. That said, the edit proved to be a very complex process which took a lot of time. Although it was shot quite formally, it was not a mathematical process of laying up each shot for a certain period of time. The only choices to make were where to cut in and out of each shot, which could greatly affect the overall rhythm of the film. As the film was of such a long duration it took time to work this out.

What does being an Australian filmmaker mean to you?

DE: It's an interesting question. I haven't really grappled with the question much internally before. I often find it hard to label myself as a filmmaker, let alone an Australian filmmaker, as it seems to connote a professional type of filmmaker. I don't see myself as a professional filmmaker, as in someone who can pick up a script and go and shoot it, on contract. I'm interested in trying things out with film, doing things I'm interested in, in that sense, an amateur.

That said, my films have been very much linked to setting, and the world around where I live. I find, even in the suburbs of Australia, where I grew up and spent a long time driving around, a great beauty – whether it be in the sky or the colours or in the trees that is uniquely Australian. The people I know and include in films are Australian. I see other people go and make films overseas. At this stage, I couldn't imagine doing that.

ENDNOTES

1   http://www.sensesofcinema.com/2022/festival-reports/stuck-in-traffic-iffr-2022/

FRANKLIN

91 mins
Director: *Kasimir Burgess*
Writers: *Kasimir Burgess, Claire Smith, Natasha Pincus*
Featuring: *Oliver Cassidy, Bob Brown, Hugo Weaving (voice)*
Producers: *Oliver Cassidy, Chris Kamen*
Composer: *Luke Altmann*
Cinematography: *Benjamin Bryan*
Editing: *Johanna Scott*

In 2022, *Franklin* was nominated for Best Documentary, Best Editing in a Documentary, and Best Sound in a Documentary at the AACTA Awards.

INTERVIEW
CO-WRITER & DIRECTOR
KASIMIR BURGESS

In Heather Rose's *Bruny*, the main protagonist, Astrid Coleman, asks herself amidst the aftermath of a destructive event: "Why are Tasmanians so good at protesting?" Within Kasimir Burgess' monumentally powerful documentary *Franklin*, which presents the history of the activist movement that saved the Franklin River from being dammed, the answer is clear: Tasmanians are so good at protesting because the land that they live with is not a resource for plundering, but rather a place to appreciate for the brief time that we are fortunate enough to exist in its presence. Many of the trees in the region surrounding the Franklin River predate the invasion of Australia, weathering time and humanity for hundreds of years.

The act of environmental protests is entwined with the identity of being Tasmanian, with stories of the island state tinged with triumphant bouts of activism that have protected the magnificent landscape the region has to offer. Tasmania is equally defined by those who stand in the face of the activists and encourage the never-satiated hunger of capitalism. For activist Oliver Cassidy, part of his identity comes from his father Michael Cassidy who was on the frontline to stop the mighty Franklin River from being destroyed and mangled into being a hydroelectric dam in the early eighties, and it's his solo journey along the Franklin that Burgess documents.

Kasimir's eye as a filmmaker has often been a deeply empathetic and curious one. Whether it be the essay on grief and destruction within his 2014 film *Fell*, or the explorative portrayal of one of Australia's most complicated public figures in *The Leunig Fragments*, his focus as a filmmaker has always been on the inner self, poking and engaging with the notion of what it means to human in the world today. *Franklin* sees a marriage of the themes within both of those films masterfully, with Burgess eager to expose and explore nature, while also investigating the souls of the people who have fought to save and protect it.

This interview was recorded by Andrew F. Peirce in July 2022.

FRANKLIN

How did the pandemic impact your plans to shoot this?

Kasimir Burgess: We managed to find a window of opportunity in the middle of the pandemic and get over there. During quarantine, I started editing. That two weeks in the hotel were some of the most productive in the whole time, getting my head around Tom Haydon's, Michael Cordell's, and Roger Scholes' beautiful, yet extensive archive from their experiences during the blockade and throughout the campaign. It was invaluable. Then going remote on the river, I think that was ideal, away from it all and isolating in quite an extreme way.

Did you go down the river alongside Oliver and the cinematographer [Benjamin Bryan]?

KB: And the producer [Chris Kamen] and drone operator [Luke Tscharke]. We, as a team, were trying to give Oliver as much space as possible for his experience to be authentic and to be connected with nature rather than an annoying director.

I found the cinematography and the observance of nature in Fell (2014), and then the observance of humanity and personality with The Leunig Fragments (2019), they're combined perfectly here with Franklin where you're observing and looking at the world around you in this really wonderous manner. Revisiting Fell and Leunig and then watching Franklin, this feels like a culmination of your filmography.

KB: Thank you. Some of those motifs and themes that run throughout those films [are] similar and maybe in harmony. I definitely have a connection, an affinity, a love of nature and a breaking heart for what's happening to our forests and our rivers, our air and our Earth. I think that the thread, if there are any, throughout my work and certainly preoccupation, it's hard for me to comment on that. It's almost like it needs a voice from the outside. That you've spotted that is impressive. I haven't heard anyone draw that line.

A powerful moment is when Bob and a few other people are talking about the pivotal change in Australia and seeing Rock Island and being able to share that image. The strong emotion in that scene comes from feeling like we're there. The cinematography immerses you so completely in what's going on. I haven't been to Tasmania myself, but I felt like I'd been there because of what I was experiencing.

KB: That was so good to be there. I felt like I would recognise it. It's so iconic from Scholes and Haydon and some other films and [I felt like I] had been there with that grainy 16mm footage. But being there in the flesh was very different. We all sat there in quiet, as Mike Cassidy writes. The trip was very

INTERVIEW | KASIMIR BURGESS

fast, we had to move down the river constantly in motion, getting coverage. But that was one moment where we stopped still for a little bit and took it in. Put the camera down even. It's an image that was spread far and wide. It was in mailboxes and posters, and it came to represent the beauty of the place. It interested me that a single image like that from an inspired artist [Peter Dombrovskis] could make a difference.

Were you a kid when the Franklin River protests were occurring?

KB: I was three or four years old. It was a seven-year campaign [and] I was alive at the tail end of the blockade. I do remember things, seeing a few news reports and that kind of thing, but it didn't really sink in. There was one image of a massive line of protesters on TV I remember seeing at my grandparents like a river snaking off into infinity and hearing that it was the biggest protest in Australian history. Even as a three- or four-year-old, it made an impression, but it wasn't til I was thirty that Chris Kamen, the producer, brought to my attention just how extraordinary the story really was and then to dig deeper into some of its personalities and facets.

How did you sequentially organise the narrative?

KB: We were lucky in that way, it has its own momentum, highs and lows and twists and turns. Just the history story that it is, I guess. The challenge was to marry that with Oliver's more personal journey. His existential searching through grief and self-discovery upon the river as he reflected on his nature, nature, and his father. That more meditative journey on the river had, at times, quite a different energy to the history-driven story. That was a big challenge to work with those different tones and rhythms and bring the two together, but I knew that I didn't want to tell the dry history version. It needed something more personal and more emotional for me to engage an audience and for me to want to invest that much time and energy in it.

At what point did Oliver's story come into the fold?

KB: From the very beginning. Chris and Oliver came together and had an idea perhaps of the story [even before I came on board] and Oliver's trip upon the river could be the backbone of the story. I was grateful to have them and their knowledge, which is far greater than mine when it comes to all the beats in the history. Chris and Oliver have an encyclopaedic knowledge of all the moments in the campaign and the blockade. Chris had studied that in high school, and then later in law. Chris and I had worked together on shorts and things, *Directions* [2008] and *Lone Rider* [2007], so we had a good friendship and working relationship. He said something about how it was "Malick-esque, it was in your ballpark." I think he was just saying, "There's nature, there's politics, there's a nice emotional coming-of-age story." Lots of ingredients that I could play with in my mind, trying to work out how they could all coexist and inform each other and then form into one cohesive whole.

I imagine that having those different narratives makes it a bit easier to manipulate in the edit room. You've got something to cut to rather than the main story.

KB: It was important for me to have moments where we're celebrating what Mike and Bob [Brown] and all these activists helped save. Existing in nature and to do that felt like quite a statement in its own way. We're just enjoying Rock Island bend or this tree or this rock formation

[it] felt like a necessary part of the story, rather than just, "It's great that it was saved," and a few fleeting epic visuals. We just wanted to sit in that space and time and feel the spirit of the place.

With that in mind, one of the motifs that is brought up is about how the resonance of the past lingers in the present. As you're filming the journey along the Franklin, the sense of the ancestors of Australia is there, but I wonder if the feeling and the echoes of the protests are there as well in the surroundings?

KB: It's really only at the very end of the river when it broadens out and it's the Franklin and Gordon, that you start to spot signs and you visit the places where they were protesting. The river itself was such a difficult journey [for] Mike Cassidy and Bob Brown. There are others, but the majority of it took place at the very end of the trip. Bob Brown made a few great short films, [there's] a beautiful 12-minute Super 8 shot on the river and there are so many moments from that film that I recognise. It feels like a dream.

They went down in summer, and the cinematography is poetic. It's got this psychedelic synth to it that just makes you fall in love with the place. Then seeing it with your own eyes and filming it in glassy, 4k resolution you have all these layers of connection to the place, and they all blend your memory of it with your memory of the various films. They're like sedimentary layers, they just layer up and layer up and they're informing consciously and unconsciously your interpretation of it and how you depict it.

I feel like it was Mike and Bob's observations along the river both in diary form, photos, and Super-8 that gave me a haunting connection to the place and a sense of the place. It was almost like a déjà vu through Mike and Bob's experience of the river. It was quite uncanny and beautiful. Bob's still alive, obviously, but it does feel like you're following a ghost with regards to Mike

INTERVIEW | KASIMIR BURGESS

because it was one of the big experiences in his life. Oliver told me at some point that he feels like if Dad's spirit is anywhere, it's on the Franklin.

It's an interesting companion to Jennifer Peedom's River. There was a beautiful resonance in your film to that one. The moment in Jen's film where there's footage of dams being blown up and rivers being revived, made me think of what was at stake for the Franklin.

KB: I watched a few hours of those images of dams being made just to try to get my head around it as well. It's sort of "Oh well, it's just the river getting bigger, right?" But it's not til you see that all the [surrounding] nature dies, and a lot of the natural curves are completely reshaped, that you start to get a sense of that destruction of the place, as well as its physical geographical facets. That was an eye-opener for me.

The score is immersive and beautiful. How did you go about creating it?

KB: I worked closely with Luke Altmann, our lovely composer. The first film he ever did was *Fell*, then his second was *The Leunig Fragments*, then his third was *Franklin*. We've developed a shorthand. I put in temp [music], which is the usual practice, just to describe a general feeling of it, and then he'll look at that and then sometimes throw it away and put forward a suggestion of something better. Sometimes we struggled on a scene, and it could take months and months to get the right thing, and then other times he was right from the beginning, which was great.

Sometimes Luke would make a piece of music for a section, and this happened quite a bit. I'll line up the timecode and I'll be like, "You know what, this will be way better over here." [I find] it's sometimes better when you find a piece that's not annotating too specifically, it's less cliched and less literal. You can find something happy to go with something sad. It's surprising what ended up being moved around and where the rightful home is. It often confounds and delights Luke and I, and we're both open to sculpting the score right up to the last minute to make sure you have the right feeling.

One of the notes that I discussed with Luke was "Let's keep it organic with wood instruments in the forest and not get electronic and too fancy." There's one big piece over Rock Island bend, that's the Adelaide Symphony Orchestra (ASO), and that's the one time we blew most of the budget on that. That was the one-time Luke and I felt the need for a much bigger, more immersive and nuanced sound down there. Everything else is understated. That ASO piece around Rock Island bend goes for like nine minutes. When we're talking about Dombrovskis' photo, that feels like the heart of the story there. A piece of art can, you hope, can make a difference.

FRANKLIN

One of the things that I appreciated about Franklin is that in comparison to other films about protests and activism, this doesn't carry the tone of 'we ought to be sad and we've got to change things.'

KB: That big wrap-up at the end, that big didactic moment where you're looking at the ice melt, children in third world countries dying. We actually had one of those scenes.

Did you have a discussion about it?

KB: It was like "Maybe this story is powerful enough, that the message or the intent is clear enough." That protest and activism is important and can transform the world. It didn't feel necessary anyway. Oliver, and the producers, and I, and co-editor Johanna [Scott], you're so close to it. Does that exposition need to be there or is it just inherent in the fabric of the film? When you're filming, when you're just sitting in nature, it does feel like quite a statement, quite political in its own way. Simply acknowledging and valuing what's currently present, what's still alive in the moment.

It sounds silly to say almost, but it feels like a brave choice to make because it's the expected resolution. For a lot of us, we get that message every single day when we open our news apps and read about what's in the world. We know about it, so not having that reminder was comforting. It made it resonate a lot stronger for me at least.

KB: And to not be bashed over the head with it. We did want an uplifting end. I mean, we're looking at a tortured tree that's been desecrated by some of the workers there, but it's still alive. Like our earth, desecrated, but somehow still alive. It feels like if you're looking closely enough that that contains the same message as you might do in a five-minute wrap-up of the global environmental situation. You can do that in one tree.

And we noticed that my last three films finished with an image of a tree.

Is that a conscious choice?

KB: Well, it is. It's just for me, really. It was just the way that it happened. You touched upon it before, saying there are some clear motifs in the films.

Let's lean into that question then about what it means to be an Australian maker and whether you have a body of work in mind as you're creating things.

KB: Probably no tree at the end of the next one. I can see a pattern emerging for sure.

INTERVIEW | KASIMIR BURGESS

It just seems impossible to create a story that doesn't include some love for the earth and a celebration of what we have, doesn't it? And an idea that it's worthwhile to protect it moving forward for generations to come. I love doing it and the journey that it takes me upon and the collaboration the friendships that are forged, what you learn about yourself and about humanities is great, which makes for a pretty cool job.

... AND THE KING: BAZ LUHRMANN'S ELVIS AND THE AUSTRALIANNESS OF IT ALL

ESSAY
ANDREW F. PEIRCE

For the purpose of this piece, the term 'the government' covers both state and federal governments. Additionally, while the term 'the arts' applies equally to film and TV, music, theatre, gaming, and literature, here it is used exclusively to refer to the film and television sector.

One of the key questions I asked Australian filmmakers for this book is what it means to be an Australian creative working today and whether the Australian identity plays a part in their work. Behind that line of questioning was a desire to understand the importance of hearing Australian voices on screen, and seeing Australian stories play out from an Australian perspective.

There is another side of the Australian film industry, and it's one where international stories are told by Australian filmmakers with Australian film financing, often shot in Australia. While they may feature international actors telling a non-Australian story, they are still Australian films.

One such film is Baz Luhrmann's *Elvis*, the musical drama on the life of Elvis Presley which became the king of the box office in Australia in 2022.

Baz Luhrmann's *Elvis* presents the life of Elvis Presley, aka 'the King', as seen through the life of his controlling and manipulative manager Colonel Tom Parker (Tom Hanks). While Hanks struggles to match the tonal variance of a Luhrmann epic, with the screen legend giving one of his hammiest performances, it's Austin Butler as Elvis who inhibits the legend in a way that suggests that he's become possessed by the King himself. Luhrmann fills out the cast for this American tale with a few familiar Aussie faces, including Baz regulars Richard Roxburgh and David Wenham, who join Olivia DeJonge, Kodi Smit-McPhee, Helen Thomson, Xavier Samuel, and Luke Bracey, and others in the mix.

Elvis swiftly became the fourth highest grossing Australian film (domestic) to date[1], bringing the number of Luhrmann flicks in the top ten to four, with it joining second ranked *Australia* (2008), seventh ranked *Moulin Rouge!* (2001), and eighth ranked *The Great Gatsby* (2013). Just outside the top ten is Luhrmann's debut *Strictly Ballroom* (1992), ranked twelfth

... AND THE KING

on the list. The only Luhrmann flick to not feature on the list is *Romeo + Juliet* (1996), which is not considered an Australian film[2].

Outside of *Romeo + Juliet*, Luhrmann's feature film work has predominantly been filmed in Australia, with locations being meticulously transformed into decidedly non-Australian locales; Balmain, NSW became West Egg and New York for *The Great Gatsby*, while Miami, a coastal suburb in the City of Gold Coast, transformed into Memphis, Las Vegas, and more, for *Elvis*.

Baz had shot both *Moulin Rouge!* and *The Great Gatsby* in Sydney's Fox Studios, but when Disney took it over and turned it into Disney Studios, the option to shoot in NSW was off the table, leading Luhrmann to turn north. With an image of the Gold Coast being the land of metre maids in his mind, he met with Former Premier of Queensland Annastacia Palaszczuk to discuss the notion of shooting in the burgeoning film region and found a 'paradise' of possibility.

The Gold Coast is home to one of the largest studio lots in the Southern Hemisphere: The Village Roadshow studios. Boasting nine sound stages and a range of production facilities, the studios have become a hotbed of activity, with the Legendary Pictures produced *Kong* and *Godzilla* films being shot there, and Academy Award winner Ron Howard opting to make it his home away from home, shooting *Thirteen Lives* (2022) and *Eden* (undated) on the Goldie.

The existence of the Village Roadshow studios feels like the natural evolution of the early nineties when Luhrmann lobbied then Prime Minister Paul Keating for a film studio to be built in the heart of Sydney, an act that ultimately helped guide the way for the Fox Studios facility, and helped inform Keating's four-year, $250 million Creative Nation strategy. Now, there are film studios in almost every state, with soil being turned on Perth's film studio in 2024, and current AACTA President Russell Crowe pledging support for a fully integrated feature-film production and post-production complex in Coffs Harbour.

Luhrmann is a multi-Academy Award nominated filmmaker[3] whose work has reached a global box office total of US$1.2 billion (unadjusted for inflation). With Warner Bros. as the key production company, and *Elvis* boasting a reported budget of US$85 million, Bazmark Inq (Luhrmann's company) sought to go through the funding application route to make the film in Australia.

For Luhrmann's partner and collaborator, Catherine Martin, there's a level of importance that comes with making a film in Australia:

> The Australian Government is very generous in its support of movies and has been to us. I think that we have worked with Australian crews and valued those relationships over twenty years. The skill and artistry of those people is irreplaceable. Similarly, the ability to get such a great Australian cast, whether it's Helen Thomson, David Wenham,

or Richard Roxburgh, they're all so extraordinary. It's nice to come home and be able to use all these homegrown resources. It's very satisfying. Baz and I are very proud that we can make movies of all scales here and that we have the resources to do so.[4]

The following exploration into how *Elvis* may have received support from government funding bodies comes with a few caveats.

Firstly, Australia has restrictive tax secrecy laws that mean that there is no way to glean which companies received rebates and how much they received. However, I was able to gather publicly available information from each of the government funding body websites which provides information about films that are wholly or partially produced within Australia that received support via their various incentives.

Secondly, while the following provides a rundown of the financial support *Elvis* received and its subsequent awards recognition, it is by no means an extensive exploration of screen body funding within Australia. For further reading, I recommend the work of Michael West Media[5], an independent journalist who has written about the way taxpayer funds have been used to prop up Hollywood studio productions. Additional reading includes Kelly Burke's complementary piece on The Guardian[6] about how the Albanese government aims to continue providing rebates to Hollywood, which works in collaboration alongside the extensive coverage provided by Inside Film and ScreenHub where the role of government support for the arts is explored on a regular basis.

Thirdly, links have been provided where possible to reflect where the information was gathered from. As these are stored on the internet, they may not be active by the time you read this book. If you are unable to access the links, I recommend using the Internet Archive to view a snapshot of the site from the time when I accessed the information.

It's also worth noting the emotional toll that comes with seeking funding from the different incentives mentioned below. Each one often requires pages upon pages of evidence to justify why your project not only needs government support, but also that it's a project worthy of receiving said support. The Australian film industry is a small one, so there can also be that unspoken knowledge that you're competing against friends and colleagues for the same funding. Compared to smaller films that may only have one or two producers doing the leg work of ensuring applications are complete and submitted on time, a production like *Elvis* would have a dedicated team whose sole focus is the application process.

After COVID, the topic of burnout is one that is only just being safely addressed within the wider working community, creative or otherwise. The hustle mindset is thankfully being dismantled and disrupted across different industries, and if mental and physical health protocols are implemented safely, then it should create less stress across the board.

... AND THE KING

Now onto the way BazMark may have approached different government funding bodies for support.

In Australia, the term 'collaboration' is often used to describe the relationship between the arts and governments. In reality, if you're a filmmaker working today seeking to get a project off the ground, you have little choice but to run the gambit of trying to get your film funded by the national funding body, Screen Australia, or via one of the state funding bodies. If either of these avenues comes up short, then the only other option is to seek financial support through private investors, philanthropists, crowdfunding, the bank of "mum and dad", or riskier methods like the Kevin Smith route of maxing out credit cards or taking out unsecured loans[7].

For *Elvis*, Bazmark received support from seven of the available nine[8] government and local funding bodies, but to begin with we will focus on the support they received from the Queensland Government, Screen Queensland, and the Australian Government's Producer Offset program[9].

As per the Screen Australia website[10]:

> *The Producer Offset is a refundable tax offset (rebate) for producers of Australian feature films, television and other projects. Because it's underpinned by income tax legislation, it represents a source of funds for producers of eligible Australian projects.*

It's easy to get stuck in the mud regarding the different thresholds and offsets, especially when we note that on 13 December 2023 the Federal Government made changes to the Producer Offset as part of the MYEFO, so with that in mind, let's take a quick squiz under section 2.1 Eligible Applicants in the Producer Offset Guidelines[11] to see what qualifies as an 'eligible Australian project':

> *2.1.1 The Company*
> *(a) To be eligible for the Producer Offset, an applicant must be either:*
> *(i) an Australian resident company, being:*
> *A. or a company incorporated in Australia; or*
> *B. if not incorporated in Australia, a company having its central management and control (CMC) in Australia, or its voting power controlled by shareholders who are residents of Australia. (Taxation Rule TR 2018/5 and PCG 2018/9 provides guidance for when a foreign incorporated company is an Australian tax resident);*
> *Or*
> *(ii) a foreign resident company with an ABN operating through a permanent establishment in Australia. (Taxation ruling TR 2002/5, as amended by TR 2002/5A, 5A2 and 5A3, provides guidance about whether a foreign resident company has a place at or through*

which it carries on business for the purposes of the definition of 'permanent establishment').

(b) Individuals, partnerships, sole traders and a company which is acting in the capacity of a trustee of a trust are ineligible for the Producer Offset.

Cutting through the legalese jargon, and noting the changes implemented by the Albanese Government in the 2023-24 Budget and 2023-24 MYEFO[12], the Producer Offset effectively provides a 40 per cent rebate for feature film productions, and a 30 per cent rebate for productions on other platforms, which is calculated as a percentage of a production's qualifying Australian production expenditure.

Technically the offset can be accessed by Australian filmmakers, but there was a catch for films made during the time *Elvis* was produced: to qualify, a feature film must have had a budget of at least AU$15m, which effectively locked out most of the local market. According to Screen Australia[13], during the 2020/21 financial year there were 47 feature films produced in Australia. Of those 47 features, three feature films had a budget of between AU$10m-20m, with six having a budget over AU$20m. Because of the breakdown in figures, it is not possible to determine which of the three feature films had a budget of over AU$15m.

When the majority of feature films produced in Australia fall well outside the offset scope, it becomes clear just how difficult it is for local productions to gain much needed funding body support. This also applies to multi-million-dollar productions like Leah Purcell's *The Drover's Wife* and Thomas M. Wright's *The Stranger* where their budgets sit just below the required threshold. These are feature films that, if made in the Hollywood system, would otherwise be considered major studio productions. In Australia, they exist in a grey area as major productions that stand as the bread-and-butter output of the Australian film industry, however their budgets aren't significant enough to garner the support that global productions shot in Australia manage to receive.

While it is not an expectation for productions to publicise that they are the recipient of the Producer Offset, titles such as *Mad Max: Fury Road* (2015), *Hacksaw Ridge* (2016), and *Peter Rabbit* (2018) have each publicly acknowledged they received support through the scheme, while on the Screen Australia website, stills from *Elvis*, *The Great Gatsby*, and *The Railway Man* (2013) are used as examples of productions that have received support.

There is an argument to be made that the government funding bodies support these features because they stand as safe projects that almost guarantee a return on investment, and within that safe environment a productive film industry in Australia is nurtured; as if to say, 'If that means the film industry in Australia becomes an industry for hire without its own cultural identity, then so be it.'

... AND THE KING

From an outsider's perspective, the perception is that unless your film features Leonardo DiCaprio raising a glass of champers in the air with a twinkle in his eye or a bevy of digital bunnies bouncing around to Len's 'Steal My Sunshine', you're going to be hard pressed to gain much needed financial support to create a film that can financially compete on a Hollywood level.

As an aside: Screen Australia also has treaties and MOUs with partner countries[14] to create official co-productions which benefit both partners. These films are often noted as being co-productions, with films like *The Power of the Dog* (UK), *Dirt Music* (UK), *Animals* (Ireland), and *The Australian Dream* (UK), with the percentage of funding (usually more than 50%) being used to determine if it can wear the label of being an "Australian film" or not.

Thus, with its Producer Offset in the bag for *Elvis*, Bazmark was then also able to apply to the state funding bodies for support. *Elvis* was shot in Queensland, which was able to provide dual support by way of Screen Queensland and the Gold Coast Film Commission (GCFC).

At the Australian Premiere of *Elvis*, Baz Luhrmann said[15]:

> Magic, magic, magic. 'The Goldie' [Gold Coast] is golden.
> I say it because we're buying space here, we'll make more movies here, it's a special part of the world.

That magic is in part thanks to the GCFC's Screen Attraction Program, 'an incentive that is agreed to prior to the production being undertaken on the Gold Coast.[16]' GCFC is the only local government in Australia to provide a Screen Attraction Program that includes financial incentives.

The eligibility requirements for the program are[17]:
- *Screen productions can be feature films, television programs (including drama, documentaries, factual, reality, entertainment series), games, animation, SVOD and online content.*
- *Applicants can be international, national or Gold Coast productions or post-production, games, animation and visual effects studios with a track record of successfully delivering and screening completed projects.*
- *Productions must have an Australian broadcast or screening in place or under negotiation.*
- *Applications must be made by the company responsible for undertaking the activities of production.*
- *The production and/or post-production office of the program must be located on the Gold Coast.*
- *A minimum Gold Coast production or post-production expenditure of $750,000.*
- *Applications must be made prior to the completion of pre-production.*

Assessment criteria
- *Number of Gold Coast employees being a minimum of 50% of total crew roles*
- *Value of Gold Coast investment*

ESSAY | ANDREW F. PEIRCE

With the film shoot set to take place in COVID locked down[18] Queensland, Bazmark also sought support from Screen Queensland who provide an array of incentives for productions. They include, but are not limited to[19]:
Production Attraction Incentive Benefits:
- *The Queensland Government via Screen Queensland offers a Production Attraction incentive for productions with a minimum spend of AU$3.5 million within the state.*
- *A further incentive is available from the City of Gold Coast to productions that spend a minimum of AU$750,000 in the region.*
- *These incentives can be used in conjunction with the Australian Government's Location Offset, Producer Offset and PDV Offset.*

State Payroll Tax Rebate Benefits:
- *Available to productions that have paid the 4.75 per cent Queensland Payroll Tax.*

The Revolving Film Financing Fund Benefits:
- *Provides secured loans to cash-flow the Producer Offset, distribution guarantees and pre-sales.*
- *Post, Digital and Visual (PDV) Incentive*
- *And more*

In researching the various incentives that *Elvis* could have utilised, it is not clear whether they were able to utilise both of the Production Attraction Incentives provided by the Queensland Government via Screen Queensland and the incentive provided by City of Gold Coast, but given that both Screen Queensland and the GCFC note *Elvis* as a production that received their support on their websites, it can be assumed that this is the case. It's worthwhile noting that both the GCFC and Screen Queensland credit productions like *Ticket to Paradise* (2022), *Thirteen Lives* (2022), *Spiderhead* (2022), and *Godzilla vs Kong* (2021) as recipients of the incentives on offer.

Given the level of support *Elvis* received from the Queensland government and its funding bodies, it made sense then that Baz would recognise the support from Former Premier of Queensland Annastacia Palaszczuk in his Best Film acceptance speech at the 2022 AACTA Awards[20], saying:

> *A big last shout out to Annastacia Palaszczuk, because honestly, she was kind of a producer on the film. She stood by us through thick and thin when COVID came.*

Additional support for *Elvis* was delivered by other states funding bodies, each of which provided PDV and VFX support. These bodies include ScreenWest (Double Barrel Productions), the South Australian Film Corporation (Rising Sun Pictures, MPC, Resin), VicScreen (Framestore, Luma Pictures), and Screen NSW, making *Elvis* a truly national, collaborative film made by the Australian film industry.

... AND THE KING

It's worthwhile making the distinction between 'the Australian film industry' and the 'film industry in Australia' clear. The Australian film industry is the industry that produces Australian films, both government supported and independently produced, whereas the film industry in Australia provides a place for films to be made, and as outlined above can also receive government support in both pre- and post-production.

This is in part why the question of 'What is an Australian film?' is a deeply conflicted and complicated one. It's also a question that can't reasonably or clearly be answered, given the manner that one production can have tendrils in each state by receiving incentive support across the board. This level of support sees notable Hollywood productions like the Australian-shot *Mortal Kombat* (2017) or Marvel's *Thor: Ragnarok* (2017) somehow fall under the purview of being deemed 'Australian movies,' as determined by AACTA.

Hollywood accounting is a dark art unto itself, with the industry regularly seeking any tax breaks that they can utilise globally and domestically. Within America, at least eighteen states compete for their slice of the film industry, with regions like Louisiana, Georgia, and Arizona each providing incentives for productions to shoot away from the hills of Hollywood. The same applies to nations like Canada, the UK, Aotearoa-New Zealand, and of course, Australia.

This endless search for the best tax incentives a nation can offer at times leads Australia to feel like Hollywood's Southern Hemisphere backlot, with productions like David Leitch's *The Fall Guy* (2024) and Wes Ball's *Kingdom of the Planet of the Apes* (2024) shifting south to take advantage of the government incentives on offer. While Hollywood productions can bring an increase in employment and skill opportunities for local crews, it also means that they rely on the decision of Hollywood executives who may decide to pull the plug on industry boosting projects like Sam Esmail's proposed US$188 million Apple TV+ remake of *Metropolis*, which was cancelled due to the 2024 writers' strike[21].

When the AACTA Awards screened from the Gold Coast in 2024, a preshow reel played proudly presenting the 'Australian productions' in the year to come. Concerningly, the films presented were mostly American productions: *The Fall Guy, Kingdom of the Planet of the Apes, Mortal Kombat 2* (undated), *Godzilla x Kong*, with Robert Connolly's *Force of Nature: The Dry 2* (2024) sitting as the rare truly Australian feature-film production on the horizon.

While these titles are the bread-and-butter fodder for cinema going audiences, unless they stick around for the credits, the average punter is unlikely to recognise that the flick they've just munched a box of popcorn through was partially financed by, post-produced or predominantly shot in Australia. The film industry in Australia has effectively become a bunyip in King Kong's clothing, so much so that when we are given the opportunity to create large-scale feature films like *Mad Max: Fury Road*, the lead characters are portrayed by poms and seppos.

A decade of culture adverse, employment and budget focused LNP Federal governments has led the current state of film and TV production in Australia to become an industry for hire, with the number one name on the government call sheet being 'Jobson Grothe'. However, with the arrival of the Albanese government, and the return of Hon Tony Burke MP to the portfolio of Minister for the Arts, cultural change is on the horizon with the announcement of the arts policy: *Revive: A Place for Every Story, A Story for Every Place*. More on that later.

Although Australia is still perceived to be a nation of labourers and miners, it does have a healthy community of film and video production practitioners, with some 15,872 people reported to be employed by the sector in the 2021 Census[22]. It's that active industry group that was behind Russell Crowe's decision to take on the reigns of his 2021 thriller *Poker Face*, saying[23]:

> *I'm making that decision [...] that if I say no, [...] 280 crew people in Australia simply lose their job. We're in a pandemic. The city's going into a lockdown. The difference between them staying employed and not is why I'm saying yes.*
> *If we're going to make this film, we're going to make it in Australia, we're going to make it with largely an Australian cast, then let's just have this be an Australian story.' It's an urban Australian story ... I just don't see there is any valid reason that you can't tell a contemporary urban Australian story without having to have a kangaroo involved.*

That focus on jobs and industry support was a key part of the 2019 press release announcing the Queensland-based shoot for *Elvis*[24], where it was noted that the production was expected 'to employ 900 Queenslanders in behind-the-scenes roles.'

While the Australian film industry has been in operation since the dawn of cinema, in many ways, it's still in its nascent state, and is unlikely to ever reach parity with the studio-driven financial system of America. American productions are often seen as the benchmark for how Australian filmmakers should measure their success and creative output, carrying across the reality that many American films are crewed up teams who workday in, day out on major studio productions, giving them the ability to swap over to indie films with a deeper knowledge base. The mindset being that Australian crews can then transfer those Hollywood-level skills to lower budget location productions, effectively creatively upskilling Australian films.

It's easy for me to sit here and advocate for cultural safety and to say that the film industry in Australia is not just an industry for hire, it would be ignorant to not recognise the personal and financial choice that comes when Disney calls with buckets of money on offer, while on the other line is a local filmmaker who barely has $100,000 to their name. As an award-winning director once mentioned to me, the reason they work overseas as a director for hire is that they can earn ten times more doing a five-week stint on a Hollywood production in Romania than they would guiding their own project at home. And while they would prefer to be at home telling Australian stories, the financial choice is clear: America is where the money is, even if that money is spent here in Australia.

There is a growing trend that has seen established Australian actors in Hollywood returning home to continue their film careers, utilising their notoriety to get productions off the ground just down the road from their home. Since *Thor: Ragnarok*, many of Chris Hemsworth's productions have been shot on the East coast, or at least in neighbouring countries, with *Spiderhead*, *Furiosa* (2024), and the TV series *Shark Beach with Chris Hemsworth* all being produced locally. Other talent who have decided to solely work in Australia or increase their output here include Simon Baker, Hugo Weaving, Eric Bana, and Nicole Kidman.

These actors come with a certain level of cultural heft to their name, meaning that filmmakers like Mark Leonard Winter can get *The Rooster* (2023) off the ground on the strength of Weaving's bona fides or Ivan Sen can secure funding for his black and white neo-noir film *Limbo* (2023) thanks to Simon Baker's involvement. While both films were made with shoestring budgets and limited crews, they received the attention of audiences in part thanks to the familiarity of their lead actors.

Which brings us to the AACTA Awards.

First, a short history lesson. The AACTAs were instituted in 2011, born out of the Australian Film Institute (AFI) Awards[25]. The creation of the AFI, and by virtue, AACTAs, is diametrically opposed to the foundation of the Academy Awards, which were created in an act of union-busting by Louis B. Mayer[26]. The AFI was formed in 1958 as part of the Melbourne Film Festival (later known as MIFF) 'as a way to improve the impoverished state of Australian cinema.'[27] Its existence was an act of recognition of the importance of Australian screen culture.

After industry consultation, the AACTAs were formed as an 'Australian Academy.' It's a term which has led the award to rarely be referred to as an 'AACTA Award,' instead being dubbed the 'Aussie Oscars,' even during the ceremony where presenters have announced 'the winner of the Aussie Oscar' before naming the recipient. While Australia as a nation has often maintained an underdog status in the world, the term 'the Aussie Oscars' can feel at times like an attempt to delegitimise the awards, noting that the BAFTAs are rarely referred to as the British Oscars or the Goya Awards the Spanish Oscars, but are acknowledged as prestigious entities in their own right.

However, the notion of being the 'Australian Academy' has shaped the way the AACTAs have positioned themselves as the leading organisation that honours and celebrates Australian film and television practitioners.

As per the AACTA overview[28]:

> The primary role of the Australian Academy of Cinema and Television Arts (AACTA), a not-for-profit organisation, is to recognise, encourage, promote and celebrate film and television excellence in Australia, connecting Australian and international audiences with great Australian screen content. The Academy serves as Australia's most prestigious film and television membership body, bringing together and representing screen professionals from a cross-section of the screen industry in order to further screen excellence in Australia. Australia has produced some of the best screen performers, practitioners and productions in the world, and the Academy remains committed to promoting, within Australia and internationally, Australia's best and brightest screen professionals and the great Australian stories which they tell on the big and small screens.

And as per the About AACTA section of the website[29]:

> We believe in celebrating and supporting every aspect of Australian screen creativity, and we are committed to recognising our nation's growing contribution to global pop culture. We are proud of the role we play in generating sales and jobs for our industry and creatives at home and abroad, helping to fuel the Australian screen industry's $3bn contribution to the national economy each year, generating $250m in exports and supporting 25,000 jobs, as we take Australian screen culture, craft, creativity, entertainment and business to the world.

Unlike the Academy of Motion Pictures Arts and Sciences (AMPAs) or the BAFTAs, the AACTAs have not announced the membership figures. When approached for information on membership numbers, AACTA did not provide a response. Given, at time of writing, the AFI were at risk of regulatory breach after failing to lodge financial statements with the Australian Charities and Not-for-profits Commission on time[30], I can understand that they may have more pressing issues on hand than answering queries from a film critic about membership or voting rules.

While the saying 'awards don't matter' does apply to most glitzy industry-led awards groups, the reality is that what wins at the AACTAs can determine the shape of Australian film and TV for the years to come. With a peer decided golden trophy in your hands, the chances of your next project getting that all-too-vital funding body support suddenly increases. Failing that, a nomination looks neat on the resume too.

... AND THE KING

This is a notion that AACTA is well aware of, stating on the Membership section of the site[31]:

> With 75% of AACTA Award winners receiving new opportunities and a third receiving new funding following their win, your vote makes a difference!

Membership for the AACTAs are made up of three tiers:

- *Professional:* Open to accredited screen professional and industry practitioners;
- *General:* Available to everyone; and
- *Youth:* Provides access to a range of resources for students and film fans under 25.

As of 2021[32], all members are eligible to vote in the awards, with the General and Youth member votes weighted at 0.5[33], and the Technical Craft Awards restricted to votes from the Professional membership group. At time of publication, membership fees[34] vary from $25 to $140, providing members with access to the AACTA TV platform, ScreenFest Events, masterclasses, cinema & film festival discounts, and development initiatives, alongside voting rights. For General members, being able to help decide the winner of the AACTAs is a fun and entertaining way to interact with the Australian film community. Savvy film productions might also be able to enlist family and friends to become members to support their films when voting time opens.

For a film to be eligible for the AACTA Awards, it must be released publicly with the following stipulations[35]:

> 7.3 (i) A commercial cinema, in a minimum of two Australian capital cities including Sydney or Melbourne, for a run of at least seven consecutive days; or
> (ii) An approved Qualifying Australian Film Festival along with a minimum of four separate screenings (paid admission) at a commercial cinema across a minimum of two Australian Capital cities with one city being Melbourne or Sydney;
> (iii) or An approved Qualifying VOD/SVOD platform or broadcast on Free to Air;
> (iv) or Have a release strategy that otherwise satisfies AACTA, at its discretion.

Unlike the AMPAs, the AACTAs do not have a rule in place regarding campaigning for awards, meaning that submitting members can, if they choose to, petition fellow members for votes, engage in blanket 'for your consideration' social media campaigns, and hold exclusive screening events with cast and crew in attendance. This is considered normal awards season behaviour.

If a filmmaker wishes to submit their film, then they're presented with staggered submission fees depending on the budget of their work:

For Feature Films[36]:
Budget under $500k - $599; Budget $500k to $2M - $1350; Budget $2M to $4M - $1799; Budget over $4m - $2299

For Documentaries[37]:
Budget under $500k - $550; Budget $500K to $1M - $700; Budget over $1M - $900

For Short Films[38]:
$150 (Full); $70 (Student)

While the AACTA Awards are not considered an essential aspect of the film-to-audience life cycle for an Australian filmmaker, they do play a role in facilitating a continued connection with the Australian film industry for those who work within it. For the self-funded filmmakers who have nurtured their production from concept to creation, including paying out of pocket expenses for festival submissions, screenings, and marketing, the notion of engaging with yet another organisation that requires payment of some kind to participate in can be a difficult one.

The Australian film industry does not operate within a studio system like Hollywood does. There, the term 'independent' production is used to define any film that is made without the support of an organisation that can provide the financial foundations that will see a film run from concept to creation to release. Logically, one could say that due to the ties that governments have to screen funding bodies, they supplant the 'studio system' in Australia, and therefore, every film that does not receive government support is an 'indie film.'

However, determining what constitutes an Australian 'indie' film is partly difficult to define since filmmakers can receive part (i.e., less than 50%) funding for their production from government bodies. Additionally, applications for funding can be submitted prior to or during the post-production period, allowing filmmakers to gain additional funds for that VFX shot they require, or to polish the sound mix.

Therefore, under the purview of AACTA, it is not possible to reach a clear definition of what constitutes an 'independent' production in Australia. For AACTA, the distinction between an independent film and a non-independent film becomes a purely financial one, meaning that films that are over 60-minutes long and with a budget under AU$2 million are eligible for all awards, including the Best Indie Film award.

Screen Australia tracks the number of Australian feature films by budget ranges[39], noting that for the 2022/23 financial year, of the 31 productions registered, 48% cost between AU$1-5 million. It's hard not to raise an eyebrow at the number of titles presented on this list, especially when there

... AND THE KING

is only one title registered that came in with a budget under AU$1 million. Screen Australia does not provide a rundown of each title, however, as per the fine print on the report notes, it 'includes only feature films first released, or with an intended first release, in Australian cinemas.'

It can be read then that this does not include the many independent feature films which screened exclusively at film festivals, like *The Lonely Spirits Variety Hour* or *Bassendream*, or via the rebirth of Australia film co-ops and communities, like Moviejuice in Adelaide, Black Maria Film Club in Perth, BORLFF in Brisbane, Unknown Pleasures and Kinotopia in Melbourne.

These films fit into the category 'free-range film' - a term coined by director Maria Nieto to recognise that these are films that are made outside of the institutional industry apparatus[40]. By their very nature, they're also films that tend to fall out of the purview of Screen Australia due to not receiving support or fitting into their monitoring criteria, and the AACTAs, with many filmmakers either not having the funds to submit their film, or not seeing a benefit in putting in for contention.

This distinction matters because it helps outline the fact that there are essentially two Australian film industries operating at once: the government supported industry where everything from *Elvis* to *Sweet As* are created, and the free-range film industry where films such as Gabriel Bath's *Ships That Bear* (2023) or Sarah Legg's *Cherubhead* (2022) are born. While they may not have the government support that their cinematic siblings do, free-range films like *Ships That Bear* and *Cherubhead* are no less valuable. As many cineastes will attest, it's when you wade into the wealth of truly indie films where you are able to find genuine cinematic gold.

Operating in the grey area outside of the screen funding bodies and these free-range filmmakers are the various funding initiatives driven by localised film festivals like the Adelaide Film Festival and MIFF. The Adelaide Film Festival Investment Fund (AFFIF) was established in 2003 and saw the festival become an active participant in creating new work. AFFIF was the first fund of its kind in Australia, leading to the support of over 110 screen projects, including work by Goran Stolevski, Sarah Watt, Rolf de Heer, Warwick Thornton, Granaz Moussavi, and more. In Victoria, the MIFF Premiere Fund was established in 2007 and 'offers minority co-financing to new Australian quality theatrical (narrative and documentary) feature films'[41], and has supported filmmakers like Rhian Skirving, Sean Byrne, Ana Kokkinos, Thomas M. Wright, Justin Kurzel, and Alena Lodkina, who all premiered their films at MIFF.

The one thing that all of these films share is that they're the result of a collaborative effort. When the newly minted Hon Tony Burke MP, Minister for the Arts (2022-) took to the stage at the close of the 12th AACTA Awards on 7 December 2022 to present the award for Best Film, he said:

> *Everything that you do is about collaboration, and the fact that Australian creatives are involved in that collaboration*

ESSAY | ANDREW F. PEIRCE

helps us see ourselves, helps us know each other, and lets the world recognise us.

After a clip reel that showed an array of Aussie accents in Aussie stories (*Here Out West*, *Sissy*, *The Drover's Wife*, and *The Stranger*), Burke announced the winner: Baz Luhrmann's *Elvis*.
Accepting his award remotely, Baz said:

As the Minister said, this is an industry that is robust and that is being supported and is flourishing. It really is about collaboration.

Elvis is the creative result of a 900-strong nation-wide behind the scenes crew who collectively worked through some of the toughest years that global creative industries have experienced. It's the end result of a shared vision that was in part made possible thanks to the government funding bodies that kept people employed. It is presumed too that many of the 900 cast and crew who worked on it are AACTA members. With that in mind, while *Elvis* is a truly American story, its Australian-ness is never really in question.

Naturally, that then becomes the biggest sticking point for Australia's Oscars: what exactly quantifies an Australian film?

When the AFI started bestowing the award for Best Film in the seventies, it did so by celebrating genuinely Australian stories like Ken Hannam's *Sunday Too Far Away* (1975), Phillip Noyce's *Newsfront* (1978), and Gillian Armstrong's *My Brilliant Career* (1979). These narratives had something to say about the Australia of the past, and in doing so, they commented on the Australia of the present.

As the AFI transitioned into AACTA, it brought about a globalist scope that positioned the awards group as an Oscar precursor. It can be perceived that wins at the AACTAs might have helped push films like *Mad Max: Fury Road*, *Hacksaw Ridge*, and *Lion* towards their eventual Best Picture nominations, however it's likely that their Hollywood pedigree helped more than the Aussie Oscar did.

In a bid to maintain their presence in the global awards conversation, the AACTAs shifted their 2023 awards ceremony to February 2024, weeks ahead of the 96th Academy Awards where local legend turned Hollywood royalty Margot Robbie was nominated for producing *Barbie* (2023). To secure the presence of Robbie and the social media coverage that comes with her, the 13th AACTA Awards effectively became a night of celebrating Barbie herself as Margot took home the AACTA International Award for Best Lead Actress in Film, and screen legend Cate Blanchett dressing up in an oversized bright pink outfit to present Robbie with the Trailblazer Award[42], a 'discretionary award' that is 'determined by the AFI | AACTA Board and President.' As per the AACTA website:

... AND THE KING

> *The Trailblazer Award recognises the multi-disciplinary achievements of talented individuals, acknowledging their valuable contribution to promoting Australian screen excellence both in Australia and abroad.*

Previous recipients who have managed to 'promote Australian screen excellence' (definition pending) include global names like Chris Hemsworth, Simon Baker, Isla Fisher, and Rose Byrne.

While the Australian film industry in the seventies and eighties is a vastly different landscape compared to the Australian film industry of today, it's difficult to see how previous winners like Paul Cox's *Lonely Hearts* (1982) or Gil Brealey's *Annie's Coming Out* (1984) would be able to stand out against the array of Hollywood productions that have started to dominate the AACTA Awards of today.

To be clear, it would be a destructive, insular act if the film industry in Australia shut off the eligibility for Hollywood produced, international narrative, Australian financed and shot films like *Elvis*, *Hacksaw Ridge*, and *Three Thousand Years of Longing* to compete for the AACTA Awards. As this book has hopefully presented, Australian stories do not always need to be focused on Australia, its culture, and the people who live with it.

However, within the Australian film industry, the cultural dominance of non-Australian stories presents a complicated landslide that can make it difficult for Australian stories to stand out. After all, these are films that have the financial heft of Hollywood behind them to produce and market. They are also the movies that the film industry in Australia has come to rely on as a place to continually employ cast and crew. Without these films, the presence of a productive film industry in Australia would be in doubt.

Which means that the Australian film industry must think smarter and find ways for Australian voices and stories to stand out.

One way would be for the Australian film industry to take a page out of its artistic companions book and create an annual award akin to the prestigious Miles Franklin Literary Award, an annual literary prize awarded to 'a novel which is of the highest literary merit and presents Australian life in any of its phases.[43]' The act of recognising films that have the highest cinematic merit and depict Australian life in any of its phases reinforces the value and importance of seeing Australian stories on screen. If the AACTAs were to introduce an award akin to the Miles Franklin Literary Award, it would provide a shared space for both non-Australian narrative films and Australian narrative films to be recognised during the ceremony.

A year after *Elvis* triumphed at the AACTAs, Danny and Michael Philippou stretched out a porcelain hand to the world and scared the living shit out of them with their grotty horror debut film *Talk to Me* (2023), which took home eight AACTA Awards including Best Picture and Best Director.

This nasty flick spent years in pre-production with the brother's facing studio after studio who told them to remove the Australianness out of the script. Each time they heard that, it made them stick their heels into the sand further and solidify the Aussie lingo and the Strine accent that helped make the film the bloody ripper that it is.

In their acceptance speech (which opens in the most Aussie way possible with Danny getting to the mic and uttering 'Shit. Fuck. Oh, sorry,' in shock), Michael acknowledges the support of Causeway Films, an Aussie production company who has helped bring both distinctly Australian films like *The Babadook, Blaze, Of an Age,* and *Talk to Me* to life, while also finding a way to support global stories told by Australian filmmakers, like they did with Rodd Rathjen's *Buoyancy* (2019) and Goran Stolevski's *You Won't Be Alone*.

Michael continued his speech by thanking his cast and crew[44]:

> *We were able to do it our way, the Aussie way. It was the best decision we ever made. So, everyone, let's keep working together, helping each other, and showing the world that Australia is batshit fucking crazy, but we make cool arse shit.*

Then they walk off stage, hugging host Rebel Wilson and shaking the hand of Ron Howard again.

When *Talk to Me* won Best Film, producer Samantha Jennings took to the stage and gave a speech which further embraced the Australianness of the production, and voiced genuine awe that not only would Australian audiences want to see an Aussie horror flick in cinemas, but they would continue to do so when *Barbie* was released into the world. She closes her speech saying:

> *It has just been insane, the last year. We're just this little Australian film, to watch it just go out into the world and to have people in [...] far-flung corners of the world watch it and love it and feel like it was relevant to them and exciting to them, [...] that's why we do what we do and that's what makes it worth it, so we have to keep doing it, because Australian cinema matters. And that's why we're all here.*

I want to stress; this is not an 'us' versus 'them' debate. There used to be a time where international filmmakers would look to Australia and say, 'I want to make stories about that place'. It's how we ended up with filmmakers like Canadian Ted Kotcheff (*Wake in Fright*), Brit Nicolas Roeg (*Walkabout*), and American Stanley Kramer (*On the Beach*), seeing both the cultural and location opportunities of presenting Australian stories from an international perspective.

Australian filmmakers like Baz Luhrmann, Jocelyn Moorhouse, Alex Proyas, Peter Weir, Gillian Armstrong, and George Miller are once in a generation talents, but they're also the results of creative systems that supported them in testing out their vision and facilitating pathways to audiences.

... AND THE KING

Their work has shifted a global understanding of what Australian cinema can be. By supporting them, generations of filmmakers have sought to replicate and become the Baz, Alex, or George of the future. They can only do that if there is an ecosystem that nurtures that vision.

Which brings me back to the Albanese government's cultural vision for Australia[45]:

> Revive
> A Place for Every Story, A Story for Every Place.

Revive was published on 9 February 2023 and is an aspirational read, full of hope and a clear vision for what the future could hold.

It's a National Cultural Policy that's held up by five pillars:

> Pillar 1 – First Nations First
> Pillar 2 – A Place for Every Story
> Pillar 3 – Centrality of the Artist
> Pillar 4 – Strong Cultural Infrastructure
> Pillar 5 – Engaging the Audience

and it contains sentences like:

> 'A responsible and secure nation welcomes stories that wake it up.'

and

> 'It is not the role of governments to create culture. Let's leave that to the artists, makers, and storytellers - the creative practitioners.'

and

> 'The government's role is to invest in our creative infrastructure. To preserve the structures and facilities that make cultural memory possible: our libraries and museums, our galleries and archives, our national broadcasters.'

This is a policy which has a vision for years to come, and as such, its impact will only truly be known years down the line, not a year after it has launched. It talks of supporting Australian artists, of listening to, engaging with, and supporting First Nations voices, it talks about creating pathways to audiences.

An immediate action result from Revive is the requirement for streaming services to have 'Australian content' quotas applied on their output from as early as 1 July 2024. This leads to a further blurring of what constitutes an Australian production. Are the productions which are funded and created by Hollywood based studios (i.e., Netflix or Amazon) and are made in Australia with Australian actors telling Australian stories truly Australian?

ESSAY | ANDREW F. PEIRCE

This is where those federal, state, and council rebates come into stronger effect, as they prop up Australian film and TV to build an active industry. Your tolerance for how much taxpayer funding is spent on these productions may vary, and I'll leave it up to you to determine whether this passes the pub test or not, however it is a structural aspect of how Australian screen culture is produced and is not going away any time soon.

This is a buzzing gnat of an issue, fast moving and hard to grab hold of. When you do feel you've finally squashed the annoying problem, fifty more are floating nearby to fill the space. On paper, *Revive* will provide some stability and support to a fractured system, but whether it provides a framework for the arts industry to become agile enough to pivot safely through the rising threat of AI (generative or otherwise) and automated creative systems or to sustain the tumbling institutions within the ever-crumbling state of Hollywood, remains to be seen.

It's hard not to feel sceptical or to feel like we've been here before. Because we have been here before. Many times. Tony Burke himself had a cultural policy which had a vision for the Australian arts, before subsequent LNP governments defunded and cut the budgets of national broadcasters and more.

Then, before that, we're brought full circle back to Paul Keating and the Creative Nation policy launch in the early 1990s, where Keating said in his speech[46]:

> *Creative Nation does not attempt to impose a cultural landscape on Australia but to respond to one which is already in bloom. I hope that in time this statement will be seen as the day we drew a line under our post-colonial era and said good-bye to it.*

While this book does carry a sense of anti-Americana, it's important to note that this argument is not driven by the excoriating fire of nationalism. Australia is a conflicted nation that requires breathing room to adjust and navigate through the continually unresolved trauma left by the act of colonisation on this land and its custodians. On a cultural level, that can be difficult to engage with when the dominant cultural presence is that of a nation going through its own internal conflicts.

This is not the space to sensitively approach the failure of the Albanese government's referendum on the Voice to the Parliament, but with that in mind, it is clear that as a nation Australia needs to undergo a major cultural shift. The concept of 'reconciliation' in Australia is dead. After all, it's impossible to engage in reconciliation if there was no conciliation in the first place.

Significant work goes into creating a nation's history and while this responsibility does not solely fall on the artists of Australia, they can play a part in ensuring that we affirmatively strike a line under our post-colonial

... AND THE KING

era, ensuring that we engage in acts of decolonisation, and that we start building a future that puts First Nations culture first.

If we consider a future where *Revive* is in functionally active, and there is a place for every story, and a story for every place, then ideally that means we will find ourselves in a new world where we can have the Baz Luhrmann sequined biopics, the observational coming-of-age stories from Alena Lodkina and Jub Clerc, the shed-shot quirky comedy from Platon Theodoris, the environmental documentary work of Jennifer Peedom, while the next Ted Kotcheff or Nicolas Roeg might look to Australia and say, 'Hey, I want to make a film about that place.'

In an attempt to push cynicism aside and not close this book on a dour note, it's important to remind that even though the screen funding bodies exist and that there's a legion of free-range filmmakers shifting the scope of what Australian cinema can be, their films desperately need you: the audience.

Your support for Australian cinema by way of buying a movie ticket, attending a film festival, purchasing a film on physical media, or simply logging your latest Aussie film watch on Letterboxd, means that you keep Australian screen culture alive. Become an active audience member; talk about what you have seen, whether it's good or bad, and let people know that it exists. Heck, go one step further and let the filmmaker know that you appreciate what they've created.

Australian films live on long after the credits have rolled. They take flight in the form of discussions in the cinema foyer that then give way to conversations months or years later when a thought sparks a memory, flashing to the front of our mind as a reminder of who we are. Those memories conjure visions of my grandmother dancing down the aisle to *Strictly Ballroom*, her waltzing feet carrying her all the way home.

There's a reason why our cinemas are often referred to as our churches. They're sanctuaries. Our place for silent communion. That happens because of the films that we see within their darkened rooms, films that make us feel seen or alive like nothing else ever can. It's my grandfather wanting to see more of Edinburgh in a *Trainspotting* sequel, or my recognition of the Australia that I knew as a kid in *Welcome to Woop Woop*.

It's home.

And that matters more than anything else.

ESSAY | ANDREW F. PEIRCE

ENDNOTES

1 Top 100 Australian Feature Films of All Time https://www.screenaustralia.gov.au/fact-finders/cinema/australian-films/feature-film-releases/top-australian-films - Accessed 1 April 2024.
2 Romeo + Juliet was US financed, shot in Mexico, and did not feature any Australians in its main cast.
3 Baz received Best Picture nominations for producing Moulin Rouge! and Elvis, with his films collectively receiving a total of 21 nominations with four wins.
4 Interview with Catherine Martin recorded in June 2022
5 Fall Guys: a generation of film-makers gutted by Australia bowing as Hollywood's backlot, Michael West Media - Michael West https://michaelwest.com.au/fall-guys-a-generation-of-film-makers-gutted-by-australia-bowing-as-hollywoods-backlot/?mibextid=Zxz2cZ, Accessed 23 April 2024
6 Australia is spending millions to lure Hollywood productions. But is it worth it?, The Guardian - Kelly Burke https://www.theguardian.com/film/2023/may/25/australia-is-spending-millions-to-lure-hollywood-productions-but-is-it-worth-it, Accessed 23 April 2024
7 Naturally, in this economy, we do not recommend this option.
8 In Australia, there are currently nine state and local government funding bodies. They are: Screen Australia, Screen Queensland, Screen NSW, Screen Tasmania, Screen Territory (NT), ScreenWest, South Australian Film Corporation, Vicscreen, Gold Coast Film Commission. https://www.ausfilm.com.au/why-film-in-australia/work-with-the-best/federal-state-local-government-agencies/ Accessed 2 April 2024
9 Synopsis for Elvis on Bazmark website: https://www.bazmark.com/ Accessed 1 April 2024
10 https://www.screenaustralia.gov.au/funding-and-support/producer-offset Accessed 1 April 2024
11 Producer Offset Document Library https://www.screenaustralia.gov.au/funding-and-support/producer-offset/document-library Accessed 1 April 2024
12 https://treasury.gov.au/consultation/c2024-489332 Accessed 1 April 2024
13 Australian Theatrical Feature Production Budget Ranges, Screen Australia - https://www.screenaustralia.gov.au/fact-finders/production-trends/australian-features/budget-ranges#:~:text=Proportions%20of%20films%20in%20various%20budget%20ranges&text=When%20adjusted%20for%20inflation%2C%20the,%2410%20million%20-%20accounted%20for%202021%25. - Accessed 23 April 2024
14 At time of publication, Australia has treaties with Canada, China, Germany, India, Ireland, Israel, Italy, Korea, Malaysia, Singapore, South Africa, United Kingdom, and MOUs with France and Aotearoa-New Zealand: https://www.screenaustralia.gov.au/funding-and-support/co-production-program/partner-countries Accessed 1 April 2024
15 https://www.ausfilm.com.au/news/queensland-all-shook-up-at-elvis-australian-premiere/ Accessed 31 March 2024
16 https://www.ausfilm.com.au/why-film-in-australia/work-with-the-best/federal-state-local-government-agencies/film-gold-coast/ Accessed 1 April 2024
17 https://www.goldcoast.qld.gov.au/Invest-do-business/Supporting-business/Business-incentives-investment-programs/Gold-Coast-Film-Commission/Screen-Attraction-Program Accessed 1 April 2024

... AND THE KING

18. For the purpose of this article, I have not included a breakdown of the government COVID support that Elvis may have received.
19. https://www.ausfilm.com.au/why-film-in-australia/work-with-the-best/federal-state-local-government-agencies/screen-queensland/ Accessed 1 April 2024
20. Elvis wins Best Film | 2022 AACTA Awards - https://www.youtube.com/watch?v=Uth07EHBHfk
21. Massive TV production planned for Australia cancelled due to writers' strike - Karl Quinn, The Sydney Morning Herald https://www.smh.com.au/culture/tv-and-radio/big-budget-tv-series-metropolis-planned-for-australia-cancelled-20230620-p5dhy7.html
22. Employment Trends Summary. Number of People Working in Audiovisual Industries https://www.screenaustralia.gov.au/fact-finders/people-and-businesses/employment-trends/summary Accessed 2 April 2024
23. 'What the f**k': Why Russell Crowe blatantly shut down original plan for Poker Face - Chantelle Francis, Daily Mail https://www.couriermail.com.au/entertainment/movies/what-the-fk-why-russell-crowe-blatantly-shut-down-original-plan-for-poker-face/news-story/9e78566a904de28b414b102d66bef81b
24. Baz Luhrmann's Untitled Elvis Project to be filmed in Queensland - Screen Queensland https://screenqueensland.com.au/sq-news/baz-luhrmanns-untitled-elvis-project-to-be-filmed-in-queensland/
25. For more on the history of the AFI, seek out Shining a Light: 50 Years of the Australian Film Institute by Lisa French and Mark Poole, ISBN 1 876467 20 7
26. The Oscars in Labor History: Union-Busting IIs at the Roots of the Ceremony - Sophie Hayssen, Teen Vogue - https://www.teenvogue.com/story/oscars-union-busting
27. 'Film for the intelligent layman': The origins of the Sydney and Melbourne Film Festivals (1952-1958), Cathay Hope and Adam Dickerson https://web.archive.org/web/20110806041949/http://www.latrobe.edu.au/screeningthepast/19/sydney-melbourne-film-festivals.html
28. AACTA Overview https://www.aacta.org/about-us/ Accessed 2 April 2024
29. About AACTA https://www.aacta.org/about-us/about-aacta/ Accessed 31 March 2024
30. Australian Film Institute risks regulatory breach after failing to lodge financial statements on time - Brendan Swift, IF.com.au https://if.com.au/australian-film-institute-risks-regulatory-breach-after-failing-to-lodge-financial-statements/
31. 2024 AACTA Rule Book - Accessed 2 April 2024
32. AACTA adjusts voting framework, unveils documentary entries - Jackie Keast, IF.com.au https://if.com.au/aacta-adjusts-voting-framework-unveils-documentary-entries/
33. AACTA Awards Voting - https://www.aacta.org/aacta-awards/voting-2022/ Accessed 2 April 2024
34. AACTA Membership Overview - https://www.aacta.org/membership/ Accessed 2 April 2024
35. 2024 AACTA Rule Book - Accessed 2 April 2024
36. https://www.aacta.org/aacta-awards/entries-open/film/ - Accessed 30 March 2024
37. https://www.aacta.org/aacta-awards/entries-open/documentary/ - Accessed 30 March 2024
38. https://www.aacta.org/aacta-awards/entries-open/short-film/ - Accessed 30 March 2024
39. https://www.screenaustralia.gov.au/fact-finders/production-trends/australian-features/budget-ranges - Accessed 2 April 2024

40 Producer Data: The Numbers Don't Lie (The Truth about Independent Film Revenue) - Naomi McDougall Jones, Liz Manashil, Filmmaker Magazine https://filmmakermagazine.com/120384-truth-about-independent-film-revenue/
41 MIFF Premiere Fund - https://miff.com.au/premierefund - Accessed 28 April 2024
42 AACTA Awards - Trailblazer Award https://www.aacta.org/aacta-awards/trailblazer-award/
43 Miles Franklin Literary Award, AustLit https://www.austlit.edu.au/austlit/page/v254
44 Danny and Michael Philippou win Best Direction In Film at the AACTA Awards https://www.youtube.com/watch?v=tCIj7oAOscQ&t=19s
45 National Cultural Policy—Revive: a place for every story, a story for every place https://www.arts.gov.au/publications/national-cultural-policy-revive-place-every-story-story-every-place
46 Address by the Prime Minister, the Hon P J Keating MP - Commonwealth Cultural Policy Launch Tuesday 18 October https://pmtranscripts.pmc.gov.au/release/transcript-9384

ACKNOWLEDGEMENTS

This book would not be possible without the support and guidance from my partner Carley Tillett. Thank you for listening to me in the late hours of the night when I would ramble on about the great interview I had that day, or as I recounted the emotional impact of the film that I'd seen, or when I went down rambling tracks about the grand ideas I had for this book. Your guidance, patience, and support for my work is presented in an unceasing enthusiasm for my passion. The world would be a much better place if everyone had someone like Carley in their corner supporting them.

I have to thank my dogs Monty and Lawrie, while you can't read this book, I do hope you understand the strength you give me by being by my side every day. To George and Cheese, who we lost during the writing of this book, your presence will always be in my mind. And to Zac the Cat, my black panther, thank you for your purring presence.

Thank you to Kate Separovich who agreed to write the introduction to this tome long before I had ever finished drafting the words. Your trust in me is valued and appreciated, as is your support and for the local WA film industry.

To my friend, colleague, and fellow film critic, Nadine Whitney, thank you for being the ear that I needed when I was unsure whether this whole writing thing was for me. You've reminded me that what we do as writers matters.

Thank you to Bianca Kartawiria for being the first reader and providing essential feedback in the editing process. You helped shape this shaggy beast into shape.

Thanks to Jelena Sinik and Nicolette Axiak for the stunning cover art. You took my vague idea and turned into a work of art. I'm forever grateful for your creative vision.

Thanks to my fellow critics, wherever you are in the world. You frequently set the benchmark for what I aim to work towards.

To the filmmakers and patrons of cinema who gave their time for this book, thank you. You trusted me with your words and vision and helped me present the state of Australian cinema how it deserves to be presented: alive and thriving.

Thank you to the publicists who connected me with many of the people interviewed for this book. Your work is often an unseen side of the film industry, but without your presence, it would stand still.

I must once more thank my grandparents. You'll never read this book, but I know deep inside that you both knew I had it in me to write it and bring it to life. I lost my grandfather during the writing of this book, and on the day of his passing I watched his favourite film, *The Mask*. I can still hear him laughing now.

Finally, during the writing of this book the world lost some great voices who have influenced the world of cinema and have been major inspirations for my own work: Jennifer Ross, Lee Gambin, David Tiley, Cam McCarthy, Anthony Horan, Grant Page, and Scott Wampler. A world without their voices is difficult to fathom, but we can continue singing their songs and stomping their beat.

GLOSSARY

AFTRS: Australian Film Television and Radio School

AIDC: Australian International Documentary Conference

BFA: Bachelor of Fine Arts Degree

Big Print: Screenplay directions

Bio Box: The room used for projectionists to operate audio visual equipment, aka the projection booth

DCP: Digital Cinema Package, a file used to store and convey digital cinema, audio, image and data streams. Traditionally used for cinema projection.

DoP: Director of Photography, Cinematographer

FIFO: Fly in, fly out workers. Usually associated with mining workers in Australia.

HoD: Head of Department

Hollywood accounting or bookkeeping: the opaque or creative set of accounting methods used by the film, video, television and music industry to budget and record profits for creative projects.

IB Technicolour: IB abbreviates 'imbibition', a dye-transfer operation that allows for the use of dyes that are more stable and permanent than those formed in ordinary chromogenic colour printing.

Keys: Chroma key compositing, or chroma keying, is a visual-effects and post-production technique for layering two or more images or video streams together based on colour hues.

LNP: Liberal National Party

Malpa: A Pintupi/Warlpiri/Luritja word which means 'friends of the journey'

MEAA: Media, Entertainment and Arts Alliance

MOUs: Memorandum of Understanding

MYEFO: Mid-Year Economic and Fiscal Outlook

NIDA: National Institute of Dramatic Art

NIXCO: A public relations company led by company director Fiona
Nix

Ob-doc: Observational Documentary

P&A: Print and Advertising

PDV: Post, Digital and Visual Effects, usually referred to in relation to the PDV Offset - a 30 per cent rebate for work on post, digital and visual effects production in Australia, regardless of where a project is filmed.

PoC: People of colour

Shift72:   An online, on-demand platform used to securely provide MIFF films to virtual attendees

SVOD: Subscription Video on Demand

VOD: Video on Demand

INDEX

INTERVIEWS

Axiak, Nicolette, 419–427
Baretto, Tim, 95–103
Barlow, Hannah, 299–309
Barr, Tristan, 245–249
Begg, Zanny, 447–453
Berger, Gus, 573–579
Boreham, Craig, 375–383
Burgess, Kasimir, 653–659
Castle, Jane, 455–462
Chambers, Tania, 55–63
Champeaux, Nic, 205–214
Cohen, Danny, 615–622
Cordery, Daniel, 205–214
Cossar, Al, 545–555
Courtin-Wilson, Amiel, 521–527
Daw, Jonathan, 139–147
Dean, Bentley, 41–47
Duan, William, 437–445
Easteal, David, 645–650
Eeles, Matthew, 105–117
Ferraro, Nicole, 65–71
Finney, Adam, 293–297
Graham, Patrick, 165–175
Hartley, Mark, 605–609
Harvey, John, 581–586
Hüa, Jayden Rathsam, 501–506
Kern, Sara, 467–471
Lamphee, Jennifer, 149–155
Levine, Judi, 55–63
Lodkina, Alena, 535–542
Lynch, Derik, 165–175
Martin, Catherine, 279–280
Martiri, Luisa, 237–242
McKenzie, Luke, 485–488
Miller, Natalie, 635–643
Modini, Tanya, 237–242
Moussavi, Granaz, 157–162
Murphy, Rob, 595–603
Nagle, George-Alex, 349–358
Newell, Maya, 401–406
Njoo, Simon, 189–195
Onus, Tiriki, 389–394
Paez, Diana, 589–593
Pendragon. Lachlan, 269–276
Poole, Brodie, 123–129
Proyas, Alex, 491–499
Riederer, Karin, 139–147
Rifici, Rick, 33–39
Roache-Turner, Kiah, 473–484
Ross, Jennifer, 429–434
Senes, Kane, 299–309
Sen, Ivan, 251–257
Sinik, Jelena, 419–427
Skirving, Rhian, 581–586
Smith, David Vincent, 73–83
Stolevski, Goran, 629–633
Stone, Georgie, 397–400
Target, Simon, 409–417
Tarwin, Ben, 349–358
Theodoris, Platon, 327–347
Thorne, Matthew, 165–175
Vanderwalt, Lesley, 259–267
Vaughan, James, 509–518
Vengurlekar, Nitin, 327–334
von Hofman, Alexander, 89–93
Webster, Renée, 49–53

Wilkinson, Josh, 131–136
Williams, Mark, 361–363
Wilson, Aaron, 365–373
Wilson, Martin, 65–71
Wright, Thomas M., 197–203
Young, Michelle, 139–147
Zarkesh, Anousha, 181–188

REVIEWS

Ablaze, 385–387
Anonymous Club, 611–614
The Stranger, 177–179
General Hercules, 119–121
He Ain't Heavy, 85–87
Here Out West, 310–313
Petrol, 529–534
The Lost City of Melbourne, 569–571
The Stranger, 176
Moja Vesna, 465–466
Of an Age, 625–627

ESSAYS

The Lonely Spirits Variety Hour, 315–334
...and the King: Baz Luhrmann's Elvis and the Australianness of it All, 660–683

A - Z

1% 106
4D cinema 576
100% Wolf 61
101 Days of Lockdown 418–427
1984 162
2040 563–564

AACTA 662–680
AACTA Awards 30, 668, 670, 674
ABC (Australian Broadcasting Corporation) 161, 162, 188, 313, 337, 532, 543, 545, 560, 637, 648
Ablaze 26, 384–395
Academy Award 41, 201, 259, 269, 462, 662
Academy Awards 21, 31, 268, 269, 276, 279, 670, 675
Acute Misfortune 177, 179, 197, 198, 199, 201, 202
Adelaide Film Festival (AFF) 160, 167, 674

Investment fund 674
Adore 34
A Few Less Men 60
Aftersun 466, 641
AFTRS 140, 145, 501, 531, 689
Age of Rage - The Australian Punk Revolution 428–435
Akbar, Travis 385, 386
Albanese government 27, 663, 669, 678, 679
Albany 71, 108, 109
Alien 89, 92
Alvin's Harmonious World of Opposites 315–347
A Man Escaped 76
Amazon 678
American Werewolf in London 606
Anangu 139–147
Anderson, Robin 119
Annie 66, 335, 676
Anonymous Club 559–560, 565, 610–622
An Ostrich Told Me the World is Fake and I Think I Believe It 268–277
Ansett 100
Apatow, Judd 210
Apocalypse Now 474, 475, 483
A Private Function 15, 29
Armfield, Neil 86
Armstrong, Gillian 638, 675, 677
Arnhem Land 45, 188
Artificial Intelligence (AI) II, 27, 491, 498, 679
Ashton, Jeremy 32, 41
Assange, Julian 161, 162, 217–235
Astor 102, 570
A Ticket in Tatts 545, 548
ATOM Awards 101
Australiana 18, 22, 29, 119, 123, 135, 242, 320, 321, 324, 333, 353, 502, 505
Australian Centre for Moving Image (ACMI) 545, 551, 639, 643
Australian Cinematographers Society 59
Australian Council for the Arts (AusCA) 514, 515
Australian Directors Guild Award 48, 364
Australian Film Institute (AFI) 636, 670, 671, 675
Avanca Film Festival 349
Axiak, Nicolette II, 418–427, 685

Babyteeth 86
Bad Taste 475
Baker, Simon 114, 670, 676
Bana, Eric 670
Barbie 675, 677
Baretto, Tim 94–103
Barlow, Hannah 298–309

693

INDEX

Barnett, Courtney 559, 610–623
Barr, Tristan 244
Barton, Del Kathryn 237
Basha, George 312
Bassendream 94–103, 674
Bastardy 521
Bate, Matthew 118, 396
Bath, Gabriel 674
BazMark 664
BeDevil 202
Before the Dream 101
Begg, Zanny 446–453
Beijing International Film Festival 508
Bell, Jon 26, 189, 195, 385
Below 110
Beresford, Bruce 18, 226
Berger, Gus 545, 549, 558, 568–579
Berger, Katherine 339
Biden, Joe 223, 231
Black ANZAC 386
Black Chicks Talking 26
Black Dynamite 210
Blacklight 360–363
Black Maria Film Collective 531, 674
Blade Runner 254, 474
Blair, Wayne 26, 384, 385
Blanchett, Cate 188, 434, 642, 675
Blaze 237, 677
Bliss 224
Blood Moon 607
Blue Heelers 115
Bluey 28, 31, 140
Blu-ray 205, 206, 209, 213, 606
Bonsai Films 642
Boreham, Craig 374–383
Boston Film Festival 349
Boyle, Michael 67
Bran Nue Dae 26
Breath 34, 37
Bridesmaids 300, 301
Brisbane International Film Festival (BIFF) 337, 338, 557, 640, 643
Brisbane Only Repulsive Liquid Film Festival (BORLFF) 674
British Academy of Film and Television Arts (BAFTA) 670, 671
British Film Institute (BFI) Film Festival 337
Broome 71, 108, 188
Brown, Bryan 114
Bucharest Short Film Festival 349
Buoyancy 75, 677
Burgess, Kasimir 558, 652–659
Busan International Film Festival (BIFF) 338
Buxton, Nina 237
Bye Bye Africa 27
Byrne, Sean 674

Cage, Nicolas 108
Calendar Girls 55
Call Me Mr. Brown 116
Camera
  360 camera 43
  Aaton XTR 97
  ARRI Alexa 517, 539
  Bolex 190, 335
  Canon 5D Mark II 461
  Drone 68, 125, 247, 373, 409–417, 482–483, 654
  DSLR 431
  Éclair 16mm 335
  GoPro 43, 44, 412
  Kodak Vision3 97, 619
Campbell, Salliana Seven 283–291
Campion, Jane 203
Canberra 303, 361, 362
Candy 86
Cannes Film Festival 74, 82, 176, 203, 307, 475, 549, 550, 637, 638, 641
Canopy 366, 370, 373
Cargo 77
Carpenter, John 256
Carrie 300
Carter, Arnold Luke 109
Casting JonBenet 450
Castle, Jane 454–463
Chambers, Tania 48–63
Champeaux, Nic 204–215
Chan, Jackie 18, 473
Chan-wook, Park 81
Charles, Uncle Jack 386, 521
Charlie's Country 202
Chauvel, Charles 190, 386
Cherubhead 111, 674
Chopper 312
CinefestOz 70
Cinema Australia 105–117
Cinema Nova 549, 600, 635–643
Clerc, Jub 26, 59, 385, 680
Clermont-Ferrand International Short Film Festival 349, 351
Cloak and Dagger 606
Cloud City Chaos 68
Cohen, Danny 559, 610–622
Cold War 76
Cole, Beck 26
Connolly, Bob 119
Connolly, Robert 668
Contact 41, 42
Continuous Pictures 245
Cook, Lincoln James 109
Cordery, Daniel 204–215
Cossar, Al 545–555
Country Women's Association (CWA) 410, 411, 415
Count, Tim 32, 64, 68
Courtin-Wilson, Amiel 203, 510–511, 520–527, 536
COVID pandemic
  Creativity and 426
  Duration of lockdowns 421, 532, 557
  Filmmaking and 38, 42, 45, 78,

89, 167, 169, 223, 256, 259, 261, 275, 279, 320, 339, 361, 371, 377, 415, 431, 565, 573, 574, 579, 582, 583, 592, 608, 654, 667, 669
  Impact on audiences 71, 366, 545, 546, 550, 558, 561, 562, 637, 641
  Isolation and loneliness 381, 415
  Living during 174, 295, 296, 409, 419, 420, 532, 579, 581, 582
  Screenings during 110, 111, 351, 559, 562, 641, 645
  Supportive collaborators and 423, 607
Cows 409, 415
Criterion Channel 531
Crocodile Dundee 18, 20, 21, 31, 505
Crowe, Russell 21, 662, 669, 682
Curtin University 97

Damon, Annika 118
Dark City 265, 266, 267, 491, 494, 495
Davis, Garth 203, 227, 617
Daw, Jonathan 138–147
Dean, Bentley 33–47, 558
de Heer, Rolf 103, 202, 225, 549, 674
Dendy Cinemas 312
DePalma, Brian 537
Destination NSW 355
Disney 27, 28, 494, 662, 669
Doc Society 405
Do, Khoa 312
Double Barrel Productions 667
Dreamland 251
Dreamlife Youth Committee 406
Drift 34
Drive 210, 643, 699
Duan, William 436–445
DuVernay, Ava 74

Early Man 271
Easteal, David 644–650
Easter Parade 70
Edgerton, Nash 80, 195
Edillo, Carl 311
Edith Cowan University (ECU) 95, 97, 101
Eeles, Matthew 105–117
Efron, Zac 148, 149
Elect Lincoln 109
Elton, Ben 114
Elvis 29, 71, 261, 278–281, 558, 563, 660–683
Eno, Brian 216, 234
Event Cinemas 312
Evie 88–93
Evil Dead 475, 483

694

Facebook 210, 211, 293, 294, 296, 431, 432, 564, 575
Facing Monsters 32–47, 558
Falling For Figaro 55, 61, 563
Farscape 267
Faster, Pussycat! Kill! Kill! 322
Fauda 412
Ferraro, Nicole 64–71
Festival of the Antipodes (Du Cinema Des Antipodes) 345
Film Format
  Cinerama 595, 597, 601
  Super 8 335, 656
  Super-8 430, 656
Film Formats
  Ultra Panavision 597, 601
film noir 254
Film Stock
  16mm 97, 335, 336, 458, 559, 619, 654
  35mm 97, 336, 601
  65mm 265, 602
  70mm 597, 601, 602
  IB technical upgrade 596
  Technicolor 596
Film Threat Magazine 190
Film Victoria. See VicScreen
Finke: There and Back 26
Finney, Adam 292–297
First Footprints 41, 42, 45
First Nations 15, 23, 25, 26, 28, 41, 178, 386, 401, 402, 462, 512, 513, 532, 562, 586, 678, 680
flipbook animations 269
For Now 302
Foulkes, Mirrah 195
Fox Studios 662
Framestore 667
Franklin 12, 557, 558, 563, 565, 652–659
Fraser, Lilias 454, 455
Frater, Jim 64, 67
Freddy Got Fingered 207
Fremantle 33, 60, 61, 69, 108
Friday the 13th 300
Friends and Strangers 508–519, 541
Friends of Mine 530
Funding
  Crowd- 102
  Gold Coast Film Commission (GCFC) 666
  Screen Australia 55, 58, 59, 81, 456, 674
  Screen Australia Gender Matters 59
  ScreenWest 59, 107, 667
  Self- 510, 512
  South Australian Film Corporation (SAFC) 161, 167, 667
  VicScreen 390, 547, 554, 667

Gayby Baby 401, 405
Gender Matters Taskforce 55, 58
General Hercules 118–137

GenreBlast Film Festival 205, 206
Gerwig, Greta 270
Ghosthunter 217, 218, 220, 225, 226, 229
Giallo 300, 502
Giardina, Ross 148
Girl at the Window 604–609
Gold 148–155
Gold Coast Film Commission (GCFC) 667. See also Funding
Gold Coast Film Festival 557, 643
Goldstone 251, 253, 254, 257
Golovko, Dmitri 88
Goodfellas 475
Good Night 72–83
Graham, Patrick 164–175
Gray, Anna 149
Great White 65, 68
Greenfield 107
Green, Kitty 203, 450, 453
green screen 487, 495
Green, Tom 207
Gremlins of the Clouds 491
Griffiths, Rachel 114
Griffith University (Queensland Conservatorium of Music) 284
Gulpilil, David 22, 257

Hacksaw Ridge 201, 665, 675, 676
Hafekasi 629
Hail 510, 521, 525, 526, 536
Hale, Ian 71, 105
Halloween 300
Halsted, Beth 148, 149, 282
Harlequin 608
Hartley, Mark 473, 604–609
Harvard University 640
Harvey, John 580, 581–586
Hayes, Anthony 148, 149
Haywood, Chris 116
Head On 375
He Ain't Heavy 73, 76, 84–87
Hearts and Bones 217, 225, 226, 229
Heatwave 449
Helping Minds 65
Here I Am 26
Here Out West 310–313, 354, 355, 675
Heretic Foundation 490–499
Hi8 camera 474, 475
Hicks, Scott 116
High Ground 181, 188
Hill, Damian 115
Hitchcock, Alfred 17, 69
Hogan, Paul 18, 20, 22, 31, 434
Hollywood 26, 29, 70, 149, 150, 207, 210, 255, 361, 486, 492, 494, 495, 496, 499, 510, 554, 558, 559, 562, 608, 643, 663, 665, 666, 668, 669, 670, 673, 675, 676, 678, 679, 681, 689
Housos 311

Howard, Ron 662, 677
How to Please a Woman 48–63, 108, 181, 185, 186, 187, 563
How to Thrive 563
Hoyts 12, 19, 312, 337, 548, 551
Hüa, Jayden Rathsam 500–507
Human Rights Arts & Film Festival 550

IMAX 547, 548
I Met a Girl 61
immigrant 160, 242, 365, 371, 372, 465, 466, 467
Impostor Syndrome 114, 115, 266
Independent Film 29, 65, 339, 379, 673
Indigenous New Wave 25, 26, 385
In My Blood It Runs 401, 402, 405
Inside Film 663
Invisible Boys 55
I, Robot 491, 494
Ithaka 12, 216–235

Jackson, Peter 475, 476
Jakarta Institute of Arts 336
Jasper Jones 181
Jeonju International Film Festival 508
Jindabyne 224
Joan of Arc 450
Johnson, Karen 216, 228, 231
Juanita Nielsen NOW 446–453
Jurassic Park 18, 90, 91
Jurassic World 90

Kalgoorlie 71, 108, 119–137, 338
Keating, Paul 662, 679, 683
Kelly, Paul 95, 100
Kennedy Miller Mitchell 234, 259
KenTacoHut 26
Kent, Jennifer 189, 194, 195, 203
Kern, Sara 464–471
Kiarostami, Abbas 157
Kickstarter 302
Kidman, Nicole 308, 434, 670
Kill Me Three Times 55, 60
Kimberley 108
Kinotopia 674
Knowing the Score 641, 642
Kodak 97, 597, 619
Kotcheff, Ted 677, 680
Kramer, Stanley 677
Kukaputju 138–147
Kurzel, Justin 179, 197, 203, 674

695

INDEX

Ladies in Black 149
La Flor 551
Lahiff, Sean 148
"La Jetée" 352
Lakemba 337, 338
Lamphee, Jennifer 148–155, 282
Lantana 224
Last Cab to Darwin 303
Lawrence, Ben 216–235
Lawrence, Ray 224
Legendary Pictures 662
Legg, Sarah 111, 674
Leslie, Ewen 111, 176, 184
Letterboxd 209, 680
Levine, Judi 48–63
Lieutenant Jangles 7, 204–215
Life is but a Dream 81
Lindsay, Meredith 88, 93
Lion 227, 675
Little Fish 312
Little Tornadoes 364–373
Little Women 270
Loach, Ken 87
Locarno Film Festival 542
Lodkina, Alena 203, 510, 511, 525, 528–543, 545, 552, 674, 680
Lonesome 374–383
Longford Cinema 635, 636, 638
Lord, Kim 68, 69
Lord of the Rings 483
Love and Other Catastrophes 548
Loveland 250–257
Luhrmann, Baz 29, 105, 278, 279, 281, 308, 558, 660, 661, 666, 675, 677, 680, 682
Luma Pictures 667
Lynch, David 479, 529, 534
Lynch, Derik 164–175

Mac and Me 322, 324
Mad Max 26, 77, 259, 267, 362, 474, 475, 476, 478, 665, 669, 675
Mann, Michael 537
Man on Earth 520–527
Manslaughter 386
Martin, Atticus 88
Martin, Catherine 278–281, 662
Martin, Jaydon 118, 120, 126
Martin, Lukas William 88
Martiri, Luisa 236–243
Marungka Tjalatjunu 164–175
Marvel 27, 71, 304, 366, 495, 497, 514, 668
Mask of the Evil Apparition 491, 495
Maslin, Sue 389, 557–567
Mate 348–359
McDonough, Lauren 67
McKenzie, Luke 472, 485–488
McLaren, Joe 118, 120
McQueen, Steve 74, 77
Mean Girls 300, 301
Media, Entertainment and Arts

Alliance (MEAA) 641, 689
Meet Me in St Louis 70
Melbourne International Film Festival (MIFF) 8, 164, 203, 327, 365, 535, 542, 544–555, 577, 600, 642, 670, 674
MeToo 57
Miami Connection 209
Michôd, David 195, 203, 307
Midnight Film Festival 308
migrant 312, 368, 371, 440, 470, 471, 537, 589, 590
Miguelito 228
Miller, George 18, 258, 259, 475, 487, 677
Miller, Natalie 634–643
Mimi 257
Mini DV 430
Modini, Tanya 236–243
Moffatt, Tracey 202
Moja Vesna 464–471
Molly & Mobarak 459
Moorhouse, Jocelyn 677
Morehouse, Jocelyn 638
Morgan, Alec 384, 385, 386, 389, 390, 391
Morris, Ben 68
Morrison, Scott 110, 353, 416
Moulin Rouge! 279, 308, 661, 662, 681
Moussavi, Granaz 157–162, 674
Moviejuice 531, 674
MPC 667
Mr. Accident 181
Mrs. Fang 524
Mt Trolla 246, 247
MTV Awards 336
MUBI 531
mumblecore 302
Muriel's Wedding 115, 300, 301
Murphy, Rob 573, 594, 595–603
Murphy, Shannon 86
Mwah 237
Mystery Road 26, 187, 188, 251, 253, 257
My Tehran for Sale 158

Naderi, Amir 157, 158, 160
Nagle, George-Alex 348–359
Namatjira Project 459
Napoléon 600
Natalie Miller Fellowship 639, 640
National Association of Cinema Operators-Australasia 640
National Film and Sound Archive of Australia (NFSA) 385, 387, 391, 458, 567
National Institute of Dramatic Art (NIDA) 302, 627, 690
Neighbours 99, 400, 403
Netflix 202, 222, 376, 404, 406, 412, 434, 494, 561, 678
Neurodivergent 324, 325

Newell, Maya 396–407
New York Film Academy (NYFA) 301, 302
New York Film Academy (NYFA) 301, 302
Ngayuku Papa: Bluey and Big Boy 140
Ngayuku Papa: Tiny 140
Nieto, Maria 674
Nightmare Alley 280
Night of the Living Dead 475
Nitram 179, 553
Njoo, Simon 176, 189–195
Nolan, Christopher 597
non-binary 56, 240, 399, 400, 401
Not Quite Hollywood 209, 473, 605, 608, 609
Nott, Ben 48, 60
Noyce, Phillip 449, 675
NT Travelling Film Festival 145
Nuestras Voces 588–593

Of an Age 552, 553, 624–633, 677
Off Country 580–586
One Hundred a Day 639
On the Beach 677
Onus, Tiriki 26, 384–395
Onus, William T. (Bill) 26, 384, 385, 389, 394
Overlook Film Festival 299
Ozploitation 26, 205, 209, 249, 473, 483, 487, 605, 607

Pacific Rim: Uprising 149
Paez, Diana 589–593
Palm Beach 312
ParaSoul 337
Parker, Jess 82, 84
Parks and Recs 74
Partos, Antony 148
Patrick 605, 607, 608, 609
Pavlovic, Nina 118
Peedom, Jennifer 189, 193, 195, 228, 558, 559, 657, 680
Pendragon, Lachlan 268–277
Perkins, Rachel 23, 26, 181, 187, 385
Perth International Film Festival 49, 559
Petrol 203, 528–543, 545
Philippou, Danny 28, 676, 683
Philippou, Michael 28, 676, 683
Phillips, Sally 48, 49, 50
Pieces 65–71
Planet of the Apes 262, 668
Poole, Brodie 118, 119, 123–129
Pools 242
Popescu, Stefan 339
Portable Film Festival 545, 550
Potts, Lewis 84
Priscilla 115
Projecting Natalie Miller

634–643
Proyas, Alex 491–499, 677
Pub: The Movie 430
Punching Darts 109
Purcell, Leah 26, 282, 283, 291, 310, 665

Queensland University of Technology (QUT) 237, 238, 376
queer 49, 56, 165, 172, 375, 376, 379, 380, 381, 382, 383, 437, 441, 442, 444, 625, 629

Rabat International Author Film Festival 349
Raimi, Sam 475, 476, 483
Raindance Film Festival 330
Rake 185, 187
Rams 75, 303
Rapsey, Brian 314, 320, 331, 339
Rats in the Ranks 119, 459
Razorback 307
Real Stories 65
Red Dragon 34
Redfern Now 187, 188
referendum 679
Resin Visual Effects Studio 667
Revelation International Film Festival (Rev) 102, 103, 322, 325, 326, 327, 338
Revive 27, 28, 561, 562, 669, 678, 679, 680
Riederer, Karin 138–147
Rifici, Rick 32–47
Rising Sun Pictures 667
River 26, 61, 188, 189, 193, 194
River, Dylan 26, 385
RMIT 189
Roache-Turner, Kiah 472–489
Roache-Turner, Tristan 473–489
Road of The Dead 478, 484
Road Warrior 478
Roeg, Nicolas 677, 680
Romero, George A 475
Rosenzweig, Robert (Bob) 520, 521, 521–527, 522
Ross, Jennifer 428–435
Rotoscope 304
Rotterdam International Film Festival 508
Rowe, Kristie 64, 69
Rowe, Tess 70

Samson and Delilah 26, 77, 202
Sapporo International Short Film Festival 349
Sargeant, Jack 326, 339
SBS 237, 337, 526, 560, 581
Scarecrow Studios 305
Schepisi, Fred 18, 226, 638, 639
Schmidt, Ruby 118

Schwarz, John 148
Schwarz, Michael 148
Scoff 55
Scorsese, Martin 479
Scott, Ridley 89, 254
Scream 300, 305, 331
Screen Australia 55, 59, 63, 82, 188, 402, 404, 641, 664, 665, 666, 673, 674. See also Funding
ScreenHub 663
Screen New South Wales 667. See also Funding
Screen Queensland 664, 666, 667, 681, 682. See also Funding
ScreenWest 55, 105. See also Funding
Senes, Kane 298–309
Sen, Ivan 26, 202, 250–257, 385, 547, 670
Senses of Cinema (journal) 648
Separovich, Kate 10–13, 72, 79, 88, 89, 685
Sharmill Films 635, 636, 641
Ships That Bear 674
Shipton, Gabriel 216, 229–234
Ship to Shore 111, 112
Shorts International 337
Sight and Sound Magazine 508, 509, 645
Silvestrin, Lawrie 64, 67, 68
Simpsons 21, 126
Singapore International Film Festival (SGIFF) 338
Sinik, Jelena II, 418–427, 685
Sissy 12, 298–309, 675
Sissy Screens 375
Sitges Film Festival 299
Skirving, Rhian 581–586, 674
Slamdance Film Festival 339
Slawinski, Scott 68
Smith, David Vincent 72–83, 84–87
Smith, Geoffrey 32, 42, 594
Smyth, Polly 148
Snapshot 609
Snowtown 197
Soldiers of the Cross 577
Son of a Gun 106
Son of Rambow 270
Soto, John 106
South Australian Film Corporation (SAFC) 681. See also Funding
South by Southwest Film Festival (SXSW) 299, 308
South Carolina Underground Film Festival 205
Sowada, Richard 326, 339
Spider, Bear, Shark 80
Spielberg, Steven 89, 530
Spirits of the Air 491
Splice Here: A Projected Odyssey 573, 594–603
Stan 640
Star Wars 247, 599, 636
Stingers 115
St. Kilda Film Festival (SKFF) 338

Stolevski, Goran 203, 552, 553, 624–633, 674, 677
Stone, Georgie 397–407
Stop-motion 139–147, 269–277, 480
Storyboard 36, 208, 272, 273, 476, 607
Strange Colours 535, 536, 538, 541
Strictly Ballroom 18, 267, 661, 680
Struggle Street 311, 312
StudioCanal 640
Subject 244–249
Sundance 75, 82, 339, 550
Sun Moon & Thalia 109
Sunrise 315, 319, 338, 339
Sun Theatre 595
Sushi Noh 500–507
Sweet As 26, 59, 108, 674
Sweet Country 181
Sydney Film Festival 140, 145, 164, 173, 308, 312, 402
Sydney Underground Film Festival (SUFF) 325, 326, 338, 339

TAFE 73, 74, 97, 432
Talk to Me 28, 676, 677
Tambo 386
Tangki 138–147
Tanna 41, 42, 45
Tanner, Josh 493
Tapaya, Tjunkaya 138, 139
Target, Simon 408–417
Tarkovsky 81, 539, 638
Tarwin, Ben 348–359
Taxi Driver 480
Team America 207
Teenage Kicks 375, 376, 377, 382
Ten Canoes 202
The Artful Dodger 262
The Babadook 76, 189, 195, 307, 677
The Backlot 71, 105
The Batman 514
The Beach 188
The Beehive 447, 449, 450, 452
The Blues Brothers 576
The Bold Type 306
The Boys 202, 312
The Castle 26
The City of Ladies 450
The Combination 312
The Crow 491
The Dirty Three 131, 132, 553
The Dreamlife of Georgie Stone 396–407
The Dressmaker 564, 567
The Drover's Wife 248, 282–291, 563, 665, 675
The Dry 86, 668
The English Surgeon 42
The Fall Guy 262, 668
The Finished People 312

INDEX

The Full Monty 55
The Great Gatsby 279, 661, 662, 665
The Heights 67, 69
The Home Song Stories 181
The Howling 606
The Kelly Gang 577
The Killing of Angel Street 449
The Lonely Spirits Variety Hour 29, 248, 314–347, 552, 674
The Lost City of Melbourne 545, 549, 558, 560, 565, 569–571, 573–579, 642
The Loved Ones 307
The Merchant of Venice 335
The Moogai 26, 189
The Moths Will Eat Them Up 236–243
The New Boy 181, 188
Theodoris, Platon 29, 314–347, 552, 680
The Plains 553, 644–650
The Power of the Dog 203, 666
The Quiet Girl 466
The Rocky Horror Picture Show 576
The Room 641
The Rover 77, 307
The Saddle Club 306
The Sapphires 26
The Sea Inside 345
The Sessions 52, 55
Thessaloniki Documentary Film Festival 118, 216
Thessaloniki International Short Film Festival 349
The Story of the Kelly Gang 12, 569, 577
The Stranger 12, 176–203, 665, 675
The Surfer 108
The Sword in the Stone 335
The Wizard of Oz 335, 598
The Wolverine 149, 155
The X Files 325
Thirst 608
Thor: Love and Thunder 361
Thornbury Picture House 570, 574, 579
Thorne, Matthew 164–175
Thornton, Warwick 25, 26, 31, 181, 202, 227, 257, 385, 674
Three Summers 114
Three Thousand Years of Longing 258–267, 676
Tjanpi 139, 140, 141, 143, 145, 146, 147
Tokyo-ga 618
Toomelah 26, 202, 251
Top Gun Maverick 71
Torino Underground Cinefest 349
Total Control 181
Tourism Australia 21
Tracks 77
Trainspotting 19, 680

Transgender 397, 401, 406
Travelling Film Festival 143, 145
Triangle of Sadness 636, 641, 642
Trump, Donald 223, 231
Tui Ná 436–445

UK Film Festival 349
Umbrella Entertainment 112, 205, 206, 209, 210, 213, 248
Un Chien Andalou 352
Under the Skin 201
University of Melbourne (VCA) 247, 547
University of New South Wales (UNSW Sydney) 301, 335, 336, 419
University of Technology Sydney (UTS) 190
University of Western Australia 67
Unknown Pleasures 531, 674

Valhalla Cinema 190, 474, 576, 638, 643
Vancouver Film Festival 158
Vancouver International Film Festival (VIFF) 338
Vanderwalt, Lesley 259–267
Vaughan, James 508–519, 525, 531, 541
Vegas 157, 158, 662
Vegas: Based on a True Story 157
Vengurlekar, Nitin 314, 319, 327–334
Venice International Film Festival 157, 335
VFX 89, 241, 304, 305, 491, 493, 495, 622, 667, 673
VHS 17, 335, 430, 599
VicScreen 639, 640, 641. See also Funding
Vidiverse 490–499
Village Roadshow 662
Vimeo 492
Voice to the Parliament 679
von Hofmann, Alexander 88–93

Waiting 157
Waititi, Taika 74
Wake in Fright 307, 677
Walkabout 677
Wallace and Gromit 270
Walton, Tasma 48, 49, 112, 113
WA Made Film Festival 104–117
Warner Bros. 662
warrawong... the windy place on the hill 408–417
WA Salvage 95, 99, 100
Watch the Sunset 245, 248

Water Rats 115
Watt, Sarah 115, 674
Weaving, Hugo 226, 250, 652, 670
Webb, Antony 84
Webster, Renée 49–63, 181
Weir, Peter 226, 677
Welcome to Woop Woop 20, 324, 680
We're Not Here to Fuck Spiders 491, 497
West Coast Visions 59, 75, 82
Western Sydney 225, 311, 312, 313, 349, 354, 355, 453, 513
When Pomegranates Howl 156–163
When the Camera Stopped Rolling 454–463
Where is My Darling? 292–297
White Justice 393, 394
Whitney, Nadine 177, 465, 569, 685
WikiLeaks 220, 222, 223, 234
Wilkinson, Josh 118, 128, 131–136
Williams, Mark 360–363
Willy Wonka and the Chocolate Factory 335, 598
Wilson, Aaron 364–373
Wilson, Martin 64–71
Wilson, Monique 64, 65, 69
Wilson, Rebel 677
Wilson, Ted 510, 511, 515, 677, 680
Wine Lake 315, 319, 330, 331, 339, 343
Winterbottom, Michael 225
Wolf Creek 149, 307
Wotton, Ben 89, 93
Wright, Andy 201
Wright, Thomas M. 177–179, 181, 197–203, 552
Wyrmwood: Apocalypse 472–489
Wyrmwood: Road of the Dead 473, 476, 485

Young Einstein 11, 18, 21, 22
Young, Michelle 138–147
YouTube 28, 81, 112, 210, 285, 305, 325, 330, 491, 492
You Won't Be Alone 82, 552, 625, 630, 677

Zarkesh, Anousha 181–188
Zombies 24, 473, 475, 478, 481, 485
Zubrycki, Sam 228
Zubrycki, Tom 384, 389, 391

Image: Busselton Drive-in Outdoor Cinema 2023, Andrew F. Peirce

www.ingramcontent.com/pod-product-compliance
Lightning Source LLC
Chambersburg PA
CBHW031352160426
42811CB00092B/101